Criminal Law 4th Edition

Edition
4

Criminal Law

Joel Samaha
University of Minnesota

West Publishing Company
Minneapolis/St. Paul ▼ New York ▼ Los Angeles ▼ San Francisco

West's Commitment to the Environment

In 1906, West Publishing Company began recycling materials left over from the production of books. This began a tradition of efficient and responsible use of resources. Today, up to 95 percent of our legal books and 70 percent of our college texts are printed on recycled, acid-free stock. West also recycles nearly 22 million pounds of scrap paper annually—the equivalent of 181,717 trees. Since the 1960s, West has devised ways to capture and recycle waste inks, solvents, oils, and vapors created in the printing process. We also recycle plastics of all kinds, wood, glass, corrugated cardboard, and batteries, and have eliminated the use of styrofoam book packaging. We at West are proud of the longevity and the scope of our commitment to our environment.

Production, Prepress, Printing and Binding by West Publishing Company.

Copyediting: Chris Thillen
Composition: Parkwood Composition Services, Inc.
Index: Schroeder Indexing Services
Interior design: David J. Farr, Imagesmythe, Inc.

COPYRIGHT © 1983,
1987, 1990   By WEST PUBLISHING COMPANY
COPYRIGHT © 1993   By WEST PUBLISHING COMPANY
                          610 Opperman Drive
                          P.O. Box 64526
                          St. Paul, MN 55164-0526

Printed in the United States of America

00 99 98 97 96 95 94 93   8 7 6 5 4 3 2 1 0

Library of Congress Cataloging-in-Publication Data

Samaha, Joel.
    Criminal law / Joel Samaha. — 4th ed.
       p.   cm.
    Includes index.
    ISBN 0-314-00774-1 (hard)
    1. Criminal law—United States—Cases.   I. Title.
  KF9218.S26   1993
  345.73—dc20
  [347.305]
                                                        92-16021
                                             ⊗   CIP

▼ *About the Author* ▼

Professor Joel Samaha teaches Criminal Law, Criminal Procedure, and Introduction to Criminal Justice at the University of Minnesota. He is both a lawyer and a historian whose primary research interest is the history of criminal justice. He received his B.A. (1958), J.D. (1961), and Ph.D. (1972) from Northwestern University. Samaha also studied at Cambridge University, England (1969–70), while doing research for his first book, *Law and Order in Historical Perspective* (1974), a quantitative and qualitative analysis of law enforcement in pre-industrial society.

Professor Samaha was admitted to the Illinois Bar in 1962. He taught at UCLA before coming to the University of Minnesota in 1971. At the University of Minnesota, he served as chairman of the Department of Criminal Justice Studies from 1974 to 1978. Since then he has returned to teaching, research, and writing full time. He has taught both television and radio courses in criminal justice, and has co-taught a National Endowment for the Humanities seminar in legal and constitutional history. He was named Distinguished Teacher at the University of Minnesota, a coveted award, in 1974.

Professor Samaha is an active scholar. In addition to his monograph on pre-industrial law enforcement and a transcription with scholarly commentary of English criminal justice records during the reign of Elizabeth I, he has written numerous articles on the history of criminal justice, published in such scholarly journals as *Historical Journal, American Journal of Legal History, Minnesota Law Review, William Mitchell Law Review,* and *Journal of Social History.* In addition to his best-seller, *Criminal Law, Fourth Edition,* he has written two other successful textbooks, *Criminal Justice,* in press for its third edition, and *Criminal Procedure,* now in its second edition.

▼ *For My Sons and Students* ▼

▼ Contents ▼

Table of Cases **xiii**
Preface **xv**

▼ Chapter One
The Nature and Origins of Criminal Law 2

Introduction 5
The Nature of Criminal Law 7
    The Characteristics of Criminal Law **7**
    Variety of Crimes and Punishments **8**
    "Rational Criminal Law" and the Model Penal Code **9**
    The General and Special Parts of Criminal Law **10**
Sources of Criminal Law 11
    The Common-Law Origins of Criminal Law **11**
    Criminal Codes **13**
    Common Law Crimes and Modern Criminal Law **15**
    How to Read, Analyze, and Find Cases **15**
Classifying and Grading Crimes 22
    Crime, Tort, and Nonlegal Responses to Social Harms **22**
    Felony, Misdemeanor, and Violation **24**
    Wrongs *Mala in Se* and *Mala Prohibita* **24**
    Classifications According to Subject **26**
Perspectives on Crime and the Criminal Law 27
    Ideological Perspective **27**
    Irrational Forces Perspective **29**
    Historical Perspective **30**
    Ethical Core Perspective **31**
Summary 33

▼ Chapter Two
The General Principles of Criminal Law 40

Introduction 42
The Principle of Legality 43
Constitutional Limits 43
    The *Ex Post Facto* Prohibition **44**
    Void for Vagueness **44**
    Equal Protection of the Laws **49**
    The Right to Privacy **54**
    The Right to Free Speech and Expressive Conduct **61**

The Principle of Punishment 66
   Retribution **67**
   Prevention **71**
   Trends in Punishment **75**
   Proportionality **76**
Summary 83

▼ **Chapter Three**
   The General Principles of Criminal Liability 90

Introduction 92
***Actus Reus* 93**
   Status or Condition as Action **94**
   Thoughts and Action **98**
   Voluntariness **99**
   Verbal Acts **102**
   Omission **102**
   Possession **109**
   Summary of *Actus Reus* **114**
***Mens Rea* 114**
   Determining *Mens Rea* **114**
   Defining *Mens Rea* **115**
      Purpose **117**
      Knowing **119**
      Subjective and Objective Standards **121**
      Recklessness and Negligence **122**
      Strict Liability **127**
Concurrence 131
Causation 132
Grading Offenses 140
Summary 141

▼ **Chapter Four**
   Parties to Crime: The Doctrine of Complicity 146

Introduction 148
Parties to Crime 148
   Actus Reus of Parties before and during Crime **150**
   Mens Rea of Parties before and during Crime **155**
   Complicity following Crime **159**
Vicarious Liability 162
   Vicarious Liability and Business Crime **163**
   Vicarious Corporate Liability for Real Crime **169**
   Vicarious Individual Liability for Corporate Crime **170**
Summary 174

▼ **Chapter Five**
Uncompleted Crimes: Attempt, Solicitation, and Conspiracy 178

Introduction 180
Attempt 180
    Rationale of Attempt Law **182**
    Material Elements in Attempt **182**
    Attempt *Mens Rea* **183**
    Attempt *Actus Reus* **186**
    Legal and Factual Impossibility **191**
    Renunciation **202**
    Summary of Attempt **207**
Conspiracy 207
    Material Elements in Conspiracy **207**
    Conspiracy *Actus Reus* **208**
    Conspiracy *Mens Rea* **210**
    The Objective of the Conspiracy **214**
    Parties to Conspiracy **214**
    Summary of Conspiracy **220**
Solicitation 221
Summary 225

▼ **Chapter Six**
Defenses to Criminal Liability: Justifications 230

Introduction 232
Self-Defense 234
    Elements of Self-Defense **239**
    The Retreat Doctrine **247**
Defense of Others 250
General Principle of Necessity 251
Execution of Public Duties 260
Resisting Unlawful Arrest 264
Defense of Homes and Property 266
Consent 269
Summary 273

▼ **Chapter Seven**
Defenses to Criminal Liability: Excuses 278

Introduction 280
Duress 280
Intoxication 286
Mistake 290
Age 295

Entrapment 299
Insanity 302
    Right-Wrong Test **303**
    Irresistible Impulse Test **309**
    Substantial Capacity Test **311**
    Burden of Proof **313**
Diminished Capacity 319
Syndromes 322
Summary 324

▼ **Chapter Eight**
Crimes Against Persons I: Criminal Homicide 330

Introduction 332
Criminal Homicide *Actus Reus* 333
    The Beginning of Life **333**
    The End of Life **338**
Causing Another's Death 342
Criminal Homicide *Mens Rea* 345
Types and Degrees of Criminal Homicide 345
    First-Degree Murder **345**
    Felony Murder **352**
    Second-Degree Murder **358**
    Corporate Murder **361**
    Summary of Murder **364**
    Manslaughter **364**
        Voluntary Manslaughter **365**
        Involuntary Manslaughter **372**
    Negligent Homicide **376**
Summary 382

▼ **Chapter Nine**
Crimes against Persons II: Criminal Sexual Conduct, and Others 388

Introduction 390
Criminal Sexual Conduct 390
    History of Rape **391**
    The *Actus Reus* of Rape **396**
    The *Mens Rea* of Rape **404**
    Statutory Rape **405**
    Criminal Sexual Conduct with Children **408**
    Marital Rape Exception **409**
    Criminal Sexual Conduct Statutes **411**

Grading Rape **412**
Summary of Rape and Criminal Sexual Conduct **413**
Battery 413
The *Actus Reus* of Battery **414**
The *Mens Rea* of Battery **414**
The Harm in Battery **417**
Assault 418
False Imprisonment 423
Kidnapping 424
Summary 430

▼ Chapter Ten
Crimes Against Habitation: Burglary and Arson 434

Introduction 436
Burglary 436
Burglary *Actus Reus* **438**
Dwelling Requirement **442**
Burglary *Mens Rea* **447**
Grading Burglary **448**
Rationale of Burglary Law **449**
Proposed Reforms to Burglary Law **450**
Arson 451
History and Rationale **451**
Burning: The Arson *Actus Reus* **451**
Arson *Mens Rea* **453**
Property in Arson **454**
Summary of Arson **455**
Summary 455

▼ Chapter Eleven
Crimes against Property 458

Introduction 460
History of Theft 461
Larceny 462
Larceny *Actus Reus* **462**
Larceny Material Circumstances **466**
Larceny *Mens Rea* **471**
Summary of Larceny **471**
Embezzlement 471
False Pretenses 472
Consolidated Theft Statutes 476
Receiving Stolen Property 477
Forgery and Uttering 481
Forgery **482**

Uttering **484**
Robbery and Extortion 484
Robbery **485**
Degrees of Robbery **488**
Extortion **488**
Summary 491

▼ **Chapter Twelve**
Crimes against Public Order and Morals 494

Introduction 496
Crimes Against Public Order 498
Driving While Intoxicated **498**
Nuisance **505**
Coarse and Indecent Language **511**
Fighting Words **513**
Threats **519**
Group Disorderly Conduct **521**
Hate Crimes **530**
Crimes of Condition **535**
Public Morals Offenses 544
Fornication and Illicit Cohabitation **546**
Prostitution **546**
Solicitation and Promotion of Prostitution **548**
Sodomy and Related Offenses **550**
Summary 554

Appendix **559**
Glossary **563**
Index **569**

▼ *Table of Cases* ▼

The principal cases are in italic type. Cases cited or discussed in the text are roman type. References are to pages. Cases cited in principal cases and within other quoted materials are not included.

Aguillard, State v., 275
Alexander, State v., 36
Ameker, State v., 227
Anderson, People v., 385
Arnold, Rex v., 311, 328
Bailey, Rex v., 457
Baker v. Commonwealth, 227
Barber, State v., 489
Barnes v. Glen Theatre, Inc., 66
Barraza, People v., 327
Beard v. United States, 241, 275
Beasley v. State, 385
Beaudry, State v., 164
Berry, People v., 369, 385
Bishop v. State, 267
Block, State v., 498
Bonds, State v., 404, 433
Borak, People v., 393
Bowers v. Hardwick, 55, 86, 87, *551*
Brackett, People v., 134
Brawner, United States v., 327
Brent v. State, 327
Brown, State v., 270
Brown v. State, 375, 392
Brown, United States v., 208
Buck v. Bell, 86
Burley, People v., 439
Burrows v. State, 327
Buyle, People v., 439
Calder v. Bull, 86
Calley, United States v., 284
Campbell, People v., 386
Campbell v. State, 385
Cascio v. State, 433
Casey, People v., 557
Casper, State v., 144
Celli, State v., 256, 260
Chambers, People v., 439
Chaplinsky v. New Hampshire, 87, 515
Chessman, People v., 425, 429, 433
Chism, State v., 159, 160
City of (see name of city)
Clark, State v., 113
Coker v. Georgia, 87
Colavecchio, People v., 328
Commonwealth v. _____ (see opposing party)
Craig, People v., 557
Crane, State v., 385
Crenshaw, State v., 305
Crow v. State, 457
Cruz v. State, 300
Cunningham, Regina v., 143
Dabney v. State, 386
Damms, State v., 192
Davis v. Peachtree City, 176
Davis, People v., 228, 385, 440
Davis, State v., 227, 478, 481
Dawkins v. State, 113
Dennis v. United States, 87
Direct Sales Co. v. United States, 227

Dover, People v., 255, 275
Dudley and Stephens, Queen The v., 255, 275
Durham v. United States, 308, 309, 327
Edina, City of v. Dreher, 506
Ely, State v., 433
Eulo, People v., 338
Evans, People v., 397
Faulkner, Regina v., 143
Feinberg, Commonwealth v., 372
Fierro, State v., 384
Flory, State v., 386
Foster, State v., 159
Frazier v. State, 242, 275
Fulcher, State v., 429
Furr, State v., 223
Gallegos, People v., 320
Gauze, People v., 444
George v. State, 101
Gitlow v. New York, 61, 87
Gladstone, State v., 155
Goetz, People v., 235
Golston, Commonwealth v., 342, 385
Goode, State v., 275
Goodman v. State, 385
Grant, State v., 385
Gray v. State, 227
Greer, United States v., 176
Gregg v. Georgia, 385
Griswold v. Connecticut, 55, 86
Hagen, State v., 512
Hales v. Petit, 142
Hall, State v., 290, 327, 385, 439
Harmelin v. Michigan, 77
Harris, People v., 185
Harris, Regina v., 457
Harrod v. State, 423
Haupt v. United States, 143
Hauptmann, State v., 433
Henriott v. State, 500
Hernandez, People v., 405, 407
Hixson v. State, 474
Hopkins v. State, 327
Houston, City of v. Hill, 66, 516, 517, 519
Hudson, United States v., 14, 36
Hughes v. State, 110
Humphries, State v., 433
Hutto v. Davis, 78
Hyam v. Director of Public Prosecutions, 139
Iowa City v. Nolan, 169
Jackson, State v., 121
Jantzi, State v., 120
J.A.T. v. State, 414, 415
Jenkins v. State, 118
Jerrett, State v., 102
Jiminez, People v., 443
Johnson, People v., 206, 275
Jones, Commonwealth v., 486
Jones v. Commonwealth, 557
Jones v. United States, 314
Keeler v. Superior Court, 15, 16, 18
Kemp, Regina v., 327

Kennamore, State v., 275
Kibbe, People v., 138
Kimball, People v., 183
King, The v. Cogdon, 99
Kizer v. Commonwealth, 409
Koczwara, Commonwealth v., 176
Kolender v. Lawson, 86, 537
Konz, Commonwealth v., 106
Kraft, State v., 83
Krulewitch v. United States, 227
Lanzetta v. New Jersey, 45, 86
Lauria, People v., 211
Lavary, State v., 215
Le Barron v. State, 203, 205
Lewis v. City of New Orleans, 513, 557
Lewis v. State, 159
Lonschein, People ex rel. v. Warden, 86
Lynch v. State, 452
Lynch, State v., 514, 516, 518, 519
Maine v. Austin, 264
Mandujano, United States v., 227
Manning's Case, 386
Marks, State v., 119
Mast, State v., 521
Matthews v. United States, 327
Mattis v. Schnarr, 275
McDougherty, United States v., 82
McDowell, State v., 128
McFeely, State v., 37
McGraw, State v., 468
McIntosh v. State, 447
McKeiver, State v., 353, 385
McLaughlin, State v., 429
McLaughlin v. Florida, 54
Mellenberger, State v., 36
Merrill, State v., 334
Metzger, State v., 45
Michael M. v. Superior Court of Sonoma County,
    49, 50, 86
Miller, People v., 439
Miller, State v., 386, 530
Minster, State v., 342
Mlinarich, Commonwealth v., 433
M'Naghten's Case, 304, 309, 311, 327
Moe, State v., 257
Moore, United States v., 420
Moran v. People, 433
Morgan, Regina v., 404, 433
Moss v. Commonwealth, 439
Munoz, People v., 327
Musser, State v., 214
Musser v. Utah, 227
Myrick, State v., 457
Nalls v. State, 457
Nilsen, State v., 327
Noren, State v., 352, 385
O'Brien, State v., 252
O'Dell, State v., 385
O'Farrell, State v., 457
Oliver, People v., 103
Olivo, People v., 463
Ostrosky v. State, 327
Palmore v. State, 386
Papachristou v. City of Jacksonville, 79, 536, 557
Park, United States v., 170
Parsons v. State, 310, 328
Peaslee, Commonwealth v., 186
Pembletonn, Regina v., 143
Penman, People v., 326
Penry v. Lynaugh, 83
Peoni, United States v., 176
People v._____(see opposing party)
People ex rel. v._____(see opposing party
    and relator)
Perry, State v., 98
Phillips, People v., 385

Poplar, People v., 155, 176
Porter, Rex v., 303
Powell v. Texas, *95,* 290, 327
Preslar, State v., 144
Proffitt v. Florida, 385
Quarles, State v., 247
Queen v._____(see opposing party)
Randolph, State v., 407, 433
Rasinski, State v., 377
Ravin v. State, 36, 56
Reed, State v., 433
Regina v._____ (see opposing party)
Reiff, Commonwealth v., 327
Rex v._____(see opposing party)
Reynolds v. State, 432
Riedl, State v., 282
Rizzo, People v., 187, 191
Robinson v. California, 63, 88, 95, 143, 290
Rocker, State v., 117
Roe v. Wade, 86, 333, 384
Rummell v. Estelle, 80
Satterwhite v. Commonwealth, 433
Schenck v. United States, 87
Schleifer, State v., 228
Schmidt, People v., 327
Schnopps, Commonwealth v., 369, 371
Schroeder, State v., 275
Seattle, City of v. Webster, 540
Shamp, State v., 433
Sherman v. United States, 327
Sine, People, v., 439
Skinner, People v., 311, 312
Skinner, State v., 49
Snowden, State v., 347, 349
Snyder, People v., 291, 292
Solem v. Helm, *78, 79,* 80, 82, 88
Spillman, State v., 176
Stanford v. Kentucky, 83
Stanley v. Georgia, 55
Staples, People v., 207
Stasio, State v., 188, 290
State v._____(see opposing party)
Stewart, State v., 242
Strong, People v. 123
Tennessee v. Garner, 260, 261
Texas v. Johnson, 6
Thacker v. Commonwealth, 185
Thomas v. Commonwealth, 519
Thomas, People v., 3, 358, 359, 360
Thomas, United States v., 198, 199
Thompson v. City of Louisville, 509, 511
Townsend v. Commonwealth, 239
Tuzon, State v., 385
Ulvinen, State v., 151
United States v._____(see opposing party)
Wadley, Commonwealth v., 439
Walden, State v., 151
Wall, United States v., 526
Walter, Commonwealth v., 547
Warden, People ex rel. Lonschein v., 86
Warner-Lambert Co., People v., 126
Washington, People v., 371, 386
Watson, State v., 366, 368
Weathington, People v., 502
Weaver, State v., 48
Weems v. United States, 76, 77, 88
Weisengoff, State v., 385
Wesson, State v. 553
Williams, People v., 275
Williams v. State, 218
Wilson v. State, 493
Wolff, People v., 295, 298, 385
Woodson v. North Carolina, 385
Young v. New York City Transit Authority, 66,
    544
Young v. State, 188, 227

Criminal Law, broadly speaking, examines the ordinary phenomena of life under extraordinary circumstances. Who pays attention to a moving hand or the intention to move it, or the consequences of moving it, if the object is to pick up a cup of coffee? If the hand clenches into a fist and strikes a blow at another person, then the event takes on great moral and legal significance. The blow, the intention for it, and the results of it, as well as the possible justification or excuse for moving the hand that struck the blow, determine whether the person was either "wrong" in the moral sense, or committed a crime, or both. The principles of *mens rea, actus reus,* concurrence, and causation, as well as the defenses of justification and excuse, address ordinary phenomena and relationships when they violate the criminal law. The basic principles of criminal liability take into account the actions, intentions, and the relationships of life, and the consequences of them. The doctrines of criminal law bring into bold relief the role of unfinished business and teamwork in social life. The defenses to criminal liability focus on justification and excuse. Under ordinary circumstances, these phenomena go largely unnoticed.

Criminal Law, fourth edition, like the previous editions, takes a broad approach to the study of criminal law. It stresses the general principles and doctrines of criminal law, not simply the rules applicable to a single jurisdiction. The diversity of criminal law according to place and its changes over time require students to concentrate on basic principles that remain constant over wide spaces and periods of time. New developments, and variations among jurisdictions, amply demonstrate both the durability and the utility of the principles of criminal law. Like its predecessors, *Criminal Law,* fourth edition, invites students to participate actively in learning rather than passively absorbing information. It emphasizes that reasonable minds can differently interpret and apply the general principles and doctrines of criminal law. The text not only explains the principles and doctrines but also presents contrasting formulations and applications among jurisdictions, demonstrating that criminal law offers no single "right" or "wrong" application of principles and doctrines, no uniform interpretation of rules.

Cases highlight and illustrate the general principles and doctrines in the context of real life. They demonstrate how courts arrive at different conclusions, according to the courts' interpretations of the principles and the application of the principles to the particular facts of individual cases. Seeing criminal law in action stimulates students to think about, formulate, and apply the principles themselves. In the discussions and examinations in my own criminal law course, I require students to act as legislators, judges, and jurors. They must demonstrate that they understand the principles and doctrines first by formulating or stating principles, doctrines, or rules and then by applying their formulations and statements to the facts of either hypothetical or real cases. The stress upon the relationship of general principles to specific facts remains central to *Criminal Law,* fourth edition.

I have edited the cases, many new or revised for this edition, to suit the particular needs of undergraduates and other students not technically trained in law. The case excerpts remain distinct from the text, which stands on its own as a narrative. Instructors can either omit the cases from assignments or use them as examples of the principles, doctrines, and rules examined in the text. The text narrative states all the main points coherently; the cases, however, enrich and elaborate upon the text. Each case follows the discussion in text of the principle, doctrine, or rule that the case elucidates. A case question introduces each case, to focus attention on the point the case addresses. Case excerpts identify the crime charged, a brief procedural history of the case, and, if known, the sentence imposed. In the exact language of the court, the excerpt states the facts of the case, followed by the court's decision and the arguments to support the decision. A case discussion follows the case excerpt. The case discussion aims to provoke students to think about the rule, doctrine, or principle the case addresses; to evaluate the decision and arguments of the court; and, where appropriate, to propose alternative decisions and arguments.

The chapters in the text follow the traditional arrangement. The first seven chapters examine the general part of the criminal law. The general part includes the overarching principles of criminal law, the general principles of criminal liability, the doctrines of complicity and incomplete crimes, and the defenses of justification and excuse. The remaining five chapters examine the special part of the criminal law, including chapters on the crimes against persons, habitation, property, and public order and morals. Chapter 1 examines the nature and origins of American criminal law. Chapter 2 discusses the overarching principles of legality, punishment, and the constitutional limits on criminal law. Chapter 3 presents the general principles of criminal liability—*actus reus, mens rea,* concurrence, and, where relevant, causation and resulting harm. Chapters 4 and 5 examine the doctrines of complicity or parties to crime, including the law of accomplices, accessories, and vicarious liability. Chapter 5 discusses the three inchoate offenses—attempt, conspiracy, and solicitation. Chapters 6 and 7 address the defenses, that is, the principles of justification and excuse. Chapters 8 and 9 include the crimes against persons, chapter 10 the crimes against habitation, chapter 11 the crimes against property, and chapter 12 the crimes against public order and morals.

The logic of the arrangement is to treat first the principles and doctrines that apply to the specific crimes, and then to apply the general principles and doctrines to the elements of specific crimes. For just one example, chapter 3 sets out the general principles of liability; chapter 8 examines the *actus reus, mens rea,* concurrence, causation, and resulting harm to the crime of homicide. The specific crimes section begins with the most serious crime against the person, homicide, and then moves through the other serious felonies against the person to felonies against habitation and property, and ends with a discussion of some of the many misdemeanors falling under the rubric of crimes against public order and morals. However, I have written the chapters so that each can stand alone. This allows the instructor to teach criminal law in a variety of ways to suit individual tastes. For example, an instructor could begin with chapter 8, "Homicide," stressing the elements of the crime, then turn to chapter 3 to examine the general principles that the elements of homicide represent, then to chapter 5 to treat attempted murder, and then chapter 6 to examine the defense of self-defense. Another instructor might begin with the least serious offenses found in chapter 12 and move back through the chapters in order to follow a logic of least serious to most serious crimes. Some instructors focus heavily on the general part of the criminal law, using parts of the chapters on specific crimes as examples of general principles. Others stress the elements of specific crimes. *Criminal Law,* fourth edition, allows instructors to tailor the text and case excerpts to suit their individual style.

Chapter Outlines, Chapter Main Points, and Key Terms at the beginning of each chapter provide a road map for students to follow. Students tell me that they use these devices both as a guide to what to look for before they read each chapter and as a review of what they have learned after reading each chapter. **Questions for Review and Discussion** provide reinforcement to review of the main points in each chapter. The annotated **Suggested Readings** introduce the serious student to a deeper examination of the topics covered in each chapter. A completely revised **Test Bank** and **Instructor's Manual** accompany *Criminal Law,* fourth edition.

The success of the first three editions of *Criminal Law* permits me to enhance and enrich this proven general approach to the study of criminal law. *Criminal Law,* fourth edition, includes new cases, accounts for recent developments, and expands the coverage of criminal law found in previous editions. The coverage of constitutional issues in criminal law has also been expanded, including an entirely new section on the limits of the First Amendment on making speech and expressive conduct crimes. The coverage of public order and morals offenses has grown; it now includes a new section on driving while intoxicated and hate crimes, and an expanded section on group disorderly conduct.

Criminal Law, fourth edition, also contains an entirely new feature, **Note Cases.** Like the main case excerpts, these cases are real, not hypothetical. They follow the **Case Discussion** of the main case excerpts. Much briefer and often written in the author's words, the note cases show variations in the application of principles either by different interpretations given to the principles by different courts, or by variations on the facts of the main case excerpt and those of the note case. Like the main case excerpts, the purposes of the note cases include deepening the understanding of the principles of criminal law explained in the text and provoking a richer discussion of the principles.

In addition to entirely new sections and features, *Criminal Law,* fourth edition, contains about half new or re-edited cases. This edition sometimes expands the portions of court opinions included in the case excerpts where such enlargement contributes to a deeper understanding of the principles of criminal law and a richer discussion of these principles. Although in some instances slightly longer than the excerpts in previous editions, the excerpts retain their original purpose of amplifying these principles by showing their application to specific real-life cases in a form readily understandable and manageable to students not trained in law.

I have received invaluable help in improving *Criminal Law* for this fourth edition. Excellent advice, even when not always accepted, came from the remarkably thorough reviews of Kathleen J. Block, Diane M. Daane, Donald A. Downs, Richard C. Frey, Jona Goldschmidt, Louis Holscher, Robert A. Partel, and R. Bankole Thompson. *Criminal Law,* fourth edition, also benefits from the advice of reviewers of previous editions, including that generously provided by Jerry Dowling, Richard Gwen, Robert Harvie, Julius Koefoed, James Maddex, Leon Manning, William Michalek, William Pelkey, Gregory Russell, Susette Talarico, James Todd, Donald Wallace, and Wayne Wolff. Two people at West Publishing Company worked unstintingly to make *Criminal Law,* fourth edition, a better book. Poh Lin Khoo carefully produced the book, in the face of an author who too rarely and with too little patience paid heed to important details. As in every edition from the first, Mary Schiller encouraged me throughout, giving me invaluable suggestions; when necessary, she prodded me to make changes that definitely improved the book. Finally, I acknowledge a continuing debt to my students, who listened to my ideas and read all of the new material in manuscript before it reached the printed page, and who without realizing it improved the book by their enthusiasm for the study of criminal law. The strengths of the book owe much to all of the above; its shortcomings, of course, I accept as fully mine.

Joel Samaha
University of Minnesota
June 3, 1992

Chapter

1

The Nature and Origins of Criminal Law

▼ *Chapter Outline* ▼

I. Introduction

II. The Nature of Criminal Law
   A. The Characteristics of Criminal Law
   B. Variety of Crimes and Punishments
   C. "Rational Criminal Law" and the Model Penal Code
   D. The General and Special Parts of Criminal Law

III. Sources of Criminal Law
   A. The Common-Law Origins of Criminal Law
   B. Criminal Codes
   C. Common-Law Crimes and Modern Criminal Law
   D. How to Read, Analyze, and Find Cases

IV. Classifying and Grading Crimes
   A. Crime, Tort, and Nonlegal Response to Social Harms
   B. Felony, Misdemeanor, and Violation
   C. Wrongs *Mala in Se* and *Mala Prohibita*
   D. Classifications According to Subject

V. Perspectives on Crime and the Criminal Law
   A. Ideological Perspective
   B. Irrational Forces Perspective
   C. Historical Perspective
   D. Ethical Core Perspective

VI. Summary

1. Criminal law is the study of ordinary phenomena under extraordinary circumstances.

2. Criminal law is a method for reducing *some* harms to society.

3. Criminal law consists of both the extent and the limits of government power to reduce and punish *some* harmful conduct under *some* circumstances.

4. Criminal law is a list of commands applicable to everyone, the failure of which to obey carries punishment.

5. Conviction of a crime carries with it the community's formal moral condemnation.

6. In the United States, there are fifty separate state criminal codes and a federal criminal code.

7. A rational criminal law rests on general principles applicable to specific crimes, graded according to seriousness and blameworthiness, and carrying only the amount of punishment necessary to prevent and punish the crime.

8. The general part of criminal law consists of principles and doctrines that apply to all specific crimes.

9. The special part of criminal law defines specific crimes.

10. American criminal law originates in constitutions, statutes, and the common law; and in judicial opinions interpreting constitutions, statutes, and the common law.

11. Even where the common law has been abolished, its influences remain in defining statutory crimes and the defenses.

12. Crimes are classified according to several schemes—penalties, inherent "evil," and subject matter.

13. The ideological, irrational, historical, and ethical core perspectives enrich our understanding of how and why the principles, doctrines, and rules of criminal law originated.

▼ Chapter Key Terms ▼

affirm—To uphold a trial court's decision.

appellant—A party who appeals a lower court decision.

appellate court—A court that reviews decisions of trial courts.

appellee—The party appealed against.

citation—A reference to the published report of a case.

civil law—The law that deals with private rights and remedies.

collateral attack—A proceeding asking an appellate court to rule against the trial court's jurisdiction to decide a question or case.

common law—All the statutes and case law background of England and the colonies before the American Revolution, based on principles and rules that derive from usages and customs of antiquity.

common-law crimes—Crimes originating in the English common law.

concurring opinion—An opinion that joins the court's result but not its reasoning.

damages—Money awarded in civil lawsuits for injuries.

defendant—The person against whom a civil or criminal action is brought.

discretion—Freedom to decide outside of written rules.

dissent—The opinion of the minority of justices.

distinguish cases—To find that facts differ enough from those in a prior case to release judges from the precedent of the decision in that case.

felonies—Serious crimes generally punishable by one year or more in prison.

habeas corpus petition—A request for a court to review an individual's detention by a state or local government.

holding—The legal principle or rule that a case enunciates.

information—A document drawn up by a prosecutor formally charging a suspect with a crime.

jurisdiction—Territory or subject matter under the control of a government body.

majority opinion—The opinion of the majority of justices.

malum prohibitum—A crime not inherently bad.

malum in se—A crime inherently bad.

misdemeanor—A minor crime for which the penalty is usually less than one year in jail or a fine.

Model Penal Code—The code developed by the American Law Institute to guide reform in criminal law.

opinion—The holding and/or reasoning of a court.

plaintiff—The person who sues another party in a civil action.

plurality opinion—An opinion that announces the result of the case but whose reasoning does not command a majority of the court.

precedent—Prior court decisions that guide judges in deciding future cases.

reasoning—The reasons a court gives to support its holding.

remand—To send a case back to a trial court for further proceedings consistent with the reviewing court's decision.

reverse—To set aside the decision of the trial court.

stare decisis—The principle that binds courts to stand by prior decisions and to not disturb settled points of law.

statutes—Rules or doctrines enacted by legislatures.

tort—A legal wrong for which the injured party may sue the injuring party.

violation—A minor legal infraction subject to a small fine.

writ of prohibition—An order from an appellate court to a lower court ordering it to cease proceedings until the appellate court can resolve a matter not within the lower court's authority.

▼ INTRODUCTION

Pick up your pen and take notes during a lecture; enjoy the company of your friends at a rock concert; explain to your professor that you missed class because you took an accident victim to the hospital—phenomena so common that you hardly give them a thought. However, change the circumstances and these same phenomena will interest you greatly. "Depend on it, when a man knows he is going to be hanged, it concentrates his mind wonderfully," wrote the famous eighteenth-century English essayist Samuel Johnson. Pick up a gun and shoot your enemy; join together with cohorts and rob a bank; explain that you shot an intruder who attacked you in your home. Then the phenomena take on immense significance. Criminal law examines the ordinary phenomena of action, intention, relationships, justifications, and excuses under the extraordinary circumstances that define them as crimes and determines their seriousness and the sanctions they receive. These concepts under the variety of extraordinary circumstances in which they occur will provide you with a fascinating and challenging opportunity to concentrate *your* minds wonderfully.[1]

Consider the ordinary phenomena and the extraordinary circumstances under which they occurred in the following cases. Without drawing on any specific knowledge you may have about actual criminal law, what phenomena and circumstances do you think ought to make the actors guilty of crimes? Rank the examples from most to least serious. For those hypothetical cases that you believe do not describe crimes, do you think the state should take *some* action? What kind? Should the law allow the "victims" to sue the person who injured them? What should be the outcome of such lawsuits? Do some actors deserve condemnation by families and friends, even though they have not committed crimes and are not subject to other state intervention or private lawsuits? Do any deserve no sanction? Do any deserve praise or other reward? Can you state specifically why you answered the questions the way you did?

1. Sheila hates Rosemary because Rosemary is rich, charming, and beautiful, but most of all because she is more intelligent, aggressive, and successful than Sheila. Sheila reaches the breaking point in her long, controlled hostility when a prestigious medical school accepts Rosemary, while the law school at the same university rejects Sheila. Enraged, Sheila decides to murder Rosemary. Sheila carefully awaits the appropriate time and gets her chance when Rosemary invites Sheila to a celebration party. Sheila takes a deadly drug from the medical center where she works, conceals it in her pocket, and puts it in Rosemary's drink. Then she watches with immense pleasure as Rosemary writhes in pain and dies a slow, agonizing death.

2. Tom's wife suffers excruciating pain from what the doctors say is terminal bone cancer. The family has exhausted its insurance coverage and savings in order to keep her alive. For the past few weeks now, every time Tom sees his wife, she pleads, "Tom, please put me out of my misery. I can't take this anymore." Tom loves his wife dearly and cannot bear her pain. An avid hunter, he takes one of his guns and shoots her in the head, killing her instantly.

3. Driving down an icy city street, David accelerates rapidly as he approaches a particularly slick spot, hoping for the thrill of feeling the car spinout. As it does, David sees a pedestrian, a frail ninety-year-old man, crossing the street in front of him. He tries to swerve away but cannot. He hits the old man, seriously injuring him. "Oh, my God!" cries David. "This is the last thing I wanted to happen." Two days later, while still in the hospital for treatment of his injuries, the man dies of a heart attack.

4. Kim is drowning in a lake. Steve, his lifelong enemy, sees Kim struggling but walks on, laughing at the thought of getting Kim out of the way. Kim drowns.

5. Every night when he gets home from work, Marty watches hard-core child pornography videos. He finds them highly erotic, especially when they involve sex between older guys like Marty and very young girls, particularly those under twelve years. After getting his "release," he usually falls into a deep sleep until time to get up for work the next morning.

6. Michael really likes women and is a demonstrative person. He goes into a singles' bar where he is immediately drawn to Theresa. Michael puts his arm around her waist and introduces himself. Theresa, offended by a stranger touching her, says firmly, "Stop that!" Michael does not remove his arm, saying, "Don't be such a prude, I'm just trying to be friendly."

7. Adam sees a radio in a department store that he wants. When the clerk walks away, Adam takes the radio. His friend Steve watches Adam take the radio. Outside the store, Steve says, "That was really good work Adam; I always enjoy a good rip-off."

8. Bill is addicted to cocaine.

9. Jessica smokes marijuana on weekends.

10. Kristen hates men and takes advantage of any opportunity to destroy them. She focuses on Lucas, presently vulnerable because he has just broken up with Allison. As soon as she succeeds in getting Luke to fall in love with her, Kristen rejects him, revealing how he was merely a foil to express her hate for men. Broken-hearted and thoroughly distraught, Luke loses his highly successful video business, goes bankrupt, acquires enormous medical bills for treatment of a nervous breakdown, and ends up an alcoholic.

11. A major pharmaceutical corporation introduced to the U.S. market a drug used to treat hypertension. The company knew the drug had been reported to cause death and liver damage in French patients. The corporation labeled the product saying that no cause-and-effect relationship existed between the drug and liver damage. After the drug was linked to thirty-six deaths and more than five hundred cases of liver and kidney damage, the corporation withdrew the drug from the market.

12. Hilary, a gynecologist, recommends a hysterectomy for Jane, who suffers from back pains. After the surgery, the pain continues. Another doctor discovers that the source of Jane's pain is her left leg being shorter than her right leg. He recommends platform shoes, and Jane's pain disappears.

13. John, a respected surgeon in a major hospital, refuses to take an AIDS test.

14. Sonya burns the American flag while chanting, "I hate America."

15. Jane, a respected black professor, allows only black women to enroll in her class in a private college. She believes whites are inferior and will corrupt black students. She maintains that black men have had too many advantages, and now it's time to let black women have some.

16. Kevin dances nude in a local tavern. A sign outside the bar reads: "All male strippers. Adults welcome."

▼ THE NATURE OF CRIMINAL LAW

Murder, rape, robbery, burglary, child abuse, cancer, unemployment, poor productivity, illiteracy, poverty, misleading advertising, cheating, lying, mistreatment of friends, and rejection of lovers all harm both individual victims and society as a whole. Society relies on both private and public mechanisms to reduce these harms. The methods include moral and ethical standards, education, private and public aid, government regulation, private lawsuits, and criminal law. In the broadest sense, all law, including criminal law, is a method or process—"a way of doing things"—to secure compliance with community standards. Criminal law is not a tool for building either a perfect society or a society free of crime. Rather, it aims to establish minimum standards and optimum compliance with those standards.[2]

The law of private wrongs, usually called personal injury law, or **torts,** focuses on lawsuits in which one person sues another to recover money. Criminal law centers on the government's power to define, prosecute, and punish crime. Criminal law is the harshest, most cumbersome, and most expensive social control mechanism. These qualities limit the use of criminal law as a tool for social control; it is a last resort in the effort to prevent, prohibit, and punish social harms. Remember this limit as you study criminal law.

The Characteristics of Criminal Law

Criminal law consists of the power of government to prevent and punish some, but not all, harmful conduct under some, but not all, circumstances. The interests of economy, effectiveness, and individual autonomy limit that power, however. The study of criminal law therefore examines both the extent and the limits of government power.

In addition to this general character, criminal law has six fundamental characteristics: (1) It is a list of commands, of dos and don'ts telling citizens what they must do or refrain from doing. Common don'ts include "Do not murder, rape, rob, steal, panhandle, fornicate outside marriage, or urinate in public." Common dos include "Pay your taxes, support your children, report child abuse." (2) These commands are formally enacted into and established by law. Only commands enacted by legislatures or established in the common law (see text following) qualify as crimes. (3) The law prescribes a punishment to accompany the crime. Crimes are not bare commands; failure to obey them carries legally defined painful consequences. (4) Once enacted or established, these dos and don'ts apply to everyone within the **jurisdiction,** or territory under the authority of the body that enacted or established the crime. The commands, therefore, "speak to [all] members of the community ... in the community's behalf, with all the power and prestige of the community behind them." (5) Crimes constitute injuries both to individual victims and to society generally. A mugging injures not only its immediate victim, it puts the whole community in fear; forgery cheats not only the object of the forgery, it undermines public confidence in a variety of transactions necessary to life in modern society.[3]

These five characteristics are not peculiar to criminal law. They also describe **civil law,** or the law concerned with private rights and remedies, especially the law of contracts, property, and torts. Civil law operates by commands enacted and established. Complex laws govern contracts, property rights, and torts. Unpleasant consequences befall losers in private lawsuits: they have to pay money, perform duties, or give up employment. Society also has an interest in seeing contracts performed, in protecting the rights of property, and in preventing personal injuries covered by tort law.

Criminal law, however, possesses a sixth characteristic, one that all other branches of law lack. (6) Conviction of crime carries with it the community's formal moral condemnation.

> The essence ... lies in the criminal conviction itself. One may lose more money on the stock market than in a court-room; a prisoner of war camp may well provide a harsher environment than a state prison; death on the field of battle has the same characteristics as death by sentence of law. It is the expression of the community's hatred, fear, or contempt for the convict which alone characterizes physical hardship as punishment.[4]

Variety of Crimes and Punishments

Throughout this book, you will frequently see the term *criminal law* in the singular. This is not strictly accurate. An outstanding characteristic of American criminal law is its variety. There are fifty state criminal codes, a federal criminal code, and innumerable city ordinances containing myriad violations. The use of the term *criminal law* in the singular refers to the similarities in most state codes. They all include the most serious crimes—murder, rape, robbery, burglary, arson, theft, and assault. They all allow the most common defenses—self-defense and insanity. And they all punish serious crimes by imprisonment. However, they define differently the conduct crimes encompass. For example, in some jurisdictions, burglary requires actual unlawful breaking and entering; in others, it requires only entering without breaking; and in still others, it requires merely unlawfully remaining in a building entered lawfully, such as hiding until after closing time in a department store restroom lawfully entered during business hours (see chapter 10 on burglary).

The defenses to crime also vary across state lines. In some states, insanity may require proof *both* that defendants did not know what they were doing and that they did not know that it was wrong to do it. In other states, it suffices to prove *either* that defendants did not know what they were doing *or* that they did not know that it was wrong. Some states permit using deadly force to protect homes from intruders; others require proof that the occupants in the home were in danger of serious bodily harm or death before occupants can shoot intruders (see chapter 6 on deadly force).

Criminal penalties also differ widely among jurisdictions. Several states prescribe death for some convicted murderers; others, life imprisonment. Hence, where murderers kill determines whether those murderers will live or die. It also determines how they will die: by electrocution, lethal injection, the gas chamber, hanging, or even the firing squad.

The death penalty is only the most dramatic example of disparate penalties, and it affects only a few individuals. Other less dramatic examples affect far more people. Some states subject those who engage in "open and notorious" sexual intercourse to fines; others make the mere fact of cohabitation outside marriage punishable by three to five years' imprisonment. Some states imprison individuals who possess small quantities of marijuana; others protect private marijuana use as a constitutional right.[5]

These disparities in crime and punishment among jurisdictions stem from several sources having to do with the type of community, the period in time, and the social problems of particular localities. In Texas, for example, stealing property valued between $750 and $20,000 is a third-degree felony. It is also a third-degree felony theft to steal crude petroleum oil "regardless of the value"[6] (see chapter 11 on crimes against property).

"Rational Criminal Law" and the Model Penal Code

The phrase "rational criminal law" appears frequently in this text. It refers to a criminal law limited by four criteria: (1) it is based on general principles and doctrines, not on the discretion and personal philosophies of legislators and judges; (2) these general principles apply to all specific crimes; (3) it grades punishment according to the seriousness of the harm and the blameworthiness of the conduct; and (4) it prescribes no greater penalty than punishment and prevention require.

A rational criminal law emphasizes criminal law as a limited method, a method of last resort. If informal private sanctions secure compliance, criminal law has no role to play. If informal sanctions fail and civil actions can secure compliance, then criminal law should not apply. If civil actions fail and criminal law becomes necessary to obtain social ends, and if a lesser penalty will punish and prevent crime as effectively as a greater penalty, then a rational criminal law relies on the lesser penalty. Rational criminal law rests on values of individual autonomy and economy. Government should intervene in human actions only when absolutely necessary and should expend no more money and power than is required to obtain social goals embodied in the prevention and punishment of antisocial conduct.[7]

The American Law Institute's **Model Penal Code** has greatly advanced the pursuit of a rational criminal code. The American Law Institute (ALI) is a private association whose membership includes eminent lawyers, judges, and professors. Founded in 1923, it works to clarify and improve the law. In 1950, with Rockefeller Foundation aid, it undertook a major effort to guide reform in American criminal law. The ALI created a large advisory committee drawn from all disciplines concerned with criminal justice and charged it with drafting a model penal code. For ten years, these specialists met and drafted, redrafted, and finally in 1961 completed the *Model Penal Code and Commentaries,* a learned and influential document.[8]

As its title indicates, the code is a model to guide actual legislation. Jurisdictions vary in which specific provisions meet their needs. By 1980 and 1985, when the ALI published an updated code and commentary, thirty-four states had enacted widespread criminal law revision and codification based on its provisions; fifteen hundred courts had cited its provisions and referred to its commentary. The Model Penal Code fulfills the criteria outlined earlier for a rational criminal code, but it is not the final word on the subject. When you encounter its provisions in the text, feel free to disagree with it; when you do disagree, devise your own scheme for a rational criminal law.

The General and Special Parts of Criminal Law

Criminal law is divided into a general part and a special part. The general part covers the general principles and doctrines that apply to all crimes. The principles relate to legality, punishment, and the requirements for criminal liability (see chapters 2 and 3). The doctrines refer to tenets that may apply to all crimes, but are not necessarily present in all cases. The doctrines include liability for complicity, such as that exhibited by accomplices and accessories (chapter 4); liability for uncompleted crimes, such as attempt and conspiracy (chapter 5); and the defenses to criminal liability, such as insanity and self-defense (chapters 6 and 7).[9]

The special part of criminal law defines the specific crimes—murder, rape, robbery, theft, and disturbing the peace, for example (see chapters 8 through 12). These definitions must agree with the principles and, where relevant, the doctrines in the general part. For example, the general principle *actus reus* bases criminal liability on action—on what people do, not on what they think or who they are. The acts defined in specific crimes apply this general principle, such as the act of killing in the crime of murder, breaking and entering in burglary, taking another's property in theft. Similarly, criminal liability, at least for serious crimes, requires a *mens rea,* or a mental element. Particular crimes have individual mental element requirements, such as the intent to kill in the crime of murder, to permanently deprive another of property in theft, and to take property by fear or force in robbery.

▼ SOURCES OF CRIMINAL LAW

The United States Constitution created a complex structure in order to balance the need for government power to control the governed with the restraints on that power intended to oblige government to control itself. According to James Madison, the great eighteenth-century American political theorist:

> If men were angels, no government would be necessary. If angels were to govern men, neither external nor internal controls on government would be necessary. In framing a government which is to be administered by men over men, the great difficulty is this: You must first enable the government to control the governed; and in the next place, oblige it to control itself.[10]

This complex structure complicates the study of criminal law. It separates legislative, judicial, and executive powers, and it divides power between federal and state governments. State constitutions, in turn, devolve the power to enact ordinances to municipalities within their borders.

Criminal law stems from federal and state constitutions, federal and state criminal codes, municipal ordinances, the common law derived from England prior to the Revolution, and judicial decisions interpreting and applying the common law and statutes. Treason is the only specific crime defined in constitutions. The federal criminal code, enacted by the United States Congress, includes all the offenses against the United States government. Municipal ordinances include long lists of minor violations, such as traffic offenses, and a wide range of misbehavior in parks, on public transportation, and other public places.

The bulk of criminal law originates in the separate criminal codes of the fifty states. Most of the law you will read about in this book appears in the judicial decisions that interpret and apply the crimes defined in these state codes.

The Common-Law Origins of Criminal Law

State criminal codes did not spring full grown from state legislatures. They derived from a long history of offenses called the **common-law crimes,** crimes that originated in the ancient customs transformed by the English common-law courts into written law in their judicial decisions. We are used to legislatures creating crimes, but this was not always so. Before legislatures existed, social order depended on obedience to unwritten rules—the *lex non scripta*—based on local community customs and mores. These traditions were passed on from generation to generation, and altered from time to time in order to meet changed conditions. In England, from which American law descended, these unwritten rules were eventually incorporated into court decisions. These incorporated traditions became the **common law.**

The 18th century English jurist Sir William Blackstone, whose *Commentaries on the Laws and Customs of England* was the only law book most American lawyers read until well into the nineteenth century, described the common law as follows:

As to general customs, or the common law, properly so called, this is that law, by which proceedings and determinations in the king's ordinary courts of justice are guided and directed. This, for the most part, settles ... the several species of temporal offenses, with the manner and degree of punishment ...; [A]ll these are doctrines that are not set down in any written statute or ordinance, but depend merely upon immemorial usage, that is, upon the common law, for their support.[11]

By the seventeenth century, the courts had created a substantial list of common-law felonies and misdemeanors. Most have familiar names today, and many have retained the core of their original meaning, although most have adapted to meet modern conditions. The common-law felonies included murder, suicide, manslaughter, burglary, arson, robbery, larceny, rape, sodomy, and mayhem. The common-law misdemeanors included (and in some jurisdictions still include) assault, battery, false imprisonment, libel, perjury, corrupting morals, and disturbing the peace.[12]

Exactly how it began lies shrouded in obscurity, but like the traditions it incorporated, the common law grew and changed to meet new conditions. At first, its growth depended mainly on judicial decisions. The courts formulated basic principles, rules, and standards based on the common law. They considered these the law of the land. Judges felt bound to follow these common-law principles, standards, and rules, and interpreted new cases according to them. As judges decided more cases according to them, the law became more elaborate and complete. These prior decisions they called **precedent.** They devised the principle of *stare decisis* that bound them to follow precedents established in prior court decisions. The late Supreme Court Justice, Benjamin Cardozo, in a lecture about precedent and *stare decisis,* explained why he relied on prior scholars' work in preparing his lecture. In doing so, he also explained precedent itself.

It is easier to follow the beaten track than it is to clear another. In doing this, I shall be treading in the footsteps of my predecessors, and illustrating the process that I am seeking to describe, since the power of precedent, when analyzed, is the power of the beaten path.[13]

You will realize the importance of precedent and *stare decisis* in the cases excerpted throughout this book. Court opinions contain many references to prior cases, relying on them to decide the case under review. Sometimes, an opinion expresses regret about a decision, but explains that prior decisions—precedent and *stare decisis*—bind the court to follow the prior cases. *Stare decisis* does not prevent courts from *ever* changing precedent. Courts **distinguish cases;** that is, they decide, or "find" that the prior case is not similar enough to bind the present court to its decision. Precedent binds courts only in cases with similar facts. For example, a court might find the battered woman syndrome relevant in a case where a battered wife kills her husband following his threats to kill her while he is lying on his bed awake. But the court might find otherwise if the battered wife kills him while he is asleep. This the court calls distinguishing the case "on its facts," or limiting a holding to the facts of the prior case (see chapter 6 on self-defense).

Courts can also overrule precedent, although they do it rarely and reluctantly. If a court finds that a prior court decided a case wrongly, it can overrule the precedent. In one case, a court had earlier ruled that a defendant who obtained money by false pretenses had this defense: the victim was also engaged in crime. Later, it reconsidered its decision. Most jurisdictions did not allow the defense of criminality of the victim, and in any event it is a bad rule to allow one wrongdoer to escape punishment simply because the victim was also engaged in wrongdoing. That court overruled its precedent and denied the defense.[14]

As legislatures became more established, **statutes** were added to the common law, partly to clarify existing common law, partly to fill in blanks left by the common law, and partly to adjust the common law to new conditions. Court decisions interpreted these statutes according to common-law principles and past decisions. These judicial decisions interpreting the statutes became part of the growing body of precedent making up the common law.

The English colonists brought this common law with them to the New World, and incorporated the common-law crimes into their legal systems. Following the American Revolution, the thirteen original states, in turn, incorporated the common law into their new state legal systems. Virtually every new state after that enacted "reception statutes," adopting or receiving the English common law. The Florida statute, for example, reads:

> The Common Law of England in relation to crimes ... shall be of full force in this state where there is no existing provision by statute on the subject.[15]

Criminal Codes

Periodically, reformers have called for abolishing the common law in America. The first such effort appeared in 1648, the work of the first generation of English Puritans to arrive in New England. *The Laws and Liberties of Massachusetts* codified the criminal law, defining crimes and prescribing punishments. The authors put their case for a code:

> So soon as God had set up political government among his people Israel he gave them a body of laws for judgment in civil and criminal causes.... For a commonwealth without laws is like a ship without rigging and steerage.[16]

Although the code included offenses, some capital, that sound odd in today's world (witchcraft, cursing parents, blasphemy, idolatry, and adultery), others, such as rape—

> If any man shall ravish any maid or single woman, committing carnal copulation with her by force, against her own will, that is above ten years of age he shall be punished either with death or some other grievous punishment—

and murder—

> If any man shall commit any wilful murder, which is manslaughter, committed upon premeditate malice, hatred, or cruelty not in a man's necessary and just defense, nor by mere casualty against his will, he shall be put to death—

do not strike us as all that strange or out of place.[17]

Hostility to English institutions following the American Revolution led reformers to call again for codes to replace the "English" common law. The eighteenth-century Enlightenment, with its emphasis on natural law and order, inspired reformers to put aside the piecemeal, common law scattered throughout judicial decisions, and to replace it with criminal codes that implemented the natural law of crimes. Despite anti-British feeling, Blackstone's *Commentaries* remained popular with reformers who hoped to transform Blackstone's complete and orderly outline of criminal law into criminal codes.

Reformers contended that judge-made law was not only disorderly and incomplete but also antidemocratic. They maintained that legislatures, which they believed reflected the popular will, should make laws, not aloof judges out of touch with public opinion. Thomas Jefferson proposed a reformation of Virginia's penal code that reflected these influences. The Proposed Virginia Code never passed the Virginia legislature, not because it codified the law but because it recommended too many drastic reductions in criminal punishments.[18]

Reformers' fears of judicial oppression seemed realized when a federal court in Connecticut attempted to create a new common law of libel early in the nineteenth century. The defendants were indicted for

> a libel against the President and Congress of the United States, contained in the Connecticut Courant of 7th May, 1806, charging them with having in secret voted $2,000,000 as a present to Bonaparte, for leave to make a treaty with Spain.

No statute made such conduct an offense. In *United States v. Hudson and Goodwin,* the United States Supreme Court only partially alleviated reformers' fear of judge-made law. The Court denied the *federal* courts the power to create common-law crimes. The Supreme Court held that federal courts were not

> vested with jurisdiction over any particular act done by an individual in supposed violation of the peace and dignity of the sovereign power. The legislative authority of the Union must first make an act a crime, affix a punishment to it, and declare the court that shall have jurisdiction over the offense.

However, *United States v. Hudson and Goodwin* did not prohibit *state* courts from creating common-law crimes.[19]

The codification movement had an uneven history, but the concept of common-law crimes retreated throughout the nineteenth century. During the twentieth century, the codification movement strengthened. The American Law Institute supported codification, and the earliest drafts of the Model Penal Code abolished common-law crimes:

> § 1.05 All Offenses Defined by Statute. (1) No conduct constitutes an offense unless it is a crime or violation under this Code or another statute of this State.

Common Law Crimes and Modern Criminal Law

Since the American Law Institute adopted § 1.05, twenty-five states have abolished the common-law crimes and ten others have proposed to do so. Several states, however, still recognize the common law of crimes: Florida, Idaho, Mississippi, New Mexico, North Carolina, Rhode Island, and Washington. Others do so at least in part: Connecticut, Nevada, Virginia, and possibly Oregon.[20]

Abolishing the common-law crimes does not render the common law irrelevant. Most states that have abolished common-law offenses (these states are called code jurisdictions) retain the common-law defenses, such as self-defense and insanity. Furthermore, statutes frequently contain the terms murder, manslaughter, robbery, burglary, rape, and assault without defining them, and courts turn to the common law to determine the meanings of those terms. For example, the 1975 Alabama Criminal Code provides as follows:

> Any person who commits ... voluntary manslaughter, shall be guilty of a felony. Voluntary manslaughter is punishable as a Class 5 felony.[21]

California, a code state, included the common-law felonies in that code. The California Supreme Court reviewed the common law to determine the meaning of its murder statute in *Keeler v. Superior Court,* which is excerpted in this chapter. First, however, you need some guidance in reading *Keeler* and the other case excerpts that appear throughout the book.

How to Read, Analyze, and Find Cases

Cases bring the criminal law to life; they involve real people accused of actual crimes. In the cases, courts apply the abstract general principles, doctrines, and rules to events in real life. Cases give practical effect to abstract propositions. Notice that the cases in this book are excerpts, that is, edited versions of the printed reports of the cases. You can tell where I have deleted material by the ellipses (... or ....); material I have added is in brackets ([ ]).

In most cases that you will read, a jury (or in cases without juries, the trial court judge) has already convicted the accused. The convicted defendant has asked a higher court to review the trial court's decision and/or the jury's guilty verdict. (See Figure 1.1 on p. 16.) Notice that you will never read a review of a jury's "not guilty" verdict. In American criminal law, a jury's acquittal is final and not subject to review.

The review of criminal convictions takes several forms. Convicted defendants may ask the trial court for a new trial. If this fails, they may appeal a trial court's decision directly to an **appellate court** (in most cases a state supreme court) but sometimes to an intermediate appellate court. These appeals are called appellate cases, those who appeal them are called **appellants,** and parties appealed against are called **appellees.** Convicted defendants are most often appellants in criminal cases. Convicted defendants may challenge the trial court's jurisdiction, or the legality of a

▼ **Figure 1.1** ▼
Criminal Court Structure

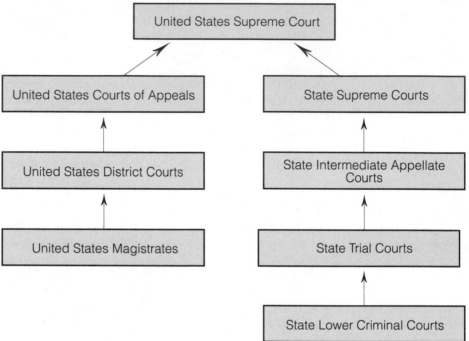

detention in state prisons, by a procedure called **collateral attack.** The most widely known among the public, although not the only mechanism of collateral attack, is the **habeas corpus petition.** In this petition, prisoners ask for a court order demanding that the agency detaining the prisoner demonstrate that the agency has lawfully detained the prisoner. Most case excerpts in this book are appellate cases in which convicted defendants are appellants and states are appellees. Defendants have appealed their convictions; they are asking appellate courts to overturn, or reverse, their convictions.

The case excerpts focus on the principles, doctrines, and rules of criminal law. You should read them with that in mind, asking yourself as you read, what principle, doctrine, or rule does this case elucidate and apply, and to what specific relevant facts does the principle, doctrine, or rule apply?

The case excerpts begin with the title of the case and its **citation,** the reference to the published report where it appears in full. The name of the judge who wrote the court's opinion follows. Then appear the facts of the case, the critical beginning point for understanding the principles, doctrines, and rules at issue. Finally, the court's opinion appears. The opinion contains two essential ingredients: (1) the court's **holding**—the legal rule that the case enunciates; and (2) the court's **reasoning**—the reasons it gives to support its holding. Occasionally, such as in *Keeler,* both a **majority opinion** and a **dissent,** or minority opinion, appear. A majority opinion, as its name indicates, represents the majority of the justices on the court. For an opinion to become law, a majority of justices must vote for it. Although the majority opinion constitutes the law of the case, the dissent usually presents a plausible alternative resolution to the question of the case.

Dissents of former times frequently become the law of later times. In criminal procedure law, for example, many dissents of the 1960s have become the law of the 1990s, and before that the dissents of the 1930s became the law of the 1960s. Occasionally, most always in the United States Supreme Court, **concurring opinions** appear. In concurring opinions, justices agree with the judgment of the court but not the reasons. This can lead to a **plurality opinion,** an opinion in which a majority stands behind the result in the case, but a majority cannot agree on the reasons for the result.

To get the most from the cases, concentrate on answering the following questions about each case excerpt:

1. What are the facts? To determine the facts relevant for the purposes of the principles, doctrines, and rules of criminal law, answer these questions:
    a. What, if anything, did the defendant do?
    b. What, if anything, did the defendant intend to do?
    c. What harm, if any, befell the victim?
    d. If harm resulted from the defendant's actions, did the actions cause the harm?
    e. Did the defendant have a justification or excuse?
2. What is the legal issue in the case? That is, what question or problem regarding the principles, doctrines, and rules of criminal law does the case raise?
3. What is the court's holding? In other words, what answer does the court give to the problem raised in the case?
4. What is the court's **opinion,** that is, what reasons does the court give for its decision and holdings? How did it arrive at the conclusions it reached? The court's reasoning, or opinion, applies the general principle, doctrine, and rule to the facts of the case.
5. Did the court **affirm** (agree with and uphold) the trial court's decision, or **reverse** it (set it aside and substitute its own decision), reverse it in part (partially reverse and partially affirm it), or **remand** it (send the case back to the trial court for further proceedings in accord with the appellate opinion)?

You cannot answer all these questions in every case, especially at this point. The answers depend on knowledge you will accumulate as the text introduces new principles, doctrines, and rules. Furthermore, courts do not follow the same order the questions do. Finally, not all the questions just asked in item 1 arise in every case.

Developing the skills needed to sort out the elements of the case excerpts requires practice, but is worth the effort. Answering the questions given here can challenge you to think not only about the basic principles, doctrines, and rules of criminal law, but also about your values concerning life, property, privacy, and morals.

For those who wish to go further and read the full cases excerpted in the text, or who wish to read cases referred to in the text or the cases, I have included the case citation. You will notice that numbers, letters, and punctuation follow the title of a case in the excerpts, or in the endnote referencing cases in the text. These symbols tell you where to locate the full case report.

For example, in the first excerpt that follows this section, just after the title of the case, *Keeler v. Superior Court,* you read "87 Cal.Rptr. 481, 470 P.2d 617 (Cal.1970)." This means you can find this case reported in two places, the *California Reporter* (Cal. Rptr.) and the *Pacific Reports, second series* (P.2d). These are multivolume sets that report the appellate cases in California. The *California Reporter,* as the name indicates, reports only California appellate cases. The *Pacific Reports* report cases for a region. The number *preceding* the title indicates in which volume of the reports the case appears. *Keeler* appears in volume 87 of the *California Reporter* and in volume 470 of the *Pacific Reports, second series.* The number *following* the title of the reports indicates on which page of the volume the case appears. *Keeler* appears on page 481, volume 87 of the *California Reporter* and on page 617 of volume 470 of the *Pacific Reports, second series.* The symbols inside the parentheses include the state court opinion reported and the year the court issued its opinion. Hence, the California Supreme Court decided *Keeler v. Superior Court* in 1970. You can tell if the court was the highest or an intermediate appellate court by the abbreviation. For example, if this were a Minnesota Court of Appeals case, the abbreviation would read, "Minn.App."

CASE

Did He "Murder" the Fetus?

Keeler v. Superior Court
87 Cal.Rptr. 481, 470 P.2d 617 (Cal.1970)

Mosk, Justice

FACTS
Petitioner and Teresa Keeler obtained an interlocutory decree of divorce on September 27, 1968. They had been married for 16 years. Unknown to petitioner, Mrs. Keeler was then pregnant by one Ernest Vogt, whom she had met earlier that summer. She subsequently began living with Vogt in Stockton, but concealed the fact from petitioner. Petitioner was given custody of their two daughters, aged 12 and 13 years, and under the decree Mrs. Keeler had the right to take the girls on alternate weekends.

On February 23, 1969, Mrs. Keeler was driving on a narrow mountain road in Amador County after delivering the girls to their home. She met petitioner driving in the opposite direction; he blocked the road with his car, and she pulled over to the side. He walked to her vehicle and began speaking to her. He seemed calm, and she rolled down her window to hear him. He said, "I hear you're pregnant. If you are you had better stay away from the girls and from here." She did not reply, and he opened the car door; as she later testified, "He assisted me out of the car.... (I)t wasn't roughly at this time." Petitioner then looked at her abdomen and became "extremely upset." He said, "You sure are. I'm going to stomp it out of you." He pushed her against the car, shoved his knee into her abdomen, and struck her in the face with several blows. She fainted, and when she regained consciousness petitioner had departed.

Mrs. Keeler drove back to Stockton, and the police and medical assistance were summoned. She had suffered substantial facial injuries, as well as extensive bruising of the abdominal wall. A Caesarian section was performed and the fetus was examined in utero. Its head was found to be severely fractured, and it was delivered still-born.... Both Mrs. Keeler and her obstetrician testified that fetal movements had been observed prior to February 23, 1969.... The expert testimony ... concluded "with reasonable medical certainty" that the fetus had developed to the stage of viability, i.e., that in the event of premature birth on the date in question it would have had a 75 percent to 96 percent chance of survival.

An **information** [a formal charge drawn up by the prosecutor] was filed charging petitioner ... with committing the crime of murder in that he did "unlawfully kill a human being, to wit Baby Girl Vogt, with malice aforethought."... His motion to set aside the information for lack of probable cause was denied, and he now seeks a **writ of prohibition** [an order from an appellate court to a lower court ordering it to cease proceedings until the appellate court can resolve a matter not within the lower court's authority] ... Pending our disposition of the matter, petitioner is free on bail.

OPINION

I

Penal Code § 187 provides: "Murder is the unlawful killing of a human being, with malice aforethought." The dispositive question is whether the fetus which petitioner is accused of killing was, on February 23, 1969, a "human being" within the meaning of this statute.... We therefore undertake a brief review of the origins and development of the common law of abortional homicide.... From that inquiry it appears that by the year 1850—the date with which we are concerned—an infant could not be the subject of homicide at common law unless it had been born alive.... Perhaps the most influential statement of the "born alive" rule is that of Coke, in mid-17th century: "If a woman be quick with childe and by a potion or otherwise killeth it in her wombe, or if a man beat her, whereby the childe dyeth in her body, and she is delivered of a dead childe, this is a great misprision (i.e., misdemeanor), and no murder; but if the childe be born alive and dyeth of the potion, battery, or other cause, this is murder; for in law it is accounted a reasonable creature ... when it is born alive." (3 Coke, Institutes 58 (1648) ...

We hold that in adopting the definition of murder in Penal Code § 187 the Legislature intended to exclude from its reach the act of killing an unborn fetus.

II

The People urge, however, that the sciences of obstetrics and pediatrics have greatly progressed since 1872, to the point where with proper medical care a normally developed fetus prematurely born at 28 weeks or more has an excellent chance of survival, i.e., is "viable"; that the common law requirement of live birth to prove the fetus had become a "human being" who may be the victim of murder is no longer in accord with scientific fact, since an unborn but viable fetus is now fully capable of independent life; and that one who unlawfully and maliciously terminates such a life should therefore be liable to prosecution for murder under § 187.

We may grant the premises of this argument; indeed, we neither deny nor denigrate the vast progress of medicine in the century since the enactment of the Penal Code. But we cannot join in the conclusion sought to be deduced: we cannot hold this petitioner to answer for murder by reason of his alleged act of killing an unborn—even though viable—fetus. To such a charge there are ... insuperable obstacles....

[A] fundamental principle of our tripartite form of government ... [is] that subject to the constitutional prohibition against cruel and unusual punishment, the power to define crimes and fix penalties is vested exclusively in the legislative branch.... The courts cannot ... create an offense by enlarging a statute, by inserting or deleting words, or by giving the terms used false or unusual meanings.... "Constructive crimes—crimes built up by courts with the aid of inference, implication, and strained interpretation—are repugnant to the spirit and letter of ... American criminal law."

Applying these rules to the case at bar, we would undoubtedly act in excess of the judicial power if we were to adopt the People's proposed construction of § 187....

[In a footnote, the court said: "We intimate no view whatever on the advisability of such action. It is a matter of historical record, however, that the feticide statutes discussed herein all date from the middle of the 19th century; that no such legislation has been adopted in the United States in recent years; and that a number of states formerly with feticide statutes in force have declined to reenact them in revising on codifying their laws...."]

For a court to simply declare, by judicial fiat, that the time has now come to prosecute under § 187 one who kills an unborn but viable fetus would indeed be to rewrite the statute under the guise of construing it. Nor does a need to fill an asserted "gap" in the law between abortion and homicide ... justify judicial legislation of this nature: to make it "a judicial function 'to explore such new fields of crime as they may appear from time to time' is wholly foreign to the American concept of criminal justice" and "raises very serious questions concerning the principle of separation of powers."...

Let a peremptory writ of prohibition issue restraining respondent court from taking any further proceedings ... charging petitioner with the crime of murder. McComb, Peters, and Tobriner, JJ., and Peek, J. pro tem., concur.

DISSENT
Burke, Acting Chief Justice

... The majority opinion suggests that we are confined to common law concepts, and to the common law definition of murder or manslaughter. However, ... those words [human being] need not be frozen in place as of any particular time, but must be fairly and reasonably interpreted by this court to promote justice and to carry out the evident purposes of the Legislature in adopting a homicide statute.... "The idea that the doctrine ... is a part of the common law adopted by our statute, and beyond the power of the court to change or modify, is founded upon a misconception of the extent to which the common law is adopted by such statutory provisions, and a failure to observe some of the rules and principles of the common law itself.... The true doctrine is that the common law by its own principles adapts itself to varying conditions, and modifies its own rules so as to serve the ends of justice under the different circumstances...."

The common law reluctance to characterize the killing of a quickened fetus as a homicide was based solely upon a presumption that the fetus would have been born dead. This presumption seems to have persisted in this country at least as late as 1876. Based upon the state of the medical art in the 17th, 18th and 19th centuries, that presumption may have been well-founded However, as we approach the 21st century, it has become apparent that "This presumption is not only contrary to common experience and the ordinary course of nature, but it is contrary to the usual rule with respect to presumptions followed in this state."

There are no accurate statistics disclosing fetal death rates in "common law England," although the foregoing presumption of death indicates a significantly high death experience. On the other hand, in California the fetal death rate [i.e., fetal deaths of 20 weeks or more gestation] in 1968 is estimated to be 12 deaths in 1,000, a ratio which would have given Baby Girl Vogt a 98.8 percent chance of survival. (California Statistical Abstract (1969) Table E–3, p. 65.) If, as I have contended, the term "human being" in our homicide statutes is a fluid concept to be defined in accordance with present conditions, then there can be no question that the term should include the fully viable fetus....

What justice will be promoted, what objects effectuated, by construing "human being" as excluding Baby Girl Vogt and her unfortunate successors? Was defendant's brutal act of stomping her to death any less an act of homicide than the murder of a newly born baby? No one doubts that the term "human being" would include the elderly or dying persons whose potential for life has nearly lapsed; their proximity to death is deemed immaterial.

There is no sound reason for denying the viable fetus, with its unbounded potential for life, the same status ... There is no good reason why a fully viable fetus should not be considered a "human being." [under our statutes] ... To so construe them would not create any new offense....

Case Discussion

What did Mr. Keeler do that brought about the charge of murder against him? What did he intend to do? What harm did his actions cause? Why does he, or his lawyer, argue that he should not be tried and convicted of murder? What rules or principles did the court announce in the case? Why did the California court review all of the history it surveyed? Should it matter what the law was so long ago? What specific reasons did the court give for its holding? Do you agree with the majority or the dissent? Why? Shortly after this opinion, the California legislature revised its murder statute to read: "Murder is the unlawful killing of a human being, or a fetus, with malice aforethought." Did the legislature do the right thing? Was this the way to resolve the problem?[22]

Jurisdictions retaining the common-law crimes (these are called common-law jurisdictions) have created many offenses, particularly misdemeanors, that extend far beyond the common-law felonies. All of the following are crimes without statutes in some states: committing conspiracy, attempt, and solicitation; uttering grossly obscene language in public; burning a body in a furnace; keeping a house of prostitution; maliciously killing a horse; being a common scold; negligently permitting a prisoner to escape; discharging a gun near a sick person; being drunk in public; using libel; committing an indecent assault; and eavesdropping.[23]

Three problems arise in common-law jurisdictions. First, what if statutes do not prescribe penalties for individual common-law crimes? Statutes prescribing general penalties for felonies and misdemeanors alleviate this problem in some states. The problem remains when the common law does not designate an offense a felony or misdemeanor. Some states solve this problem by enacting statutes that define all common-law offenses as misdemeanors.

Second, if both statutes and common law cover the same conduct, which takes precedence? Some states construe statutes narrowly, that is, the words of the statute must either specifically repeal the common law or preempt the entire field of law covered by the common-law crimes. So, where a state conspiracy statute listed five criminal conspiracies while the common law listed many more, the court held that the statute was not meant to take over the whole field of conspiracy; hence, the conspiracies not listed in the statute remained common-law crimes.[24]

Third, what conduct constitutes common-law crimes? Courts approach this subject from two perspectives. Some courts eagerly define new crimes without precedent; others do so only reluctantly. The perspective that courts adopt depends on their view of the common law. If they believe that decid-ed cases merely illustrate broad principles of the unwritten common law, then defining new offenses requires no precedent. According to this view, the common law can expand to meet new conditions. Courts do not invent new crimes; they only apply existing common-law principles to new prob-lems. Courts following this view of the common law are likely to define new crimes without precedent. Other courts view the decisions themselves as embodying the whole of common law. These courts maintain that American courts cannot define new crimes. Therefore, they depend on spe-cific precedent to justify expanding the scope of common-law crimes.

▼ CLASSIFYING AND GRADING CRIMES

Criminal law covers a broad range of conduct, encompassing everything from murder to spitting on the street. In Palo Alto, California, for example, "harboring overdue library books" is punishable by thirty days in jail! In Minnesota, it is a crime to fornicate with a bird. In some places, it is a crime to park a pickup truck in your own driveway, hang laundry out on a clothesline, or eat on a bus (see chapter 12 on public order and morals offenses).

Despite its breadth, criminal law punishes only some harms to people and their property, reputations, and relationships. Many injuries, deaths, and property losses are not included in the criminal law. Most harms caused by corporations are not within the scope of criminal law. They are considered "business matters," best managed by informal (or at least noncriminal) pro-ceedings such as private lawsuits. Reformers have long recommended extending the criminal law to corporations, and one recent development in criminal law is expanding corporate criminal liability.[25]

Furthermore, criminal justice officials have traditionally treated harms that individuals inflict on their relatives and friends as "family matters," even though they are crimes. Counselors, social service agencies, or families themselves have had to deal with them. Recently, attitudes and criminal law enforcement practices have begun to change. Crimes committed against friends, lovers, and family are no longer so widely considered family mat-ters; increasingly, police arrest, and prosecutors charge, the perpetrators of such crimes.[26]

Despite new efforts and a few notorious cases receiving publicity, everyday practice in criminal law still mainly involves harms inflicted by individuals on strangers. Corporate harms and harms inflicted upon friends, lovers, and family remain largely outside formal criminal law.

Crime, Tort, and Nonlegal Responses to Social Harms

Fair and effective social control calls for grading social harms as well as establishing a measured response to them. Not all immoral, reprehensible, and indecent conduct is criminal, nor should it be. A "creep" is not neces-sarily a criminal! society draws lines between mere immoralities, torts, and crimes. A measured response calls for leaving some wrongs entirely to wrongdoers' consciences.

Some conduct, while reprehensible, does not demand a criminal law response; private sanctions suffice. Appropriate private sanctions include suspending students who cheat on exams, exacting a penance for church-goers who lie to their friends, and censuring peers who maliciously reject their lovers.

Some harms may call for legal redress, but not a criminal law response. Law is divided into two basic parts: civil law and criminal law. Civil law provides private and individual redress, by which injured persons sue those who have injured them. The formal title to a civil action reflects these individual and private qualities—for example, *Marconi* (**plaintiff,** or injured person who brings the suit) *v.* (versus or against) *Yu* (**defendant,** or the person sued). **Torts,** the technical term for personal injuries for which the injured party can sue the injuring party, are common civil actions that complement criminal law. The primary object of a civil action is to recover money, known legally as **damages.** Damages are not fines; damages compensate injured individuals, whereas fines are penalties paid to the state. Although tort actions can include punitive damages, the primary purpose of damages is to restore injured persons to their position before injury, not to punish defendants for hurting plaintiffs. Damages cover medical expenses, lost wages, disability, and sometimes pain and suffering.

Criminal law treats society as a whole as the injured party, because harms to individuals and their property undermine social security, harmony, and well-being. The government prosecutes criminal defendants to protect the social interest in harmony, order, and security. The titles of criminal cases—*State v. Wenz, People v. Twohy, Commonwealth v. McDonald,* or *United States v. Storlie*—denote the societal nature of criminal prosecution. The stigma attached to criminal conviction and incarceration is far greater than that associated with losses in private lawsuits, even though the financial cost may be lower.

Civil actions and criminal prosecution are not mutually exclusive responses to social harms. States may prosecute, injured parties sue, friends censure, and conscience pang the same person, all for a single event. Most crimes are also torts: burglary is the tort of trespass, theft is the tort of conversion, and assault is both civil and criminal. Burglary victims can sue burglars for trespass, and states can prosecute burglars for burglary. The double jeopardy clause in the United States Constitution—"no person shall … be subject for the same offence to be twice put in jeopardy of life or limb"—does not prohibit tort and criminal actions for the same conduct. Defendants in tort actions do not lose "life or limb"; they can only lose money.

As you study criminal law, keep this range of alternative responses—personal and private sanctions, tort, and criminal prosecution—in mind. Rational law appropriately grades social harm among crimes, torts, and private condemnation. The most serious harms are designated as crimes. Murder, rape, robbery, and burglary are obvious examples; they call for society's strongest response. Imprisonment and sometimes death, the consequences for committing serious crimes, evidence the gravity of criminal law. Criminal law is society's last resort in dealing with social harms. Where something less will do, common sense requires that something less be done. Thus, if friends' disapproval makes avaricious people less greedy, then making avarice a crime does not make sense.[27]

Felony, Misdemeanor, and Violation

Criminal law grades offenses according to several schemes. One scheme focuses on the penalties imposed. From most severe to least severe, the penalty categories are capital felonies, felonies, gross misdemeanors, petty misdemeanors, and violations. In some states, capital felonies are punishable by death; in states without the death penalty, capital offense can mean life imprisonment without parole. In the United States, aggravated murder is currently the only capital felony punishable by death. However, some states have recently enacted life-without-parole statutes for some drug law violations. Michigan, for example, punishes the possession of more than 650 grams of cocaine with life imprisonment without parole.[28]

The broad distinction between felonies and misdemeanors is that felony convictions are punishable by incarceration in state prisons, whereas misdemeanors are punishable by incarceration in local jails or by fines. Noncapital **felonies** in most jurisdictions are punishable by imprisonment for between one year and life. **Misdemeanors** are punishable by jail sentences, fines, or both. Although disparity exists among jurisdictions, gross misdemeanors typically carry maximum penalties of close to one year, ordinary misdemeanors are usually punishable in the ninety-day range, and petty misdemeanors receive up to thirty days. In most jurisdictions, **violations** that are punishable by fines only—mainly traffic offenses—are not designated criminal convictions.[29]

One problem with grading is the large number of offenses and penalties that exist in the criminal codes of most jurisdictions. At one time, Oregon, for instance, had 1,413 separate offenses and 466 different sentencing levels. Some maintain that this multitude of crimes and penalties creates "anarchy in sentencing." It also inhibits rational thinking about sentencing, builds sentencing disparities in practice, and prevents systematic sentencing reform. Furthermore, chaotic sentencing patterns undermine public confidence in, and respect for, the criminal law and its administration. According to one expert:[30]

> The human mind cannot draw an infinite number of distinctions about crime. You can see the most serious crimes and the less serious ones, and you can see some gradations in between. And there may be some difference of opinion whether you can see three or four or six or seven categories. But there is a finite number that it is prudent to attempt to perceive.[31]

The Model Penal Code divides crimes into six categories: three degrees of felonies, misdemeanors, petty misdemeanors, and violations. (See table 1.1.)

Wrongs Mala in Se *and* Mala Prohibita

Another classification scheme divides crimes between inherently evil conduct, **malum in se,** and merely prohibited conduct, **mala prohibita.** The serious felonies—murder, rape, robbery, burglary, arson, larceny—are classified as evil by their very nature. Killing another without justification or excuse, raping, robbing, burglarizing, and stealing are bad even if they were not crimes under the law. On the other hand, the long list of violations that attend regulating modern urban industrial society, such as traffic

▼ Table 1 ▼
Degrees of Felonies
Model Penal Code, Art. 6 § 6.01

Distribution of Offenses

The Model Code contains 141 crimes and violations, divided as follows: 50 felonies, 84 misdemeanors and petty misdemeanors, and 7 violations. The 50 felonies are distributed among the three classes authorized by this section in the following manner:

First-Degree Felonies

Offenses Involving Danger to the Person
 Murder
 Kidnapping
 Rape
Offenses against Property
 Robbery

Second-Degree Felonies

Offenses Involving Danger to the Person
 Manslaughter
 Causing or aiding suicide
 Aggravated assault
 Kidnapping
 Rape
 Deviate sexual intercourse by force
Offenses against Property
 Arson
 Causing catastrophe
 Burglary
 Robbery
 Forgery
Offenses against the Family
 Abortion

Third-Degree Felonies

Offenses Involving Danger to the Person
 Negligent homicide
 Aggravated assault
 Terroristic threats
 Felonious restraint
 Interference with custody of children
 Criminal coercion
 Gross sexual imposition
 Deviate sexual intercourse by imposition
 Corruption of minors
Offenses against Property
 Reckless burning or exploding
 Causing catastrophe
 Criminal mischief
 Burglary
 Theft
 Forgery

(Continued)

▼ Table 1 ▼
Degrees of Felonies (Continued)

Fraudulent destruction, removal, or concealment of recordable instruments
Credit card fraud
Offenses against the Family
  Polygamy
  Incest
  Abortion
  Self-abortion
  Pretended abortion
Offenses against Public Administration
  Bribery in official and political matters
  Threats and other improper influence in official and political matters
  Perjury
  Tampering
  Witness or informant taking bribe
  Tampering with public records or information
  Hindering apprehension or prosecution
  Aiding consummation of crime
  Escape
  Bail jumping, and so on
Offenses against Public Order and Decency
  Riot
  Promoting prostitution

codes, building codes, and health regulations, are illegal, but most do not consider them inherently bad. Society does not label drivers who make illegal left turns or park in no-parking zones bad, even though they have broken the law.

Classifications According to Subject

At least as early as the sixteenth century, some criminal law commentators classified crimes according to their subject matter. This scheme still influences the classification of crimes. This book follows that scheme, organizing the special part of the criminal law into these subject classifications:

☐ Crimes against the state, including treason and sedition
☐ Crimes against persons, including murder, manslaughter, rape, kidnapping, assault, and battery
☐ Crimes against habitation, including burglary and arson
☐ Crimes against property, including larceny, embezzlement, false pretenses, malicious mischief, and robbery (really a combination of a crime against a person and property)
☐ Crimes against public order, including disorderly conduct and public drunkenness
☐ Crimes against the administration of justice, including obstruction of justice and bribery
☐ Crimes against public morals, including prostitution, fornication, and profanity.

▼ PERSPECTIVES ON CRIME AND THE CRIMINAL LAW

Prosecutors, defense attorneys, and judges view crime and criminal law from the perspective of practitioners. They accept the existing definitions of crime in the criminal law, and proceed from there to argue and decide cases. The remaining chapters in this book concentrate on the legal definitions, and the general principles and doctrines that limit the power of the state to create criminal law. Other disciplines focus on why and how the definitions came to be: Why is some conduct and harm defined as criminal and some not? You should keep these perspectives in mind as you study the topics in the remainder of the book. They do not contradict the legal definition of crime. Rather, these perspectives enrich our understanding of criminal law by going beyond the definitions of principles, doctrines, and rules to an examination of when, how, and why they developed.

Ideological Perspective

[handwritten: Crimes are political becaup they come from a state legislature]

Political scientists and sociologists study the political influences on the formation and administration of criminal law. All crimes are political in the sense that the legislatures that enact criminal codes are not neutral bodies. Also, community standards informally, and perhaps imperceptibly, influence judges when they interpret the law. Statutes outline broad categories of conduct, permitting judges room in which to fit particular cases. In applying broad categories to individual cases, judges' own ideas and community standards influence their decisions; applying criminal law to individual cases is never a value-neutral exercise.[32]

Two opposing theories inform the ideological perspective. The democratic-consensus theory, originating in the insights of the great sociologist Emile Durkheim, holds that elected representatives define crime. The criminal law expresses the will of the people through their elected representatives. Criminal law represents society's stand against conduct that violates its values and describes what punishments society inflicts on those who flout its values. This reading of the legislative process rests on two assumptions: First, politics and laws reflect consensus; people work together and compromise their individual interests so the state can work efficiently and effectively to satisfy the majority's collective needs. Second, criminal statutes embody the people's will. Recent research suggests that criminal codes express neither the will of the people nor the will of their legislators; instead, criminal justice professionals write most criminal laws.[33]

The conflict-elitist theory assumes that society operates according to conflict, not consensus. Interest groups, each ensconced in a bailiwick, come out fighting for their selfish interests—interests promoted only at the expense of other groups' interests. The most powerful interest group wins every major contest and then imposes its values on the rest of society. The rich and powerful use the legal system to protect their wealth and secure their dominant position of power. The ruling elite brandish the criminal laws as weapons to coerce weaker elements of society into submission.[34]

The conflict-elitist theory is considerably more complicated than this brief summary suggests. The criminal process is rarely so personal and purposely exploitative. Furthermore, the ruling elite often disagree over which criminal laws best serve their interests; nor do all laws by any means promote the dominant class's interests, at least not in the short term.[35]

Both theories are true to some extent. Without question, much criminal law exhibits consensus. Most people, for example, agree that murder, rape, and robbery should be crimes; in fact, widespread agreement exists about the seriousness of more than one hundred crimes. Legislatures represent most people when they enact these statutes, as do judges when they apply them. Much criminal law, however, does not represent consensus. Historically, the powerful have used vagrancy laws to keep in their place certain elements of society—the poor, the unattached, and others on the fringes of "respectable" society. Vagrancy legislation therefore supports the claim of the conflict-elitist theory that criminal law results from the ruling class's effort to keep the "lower orders" in line. Similarly, recent ordinances against "aggressive panhandling," sleeping on park benches, and camping within city limits represent efforts of the middle class to control the growing numbers of homeless people.[36]

Both theories are naive in some respects. The democratic-consensus theory fails to account for the powerful effects that money, class, race, and other social factors have on both the political and the legal processes. Decisions throughout every stage of the criminal process—reporting crimes; arresting suspects; prosecuting, trying, and convicting defendants; and sentencing or releasing offenders—require judgments. The amount of freedom that victims, police officers, prosecutors, judges, or juries have in making these decisions is called **discretion.**[37]

A debate as old as law itself exists concerning how much leeway law officers and the public should have in enforcing criminal law. Good reasons support tempering the letter of the law with flexibility to do justice in individual cases. In his advice to new judges, Sir Nicholas Bacon, a sixteenth-century English lord chancellor, stressed that legislators could not possibly write statutes clear enough or complete enough to cover all cases. Because of this,

> the judge is not always so narrowly to weigh the words of the law, but sometimes in respect of the person, place, time and occasion or other circumstance to qualify and moderate such extremities as the particular words of the law written may offer.

Sir Nicholas was no fool. Realizing that discretion was equally a means to evil as well as good, he warned his new judges accordingly:

> For albeit his knowledge be never so great and his discretion equal to it, if he will suffer them to be subject and governed by fear, by love, by malice or gain, then shall all his judgments be such as his affections be and not such as knowledge and discretion doth require.[38]

Class, wealth, power, and prejudice influence the operation of the law, perhaps even more than they influence its formulation. Selective enforcement has characterized the administration of criminal law from as early as the sixteenth century. For example, in one English town in the 1570s, poor, wandering people without family or other community ties were arrested more often, prosecuted more vigorously, and punished more harshly than were "respectable," established residents.[39]

Discretion creates a gap between what law books *say* and what law officers *do* because class, race, economics, and politics affect it. Victims who never report crimes, suspects whom police could arrest but do not, arrested suspects whom prosecutors could charge but do not, and offenders who could be punished but are not—they, as much as any statute or universal moral code, shape the criminal law. Commenting on social forces and their current impact on the administration of justice, the late criminologist Donald R. Cressey concluded that

> [t]here is a great deal of evidence that current statutes calling for punishment of lawbreakers are not administered uniformly, or with celerity or certainty. This suggests that the actual reactions to crime are not really reflected in the laws governing the administration of justice. Statutes are so severe they must be mitigated in the interests of justice, and in order to maintain the consent of the governed. The following conclusions have been drawn by so many investigators that they may be accepted as factual:
>
> 1. Blacks are more likely to be arrested than whites.
> 2. Blacks are more likely to be indicted than whites.
> 3. Blacks have a higher conviction rate than whites.
> 4. Blacks are usually punished more severely than whites, but this is not true for all crimes, especially those in which a black person victimizes a black person.
> 5. Blacks are less likely to receive probation and suspended sentences.
> 6. Blacks receive pardons less often than do whites.
> 7. Blacks have less chance of having a death sentence commuted than do whites.[40]

The conflict-elitist theory, no more than the democratic-consensus theory, fully explains criminal laws origins and nature. Just as the democratic-consensus theory minimizes the pluralistic conflict of interests in society, the conflict-elitist theory ignores the very real core of values about which wide agreement exists. The same sixteenth-century English town that favored established members of the community over poor, wandering strangers also exhibited wide consensus on some values. Town officials adhered to the principle of legality in the administration of justice, enforcing procedural safeguards such as rules of proof requiring reliable witnesses to bring charges and testify in court against the accused. They also firmly recognized that despite the letter of the law prescribing death as a punishment for all felonies—from murder to the theft of a chicken—only murderers and some other violent criminals should hang for their crimes. This consensus persists today.

Irrational Forces Perspective

Both the conflict-elitist and the democratic-consensus theories possess one major flaw. Neither allows room for chance or for the irrational or emotional elements in human behavior. Behaviorists cannot accurately predict what people will do; individuals rarely act strictly according to democratic-consensus and conflict-elitist theories. Police officers on patrol, for example, may arrest citizens as much because they are tired, irritable, or bored as because they revere law and order.

Irrational forces give rise to more than erratic individual decisions. They affect criminal codes as well, as sex psychopath laws illustrate. Shortly after World War II, a small spate of brutal sex crimes generated public fear. One ghoulish man dismembered and killed several young girls after sexually assaulting them. In response, most states hastily passed sex psychopath statutes, enabling states to confine potential sex offenders indefinitely without a trial. Some experts questioned the effectiveness, propriety, and constitutionality of these statutes. Critics argued that the statutes were unconstitutional because they denied procedural safeguards to those affected by them. Furthermore, they rested on shaky confidence in predictive capacity, since identifying in advance who will commit sex offenses is virtually impossible.[41]

Considerable empirical evidence since the passage of sex psychopath legislation has demonstrated its shortcomings. Despite this knowledge, the laws remain largely in force today. Fear and panic explain their enactment. Any complete explanation of the nature and origins of criminal law must account for the unpredictable, irrational, and chance elements in human behavior.[42]

Historical Perspective

The great jurist Oliver Wendell Holmes maintained that in understanding the law, "a page of history is worth a volume of logic." He meant that real life experience, not abstract reasoning, creates law. Most crimes originate in the circumstances of time and place. In addition to law's response to time and place, lawyers' reverence for precedent enhances history's strength. Imbued with the importance of precedent, lawyers approach change in the law cautiously. As a result, the present criminal law retains laws that were once believed necessary but are no longer relevant. One legal historian noted that the ghosts of the past stalk silently through our courts and legislatures, ruling our modern law by means of outdated and irrelevant but venerated ancient principles and doctrines. Thus, history plays a powerful part in maintaining, in today's criminal law, that which yesterday's social, economic, political, and philosophical considerations created.[43]

The development of the modern law of theft illustrates the historical perspective on criminal law. In early times, larceny—forcibly taking and carrying away another's cattle—was the only theft. The original crime resembles the modern law of robbery—taking another's property by force or by threat of force (see chapter 11). Later, larceny came to include taking another's property by stealth (from which our word *stealing* descends). Getting another's property by trickery was not a crime; it was shrewd or clever. Neither was taking property left for safekeeping (examples would be taking a car left in an attended parking lot, or clothes left at a dry cleaner's); it was the owner's folly. Hence, only stealing or forcibly taking another's property constituted larceny; cheating was not a crime.[44]

Such was the law of theft in medieval England before commerce and industry had advanced beyond the most rudimentary stages. Most people lived in small communities, rarely dealt with strangers, and had few personal property items available to misappropriate. Furthermore, larceny was a felony, punishable by death. Judges were reluctant to expand the definition of larceny if doing so meant hanging more property offenders.

The complexities of modern life changed all this. More people, personal property, and strangers; a greater need to leave property and money with strangers; and less bloody punishments for larceny all led to alterations in theft law. Larceny came to include the theft of most movable personal property, such as jewels, furniture, clothing, and utensils. Then it was expanded to include the stealing of paper instruments representing ownership, such as checks, bank notes, and deeds. Finally, new crimes were created to embrace more misappropriations than the taking of property by force and stealth. Misappropriating money entrusted to another became embezzlement; tricking another out of money became false pretenses; both became felonies.

Theft law developed to meet the needs of a complex society and to ameliorate a harsh criminal law; these historical facts explain theft law. In the past twenty years, thirty states have overcome this history by consolidating larceny, embezzlement, false pretenses, and other theft offenses into one crime. The remaining twenty states cling to a host of theft offenses, of which the arcane larceny, embezzlement, fraud, and false pretenses are only the most common.

To cite one more example, the criminal law enacted in seventeenth-century New England to secure Puritan religious values, despite its clear irrelevance to modern behavior, remains surprisingly intact. For example, until their recent demise in the face of a constitutional assault on their validity, vagrancy statutes were based on the needs of sixteenth-century England. Yet, as recently as 1971, American vagrancy statutes copied their sixteenth-century English legal forbearers verbatim. Fornication, profanity, and curfews still remain on the books, although they are rarely enforced. The retention of these "morals" offenses demonstrates that the past rules the present in criminal law.[45]

oure law. is a Out spray

Ethical Core Perspective

The historical, irrational, political, and legal theories all rest on the assumption that environment determines criminal law. Crime does not reflect permanent values; it is relative to time and place. In other words, irrational outbursts, ideology, social conditions, and other circumstances shape what society condemns in its criminal law. What one age considers evil, another may tolerate, even promote as good.

Philosophers take a fundamentally different approach, assuming that crime represents universal, permanent, inherent evil in codified form. According to this theory, lawmaking, politics, history, and emotional outbursts do not affect this ethical core of criminal law.

The ethical core theory stems in part from religion. For example, some proponents maintain that criminal law reflects the Ten Commandments: "Thou shalt not kill" and "Thou shalt not steal" illustrate this view. Other commandments, however, do not comport with modern criminal law. "Thou shalt not covet thy neighbor's wife" violates the basic principle that the state cannot punish thoughts unaccompanied by action. Moreover, consensus supports only some commandments; deep controversy surrounds others (see chapter 3).

The ethical core theory is not always articulated in strictly religious form; sometimes it is cast in general moral terms. For instance, criminal law manifests the universally high value placed on the rights to life, liberty, and property. The English common law first enshrined these rights; then Americans entrenched them in constitutions, statutes, and court decisions. The ethical core theory strikes a responsive chord in those who accept that life, liberty, and property are widely valued, uniformly defined, and universally protected by law. But the theory does not fully match reality. The enormous body of regulatory offenses—traffic offenses, for example—does not fit the theory. Driving seventy-five miles per hour in a sixty-five-mile-an-hour zone may violate the law, but few would call it inherently evil, violating some ethical core of values. On the other hand, although Kristen is breaking Lucas's heart (recall the hypothetical cases on pages 6–7), the law does not make it a crime.

Some critics argue that equating values or notions of good and bad with crime, as the ethical core theory does, is both dangerous and improper. Professor Louis B. Schwartz criticized the statement of purpose in the Federal Criminal Justice Reform Act of 1973 on the ground that

> the bill injects a new, false, and dangerous notion that the criminal code "aims at the articulation of the nation's public values" and its vindication through punishment. A criminal code necessarily falls far short of expressing the nation's morality. Many things are evil or undesirable without being at all appropriate for imprisonment: lying, overcharging for goods and services, marital infidelity, lack of charity or patriotism. Nothing has been more widely recognized in modern criminal law scholarship than the danger of creating more evil by ill-considered use of the criminal law than is caused by the target misconduct. Accordingly, the failure to put something under the ban of the penal code is not an expression of a favorable "value" of the non-penalized behavior. It is a fatal confusion of values to see the Criminal Code as anything but a list of those most egregious misbehaviours, which according to a broad community consensus, can be usefully dealt with by social force.[46]

Several of the hypothetical cases presented early in this chapter illustrate other weaknesses in the ethical core theory. They demonstrate that the meaning of life, liberty, and property is by no means settled. Controversy surrounds issues such as whether looking at pornography, smoking marijuana, or even using heroin should be crimes. What constitutes life and property, not to mention liberty? Should these be protected by the criminal law, and to what extent? The answers vary from place to place and over time.

One major theme in criminal law is the need to reconcile stability with change. Changed conditions, new knowledge, and shifts in ideals all require that in the late twentieth century the law advance beyond what it was in the eighteenth or nineteenth centuries. Stealing a chicken was once a capital offense. Wives who scolded their husbands were considered criminals in the not-too-distant past. Most of the adult population in India can remember a time when a widow's burning herself to death after her husband died was considered the highest form of love. Recent cases involving people whose hearts are beating and who are still breathing but whose brains have stopped functioning have raised new questions about the meanings of life and death. A term has even been created to describe the new dilemma: brain death. Equally controversial is the heated debate over whether a fetus is property subject to contract law, and whether it is a life for purposes of criminal law (see chapter 8).

General Moral Background

▼ *Summary* ▼

Criminal law examines the ordinary phenomena of action, intention, relationships, causation, justification, and excuse under the extraordinary circumstances that result in social harm. Criminal law is a method, or way of doing things, that aims to reduce crime and punish criminals. It is a list of commands, or dos and don'ts, written into law, with penalties attached that apply to everyone in the jurisdiction, or authority of the government making the law. Criminal law shares these qualities with other forms of law, but it has another distinctive feature—criminal conviction carries with it the formal moral condemnation of the community. A rational criminal law rests on fundamental principles, universally applied, that grades and punishes crimes according to their seriousness and blameworthiness. It acts economically to use only sufficient punishment to reduce crime and punish criminals. Criminal law, therefore, is a limited instrument of social control. It consists of both government power and limits on that power.

The United States does not have a unified criminal law. Each of the fifty states has its own criminal law, and the federal government has a separate criminal code. The states and federal criminal codes share similarities in general terms, but the specific definitions of crimes—and the penalties attached—differ widely across jurisdictions.

Criminal law has two parts. The general part establishes the general principles of criminal law that apply to all crimes. It also sets forth the doctrines that may apply to all crimes, such as accomplice liability, attempts, justifications, and excuses. The special part includes the rules, or definitions of specific crimes.

American criminal law originates in several sources. The United States Constitution and the state constitutions define the crimes against the nation and state, specifically treason. Statutes define crimes; in fact, most criminal law today originates in statutes, primarily state criminal codes. Definitions of crimes in statutes, and defenses to crimes, require reference to the common law, another major source of criminal law. Some states have retained the common-law crimes; others have abolished the common-law crimes but retained the common-law defenses. All, however, require reference to the common law for definition of terms. A final source of criminal law is judicial opinions interpreting constitutions, statutes, and the common law.

Crimes are classified according to several schemes. One scheme, the felony, misdemeanor, violation scheme, organizes crimes according to the penalty. Capital felonies are punishable by death or life imprisonment without parole. Felonies are punishable by incarceration in prisons for one year or more. Misdemeanors are punishable by fine or incarceration in local jails for up to one year. Violations, often not designated crimes at all, are punishable by fine only. Another classification scheme ranks crimes according to their "badness" or "evil." Crimes *mala in se* are inherently evil, like rape and murder. Crimes *mala prohibita,* such as parking violations, are illegal but not evil. Another scheme classifies crimes according to their subject matter, including crimes against the state, crimes against the person, crimes against habitation, crimes against property, crimes against the administration of justice, crimes against public order, and crimes against public morals.

Studying the principles, doctrines, and rules of criminal law reveals what the criminal law consists of. However, it does not tell us how or why the criminal law established the principles, doctrines, and rules. Sociology, political science, psychology, history, and philosophy shed light on the rationale, policies and values of the criminal law and how they developed in the context of specific times and places. In this we find that criminal law did not spring full-grown from rational minds. Social forces, political power, emotions, past traditions and practices, and philosophy have shaped the criminal law.

▼ *Questions for Review and Discussion* ▼

1. Why can we say criminal law is the study of ordinary phenomena under extraordinary circumstances?

2. Why do we say criminal law is a method, or way of doing things?

3. Describe the major characteristics of criminal law. How do they compare and contrast with other branches of law? What is most distinctive about criminal law compared to other branches of law?

4. Why is the term *criminal law* somewhat of a misnomer?

5. Explain the major characteristics of a "rational criminal law." Should a criminal law be rational? Why?

6. Describe the general and special parts of the criminal law.

7. What are the major sources of American criminal law?

8. What is the importance of the common law today? Should states abolish the common law? Can they, even if they want to do so? Explain.

9. Describe the major classification schemes for organizing and grading crimes. Which makes the most sense to you? Explain your answer.

▼ *Suggested Readings* ▼

1. Wayne R. LaFave and Austin W. Scott, Jr., *Criminal Law,* 2d ed. (St. Paul: West Publishing Company, 1986). An updated version of a classic law school textbook, *Criminal Law* is a good place for the undergraduate to search further into the problems of criminal law.

2. Rollin M. Perkins and Ronald N. Boyce, *Criminal Law,* 3d ed. (Mineola, N.Y.: Foundation Press, 1982). This is a law school hornbook (textbook) covering the general and special parts of criminal law. It is an excellent, up-to-date reference book for anyone who wishes to pursue in further detail topics suggested here.

3. George P. Fletcher, *Rethinking Criminal Law* (Boston: Little, Brown, 1978). A provocative effort to write a comprehensive theory of criminal law, Fletcher's book is challenging and difficult but well worth the serious student's efforts.

4. Lawrence M. Friedman, *A History of American Law* (New York: Simon and Schuster, 1973). Friedman has written an interesting history of American law for the general public. Although it covers all law, sections on criminal law are clearly set apart and can be read separately without difficulty.

5. American Law Institute, *Model Penal Code* (Philadelphia: American Law Institute, 1954–61); and American Law Institute, *Model Penal Code and Commentaries* (Philadelphia: American Law Institute, 1980, 1985). These are excellent works full of the latest scholarship, thoughtful analyses, and commentary by some of the leading judges, lawyers, and academics in American law. The works present, in imposing fashion, the democratic-consensus approach to criminal law; but their value stretches well beyond. They contain the most comprehensive coverage of American criminal law in existence.

6. Lawrence M. Friedman, *American Law* (New York: Norton, 1984). This is a general introduction to American law, filled with anecdotes and discussion intended to explain the nature and processes of American law to the general reader. It is a vivid picture of American law and its role in American life, well worth the time spent reading it.

7. Jerome Hall, *General Principles of Criminal Law,* 2d ed. (Indianapolis: Bobbs-Merrill, 1960). Hall covers the general principles and doctrines of criminal law, arranging them into a theory of criminal law. This text is a classic in the literature of criminal law.

8. Leo Katz, *Bad Acts and Guilty Minds* (Chicago: University of Chicago, 1987). The author presents an interesting, thought-provoking look at the philosophy of criminal law. He focuses on the basic problems of criminal law, using real cases from several countries, many challenging hypothetical cases, and critical suggestions.

9. Henry M. Hart, Jr., "The Aims of the Criminal Law," *Law and Contemporary Problems* 23(1958):104–441. This essay is the best brief statement about the nature of criminal law and its characteristics.

10. Jeffrey H. Reiman, *The Rich Get Richer and the Poor Get Prison,* 2d ed. (New York: Wiley, 1984). In this book, Reiman forcefully presents the conflict-elitist theory.

▼ *Notes* ▼

1. Leo Katz, *Bad Acts and Guilty Minds* (Chicago: University of Chicago Press, 1987), p. 300.

2. Joel Feinberg, *Harm to Others* (New York: Oxford University Press, 1984). In chapter 1, Feinberg elaborates on the concept of harm and its relation to the criminal law. See also-Henry M. Hart, Jr., "The Aims of the Criminal Law," *Law and Contemporary Problems* 23 (1958):401–41.

3. These characteristics modify and expand on those listed in Henry M. Hart, Jr.'s classic, "The Aims of the Criminal Law," *Law and Contemporary Problems* 23 (1958):403–405.

4. Ibid., p. 405.

5. Ravin v. State, 537 P.2d 494 (Alaska 1975), excerpted in chapter 2.

6. Texas Penal Code, § 31.03(5) (a)(i) (St. Paul: West Publishing Co., 1988).

7. Herbert Packer, "The Aims of the Criminal Law Revisited: A Plea for a New Look at "Substantive Due Process," *Southern California Law Review* 44 (1970–71):490–98.

8. A useful survey of the Model Penal Code written by its leading light can be found in Herbert Wechsler, "The Model Penal Code and the Codification of American Criminal Law," Roger Hood, ed., *Crime, Criminology, and Public Policy* (London: Heineman, 1974), pp. 419–68; American Law Institute, tentative drafts 1–13 (Philadelphia: American Law Institute, 1954–61).

9. See Jerome Hall, *The General Principles of Criminal Law,* 2d ed. (Indianapolis: Bobbs-Merrill, 1960), pp. 16–26, for a detailed discussion of the differences among principles, doctrines, and rules.

10. James Madison, "Federalist No. 51," in Jacob E. Cooke, ed., *The Federalist,* no. 51, (Middletown, Conn.: Wesleyan University Press, 1961), p. 349.

11. Blackstone, *Commentaries,* book IV.

12. Wayne R. LaFave and Austin W. Scott, Jr., *Criminal Law* (St. Paul: West Publishing Co., 1972), p. 59.

13. The Growth of the Law (New Haven, Conn.: Yale University Press, 1924), p. 62.

14. State v. Mellenberger, 95 P.2d 709 (Oregon 1939) overruling *State v. Alexander,* 148 P. 1136 (Oregon 1915).

15. West's Florida Statutes Annotated (1991), Title XLVI, § 775.01.

16. Max Farrand, editor, *The Laws and Liberties of Massachusetts* (Cambridge: Harvard University Press, 1929), p. A2.

17. Ibid., pp. 5, 6.

18. Julian P. Bond, ed., *The Papers of Thomas Jefferson,* vol.2 (Princeton: Princeton University Press, 1950) reprints this proposed code and Jefferson's fascinating notes about it. Also, Kathryn Preyer's recent "Crime, the Criminal Law and Reform in Post-Revolutionary Virginia," *Law and History Review* 1 (1983): 53–85, contains an informative discussion about Jefferson's code.

19. 11 U.S. (7 Cranch) 32, 3 L.Ed. 259 (1812).

20. American Law Institute, *Model Penal Code and Commentaries,* part I, §§ 1.01 to 2.13 (Philadelphia: American Law Institute, 1985), pp. 75–80.

21. § 13A-1-4, Code of Alabama 1975.

22. West's California Penal Code (St. Paul: West Publishing Company, 1988) § 187(a).

23. Wayne R. LaFave and Austin Scott, Jr., *Criminal Law,* 2d ed. (St. Paul: West Publishing Co., 1986), pp. 68–69.

24. *State v. McFeely,* 25 N.J. Misc. 303, 52 A.2d 823 Quar.Sess. 1947).

25. See, for example, "Business and the Law: Criminal Onus on Executives," *New York Times* (March 5, 1985); "Can a Corporation Commit Murder?" *New York Times* (May 19, 1985). For useful introductions to this problem, see Jeffrey H. Reiman, *The Rich Get Richer and the Poor Get Prison,* 2d ed. (New York: Wiley, 1984); and William Chambliss and Robert Seidman, *Law, Order, and Power* (Reading, Mass.: Addison-Wesley, 1982), chapter 7.

26. For an unsettling look at how it took twenty years, a change in attitude, and a great deal of individual pressure on public officials in order to bring an egregious case of child murder to trial, see Barry Siegel's gripping *A Death in White Bear Lake: The True Chronicle of an All-American Town* (New York: Bantam Books, 1990).

27. For two excellent discussions of rational grading, see American Law Institute, *Model Penal Code and Commentaries,* vol. 1 (Philadelphia: American Law Institute, 1985), pp. 1–30; and for the general reader, Norval Morris and Gordon Hawkins, *The Honest Politician's Guide to Crime Control* (Chicago: University of Chicago Press, 1969), chapter 1.

28. For an excellent discussion of capital crimes and punishment, see Hugo Adam Bedau, ed., *The Death Penalty in America,* 3d ed. (New York: Oxford University Press, 1982).

29. For a thorough summary of the wide disparity in existing misdemeanor classification, see American Law Institute, *Model Penal Code and Commentaries* (Philadelphia: American Law Institute, 1985), pp. 1–30.

30. American Law Institute, *Model Penal Code and Commentaries,* vol. 3 (Philadelphia: American Law Institute, 1985), part I, pp. 34–38.

31. Ibid, p. 34.

32. An excellent discussion of some of these matters appears in David W. Neubauer, *Criminal Justice in Middle America* (Morristown, NJ: General Learning Press, 1974), pp. 86–105. For an earlier but provocative analysis, see Jerome Frank, *Courts on Trial: Myth and Reality in American Justice* (Princeton: Princeton University Press, 1949), chapter 14.

33. Emile Durkheim, *The Division of Labor in Society* (New York: Free Press, 1933), pp. 73–80; the insight concerning policy formulation stems from Timothy Lenz's research. Department of Political Science, University of Minnesota.

34. George B. Vold and Thomas J. Bernard, *Theoretical Criminology,* 3d ed. (New York: Oxford University Press, 1986); chapters 14 through 16 develop these points fully.

35. For good introductions to this theory, see Richard Quinney, *Criminology,* 2d ed. (Boston: Little, Brown, 1979), pp. 120–25; and William Chambliss and Robert Seidman, *Law, Order, and Power,* 2d ed. (Reading, Mass.: Addison-Wesley, 1982), pp. 171–207.

36. Peter Rossi et al., "The Seriousness of Crimes: Normative Structure and Individual Differences," *American Sociological Review* 39 (1974):224–37; William J. Chambliss, "The Law of Vagrancy," in *Criminal Law in Action,* 2d ed., edited by William J. Chambliss (New York: Macmillan, 1984), pp. 33–42.

37. The definitive work on discretion is Kenneth Culp Davis, *Discretionary Justice* (Baton Rouge, La.: Louisiana State University Press, 1969).

38. Sir Nicholas Bacon, quoted in Joel Samaha, "Hanging for Felony," *Historical Journal* (1979):75.

39. Ibid., pp. 769–71.

40. Edwin H. Sutherland and Donald R. Cressey, *Criminology,* 10th ed., rev. (Philadelphia: Lippincott, 1978), pp. 333–34.

41. Edwin Sutherland, "The Sexual Psychopath Laws," *Journal of Criminal Law, Criminology, and Police Science* 40 (1950):543–54.

42. Francis A. Allen, *The Borderland of Criminal Justice* (Chicago: University of Chicago Press, 1964), p. 15.

43. Holmes's famous aphorism appears in *New York Trust Company v. Eisner,* 256 U.S. 345 (1921), 349.

44. See Rollin M. Perkins and Ronald N. Boyce, *Criminal Law,* 3d ed. (Mineola, N.Y.: Foundation Press), pp. 289–92; and American Law Institute, *Model Penal Code and Commentaries,* vol. 2 (Philadelphia: American Law Institute, 1980), pp. 128–30. For a full and interesting treatment of the relationship of history and society to theft, see Jerome Hall, *Theft, Law, and Society* (Indianapolis: Bobbs-Merrill, 1952).

45. Joel Samaha, "John Winthrop and the Criminal Law" *William Mitchell Law Review* (1989):217.

46. Quoted in Sanford Kadish and Manfred Paulson, *Criminal Law and Its Processes,* 3d ed. rev. (Boston and Toronto: Little, Brown, 1975), p. 40.

Chapter
2

The General Principles of Criminal Law

▼ *Chapter Outline* ▼

   I. Introduction
  II. The Principle of Legality
 III. Constitutional Limits
    A. The *Ex Post Facto* Prohibition
    B. Void for Vagueness
    C. Equal Protection of the Laws
    D. The Right to Privacy
    E. The Right to Free Speech and Expressive Conduct
 IV. The Principle of Punishment
    A. Retribution
    B. Prevention
    C. Trends in Punishment
    D. Proportionality
  V. Summary

1. The general principles refer to the balance of government power and to the limits of that power to define crimes.

2. The general principles of criminal law apply to the general principles of liability, justification, and excuse, to the doctrines of complicity and incomplete crimes, and to the rules defining specific crimes.

3. The principle of legality requires that criminal laws proscribe conduct and prescribe punishments clearly and in advance of prosecution.

4. The *ex post facto* prohibition protects against making conduct criminal after it occurs and against applying arbitrary government power.

5. The void for vagueness doctrine requires that laws give fair warning to citizens and prevent undue discretionary discrimination by law enforcement officers.

6. Equal protection prohibits classifications based on unacceptable criteria (such as race), requires a rational basis for most classifications, and looks with special care at gender-based classifications.

7. The right to privacy is based on the idea that citizens in free societies should be "left alone" from government interference.

8. Government cannot make speech or expressive conduct criminal except when they present a "clear and present danger" to legitimate government ends.

9. The principle of punishment refers both to the purposes of punishment and to its proportionality.

10. The major purposes of punishment are retribution and prevention.

11. Retribution looks back and punishes the crime because it is right to punish it; prevention looks forward to prevent crimes in the future.

12. The principle of proportionality refers mainly to death penalty cases, but also to imprisonment in exceptional cases.

Knew this for test

▼ *Chapter Key Terms* ▼

criminal punishment—(1) Pain or other unpleasant consequence (2) inflicted for breaking a specific law and (3) administered by the state (4) for the primary purpose of hurting criminal offenders, not helping them.

culpability—Blameworthiness for criminal conduct.

due process clauses—Government cannot deny citizens life, liberty, or property without notice, hearing, and other established procedures.

ex post facto **laws**—Laws passed after the occurrence of the conduct constituting the crime.

general deterrence—Preventing crime by threatening potential law-breakers.

incapacitation—Punishment by imprisonment, mutilation, and even death.

nulla poena sine lege—Punishment without a specific law.

nullum crimen sine lege—No crime without a specific law.

principle of legality—No crime or punishment without notice and hearing.

proportionality—Punishment in relation to the person and conduct.

rehabilitation—Prevention of crime by treatment.

retribution—Punishment based on just deserts.

special deterrence—Aims at individual offenders, hoping to deter their future conduct by the threat of punishment.

void-for-vagueness principle—Statutes violate due process if they do not clearly define crime and punishment in advance.

writ of certiorari—Discretionary Supreme Court order to review lower court decisions.

▼ INTRODUCTION

The general principles of criminal law balance the power and limits of government to define crimes. Criminal law protects against the social harms caused by criminals who invade law-abiding citizens' life, liberty, and property. But it also takes into account that defining conduct as criminal and using government power to enforce the criminal law also limits life, liberty, and property. The general principles of criminal law seek to allow government sufficient power to reduce and punish crime without entrenching too much on the lives, liberty, privacy, and property of private citizens. Do not think that criminal law and its enforcement create costs only for guilty people, nor that limiting the reach of criminal law protects only criminals. It also demarks the amount of privacy, liberty, and security for all citizens. Winston Churchill, the great English prime minister, once said you can measure the quality of a civilization by its criminal laws.

The principles of criminal liability define the extent and limits of government power by requiring conduct as the basis of liability. The doctrines define the limits of liability based on complicity and crimes initiated but not completed. The principles of justification and excuse, as their names imply, permit acquittal when conduct otherwise criminal is justified or excusable. The definitions of the specific crimes against persons, habitation, property, public administration of justice, public order, and public morals limit liability to precise conduct included in the definitions.

Overarching the principles of liability, justification, and excuse; the doctrines of complicity and incomplete crimes; and the definitions of specific crimes are the principle of legality, several provisions in the United States Constitution, its Bill of Rights, and in parallel state constitutions and state bills of rights. We leave the discussion of the principles of liability, justification, and excuse; of the doctrines of complicity and incomplete crimes; and of the definitions of specific crimes to later chapters. In this chapter, we examine the principle of legality and some of the constitutional limits on the power of the government to create crimes.

▼ THE PRINCIPLE OF LEGALITY

The essence of the **principle of legality** is that the government cannot punish citizens without specific laws forewarning citizens that the government will punish specific conduct in a particular manner. Legality encompasses all the following: (1) ***nullum crimen sine lege*** (nothing is a crime without a specific law defining it as such); (2) the constitutional **void-for-vagueness principle,** that legislatures must draft laws clear enough for ordinary citizens and law enforcement officers to understand; (3) the constitutional prohibition against ***ex post facto*** **laws** (laws passed after the occurrence of the conduct); and (4) ***nulla poena sine lege*** (the principle that no punishment is administered without specific authority in law).

▼ CONSTITUTIONAL LIMITS

The United States Constitution's prohibitions against *ex post facto* laws and vagueness in criminal statutes, and its guarantee of equal protection of the laws, embody most of the principle of legality. These constitutional principles reflect the eighteenth-century Enlightenment's philosophical commitment to the rule of law, particularly to codification. However, the basic idea that the law must define the crime and penalty in advance enjoys a long history. The ancient Greeks prohibited *ex post facto* laws, and the Roman Civil Law read: "[A] penalty is not inflicted unless it is expressly imposed by law, or by some other authority." In the fierce struggle between king and Parliament in seventeenth-century England, the great jurist Lord Edward Coke said:

> [I]t is against the law, that men should be committed [to prison], and no cause shewed ... it is not I, Edward Coke, that speaks it, but the Records that speak it; we have a national appropriate Law to this nation.[1]

The Ex Post Facto *Prohibition*

The Constitution's framers considered the *ex post facto* principle so important that they wrote it into the main body of the Constitution before adding the Bill of Rights. (The Bill of Rights includes most of the provisions affecting criminal law.) According to the Supreme Court, which addressed the question as early as 1798, the *ex post facto* clause prohibits the following: (1) laws that make a crime of and punish conduct done before their passage; (2) laws that aggravate a crime after it was committed; (3) laws that increase the punishment for a specific crime after the crime was committed; and (4) laws that alter the rules of evidence to convict a defendant, receiving less or different testimony than the law required when the offense was committed.[2]

The *ex post facto* prohibition has two major goals: to give fair warning to citizens and to prevent arbitrary action by government. Since ignorance of the law does not ordinarily excuse criminal liability, guarding against arbitrary government action is the more important purpose. The *ex post facto* prohibition does not apply to changes in the law that *benefit* defendants. For example, if a law reduces from first- to second-degree murder killings that occur during the commission of other felonies, that law can be retroactive because it benefits defendants. Similarly, laws that reduce the penalty for particular crimes can be retroactive. For example, a defendant who committed a capital murder before the enactment of a statute abolishing capital punishment cannot suffer the death penalty. Some statutes have "savings clauses" specifically excluding retroactivity. In these cases, reductions in crime and punishment do not benefit defendants; the law that was in effect when the crime was committed governs.[3]

Void for Vagueness

The Constitution does not specifically prohibit vague laws. However, courts' refusal to enforce vague and uncertain laws has a long history. At common law, judges refused to enforce vague statutes. The United States Supreme Court in early cases refused to enforce uncertain laws, on the ground that they violated the separation of powers by placing the burden of law making on the judiciary. In other words, vague laws require judges to define the law, which is the legislature's responsibility. The Supreme Court also struck down vague laws on the ground that they denied defendants in criminal cases their Sixth Amendment right to know "the nature and cause of the accusation" against them.

Eventually, the Court settled on the void-for-vagueness doctrine, ruling that vague laws violate the **due process clauses** of the Fifth Amendment in federal statutes and the Fourteenth Amendment in state statutes. The clauses read:

> No person ... shall ... be deprived of life, liberty or property without due process of law. [Amendment V, U.S. Constitution] No *state* ... shall ... deprive any person of life, liberty, or property, without due process of law. [Amendment XIV, U.S. Constitution] (Emphasis added).

The due process clause has both substantive and procedural dimensions. In the procedural sense, it requires that government follow established practices in criminal law enforcement, trial, and punishment. In the substantive sense, due process limits the power of government to encroach upon citizens' lives, liberty, or property. We see these dimensions in the following sections on privacy and free speech, and again in the crimes against public order and morals in chapter 12. Here, we focus on the procedural requirement stipulating that legislatures specifically define criminal conduct.

In early cases, the Supreme Court focused on fair warning to citizens. In *Lanzetta v. New Jersey,* for example, the Supreme Court struck down a statute that made it a crime to be a member of a "gang." After holding that the word *gang* was too vague to give fair warning, the Court commented on the fair warning idea:

> No one may be required at peril of life, liberty, or property to speculate as to the meaning of penal statutes. All are entitled to be informed as to what the State commands or forbids.... [A] statute which either forbids or requires the doing of an act in terms so vague that men of common intelligence must necessarily guess at its meaning and differ as to its application, violates the first essential of due process of law.[4]

More recently, the Court has ruled that in addition to defining a statute "with sufficient definiteness that ordinary people can understand what conduct is prohibited," it must do so in a manner that does not encourage arbitrary and discriminatory law enforcement. Hence, the doctrine has two prongs. The first points to ordinary people, requiring that they receive fair warning about the possible criminality of their conduct; the other points to criminal justice officials, requiring that the law prevent the abuse of discretion. The Court has gone so far as to hold that the

> more important aspect of the vagueness doctrine is not actual notice, but the other principal element of the vagueness doctrine—the requirement that a legislature establish minimal guidelines to govern law enforcement.[5]

What constitutes a law vague enough to violate the due process clause? Words are not precise like numbers; they cannot define as clearly. Furthermore, lawmakers cannot foresee all the variations that might arise under statutes; ambiguity inheres in all laws. As a result, no litmus test can mark a law "vague." The Nebraska supreme court applied the void for vagueness doctrine to a Lincoln, Nebraska, ordinance in the case of *Metzger v. State.*

CASE

Was the Ordinance Void for Vagueness?

State v. Metzger
211 Neb. 593, 319 N.W.2d 459 (1982)

Heard before Krivosha, C.J., and Boslaugh, McCown, Clinton, White, Hastings, and Caporale, JJ.
  Krivosha, Chief Justice

FACTS

... Douglas E. Metzger, was convicted in the municipal court of Lincoln, Nebraska, of violating § 9.52.100 of the Lincoln Municipal

(handwritten margin note: 1) People must know what the law is about 2) law enforcement can't be arbitrary on your arrest. Prosecution on arrest)

Code. The judgement was affirmed by the District Court for Lancaster County, Nebraska, and Metzger has appealed to this court.... [W]e reverse and dismiss....

Metzger lived in a garden-level apartment located in Lincoln, Nebraska. A large window in the apartment faces a parking lot which is situated on the north side of the apartment building. At about 7:45 a.m., on April 30, 1981, another resident of the apartment, while parking his automobile in a space directly in front of Metzger's apartment window, observed Metzger standing naked with his arms at his sides in his apartment window for a period of 5 seconds. The resident testified that he saw Metzger's body from the thighs on up.

The resident called the police department and two officers arrived at the apartment at about 8 a.m. The officers testified that they observed Metzger standing in front of the window eating a bowl of cereal. They testified that Metzger was standing within a foot of the window and his nude body, from the mid-thigh on up, was visible.

OPINION

... The pertinent portion of § 9.52.100 ... under which Metzger was charged, provides as follows: "It shall be unlawful for any person within the City of Lincoln ... to commit any indecent, immodest or filthy act in the presence of any person, or in such a situation that persons passing might ordinarily see the same."...

The ... basic issue presented to us by this appeal is whether the ordinance, as drafted, is so vague as to be unconstitutional. We believe that it is. There is no argument that a violation of the municipal ordinance in question is a criminal act. Since the ordinance in question is criminal in nature, it is a fundamental requirement of due process of law that such criminal ordinance be reasonably clear and definite. Moreover, a crime must be defined with sufficient definiteness and there must be ascertainable standards of guilt to inform those subject thereto as to what conduct will render them liable to punishment thereunder.

The dividing line between what is lawful and unlawful cannot be left to conjecture. A citizen cannot be held to answer charges based upon penal statutes whose mandates are so uncertain that they will reasonably admit of different constructions. A criminal statute cannot rest upon an uncertain foundation. The crime and the elements constituting it must be so clearly expressed that the ordinary person can intelligently choose in advance what course it is lawful for him to pursue. Penal statutes prohibiting the doing of certain things and providing a punishment for their violation should not admit of such a double meaning that the citizen may act upon one conception of its requirements and the courts upon another.

A statute which forbids the doing of an act in terms so vague that men of common intelligence must necessarily guess as to its meaning and differ as to its application violates the first essential elements of due process of law. It is not permissible to enact a law which in effect spreads an all-inclusive net for the feet of everybody upon the chance that, while the innocent will surely be entangled in its meshes, some wrongdoers may also be caught. *State v. Adkins,* 196 Neb. 76, 241 N.W.2d 655 (1976).

In State ex rel. *English v. Ruback,* 135 Neb. 335, 281 N.W. 607 (1938), this court laid down guidelines to assist in determining whether a statute defining an offense is void for uncertainty. In *Ruback,* we said: "'The test to determine whether a statute defining an offense is void for uncertainty (1) is whether the language may apply not only to a particular act about which there can be little or no difference of opinion, but equally to other acts about which there may be radical differences, thereby devolving on the court the exercise of arbitrary power of discriminating between the several classes of acts. (2) The dividing line between what is lawful and what is unlawful cannot be left to conjecture.'"

In the case of *Papachristou v. City of Jacksonville,* 405 U.S. 156, 162, 92 S.Ct. 839, 31 L.Ed.2d 110 (1972), the U.S. Supreme Court said: "Living under a rule of law entails various suppositions, one of which is that '[all persons] are entitled to be informed as to what the State commands or forbids.'" In *Papachristou,* the U.S. Supreme Court declared a vagrancy statute of the city of Jacksonville, Florida, invalid for vagueness, saying: "This aspect of the vagrancy ordinance before us is suggested by what this Court said in 1876 about a broad criminal statute enacted by Congress: 'It would certainly be dangerous if the legislature could set a net large enough to catch all possible offenders, and leave it to the courts to step inside and say who could be rightfully detained, and who should be set at large.'"

Several other jurisdictions which have viewed ordinances with the same general intent in mind have reached similar conclusions. In the case of *State v. Sanders,* 37 N.C.App. 53, 245 S.E.2d 397 (1978), the South Carolina Court of Appeals was presented with a statute making it a misdemeanor for members of the opposite sex to occupy the same bedroom at a hotel for "any immoral purpose." In finding the ordinance too vague and indefinite to comply with constitutional due process standards, the court said: "A criminal statute or ordinance must be sufficiently definite to inform citizens of common intelligence of the particular acts which are forbidden. G.S. 14–186 [the statute] fails to define with sufficient precision exactly what the term 'any immoral purpose' may encompass.

The word immoral is not equivalent to the word illegal; hence, enforcement of G.S. 14–186 may involve legal acts which, nevertheless, are immoral in the view of many citizens. One must necessarily speculate, therefore, as to what acts are immoral. If the legislative intent of G.S. 14–186 is to proscribe illicit sexual intercourse the statute could have specifically so provided."

And in the case of City of *Detroit v. Sanchez,* 18 Mich.App. 399, 171 N.W.2d 452 (1969), the Michigan Court of Appeals was asked to determine whether an ordinance prohibiting ogling, insulting, annoying, following, or pursuing any person in any public street in the city was overbroad. In holding the ordinance void, the Michigan court said: "We are compelled to decide thus because this provision of the ordinance is unconstitutionally vague.

By 'vague' we do not mean here that sort of vagueness … [in which] the ordinance is put in terms which require men of common intelligence to guess as to its meaning and differ as to its application. The vagueness which invalidates this ordinance is its overbreadth of coverage rather than imprecise terminology or phraseology. The conviction cannot be sustained, because the ordinance makes criminal innocent as well as culpable conduct."

Holding

The ordinance in question makes it unlawful for anyone to commit any "indecent, immodest or filthy act." We know of no way in which the standards required of a criminal act can be met in those broad, general terms. There may be those few who believe persons of opposite sex holding hands in public are immodest, and certainly more who might believe that kissing in public is immodest. Such acts cannot constitute a crime. Certainly one could find many who would conclude that today's swimming attire found on many beaches or beside many pools is immodest. Yet, the fact that it is immodest does not thereby make it illegal, absent some requirement related to the health, safety, or welfare of the community.

The dividing line between what is lawful and what is unlawful in terms of "indecent," "immodest," or "filthy" is simply too broad to satisfy the constitutional requirements of due process. Both lawful and unlawful acts can be embraced within such broad definitions. That cannot be permitted. One is not able to determine in advance what is lawful and what is unlawful. We do not attempt, in this opinion, to determine whether Metzger's actions in a particular case might not be made unlawful, nor do we intend to encourage such behavior. Indeed, it may be possible that a governmental subdivision using sufficiently definite language could make such an act as committed by Metzger unlawful. We simply do not decide that question at this time because of our determination that the ordinance is so vague as to be unconstitutional.

We therefore believe that § 9.52.100 of the Lincoln Municipal Code must be declared invalid. Because the ordinance is therefore declared invalid, the conviction cannot stand.

Reversed and Dismissed.

DISSENT
Boslaugh, Justice, dissenting.

The ordinance in question prohibits indecent acts, immodest acts, or filthy acts in the presence of any person. Although the ordinance may be too broad in some respects... [t]he exhibition of [Metzger's] genitals under the circumstances of this case was, clearly, an indecent act. Statutes and ordinances prohibiting indecent exposure generally have been held valid. I do not subscribe to the view that it is only "possible" that such conduct may be prohibited by statute or ordinance.

Clinton and Hastings, JJ., join in this dissent.

Case Discussion

Does the dissent have a point when he argues that displaying genitals when others can see them is clearly an indecent act? Or does the ordinance refer to intentionally exposing genitals, or "flashing"? Should courts guess what legislatures mean, or should they construe the words as narrowly as possible, or strike down laws, as this court did? Explain.

Note Cases

1. Graham struck Suzanne Olson on the face, legs, and arms with "a four-foot metal floor lamp with a large metal base." A Minnesota statute provides: "Whoever assaults another with a deadly weapon ... may be sentenced to imprisonment for not more than five years or to payment of a fine of not more than $5,000 or both." The statute defines dangerous weapon as "any device or instrumentality which, in the manner it is used or intended to be used, is calculated to produce death or great bodily harm." Did the statute invite arbitrary law enforcement due to its vagueness? No, said the court:

> Due process does not ... require impossible standards of clarity. It would be impossible to specify any and all objects capable of producing death or great bodily harm when used to inflict injury on another.... Whether the lamp as allegedly used in this case does constitute a dangerous weapon is for the jury to determine. *State v. Graham,* 366 N.W.2d 335 (Minn.1985)

2. A statute makes it a felony to possess a "switchblade or gravity knife." Is it void for vagueness? The court ruled that it was not, because "The term has a readily ascertainable and consistent definition. As commonly understood, a gravity knife is one in which the blade opens, falls into place, or is ejected into position by the force of gravity or by centrifugal force." *State v. Weaver,* 736 P.2d 781 (Alaska 1987)

3. A statute provides: "Whoever has in his possession any device, gear, or instrument specially designed to assist in shoplifting ... may be sentenced to ... not more than three years of imprisonment and to payment of a fine of not more than $5,000, or both." Danny Skinner wore a long blue trench coat into a discount store. The coat had a hidden pocket beneath the lining. He argued that the statute was void for vagueness because it did not specify what items qualified as "specially designed" shoplifting gear, by whom the device must be specifically designed, whether the item must be purchased from a manufacturer or altered after purchase, and whether common items of everyday use can qualify as shoplifting gear. Was the statute void for vagueness? The court ruled that the statute was not void for vagueness, because: "The statute puts individuals on notice of the prohibited conduct, possession of 'gear specially designed to assist in shoplifting'. The language is clear and can be understood by an ordinary person." Is it as clear as the court says? *State v. Skinner,* 403 N.W.2d 912 (Minn.1987)

Equal Protection of the Laws

The Fourteenth Amendment to the United States Constitution provides that "no state shall deny to any person within its jurisdiction the equal protection of the laws." The equal protection clause does not require that the government treat all citizens exactly alike. The common law and numerous statutes classify (that is, single out for special treatment) certain persons and conduct. For example, statutes in some jurisdictions classify embezzlement by public officials as a more serious crime than embezzlement by private citizens; virtually every state labels premeditated killings as more heinous than negligent homicides; and several states punish habitual offenders more severely than first-time offenders. Hence, the criminal law frequently distinguishes according to occupation, state of mind, and type of person.

Other statutes exempt particular conduct or groups from criminal liability. For example, Sunday closing laws typically exempt from coverage small businesses or sales of necessary items. All these and many more classifications comport with the equal protection clause.

In these kinds of classifications, the equal protection challenge to a statute is "the usual last resort of constitutional arguments." With good reason. The Supreme Court upholds most of these kinds of statutory classification schemes, striking down only statutory classifications without a "reasonable basis." And, it requires defendants to prove the lack of a reasonable basis.[6]

The Supreme Court scrutinizes classifications based on race and gender more carefully. According to the Supreme Court, a statute violates the equal protection clause if it

> invidiously classifies similarly situated people on the basis of the immutable characteristics with which they were born. Thus, detrimental racial classifications by government *always* [emphasis added] violate the Constitution, for the simple reason that, so far as the Constitution is concerned, people of different races are always similarly situated.[7]

Gender classifications stand between general classifications and race classifications. Unlike race classifications, they are not always unconstitutional. On the other hand, they bear closer scrutiny than other classifications. The Supreme Court has had difficulty deciding exactly how carefully to scrutinize gender classifications in criminal statutes. The plurality, but not a majority of the justices, in *Michael M. v. Superior Court of Sonoma County* agreed that gender classifications must have a "fair and substantial relationship" to legitimate state ends. The plurality applied that test to California's gender based statutory rape law.

CASE

Was the Gender Classification "Reasonable"?

Michael M. v. Superior Court of Sonoma County

450 U.S. 464, 101 S.Ct.
1200 67 L.Ed.2d 437 (1981)

Justice Rehnquist announced the judgment of the Court and delivered an opinion, in which the chief justice, Justice Stewart, and Justice Powell joined.

FACTS

... In July 1978, a complaint was filed in the Municipal Court of Sonoma County, Cal., alleging that petitioner, then a 17½-year-old male, had had unlawful sexual intercourse with a female under the age of 18, in violation of § 261.5 [California's statutory rape law, which defines unlawful sexual intercourse as "an act of sexual intercourse accomplished with a female not the wife of the perpetrator, where the female is under the age of 18 years"]. The evidence adduced at a preliminary hearing showed that at approximately midnight on June 3, 1978, petitioner and two friends approached Sharon, a 16 ½-year-old female, and her sister as they waited at a bus stop. Petitioner and Sharon, who had already been drinking, moved away from the others and began to kiss. After being struck in the face for rebuffing petitioner's initial advances, Sharon submitted to sexual intercourse with petitioner. Prior to trial, petitioner sought to set aside information on both state and federal constitutional grounds, asserting that § 261.5 unlawfully discriminated on the basis of gender. The trial court and the California Court of Appeal denied petitioner's request for relief and petitioner sought review in the supreme court of California.

Prior to trial, petitioner sought to set aside the information [the document charging Michael M. with statutory rape] on both state and federal constitutional grounds, asserting that § 261.5 unlawfully discriminated on the basis of gender. The trial court and the California Court of Appeal denied petitioner's request for relief and petitioner sought review in the Supreme Court of California. The [California] Supreme Court held that "§ 261.5 discriminates on the basis of sex because only females may be victims, and only males may violate the section." The court then subjected the classification to "strict scrutiny," stating that it must be justified by a compelling state interest. It found that the classification was "supported not by mere social convention but by the immutable physiological fact that it is the female exclusively who can become pregnant." Canvassing "the tragic human costs of illegitimate teenage pregnancies," including the large number of teenage abortions, the increased medical risk associated with teenage pregnancies, and the social consequences of teenage childbearing, the court concluded that the State has a compelling interest in preventing such pregnancies. Because males alone can "physiologically cause the result which the law properly seeks to avoid," the court further held that the gender classification was readily justified as a means of identifying offender and victim.

For the reasons stated below, we affirm the judgment of the California supreme court.

PLURALITY OPINION

... Unlike the California supreme court, we have not held that gender-based classifications are "inherently suspect" and thus we do not apply so-called "strict scrutiny" to those classifications. Our cases have held, however, that the traditional minimum rationality test takes on a somewhat "sharper focus" when gender-based classifications are challenged.... A legislature may not "make overbroad generalizations based on sex which are entirely unrelated to any differences between men and women or which demean the ability or social status of the affected class." But because the Equal

Protection Clause does not "demand that a statute necessarily apply equally to all persons" or require "'things which are different in fact to be treated in law as though they were the same,'" this Court has consistently upheld statutes where the gender classification is not invidious, but rather realistically reflects the fact that the sexes are not similarly situated in certain circumstances. As the Court has stated, a legislature may "provide for the special problems of women."

Applying those principles to this case, the fact that the California Legislature criminalized the act of illicit sexual intercourse with a minor female is a sure indication of its intent or purpose to discourage that conduct.... The justification for the statute offered by the State, and accepted by the Supreme Court of California, is that the legislature sought to prevent illegitimate teenage pregnancies....

We are satisfied not only that the prevention of illegitimate pregnancy is at least one of the "purposes" of the statute, but also that the State has a strong interest in preventing such pregnancy. At the risk of stating the obvious, teenage pregnancies, which have increased dramatically over the last two decades, have significant social, medical, and economic consequences for both the mother and her child, and the State. Of particular concern to the State is that approximately half of all teenage pregnancies end in abortion. And of those children who are born, their illegitimacy makes them likely candidates to become wards of the State.

We need not be medical doctors to discern that young men and young women are not similarly situated with respect to the problems and the risks of sexual intercourse. Only women may become pregnant, and they suffer disproportionately the profound physical, emotional and psychological consequences of sexual activity. The statute at issue here protects women from sexual intercourse at an age when those consequences are particularly severe....

The question thus boils down to whether a State may attack the problem of sexual intercourse and teenage pregnancy directly by prohibiting a male from having sexual intercourse with a minor female. We hold that such a statute is sufficiently related to the State's objectives to pass constitutional muster.

Because virtually all of the significant harmful and inescapably identifiable consequences of teenage pregnancy fall on the young female, a legislature acts well within its authority when it elects to punish only the participant who, by nature, suffers few of the consequences of his conduct. It is hardly unreasonable for a legislature acting to protect minor females to exclude them from punishment. Moreover, the risk of pregnancy itself constitutes a substantial deterrence to young females. No similar natural sanctions deter males. A criminal sanction imposed solely on males thus serves to roughly "equalize" the deterrents on the sexes....

There remains only petitioner's contention that the statute is unconstitutional as it is applied to him because he, like Sharon, was under 18 at the time of sexual intercourse. Petitioner argues that the statute is flawed because it presumes that as between two persons under 18, the male is the culpable aggressor. We find petitioner's contentions unpersuasive. Contrary to his assertions, the statute does not rest on the assumption that males are generally the aggressors. It is instead an attempt by a legislature to prevent illegitimate teenage pregnancy by providing an additional deterrent for men. The age of the man is irrelevant since young men are as capable as older men of inflicting the harm sought to be prevented....

Accordingly, the judgment of the California Supreme Court is Affirmed.

[Concurring opinions of Justices Stewart and Blackmun omitted. They stressed the importance of the State's goal of preventing unwanted pregnancies.]

DISSENT

Justice Brennan, with whom Justices White and Marshall join, dissenting.

... I am convinced that there is only one proper resolution of this issue: the classification must be declared unconstitutional. I fear that the plurality opinion and Justices Stewart and Blackmun reach the opposite result by placing too much emphasis on the desirability of achieving the State's asserted statutory goal—prevention of teenage pregnancy—and not enough emphasis on the fundamental question of whether the sex-based discrimination in the California statute is substantially related to the achievement of that goal....

[A] statute containing a gender-based classification cannot withstand constitutional challenge unless the classification is substantially related to the achievement of an important governmental objective....

The burden is on the government to prove both the importance of its asserted objective and the substantial relationship between the classification and that objective. And the State cannot meet that burden without showing that a gender-neutral statute would be a less effective means of achieving that goal.

The State of California vigorously asserts that the "important governmental objective" to be served by § 261.5 is the prevention of teenage pregnancy.... But even assuming that prevention of teenage pregnancy is an important governmental objective and that it is in fact an objective of § 261.5, California still has the burden of proving that there are fewer teenage pregnancies under its gender-based statutory rape law than there would be if the law were gender neutral. To meet this burden, the State must show that because its statutory rape law punishes only males, and not females, it more effectively deters minor females from having sexual intercourse....

[A] [s]tate's bare assertion that its gender-based statutory classification substantially furthers an important governmental interest is not enough to meet its burden of proof under *Craig v. Boren.* Rather, the State must produce evidence that will persuade the court that its assertion is true. See *Craig v. Boren,* 429 U.S., at 200–204, 97 S.Ct., at 458–460. The State has not produced such evidence in this case....

[T]he experience of other jurisdictions, and California itself, belies the plurality's conclusion that a gender-neutral statutory rape law "may well be incapable of enforcement." There are now at least 37 States that have enacted gender-neutral statutory rape laws.... California has introduced no evidence that those States have been handicapped by the enforcement problems the plurality finds so pervasive. Surely, if those States could provide such evidence, we might expect that California would have introduced it....

Common sense ... suggests that a gender-neutral statutory rape law is potentially a greater deterrent of sexual activity than a gender-based law, for the simple reason that a gender-neutral law subjects both men and women to criminal sanctions and thus arguably has a deterrent effect on twice as many potential violators. Even if fewer persons were prosecuted under the gender-neutral law, as the State suggests, it would still be true that twice as many persons would be subject to arrest. The State's failure to prove that a gender-neutral law would be difficult to enforce, should have led this Court to invalidate § 261.5.

Until very recently, no California court or commentator had suggested that the purpose of California's statutory rape law was to protect young women from the risk of pregnancy. Indeed, the historical development of § 261.5 demonstrates that the law was initially enacted on the premise that young women, in contrast to young men, were to be deemed legally incapable of consenting to an act of sexual intercourse. Because their chastity was considered particularly precious, those young women were felt to be uniquely in need of the State's protection. In contrast, young men were assumed to be capable of making such decisions for themselves; the law therefore did not offer them any special protection.

It is perhaps because the gender classification in California's statutory rape law was initially designed to further these outmoded sexual stereotypes, rather than to reduce the incidence of teenage pregnancies, that the State has been unable to demonstrate a substantial relationship between the classification and its newly asserted goal. But whatever the reason, the State has not shown that Cal.Penal Code § 261.5 is any more effective than a gender-neutral law would be in deterring minor females from engaging in sexual intercourse. It has there-fore not met its burden of proving that the statutory classification is substantially related to the achievement of its asserted goal.

I would hold that § 261.5 violates the Equal Protection Clause of the Fourteenth Amendment, and I would reverse the judgment of the California Supreme Court. [Justice Stevens's dissent omitted.]

Case Discussion

Do you agree that distinguishing between men and women in statutory rape cases is a reasonable device to protect against teenage pregnancies? Or does the classification deny men the equal protection of the laws? Should the Court require proof that there is some basis, however much, for the gender classification, or should it leave the question of how to deal with the problem of teenage pregnancies and abortions to the wisdom of the California legislature? Should defendants have to prove there is no reasonable basis for the legislation, or should the government have to prove there is a reasonable basis for punishing young men? Has the State proved that punishing only young men only works? Is the dissent's "common sense" argument about gender-neutral statutes right?

Note Cases

1. A Florida statute provided: "Any negro man and white woman, or any white man and negro woman, who are not married to each other, who shall habitually live in and occupy in the nighttime the same room shall each be punished by imprisonment not exceeding twelve months, or by fine not exceeding five hundred dollars." Florida convicted McLaughlin under the statute. He challenged the statute on the grounds that it invidiously discriminated on the basis of race.

A majority of the U.S. Supreme Court held, "Normally, the widest discretion is allowed the legislative judgment in determining whether to attack some, rather than all, of the manifestations of the evil aimed at; and normally that judgment is given the benefit of every conceivable circumstance which might suffice to characterize the classification as reasonable rather than arbitrary and invidious. But we deal here with a classification based upon the race of the participants, which must be viewed in light of the historical fact that the central purpose of the Fourteenth Amendment was to eliminate racial discrimination emanating from official sources in the States. This strong policy renders racial classifications 'constitutionally suspect,' and subject to the 'most rigid scrutiny,' and 'in most circumstances irrelevant' to any constitutionally acceptable legislative purpose."

"We deal here with a racial classification embodied in a criminal statute. In this context, where the power of the State weighs most heavily upon the individual or the group, we must be especially sensitive to the policies of the Equal Protection Clause.... Our inquiry, therefore, is whether there clearly appears ... some overriding statutory purpose requiring the proscription of the specified conduct when engaged in by a white person and a Negro, but not otherwise. Without such justification the racial classification ... is reduced to an invidious discrimination forbidden by the Equal Protection Clause."

"There is involved here an exercise of the state police power which trenches upon the constitutionally protected freedom from invidious official discrimination based on race. Such a law, even though enacted pursuant to a valid state interest, bears a heavy burden of justification, as we have said, and will be upheld only if it is necessary, and not merely rationally related, to the accomplishment of a permissible state policy."

Two justices went further. Justice Stewart wrote for himself and Justice Douglas: "I concur in the judgment and agree with most of what is said in the Court's opinion. But the Court implies that a criminal law of the kind here involved might be constitutionally valid if a State could show 'some overriding statutory purpose.' This is an implication in which I cannot join, because I cannot conceive of a valid legislative purpose under our Constitution for a state law which makes the color of a person's skin the test of whether his conduct is a criminal offense.

These appellants were convicted, fined, and imprisoned under a statute which made their conduct criminal only because they were of different races.… There might be limited room under the Equal Protection Clause for a civil law requiring the keeping of racially segregated public records for statistical or other valid public purposes. But we deal here with a criminal law which imposes criminal punishment. And I think it is simply not possible for a state law to be valid under our Constitution which makes the criminality of an act depend upon the race of the actor. Discrimination of that kind is invidious per se." *McLaughlin v. Florida,* 379 U.S. 184 (1964)

2. Colorado prohibits the possession, use, and sale of "narcotic drugs." It defines narcotic drug as "coca leaves, opium, cannabis, [i.e., marijuana] isonipecaine, amidone, isoamidone, ketobemidone, and every other substance neither chemically nor physically distinguishable from them, and any other drug to which the federal narcotic laws may apply."

Stark was convicted of possessing marijuana and argued that the classification of cannabis in the same category as addicting narcotic drugs denied him the equal protection of the law. Was he right? The Colorado supreme court said no: "We recognize the differences of opinion exist as to whether cannabis causes physical or psychological addition. This fact is not material in determining what drugs may be included within the classification of 'narcotic drugs' in an exercise of police powers by a state. The important and pivotal consideration is whether the classification bears a reasonable relation 'to the public purpose sought to be achieved by the legislation involved.' Clearly, the use of marijuana and other drugs identified in the Colorado statute presents a danger to the public safety and welfare of the community since they are clearly related to each other and to the commission of crime." *People v. Stark,* 400 P.2d 923 (1965)

The Right to Privacy

The United States Constitution nowhere mentions a right to privacy. However, the Supreme Court has read a *limited* right to privacy into the Constitution. The constitutional right to privacy arises out of an amalgam of the First Amendment right to free expression and association, the Third Amendment prohibition against quartering soldiers in private homes, the Fourth Amendment right to be secure in one's person, house, and effects, and the Ninth Amendment, which provides:

> The enumeration in the Constitution, of certain rights, shall not be construed to deny or disparage others retained by the people.

According to the Court, these amendments protect "against all governmental invasions of the sanctity of a man's home and the privacies of life." The right to privacy reflects the notion that a free society guarantees that its citizens will be "left alone," particularly by the government. The federal right to privacy has generated high controversy, particularly when applied to abortion and sexual preference.[8]

Unlike the United States Constitution, several state constitutions—such as those of Alaska, Hawaii, and Florida—contain specific provisions guaranteeing their citizens the right to privacy. The Florida Declaration of Rights provides:

> Every natural person has the right to be let alone and free from governmental intrusion into his private life.[9]

The Supreme Court has restricted the right to privacy mainly to intimate relationships inside family and home. Hence, in the leading case on the point, *Griswold v. Connecticut,* the Court struck down a statute making it a crime for married couples to use contraceptives. Justice Douglas, writing for the majority, said that the prohibition against contraceptives

> operates directly on an intimate relation of husband and wife.... The present case ... concerns a relationship lying within the zone of privacy created by several different fundamental constitutional guarantees. And it concerns a law which, in forbidding the *use* of contraceptives rather than regulating their manufacture or sale, seeks to achieve its goals by means having a maximum destructive impact upon that relationship. Such a law cannot stand.[10]

Four years later, in *Stanley v. Georgia,* the Supreme Court struck down a statute that made it a crime to possess pornography within the privacy of a home. It appeared to some that the Court had permanently locked the criminal law out of private homes, believing that the Court's holding meant that whatever citizens do within their homes is not the law's business. The Court has not, however, ruled that the right to privacy so restricts the criminal law.[11]

In 1986, in *Bowers v. Hardwick,* the Court upheld Georgia's sodomy statute against a challenge that what consenting adult homosexuals do in the privacy of their own homes cannot be made a crime by the state. Hardwick and a friend left a gay bar and went to Hardwick's house. They passed a sleeping guest in the living room. Atlanta police, who had followed Hardwick and his friend from the bar, awoke the guest and entered Hardwick's home with the guest's permission but without Hardwick's knowledge. The police surprised Hardwick in his bedroom, where he was engaged in sodomy with his friend, an adult. The police arrested Hardwick for violating Georgia's sodomy statute. In an ensuing law suit, Hardwick argued that:

> the Georgia statute violated [Hardwick's] fundamental rights because his homosexual activity is a private and intimate association that is beyond the reach of state regulation by reason of the Ninth Amendment.[12]

The court held that the right of privacy does not prevent states from making homosexual conduct criminal, even within the privacy of homes. (See chapter 12 on sodomy for full excerpt.)

In *Ravin v. State,* the Alaska Supreme Court addressed the question of whether Alaska's right to privacy provision—"[t]he right of the people to privacy is recognized and shall not be infringed"—protected Ravin from prosecution for possession of marijuana in the privacy of his home. Alaska makes possession of marijuana a crime.[13]

CASE

Does He Have a "Right" to Possess Marijuana in His Home?

Ravin v. State
537 P.2d 494 (Alaska 1975)

Rabinowitz, Chief Justice

FACTS

... Ravin was arrested on December 11, 1972 and charged with violating AS [Alaska Statute] 17.12.010, [which] provides: Except as otherwise provided in this chapter, it is unlawful for a person to manufacture, compound, counterfeit, possess, have under his control, sell, prescribe, administer, dispense, give, barter, supply or distribute in any manner, a depressant, hallucinogenic or stimulant drug. [AS 17.12.150 defines 'depressant, hallucinogenic, or stimulant drug' to include all parts of the plant Cannabis Sativa L.]

Before trial Ravin attacked the constitutionality of AS 17.12.010 by a motion to dismiss in which he asserted that the State had violated his right of privacy under both the federal and Alaska constitutions.... Lengthy hearings on the questions were held before District Court Judge Dorothy D.

Tyner, at which testimony from several expert witnesses was received. Ravin's motion to dismiss was denied by Judge Tyner. The superior court then granted review and after affirmance by the superior court, we, in turn, granted Ravin's petition for review from the superior court's affirmance.

OPINION

Here Ravin raises two basic claims: first, that there is no legitimate state interest in prohibiting possession of marijuana by adults for personal use, in view of the right to privacy....

Ravin's basic thesis is that there exists under the federal and Alaska constitutions a fundamental right to privacy, the scope of which is sufficiently broad to encompass and protect the possession of marijuana for personal use....

Ravin's argument that he has a fundamental right to possess marijuana for personal use rests on both federal and state law, and centers on what may broadly be called the right to privacy ... [which] was recently made explicit in Alaska by an amendment to the state constitution.

In Ravin's view, the right to privacy involved here is an autonomous right which gains special significance when its situs is found in a specially protected area, such as the home. Ravin begins his privacy argument by citation of and reliance upon

Griswold v. Connecticut, 381 U.S. 479, 85 S.Ct. 1678, 14 L.Ed.2d 510 (1965), in which the Supreme Court of the United States struck down as unconstitutional a state statute effectively barring the dispensation of birth control information to married persons. Writing for five members of the Court, Mr. Justice Douglas noted that rights protected by the Constitution are not limited to those specifically enumerated in the Constitution:

"In order to secure the enumerated rights, certain peripheral rights must be recognized. In other words, the 'specific guarantees in the Bill of Rights have penumbras, formed by emanations from those guarantees that help give them life and substance.' Certain of these penumbral rights create 'zones of privacy,' for example, First Amendment rights of association, Third and Fourth Amendment rights pertaining to the security of the home, and the Fifth Amendment right against self-incrimination."

The Supreme Court of the United States then proceeded to find a right to privacy in marriage which antedates the Bill of Rights and yet lies within the zone of privacy created by several fundamental constitutional guarantees....

[The Court proceeded to review several other important Supreme Court opinions concerning the right to privacy.]

These Supreme Court cases indicate to us that the federal right to privacy arises only in connection with other fundamental rights, such as the grouping of rights which involve the home. And even in connection with the penumbra of home related rights, the right of privacy in the sense of immunity from prosecution is absolute only when the private activity will not endanger or harm the general public.

The view is confirmed by the Supreme Court's abortion decision, *Roe v. Wade,* 410 U.S. 113, 93 S.Ct. 705, 35 L.Ed.2d 147 (1973). There appellant claimed that her right to decide for herself concerning abortion fell within the ambit of a right to privacy flowing from the federal Bill of Rights. The Court's decision in her favor makes clear that only personal rights which can be deemed "fundamental" or "implicit in the concept of ordered liberty" are protected by the right to privacy. The Supreme Court found this right "broad enough to encompass a woman's decision whether or not to terminate her pregnancy," but it rejected the idea that a woman's right to decide is absolute. At some point, the state's interest in safeguarding health, maintaining medical standards, and protecting potential life becomes sufficiently compelling to sustain regulations. One does not, the Supreme Court said, have an unlimited right to do with one's body as one pleases.

The right to privacy which the Court found in *Roe* is closely akin to that in *Griswold;* in both cases the zone of privacy involves the area of the family and procreation, more particularly, a right of personal autonomy in relation to choices affecting an individual's personal life....

In Alaska this court has dealt with the concept of privacy on only a few occasions. One of the most significant decisions in this area is *Breese v. Smith,* 501 P.2d 159 (Alaska 1972), where we considered the applicability of the guarantee of "life, liberty, the pursuit of happiness" found in the Alaska Constitution, to a school hairlength regulation. Noting that hairstyles are a highly personal matter in which the individual is traditionally autonomous, we concluded that governmental control of personal appearance would be antithetical to the concept of personal liberty under Alaska's constitution.

Since the student would be forced to choose between controlling his own personal appearance and asserting his right to an education if the regulations were upheld, we concluded that the constitutional language quoted above embodied an affirmative grant of liberty to public school students to choose their own hairstyles, for "at the core of (the concept of liberty) is the notion of total personal immunity from governmental control: the right 'to be let alone.'" That right is not absolute, however; we also noted that this "liberty" must yield where it "intrude(s) upon the freedom of others."

Subsequent to our decision in *Breese,* a right to privacy amendment was added to the Alaska Constitution. Article I, § 22 reads:

The right of the people to privacy is recognized and shall not be infringed. The legislature shall implement this section. The effect of this amendment is to place privacy among the specifically enumerated rights in Alaska's constitution. But this fact alone does not, in and of itself, yield answers concerning what scope should be accorded to this right of privacy.

We have suggested that the right to privacy may afford less than absolute protection to "the ingestion of food, beverages or other substances." *Gray v. State,* 525 P.2d 524, 528 (Alaska 1974)....

[I]n our view, the right to privacy amendment to the Alaska Constitution cannot be read so as to make the possession or ingestion of marijuana itself a fundamental right. Nor can we conclude that such a fundamental right is shown by virtue of the analysis we employed in *Breese.*

In that case, the student's traditional liberty pertaining to autonomy in personal appearance was threatened in such a way that his constitutionally guaranteed right to an education was jeopardized. Hairstyle, as emphasized in *Breese,* is a highly personal matter involving the individual and his body....

Few would believe they have been deprived of something of critical importance if deprived of marijuana, though they would if stripped of control over their personal appearance.... Therefore, if we were employing our former test, we would hold that there is no fundamental right, either under the Alaska or federal constitutions, either to possess or ingest marijuana.

The foregoing does not complete our analysis of the right to privacy issues. For in *Gray* we stated that the right of privacy amendment of the Alaska Constitution "clearly it shields the ingestion of food, beverages, or other substances," but that this right may be held to be subordinate to public health and welfare measures. Thus, Ravin's right to privacy contentions are not susceptible to disposition solely in terms of answering the question whether there is a general fundamental constitutional right to possess or smoke marijuana.

This leads us to a more detailed examination of the right to privacy and the relevancy of where the right is exercised. At one end of the scale of the scope of the right to privacy is possession or ingestion in the individual's home. If there is any area of human activity to which a right to privacy pertains more than any other, it is the home. The importance of the home has been amply demonstrated in constitutional law....

[The Court then discussed the meaning of the right to privacy in the U.S. Constitution, its Bill of Rights, and cases interpreting them.]

In Alaska we have also recognized the distinctive nature of the home as a place where the individual's privacy receives special protection....

Privacy in the home is a fundamental right, under both the federal and Alaska constitutions. We do not mean by this that a person may do anything at anytime as long as the activity takes place within a person's home. There are two important limitations on this facet of the right to privacy. First, we agree with the Supreme Court of the United States, which has strictly limited the ... guarantee to possession for purely private, noncommercial use in the home. And secondly, we think this right must yield when it interferes in a serious manner with the health, safety, rights and privileges of others or with the public welfare.

No one has an absolute right to do things in the privacy of his own home which will affect himself or others adversely. Indeed, one aspect of a private matter is that it is private, that is, that it does not adversely affect persons beyond the actor, and hence is none of their business. When a matter does affect the public, directly or indirectly, it loses its wholly private character, and can be made to yield when an appropriate public need is demonstrated.

The privacy amendment to the Alaska Constitution was intended to give recognition and protection to the home. Such a reading is consonant with the character of life in Alaska. Our territory and now state has traditionally been the home of people who prize their individuality and who have chosen to settle or to continue living here in order to achieve a measure of control over their own lifestyles which is now virtually unattainable in many of our sister states.

Thus, we conclude that citizens of the State of Alaska have a basic right to privacy in their homes under Alaska's constitution. This right to privacy would encompass the possession and ingestion of substances such as marijuana in a purely personal, non-commercial context in the home unless the state can meet its substantial burden and show that proscription of possession of marijuana in the home is supportable by achievement of a legitimate state interest.

This leads us to the second facet of our inquiry, namely, whether the State has demonstrated sufficient justification for the prohibition of possession of marijuana in general in the interest of public welfare; and further, whether the State has met the greater burden of showing a close and substantial relationship between the public welfare and control of ingestion or possession of marijuana in the home for personal use....

[The Court reviewed voluminous studies on the dangers of marijuana.]

The state is under no obligation to allow otherwise "private" activity which will result in numbers of people becoming public charges or otherwise burdening the public welfare. But we do not find that such a situation exists today regarding marijuana. It appears that effects of marijuana on the individual are not serious enough to justify widespread concern, at least as compared with the far more dangerous effects of alcohol, barbiturates and amphetamines.

Moreover, the current patterns of use in the United States are not such as would warrant concern that in the future consumption patterns are likely to change....

Given the relative insignificance of marijuana consumption as a health problem in our society at present, we do not believe that the potential harm generated by drivers under the influence of marijuana, standing alone, creates a close and substantial relationship between the public welfare and control of ingestion of marijuana or posses-

sion of it in the home for personal use. Thus we conclude that no adequate justification for the state's intrusion into the citizen's right to privacy by its prohibition of possession of marijuana by an adult for personal consumption in the home has been shown. The privacy of the individual's home cannot be breached absent a persuasive showing of a close and substantial relationship of the intrusion to a legitimate governmental interest. Here, mere scientific doubts will not suffice. The state must demonstrate a need based on proof that the public health or welfare will in fact suffer if the controls are not applied.

The state has a legitimate concern with avoiding the spread of marijuana use to adolescents who may not be equipped with the maturity to handle the experience prudently, as well as a legitimate concern with the problem of driving under the influence of marijuana. Yet these interests are insufficient to justify intrusions into the rights of adults in the privacy of their own homes. Further, neither the federal or Alaska constitution affords protection for the buying or selling of marijuana, nor absolute protection for its use or possession in public. Possession at home of amounts of marijuana indicative of intent to sell rather than possession for personal use is likewise unprotected.

In view of our holding that possession of marijuana by adults at home for personal use is constitutionally protected, we wish to make clear that we do not mean to condone the use of marijuana. The experts who testified below, including petitioner's witnesses, were unanimously opposed to the use of any psychoactive drugs. We agree completely. It is the responsibility of every individual to consider carefully the ramifications for himself and for those around him of using such substances. With the freedom which our society offers to each of us to order our lives as we see fit goes the duty to live responsibly, for our own sakes and for society's. This result can best be achieved, we believe, without the use of psychoactive substances....

The record does not disclose any facts as to the situs of Ravin's arrest and his alleged possession of marijuana. In view of these circumstances, we hold that the matter must be remanded to the district court for the purpose of developing the facts concerning Ravin's arrest and circumstances of his possession of marijuana. Once this is accomplished, the district court is to consider Ravin's motion to dismiss in conformity with this opinion.

Remanded for further proceedings consistent with this opinion.

CONCURRING OPINION

Boochever, Justice (concurring, with whom Connor, Justice, joins).

... While we must enforce the minimum constitutional standards imposed upon us by the United States Supreme Court's interpretation of the Fourteenth Amendment, we are free, and we are under a duty, to develop additional constitutional rights and privileges under our Alaska Constitution if we find such fundamental rights and privileges to be within the intention and spirit of our local constitutional language and to be necessary for the kind of civilized life and ordered liberty which is at the core of our constitutional heritage. We need not stand by idly and passively, waiting for constitutional direction from the highest court of the land. Instead, we should be moving concurrently to develop and expound the principles embedded in our constitutional law....

Since the citizens of Alaska, with their strong emphasis on individual liberty, enacted an amendment to the Alaska Constitution expressly providing for a right to privacy not found in the United States Constitution, it can only be concluded that that right is broader in scope than that of the Federal Constitution. As such, it includes not only activities within the home and values associated with the home, but also the right to be left alone and to do as one pleases as long as the activity does not infringe on the rights of others. Thus, the decision whether to ingest food, beverages or other substances comes within the purview of that right to privacy.

Case Discussion   Is the right to privacy a "fundamental right"? What harms might justify limiting the right to privacy? Is it true that possessing marijuana at home does not harm anyone? What harms justify limiting the right to privacy? Would the government have to prove the harm to society? Or would defendants have to prove that their conduct did not harm society? If you were compiling a list, what could citizens do in the privacy of their homes that government could not make a crime? What criteria would you establish for determining what falls within the right to privacy, and what does not? Would you extend the privacy right to motor homes? To motel rooms? To cars?

Note Case   Florida prosecuted Borras for possession of marijuana in his home. Borras argued that "the primary purpose of smoking marijuana is the 'psychological reaction' it produces in the user and that by smoking marijuana he was 'merely asserting the right to satisfy his intellectual and emotional needs' in the privacy of his own home."

The Florida Supreme Court ruled: "This Court is aware that commission of other types of crime, particularly violent crimes, has an emotional effect on the perpetrator. This, however, does not give a constitutional right to commit the crime.... Marijuana is a harmful, mind-altering drug. An individual might restrict his possession of marijuana to the privacy of his home, but the effects of the drug are not so restricted. The interest of the state in preventing harm to the individual and to the public at large amply justifies the outlawing of marijuana, in private and elsewhere." *Borras v. State,* 229 So.2d 244 (Fla.1969)

The Right to Free Speech and Expressive Conduct

The First Amendment provides that Congress shall make no law ... abridging the freedom of speech. Although the Amendment directs its prohibition to Congress, the Supreme Court long ago applied the prohibition to the States. In *Gitlow v. New York,* the Court ruled that a state law abridging free speech denied a citizen liberty without due process of law under the Fourteenth Amendment.

Despite the seeming unqualified language in the Amendment—"no law"—statutes can restrict speech that creates a "clear and present danger" of evils that legislatures have a right to prevent. (See chapter 12, "Fighting words.")[14]

According to the Supreme Court:

> There are certain well-defined and narrowly limited classes of speech, the prevention and punishment of which has never been thought to raise any Constitutional problem. These include the lewd and obscene, the profane, the libelous, and the insulting or "fighting" words—those which by their very utterance inflict injury or tend to incite an immediate breach of their peace.

For example, Justice Holmes wrote:

> The most stringent of free speech would not protect a man in falsely shouting fire in a theatre and causing a panic.[15]

On one hand, the Court has interpreted the First Amendment to limit speech that threatens certain evils. On the other hand, it has expanded the meaning of "speech" beyond words alone. The word speech, as the Court has interpreted it, includes "expressive conduct," such as wearing black arm bands to protest war, "sitting in" to protest racial segregation, picketing to support strikes. The Court grappled with the problem of flag burning as expressive conduct in *Texas v. Johnson.*

CASE

Did the Statute Violate the Constitution?

Texas v. Johnson
491 U.S. 397, 109 S.CT. 2533 (1989)

Brennan, J., delivered the opinion of the Court, in which Marshall, Blackmun, Scalia,

and Kennedy, JJ., joined. Kennedy, J., filed a concurring opinion. Rehnquist, C.J., filed a dissenting opinion, in which White and O'Connor, J.J., joined. Stevens, J., filed a dissenting opinion. Justice Brennan delivered the opinion of the Court.

FACTS
While the Republican National Convention was taking place in Dallas in 1984, respondent Johnson participated in a political demonstration dubbed the "Republican War Chest Tour." As explained in literature dis-

tributed by the demonstrators and in speeches made by them, the purpose of this event was to protest the policies of the Reagan administration and of certain Dallas-based corporations. The demonstrators marched through the Dallas streets, chanting political slogans and stopping at several corporate locations to stage "die-ins" intended to dramatize the consequences of nuclear war. On several occasions they spray-painted the walls of buildings and overturned potted plants, but Johnson himself took no part in such activities. He did, however, accept an American flag handed to him by a fellow protestor who had taken it from a flag pole outside one of the targeted buildings.

The demonstration ended in front of Dallas City Hall, where Johnson unfurled the American flag, doused it with kerosene, and set it on fire. While the flag burned, the protestors chanted, "America, the red, white, and blue, we spit on you." After the demonstrators dispersed, a witness to the flag-burning collected the flag's remains and buried them in his backyard. No one was physically injured or threatened with injury, though several witnesses testified that they had been seriously offended by the flag-burning.

Of the approximately 100 demonstrators, Johnson alone was charged with a crime. The only criminal offense with which he was charged was the desecration of a venerated object in violation of Tex.Penal Code Ann. § 42.09(a)(3) (1989).[16] After a trial, he was convicted, sentenced to one year in prison, and fined $2,000. The Court of Appeals for the Fifth District of Texas at Dallas affirmed Johnson's conviction, but the Texas Court of Criminal Appeals reversed, holding that the State could not, consistent with the First Amendment, punish Johnson for burning the flag in these circumstances.... We granted certiorari, and now affirm.

OPINION

... The First Amendment literally forbids the abridgment only of "speech," but we have long recognized that its protection does not end at the spoken or written word. While we have rejected "the view that an apparently limitless variety of conduct can be labeled 'speech' whenever the person engaging in the conduct intends thereby to express an idea, we have acknowledged that conduct may be sufficiently imbued with elements of communication to fall within the scope of the First and Fourteenth Amendments."...

Especially pertinent to this case are our decisions recognizing the communicative nature of conduct relating to flags. Attaching a peace sign to the flag, *Spence [v. Washington]*, 418 U.S. 405 (1974); saluting the flag, *Barnette*, 319 U.S., at 632, 63 S.Ct., at 1182; and displaying a red flag, *Stromberg v. California*, 283 U.S. 359, 368–369, 51 S.Ct. 532, 535–36, 75 L.Ed. 1117 (1931), we have held, all may find shelter under the First Amendment. That we have had little difficulty identifying an expressive element in conduct relating to flags should not be surprising. The very purpose of a national flag is to serve as a symbol of our country; it is, one might say, "the one visible manifestation of two hundred years of nationhood."... Pregnant with expressive content, the flag as readily signifies this Nation as does the combination of letters found in "America."

We have not automatically concluded, however, that any action taken with respect to our flag is expressive. Instead, in characterizing such action for First Amendment purposes, we have considered the context in which it occurred. In *Spence,* for example, we emphasized that Spence's taping of a peace sign to his flag was "roughly simultaneous with and concededly triggered by the Cambodian incursion and the Kent State tragedy."...

Johnson burned an American flag as part—indeed, as the culmination—of a political demonstration that coincided with the convening of the Republican Party and its renomination of Ronald Reagan for President. The expressive, overtly political nature of this conduct was both intentional and overwhelmingly apparent. At his trial,

Johnson explained his reasons for burning the flag as follows: "The American Flag was burned as Ronald Reagan was being renominated as President. And a more powerful statement of symbolic speech, whether you agree with it or not, couldn't have been made at that time. It's quite a just position [juxtaposition]. We had new patriotism and no patriotism." In these circumstances, Johnson's burning of the flag was conduct "sufficiently imbued with elements of communication," to implicate the First Amendment....

Texas claims that its interest in preventing breaches of the peace justifies Johnson's conviction for flag desecration. However, no disturbance of the peace actually occurred or threatened to occur because of Johnson's burning of the flag. Although the State stresses the disruptive behavior of the protestors during their march toward City Hall, it admits that "no actual breach of the peace occurred at the time of the flagburning or in response to the flagburning."...

The State's position, therefore, amounts to a claim that an audience that takes serious offense at particular expression is necessarily likely to disturb the peace and that the expression may be prohibited on this basis. Our precedents do not countenance such a presumption. On the contrary, they recognize that a principal "function of free speech under our system of government is to invite dispute. It may indeed best serve its high purpose when it induces a condition of unrest, creates dissatisfaction with conditions as they are, or even stirs people to anger."...

Nor does Johnson's expressive conduct fall within that small class of "fighting words" that are "likely to provoke the average person to retaliation, and thereby cause a breach of the peace." *Chaplinsky v. New Hampshire,* 315 U.S. 568, 574, 62 S.Ct. 766, 770, 86 L.Ed. 1031 (1942). No reasonable onlooker would have regarded Johnson's generalized expression of dissatisfaction with the policies of the Federal Government as a direct personal insult or an invitation to exchange fisticuffs.

We thus conclude that the State's interest in maintaining order is not implicated on these facts. The State need not worry that our holding will disable it from preserving the peace. We do not suggest that the First Amendment forbids a State to prevent "imminent lawless action."...

If there is a bedrock principle underlying the First Amendment, it is that the Government may not prohibit the expression of an idea simply because society finds the idea itself offensive or disagreeable. We have not recognized an exception to this principle even where our flag has been involved. In *Street v. New York,* 394 U.S. 576, 89 S.Ct. 1354, 22 L.Ed.2d 572 (1969), we held that a State may not criminally punish a person for uttering words critical of the flag....

In holding in *Barnette* that the Constitution did not leave this course open to the Government, Justice Jackson described one of our society's defining principles in words deserving of their frequent repetition: "If there is any fixed star in our constitutional constellation, it is that no official, high or petty, can prescribe what shall be orthodox in politics, nationalism, religion, or other matters of opinion or force citizens to confess by word or act their faith therein."...

We are fortified in today's conclusion by our conviction that forbidding criminal punishment for conduct such as Johnson's will not endanger the special role played by our flag or the feelings it inspires. To paraphrase Justice Holmes, we submit that nobody can suppose that this one gesture of an unknown man will change our Nation's attitude towards its flag....

We can imagine no more appropriate response to burning a flag than waving one's own, no better way to counter a flagburner's message than by saluting the flag that burns, no surer means of preserving the dignity even of the flag that burned than by—as one witness here did—according its remains a respectful burial. We do not consecrate the flag by punishing its desecration, for in doing so we dilute the freedom that this cherished emblem represents.

Johnson was convicted for engaging in expressive conduct. The State's interest in preventing breaches of the peace does not support his conviction because Johnson's conduct did not threaten to disturb the peace. Nor does the State's interest in preserving the flag as a symbol of nationhood and national unity justify his criminal conviction for engaging in political expression. The judgment of the Texas Court of Criminal Appeals is therefore Affirmed.

CONCURRING OPINION

Justice Kennedy, concurring.

... The hard fact is that sometimes we must make decisions we do not like. We make them because they are right, right in the sense that the law and the Constitution, as we see them, compel the result. And so great is our commitment to the process that, except in the rare case, we do not pause to express distaste for the result, perhaps for fear of undermining a valued principle that dictates the decision. This is one of those rare cases. Our colleagues in dissent advance powerful arguments why respondent may be convicted for his expression, reminding us that among those who will be dismayed by our holding will be some who have had the singular honor of carrying the flag in battle. And I agree that the flag holds a lonely place of honor in an age when absolutes are distrusted and simple truths are burdened by unneeded apologetics....

The case here today forces recognition of the costs to which [our] ... beliefs commit us. It is poignant but fundamental that the flag protects those who hold it in contempt.... So I agree with the Court that he must go free.

DISSENT

Chief Justice Rehnquist, with whom Justice White and Justice O'Connor join, dissenting.

... The flag symbolizes the Nation in peace as well as in war. It signifies our national presence on battleships, airplanes, military installations, and public buildings from the United States Capitol to the thousands of county courthouses and city halls throughout the country. Two flags are prominently placed in our courtroom. Countless flags are placed by the graves of loved ones each year on what was first called Decoration Day, and is now called Memorial Day. The flag is traditionally placed on the casket of deceased members of the Armed Forces, and it is later given to the deceased's family....

With the exception of Alaska and Wyoming, all of the States now have statutes prohibiting the burning of the flag. Most of the state statutes are patterned after the Uniform Flag Act of 1917, which in § 3 provides: "No person shall publicly mutilate, deface, defile, defy, trample upon, or by word or act cast contempt upon any such flag, standard, color, ensign or shield."

The American flag ... throughout more than 200 years of our history, has come to be the visible symbol embodying our Nation. It does not represent the views of any particular political party, and it does not represent any particular political philosophy. The flag is not simply another "idea" or "point of view" competing for recognition in the marketplace of ideas. Millions and millions of Americans regard it with an almost mystical reverence regardless of what sort of social, political, or philosophical beliefs they may have. I cannot agree that the First Amendment invalidates the Act of Congress, and the laws of 48 of the 50 States, which make criminal the public burning of the flag....

[T]he public burning of the American flag by Johnson was no essential part of any exposition of ideas, and at the same time it had a tendency to incite a breach of the peace. Johnson was free to make any verbal denunciation of the flag that he wished; indeed, he was free to burn the flag in private. He could publicly burn other symbols of the Government or effigies of political leaders. He did lead a march through the streets of Dallas, and conducted a rally in front of the Dallas City Hall. He engaged in a "die-in" to protest nuclear weapons. He shouted out various slogans during the march, including: "Reagan, Mondale which will it be? Either one means World War III"; "Ronald Reagan, killer of the hour, perfect example of U.S. power"; and "red, white and blue, we spit on you, you stand for plunder, you will go under." For none of these acts was he arrested or prosecuted; it was only when he proceeded to burn publicly an American flag stolen from its rightful owner that he violated the Texas statute....

The Texas statute deprived Johnson of only one rather inarticulate symbolic form of protest—a form of protest that was profoundly offensive to many—and left him with a full panoply of other symbols and every conceivable form of verbal expression to express his deep disapproval of national policy....

But the Court today will have none of this. The uniquely deep awe and respect for our flag felt by virtually all of us are bundled off under the rubric of "designated symbols," that the First Amendment prohibits the government from "establishing." But the government has not "established" this feeling; 200 years of history have done that. The government is simply recognizing as a fact the profound regard for the American flag created by that history when it enacts statutes prohibiting the disrespectful public burning of the flag....

Surely one of the high purposes of a democratic society is to legislate against con-

duct that is regarded as evil and profoundly offensive to the majority of people—whether it be murder, embezzlement, pollution, or flag burning.... Uncritical extension of constitutional protection to the burning of the flag risks the frustration of the very purpose for which organized governments are instituted. The Court decides that the American flag is just another symbol, about which not only must opinions pro and con be tolerated, but for which the most minimal public respect may not be enjoined. The government may conscript men into the Armed Forces where they must fight and perhaps die for the flag, but the government may not prohibit the public burning of the banner under which they fight. I would uphold the Texas statute as applied in this case.

Justice Stevens, dissenting.

... The ideas of liberty and equality have been an irresistible force in motivating leaders like Patrick Henry, Susan B. Anthony, and Abraham Lincoln, schoolteachers like Nathan Hale and Booker T. Washington, the Philippine Scouts who fought at Bataan, and the soldiers who scaled the bluff at Omaha Beach. If those ideas are worth fighting for—and our history demonstrates that they are—it cannot be true that the flag that uniquely symbolizes their power is not itself worthy of protection from unnecessary desecration. I respectfully dissent.

Case Discussion

What distinguishes speech from expressive conduct? Can conduct actually say more than words? Were Johnson's actions speech? Expressive conduct? Conduct? How does the Court distinguish them? How would you? Does the emotion created over flag burning prove that it is expression? If so, should the government have the power to control the passions it arouses? What role, if any, does criminal law have to play in flag burning? What does Justice Kennedy mean by saying that the painful decision in the case must rest with the judiciary alone? Does Chief Justice Rehnquist have a point that this decision flouts the will of the majority of Americans who want flag burners punished? What is your position on the matter? If you think Johnson committed a crime, how serious was the crime?

Note Cases

1. The New York Transit Authority, which has the authority to make rules equivalent to laws, made it unlawful to panhandle or beg in the New York subways. Several homeless people argued that the rule violated their right to free speech. The United States Second Circuit Court of Appeals ruled: "Common sense tells us that begging is much more 'conduct' than it is 'speech.'" The court acknowledged that the conduct had an element of expression in it, but said: "The only message that we are able to espy as common to all acts of begging is that beggars want to exact money from those whom they accost. Such conduct, therefore, is subject to regulation." Research and other experts indicated that panhandlers and beggars frighten passengers; this provides adequate grounds to regulate them. *Young v. New York City Transit Authority,* 903 F.2d 146 (1990)

2. An Indiana statute prohibits nude dancing in public. Glen Theatre, a bar that featured nude dancing, sought an injunction against enforcing the law, arguing that it violated the First Amendment. The law permitted erotic dancing, so long as the dancers wore "G-strings" and "pasties." It prohibited only *totally* nude dancing. Dancers can express themselves erotically without total nudity. The United States Supreme Court ruled that it did not unduly restrict expressive conduct. *Barnes v. Glen Theatre, Inc., et al.,* 1991 WL 106079 (1991)

3. Raymond Hill, a "gay activist troublemaker," witnessed a friend intentionally stop traffic on a busy Houston, Texas, street so that a car could enter traffic. Two officers approached Hill's friend to talk to him. Hill began shouting at the officers to divert their attention. First he shouted, "Why don't you pick on somebody your own size?" After Officer Kelley responded, "Are you interrupting me in my official capacity as a Houston police officer?" Hill shouted, "Yes, why don't you pick on somebody my size?" The police arrested Hill for "wilfully or intentionally interrupting an officer by verbal challenge during an investigation." A Houston ordinance makes it unlawful to "in any manner oppose, molest, abuse or interrupt any policeman in the execution of his duty." Hill argued that the ordinance violated his right to free speech. The United States Supreme Court agreed. *City of Houston v. Hill,* 482 U.S. 451 (1987). (See chapter 12 on fighting words for full excerpt.)

▼ THE PRINCIPLE OF PUNISHMENT

Criminal law not only proscribes—that is, prohibits—conduct, but it also *prescribes,* or assigns, punishment. The principle includes both the purposes of punishment and its **proportionality**—the nature and amount of punishment in relation to the person and conduct punished.

Punishment takes many forms. A parent who grounds a teenager, a club that expels a member, a church that excommunicates a parishioner, a friend who rejects a companion—all punish because they intentionally inflict pain or other unpleasant consequences on their objects. None of these examples involve criminal punishment. **Criminal punishment** requires the following elements: (1) pain or other unpleasant consequences (2) prescribed by law and (3) administered intentionally (4) by the state. The last three elements are self-explanatory; the first requires elaboration.

The phrase "pain or other unpleasant consequences" is both broad and vague. It does not define the kind and amount of pain. A violent mental patient indefinitely confined to a padded cell in a state security hospital suffers more pain than a person incarcerated for five days in the county jail for disorderly conduct. Nevertheless, only the jail sentence is criminal punishment. The difference lies in the purpose. Hospitalization, at least formally, aims to treat and cure; the pain accompanying treatment is incidental to, not a reason for, the hospitalization. On the other hand, punishment—the intentional infliction of pain—is the reason for the jail inmate's incarceration.

This distinction between criminal punishment and treatment is rarely clear cut. Many persons in maximum-security hospitals are convicted criminal offenders, but the government sentences other convicted criminals to prison for "treatment" and "cure." Furthermore, pain and pleasure do not always distinguish punishment from treatment. Shock treatment and padded cells inflict more pain than confinement in some minimum-security federal prisons with their "country club" atmospheres. When measured by pain, punishment may often be preferable to treatment. Indeed, some critics maintain that the major shortcoming of treatment is that "helping" a patient justifies extreme measures: massive surgery, castration, and lobotomy.[17]

Professor Herbert Packer resolved the dilemma of treatment and punishment by adding a fifth element to criminal punishment, suggesting that its dominant purpose is not to make offenders better, but to inflict "deserved pain" and prevent crimes. Although criminal punishment aims primarily to hurt and not help offenders, treatment can also deter crime. Rehabilitation assumes deterrence as a utilitarian aim of rehabilitation. New York clearly asserted this aim in its 1967 Revised Penal law:[18]

> The general purposes of this chapter are to insure public safety by preventing the commission of offenses through the deterrent influence of the sentences authorized, [and] the rehabilitation of those convicted.[19]

Two basic justifications underlie all criminal punishment: retribution and prevention. Retribution looks back to the crime committed, punishing it because it is right to do so. Prevention looks forward, punishing offenders in order to prevent crimes in the future. Prevention takes three forms: general deterrence, incapacitation, and rehabilitation.

Retribution

Striking out to hurt what hurts us is a basic human impulse. In one commentator's words, "It is what makes us kick the table leg on which we stub our toe." This impulse captures the idea of **retribution,** which appears in the Old Testament:

> When one man strikes another and kills him, he shall be put to death. When one man injures and disfigures his fellow-countryman, it shall be done to him as he had done; fracture for fracture, eye for eye, tooth for tooth.[20]

Retribution rests on the assumption that hurting the wicked is right. As forcefully stated by Sir James F. Stephen, a nineteenth-century judge and historian of the criminal law, the wicked deserve to suffer for their evil deeds.

> [T]he infliction of punishment by law gives definite expression and a solemn ratification and justification to the hatred which is excited by the commission

▼ **Table 2.1** ▼
Typical Sentences
"What Types of Sentences Usually Are Given to Offenders?"

Death Penalty

For the most serious crimes such as murder, the courts in most states may sentence an offender to death by lethal injection, electrocution, exposure to lethal gas, hanging, or other method specified by state law.

☐ As of 1985, 37 states had laws providing for the death penalty.
☐ Virtually all death penalty sentences are for murder.
☐ As of year-end 1985, 50 persons had been executed since 1976, and 1,591 inmates in 32 states were under a sentence of death.

Incarceration

Incarceration is the confinement of a convicted criminal in a federal or state prison or a local jail to serve a court-imposed sentence. Confinement is usually in a jail, administered locally; or in a prison, operated by the state or federal government. In many states offenders sentenced to 1 year or less are held in a jail; those sentenced to longer terms are committed to a state prison. More than 4,200 correctional facilities are maintained by federal, state, and local governments. They include 47 federal facilities, 922 state-operated adult confinement and community-based correctional facilities, and 3,300 local jails, which usually are county operated.

On any given day in 1985, about 503,000 persons were confined in state and federal prisons. About 254,000 were confined in local jails on June 30, 1985.

Probation

Probation is the sentencing of an offender to community supervision by a probation agency, often as a result of suspending a sentence to confinement. Such supervision normally entails specific rules of conduct while in the community. If the rules are violated, a sentence to confinement may be imposed. Probation is the most widely used correctional disposition in the United States.

☐ State or local governments operate more than 2,000 probation agencies.
☐ At year-end 1985, nearly 1.9 million adults were on probation, or about 1 of every 95 adults in the nation.

Split Sentences, Shock Probation, and Intermittent Confinement

These are penalties that explicitly require the convicted person to serve a brief period of confinement in a local, state, or federal facility (the "shock") followed by a period of probation. This penalty attempts to combine the use of community supervision with a short incarceration experience. Some sentences are periodic rather than continuous; for example, an offender may be required to spend a certain number of weekends in jail.

In 1984 nearly a third of those receiving probation sentences in Idaho, New Jersey, Tennessee, Utah, and Vermont also were sentenced to brief periods of confinement.

Restitution and Victim Compensation

In these dispositions, the offender is required to provide financial repayment—or, in some jurisdictions, services in lieu of monetary restitution—for the losses incurred by the victim.

Nearly all states have statutory provisions for the collection and disbursement of restitution funds. A restitution law was enacted at the federal level in 1982.

Community Service

The offender is required to perform a specified amount of public service work, such as collecting trash in parks or other public facilities.

Many states authorize community service work orders. Community service often is imposed as a specific condition of probation.

Fines

A fine is an economic penalty that requires the offender to pay a specified sum of money within limits set by law. Fines often are imposed in addition to probation or as alternatives to incarceration.

☐ The Victims of Crime Act of 1984 authorizes the distribution of fines and forfeited criminal profits to support state victim-assistance programs, with priority given to programs that aid victims of sexual assault, spousal abuse, and child abuse. These programs, in turn, provide assistance and compensation to crime victims.

☐ Many laws that govern the imposition of fines are being revised. The revisions often provide for more flexible means of ensuring equity in the imposition of fines, flexible fine schedules, "day fines" geared to the offender's daily wage, installment payment of fines, and the imposition of confinement only when there is an intentional refusal to pay.

☐ A 1984 study estimated that more than three-fourths of criminal courts use fines extensively, and that fines levied each year exceed $1 billion.

SOURCE: *Report to the Nation on Crime and Justice: The Data,* Bureau of Justice Statistics, United States Justice Department, Washington, D.C., 1988, page 96.

of the offense. The criminal law thus proceeds upon the principle that it is morally right to hate criminals, and it confirms and justifies that sentiment by inflicting on criminals punishments which express it. I think it highly desirable that criminals should be hated, that the punishments inflicted upon them should be so contrived as to give expression to that hatred, and to justify it so far as the public provision of means for expressing and gratifying a healthy natural sentiment can justify and encourage it. The forms in which deliberate anger and righteous disapprobation are expressed, and the execution of criminal justice is the most emphatic of such forms, stand to the one set of passions in the same relation in which marriage stands to sexual passion.[21]

Proponents of retribution contend that it benefits not only society, as Stephen emphasized, but also criminals. Just as society feels satisfied in retaliating against, or paying back, criminals, offenders themselves benefit through expiating their evil, or paying their debt to society. Retaliation, by which society pays back criminals, and expiation, through which criminals pay back society, are both central to retribution. Retribution assumes that offenders are free to choose between committing and not committing crimes. Because offenders have this choice, society can blame them for making the wrong choice. This blameworthiness is called **culpability.** Culpability means that offenders are responsible for their actions and must suffer the consequences if they act irresponsibly.

Retribution has several appealing qualities. First, it assumes free will, or human autonomy. This assumption upholds a basic value—that individuals have the power to determine their own destinies and are not at the mercy of uncontrollable forces. Retribution also makes sense because it seems to accord with human nature. Hurting that which hurts and hating wrongdoers—especially murderers, rapists, robbers, and other violent criminals—appear to be natural impulses.[22]

From the Old Testament's philosophy of taking an eye for an eye, to the nineteenth-century Englishman's claim that it is right to hate and hurt criminals, to the modern idea of "lock 'em up and throw away the key," the desire for retribution has run strong and deep in both religion and criminal justice. This long tradition endorses retribution, especially in the average person's mind. The sheer tenacity of the principle seems to validate its use in modern criminal justice.

Retributionists maintain that retribution rests not only on long use but also on a firm jurisprudential (legal philosophical) foundation. Two reasons support this claim, the first centering on culpability, the second on justice.

Retribution requires culpability—it requires that criminals choose and intend to harm their victims. Accidents do not qualify for retribution. Hence, people who load, aim, and fire guns into their enemies' chests deserve punishment; hunters who lay down and leave loaded guns that fire and kill companions who bump them do not deserve punishment. Civil law can deal with careless people; the criminal law ought to punish only people who purposely perpetrate harm. Retribution focuses the criminal law on culpable behavior.

Retributionists also claim that justice is the only proper measure of punishment. Justice is a philosophical concept whose application depends on culpability. Only those who deserve punishment can receive it, or it is unjust. Similarly, only justice qualifies to determine the quality and quantity of punishment—the culpable defendant's just deserts.

It is difficult to translate abstract justice into concrete penalties. What are a rapist's just deserts? Is castration justice? How many years in prison is robbery worth? How much offender suffering will repay the pain of a maimed aggravated assault victim? The pain of punishment cannot be equivalent to the suffering caused by the crime. Furthermore, critics, such as Henry Wiehofen, contend that retribution is the last holdout of barbarism.

> All of this abstract philosophizing about punishment as requital for crime has a musty smell about it, a smell of the professor's study. The people who have the responsibility for fighting crime and dealing with criminals have learned that it is pointless to talk about "how much punishment" is deserved. In the nineteenth century [it] had its appeal. [But] the modern behavioral sciences have shown that armchair abstractions about the "justice" of retribution by philosophers who reject human experience are sadly defective in human understanding, not to say human sympathy. The retributive approach is too subjective and too emotional to solve problems that have their roots in social conditions and the consequent impact on individual personality.[23]

Wiehofen denies that the urge to retaliate inheres in human nature; the law ought to reject any demand for vengeance. Furthermore, he argues that retributionists merely assume, but do not have proof, that a bloodthirsty human nature craves vengeance.

The determinists reject the freewill assumption that underlies retribution. They suggest that forces beyond human control determine individual behavior. Social scientists have shown the relationship between social conditions and crime. Psychiatrists point to subconscious forces, beyond the conscious will's control, that determine criminal conduct. A few biologists link violent crime to an extra Y chromosome. Determinism undermines the theory of retribution because it forecloses blame, and punishment without blame is unjust.[24]

Prevention

Retribution justifies punishment on the ground that it is right to inflict pain on criminals. Prevention inflicts pain not for its own sake, but to prevent future crimes. **General prevention,** also called **general deterrence,** aims by threat of punishment to prevent the general population who have not committed crimes from doing so. **Special deterrence** aims at individual offenders, hoping to deter their future conduct by the threat of punishment. **Incapacitation** prevents convicted criminals from committing future crimes by confining them or more rarely by altering them surgically or executing them. **Rehabilitation** hopes to prevent crime by changing individuals so that they will obey the law. These purposes all have in common the aim of preventing future crime; inflicting pain for its own sake is not the aim of prevention.

Jeremy Bentham, an eighteenth-century English law reformer, promoted deterrence. Bentham was part of, and was heavily influenced by, the intellectual movement called the Enlightenment. At the core of the movement was the notion that natural laws govern the universe and, by analogy, human society. One of these laws, hedonism, posits that human beings seek pleasure and avoid pain. A related law, rationalism, states that individuals can, and ordinarily do, act to maximize pleasure and minimize pain. Rationalism also permits human beings to apply natural laws mechanistically (that is, according to rules, not discretion).

These ideas, which are much oversimplified here, led Bentham to formulate classical deterrence theory. It states that rational human beings will not commit crimes if they know that the pain of punishment outweighs the pleasure gained from committing crimes. Prospective criminals weigh the pleasure derived from present crime against the pain from the threat of future punishment. According to the natural law of hedonism, if prospective criminals fear future punishment more than they derive pleasure from present crime, they will not commit crimes.

Deterrence is considerably more complex than Bentham's useful but oversimplified crime prevention model suggests. Threatened punishment does not always deter—it goads some to do the very thing it aims to prevent. During the Vietnam War, for example, Congress made burning draft cards a crime. Instead of avoiding such conduct, protesters turned out in scores to flout the law. Deterrence, then, has two dimensions.[25]

Deterrence proponents argue that the principle of utility—permitting only the minimum amount of pain necessary to prevent the crime—better limits criminal punishment than retribution does. English playwright George Bernard Shaw, a strong deterrence supporter, put it this way: "Vengeance is mine saith the Lord; which means it is not the Lord Chief Justice's." According to this argument, divinity enables only God, the angels, or some other divine being to measure just deserts, while social scientists can determine how much pain, or threat of pain, deters crime. With this knowledge, the state can scientifically inflict the minimum pain needed to produce the maximum crime reduction.

Deterrence proponents concede that impediments to implementing deterrence exist. The emotionalism surrounding punishment impairs objectivity. Often, prescribed penalties rest more on faith than on evidence. For example, one economist's study shows that every execution under capital punishment laws saves about eight lives by deterring potential murderers. This finding sparked a controversy having little to do with the study's empirical validity. Instead, the arguments turn to ethics—whether killing anyone is right, no matter what social benefits it produces.[26]

Deterrence proponents do not argue against the need for an inquiry into the ethics, wisdom, and humaneness of punishment, but they do maintain that empirical research necessarily precedes answers to those questions. The problem of punishment involves a division of labor. Researchers answer the empirical question What works? Policymakers answer the questions Is it wise? Is it humane? Is it legal? For instance, research might demonstrate that the death penalty for rape prevents rape, but the United States Supreme Court has declared that capital punishment for rape violates the Eighth Amendment.[27]

Even if particular punishments are constitutional, they may still be unwise public policy. For example, suppose it is found that a statute authorizing surgery to prevent erections deters male sex offenders. Even if the statute were constitutional (an issue about which there are grave doubts), the humaneness of this draconian measure should be raised. Amputating thieves' hands, an effective deterrent in some countries, is rejected on humanitarian grounds in America.

Critics find several faults with deterrence theory and its application to criminal punishment. The wholly rational, freewill individual that deterrence theory assumes exists is as far from reality as the eighteenth-century world that spawned the idea. Complex forces within the human organism and in the external environment, both of which are beyond individual control, strongly influence behavior.[28]

Human beings and their behavior are too unpredictable to reduce to a mechanistic formula. For some people, the existence of criminal law suffices to deter them from committing crimes; others require more. Information about just who these others are and of what the more consists has not been determined sufficiently so that policy can rest upon it. Furthermore, severity is not the only influence on the effectiveness of punishment. Tentative conclusions are that certainty and celerity (speed) have a greater deterrent effect than severity.[29]

Moreover, threats do not affect all crimes or potential criminals equally. Crimes of passion, such as murder and rape, are probably little affected by threats; whereas speeding, drunken driving, and corporate crime are probably greatly affected by threats. The leading deterrence theorist, Johannes Andenaes, sums up the state of our knowledge about deterrence:

> There is a long way to go before research can give quantitative forecasts. The long-term moral effects of the criminal law and law enforcement are especially

hard to isolate and quantify. Some categories of crime are so intimately related to specific social situations that generalizations of a quantitative kind are impossible. An inescapable fact is that research will always lag behind actual developments. When new forms of crime come into existence, such as high-jacking of aircraft or terrorist acts against officers of the law, there cannot possibly be a body of research ready as a basis for the decisions that have to be taken. Common sense and trial by error have to give the answers.[30]

Finally, critics maintain that even if getting empirical support for criminal punishment is possible, deterrence is unjust because it punishes for example's sake. Supreme Court Justice Oliver Wendell Holmes described the example dimension to deterrence:

> If I were having a philosophical talk with a man I was going to have hanged (or electrocuted) I should say, "I don't doubt that your act was inevitable for you but to make it more avoidable by others we propose to sacrifice you to the common good. You may regard yourself as a soldier dying for your country if you like. But the law must keep its promises."[31]

Punishment should not be a sacrifice to the common good, according to retributionists; it is just only if administered for the redemption of particular individuals. According to critics, punishment is personal and individual, not general and societal. Deterrence proponents respond that so long as offenders are in fact guilty, punishing them is personal; hence, it is just to use individual punishment for society's benefit.

Incapacitation restrains offenders from committing further crimes. At the extreme, incapacitation includes mutilation—castration, amputation, and lobotomy—or even death in capital punishment. Incapacitation in most cases means imprisonment. Incapacitation works: dead people cannot commit crimes, and prisoners do not commit them, at least not outside prison walls. Incapacitation, then, offers much to a society determined to repress crime.

> [T]he chances of a persistent robber or burglar living out his life, or even going a year with no arrest are quite small. Yet a large proportion of repeat offenders suffer little or no loss of freedom. Whether or not one believes that such penalties, if inflicted, would act as a deterrent, it is obvious that they could serve to incapacitate these offenders and, thus, for the period of the incapacitation, prevent them from committing additional crimes.[32]

Like general deterrence and retribution, incapacitation has its share of critics. Some stress the distant relationship between offense and punishment. The basic problem with incapacitation is predicting behavior, particularly violent criminal conduct. Kleptomaniacs will almost surely steal again, exhibitionists will expose themselves, and addicts will continue to use chemicals. But when will murderers, rapists or bank robbers strike again? Nobody really knows. Therefore, punishment is based, empirically, on a poor guess concerning future danger.[23]

Furthermore, critics argue, incapacitation merely shifts criminality from outside prisons to inside prisons. Sex offenders and other violent criminals can and do still find victims among other inmates; property offenders abound in trading contraband and other smuggled items. Incarceration is also expensive. According to current estimates, it costs approximately $50,000 to construct prison cells and in some states another $20,000 to feed, house, and clothe every prisoner. Finally, critics maintain that several incapacitative measures—death, psychosurgery, mutilation, and long-term incarceration—violate the Eighth Amendment.[34]

In a widely acclaimed essay, *The Limits of the Criminal Sanction,* the late Professor Herbert Packer succinctly summarized the aims of rehabilitation:

> The most immediately appealing justification for punishment is the claim that it may be used to prevent crimes by so changing the personality of the offender that he will conform to the dictates of law; in a word, by reforming him.[35]

Rehabilitation borrows much from medicine. Indeed, it is based on what has been called the medical model. In this model, crime is a "disease" that criminals have contracted. The major purpose in punishment is to "cure" criminal patients through "treatment." The length of imprisonment depends upon how long it takes to effect this cure. On its face, rehabilitation is the most humane justification for criminal punishment. Its proponents contend that treating offenders is much more civilized than punishing them.

Two assumptions underlie rehabilitation theory. First, external and internal forces beyond offenders' control determine criminality. Rehabilitationists are determinists when it comes to crime causation. Since offenders do not freely choose to commit crimes, they cannot be blamed for doing so. Second, experts can modify subjects' behavior to prevent further crimes. After treatment or rehabilitation, former criminals will control their own destinies, at least enough so that they will not commit crimes. In this respect, rehabilitationists subscribe to free will: criminals can choose to change their life habits and often do, after which society can hold them responsible for their actions.

The view that criminals are sick has profoundly affected criminal law and has generated acrimonious debate. The reason is not that reform and rehabilitation are new ideas; quite the contrary. Victorian Sir Francis Palgrave summed up a 700-year-old attitude when he stated the medieval church's position on punishment: it was not to be "thundered in vengeance for the satisfaction of the state, but imposed for the good of the offender; in order to afford the means of amendment and to lead the transgressor to repentance, and to mercy." Sixteenth-century Elizabethan pardon statutes were laced with the language of repentance and reform; the queen hoped to achieve a reduction in crime by mercy rather than by punishment. Even Jeremy Bentham, most closely associated with deterrence, claimed that punishment would "contribute to the reformation of the offender, not only through fear of being punished again, but by a change in his character and habits."[36]

Despite its long history, rehabilitation has suffered serious attacks. The most fundamental criticism is that rehabilitation is based on false, or at least unproven, assumptions. The causes of crime are so complex, and the wellsprings of human behavior as yet so undetermined, that sound policy cannot rest on treatment. A second criticism is that is makes no sense to brand everyone who violates the criminal law as sick and needing treatment.[37]

Some critics call rehabilitation inhumane because cure justifies administering large doses of pain. Noted British philosopher C. S. Lewis argued as follows:

> My contention is that good men (not bad men) consistently acting upon that position would act as cruelly and unjustly as the greatest tyrants. They might in some respects act even worse. Of all tyrannies a tyranny sincerely exercised for the good of its victims may be the most oppressive. It may be better to live under robber barons than under omnipotent moral busybodies. The robber baron's cruelty may sometimes sleep, his cupidity may at some point be satiated; but those who torment us for our own good will torment us without end for they do so with the approval of their own conscience. They may be more likely to go to Heaven yet at the same time likelier to make a Hell of earth. Their very kindness stings with intolerable insult. To be "cured" against one's will and cured of states which we may not regard as disease is to be put on a level with those who have not yet reached the age of reason or those who never will; to be classed with infants, imbeciles, and domestic animals. But to be punished, however severely, because we have deserved it, because we "ought to have known better," is to be treated as a human person made in God's image.[38]

Trends in Punishment

Historically, societies have justified punishment on the grounds of retribution, deterrence, incapacitation, and rehabilitation. But the weight given to each has shifted over the centuries. Retribution and reformation, for example, run deep in English criminal law from at least the year 1200. The church's emphasis on atoning for sins and reforming sinners affected criminal law variously. Sometimes the aims of punishment and reformation conflict in practice.

In Elizabethan England, for example, the letter of the law was retributionist: the penalty for all major crimes was death. Estimates show that in practice, however, most accused persons never suffered this extreme penalty. Although some escaped death because they were innocent, many were set free based on their chances for rehabilitation. The law's technicalities, for example, made death a virtually impossible penalty for first-time property offenders. In addition, the queen's general pardon, issued almost annually, gave blanket clemency in the hope that criminals, by this act of mercy, would reform their erring ways.[39]

Gradually retribution came to dominate penal policy, until the eighteenth century, when deterrence and incapacitation were introduced to replace what contemporary humanitarian reformers considered ineffective, brutal, and barbaric punishment in the name of retribution. By the turn of the twentieth century, humanitarian reformers concluded that deterrence was neither effective nor humane. Rehabilitation replaced deterrence as the aim of criminal sanctions, and remained the dominant justification for criminal punishment throughout the twentieth century's first sixty years. Most states enacted indeterminate sentencing laws that made prison release dependent on rehabilitation. Most prisons created treatment programs intended to reform criminals so they could become law-abiding citizens. Nevertheless, considerable evidence indicates that rehabilitation never really won the hearts of most criminal justice professionals despite their strong public rhetoric to the contrary.[40]

In the early 1970s, little evidence existed to show that rehabilitation programs reformed offenders. "Nothing works" dominated reform discussions, prompted by a highly touted, widely publicized, and largely negative study evaluating the effectiveness of treatment programs. At the same time that academics and policymakers were becoming disillusioned with rehabilitation, public opinion was hardening into demands for severe penalties in the face of steeply rising crime rates. The time was clearly ripe for retribution to come again to the fore as a dominant aim of punishment.[41]

California, a rehabilitation pioneer in the early twentieth century, reflected this shift in attitude in 1976. In its Uniform Determinate Sentencing Law, the legislature abolished the indeterminate sentence, stating boldly that "the purpose of imprisonment is punishment," not treatment or rehabilitation. Called just deserts or even simply deserts, retribution was touted as "right" by conservatives who believed in punishment's morality and as "humane" by liberals convinced that rehabilitation was cruel and excessive. Public opinion supported it, largely on the ground that criminals deserve to be punished.[42]

Since the middle of the 1980s, reformers have heralded retribution and incapacitation as the primary criminal punishments. There are, to be sure, some powerful holdouts. One was the Model Penal Code, first written in 1961 when rehabilitation dominated penal policy. After reviewing current research and debate thoroughly, its reporters decided to retain rehabilitation as the primary purpose of punishment.[43]

Proportionality

 The Eighth Amendment declares that [e]xcessive bail shall not be required, nor excessive fines imposed, nor cruel and unusual punishments inflicted.

The Supreme Court has ruled that the phrase "cruel and unusual punishments" means "not only barbaric punishments, but in some cases also sentences that are disproportionate to the crime committed."[44]

The principle of proportionality of punishment originated long before the Eighth Amendment. In 1215, three articles in the Magna Carta prohibited "excessive" fines. The principle was repeated and extended in the First Statute of Westminster in 1275. The royal courts relied on these provisions to enforce the principle in actual cases. When imprisonment became a common-law sanction, the courts extended the principle to prison terms. The English Bill of Rights in 1689 repeated the principle of proportionality in the language that later appeared in the Eighth Amendment. Three months later, the House of Lords, the highest court in England, declared that a fine of 30,000 pounds was excessive and exorbitant, against Magna Carta, the common right of the subject, and the law of the land.[45]

The Supreme Court first applied the constitutional principle of proportionality in *Weems v. United States,* in 1910. Weems was convicted of falsifying a public document. The trial court sentenced him to fifteen years in prison at hard labor in chains and permanently deprived him of his civil rights. The Supreme Court ruled that the punishment violated the proportionality requirement of the Eighth Amendment. In the 1960s, the Court reaffirmed its commitment to the principle in *Robinson v. California*, ruling that a ninety-day sentence for drug addiction was disproportionate because addiction is an illness, and it is cruel and unusual to punish persons for being sick.

> Even one day in prison would be a cruel and unusual punishment for the "crime" of having a common cold.[46]

During the 1970s, the Court considered proportionality mainly in capital cases. For example, it held that the death penalty is disproportionate for raping an adult woman. Not until the 1980s did the Court take up the application of the principle to the length of imprisonment. In 1991, the Supreme Court extended the principle of proportionality to sentences of imprisonment.

CASE

Is Life without Parole for Cocaine Possession Cruel and Unusual Punishment?

Harmelin v. Michigan
1991 WL 111151

Scalia, J., announced the judgment of the Court in which Rehnquist, C.J., and O'Connor, Kennedy, and Souter, J.J., joined, Kennedy, J., filed an opinion concurring in part and concurring in the judgment, in which O'Connor and Souter, J.J., joined. White, J., filed a dissenting opinion, in which Blackmun, and Stevens, J.J., joined. Marshall, J., filed a dissenting opinion. Stevens, J., filed a dissenting opinion, in which Blackmun, J., joined.

   Justice Scalia announced the judgment of the Court....

FACTS
Petitioner was convicted of possessing 672 grams of cocaine and sentenced to a mandatory term of life in prison without possibility of parole.[47] ... [T]he Michigan Court of Appeals ... affirmed petitioner's sentence, rejecting his argument that the sentence was "cruel and unusual" within the meaning of the Eighth Amendment. [Harmelin petitioned the United States Supreme Court for a **writ of certiorari,** a court order used by the Supreme Court as a discretionary device to decide which cases from lower courts, in this case the Michigan Court of Appeals, it wishes to review.] Petitioner claims that his sentence is unconstitutionally "cruel and unusual"... because it is "significantly disproportionate" to the crime he committed....

OPINIONS
... In *Rummel v. Estelle*, 445 U.S. 263, 100 S.Ct. 1133, 63 L.Ed.2d 382 (1980), we held that it did not constitute "cruel and unusual punishment" to impose a life sentence, under a recidivist statute, upon a defendant who had been convicted, successively, of fraudulent use of a credit card to obtain $80 worth of goods or services, passing a forged check in the amount of $28.36, and obtaining $120.75 by false pretenses. We said that ... "the length of the sentence actually imposed is purely a matter of legislative prerogative."... A footnote in the opinion, however, said: "This is not to say that a proportionality principle would not come into play in the extreme example... if a legislature made overtime parking a felony punishable by life imprisonment."

   Two years later, in *Hutto v. Davis*, 454 U.S. 370, 102 S.Ct. 703, 70 L.Ed.2d 556 (1982), we similarly rejected an Eighth Amendment challenge to a prison term of 40 years and fine of $20,000 for possession and distribution of approximately nine ounces of marijuana....

A year and a half after Davis we uttered what has been our last word on this subject to date. *Solem v. Helm,* 463 U.S. 277, 103 S.Ct. 3001, 77 L.Ed.2d 637 (1983), set aside under the Eighth Amendment, because it was disproportionate, a sentence of life imprisonment without possibility of parole, imposed under a South Dakota recidivist statute for successive offenses that included three convictions of third-degree burglary, one of obtaining money by false pretenses, one of grand larceny, one of third-offense driving while intoxicated, and one of writing a "no account" check with intent to defraud....

[The court here discussed inconsistencies in *Solem v. Helm* and *Hutto v. Davis* concerning the holdings and precedents regarding proportionality outside death penalty cases.]

It should be apparent from the above discussion that our 5-to-4 decision eight years ago in *Solem* was scarcely the expression of clear and well accepted constitutional law. We have long recognized, of course, that the doctrine of stare decisis is less rigid in its application to constitutional precedents, and we think that to be especially true of a constitutional precedent that is both recent and in apparent tension with other decisions. Accordingly, we have addressed anew, and in greater detail, the question whether the Eighth Amendment contains a proportionality guarantee ... and to the understanding of the Eighth Amendment before the end of the 19th century.... We conclude from this examination that *Solem* was simply wrong; the Eighth Amendment contains no proportionality guarantee.

Solem based its conclusion principally upon the proposition that a right to be free from disproportionate punishments was embodied within the "cruell and unusuall Punishments" provision of the English Declaration of Rights of 1689, and was incorporated, with that language, in the Eighth Amendment. There is no doubt that the Declaration of Rights is the antecedent of our constitutional text.... As *Solem* observed, the principle of proportionality

was familiar to English law at the time the Declaration of Rights was drafted.... When imprisonment supplemented fines as a method of punishment, courts apparently applied the proportionality principle while sentencing.... Despite this familiarity, the drafters of the Declaration of Rights did not explicitly prohibit "disproportionate" or "excessive" punishment. Instead, they prohibited punishments that were "cruell and unusuall." The *Solem* court simply assumed, with no analysis, that the one included the other. As a textual matter, of course, it does not: a disproportionate punishment can perhaps always be considered "cruel," but it will not always be (as the text also requires) "unusual."...

The language bears the construction, however—and here we come to the point crucial to resolution of the present case—that "cruelty and unusualness" are to be determined not solely with reference to the punishment at issue ("Is life imprisonment a cruel and unusual punishment?") but with reference to the crime for which it is imposed as well ("Is life imprisonment cruel and unusual punishment for possession of unlawful drugs?"). The latter interpretation would make the provision a form of proportionality guarantee. The arguments against it, however, seem to us conclusive....

Throughout the 19th century, state courts interpreting state constitutional provisions with identical or more expansive wording (i.e., "cruel or unusual") concluded that these provisions did not proscribe disproportionality but only certain modes of punishment. For example, in *Aldridge v. Commonwealth,* 4 Va. 447 (1824), the General Court of Virginia had occasion to interpret the cruel and unusual punishments clause that was the direct ancestor of our federal provision. In rejecting the defendant's claim that a sentence of so many as 39 stripes violated the Virginia Constitution, the court said: "As to the ninth section of the Bill of Rights, denouncing cruel and unusual punishments, we have no notion that it has any bearing on this case. That provision was never designed to control the Legislative right to determine ad libitum upon the adequacy of punishment, but is merely applicable to the modes of punishment."...

We think it enough that those who framed and approved the Federal Constitution chose, for whatever reason, not to include within it the guarantee against disproportionate sentences that some State Constitutions contained. It is worth noting, however, that there was good reason for that choice—a reason that reinforces the necessity of overruling *Solem*. While there are relatively clear historical guidelines and accepted practices that enable judges to determine which modes of punishment are "cruel and unusual," proportionality does not lend itself to such analysis. Neither Congress nor any state legislature has ever set out with the objective of crafting a penalty that is "disproportionate," yet as some of the examples mentioned above indicate, many enacted dispositions seem to be so—because they were made for other times or other places, with different social attitudes, different criminal epidemics, different public fears, and different prevailing theories of penology. This is not to say that there are no absolutes; one can imagine extreme examples that no rational person, in no time or place, could accept. But for the same reason these examples are easy to decide, they are certain never to occur. The real function of a constitutional proportionality principle, if it exists, is to enable judges to evaluate a penalty that some assemblage of men and women has considered proportionate—and to say that it is not. For that real-world enterprise, the standards seem so inadequate that the proportionality principle becomes an invitation to imposition of subjective values.

This becomes clear, we think, from a consideration of the three factors that *Solem* found relevant to the proportionality determination: (1) the inherent gravity of the offense, (2) the sentences imposed for similarly grave offenses in the same jurisdiction, and (3) sentences imposed for the same crime in other jurisdictions. As to the first factor: Of course some offenses, involving violent harm to human beings, will always and everywhere be regarded as serious, but that is only half the equation.

The issue is what else should be regarded to be as serious as these offenses, or even to be more serious than some of them. On that point, judging by the statutes that Americans have enacted, there is enormous variation—even within a given age, not to mention across the many generations ruled by the Bill of Rights.... In Louisiana, [for example] one who assaults another with a dangerous weapon faces the same maximum prison term as one who removes a shopping basket "from the parking area or grounds of any store ... without authorization." La.Rev.Stat.Ann.§§ 14:37; 14:68.1 (West 1986)....

The difficulty of assessing gravity is demonstrated in the very context of the present case: Petitioner acknowledges that a mandatory life sentence might not be "grossly excessive" for possession of cocaine with intent to distribute. But surely whether it is a "grave" offense merely to possess a significant quantity of drugs—thereby facilitating distribution, subjecting the holder to the temptation of distribution, and raising the possibility of theft by others who might distribute—depends entirely upon how odious and socially threatening one believes drug use to be. Would it be "grossly excessive" to provide life imprisonment for "mere possession" of a certain quantity of heavy weaponry? If not, then the only issue is whether the possible dissemination of drugs can be as "grave" as the possible dissemination of heavy weapons. Who are we to say no? The Members of the Michigan Legislature, and not we, know the situation on the streets of Detroit.... [Discussion of the other two factors in *Solem v. Helm* is omitted.]

Our 20th-century jurisprudence has not remained entirely in accord with the proposition that there is no proportionality requirement in the Eighth Amendment, but neither has it departed to the extent that *Solem* suggests. In *Weems v. United States,* 217 U.S. 349, 30 S.Ct. 544, 54 L.Ed. 793 (1910), a government disbursing officer convicted of making false entries of small sums in his account book was sentenced by Philippine courts to 15 years ... at "'hard and painful labor'" with chains fastened to the wrists and ankles at all times. Several "accessor[ies]" were superadded, including permanent disqualification from holding any position of public trust, subjection to "[government] surveillance" for life, and "civil interdiction," which consisted of deprivation of "'the rights of parental authority, guardianship of person or property, participation in the family council, [etc.]'"

Justice McKenna, writing for himself and three others, held that the [sentence] ... was "Cruel and Unusual Punishment.... The punishment was both (1) severe and (2) unknown to Anglo-American tradition." [The plurality concluded that some portions of the opinion seemed to support proportionality and some did not.]...

The first holding of this Court unqualifiedly applying a requirement of proportionality to criminal penalties was issued 185 years after the Eighth Amendment was adopted. In *Coker v. Georgia,* the Court held that, because of the disproportionality, it was a violation of the Cruel and Unusual Punishments Clause to impose capital punishment for rape of an adult woman. Four years later, in *Enmund v. Florida,* 458 U.S. 782, 102 S.Ct. 3368, 73 L.Ed.2d 1140 (1982), we held that it violates the Eighth Amendment, because of disproportionality, to impose the death penalty upon a participant in a felony that results in murder, without any inquiry into the participant's intent to kill.

Rummel v. Estelle treated this line of authority as an aspect of our death penalty jurisprudence, rather than a generalizable aspect of Eighth Amendment law. We think that is an accurate explanation, and we reassert it. Proportionality review is one of several respects in which we have held that "death is different," and have imposed protections that the Constitution nowhere else provides. We would leave it there, but will not extend it further....

The judgment of the Michigan Court of Appeals is AFFIRMED.

CONCURRING OPINION

Justice Kennedy, with whom Justice O'Connor and Justice Souter join, concurring in part and concurring in the judgment.

... I write this separate opinion because my approach to the Eighth Amendment proportionality analysis differs from Justice Scalia's. Regardless of whether Justice Scalia or the dissent has the best of the historical argument ... stare decisis counsels our adherence to the narrow proportionality principle that has existed in our Eighth Amendment jurisprudence for 80 years. Although our proportionality decisions have not been clear or consistent in all respects, they can be reconciled, and they require us to uphold petitioner's sentence.

Our decisions recognize that the Cruel and Unusual Punishments Clause encompasses a narrow proportionality principle.... Its most extensive application has been in death penalty cases.... [However,] the Eighth Amendment proportionality principle also applies to noncapital sentences.... [Justice Kennedy discusses *Solem v. Helm* and *Rummell v. Estelle* here.] ... Petitioner's life sentence without parole is the second most severe penalty permitted by law. It is the same sentence received by the petitioner in *Solem.* Petitioner's crime, however, was far more grave than the crime at issue in Solem. The crime of uttering a no account check at issue in *Solem* was "'one of the most passive felonies a person could commit.'"

Petitioner was convicted of possession of more than 650 grams (over 1.5 pounds) of cocaine. This amount of pure cocaine has a potential yield between 32,500 and 65,000 doses. From any standpoint, this crime falls in a different category from the relatively minor, nonviolent crime at issue in *Solem.* Possession, use, and distribution of illegal drugs represents "one of the greatest problems affecting the health and welfare of our population." Treasury *Employees v. Von Raab,* 489 U.S. 656, 668, 109 S.Ct. 1384, 1392, 103 L.Ed.2d 685 (1989). Petitioner's suggestion that his crime was nonviolent and victimless, echoed by the dissent, is false to the point of absurdity. To the contrary, petitioner's crime threatened to cause grave harm to society.

Quite apart from the pernicious effects on the individual who consumes illegal drugs, such drugs relate to crime in at least three ways: (1) A drug user may commit crime because of drug-induced changes in physiological functions, cognitive ability, and mood; (2) A drug user may commit crime in order to obtain money to buy drugs; and (3) A violent crime may occur as part of the drug business or culture. Studies bear out these possibilities, and demonstrate a direct nexus between illegal drugs and crimes of violence....

A penalty as severe and unforgiving as the one imposed here would make this a most difficult and troubling case for any judicial officer. Reasonable minds may differ about the efficacy of Michigan's sentencing scheme, and it is far from certain that Michigan's bold experiment will succeed. The accounts of pickpockets at Tyburn hangings are a reminder of the limits of the law's deterrent force, but we cannot say the law before us has no chance of success and is on that account so disproportionate as to be cruel and unusual punishment....

For the foregoing reasons, I conclude that petitioner's sentence of life imprisonment without parole for his crime of possession of more than 650 grams of cocaine does not violate the Eighth Amendment.

DISSENT

Justice White, with whom Justice Blackmun and Justice Stevens join, dissenting.

[The portion of Justice White's dissent refuting Justice Scalia's reading of the history of proportionality as part of the meaning of cruel and unusual is omitted.]

... [T]he Amendment as ratified contained the words "cruel and unusual," and there can be no doubt that prior decisions of this Court have construed these words to include a proportionality principle. In 1910, in the course of holding unconstitutional a sentence imposed by the Philippine courts, the Court stated: "Such penalties for such offenses amaze those who ... believe that it is a precept of justice that punishment for crime should be graduated and proportioned to [the] offense.... *Robinson v. California,* 370 U.S. 660, 82 S.Ct. 1417, 8 L.Ed.2d 758 (1962), held ... it to be cruel and unusual to impose even one day of imprisonment for the status of drug addiction."

The plurality opinion in *Gregg,* supra, 428 U.S., at 173, 96 S.Ct., at 2925, observed that the Eighth Amendment's proscription of cruel and unusual punishment is an evolving concept and announced that punishment would violate the Amendment if it "involve[d] the unnecessary and wanton infliction of pain" or if it was "grossly out of proportion to the severity of the crime."...

If Justice Scalia really means what he says—"the Eighth Amendment contains no proportionality guarantee," it is difficult to see how any of the above holdings and declarations about the proportionality requirement of the Amendment could survive....

What is more, the court's jurisprudence concerning the scope of the prohibition against cruel and unusual punishments has long understood the limitations of a purely historical analysis.... The Court therefore has recognized that a punishment may violate the Eighth Amendment if it is contrary to the "evolving standards of decency that mark the progress of a maturing society."...

In evaluating a punishment under this test, "we have looked not to our own conceptions of decency, but to those of modern American society as a whole" in determining what standards have "evolved," and thus have focused not on "the subjective views of individual Justices," but on "objective factors to the maximum possible extent."... [Justice White then proceeded to examine the sentence compared to other crimes.]

[T]here is no death penalty in Michigan; consequently, life without parole, the punishment mandated here, is the harshest penalty available. It is reserved for three crimes: first-degree murder; manufacture, distribution, or possession with intent to manufacture or distribute 650 grams or more of narcotics; and possession of 650 grams or more of narcotics. Crimes directed against the persons and property of others—such as second-degree murder, and armed robbery, do not carry such a harsh mandatory sentence, although they do provide for the possibility of a life sentence in the exercise of judicial discretion. It is clear that petitioner "has been treated in the same manner as, or more severely than, criminals who have committed far more serious crimes."

... [Furthermore,] [n]o other jurisdiction imposes a punishment nearly as severe as Michigan's for possession of the amount of drugs at issue here. Of the remaining 49 States, only Alabama provides for a mandatory sentence of life imprisonment without possibility of parole for a first-time drug offender, and then only when a defendant possesses ten kilograms or more of cocaine. Ala.Code § 13A–12–231(2)(d) (Supp.1990). Possession of the amount of cocaine at issue here would subject an Alabama defendant to a mandatory minimum sentence of only five years in prison. § 13A–12–231(2)(b). Even under the Federal Sentencing Guidelines, with all relevant enhancements, petitioner's sentence would barely exceed ten years....

Application of *Solem's* proportionality analysis leaves no doubt that the Michigan statute at issue fails constitutional muster. The statutorily mandated penalty of life without possibility of parole for possession of narcotics is unconstitutionally disproportionate in that it violates the Eighth Amendment's prohibition against cruel and unusual punishment. Consequently, I would reverse the decision of the Michigan Court of Appeals.

[Justice Marshall's dissent, Justice White's dissent, joined by Justices Blackmun and Stevens, and Justice Stevens's dissent, are omitted.]

Case Discussion Why does Justice Scalia argue that the Eighth Amendment does not apply to a mandatory life sentence without parole from the proportionality requirement? Why is death different? Overruling a prior decision rarely occurs. Why did Justices Scalia and Rehnquist decide to overrule *Solem v. Helm?* Notice that this is a case in which a majority did not agree with the opinion, although they agreed with the judgment. How did Justice Kennedy arrive at the judgment but not agree with Justice Scalia? Do you agree with Justice Scalia that proportionality applies only to death penalty cases? Do you agree with Justice Kennedy that proportionality applies to imprisonment but that this sentence was not cruel and unusual? Or, do you agree with the dissent that proportionality applies to imprisonment and that this sentence is cruel and unusual?

Note Cases *1.* McDougherty sold two pieces of cocaine base to an undercover police officer in a park approximately 690 feet from an elementary school. A statute provides for enhanced penalties for drug offenses taking place in the vicinity of schools. McDougherty was convicted and sentenced to 22 years in prison followed by 6 years of supervised release. Was the sentence cruel and unusual? The Ninth Circuit Court of Appeals said no. Because the sentence did not exceed the statutory maximum (40 years), it was not cruel and unusual. The court said: "Congress has determined that selling cocaine near a school is a very serious offense." *U.S. v. McDougherty,* 1991WL 182399 (9th Cir.Cal)

2. Kraft, 21, killed another person in a drunk-driving incident. The court sentenced him to 5 years of probation, the first 6 months of which he had to serve in jail. Kraft is suffering from terminal leukemia. Treatment for it required chemotherapy. Chemotherapy increases the risk of fatal infections.

Kraft's doctor testified that the risk of these infections would increase if Kraft was in jail. Kraft maintained that the sentence subjected him to cruel and unusual punishment. The court held: "It might be cruel and unusual punishment to sentence a person with defendant's condition to jail if the court knew the defendant would thereby be deprived of adequate medical treatment for his condition." Since the treatment was adequate, the punishment was not cruel and unusual. *State v. Kraft,* 326 N.W.2d 840 (Minn.1982)

3. Kevin Stanford committed murder on January 7, 1981, when he was approximately 17 years and 4 months of age. Stanford and his accomplice repeatedly raped and sodomized Poore during and after their commission of a robbery at a gas station where she worked as an attendant. They then drove her to a secluded area near the station, where Stanford shot her point-blank in the face and then in the back of her head. The proceeds from the robbery were roughly 300 cartons of cigarettes, two gallons of fuel, and a small amount of cash. A corrections officer testified that petitioner explained the murder as follows: "'[H]e said, I had to shoot her, [she] lived next door to me and she would recognize me.... I guess we could have tied her up or something or beat [her up] ... and tell her if she tells, we would kill her.... Then after he said that he started laughing.'" Is it cruel and unusual punishment to execute a person who commits murder while a juvenile? The Supreme Court ruled that it is not. "Of the 37 States that permit capital punishment, 15 decline to impose it on 16-year-olds and 12 on 17-year-olds. This does not establish the degree of national agreement this Court has previously thought sufficient to label a punishment cruel and unusual." *Sanford v. Kentucky,* 492 U.S. 361 (1989)

4. Johnny Paul Penry, who had the mental age of 6, raped, beat, and then stabbed Pamela Carpenter to death. Is it cruel and unusual punishment to execute a mentally retarded person? The Supreme Court ruled that it is not. The Court held, *inter alia,* that there was insufficient "objective evidence today of a national consensus against executing mentally retarded capital murderers, since petitioner has cited only one state statute that explicitly bans that practice and has offered not evidence of the general behavior of juries in this regard. Opinion surveys indicating strong public opposition to such executions do not establish a societal consensus." *Penry v. Lynaugh,* 109 S.Ct. 2934 (1989)

This is long and boring

▼ *Summary* ▼

The general principles of criminal law overarch the entire criminal law. They differ from the general principles of criminal liability, justification and excuse; from the doctrines of complicity and incomplete crimes; and from the rules defining specific crimes. The principles of liability govern the elements of crimes—the requirement of criminal conduct (the combination of act and intent), and where relevant, the element of causing a particular result. The doctrines of complicity and incomplete crimes, and the principles of justification and excuses, may or may not apply to a particular case or crime. The rules refer to individual crimes. The general principles of criminal law, on the other hand, encompass all the elements, doctrines, excuses, justifications, rules, and penalties.

The principle of legality requires that the law specifically define the crime and prescribe a penalty. The principle of legality encompasses at least three other principles: (1) the *ex post facto* prohibition against making conduct criminal after it occurs; (2) the void-for-vagueness principle, which requires the law to state with precision what conduct it prohibits; and (3) equal protection of the laws. The purposes underlying the principle of legality include (1) forewarning citizens about the conduct the law proscribes, (2) protecting against abuse of state power, and (3) assuring equal treatment by government.

The Constitution protects a number of individual rights from criminal prohibition. For example, the right to privacy, although not mentioned in the U.S. Constitution, protects some conduct. The right to free speech protects the freedom to express ideas and feelings consistent with a free society. The underlying purpose of the right to privacy and other civil rights is that the government should not interfere with conduct that either affects only the individuals who engage in it, or that promotes the free expression and exchange of ideas. Limits on making crimes out of conduct that is included in civil rights reflect the positive side of criminal law—that it ought to promote behavior that it does not prohibit. However, the Bill of Rights permits neither complete privacy nor unrestricted freedom of expression.

The principle of punishment refers both to the purposes of punishment and to punishment's proportionality—the nature and amount of punishment in relation to the crime committed. The two basic purposes for punishment are retribution—to inflict pain on the person who harmed another in order to give offenders their just deserts—and prevention. The major types of prevention are (1) deterrence, or using the threat of punishment to deter people generally from future crime; (2) incapacitation, or preventing specific offenders from committing future crimes; and (3) rehabilitation, or changing individual offenders' behavior so that they will not commit crimes in the future.

Throughout history, criminal law has reflected these purposes, but the emphasis has shifted among them over time. During most of early history, retribution predominated; during the first sixty years of the twentieth century, rehabilitation held sway; during the last two decades, retribution and incapacitation have returned to prominence. Proportionality prohibits excessive punishment. Punishments that are out of proportion to the conduct they penalize violate the Eighth Amendment. Proportionality might refer to types of penalty, such as hard labor or capital punishment, or to the degree of a particular penalty, such as the length of imprisonment or the amount of a fine.

▼ *Questions for Review and Discussion* ▼

1. What are the nature and the scope of the general principles of criminal law? How do they differ from the principles of liability, justification, and excuse, and from the doctrines and rules of criminal law?

2. Explain the principle of legality, state its purposes, and describe its origins.

3. To what situations does the *ex post facto* prohibition apply? What are the purposes of the prohibition against *ex post facto* laws?

4. What are the bases for the void for vagueness doctrine? Describe its two major purposes.

5. Explain how the Supreme Court differs in the standards it applies to determining whether classifications based upon race, gender, and most other classifications violate the requirement of equal protection of the laws.

6. What is the basic idea underlying the right to privacy, and to what kinds of cases does it ordinarily apply? What is the source of the right to privacy in the U.S. Constitution? In the states?

7. What does the free speech guarantee prevent governments from making criminal? Distinguish between speech and expressive conduct. What kinds of speech and expressive conduct can the government criminalize?

8. What distinguishes retribution from prevention?

9. Explain general deterrence, special deterrence, incapacitation, and rehabilitation. What do they all have in common?

10. Explain the proportionality principle. To what kinds of cases does it apply?

▼ Suggested Readings ▼

1. Herbert L. Packer, *The Limits of the Criminal Sanction* (Palo Alto, Calif.: Stanford University Press, 1968). Professor Packer's book is a necessary starting point for anyone seriously interested in the aims and purposes of criminal law in general and in criminal punishment in particular. Packer takes the approach that he is writing for the generalists, not the criminal justice specialist. He especially addresses what he calls the rational lawmaker, one who "stops, looks, and listens" before passing laws. The book is written in a thoughtful, clear, easy-to-read style.

2. Lois G. Forer, *Criminals and Victims* (New York: Norton, 1980). Written by a judge with many years of experience in sentencing criminal defendants, this book explores the difficulties in applying general purposes to concrete cases. Judge Forer analyzes the few alternatives judges have in sentencing, particularly the heavy emphasis on imprisonment, which she believes satisfies neither victims nor society. Well documented with interesting, challenging cases from her courtroom, the book is lively, easy to read, and provocative.

3. Andrew von Hirsch, *Doing Justice* (New York: Hill and Wang, 1976). This book is a brief, clear, and concise argument for just deserts. Based on deliberations by the Committee for the Study of Incarceration, it resulted from serious consideration of returning to retribution as the proper aim of punishment.

4. Norval Morris, *The Future of Imprisonment* (Chicago: University of Chicago Press, 1974). Morris, a criminal justice expert, has written an influential book in which he recommends a set of principles upon which punishment should rest. His principles are aimed at preserving what is best of the rehabilitative ideal in the realities of twentieth-century prisons. These ideas are argued convincingly and written clearly, so that general readers can profit from reading the book.

5. David J. Rothman, *Conscience and Convenience* (Boston: Little, Brown, 1980). Professor Rothman, a historian surveys the origins and historical development of rehabilitation in the early years of the twentieth century. This book is excellent for anyone interested in the history of the rehabilitative ideal.

6. Johannes Andenaes, "Deterrence," in *Encyclopedia of Crime and Justice,* vol. 2, ed. Sanford H. Kadish (New York: Free Press, 1983). This is a brief, excellent summary of deterrence theory, research, and the problems of applying deterrence theory in practice, written by the world's leading deterrence theorist. The article includes a valuable bibliography on deterrence, which can lead to fruitful examination of this basic justification for criminal punishment.

7. Jerome Hall, *General Principles of Criminal Law,* 2d ed. (Indianapolis: Bobbs-Merrill, 1960). This book gives the most comprehensive treatment of the general principles of legality and proportionality. Hall, a law professor, writes for the specialist, but his challenging arguments and his knowledge of history, law, and philosophy make the book well worth the effort of reading it.

▼ *Notes* ▼

1. Quotes from Roman Civil Law and Lord Coke appear in Jerome Hall, *General Principles of Criminal Law,* 2d ed. (Indianapolis: Bobbs-Merrill, 1960), pp. 31–32.

2. United States Constitution, Art. 1, § 9, cl. 3 prohibits the federal government from passing *ex post facto* laws; Art. 10 § 10, cl. 1 prohibits the states from doing so; *Calder v. Bull,* 3 U.S. (3 Dall.) 386, 390, 1 L.Ed. 648 (1798) defined *ex post facto.*

3. *People ex rel. Lonschein v. Warden,* 43 Misc. 2d 109, 250 N.Y.S.2d 15 (1964) (change from death penalty to life imprisonment retroactively effective).

4. *Lanzetta v. New Jersey,* 306 U.S. 451, 453, 59 S.Ct. 618, 619, 83 L.Ed. 888 (1939).

5. *Kolender v. Lawson,* 461 U.S. 352, 357–8 (1983).

6. *Buck v. Bell,* 274 U.S. 200, 208, 47 S.Ct. 584, 585, 71 L.Ed. 1000 (1927) (equal protection argument the last resort).

7. *Michael M. v. Superior Court of Sonoma County,* 450 U.S. 464, 477 (1981).

8. *Roe v. Wade,* 410 U.S. 113 (1973) (abortion); *Bowers v. Hardwick,* 478 U.S. 186 (1986) (sexual preference).

9. Florida Constitution, Article I, § 23.

10. *Griswold v. Connecticut,* 381 U.S. 479, 85 S.Ct. 1678, 14 L.Ed.2d 510 (1965).

11. Jed Rubenfeld, "The Right to Privacy," *Harvard Law Review* 102 (1989): 737–807. In this article, Rubenfeld includes a detailed, extended discussion of the concept and development in constitutional law of privacy.

12. *Bowers v. Hardwick,* 478 U.S. 186, 106 S.Ct. 2841, 92 L.Ed.2d 140 (1986).

13. Art. I, § 22. See note, "Alaska's right to Privacy Ten Years After *Ravin v. State:* Developing a Jurisprudence of Privacy," *Alaska Law Review* 2 (1985): 159–183, for recent developments in the right to privacy in Alaska.

14. *Dennis v. United States,* 341 U.S. 494 (1951).

15. *Gitlow v. New York,* 268 U.S. 652 (1925); *Chaplinsky v. New Hampshire,* 315 U.S. 568 (1942); *Schenck v. United States,* 249 U.S. 47.

16. Tex.Penal Code Ann. § 42.09 (1989) provides in full: "§ 42.09. Desecration of Venerated Object "(a) A person commits an offense if he intentionally or knowingly desecrates: "(1) a public monument; "(2) a place of worship or burial; or "(3) a state or national flag. "(b) For purposes of this section, 'desecrate' means deface, damage, or otherwise physically mistreat in a way that the actor knows will seriously offend one or more persons likely to observe or discover his action. "(c) An offense under this section is a Class A misdemeanor."

17. Thomas Szasz, M.D., *Law, Liberty, and Psychiatry* (New York: Collier Books, 1963).

18. Herbert Packer, *The Limits of the Criminal Sanction* (Palo Alto, Calif.: Stanford University Press, 1968), pp. 33–34.

19. *McKinney's New York Criminal Law Pamphlet* (St. Paul: West Publishing Co., 1988); New York Penal Code, § 1.05(6).

20. *Leviticus,* 24: 20.

21. *A History of the Criminal Law of England,* vol. 3 (London: Macmillan, 1883), pp. 81–82.

22. James Q. Wilson and Richard Herrnstein thoroughly discuss free will in *Crime and Human Nature,* chap. 19 (New York: Simon and Schuster, 1985); see also psychiatrist Willard Gaylin's fascinating *The Killing of Bonnie Garland* (New York: Simon and Schuster, 1982).

23. Henry E. Wiehofen, "Retribution Is Obsolete," in *Responsibility,* ed. C. Friedrich, Nomos series, no. 3 (New York: Lieber-Atherton, 1960), pp. 116, 119–20.

24. These theories are discussed at length in James Q. Wilson and Richard Herrnstein, *Crime and Human Nature.* An intriguing case study applying the theories to one criminal homicide is Andre Mayer and Michael Wheeler, *The Crocodile Man: A Case of Brain Chemistry and Criminal Violence* (Boston: Houghton Mifflin, 1982).

25. Joseph Goldstein, "Psychoanalysis and Jurisprudence," *Yale Law Journal* 77 (1968): 1071–72.

26. This topic is explored fully in Bedau, ed., *The Death Penalty in America,* chap. 4.

27. *Coker v. Georgia,* 433 U.S. 584, 97 S.Ct. 2861, 53 L.Ed.2d 982 (1977).

28. See Wilson and Herrnstein, *Crime and Human Nature,* for a full discussion.

29. Johannes Andenaes, "Deterrence," *Encyclopedia of Crime and Justice,* ed. Sanford H. Kadish (New York: Free Press, 1983), pp. 2, 593.

30. Ibid., 596, 97 S.Ct. at 2868.

31. Mark DeWolfe Howe, ed., *Holmes-Laski Letters* (Cambridge, Mass.: Harvard University Press, 1953), p. 806.

32. James Q. Wilson, *Thinking about Crime* (New York: Basic Books, 1975), p. 1.

33. See Mark H. Moore et al., *Dangerous Offenders: The Elusive Target of Justice* (Cambridge, Mass.: Cambridge University Press, 1984).

34. Sandra Gleason, "Hustling: The 'Single' Economy of a Prison," *Federal Probation* (June 1978), pp. 32–39; Samuel Walker, *Sense and Nonsense about Crime: A Policy Guide* (Monterey, Calif.: Brooks/Cole, 1985), pp. 59–61.

35. *The Limits of the Criminal Sanction,* p. 50.

36. For these early reformation ideas, see Joel Samaha, "Hanging for Felony," *Historical Journal* 21 (1979); and "Some Reflections on the Anglo-Saxon Heritage of Discretionary Justice," in Lawrence E. Abt and Irving R. Stuart, eds., *Social Psychology and Discretionary Law,* (New York: Van Nostrand, 1979), pp. 4–16.

37. See Richard D. Schwartz, "Rehabilitation," in *Encyclopedia of Crime and Justice,* pp. 1364–73.

38. "The Humanitarian Theory of Punishment," *Res Judicatae* 6 (1953):224.

39. Joel Samaha, *Law and Order in Historical Perspective* (New York: Academic Press, 1974); Samaha, "Hanging for Felony."

40. See David J. Rothman, *Conscience and Convenience* (Boston: Little, Brown, 1980), for the history of rehabilitation during the early twentieth century.

41. Robert Martinson, "What Works? Questions and Answers about Prison Reform," *The Public Interest* 35 (Spring 1974):22–54.

42. Quoted in Malcom M. Feeley, *Court Reform on Trial* (New York: Basic Books, 1983), 139; Walker, *Sense and Nonsense about Crime,* chap. 1, 5, 6, and 11.

43. See the excellent review of these issues in American Law Institute, *Model Penal Code and Commentaries* (Philadelphia: American Law Institute, 1985), pp. 3, 11–30.

44. *Solem v. Helm,* 463 U.S. 277, 284, 103 S.Ct. 3001, 3006, 77 L.Ed.2d 637 (1982).

45. Ibid., 285 103 S.Ct. at 3007.

46. *Weems v. United States,* 217 U.S. 349, 30 S.Ct. 544, 54 L.Ed. 793 (1910); *Robinson v. California,* 370 U.S. 660, 82 S.Ct. 1417, 8 L.Ed.2d 758 (1962).

47. Mich. Comp. Laws Ann. § 333.7403(2)(a)(i) (Supp. 1990–1991) provides a mandatory sentence of life in prison for possession of 650 grams or more of "any mixture containing [a schedule 2] controlled substance"; § 333.7214(a)(iv) defines cocaine as a schedule 2 controlled substance. § 791.234(4) provides eligibility for parole after 10 years in prison, except for those convicted of either first-degree murder or "a major controlled substance offense"; § 791.233b[1](b) defines "major controlled substance offense" as, *inter alia,* a violation of § 333.7403.

Chapter 3

The General Principles of Criminal Liability

▼ *Chapter Outline* ▼

I. Introduction
II. *Actus Reus*
   A. Status or Condition as Action
   B. Thoughts and Action
   C. Voluntariness
   D. Verbal Acts
   E. Omission
   F. Possession
   G. Summary of *Actus Reus*
III. *Mens Rea*
   A. Determining *Mens Rea*
   B. Defining *Mens Rea*
     1. Purpose
     2. Knowing
     3. Subjective and Objective Standards
     4. Recklessness and Negligence
     5. Strict Liability
IV. Concurrence
V. Causation
VI. Grading Offenses
VII. Summary

1. Every crime consists of several elements that the prosecution must prove beyond a reasonable doubt to convict.

2. The general principles of criminal liability are *actus reus, mens rea,* concurrence, causation, and resulting harm.

3. Actus reus includes voluntary bodily movements, failures to act, and possession.

4. Mens rea includes four mental states: purpose, knowledge, recklessness, and negligence.

5. Strict liability crimes require no *mens rea*.

6. Criminal acts must concur with criminal mental states, and in some cases, conduct must concur with, or cause, harmful results.

7. Factual causation means *sine qua non,* or "but for," causation; legal causation requires proximate or substantial cause.

8. Mens rea is a principal means of determining the seriousness of an offense; purposeful wrongdoing is the most serious, followed by recklessness, negligence, and liability without fault.

▼ *Chapter Key Terms* ▼

actual possession—On the possessor's person.

actus reus—The criminal act or the physical element in criminal liability.

causation—The substantial reason for the harm in crimes requiring a specific result.

concurrence—The requirement that *actus reus* must join with *mens rea* to produce criminal conduct, or to cause a harmful result.

constructive possession—Legal possession or custody.

culpability—Blameworthiness based on *mens rea.*

elements—The parts of a crime that the prosecution must prove beyond a reasonable doubt, such as *actus reus, mens rea,* causation, and harmful result.

factual causation—Conduct that sets a chain of events in motion.

general intent—Intent to commit the *actus reus.*

general principles of criminal liability—The theoretical foundation

for the elements of *actus reus, mens rea,* causation, and harm.

knowing possession—Awareness of the item possessed.

legal causation—Cause recognized by law to impose criminal liability.

mens rea—The mental element in crime, of which there are four mental states: purpose, knowledge, recklessness, and negligence.

mere possession—Possession without knowledge.

negligence—The unconscious creation of risk, or the mental state in which actors create substantial and unjustifiable risks of harm but are not aware of creating them.

recklessness—The conscious creation of substantial and unjustifiable risk; the state of mind in which actors know they are creating risks of harm.

strict liability—Liability without fault, or in the absence of *mens rea.*

verbal acts—Words.

▼ INTRODUCTION

Crooking a finger ordinarily provokes no attention; it is a perfectly unremarkable act under ordinary circumstances. But if you crook a finger around the trigger of a gun—with the intent to kill someone—and squeeze the trigger, and that someone dies, then the ordinary act of crooking a finger becomes the *actus reus* of murder. Stripping naked in order to take a shower is not an act worthy of much comment. However, stripping naked in a classroom transforms the act into the misdemeanor of public nudity in most jurisdictions.[1]

The general principles of liability define the ordinary phenomena of action, intention, concurrence, and causation. The specific crimes define the specific acts, mental states, extraordinary circumstances, and, where relevant, the results that transform ordinary phenomena into crimes. All crimes include at least three elements: (1) an act, sometimes called the objective element because you can measure it from the outside; (2) an intent, sometimes called the subjective element because it resides inside the person who has it; and (3) the union of act and intent. These are crimes of conduct, such as public nudity. Some crimes, such as murder, include two additional elements: (4) causation, and (5) a particular result.[2]

Elements of Crime

Two Types of Crime

Crimes of Conduct
Actus Reus + *Mens Rea* = Crime
Crimes Requiring Result
Actus Reus + *Mens Rea* + Causation + Specific Result = Crime

---

Each element provides the basis for the statement of a **general principle of criminal liability.** The act provides the basis for the principle of criminal liability called the ***actus reus,*** literally the "evil act." The intent provides the basis for the principle of ***mens rea,*** the "evil mind." The union of act and intent gives rise to the principle of **concurrence.** The element of **causation** gives rise to the principle of causation, and the particular result to the principle of harm. These general principles allow us to organize the content of the special part of the criminal law, the part that defines the specific crimes in chapters 8 through 12, into a logical, orderly, theoretical framework. For example, every crime (from murder and rape to disorderly conduct and making an illegal left turn) includes a union of *actus reus* and *mens rea*. In murder, the intent to kill unites with the act of killing; in illegal left turns, the intent to turn unites with the act of turning. The special part of the criminal law applies the general principles of *actus reus* and *mens rea,* and where relevant, applies causation and result to specific crimes.

▼ *ACTUS REUS*

The first principle of criminal liability is the requirement of action. Criminal law does not punish evil thoughts alone; it punishes only thoughts come to fruition in evil deeds. The ancient criminal law punished only "manifest criminality"; in 1562, the English court ruled that "men were not to be tried for their thoughts."*Actus reus,* however, requires more, and sometimes less, than "muscular contractions," or bodily movements. A spasm is not *actus reus;* a failure to act can be.[3]

The actus *reus* requirement serves several purposes. It helps to prove the *mens rea*. We cannot observe intentions; we can only infer them from actions. It also reserves the harsh sanction of the criminal law for cases of

actual danger, and protects the privacy of individuals. The law need not pry into citizens' thoughts unless the thinker crosses "the threshold of manifest criminality."[4]

Many axioms illustrate the *actus reus* principle: "Thoughts are free." "We are punished for what we do, not for who we are." "Criminal punishment depends on conduct, not status." "We are punished for what we have done, not for what we might do." Although simple to state as a general rule, much in the full statement of the principle of *actus reus* complicates its apparent simplicity.

Status or Condition as Action

> An act ... is a muscular contraction, and something more.... The contraction of muscles must be willed.[5]

Mere bodily movement does not qualify as *actus reus; actus reus* requires the freedom to choose action and the exercise of that freedom by acting. *Actus reus* therefore comprises two ideas: bodily movements and will. This excludes from criminal liability action resulting from involuntary bodily movements, such as reflexes, spasms, and other involuntary acts discussed in the next section. It also excludes most conditions or statuses. Some conditions result from prior voluntary acts—repeat offenders of crimes, and addicts and alcoholics who took their first fix or drink voluntarily. Other conditions result from no act at all—gender, age, race, and ethnicity. Status or condition contrasts with action: Act designates bodily movement; status means condition or a passive state. Status indicates who we are; action points to what we do.

In his novel about the imaginary land called *Erewhon,* Samuel Butler deals with the Erewhonians' criminal code, which makes it a crime to have tuberculosis. Following conviction for pulmonary consumption (tuberculosis), the judge pronounced sentence on one defendant in these words:

> [I]t only remains for me to pass such a sentence on you, as shall satisfy the ends of the law. That sentence must be a very severe one. It pains me much to see one who is yet so young, and whose prospects in life were otherwise so excellent, brought to this distressing condition by a constitution which I can only regard as radically vicious; but yours is no case for compassion: this is not your first offense: you have led a career of crime, and have only profited by the leniency shown you upon past occasions, to offend yet more seriously against the laws and institutions of your country. You were convicted of aggravated bronchitis last year: and I find that though you are but twenty-three years old, you have been imprisoned on no less than fourteen occasions for illnesses of a more or less hateful character; in fact, it is not too much to say that you have spent the greater part of your life in jail.
>
> It is all very well for you to say that you came of unhealthy parents, and had a severe accident in your childhood which permanently undermined your constitution; excuses such as these are the ordinary refuge of the criminal; but they cannot for one moment be listened to by the ear of justice. I am not here to enter upon curious metaphysical questions as to the origins of this or that— questions to which there would be no end were their introduction once tolerated, and which would result in throwing the only guilt on the tissues of the primordial cell, or on the elementary gasses. There is no question of how

you came to be wicked, but only this—namely, are you wicked or not? This has been decided in the affirmative, neither can I hesitate for a single moment to say that it has been decided justly. You are a bad and dangerous person....

I do not hesitate to sentence you to imprisonment, with hard labor, for the rest of your miserable existence.[6]

Why does the thought of sentencing someone to life imprisonment for having tuberculosis repel us? Because the defendant committed no act; the court punished him for his disease—a condition beyond his control, not an act—however dangerous in 1927 when Butler wrote his novel. In *Robinson v. California,* the Supreme Court ruled that punishing someone for addiction to heroin violates the Eighth Amendment to the United States Constitution (the cruel and unusual punishment clause—see chapter 2). According to the court, it would be cruel and unusual punishment to sentence someone to "even one day" for an illness. Why? Because a disease is not an act. What is it about the absence of an act that makes it unconstitutional to punish a condition? If addiction results from no act at all, as in the case of a "crack baby," the addict was not responsible for the addiction, and we cannot blame individuals for conditions beyond their control. If we cannot blame them, we find it wrong to punish them.

What about acts that result from conditions? In *Powell v. Texas,* the Supreme Court had to decide whether to extend the prohibition against punishing addiction to drugs to an alcoholic's act of public drunkenness.

CASE

Was His Public Drunkenness Part of a "Disease"?

Powell v. Texas
392 U.S. 514 (1968)

Mr. Justice Marshall announced the judgment of the Court and delivered an opinion in which the chief justice, Mr. Justice Black, and Mr. Justice Harlan join.

FACTS

In late December 1966, appellant was arrested and charged with being found in a state of intoxication in a public place, in violation of Vernon's Ann.Texas Penal Code, Art. 477 (1952), which reads as follows:

Whoever shall get drunk or be found in a state of intoxication in any public place, or at any private house except his own, shall be fined not exceeding one hundred dollars.

Appellant was tried in the Corporation Court of Austin, Texas, found guilty, and fined $20. He appealed to the County Court at Law No. 1 of Travis County, Texas, where a trial de novo was held. His counsel urged that appellant was "afflicted with the disease of chronic alcoholism," that "his appearance in public (while drunk was) ... not of his own volition," and therefore that to punish him criminally for that conduct would be cruel and unusual, in violation of the Eighth and Fourteenth Amendments to the United States Constitution.

The trial judge in the county court, sitting without a jury ... found appellant guilty, and fined him $50. There being no further right to appeal within the Texas judicial system, appellant appealed to this Court.

The principal testimony was that of Dr. David Wade, a Fellow of the American Medical Association, duly certificated in psychiatry.... Dr. Wade sketched the outlines of the "disease" concept of alcoholism; noted that there is no generally accepted definition of "alcoholism"; alluded to the ongoing debate within the medical profession over whether alcohol is actually physically "addicting" or merely psychologically "habituating"; and concluded that in either case a "chronic alcoholic" is an "involuntary drinker," who is "powerless not to drink" and who "loses his self-control over his drinking." He testified that he had examined appellant, and that appellant is a "chronic alcoholic," who "by the time he has reached (the state of intoxication) ... is not able to control his behavior, and (who) ... has reached this point because he has an uncontrollable compulsion to drink."

Dr. Wade also responded in the negative to the question whether appellant has "the willpower to resist the constant excessive consumption of alcohol." He added that in his opinion jailing appellant without medical attention would operate neither to rehabilitate him nor to lessen his desire for alcohol....

Appellant testified concerning the history of his drinking problem. He reviewed his many arrests for drunkenness; testified that he was unable to stop drinking; stated that when he was intoxicated he had no control over his actions and could not remember them later, but that he did not become violent; and admitted that he did not remember his arrest on the occasion for which he was being tried....

OPINION

... Appellant seeks to come within the application of the Cruel and Unusual Punishment Clause announced in *Robinson v. California,* 370 U.S. 660, 82 S.Ct. 1417, 8 L.Ed.2d 758 (1962), which involved a state statute making it a crime to "be addicted to the use of narcotics." This Court held there that "a state law which imprisons a person thus afflicted (with narcotic addiction) as a criminal, even though he has never touched any narcotic drug within the State or been guilty of any irregular behavior there, inflicts a cruel and unusual punishment...."

On its face the present case does not fall within that holding, since appellant was convicted, not for being a chronic alcoholic, but for being in public while drunk on a particular occasion. The State of Texas thus

has not sought to punish a mere status, as California did in *Robinson;* nor has it attempted to regulate appellant's behavior in the privacy of his own home. Rather, it has imposed upon appellant a criminal sanction for public behavior which may create substantial health and safety hazards, both for appellant and for members of the general public, and which offends the moral and esthetic sensibilities of a large segment of the community. This seems a far cry from convicting one for being an addict, being a chronic alcoholic, being "mentally ill, or a leper...."

Robinson so viewed brings this Court but a very small way into the substantive criminal law.... The entire thrust of *Robinson's* interpretation of the Cruel and Unusual Punishment Clause is that criminal penalties may be inflicted only if the accused has committed some act, has engaged in some behavior, which society has an interest in preventing, or perhaps in historical common-law terms, has committed some *actus reus....*

Traditional common-law concepts of personal accountability and essential considerations of federalism lead us to disagree with appellant. We are unable to conclude, on the state of this record or on the current state of medical knowledge, that chronic alcoholics in general, and Leroy Powell in particular, suffer from such an irresistible compulsion to drink and to get drunk in public that they are utterly unable to control their performance of either or both of these acts and thus cannot be deterred at all from public intoxication. And in any event this Court has never articulated a general constitutional doctrine of *mens rea.*

We cannot cast aside the centuries-long evolution of the collection of interlocking and overlapping concepts which the common law has utilized to assess the moral accountability of an individual for his antisocial deeds. The doctrines of *actus reus, mens rea,* insanity, mistake, justification, and duress have historically provided the tools for a constantly shifting adjustment of the tension between the evolving aims of the criminal law and changing religious, moral, philosophical, and medical views of the nature of man. This process of adjustment has always been thought to be the province of the States....

But formulating a constitutional rule would reduce, if not eliminate ... fruitful experimentation, and freeze the developing productive dialogue between law and psychiatry into a rigid constitutional mold. It is simply not yet the time to write the Constitutional formulas cast in terms whose meaning, let alone relevance, is not yet clear either to doctors or to lawyers.

Affirmed.

CONCURRING OPINION

Mr. Justice Black, whom Mr. Justice Harlan joins, concurring.

... Punishment for a status is particularly obnoxious, and in many instances can reasonably be called cruel and unusual, because it involves punishment for a mere propensity, a desire to commit an offense; the mental element is not simply one part of the crime but may constitute all of it. This is a situation universally sought to be avoided in our criminal law; the fundamental requirement that some action be proved is solidly established even for offenses most heavily based on propensity, such as attempt, conspiracy, and recidivist crimes. In fact, one eminent authority has found only one isolated instance, in all of Anglo-American jurisprudence, in which criminal responsibility was imposed in the absence of any act at all.

The reasons for this refusal to permit conviction without proof of an act are difficult to spell out, but they are nonetheless perceived and universally expressed in our criminal law. Evidence of propensity can be considered relatively unreliable and more difficult for a defendant to rebut; the requirement of a specific act thus provides some protection against false charges. Perhaps more fundamental is the difficulty of distinguishing, in the absence of any conduct, between desires of the daydream variety and fixed intentions that may pose a real threat to society; extending the criminal

law to cover both types of desire would be unthinkable, since "(t)here can hardly be anyone who has never thought evil. When a desire is inhibited it may find expression in fantasy; but it would be absurd to condemn this natural psychological mechanism as illegal."

In contrast, crimes that require the State to prove that the defendant actually committed some proscribed act involve none of these special problems. In addition, the question whether an act is "involuntary" is, as I have already indicated, an inherently elusive question, and one which the State may, for good reasons, wish to regard as irrelevant. In light of all these considerations, our limitation of our *Robinson* holding to pure status crimes seems to me entirely proper....

I suspect this is a most propitious time to remember the words of the late Judge Learned Hand, who so wisely said: "For myself it would be most irksome to be ruled by a bevy of Platonic Guardians, even if I knew how to choose them, which I assuredly do not." L. Hand, The Bill of Rights 73 (1958)

I would confess the limits of my own ability to answer the age-old questions of the criminal law's ethical foundations and practical effectiveness. I would hold that *Robinson v. California* establishes a firm and impenetrable barrier to the punishment of persons who, whatever their bare desires and propensities, have committed no proscribed wrongful act. But I would refuse to plunge from the concrete and almost universally recognized premises of *Robinson* into the murky problems raised by the insistence that chronic alcoholics cannot be punished for public drunkenness, problems that no person, whether layman or expert, can claim to understand, and with consequences that no one can safely predict. I join in affirmance of this conviction.

[Justice White's concurring opinion is omitted.]

DISSENT

Mr. Justice Fortas, with whom Mr. Justice Douglas, Mr. Justice Brennan, and Mr. Justice Stewart join, dissenting.

... It is settled that the Federal Constitution places some substantive limitation upon the power of state legislatures to define crimes for which the imposition of punishment is ordered.... *Robinson v. California* ... stands upon a principle which, despite its subtlety, must be simply stated and respectfully applied because it is the foundation of individual liberty and the cornerstone of the relations between a civilized state and its citizens: Criminal penalties may not be inflicted upon a person for being in a condition he is powerless to change.

In all probability, Robinson at some time before his conviction elected to take narcotics. But the crime as defined did not punish this conduct. The statute imposed a penalty for the offense of "addiction"—a condition which Robinson could not control. Once Robinson had become an addict, he was utterly powerless to avoid criminal guilt.

He was powerless to choose not to violate the law.

In the present case, appellant is charged with a crime composed of two elements— being intoxicated and being found in a public place while in that condition. The crime, so defined, differs from that in *Robinson*. The statute covers more than a mere status. But the essential constitutional defect here is the same as in *Robinson*, for in both cases the particular defendant was accused of being in a condition which he had no capacity to change or avoid.

The trial judge sitting as trier of fact found upon the medical and other relevant testimony, that Powell is a "chronic alcoholic." He defined appellant's "chronic alcoholism" as "a disease which destroys the afflicted person's will power to resist the constant, excessive consumption of alcohol."... I would reverse the judgment below.

Case Discussion
Does it make sense to punish Powell if he was drunk in public because of his alcoholism? Was his alcoholism a condition? If so, did it result from a voluntary act? Was his alcoholism a "disease?" Does the public drunkenness statute punish Powell for being "sick?" Which opinion do you agree with, the plurality or the dissent? Why?

Note Case
In *State v. Perry,* 436 P.2d 252 (1968), Perry was convicted under an Oregon statute making it a crime to be a "common prostitute." The court noted that the statute "does not purport to proscribe and make punishable a specific act of prostitution; it defines the crime in terms of the defendant's status or condition.... [E]ven if the defendant had reformed at the time of her arrest, she could still be charged with the violation of the statute on the ground that a crime once committed is not obliterated by reformation."

Was the statute valid? The court upheld the conviction, but noted: "The complexities created by the enactment of [common prostitution] ... as a crime of personal condition as distinguished from a crime of action present serious questions of their constitutionality as well as difficult problems of procedure and evidence and should prompt the legislature to [repeal the law.]" In 1971, the Oregon legislature repealed the statute.

Thoughts and Action

Consider a statute that makes it a crime to *intend* to kill another person. Why does such a statute strike us as absurd? It causes difficult enforcement problems because of the difficulty in proving it: "The thought of man is not triable, for the devil himself knoweth not the thought of man," said one medieval English judge. Furthermore, intentions do no harm. The moral law may condemn those who have immoral thoughts; the criminal law requires conduct—intention turned into action. Hence, punishing the intent to kill, even if possible to prove, fails to punish the harm the statute contemplates—another's death.[7]

Furthermore, it is difficult to distinguish mere daydreaming or fantasy from intention. The angry thought, "Ill kill you for that!" rarely turns into actual killing, or even an attempt to kill. It merely expresses anger, not the intention to do more. Punishment must await action sufficient to prove that the angry thoughts express the resolution and will to commit a crime (see chapter 5). Finally, punishing thoughts expands the meaning of crime to encompass a "mental state that the accused might be too irresolute even to begin to translate into action." Punishing thoughts is impractical, inequitable, and unjust; hence, thoughts are not criminal acts.[8]

Voluntariness

Actus reus excludes not only thoughts and statuses but also some physical movements as well. The criminal law imposes liability on those who act voluntarily of their own free will, not on those who are acted upon by outside (or even internal) forces. The bizarre case of *The King v. Cogdon* deals with sleepwalking as a criminal act.

CASE

Is Killing while Asleep a Criminal Act?

The King v. Cogdon[9]

FACTS

Mrs. Cogdon was charged with the murder of her only child, a daughter called Pat, aged nineteen. Pat had for some time been receiving psychiatric treatment for a relatively minor neurotic condition of which, in her psychiatrist's opinion, she was now cured. Despite this, Mrs. Cogdon continued to worry unduly about her. Describing the relationship between Pat and her mother, Mr. Cogdon testified: "I don't think a mother could have thought any more of her daughter. I think she absolutely adored her." On the conscious level, at least, there was no

reason to doubt Mrs. Cogdon's deep attachment to her daughter.

To the charge of murdering Pat, Mrs. Cogdon pleaded not guilty. Her story, though somewhat bizarre, was not seriously challenged by the Crown, and led to her acquittal. She told how, on the night before her daughter's death, she had dreamt that their house was full of spiders and that these spiders were crawling all over Pat. In her sleep, Mrs. Cogdon left the bed she shared with her husband, went into Pat's room, and awakened to find herself violently brushing at Pat's face, presumably to remove the spiders. This woke Pat. Mrs. Cogdon told her she was just tucking her in. At the trial, she testified that she still believed, as she had been told, that the occupants of a nearby house bred spiders as a hobby, preparing nests for them behind the pictures on their walls. It was these spiders which in her dreams had invaded their home and attacked Pat. There had also been a previous dream in which ghosts had sat at the end of Mrs. Cogdon's bed and she had said to them, "Well, you have come to take Pattie." It does not seem fanciful to accept the psychological explanation of these spiders and ghosts as the projections of Mrs. Cogdon's subconscious hostility towards her daughter; a hostility which was itself rooted in Mrs. Cogdon's own early life and marital relationship.

The morning after the spider dream she told her doctor of it. He gave her a sedative and, because the dream and certain previous difficulties she had reported, discussed the possibility of psychiatric treatment. That evening Mrs. Cogdon suggested to her husband that he attend his lodge meeting, and asked Pat to come with her to the cinema. After he had gone Pat looked through the paper, not unusually found no tolerable programme, and said that as she was going out the next evening she thought she would rather go to bed early. Later, while Pat was having a bath preparatory to retiring, Mrs. Cogdon went into her room, put a hot water bottle in the bed, turned back the bedclothes, and placed a glass of hot milk beside the bed ready for Pat. She then went to bed herself. There was some desultory conversation between them about the war in Korea, and just before she put out her light Pat called out to her mother, "Mum, don't be so silly worrying there about the war, it's not on our front door step yet."

Mrs. Cogdon went to sleep. She dreamt that "the war was all around the house," that soldiers were in Pat's room, and that one soldier was on the bed attacking Pat. This was all of the dream she could later recapture. Her first "waking" memory was of running from Pat's room, out of the house to the home of her sister who lived next door. When her sister opened the front door Mrs. Cogdon fell into her arms, crying "I think I've hurt Pattie."

In fact Mrs. Cogdon had, in her somnambulistic state, left her bed, fetched an axe from the woodheap, entered Pat's room, and struck her two accurate forceful blows on the head with the blade of the axe, thus killing her.

OPINION

Mrs. Cogdon's story was supported by the evidence of her physician, a psychiatrist, and a psychologist. The jury believed Mrs. Cogdon. The jury concluded that Mrs. Cogdon's account of her mental state at the time of the killing, and by the unanimous support given to it by the medical and psychological evidence completely rebutted the presumption that Mrs. Cogdon intended the natural consequences of her acts. It must be stressed that insanity was not pleaded as a defence because the experts agreed that Mrs. Cogdon was not psychotic. (See chapter 7.) The jury acquitted her because the act of killing itself was not, in law, regarded as her act at all.

Case Discussion   Was Mrs. Cogdon's act of killing Pattie involuntary? Could she have done anything to prevent her killing Pattie? It is widely held that it is wrong to punish those who cannot be blamed. Would it be "right" to punish Mrs. Cogdon? Why or why not?[10]

Note Cases   *1.* Decina suffered an epileptic seizure while driving his car. During the seizure, he struck and killed four children. Was the killing an "involuntary act" because it occurred during the seizure? The court said no:

> This defendant knew he was subject to epileptic attacks at any time. He also knew that a moving vehicle uncontrolled on a public highway is a highly dangerous instrumentality capable of unrestrained destruction. With this

knowledge, and without anyone accompanying him, he deliberately took a chance by making a conscious choice of a course of action, in disregard of the consequences which he knew might follow from his conscious act, which in this case did ensue. *People v. Decina,* 138 N.E.2d 799 (N.Y.1956)

2. In *George v. State,* 681 S.W.2d 43 (Tex.Crim.App.1984), George was convicted of aggravated assault. George put a gun to a friend's head and demanded a dollar. After he cocked the hammer, it "slipped off [his] thumb" and the "gun went off." George did not mean for the gun to go off. He did not intend to hurt his friend; it was an accident. In its opinion, the Texas Court of Criminal Appeals said:

> [T]here is no law and defense of accident in the present penal code," but ... the Legislature had not jettisoned the notion. "The function of the former defense of accident is performed now by the requirement of ... § 6.01(a), that, A person commits an offense if he voluntarily engages in conduct ..." If the issue is raised by the evidence, a jury may be charged that a defendant should be acquitted if there is a reasonable doubt as to whether he voluntarily engaged in the conduct of which he is accused."...
> If the hammer "slipped off [his] thumb," it had to be that the thumb holding the hammer partially back released just enough pressure for the hammer to "slip" forward. However slight, that is "bodily movement" within the meaning of § 1.07(a)(1), and there is no evidence that it was involuntary.

3. In a Danish case, Bjorn Nielson masterminded a robbery by hypnotizing his friend Palle Hardrup. While in the hypnotic trance, Hardrup held up a Copenhagen bank, shooting and killing a teller and director. Nielson was sentenced to life imprisonment because he masterminded the holdup, even though he was nowhere near the bank when the robbery took place. Hardrup was sent to a mental hospital. He was not tried for robbery because his acts during the holdup were not considered voluntary.[11]

4. Fulcher got in a fight in a bar, passed out, and was picked up by the police. He was taken to jail, where he brutally stomped on another jail inmate. He shouted ethnic slurs at the Mexican-American victim. Fulcher testified that he remembers nothing after passing out in the bar. At the trial, Doctor LeBegue testified that Fulcher suffered from a concussion incurred during the bar fight, and that it caused a brain injury that put Fulcher "in a state of traumatic automatism at the time of his attack on Hernandez ... the state of mind in which a person does not have conscious and willful control over his actions...." Was Fulcher liable? No, said the court. Unconscious automatism is an affirmative defense because

> [T]he rehabilitative value of imprisonment for the automatistic offender who has committed the offense unconsciously is nonexistent. The cause of the act was an uncontrollable physical disorder that may never recur and is not a moral deficiency. *Fulcher v. State,* 633 P.2d 142 (Wyo.1981)

5. Jerrett terrorized Dallas and Edith Parsons—he robbed them, killed Dallas, and kidnapped Edith. At trial, Jerrett testified that he could remember nothing of what happened until he was arrested, and that he had suffered previous blackouts following exposure to Agent Orange during military service in Vietnam. The trial judge refused to instruct the jury on the defense of automatism. The North Carolina supreme court reversed, and ordered a new trial. *State v. Jerrett,* 307 S.E.2d 339 (N.C.1983)

—————❦—————

Punishing involuntary acts does not satisfy the purposes of criminal law. Involuntary acts are not blameworthy, hence do not deserve punishment as retribution. Nor does punishment deter those who act without conscious choice. The government can incapacitate the "dangerous"—those who act involuntarily—but civil commitment more appropriately serves this purpose in the absence of blameworthiness.

Threatened punishment might induce individuals susceptible to involuntary acts to take precautions against harming others. Hypnotized persons can refuse hypnosis; sleepwalkers can lock their bedroom doors at night; and epileptics can take medication to control their seizures. If individuals can take measures to control involuntary movements and do not, then they are arguably blameworthy; they have committed voluntarily induced involuntary acts, a complex concept explored later in this chapter under *mens rea*.

Voluntarily induced involuntary states less bizarre than hypnosis include unconscious states that individuals know beforehand might occur. These arise frequently while driving: drowsy drivers continue to drive until they fall asleep; intoxicated persons continue to drive; persons with dangerously high blood pressure suffer strokes while driving; or epileptics have seizures while driving.

Verbal Acts

In common usage, *act* means bodily movement; however, in *actus reus,* the term encompasses more than moving arms, legs, hands, feet, and the entire body. Words constitute criminal acts in some crimes. Crimes consisting of **verbal acts** include conspiracy, solicitation, terroristic threats, some kinds of assault, and inciting to riot. These crimes are discussed in chapters on specific crimes; here it suffices to note that they constitute criminal acts under the general principle of *actus reus*. For example, if a supervisor in an office uses sexually graphic language with an employee under his or her supervision, or even comments on the attractiveness of the employee, these acts might amount to the misdemeanor of sexual harassment.

Omission

Voluntary bodily movements, voluntarily induced involuntary conduct, and words are not the only acts that may qualify as criminal under the general principle of *actus reus*. Under some circumstances, omissions—or failures to act—are also criminal. But the law imposes liability on omissions only reluctantly, preferring to punish those who act affirmatively rather than those who allow something to happen, as is the case in omissions. Some have criticized this distinction. Professor George Fletcher maintains:

> It is as much an act of will for the guards at Buckingham Palace to stand motionless as it is for tourists to stroll back and forth in front of them.

Conscious non-motion is a greater assertion of personality than casual acting. One can only be puzzled by the widespread belief that the distinction between motion and non-motion is of importance to the law.

Liability for omissions takes two forms. One is the failure to perform a legal duty, such as reporting an accident or child abuse, filing an income tax return, registering a firearm, and notifying sexual partners of HIV status. The other form is failing to intervene to prevent a serious harm, such as death or the destruction of property, from occurring.[12]

Only the failure to perform *legal* duties is a criminal omission. Legal duties can arise out of statutes, contracts, and relationships. Statutes creating legal duties include the duties to file income tax returns, to report accidents and child abuse, and to register firearms. Contracts create other legal duties. Police officers, for example, agree to perform certain public duties; failure to perform those duties, such as violating a citizen's civil rights, creates both civil and criminal liability. Relationships imposing legal duties include the parent-child relationship, the marital relationship (in some jurisdictions), the doctor-patient relationship, the employer-employee relationship, and the carrier-passenger relationship.

Failure to perform *moral* duties does not constitute the *actus reus*. According to Professors LaFave and Scott:

> Generally one has no legal duty to aid another person in peril, even when that aid can be rendered without danger or inconvenience to himself. He need not shout a warning to a blind man headed for a precipice or to an absent-minded one walking into a gunpowder room with a lighted candle in hand. He need not pull a neighbor's baby out of a pool of water or rescue an unconscious person stretched across the railroad tracks, though the baby is drowning or the whistle of the approaching train is heard in the distance. A doctor is not legally bound to answer a desperate call from the frantic parents of a sick child, at least if it is not one of his regular patients. A moral duty to take affirmative action is not enough to impose a legal duty to do so. But there are situations which do give rise to legal duties.[13]

Limiting criminal omissions to failure to perform legal duties rests on the proposition that individual conscience, peer pressure, and other informal mechanisms condemn and prevent behavior more effectively than criminal prosecution. Furthermore, prosecuting omissions unduly burdens an already overburdened criminal justice system. Finally, the criminal law cannot compel Good Samaritans to help those in need.[14] The court dealt with omission as *actus reus* in *People v. Oliver.*

CASE

Was There a Duty to Act?

People v. Oliver
258 Cal.Rptr. 138 (1989)

Strankman, Associate Justice

FACTS

Appellant met Cornejo on the afternoon of July 6, 1986, when she was with her boyfriend at a bar in the City of Pleasant Hill. She and her boyfriend purchased jewelry from Cornejo. In the late afternoon, when appellant was leaving the bar to return home, Cornejo got into the car with her, and she drove home with him. At the time, he appeared to be extremely drunk. At her house, he asked her for a spoon and went into the bathroom. She went to the kitchen, got a spoon and brought it to him. She knew he wanted the spoon to take drugs. She remained in the living room while Cornejo "shot up" in the bathroom. He then came out and collapsed onto the floor in the living room. She tried but was unable to rouse him.

Appellant then called the bartender at the bar where she had met Cornejo. The bartender advised her to leave him and come back to the bar, which appellant did.

Appellant's daughter returned home at about 5 p.m. that day with two girlfriends. They found Cornejo unconscious on the living room floor. When the girls were unable to wake him, they searched his pockets and found eight dollars. They did not find any wallet or identification. The daughter then called appellant on the telephone. Appellant told her to drag Cornejo outside in case he woke up and became violent. The girls dragged Cornejo outside and put him behind a shed so that he would not be in the view of the neighbors. He was snoring when the girls left him there. About a half hour later, appellant returned home with her boyfriend. She, the boyfriend, and the girls went outside to look at Cornejo. Appellant told the girls that she had watched him "shoot up" with drugs and then pass out.

The girls went out to eat and then returned to check on Cornejo later that evening. He had a pulse and was snoring. In the morning, one of the girls heard appellant tell her daughter that Cornejo might be dead. Cornejo was purple and had flies around him. Appellant called the bartender at about 6 a.m. and told her she thought Cornejo had died in her backyard. Appellant then told the girls to call the police and she left for work. The police were called.... Appellant told the police that Cornejo was extremely drunk when she drove him to her home. He went into the bathroom and asked for a spoon, which she gave him. Cornejo "shot up" and then collapsed. She

said she believed that he had collapsed from the injection of drugs, and that he had "hot-shotted."... An autopsy revealed that Cornejo died of morphine poisoning. The heroin (which shows up in the blood as morphine) was injected shortly before his death. Cornejo also had a .28 percent blood alcohol level. The forensic pathologist who testified at trial was reasonably certain that Cornejo's death was not caused by the alcohol.

OPINION

... The prosecution contended that appellant was criminally negligent when she failed to summon medical aid for Cornejo and then abandoned him, when she must have known he needed medical attention. At the close of the prosecution's case, defense counsel moved for a judgment of acquittal.... [H]e argued that the evidence failed to establish a duty of care owned by appellant to Cornejo because there was no special relationship between them, and that absent a duty of care there was no negligence. The trial court ruled that ... there was sufficient evidence of a duty owed. The trial court accordingly denied the motion for judgment of acquittal....

Generally, one has no legal duty to rescue or render aid to another in peril, even if the other is in danger of losing his or her life, absent a special relationship which gives rise to such duty. Further, "[t]he fact that the actor realizes or should realize that action on his part is necessary for another's aid or protection does not of itself impose upon him a duty to take such action."

In California civil cases, courts have found a special relationship giving rise to an affirmative duty to act where some act or omission on the part of the defendant either created or increased the risk of injury to the plaintiff, or created a dependency relationship inducing reliance or preventing assistance from others. Where, however, the defendant took no affirmative action which contributed to, increased, or changed the risk which would otherwise have existed, and did not voluntarily assume any responsibility to protect the person or induce a false sense of security, courts have refused to find a special relationship giving rise to a duty to act.

The Restatement Second of Torts provides guidelines as to the specific kinds of conduct which will require one to take affirmative action to render aid. § 321 provides: "(1) If the actor does an act, and subsequently realizes or should realize that it has created an unreasonable risk of causing physical harm to another, he is under a duty to exercise reasonable care to prevent the risk from taking effect....

§ 324 of the Restatement Second of Torts provides in part: "One who, being under no duty to do so, takes charge of another who is helpless adequately to aid or protect himself is subject to liability to the other for any bodily harm caused to him by (a) the failure of the actor to exercise reasonable care to secure the safety of the other while within the actor's charge...."

Neither appellant nor respondent cite any California decision involving a charge of criminal negligence which is helpful to our determination of the nature, if any, of the duty owed here. The cases cited by them in which the defendant was charged with criminal negligence involved relationships which undisputably gave rise to a duty of care. (See, e.g., *Walker v. Superior Court* (1988) 47 Cal.3d 112, 253 Cal.Rptr. 1, 763 P.2d 852 [parents who provided only prayer treatment for their seriously ill child]; *People v. Rodriguez* (1960) 186 Cal.App.2d 433, 8 Cal.Rptr. 863 [child killed by a fire after mother left children unattended in home].)

We find, however, that the rules governing the imposition of a duty to render aid or assistance as an element of civil negligence, are applicable to the imposition of a duty in the context of criminal negligence. As stated by one leading commentator on criminal law: "[T]he 'measuring stick' [of duty] is the same in a criminal case as in the law of torts. It is the exercise of due care and caution as represented by the conduct of a reasonable person under like circumstances, and this in itself is intended to represent the same requirement whatever the case may be." (Perkins & Boyce, *Criminal Law* (3d ed. 1982) ch. 7, § 2, p. 843.)

We conclude that the evidence of the combination of events which occurred between the time appellant left the bar with Cornejo through the time he fell to the floor unconscious, established as a matter of law a relationship which imposed upon appellant a duty to seek medical aid. At the time appellant left the bar with Cornejo, she observed that he was extremely drunk, and drove him to her home. In so doing, she took him from a public place where others might have taken care to prevent him from injuring himself, to a private place—her home—where she alone could provide care. To a certain, if limited, extent, therefore, she took charge of a person unable to prevent harm to himself. (Rest.2d Torts, op. cit. supra, § 324.) She then allowed Cornejo to use her bathroom, without any objection on her part, to inject himself with narcotics, an act involving the definite potential for fatal consequences.

When Cornejo collapsed to the floor, appellant should have known that her conduct had contributed to creating an unreasonable risk of harm for Cornejo—death. At that point, she owed Cornejo a duty to prevent that risk from occurring by summoning aid, even if she had not previously realized that her actions would lead to such risk. Her failure to summon any medical assistance whatsoever and to leave him abandoned outside her house warranted the jury finding a breach of that duty....The judgment is affirmed.

White, P.J., and Barry-Deal, J., concur.

Case Discussion What specific facts did the court say gave rise to a legal duty? Was the duty imposed by a relationship? A contract? A statute? Do you agree that Oliver had a legal duty to Cornejo? Should people who meet others in bars have legal duties to them? Suppose Ms. Oliver was talking to Cornejo in the bar and he collapsed? Or suppose he passed out in the car while she was driving home? Compare this case with the Genovese case that follows.

Note Cases   *1.* In *Commonwealth v. Konz,* 450 A.2d 638 (1982), Mrs. Konz was convicted of involuntary manslaughter in the death of her husband. Reverend Konz, a thirty-four-year-old diabetic, had administered daily doses of insulin to himself for seventeen years. After hearing an evangelist, Reverend Konz decided to give up insulin and rely on God to treat his diabetes. Without the insulin, his condition deteriorated. Within a few days, he died from diabetic ketoacidosis. During the entire time of last illness, Mrs. Konz was with Reverend Konz, except that she was sleeping at the moment of his death. She was charged with involuntary manslaughter for failure to intervene and prevent Reverend Konz's death. Did the marital relationship give rise to a legal duty to intervene? On appeal from her conviction, the appellate court held that the marital relationship did not give rise to a legal duty to seek medical attention.

The court reasoned that

> Recognition of such a duty would place lay persons in peril of criminal prosecution while compelling them to medically diagnose the seriousness of their spouses' illnesses and injuries. In addition, it would impose an obligation for a spouse to take action at a time when the stricken individual competently chooses not to receive assistance. The marital relationship gives rise to an expectation of reliance between spouses, and to a belief that one's spouse should be trusted to respect, rather than ignore, one's expressed preferences. That expectation would be frustrated by imposition of a broad duty to seek aid, since one's spouse would then be forced to ignore the expectation that the preference to forego assistance will be honored.

2. Michael was convicted of second-degree assault for failing to intervene to prevent his wife from beating their two-month-old baby, who suffered multiple fractures of all four lower leg bones. The trial court found:

> Mr. Michael had a legal duty to aid and assist his child if she was under the threat or risk of physical damage or assault—from any person, including his wife… Mr. Michael did not aid and did not help his daughter when she was in fact physically mistreated and abused by his wife…. Mr. Michael's failure was knowing. In other words … I find that Mr. Michael was capable of rescuing and assisting his daughter. And … he knew that he was capable and— could have rescued her…. And … he failed to act in the face of … that awareness. As a result … of his failure to act … his daughter suffered serious physical injury.

On appeal, the Alaska Court of Appeals affirmed the conviction, holding that the trial court correctly stated the law of omission. *Michael v. State,* 767 P.2d 193 (Ala.App.1988)

Not all failures to perform legal duties constitute criminal omissions. A criminal omission consists of an *unreasonable* failure to fulfill a legal duty to act. It would not apply if a sea captain allowed a crew member who had fallen overboard to drown in order to save other crew members and passengers from a dangerous storm. It would also not apply if a babysitter who could not swim did not dive into deep water to save the child he or she was watching.

A famous incident occurring in New York City raises both the questions of when a legal duty arises and what actions consist of reasonably performing a duty.

CASE

Was Their Omission a Crime?

37 Who Saw Murder Didn't Call the Police

New York Times (March 17, 1964).
Copyright © 1964 by the New York Times Company. Reprinted by permission.

For more than half an hour 38 respectable, law-abiding citizens in Queens watched a killer stalk and stab a woman in three separate attacks in Kew Gardens.

Twice the sound of their voices and the sudden glow of their bedroom lights interrupted him and frightened him off. Each time he returned, sought her out and stabbed her again. Not one person telephoned the police during the assault; one witness called after the woman was dead. But Assistant Chief Inspector Frederick M. Lussen, in charge of the borough's detectives and a veteran of 25 years of homicide investigations, is still shocked.

He can give a matter of fact recitation of many murders. But the Kew Gardens slaying baffles him—not because it is a murder, but because the "good people" failed to call the police.

"As we have reconstructed the crime," he said, "the assailant had three chances to kill this woman during a 35-minute period. He returned twice to complete the job. If we had been called when he first attacked, the woman might not be dead now."

This is what the police say happened beginning at 3:20 a.m. in the staid, middle-class, tree lined Austin Street area:

Twenty-eight-year-old Catherine Genovese, who was called Kitty by almost everyone in the neighborhood, was returning home from her job as manager of a bar in Hollis. She parked her red Fiat in a lot adjacent to the Kew Gardens Long Island Rail Road Station, facing Mowbray Place. Like many residents of the neighborhood, she had parked there day after day since her arrival from Connecticut a year ago, although the railroad frowns on the practice.

She turned off the lights of her car, locked the door and started to walk the 100 feet to the entrance of her apartment at 82-70 Austin Street, which is in a Tudor building, with stores on the first floor and apartments on the second.

The entrance to the apartment is in the rear of the building because the front is rented to retail stores. At night the quiet neighborhood is shrouded in the slumbering darkness that marks most residential areas.

Miss Genovese noticed a man at the far end of the lot, near a seven-story apartment house at 82-40 Austin Street. She halted. Then, nervously, she headed up Austin Street toward Lefferts Boulevard, where there is a call box to the 102d Police Precinct in nearby Richmond Hill.

She got as far as a street light in front of a bookstore before the man grabbed her. She screamed. Lights went on in the 10-story apartment house at 82-67 Austin Street, which faces the bookstore. Windows slid open and voices punctured the early morning stillness.

Miss Genovese screamed: "Oh, my God, he stabbed me! Please help me! Please help me!"

From one of the upper windows in the apartment house, a man called down: "Let that girl alone!"

The assailant looked up at him, shrugged and walked down Austin Street toward a white sedan parked a short distance away. Miss Genovese struggled to her feet.

Lights went out. The killer returned to Miss Genovese, now trying to make her way around the side of the building by the parking lot to get to her apartment. The assailant stabbed her again.

"I'm dying!" she shrieked. "I'm dying!"

Windows were opened again, and lights went on in many apartments. The assailant got into his car and drove away. Miss Genovese staggered to her feet. A city bus, Q i 10, the Lefferts Boulevard line to Kennedy International Airport, passed. It was 3:35 a.m..

The assailant returned. By then, Miss Genovese had crawled to the back of the building, where the freshly painted brown doors to the apartment house held out hope of safety. The killer tried the first door; she wasn't there. At the second door, 82-62 Austin Street, he saw her slumped on the floor at the foot of the stairs. He stabbed her a third time—fatally.

It was 3:50 by the time the police received their first call, from a man who was a neighbor of Miss Genovese. In two minutes they were at the scene. The neighbor, a 70-year-old woman, and another woman were the only persons on the street. Nobody else came forward.

The man explained that he had called the police after much deliberation. He had phoned a friend in Nassau County for advice and then he had crossed the roof of the building to the apartment of the elderly woman to get her to make the call.

"I didn't want to get involved," he sheepishly told the police.

The police stressed how simple it would have been to have gotten in touch with them. "A phone call," said one of the detectives, "would have done it." The police may be reached by dialing "0" for operator or SPring 7-3100.

Today, witnesses from the neighborhood, which is made up of one-family homes in the $35,000 to $60,000 range with the exception of the two apartment houses near the railroad station, find it difficult to explain why they didn't call the police.

Lieut. Bernard Jacobs, who handled the investigation by the detectives, said: "It is one of the better neighborhoods. There are few reports of crimes."...

The police said most persons had told them they had been afraid to call, but had given meaningless answers when asked what they had feared.

"We can understand the reticence of people to become involved in an area of violence," Lieutenant Jacobs said, "but where they are in their homes, near phones, why should they be afraid to call the police?"

Witnesses—some of them unable to believe what they had allowed to happen—told a reporter why.

A housewife, knowingly if quite casual, said, "We thought it was a lover's quarrel." A husband and wife both said, "Frankly, we were afraid." They seemed aware of the fact that events might have been different. A distraught woman, wiping her hands in her apron, said, "I didn't want my husband to get involved."...

A man peeked out from a slight opening in the doorway to his apartment and rattled off an account of the killer's second attack. Why hadn't he called the police at the time? "I was tired," he said without emotion. "I went back to bed."

It was 4:25 a.m. when the ambulance arrived for the body of Miss Genovese. It drove off. "Then," a solemn police detective said, "the people came out."

Case Discussion   Did the residents have a legal duty to intervene? A moral duty? On what basis? Should the "neighborly" relationship give rise to a duty? Why? Should a statute impose a duty of citizens to intervene? Why? Assuming a duty, of what does it consist? What should be the penalty for failing to intervene? Consider two other incidents. In the first, an assailant raped and beat an eighteen-year-old switchboard operator. The victim ran naked and bleeding from the building onto the street, screaming for help. A crowd of forty people gathered and watched, in broad daylight, while the rapist tried to drag her back into the building. No onlooker intervened; two police officers happened on the scene and arrested the assailant. In the second incident, eleven people watched while an assailant stabbed seventeen-year-old Andrew Melmille in the stomach on a subway. The assailant left the subway at the next stop. Not one of the eleven people on the train helped Melmille. He bled to death. Is there a legal duty to act in either of these incidents? What is the duty? How, if at all, do these incidents differ from the Genovese incident?[15]

Possession

In addition to voluntary acts and the failure to reasonably perform legal duties, the passive state of possessing some items and substances sometimes qualifies as a criminal act. Although possession itself is passive, acquiring possession requires action. If the possessor performs that action, then the possessor's act produces the possession. If a third person places an item or substance in another's possession without the receiver's knowledge, the possessor has, of course, not committed a voluntary act. But once the illegal item or substance is discovered retaining possession involves an omission—hence a criminal act. Thus, having pornography in my house is not an act, but buying it and putting it there is. Finding marijuana in my house and not disposing of it after discovery is an omission. Both can be criminal possession.

Jurisdictions differ on two questions regarding criminal possession: (1) What constitutes possession? and (2) Does criminal possession require *knowing* possession, or is mere possession sufficient? **Constructive possession** is not physical or **actual possession;** it is legal possession or custody. An owner has custody over a home but does not physically possess the cocaine that a weekend guest keeps in the host's closet. One who buys cocaine in order to use it has **knowing possession** of the cocaine. One who does a friend a favor by carrying a brown paper bag without knowing that the bag contains stolen money has what the law designates as **mere possession** of the money.

Constructive possession and mere possession give rise to difficult problems in criminal law. Constructive possession increases the chance that innocent people will be convicted. In the strongest possession cases, the defendant physically possesses the prohibited item or substance; constructive possession requires only that the prohibited item or substance fall under the constructive possessor's control. Having cocaine in my pocket more clearly demonstrates guilt than having cocaine found in my houseguest's room. Mere possession creates the possibility that the law may punish people who do not intend harm. For example, postal carriers possess narcotics they are carrying for delivery. If your professor asks you to deliver an envelope to her office, and you do so, do you criminally possess the cocaine it contains? A long line of cases rules that you do, on the ground that mere possession constitutes the *actus reus*.[16]

CASE

Did She Possess the Marijuana?

Hughes v. State

612 S.W.2d 581 (Tex.Cr.App.1981)

McCormick, Judge

This is an appeal from a conviction of possession of more than four ounces of marijuana. Punishment is imprisonment for ten years, probated, and a fine of $5,000. Appellant contends the evidence is insufficient to establish that she had possession and control of the marijuana....

FACTS

On November 19, 1976, several Houston police officers arrived at appellant's residence to execute a search warrant. The validity of the search warrant is not disputed. For safety precautions, Officer Delora Lott approached the house and fictitiously requested to use the telephone. Appellant's daughter refused to allow Officer Lott inside. When appellant came to the door, the officers identified themselves and their purpose. Appellant turned and ran from the door. The officers then forcibly entered the residence, followed appellant into a bedroom, and apprehended appellant. A pistol was found in the bathrobe appellant was wearing. Appellant and her three children were then seated in the living room....

On a coffee table, in the den, Lott discovered numerous marijuana "bricks." The total weight of the marijuana was over fifty pounds. In the bedroom where appellant was apprehended, Officer Bengley found a paper bag containing marijuana. Also found in a jacket hanging in one of the closets were a marijuana cigarette and a pipe containing marijuana residue. Appellant's residency of the house is undisputed.

At trial, Officers Lott and Herbert Lord testified ... that the large amount of marijuana located inside the house was clearly visible. The marijuana was approximately fifteen feet from the front door of the residence and plainly visible. Lott testified that the marijuana was similar to hay, but that it had a very strong and distinct odor.

OPINION

In cases involving possession of contraband, the State must show that (a) the defendant exercised, either singularly or jointly, care, custody, control, and management over the contraband, and (b) the defendant knew that what he possessed was contraband. However, where the defendant is not in exclusive possession of the premises where the contraband is found, it cannot be concluded that she knew of or controlled the contraband unless there are additional independent facts and circumstances which affirmatively link her to the contraband. This affirmative link must reasonably allow one to infer the defendant's knowledge and control of the contraband. This "affirmative link" has been established when the contraband is in plain view; the amount of marijuana found; the accessibility of the contraband to the accused; and facts showing defendant's residence at the place where the contraband is found.

The evidence, which this Court must view in the light most favorable to the verdict, is clearly sufficient to link appellant affirmatively to the marijuana. Officer Lott testified that a large amount of marijuana was in plain view on a coffee table in the den, and that it had a strong, distinct odor....

The evidence, which this Court must view in the light most favorable to the verdict, is clearly sufficient to establish appellant's knowledge. Over fifty pounds of marijuana in a den area is hard, if not impossible, to overlook....

Appellant ... specifically attacks her actual control over the marijuana.... [A]ppellant admitted her residency.... Regardless of the ownership or appellant's status regarding the house, such facts have been held sufficient to sustain possession.

Even ignoring these facts, it is clear that at the time of the search, appellant was in sole possession and control of the premises. When the officers secured the house, only appellant and her three children were inside. Appellant was wearing a bathrobe. As the only adult present, the jury can reasonably conclude that appellant had control of the premises. Appellant's conduct in refusing entry or use of the phone substantiates the care, control, and management of the home. In addition, the record is devoid of any evidence that anyone else except the "Hughes" or appellant occupied or had access to the house. Viewing this evidence most favorably, the verdict is upheld....

DISSENT

Teague, Judge, dissenting

... [A]ppellant was convicted by a jury of the felony offense of knowingly possessing more than four ounces of marijuana. The trial court assessed punishment at 10 years' confinement in the Texas Department of Corrections but probated same. A fine of $5,000 was also assessed but this was not probated by the trial judge because, "I can get to your husband that way."...

This record is totally and absolutely silent of any wrongful or unlawful activities of appellant outside the residence in question prior to the arrival of the police at the residence on the night in question. No evidence whatsoever was admitted at the guilt stage to show any relationship she may have had with "Mr. Hughes," the person named in the search warrant. There is no evidence to show how long appellant had been at the residence prior to the time the police arrived on the evening in question. From what appears, or fails to appear, in the record, appellant could have been merely a babysitter with the misfortune of having the same last name as the "Mr. Hughes" named in the search warrant. There is no evidence appellant was under the influence of any type drugs, narcotics or marijuana when the search warrant was executed. There is no proof that appellant was ever inside the "enclosed patio" where the marijuana, for which appellant was tried, was found and, even though testimony showed that one could see the marijuana as it then existed in the "enclosed patio" area of the residence, from the den or living room area of the residence, there is no evidence or testimony that this appellant was aware of its existence or could have seen it. Appellant also made no ... incriminatory statements when arrested or at any time during the evening in question.

We thus have nothing of an affirmative or of a direct nature to link appellant to the marijuana found in the "enclosed patio," for which marijuana she was charged, tried and convicted.

An accused, of course, may jointly possess marijuana with another and exclusive possession need not be shown. However, mere presence alone at a place where the contraband or marijuana is located or found, or is being used or possessed by others does not justify a finding of joint possession.... [W]here the State seeks to convict an accused on the basis of joint possession, the State must show "additional independent facts and circumstances which affirmatively link the accused to the contraband in such a manner that it can be concluded he or she had knowledge of the contraband as well as control over it."...

To recapitulate, the evidence to connect appellant to the marijuana found in the "enclosed patio," prior to the entry of the police into the residence, showed only that Officer Reynolds saw from the outside a "shadow" of what appeared to be an adult female near the front door when what appeared to be a small child was then speaking to Reynolds. Appellant is tenuously tied to the residence at best. As previously noted, neither the affidavit for the search warrant nor the search warrant are before us as neither was put into the record of this cause for appeal purposes at the trial.

In reference to the inside or the interior of the residence, bricks of marijuana were found inside an "enclosed patio," which was visible from the front door and the den or living room area of the residence. A bag containing an undisclosed amount of marijuana was found in the bedroom, the exact location therein is not shown. A pipe with residue was found inside a closet but its exact location is not shown. Appellant, when arrested, had in a pocket of her bathrobe a loaded .38 caliber pistol. A large sum of money was found in the bedroom; however, an objection to this answer was sustained by the trial court. Appellant was found and arrested in a bedroom. Three juveniles were also found inside the house. The exact location of these children inside the house after entry was made was never shown.

As to actions of appellant, upon announcement of "Houston Police Officers" or "Police," the "shadow," which was later shown to be appellant, fled to a back bedroom.

As to appellant's relationship to the residence or house, she was merely shown to be present when the search warrant was executed and was subsequently arrested wearing a bathrobe. During the trial at the guilt-innocence stage, the three female juveniles coincided with but were never identified as the three daughters of the appellant. According to Officer Reynolds, one of the children did say: "I'm going to ask my mother," although Officer Lord denied such statement was made. The "shadow" figure asserted a form of control of the premises by saying, "Go away," or having it said by a small child. Appellant has the same last name as the man named in the warrant; all of which testimony was adduced by rank hearsay.

From all of the above and after a most careful review of this record, I conclude the evidence is insufficient to sustain the conviction of appellant....

Possession means more than being where the action is; it involves the exercise of dominion and control over the thing allegedly possessed. Mere proximity is insufficient. By its very nature, possession is unique to the possessor and it is not enough to place him in the presence of other persons having possession to impart possession to him.

It is true that exclusive possession is not necessary where the parties jointly possess a drug and possession may be proved by circumstantial evidence. However, it cannot be inferred from merely being present in a place where marijuana is found that the defendant had knowledge of its presence and had dominion and control. There must be additional evidence of knowledge and control to sustain a conviction.... I would enter a judgment reversing and ordering the prosecution dismissed. I, therefore, respectfully dissent.

Case Discussion   Does the court require constructive or actual possession? Knowing or mere possession? What are all the relevant facts in determining whether Ms. Hughes "criminally possessed" marijuana? Why does the dissent disagree that Ms. Hughes criminally possessed marijuana? Do you agree? How would you define criminal possession? According to your definition, did Mrs. Hughes possess the marijuana? Explain.

Note Cases   *1.* The Omaha Police Department was engaged in a reverse sting operation. Kevan Barbour, a narcotics officer, sold crack cocaine to parties who approached him. After the purchase, Barbour signalled fellow officers, who arrested the purchasers. Earl Clark approached Officer Barbour, asking for a "twenty" ($20 worth of crack cocaine). Barbour handed Clark a sack. After examining it, Clark handed it back, saying it was "too small." Barbour then handed Clark a larger sack. According to Barbour, Clark then handed him $20. Barbour signalled for the arrest. While being arrested, Clark dropped the crack. In a trial without a jury for possessing crack cocaine, the court believed Barbour's testimony and convicted Clark.

According to Clark's testimony, he handed back the first package because it was too small. But, when given the larger package, he held it for about a minute and a half while trying to decide whether to buy it. Officer Barbour snatched the $20 from him, and signalled for the arrest. Did Clark criminally possess the smaller package? If his story is true, did Clark possess the larger package of crack? *State v. Clark,* 461 N.W.2d 576 (Neb.1990)

2. Leonard Dawkins was convicted of possession of heroin and "controlled paraphernalia." The police testified that when they entered a Baltimore, Maryland, hotel room, Leonard Dawkins held a tote bag in his hand. The police searched the bag, finding in it narcotics paraphernalia and a bottle cap containing heroin residue. Dawkins testified that the tote bag belonged to his girlfriend, who had asked him to carry the bag to her hotel room. He testified further that he had arrived only a few minutes before the police, and that he did not know what was in the bag. Dawkins' girlfriend produced a receipt for the purchase of the bag, and testified that she owned the bag. The trial court refused Dawkins' request for an instruction to the effect that knowledge was a requirement of criminal possession. The Maryland statute prohibits "possession of controlled substances." It is silent on intent, but it defines possession as "the exercise of actual or constructive dominion or control over a thing by one or more persons."

Did Dawkins criminally possess heroin and controlled substance paraphernalia, even if he did not know the bag contained them? The Maryland supreme court decided that he did not. It said in part: "[A]n individual ordinarily would not be deemed to exercise 'dominion or control' over an object about which he is unaware. Knowledge of the presence of an object is normally a prerequisite to exercising dominion or control." *Dawkins v. State,* 547 A.2d 1041 (Md.App.1988)

Criminal possession punishes *potential* harm. It aims to prevent possessors from putting prohibited items and substances to use; for example, from taking drugs, shooting guns, and using burglary tools. The law of criminal possession resembles the idea that, as the doctors say, prevention is better than cure. Some jurists believe that preventive justice is the best justice. Possession also increases the risk that criminal law will punish status and condition. People who possess drugs, burglary tools, and the like are considered dangerous. The law of criminal possession punishes them for being burglars or drug addicts, not because they have burgled a house or used marijuana.[17]

Problems with criminal possession have led to suggestions that it should encompass only knowingly possessing substances and objects that unambiguously threaten serious bodily harm. According to this view, the criminal law appropriately includes possessing guns and explosives; possessing marijuana and obscene materials does not threaten serious bodily harm and should not be included in criminal law. In addition, proponents maintain that the criminal law ought to exclude substances or items that possessors may use for either harmless or harmful purposes. These include burglary tools such as lock picks, and drug paraphernalia such as hypodermic needles and pipes.

Summary of Actus Reus

The *actus reus,* or criminal act, includes voluntary bodily movements; omissions, or failures to perform legal duties; and possession. This definition is cumbersome, but it covers the essential characteristics of the *actus reus*. The meanings of these aspects of *actus reus* vary from jurisdiction to jurisdiction. Whether sleepwalking or hypnosis are voluntary movements, whether harms resulting from failures to act on moral duties are crimes, and whether criminal possession must be knowing—these questions appreciably alter the scope of criminal law. Hence, they bear heavily on criminal policy, reflecting the basic values that a jurisdiction's criminal law aims to uphold and protect.

▼ *MENS REA*

The idea that some kind of blameworthy state of mind must accompany *actus reus* is fundamental to criminal law. The child's "I didn't mean to," captures this idea, as does Justice Holmes's pithy "Even a dog distinguishes between being stumbled over and being kicked." Since at least 1600, common-law judges required that some sort of "bad state of mind," or "evil intent," accompany criminal acts. The Latin maxim *"actus not facit ream nisi mens sit rea"* ("An act is not bad without an evil mind") expresses this idea.

Mens rea is complex, perhaps the most complex concept in criminal law. Sixty years ago, the late distinguished criminal law scholar, Professor Francis Sayre, wrote:

> No problem of criminal law is of more fundamental importance or has proved more baffling through the centuries than the determination of the precise mental element or *mens rea*.[18]

Various terminology conceptualizes and expresses *mens rea,* and proving it gives rise to difficult problems. Furthermore, it encompasses several mental states, and some mental states are more blameworthy than others.[19]

Determining Mens Rea

The only direct evidence of *mens rea* is defendants' confessions; no instruments can measure it. Electroencephalograms can record brain waves, and X-rays can photograph brain tissue; but the medieval judge's words are still true: "The thought of man is not triable, for the devil himself knoweth not the thought of man." St. Thomas Aquinas put it even more pointedly:

> No man, the framer of human law, is competent to judge only of outward acts, because man seeth those things that appear ... while God alone, the

framer of the Divine law, is competent to judge of the inward movement of wills.[20]

Since defendants rarely confess their intentions, the criminal law determines *mens rea* by circumstantial or indirect evidence. Action supplies the indirect evidence. Inferring intent from actions substitutes for observing thoughts directly; we can know indirectly what actors intend by observing directly what they did. Experience permits inferences about intentions from actions. For example, most people do not break into strangers' houses at night unless they intend to commit crimes. Thus, the acts of breaking into and entering another person's house permit the inference that the intruder intends to commit a crime while inside.

Do not confuse questions of whether and how to discover intent with the question: What mental states suffice to impose criminal liability? The principle of *mens rea,* when stated properly, defines the mental states required for criminal liability.

Defining Mens Rea

Until recently, courts and legislatures did not define *mens rea* precisely. Instead, they used a host of vague terms to identify the mental element. For example, the United States Criminal Code used seventy-nine words and phrases to define *mens rea*—a staggering number, according to the researcher who compiled the list.[21]

The cases, statutes, and commentators accepted four mental states that qualify as *mens rea:* general, specific, transferred, and constructive intent. **General intent** has various meanings. Sometimes it simply means *mens rea,* or all the mental states encompassed in *mens rea*. It can also mean an intent to do something at an undetermined time or directed at an unspecified object, such as firing a gun into a crowd, intending to kill whomever the bullet strikes; or setting a bomb to explode in a plane without regard to whom it kills. Most commonly, general intent refers to the *actus reus*—that is, to the intent to commit the act required in the definition of the crime. For example, the required act in burglary is breaking and entering, in larceny the taking and carrying away of another's property, and in rape sexual penetration. General intent refers to the intent to commit those acts.

Specific intent designates an intent to do something beyond the *actus reus*. For example, burglary requires an intent to commit a crime after breaking and entering, and larceny the intent to steal in addition to the taking and carrying away. Rape is sometimes called a general intent crime because its *mens rea* requires no more than the intent to penetrate. Usually, however, specific intent refers to crimes requiring an intent to cause a particular result, such as homicide, which requires the intent to cause death.[22]

Transferred intent refers to cases in which actors intend to harm one victim but instead harm another. For example, if Brent shoots at his enemy Tony but kills Tony's friend Lisa when she steps in front of Tony to block the shot, the law transfers Brent's intent to kill Tony to an intent to kill Lisa. Sometimes called "bad aim intent" because the cases frequently involve misfired guns, the law also transfers intent in other situations. If Claire intends to burn down Kent's house but mistakenly burns down Carmen's instead,

Claire has committed arson. Only the intent to cause similar harms transfers. The intent to assault a man by throwing a rock at him does not transfer to intending to break a window when the rock intended to hit the man hits the window instead.

Constructive intent refers to cases in which actors do not intend any harm, but should have known that their behavior created a high risk of injury. For example, if one drives above the speed limit on an icy city street and the car veers out of control, killing a pedestrian, one has the constructive intent to kill.

The Model Penal Code has refined these four types of intent in its *mens rea* provision. After enormous effort and sometimes heated debate, the drafters sorted out, identified, and defined four criminal mental states: purposeful, knowing, reckless, and negligent. These are roughly equivalent to but more elaborate and precise than general, specific, transferred, and constructive intent. The code specifies that all crimes requiring a mental element (some do not) must include one of these mental states.

§ 2.02.
General Requirements of Culpability.

1. Minimum Requirements of Culpability. Except as provided in § 2.05, a person is not guilty of an offense unless he acted purposely, knowingly, recklessly or negligently, as the law may require, with respect to each material element of the offense.

2. Kinds of Culpability Defined.

a. Purposely. A person acts purposely with respect to a material element of an offense when:

i. if the element involves the nature of his conduct or a result thereof, it is his conscious object to engage in conduct of that nature or to cause such a result; and

ii. if the element involves the attendant circumstances, he is aware of the existence of such circumstances or he believes or hopes that they exist.

b. Knowingly. A person acts knowingly with respect to a material element of an offense when:

i. if the element involves the nature of his conduct or the attendant circumstances, he is aware that his conduct is of that nature or that such circumstances exist; and

ii. if the element involves a result of his conduct, he is aware that it is practically certain that his conduct will cause such a result.

c. Recklessly. A person acts recklessly with respect to a material element of an offense when he consciously disregards a substantial and unjustifiable risk that the material element exists or will result from his conduct. The risk must be of such a nature and degree that, considering the nature and purpose of the actor's conduct and the circumstances known to him, its disregard involves a gross deviation from the standard of conduct that a law-abiding person would observe in the actor's situation.

d. Negligently. A person acts negligently with respect to a material element of an offense when he should be aware of a substantial and unjustifiable risk that the material element exists or will result from his conduct. The risk must be of such a nature and degree that the actor's failure to perceive it, considering the nature and purpose of his conduct and the circumstances known to him, involves a gross deviation from the standard of care that a reasonable person would observe in the actor's situation.

3. Culpability Required Unless Otherwise Provided. When the culpability sufficient to establish a material element of an offense is not prescribed by law, such element is established if a person acts purposely, knowingly or recklessly with respect thereto.

4. Prescribed Culpability Requirement Applies to All Material Elements. When the law defining an offense prescribes the kind of culpability that is sufficient for the commission of an offense, without distinguishing among the material elements thereof, such provision shall apply to all the material elements of the offense, unless a contrary purpose plainly appears.

The facts in actual cases often blur the distinctions among these four mental states, particularly between recklessness and negligence. Furthermore, notice that the Model Penal Code requires that the state prove **culpability,** or *mens rea,* with respect to all three of the following: (1) the act, or the nature of the forbidden conduct; (2) the attendant circumstances; (3) the result of the conduct. Hence, under the Model Penal Code, a single offense may require purpose for the nature of the conduct, recklessness with respect to the attendant circumstances, and negligence with respect to the result.[23]

Purpose   The mental state of purpose means the intention to commit a crime. Some crimes require purpose with respect to engaging in specific conduct. For example, common-law burglary requires that the burglar purposely break and enter a house, and larceny requires that the thief purposely take and carry away another's property. Other crimes require a purpose to produce a particular result; for example, in murder, the murderer's "conscious object" is the victim's death.

CASE

Did They Intend to Indecently Expose Themselves?

State v. Rocker
475 P.2d 684 (1970)

Before Richardson, C.J., Marumoto, Abe and Levinson, JJ., and Ogata, Circuit Judge, for Kobayashi, J., disqualified. Richardson, Chief Justice.
    [Rocker and a companion were convicted in a trial without a jury of creating a common nuisance.]

FACTS

... [P]olice officers of the Maui Police Department received a phone call from an anonymous person and, thereafter, on the day of the call, proceeded to the Puu Olai beach at Makena to look for nude sunbathers. On reaching their destination, the police surveyed the beach from a ridge using both their naked eyes and binoculars and saw the defendants lying on the beach completely nude, one on his stomach and the other on his back. The officers then approached the defendants and arrested them for indecent exposure. It was admitted by the police officers that defendants were not at any time engaged in any activity other than sunbathing. At the time of the arrest there were several other people on the beach where the defendants were nude.

Defendant Rocker was nude at the Puu Olai beach on other days before and after he was arrested on February 26, 1969. Defendant Cava likewise frequently sunbathed in the nude at the same beach prior to his arrest on February 26, 1969.

OPINION

[Hawaii had a common nuisance statute that incorporated indecent exposure as one kind of common nuisance.]... To create a common nuisance there must be an indecent exposure of the person in a public place where it may be seen by others if they pass by, and it need actually be seen by one person only. However, to answer the specific questions presented to us on this appeal and to clarify and examine our construction of the statute in light of recent decisions in this and other jurisdictions, a further discussion of the elements of the crime of indecent exposure is needed.

Sunbathing in the nude is not per se illegal. It must be coupled with the intent to indecently expose oneself. Intent is an element of the crime of common nuisance defined by [the common nuisance statute].... The intent necessary is a general intent, not a specific intent; i.e., it is not necessary that the exposure be made with the intent that some particular person see it, but only that the exposure was made where it was likely to be observed by others. Thus, the intent may be inferred from the conduct of the accused and the circumstances and environment of the occurrence. The criminal intent necessary for a conviction of indecent exposure is usually established by some action by which the defendant either (1) draws attention to his exposed condition or (2) by a display in a place so public that it must be presumed it was intended to be seen by others.

The defendants argue that there is no circumstantial evidence in the record from which a trier of fact could conclude that the element of intent had been proved beyond a reasonable doubt. The issue, therefore, is whether defendants' nude sunbathing at Puu Olai beach at Makena, Maui, was at a place so public that a trier of fact could infer it was intended to be seen by others. The prosecution offered testimony of one of the arresting police officers that the beach was a popular location for fishermen and was in fact one of his favorite fishing spots. Defendants testified that the public in general used the beach, that it was used by fishermen and local residents, and that they observed between 20 and 25 people on the beach over a two-month period. Although the Puu Olai beach is isolated by a hill and a ledge, away from the view of the public road and adjoining beaches, it is accessible by a well-worn path and known to be a favorite location of fishermen to cast and throw fish nets. In view of this and other evidence in the record, we cannot agree with defendants' argument that the trier of fact could not find the beach so public as to justify an inference of intent on the part of defendants to be seen by others....

Affirmed.

DISSENT

Levinson, Justice (dissenting)

... My reading of the majority opinion leads me to conclude that in order to prove a prima facie case against the defendants it was necessary for the prosecution to demonstrate that the defendants possessed a general intent to expose themselves in a place where it would be likely that they would be observed by others. To prove this, it would be enough for the prosecution to establish the defendants' awareness of sufficient facts and circumstances from which a trier of fact could infer such intent beyond a reasonable doubt. From the evidence in the record at the close of the prosecution's case I do not think that a trier of fact could be justified in inferring beyond a reasonable doubt that the defendants possessed the necessary general intent to be seen by others.

Although there was testimony that the beach was visited by fishermen there was no link established between the visits by the fishermen and visits to the beach by the defendants. Officer Matsunaga, one of the fishermen who used the beach, did not testify to ever having observed the defendants on this beach prior to arresting them. Thus, this evidence could not be used to support an inference that the defendants were aware that this beach was used by fishermen and therefore public. Nor could a trier of fact infer beyond a reasonable doubt that the defendants were aware of the "well-worn" path leading over the hill to the beach and therefore knew that they were sunbathing in an area readily accessible to the public.

One of the police officers testified that the beach was accessible by another trail which was not "well-used." There was no other evidence that would eliminate as a reasonable doubt the possibility that the defendants had used this other path and therefore inferred from its unused nature that the public would not be likely to see them. The majority opinion does not mention this possibility in assessing the adequacy of the prosecution's case. In failing to prove that the defendants were aware of the visits of the fishermen or the well-worn path I believe the State failed to prove beyond a reasonable doubt defendants' awareness of facts sufficient to establish a general intent to be seen by others.

National Advancement for the Advancement of Colon

Case Discussion

What is the *mens rea* required for indecent exposure, according to the court? What specific facts does the majority opinion rely on to affirm the conviction? Why does the dissent disagree with the conclusion that defendants had the requisite *mens rea?* Do you agree with the majority or dissent? If you were interpreting the statute, how would you define the *mens rea* of indecent exposure?

Note Case

NAACP?

Marks was convicted following a jury trial of the felony of escape from custody. After finishing work outside the prison picking potatoes, a group of prisoners were loaded into a truck to return to prison. One of the prisoners fell out. Marks jumped out to see if the other prisoner was injured. The officer in charge did not realize Marks was gone. Marks and the other prisoner waited alongside the road for authorities to pick them up. Marks "stated that he never had any intent to escape, or to avoid recapture."

Was he guilty of escape? Yes, said the court. "Appellant … does not contend that he fell out of the truck so that there would have been no intent at all on his part to perform the act. Appellant admits that he jumped out of the truck and further admitted that he was at a place where he was not supposed to be. The statute does not spell out a requirement for any specific intent to be formed by the prisoner to commit the crime of escape. It is our conclusion that no specific intent 'to evade the due course of justice' need be proven in order to establish the commission of the crime of escape.… The judgment is affirmed." *State v. Marks,* 442 P.2d 778 (1968)

Knowing   It is impossible to intend a wrong without knowing it, but it is possible to knowingly cause a harm without that action being one's conscious object. Awareness of conduct or knowledge that a result is practically certain to follow from conduct is not the same thing as having the conduct or result as a conscious object. For example, the owner of a telephone answering service provided service to women he knew were prostitutes;

hence, he knowingly provided the service. However, his purpose, or conscious object, was not to promote prostitution; it was to make a profit; hence, he did not conspire to promote prostitution.

A surgeon who removes a cancerous uterus to save a pregnant woman's life knowingly, but not purposely, kills the fetus in the womb. The fetus's death is an unwelcome, if necessary, side effect to removing the cancerous uterus. Similarly, in treason, defendants may knowingly provide aid and comfort to United States' enemies without intending to overthrow the government. Such defendants are not guilty of treason, even though they know their conduct is practically certain to contribute to overthrowing the government. Hence the need for a separate crime—providing secrets to the enemy—that requires only that defendants purposely provide such secrets. The need to distinguish between knowledge and purpose arises most frequently in attempt, conspiracy, and treason. However, as *State v. Jantzi* demonstrates, it can arise in other crimes as well.[24]

CASE

Did He Knowingly Stab the Victim?

State v. Jantzi
641 P.2d 62 (1981).

Before Gillette, P.J., Joseph, C. J., and Roberts, J. Pro Tem. Gillette, Presiding Judge.

FACTS
… Defendant testified that he was asked to accompany Diane Anderson, who shared a house with defendant and several other people, to the home of her estranged husband, Rex. While Diane was in the house talking with Rex, defendant was using the blade of his knife to let the air out of the tires on Rex's van. Another person put sugar in the gas tank of the van. While the Andersons were arguing, Diane apparently threatened damage to Rex's van and indicated that someone might be tampering with the van at that moment. Rex's roommate ran out of the house and saw two men beside the van. He shouted and began to run toward the men. Rex ran from the house and began to chase defendant, who ran down a bicycle path. Defendant, still holding his open knife, jumped into the bushes beside the path and landed in the weeds. He crouched there, hoping that Rex would not see him and would pass by. Rex, however, jumped on top of defendant and grabbed his shirt. They rolled over and Rex was stabbed in the abdomen by defendant's knife. Defendant could not remember making a thrusting or swinging motion with the knife; he did not intend to stab Rex.

OPINION
The indictment charged that defendant "did unlawfully and knowingly cause physical injury to Rex Anderson by means of a deadly weapon, to-wit: knife, by stabbing the said Rex Anderson with said knife." ORS 163.175 provides that: (1) A person commits the crime of assault in the second degree if he: (b) Intentionally or knowingly causes physical injury to another by means of a deadly or dangerous weapon;… "Knowingly is defined in ORS 161.085(8): 'Knowingly' or 'with knowledge' when used with respect to conduct or to a circumstance described by a statute defining an offense, means that a person acts with an awareness that his conduct is of a nature so described or that a circumstance so described exists."

The trial court stated: "Basically, the facts of this case are: that Defendant was letting air out of the tires and he has an open knife. He was aware of what his knife is like. He is aware that it is a dangerous weapon. He runs up the bicycle path. He has a very firm grip on the knife, by his own admission, and he knows the knife is dangerous. It is not necessary for the state to prove that he thrust it or anything else. Quite frankly, this could have all been avoided if he had gotten rid of the knife, so he 'knowingly caused physical injury to Rex Anderson.' And, therefore, I find him guilty of that particular charge."

Although the trial judge found defendant guilty of "knowingly" causing physical injury to Anderson, what he described in his findings is recklessness. The court found that defendant knew he had a dangerous weapon and that a confrontation was going to occur. The court believed that defendant did not intend to stab Anderson. The court's conclusion seems to be based on the reasoning that because defendant knew it was possible that an injury would occur, he acted "knowingly." However, a person who "is aware of and consciously disregards a substantial and unjustifiable risk" that an injury will occur acts "recklessly," not "knowingly." See ORS 161.085(9). Recklessly causing physical injury to another is assault in the third degree. ORS 163.165.

This is a slightly different situation from that presented in *State v. Jackson,* 40 Or.App. 759, 596 P.2d 600 (1979), in which there was insufficient evidence to support the charge for which the defendant was convicted, but the facts necessarily found supported conviction of a lesser offense. Here there was evidence that would have supported a finding of assault in the second degree, but the trial court specifically found the facts to be such that they only support a charge of reckless, rather than knowing, assault.

We have authority, pursuant to Article VII (Amended), § 3 of the Oregon Constitution, to enter the judgment that should have been entered in the court below. Assault in the third degree is a lesser included offense of the crime of assault in the second degree charged in the accusatory instrument in this case. See ORS 136.460. We modify defendant's conviction to a conviction for the crime of assault in the third degree.

Case Discussion   What are the facts relevant to determining Rex's *mens rea* in this case? What facts did the trial court rely on to conclude that Rex acted knowingly? How did the appellate court conclude that Rex acted recklessly? Relying on the facts, how would you characterize Rex's *mens rea?* Did he intend to kill Anderson? Did he kill Anderson knowingly? Or, did he kill Anderson recklessly? Defend your answer.

Note Case   Jackson was charged with robbery. While the victim was sitting in a bar, he noticed the light in his car go on. He ran outside to investigate. Defendant, using a tire iron, had broken open the glove box containing over $500 in currency, but had not taken it. The victim pulled the defendant from the car and the defendant hit him with a tire iron a number of times. The victim wrested the tire iron from the defendant, and the defendant fled. The trial court found that the blows were struck to effect escape rather than to complete theft. Therefore, according to the court, Jackson did not have the requisite intent to commit robbery. *State v. Jackson,* 596 P.2d 600 (Ore.1979)

Subjective and Objective Standards   Most jurisdictions measure knowledge and purpose *subjectively;* that is, they depend on the actor's actual state of mind. These jurisdictions reject an *objective* standard based on what defendants *should have* known, or on what "most people would have intended." Those who support the subjective standard argue that fairness requires that culpability for serious criminal conduct ought to rest on what defendants actually intend, not on what reasonable people would have intended. The Washington code is an exception:

> A person acts knowingly or with knowledge when:
> (i) he is aware of a fact, facts, circumstances or result ...; or
> (ii) he has information which would lead a reasonable man in the same situation to believe that facts exist.[25]

A Michigan statute also permits objective criteria in determining *mens rea,* but only for the purpose of inferring defendants' actual intent. The statute provides that a person acts

> intentionally with respect to a result or conduct ... when his conscious objective is to cause that result or engage in that conduct. In finding that a person acted intentionally with respect to a result the finding of fact may rely upon proof that such result was the natural and probable consequence of the person's act.[26]

Recklessness and Negligence   Reckless people do not purposely or knowingly cause harm; they consciously create *risks* of harm. Recklessness resembles knowledge in that both require consciousness. However, something less than certainty establishes conscious risk creation; recklessness rests on probabilities. The conscious risk creation may refer to the nature of the actor's conduct, to material attendant circumstances, or to the result.

Recklessness requires more than consciousness of ordinary risks; it requires awareness of *substantial* and *unjustifiable* risks. To reduce the unavoidable imprecision in the terms *substantial* and *unjustifiable,* the Model Penal Code proposes that fact finders determine recklessness according to a two-pronged test: (1) To what extent were defendants actually aware of how substantial and unjustifiable the risks were? (2) Does the disregard constitute so "gross [a] deviation from the standard" that a law-abiding person would observe that it deserves criminal condemnation in that situation? This standard has both a subjective and an objective component. Question 1 focuses on defendants' actual awareness; question 2 measures conduct according to how it deviates from what most people do.

Reckless wrongdoers do not have harm as a conscious objective (indeed, they may hope that no harm befalls anyone), yet they consciously create risks. A large drug company knew that a medication it sold could cause liver damage and even death; it sold the drug anyway. The company's officers, who made the decision to sell the drug, did not want to hurt anyone (indeed, they hoped no one would die or suffer liver damage); they sought only profit for the company. But they were prepared to risk their customers' deaths for that profit.[27]

Negligent wrongdoers do not consciously create risks. They *should* know they are creating substantial and unjustifiable risks, but they do not actually know. Recklessness is consciously creating risk; **negligence** is *un*consciously creating risk. The standard for negligence is objective—actors *should* have known, even though in fact they did not know, that they were creating risks. For example, a reasonable person should know that driving fifty miles per hour down a crowded street can cause harm, even though in fact the driver does not know it. The driver who should know this but does not is negligent. The driver who knows it but drives too fast anyway is reckless. Negligence, like recklessness, requires substantial and unjustifiable creation of risk.

CASE

Did He Consciously Create a Risk of Death?

People v. Strong
376 N.Y.S.2d 87, 338 N.E.2d 602 (N.Y. 1975)

Jasen, Judge

FACTS
Defendant was charged ... with manslaughter in the second degree (Penal Law, § 125,15) for causing the death of Kenneth Goings. At the trial, the defense requested that the court submit to the jury, in addition to the crime charged, the crime of criminally negligent homicide (Penal Law, § 125.10). The court refused, and the jury found defendant guilty as charged.

The record discloses that the defendant, 57 years old at the time of trial, had left his native Arabia at the age of 19, emigrating first to China and then coming to the United States three years later. He had lived in Rochester only a short time before committing the acts which formed the basis for this homicide charge. He testified that he had been of the Sudan Muslim religious faith since birth, and had become one of the sect's leaders, claiming a sizable following.

Defendant articulated the three central beliefs of this religion as "cosmic consciousness, mind over matter and psysiomatic psychomatic consciousness." He stated that the second of these beliefs, "mind over matter," empowered a "master," or leader, to lie on a bed of nails without bleeding, to walk through fire or on hot coals, to perform surgical operations without anesthesia, to raise people up off the ground, and to suspend a person's heartbeat, pulse, and breathing while that person remained conscious. In one particular type of ceremony, defendant, purportedly exercising his powers of "mind over matter," claimed he could stop a follower's heartbeat and breathing and plunge knives into his chest without any injury to the person. There was testimony from at least one of defendant's followers that he had successfully performed this ceremony on previous occasions. Defendant himself claimed to have performed this ceremony countless times over the previous 40 years without once causing an injury.

Unfortunately, on January 28, 1972, when defendant performed this ceremony on Kenneth Goings, a recent recruit, the wounds from the hatchet and three knives which defendant had inserted into him proved fatal.

OPINION
The sole issue upon this appeal is whether the trial court erred in refusing to submit to the jury the lesser crime of criminally negligent homicide. Recently, in *People v. Stanfield*, 36 N.Y.2d 467, 369 N.Y.S.2d 118, 330 N.E.2d 75, the same issue was before us and we held that where a reasonable view of the evidence supports a finding that a defendant committed this lesser degree of homicide, but not the greater, the lesser crime should be submitted to the jury....

"The essential distinction between the crimes of manslaughter, second degree, and criminally negligent homicide ... is the mental state of the defendant at the time the crime was committed. In one, the actor perceives the risk, but consciously disregards it. In the other, he negligently fails to perceive the risk. The result and the underlying conduct, exclusive of the mental element, are the same." Although in *Stanfield* we pointed out that "criminal recklessness and criminal negligence ... may ... be but shades apart on the scale of criminal culpability," it would be incorrect to infer from *Stanfield* that in every case in which manslaughter, second degree, is charged, a defendant is entitled also to an instruction as to criminally negligent homicide. In determining whether the defendant in this case was entitled to the charge of the lesser crime, the focus must be on the evidence in the record relating to the mental state of the defendant at the time of the crime.

We view the record as warranting the submission of the lesser charge of criminally negligent homicide since there is a reasonable basis upon which the jury could have found that the defendant failed to perceive the risk inherent in his actions. The defendant's conduct and claimed lack of perception, together with the belief of the victim and defendant's followers, if accepted by the jury, would justify a verdict of guilty of criminally negligent homicide. There was testimony, both from defendant and from one of his followers, that the victim himself perceived no danger, but in fact volunteered to participate. Additionally, at least one of the defendant's followers testified that the defendant had previously performed this ritual without causing injury.

Assuming that a jury would not believe that the defendant was capable of performing the acts in question without harm to the victim, it still could determine that this belief held by the defendant and his followers were indeed sincere and that defendant did not in fact perceive any risk of harm to the victim.

That is not to say that the court should in every case where there is some subjective evidence of lack of perception of danger submit the lesser crime of criminally negligent homicide. Rather, the court should look to other objective indications of a defendant's state of mind to corroborate, in a sense, the defendant's own subjective articulation. Thus, in *Stanfield,* there was evidence from which the jury could have reasonably concluded that the victim herself did not view Stanfield's actions as creating any risk of harm. Here, the evidence supporting defendant's claimed state of mind is, if anything, stronger. Therefore, on the particular facts of this case, we conclude that there is a reasonable view of the evidence which, if believed by the jury, would support a finding that the defendant was guilty only of the crime of criminally negligent homicide, and that the trial court erred in not submitting, as requested, this lesser offense to the jury. Accordingly, we would reverse and order a new trial.

DISSENT
Gabrielli, Judge (dissenting).

I dissent and conclude that there is no justification in the record for the majority's holding that "defendant's conduct or claimed lack of perception, together with the belief of the victim and defendant's followers, if accepted by the jury, would justify a verdict of criminally negligent homicide." The Appellate Division was correct in holding that "Defendant's belief in his superhuman powers, whether real or simulated, did not result in his failure to perceive the risk but, rather, led him consciously to disregard the risk of which he was aware."

At trial, it was shown, primarily from defendant's own statements to the police and testimony before the Grand Jury, that during the course of a "religious ordeal," defendant, the self-proclaimed leader of the Sudan Muslim sect of Rochester, New York, stabbed one of his followers, Kenneth Goings, a number of times in the heart and chest causing his death.

Additionally, the evidence established defendant's awareness and conscious disregard of the risk his ceremony created and is entirely inconsistent with a negligent failure to perceive that risk. Testimony was adduced that just prior to being stabbed, Goings, a voluntary participant up to that point, objected to continuance of the ceremony saying "No, father" and that defendant, obviously evincing an awareness of the possible result of his actions, answered,

"It will be all right, son." Defendant testified that after the ceremony, he noticed blood seeping from the victim's wounds and that he attempted to stop the flow by bandaging the mortally wounded Goings.

Defendant further stated that when he later learned that Goings had been removed to another location and had been given something to ease the pain, he became "uptight," indicating, of course, that defendant appreciated the risks involved and the possible consequences of his acts....

Can it be reasonably claimed or argued that, when the defendant inflicted the several stab wounds, one of which penetrated the victim's heart and was four and three-quarter inches deep, the defendant failed to perceive the risk?

The only and obvious answer is simply "no." Moreover, the record is devoid of evidence pointing toward a negligent lack of perception on defendant's part. The majority concludes otherwise by apparently crediting the testimony of defendant, and one of his followers, that at the time defendant was plunging knives into the victim, the defendant thought "there was no danger to it." However, it is readily apparent that the quoted statement does not mean, as the majority assert, that defendant saw no risk of harm in the ceremony, but, rather, that he thought his powers so extraordinary that resultant injury was impossible. Thus, the testimony does not establish defendant's negligent perception for even a grossly negligent individual would perceive the patent risk of injury that would result from plunging a knife into a human being; instead, the testimony demonstrates defendant's conscious disregard of the possible consequences that would naturally flow from his acts.

This case might profitably be analogized to one where an individual believing himself to be possessed of extraordinary skill as an archer attempts to duplicate William Tell's feat and split an apple on the head of another individual from some distance. However, assume that rather than hitting the apple, the archer kills the victim. Certainly, his obtuse subjective belief in his extraordinary skill would not render his actions criminally negligent. Both in the context of ordinary understanding and the Penal Law definition (§ 15.05, subd. 3), the archer was unquestionably reckless and would, therefore, be guilty of manslaughter in the second degree. The present case is indistinguishable....

Breitel, C.J., and Jones, Wachtler, Fuchsberg and Cooke, JJ., concur with Jasen.

J. Gabrielli, J., dissents and votes to affirm in a separate opinion. Order reversed.

Case Discussion   What precise facts bear on the question of *mens rea* in the case? What mental state did Strong have with respect to stabbing Goings? What was his mental state with respect to Goings' death? If you were deciding this case, would you call the death negligent or reckless? Why? What is the major disagreement between the majority and the dissent? Do you agree with the dissent or the majority? Why?

Note Cases   *1.* Cordell asked his friend Ingle if he could still do his "fast draw" trick. The trick was that a person, "while sitting or standing, would hold his hands extended forward several inches apart; defendant, with a pistol in a holster strapped to his body, would attempt to draw his pistol and place it between the hands of the other person before that person could clap his hands together." Ingle said yes, and tried it with a .22 caliber pistol. The pistol discharged, a bullet struck Cordell in the front of his head and killed him almost instantly. Ingle forgot he had loaded the pistol. Did Ingle recklessly kill Cordell? The court held yes:

> It seems that, with few exceptions, it may be said that every unintentional killing of a human being proximately caused by a reckless use of firearms, in the absence of intent to discharge the weapon, or in the belief that it is not loaded, and under circumstances not evidencing a heart devoid of a sense of social duty, is involuntary manslaughter. *People v. Ingle*

2. Warner-Lambert Co., manufacturer of Freshen-Up chewing gum, was indicted on six counts of manslaughter in the second degree and six counts of criminally negligent homicide. Six employees died in a "massive explosion and fire." Evidence was submitted that "an inspection of the plant by Warner-Lambert's insurance carrier on February 26, 1976 had resulted in advice to the insured that an explosive dust at concentrations above the lowest explosion level presented an explosion hazard." Evidence showed that the company, although beginning to reduce the hazard, continued to operate the plant above the lowest explosion level. Was Warner-Lambert negligent? The court said yes:

... The appellate court held: "There can be no doubt that there was competent evidence ... to establish the existence of a broad, undifferentiated risk of explosion from ambient MS dust which had been brought to the attention of defendants. It may be assumed that, if it be so categorized, the risk was both substantial and unjustifiable." *People v. Warner-Lambert Co.,* 51 N.Y.2d 295, 434 N.Y.S.2d 159, 414 N.E.2d 660 (1980)

3. Stanfield and his common-law wife, Thomasina, were not living together. After a date, they returned to Thomasina's house. Stanfield asked Thomasina if she was going out with his friend. She said no. Intending to frighten her, he took out a gun, cocked it, put it near her head, and said he was going to shoot her. Thomasina responded, "Bob, don't mess with the gun like that," and then "slapped his hand or arm." The gun discharged, killing Thomasina. Stanfield tried to revive her. When he failed, he called the police, and made a frantic call to his mother. He then ran outside and summoned a police officer on patrol. Was he reckless or negligent? The trial court refused an instruction on negligent manslaughter, and Stanfield was convicted of reckless manslaughter. The appellate court reversed:

> [C]riminal recklessness and criminal negligence with respect to a particular result—here homicide—may in a particular case, if not hypothetically or definitionally, be but shades apart on the scale of criminal culpability. And the distinction between the two mental states is less clear practically than theoretically. Indeed, the definitional cleavage the People would draw, while theoretically appealing, may be illusory in practical application. Hence it seems manifest that in a practical, if not a literal definitional sense, if one acts with criminal recklessness he is at least criminally negligent. Moreover, negligence may, in a particular case, quickly, even imperceptibly, aggravate on the scale of culpability to recklessness....
>
> Whether when the derringer was cocked ... unawareness escalated or should have escalated to awareness of the ultimate risk created—criminal recklessness—was a factual question for the jury, considering all the circumstances. *People v. Stanfield,* 330 N.E.2d 75 (N.Y.1975)

4. Cameron, a four-year veteran of the Marine Corps, has had extensive training and experience with a variety of weapons. He owns at least five weapons. At the time of the alleged crime, he and his wife had been married for eleven years. Three days before the incident, he discovered that she had been seeing another man. He planned to divorce her, but after some discussion they decided to remain together. In the late afternoon of March 13, 1979, they were in their bedroom discussing which one of them would pick up the children at the sitter's house. Cameron picked up a revolver from the nightstand and was passing it from hand to hand when it discharged and killed his wife.

The defendant was charged with second-degree murder for knowingly causing his wife's death by "shooting her in the head with a .44 Magnum revolver." Cameron testified that he forgot he had loaded the gun, and denied that he killed his wife intentionally. The state argued that because Cameron knew so much about guns, he knew of the risk of killing his wife and could not be simply negligent. The risk depended on whether the gun was loaded. The appellate court disagreed:

> Under all the circumstances, including the mental distress resulting from finding out that his wife had been unfaithful to him and the emotional strain of deciding whether or not to divorce her, we cannot say that the jury would not be justified in believing that the defendant had forgotten that he had loaded the gun. Thus, the evidence would justify a finding of guilt of negligent homicide rather than manslaughter, and it was error not to submit the issue to the jury. *State v. Cameron,* 430 A.2d 138 (N.H.1981)

Strict Liability **Strict liability** offenses constitute a major exception to the principle that every crime consists of both a physical and a mental element. Strict liability crimes require no *mens rea;* they impose liability without fault. Hence, whether a defendant's conduct was purposeful, knowing, reckless, or negligent is neither relevant nor material to criminal liability.

Two main arguments support strict liability. First, a strong public interest sometimes justifies eliminating *mens rea.* Strict liability arose during the industrial revolution when manufacturing, mining, and commerce exposed large numbers of the public to death, disability, and disease in the form of noxious gases, unsafe railroads and other workplaces, and adulterated foods and other products. Second, strict liability offenses carry minimum penalties, usually fines. The combined strong public interest and moderate penalty justify extending criminal liability to cases where there is no *mens rea,* according to supporters.[28]

Despite these arguments, strict liability has strong critics. They maintain that it is too easy to expand strict liability beyond public welfare offenses that seriously endanger the public. They also contend that strict liability weakens the force of criminal law, because too many people acting innocently are caught within its net. This brings disrespect to criminal law, which properly should punish only the blameworthy. It does no good, and probably considerable harm, to punish those who have not purposely, knowingly, or recklessly harmed others. In the end, critics maintain, strict liability does not fit well into the criminal law because it is inconsistent with the basic nature of criminal law: to serve as a stern moral code. To punish those who accidentally injure others violates that moral code.

CASE

Is She Liable without Mens Rea?

State v. McDowell
312 N.W.2d 301 (N.D.1981)

Sand, Justice

FACTS

... "On or about the 19th day of October, 1980 in Fargo, County of Cass, the defendant made or drew a check upon the State Bank of Burleigh County, Bismarck, North Dakota, in the sum of $13.50, dated October 19, 1980, made payable to the General Store and uttered and delivered the same to said General Store of Fargo, North Dakota, and at the time of such making, drawing, uttering or delivering, or at the time of presentation for payment made within one week of the original delivery thereof, said defendant did not have sufficient funds in, or credit with such bank to meet such check in full upon presentation...."

§ 6–08–16, North Dakota Century Code, provides as follows:

> *1.* Any person who for himself or as the agent or representative of another, or as an officer or member of a firm, company, copartnership, or corporation makes or draws or utters or delivers any check, draft, or order for the payment of money upon a bank, banker, or depository, and at the time of such making, drawing, uttering, or delivery, or at the time of presentation for payment if made within one week after the original delivery thereof, has not sufficient funds in or credit with such bank, banker, or depository to meet such check, draft, or order in full upon its presentation, shall be guilt of a class B misdemeanor....

OPINION

Initially we note, and it is conceded by both parties, that a culpability element is not required to constitute a violation of NDCC § 6–08–16.... [I]t is apparent that the Legislature intended that NDCC § 6–08–16 contain no culpability element. Prior to 1961 that section contained a culpability element (i.e., knowing); however, in 1961 the Legislature deleted those words and the present statute is the same as the 1961 amendment in this respect.

The defendant contends that NDCC § 6–08–16 is unconstitutional in that it does not set out a *mens rea,* intent, or culpability and in effect provides for strict criminal liability. The defendant further contends that if the statute is not unconstitutional for those reasons, then only a fine, but no incarceration penalty, may be imposed.

The State asserts that the statute, NDCC § 6–08–16, is a valid regulatory statute and that a violation of its provisions constitute a class B misdemeanor for which the penalty of a maximum of 30 days' imprisonment and a fine of $500, or both, may be imposed. NDCC § 12.1–32–01(5).

The pivotal issue we must resolve is: May the Legislature enact laws making the violation thereof a matter of strict criminal liability regardless of any *mens rea,* intent, or culpability involved? If so, is there any limitation as to the penalty which may be imposed? The secondary issue is: If the Legislature may enact such laws, may the penalty be more than a fine, or may incarceration be part of the penalty?

At common law, criminal liability required proof of both a guilty mind and the proscribed physical act. W. LaFave & A. Scott, Handbook on Criminal Law 192 (1972). The advent of modern statutory crime which has no antecedent in common law, has, to a limited degree modified the traditional rule. In *Lambert v. California,* 355 U.S. 225, 228, 78 S.Ct. 240, 242, 2 L.Ed.2d 228 (1957), the Supreme Court stated:

"We do not go with Blackstone in saying that a 'vicious will' is necessary to constitute a crime, ... for conduct alone without regard to the intent of the doer is often sufficient. There is wide latitude in the lawmakers to declare an offense and to exclude elements of knowledge and diligence from its definition." However, *Lambert v. California,* supra, makes it clear that the Legislature's "latitude" is not unlimited....

The Court in *Morissette [v. United States]* significantly observed that the industrial revolution, together with congestion of cities and crowded quarters and the wide distribution of goods, created the need for reasonable standards of quality, integrity, disclosure and care needed to protect the public health, safety, and welfare. The *Morissette* Court, in distinguishing that case from cases based upon regulatory or "public welfare offenses," which do not require proof of intent, said as follows:

"While many of these duties are sanctioned by a more strict civil liability, lawmakers, whether wisely or not, have sought to make such regulations more effective by invoking criminal sanctions to be applied by the familiar technique of criminal prosecutions and convictions. This has confronted the courts with a multitude of prosecutions, based on statutes or administrative regulations, for what have been aptly called 'public welfare offenses.' These cases do not fit neatly into any of such accepted classifications of common-law offenses, such as those against the state, the person, property, or public morals. Many of these offenses are not in the nature of positive aggressions or invasions, with which the common law so often dealt, but are in the nature of neglect where the law requires care, or inactions where it imposes a duty....

While such offenses do not threaten the security of the state in the manner of treason, they may be regarded as offenses against its authority, for their occurrence impairs the efficiency of controls deemed essential to the social order as presently constituted. In this respect, whatever the intent of the violator, the injury is the same, and the consequences are injurious or not according to fortuity. Hence, legislation applicable to such offenses, as a matter of policy, does not specify intent as a necessary element. The accused, if he does not will the violation, usually is in a position to prevent it with no more care than society might reasonably expect and no more exertion than it might reasonably exact from one who assumed his responsibilities. Also, penalties commonly are relatively small, and conviction does no grave damage to an offender's reputation. Under such considerations, courts have turned to construing statutes and regulations which make no mention of intent as dispensing with it and holding that the guilty act alone makes out the crime."...

We do not think that anyone would seriously dispute that the use of checks in commercial business activities has increased significantly and is now accepted as a method of doing and transacting business by a vast majority of the population. In many instances persons have become dependent upon the use of checks as a common practice of doing business and the business world has become accustomed to this and relies upon it. The practice becomes a part of the daily routine to the extent that if it were abruptly stopped or curtailed it would create havoc in the business world. It is an activity that needs to be carefully regulated because a violation impairs the efficiency of controls essential to the business world as well as to the public welfare. The method of regulation is to a great degree a matter that should be decided by legislative action rather than by judicial decree....

We conclude that it is proper for the Legislature to enact laws making the violation thereof a matter of strict criminal liability without a culpability requirement and that NDCC § 6–08–16 is a proper exercise of that power.

Further, we believe it is consistent with the purposes of a regulatory statute to allow the imposition of a fine or imprisonment for a violation of the offense without offending due process. The regulatory provisions would be an exercise in futility if there were no sanctions for non-compliance.... We must keep in mind that § 6–08–16 is a regulatory statute passed for the public welfare to help facilitate transactions in commercial business activities. Thus, the generally accepted functions of criminal sanctions (i.e., deterrence, punishment) are not the only consideration, and we must also consider the need to regulate and police business activities which are procured with a check.

The State, in its brief, cites us to several cases supporting imprisonment for the violation of a strict criminal liability offense. *United States v. Freed,* 401 U.S. 601, 91 S.Ct. 1112, 28 L.Ed.2d 536 (1971) (possession of unregistered firearm (hand grenades); $10,000 fine or ten years imprisonment, or both); *Williams v. North Carolina,* 325 U.S. 226, 65 S.Ct. 1092, 89 L.Ed. 1577 (1945) (bigamy; ten years imprisonment); *United States v. Dotterweich,* 320 U.S. 277, 64 S.Ct. 134, 88 L.Ed. 48 (1943) (misbranded or adulterated drugs; $1,000 fine and/or one year for first offense $10,000 fine and/or three years for subsequent offense); *United States v. Balint,* 258 U.S. 250, 42 S.Ct. 301, 66 L.Ed. 604 (1922) (unlawful drug sale; five years imprisonment); *United States v. Erne,* 576 F.2d 212 (9th Cir. 1978) (failure to collect and deposit into a bank trust account withholding and FICA taxes; one year and $5,000 fine); *United States v. Ayo-Gonzalez,* 536 F.2d 652 (5th Cir. 1976) cert. den 429 U.S. 1072, 97 S.Ct. 808, 50 L.Ed.2d 789 (illegal fishing in contiguous zone of United States, fine of not more than $100,000 or

more than one year in prison); *United States v. Flum,* 518 F.2d 39 (8th Cir. 1975), cert. den. 423 U.S. 1018, 96 S.Ct. 454, 46 L.Ed.2d 390 (attempt to board airplane with concealed dangerous and deadly weapon; one year of $1,000 fine, or both); *Holdridge v. United States,* 282 F.2d 302 (8th Cir. 1960) (re-entry into military reservation, six months or $500, or both).

In this instance a violation of NDCC § 6–08–16 is a class B misdemeanor with penalty provisions of a maximum thirty days' imprisonment and a fine of $500, or both. The severity of these penalties are substantially less than those which were upheld in the federal cases. Further, a misdemeanor conviction does not carry with it the repercussions of a felony conviction. Generally a person convicted of a felony may be prevented from exercising certain privileges. See, e.g., NDCC § 5–02–02. There are situations in which a person may be required to disclose misdemeanor convictions, but these convictions generally do not per se bar that person from exercising a privilege....

We conclude that it is constitutionally permissible to sentence an offender to the penalty of a class B misdemeanor for a violation of NDCC § 6–08–16.

Case Discussion
What was McDowell's state of mind with respect to writing the check? With respect to writing a check without funds to cover it? Do you agree that writing bad checks should not require a *mens rea?* What arguments does the court give for strict liability in this case? Should people who write bad checks go to jail? For how long? What is the reason for the court reviewing all the federal cases? Consider the long list of strict liability offenses under federal law. What do they have in common?

Note Cases
1. Two Fargo police officers found Vogel asleep in his car in a parking lot at about 1:20 a.m. The car engine was running, the headlights were on, and the doors were unlocked. Vogel was slumped over in the front seat. After knocking on the window, an officer opened the driver's door, turned off the engine and lights, and, with difficulty, roused Vogel. Vogel smelled of alcohol, appeared confused, and responded unintelligibly to questions.

The officer asked Vogel to leave his car and to be seated in the police car. Helped by an officer, Vogel unsteadily walked to the police car. Vogel was not asked to perform any field sobriety tests, but was arrested for actual physical control.

A jury convicted Vogel of the offense of actual physical control of a motor vehicle while under the influence of intoxicating liquor. The court held:

> The legislature has the authority to define and punish crimes by enacting statutes.... The legislature also has the authority to enact strict liability offenses which require no intent. See § 39–08–07, N.D.C.C. (hit and run); § 39–08–20, N.D.C.C. (driving without liability insurance); § 6–08–16, N.D.C.C. (insufficient funds). "Strict liability statutes in criminal law do not invariably violate constitutional requirements."...
>
> The legislature has defined one variation of the crime of actual physical control while under the influence of intoxicating liquor as the accused having an "alcohol concentration of at least ten one-hundredths of one percent by weight at the time of the performance of a chemical test."... We conclude that the legislature has constitutionally defined the crime. *State v. Vogel,* 467 N.W.2d 86 (N.D.1991)

2. Lucero's boyfriend repeatedly beat Lucero and her young child. Lucero never did anything about it because Eddie threatened to beat her more if she did. Lucero was charged with abusing her son, Arthur, by failing to do anything about Eddie's beating him. The court rejected her claim that she did not intend to hurt Arthur. The court held:

> The rationale for a strict liability statute is that the public interest in the matter is so compelling or that the potential for harm is so great, that public interests override individual interests.... [T]he child abuse statute ... [is] a strict liability statute because of the obvious public interest of prevention of cruelty to children. Therefore, in the strict liability crime of child abuse it makes no difference whether a defendant acted intentionally or negligently in committing the act. *State v. Lucero,* 98 N.M. 204, 647 P.2d 406 (1982)

▼ CONCURRENCE

The principle of **concurrence** requires that *mens rea* set the criminal act in motion; acts not generated by *mens rea* do not constitute criminal conduct. The Model Penal Code and jurisdictions following it subsume concurrence in causation. Some jurisdictions, however, provide specifically for concurrence in their criminal codes. California provides as follows:

> In every crime or public offense there must exist a union, or joint operation of act and intent, or criminal negligence.[29]

Therefore, if I plan to kill my enemy during a hunting expedition, and carry out my plans, I have committed murder—the intent to kill set my act of shooting her into motion. It is not murder if I shoot my enemy accidentally and rejoice afterwards because I am happy she died—the *mens rea* follows the act; hence, there is no concurrence because the *mens rea* did not set the fatal shot in motion.

Even if *mens rea* precedes action, it does necessarily constitute concurrence. For example, if I break the lock of my friend's house with her permission in order to wait for her to come home, but once inside decide to steal her new VCR, I have not committed common-law burglary because I decided to steal after breaking and entering her house. Burglary requires that the intent to steal motivate the breaking (see chapter 10).[30]

In cases where causing a particular result is an element in the crime, concurrence requires a fusion not only of act and *mens rea* but also of *mens rea* and resulting harm. This dimension to concurrence requires that the harm flowing from a defendant's conduct concur with the defendant's intent. For example, a man who ripped out a gas meter from a house in order to steal the coins in it did not batter a woman living in the house, but she became ill from the escaping gas fumes. Similarly, throwing a rock at another person is not malicious damage to property if that rock instead breaks a window. In addition, setting fire to the hold of a ship with a lighted match is not arson if the match was intended to illuminate an area so the defendant could see the rum he intended to steal. The felony murder doctrine, discussed in chapter 8, constitutes an exception to the rule that harms differing in kind from those intended do not satisfy concurrence.[31]

Actual harm that differs from intended harm only in degree satisfies the concurrence requirement. For example, if I intend to beat my enemy within an inch of his life, and he dies, then *mens rea* and harm concur. Furthermore, harm intended for one victim that falls upon another (transferred intent) also fits within the principle of concurrence. For example, shooting with the intent to kill Ellen but striking and killing Tim instead satisfies concurrence (see the following section on causation).[32]

▼ CAUSATION

The principle of **causation** applies to crimes requiring that conduct cause a particular result, such as death in homicide, fear in assault, injury in battery, and a burned building in arson. For a large number of crimes where conduct alone constitutes the crime, causation is not an element. For example, it is forgery to make a false writing, even if no one but the maker ever sees it; it is reckless driving to drive carelessly, whether or not the driver injures anyone; it is perjury to lie under oath, even if no one believes the lie. Crimes requiring injury to persons, property, reputation, public order, and morals do not pose problems if actors either harm persons or property other than those contemplated (as in the transferred intent cases discussed earlier), or cause less harm than they intend (as in attempt, discussed in chapter 5).

The law expresses the relationship between conduct and resulting harm in two ways: factual and legal. In **factual cause** ("but for" or *sine qua non* causation), the conduct sets in motion a chain of events that eventually leads to the harmful result; hence, "but for" the actor's conduct, the harm would not have occurred. **Legal cause,** or proximate cause (phrased variously as the direct, substantial, next, or efficient cause), is the cause recognized by the law to impose criminal liability.

Most cases satisfy the but-for standard. For example, if I strike and kill a pedestrian while driving recklessly, the pedestrian would be alive but for my reckless driving. Similarly, if I purposely shoot and kill my enemy, but for the shooting my victim would be alive. Problems arise, however, when something in addition to the actor's conduct contributes to the result. For example, if I intentionally stab my enemy, who dies during the negligent surgery to save her life, what caused her death? But for the stab wounds I inflicted, she would not be in surgery; however, if the surgery had not been negligent, she might not have died. What caused the pedestrian's death mentioned earlier? Both my reckless driving and the surgeon's negligence contributed to these deaths. In these cases, the question becomes: Was the defendant's conduct a sufficient—proximate—cause to impose criminal liability? Perhaps more accurately, upon whom is it more "just" to impose criminal liability—the purposeful or the negligent wrongdoer.[33]

Factual cause is necessary to impose criminal liability. Suppose I ask Peter to meet me in a dark park, where I plan to assault him. On the way, Doug, who does not know what I have planned, attacks Peter. Owing to the injuries Doug inflicted on him, Peter never comes to meet me. I have not, in fact, caused the injury I wished to inflict; hence, I am not criminally liable, even though I intended to cause such injury. In other words, factual cause does not encompass what *would* have happened, only what in fact happened as a result of action.

Factual cause is necessary but not sufficient to impose criminal liability. The prosecution must also prove legal cause, or the cause the law recognizes. Proximate cause suggests nearness in time and place. However, legal cause often refers to nearness in relation more than it refers to time and place. The law draws the line flexibly in determining when nearness in relation satisfies the legal cause requirement. Three primary policy considerations determine where to draw the line: expedience, justice, and fairness. These considerations might lead to drawing the line differently depending on the type offense, such as more remotely in intentional harm than in reckless harm. For example, in purposeful homicide, the law may define legal cause as almost congruent with factual cause. In negligent homicide, the law may look to a less remote cause. In establishing liability for the tort of wrongful death, the law may recognize a more remote cause than it would for criminal homicide.

Common-sense guidelines inform the approach to deciding whether legal cause exists in particular cases. First, the cause must be substantial. The legal maxim *"de minimus non curat lex"* ("The law does not care for trifles") expresses this idea. For example, if two assailants stab a victim simultaneously, the law does not inquire into which wound spilled the blood that actually killed the victim. On the other hand, suppose one assailant stabbed the victim in the jugular vein and blood gushed forth, while the other stabbed the victim in the hand and only a tiny amount of blood oozed out. Both wounds have hastened death, but the law ignores the wound in the hand as a minimal contribution to the death, relying rather on the substantial cause of the stab to the jugular.[34]

Second, the law does not follow the consequences set in motion by an act beyond the point where the consequences have "come to rest in a position of apparent safety." In one case, a man drove his wife out of their house into the subzero weather. She walked to her father's house, but when she arrived it was late. Not wishing to awaken her father, she curled up outside his front door, fell asleep, and froze to death. Since the husband's act in forcing his wife out into the cold had results that came to rest in a position of apparent safety, his actions did not legally cause her death.[35]

Several other common-sense considerations inform the decision about proximate cause. The search for a dominant—proximate—legal cause might uncover an intervening cause, one that either sufficiently interrupts the chain of events set in motion by the defendant's actions or that at least contributes to the death of the victim. Again suppose I injure a pedestrian while negligently driving my car. While the pedestrian is in the hospital seeking treatment, an inexperienced intern injects her with a fatal dose of a painkiller, given to him by a drunken nurse. The intern's inexperience and the drunken nurse's action at least contributed to the death, and perhaps supervened to become themselves the main, dominant, or proximate cause.

Legal or proximate cause also takes fairness into account; it excludes results so remote from action that criminal liability for criminal homicide would work an injustice. It may be unjust to hold the negligent driver accountable for the death of the pedestrian treated by the drunk nurse.

Intervening causes may be either coincidental or responses to the actions of the defendant, and they may come from the victim, third persons, or outside events. Courts rarely impose liability when the proximate cause of death is a coincidence from an outside force. If I rob a person, leaving him on a country road, and he climbs over a fence into a field where after falling asleep he is kicked in the head by a horse and dies, the horse's kick is a coincidental outside force too remote from the robbery to impose liability for criminal homicide.

Where the defendants' actions generate a direct human response, courts are more likely to impose liability. Sometimes, victims respond to defendants' actions. In one case, Wilson threatened to castrate Armstrong if he didn't hand over two $100 bills. In escaping, Armstrong ran into the Missouri River, where he drowned. The Nebraska Supreme Court affirmed Wilson's conviction for murder. The most common legal causation cases of human response involve medical personnel who treat wounded crime victims, such as *People v. Brackett*.[36]

CASE

Did He Legally Cause Her Death?

People v. Brackett
510 N.E.2d 877 (Ill.1987)

Justice Ryan delivered the opinion of the court:

The defendant, Randy Brackett, was originally charged in the circuit court of

Madison County with the rape, deviate sexual assault and aggravated battery of Mrs. Elizabeth Winslow. Approximately five weeks after the events giving rise to these charges, Mrs. Winslow died. The defendant was then additionally charged with four counts of murder. Pursuant to defendant's motion, the murder charges were severed from the original charges and separate bench trials were held. The defendant was convicted of rape and aggravated battery at the first trial. He was subsequently convicted of murder and sentenced to an extended term of 60 years. His separate appeals were consolidated in the appellate court, which affirmed the murder convictions and vacated the rape and aggravated battery convictions. (People v. Brackett *(1986), 144 Ill.App.3d 442, 449, 98 Ill.Dec. 488, 494 N.E.2d 610.)* We granted leave to appeal.

FACTS

On the evening of October 20, 1981, defendant Randy Brackett, age 21, entered the home of Elizabeth Winslow, an 85-year-old widow, for whom he had previously done yard work. During the course of that evening, he raped and severely beat Mrs. Winslow, forced her to write him a check for $125, cooked himself some food and fell asleep for a time in an arm chair. He finally left in the early hours of the morning.

The first policeman on the scene found Mrs. Winslow lying naked on the living room hide-a-bed. She was severely bruised about the face and appeared to have a broken arm and various other injuries to her body. She said she had been raped, choked and beaten.

She was admitted to the hospital, where medical examinations revealed she had a broken arm, broken rib, bruises on her face, neck, arms, trunk and inner thighs. There are no issues on appeal to this court involving the rape and aggravated battery convictions; therefore, it is unnecessary to recite the details of the physical and medical evidence involved in the proof of those charges. That evidence will be germane only to the extent that it may be involved in the issue on appeal concerning the cause of death.

Dr. Robert William Elliott was one of the doctors who treated Mrs. Winslow while she was hospitalized. Dr. Elliott had been Mrs. Winslow's physician for 20 years. He testified that prior to the events of October 21, 1981, Mrs. Winslow as a "feisty" old woman who lived alone and took care of herself. He further stated that during her stay in the hospital Mrs. Winslow became depressed and resisted efforts to feed her, and her condition progressively weakened.

After receiving maximum benefit from hospital treatment, Mrs. Winslow was transferred to a nursing home on November 13, 1981. Her prognosis was poor, according to Dr. Elliott, even though her injuries were healing. Dr. Elliott accounted for the poor prognosis by relating the effects of trauma to elderly patients and the depression of elderly patients when they are removed from their homes for any type of hospitalization. The nursing home staff noted Mrs. Winslow's continuing declining condition and reported to Dr. Elliott her refusal to eat. He, in turn, ordered a nasal gastric tube to be used to try to feed her. The staff reported back that they could not use the tube because Mrs. Winslow's nasal passages were too small, and her facial injuries made it too painful to insert. Dr. Elliott withdrew the order be-cause he did not want to cause Mrs. Winslow any further pain. It was his medical opinion that her death was imminent. He testified that, to a reasonable medical certainty, the tube could not be inserted because of her injuries.

Two days later Mrs. Winslow's family was called to the nursing home because her condition had worsened, she had become cyanotic (a condition where the extremities turn blue and the blood pressure drops) and they expected her to die. The next day, November 24, 1981, Mrs. Winslow's family was with her in the nursing home while she was being served lunch. For approximately 20 minutes a nurse's aide was feeding her small portions of pureed food on a spoon, which Mrs. Winslow was accepting without choking or gagging in any way. She eventually spit out some vegetables, which the aide interpreted to mean that Mrs. Winslow did not want any more. The aide tried to give Mrs. Winslow ice cream but she noticed Mrs. Winslow had stopped moving her mouth. The nurse's aide went to summon the nurses, who determined Mrs. Winslow had died.

There was an autopsy conducted by Dr. Steven Neurenberger. He determined her immediate cause of death to be asphyxiation, which resulted from six ounces of food being aspirated into her trachea. He found evidence of the internal abdominal bruises around the colon and kidney, a broken rib, and facial bruises. He testified that none of these injuries of themselves caused her death. He also testified as to the mechanics of clearing the trachea when food enters it. This requires a sufficient volume of air to be present in the lungs, which, when expelled, pushes the food out of the trachea and back into the mouth, thus preventing asphyxiation. He also testified that the pain associated with a broken rib generally inhibits deep breathing, which limits the amount of air available to the lungs. He further testified that the volume of food lodged in Mrs. Winslow's trachea was very large and would have been difficult for a normal, healthy person to expel. He stated the amount of food in her trachea would have led to her unconsciousness within 30 seconds, and death would have soon followed.

OPINION

In this appeal, the defendant first contends he was not proved guilty of murder beyond a reasonable doubt because there was insufficient evidence to prove a criminal agency caused Mrs. Winslow's death. He also contends that even if there was sufficient proof of causation, he had no intent to kill, nor did he know his acts created a strong probability of death, nor could he have foreseen that death was a likely consequence of blows from his bare fists. We disagree and affirm.

The State must prove that death was caused by a criminal agency. The defendant contends the State did not meet its burden of proof on this issue of causation. Briefly stated, the defendant claims that death was caused by an intervening event, namely asphyxiation, which was totally unrelated to the crimes of rape and aggravated battery, which the defendant acknowledges he perpetrated against Mrs. Winslow five weeks before she died.

It is a matter of common knowledge that a person can accidentally choke to death while eating. Moreover, that type of accidental death could be the type of intervening cause which would relieve a defendant of criminal responsibility for death. The courts in Illinois have repeatedly held that an inter-

vening cause completely unrelated to the acts of the defendant does relieve a defendant of criminal liability. The converse of this is also true: when criminal acts of the defendant have contributed to a person's death, the defendant may be found guilty of murder. It is not the law in this State that the defendant's acts must be the sole and immediate cause of death.

In this case, the initial trier of fact was the circuit judge. He ruled on the issue of causation. His findings of fact and judgment specifically held that the defendant's acts were a contributing cause of Mrs. Winslow's death, in that the defendant, through his criminal acts, set in motion a chain of events which culminated in her death. The appellate court affirmed his ruling on causation....

Cases concerning unrelated, intervening causes of death have been problematic in the law for hundreds of years. By the mid-1700's the doctrine was well established that "if a man receives a wound, which is not in itself mortal, but either for want of helpful applications, or neglect thereof, it turns to a gangrene, or a fever, and that gangrene or fever be the immediate cause of his death, yet, this is murder or manslaughter in him that gave the stroke or wound, for that wound, tho [sic] it were not the immediate cause of his death, yet, if it were the mediate cause thereof, and the fever or gangrene was the immediate cause of his death, yet the wound was the cause of the gangrene or fever and so consequently is causa causati." [1 Hale, Pleas of the Crown 428 (S. Emlyn Ed.).]

In our technological age, we have come to expect scientific explanations for all types of physical phenomena. In cases such as this, where the causal links are not immediately apparent, we frequently look to medical experts to assist the trier of fact in determining whether the defendant's acts constitute a contributing factor to the victim's death. In this case the trier of fact heard factual testimony and opinion testimony from the victim's treating physician, the pathologist who performed the autopsy and the nursing home staff. (We are mindful that the weight of medical experts' opinions is gauged by the reasons given for their conclusions and the factual details they marshall to support them.)

We are not prepared to say, after a careful review of the record in this case, that the medical evidence and opinions presented to the trier of fact were so unsupported that the trier of fact was left to form his decisions on causation based upon nothing more than speculation and inference. Here there was uncontradicted evidence that the ability to expel food lodged in the trachea is directly related to the volume of air present in the lungs. The victim, due to her broken rib, was not able to breathe deeply, nor would she have had the capacity to expel the food. There was further uncontradicted evidence that the nasal feeding tube could not be used because of the beating the victim had received.

Consequently, the nursing home staff was unable to use a feeding method that would have avoided the possibility of choking. Also, the victim's depressed, weakened, debilitated state was the direct result of the trauma associated with the attack upon her, and there was uncontradicted evidence to that effect. It was Dr. Elliott's opinion that she became too weak even to swallow.

Contrary to the defendant's contentions, we believe this is precisely the kind of case where the defendant takes his victim as he finds him. There are many cases in this State where the victim's existing health condition contributed to the victim's death. However, [so long as the defendant's acts contribute to the death there is still sufficient proof of causation, despite the preexisting health condition]. It appears to this court that a person's advanced age is as significant a part of his existing health condition as diabetes or hardening of the arteries.

The trial court placed great weight on the testimony of Dr. Elliott, as it was entitled to do. It was his testimony that this victim's advanced age affected her recuperative powers. Viewing all the evidence in a light most favorable to the prosecution, there was no reversible error on the issue of causation.

The trier of fact was entitled to find that the defendant, a 21-year-old male, 6 feet 3 inches tall and 170 pounds, who battered and raped an 85-year-old woman, set in motion a chain of events which contributed to her death....

The defendant argues that the appellate court ignored a long-standing principle in this State, that death is not ordinarily contemplated as a natural consequence of blows from bare fists. He therefore asserts he could not know that blows from his bare fists created a strong probability of death or great bodily harm, as charged under § 9–1(a)(2). We do not see that the appellate court ignored this principle.

While Illinois cases do stand for the proposition the defendant recites, these same cases also stand for the proposition that death may be the natural consequence of blows with bare fists where there is great disparity in size and strength between the two parties. Given the disparity in size and strength between the defendant and Mrs. Winslow, we find it difficult to give credibility to this argument that the defendant, who battered this victim with enough force to break bones, did not know that his acts created a strong probability of death or great bodily harm.

Finally, the defendant argues that Mrs. Winslow's death by asphyxiation was not a foreseeable consequence of his felonious acts. There are often cases in which the precise manner of death will not be foreseeable to the defendant while he is committing a felony. This does not relieve the defendant of responsibility. There are cases where the immediate cause of death was meningitis, or pneumonia, or a heart condition. In each of these cases the defendant's felonious acts contributed to the victim's demise, and in each of these cases the defendant could not foresee the exact manner in which the victim would die. We hold here that the defendant did not have to foresee that this victim would die from asphyxiation in order to be guilty of felony murder.

For the reasons stated, the defendant's conviction is affirmed. Judgment affirmed.

Case Discussion   What was the factual cause of Mrs. Winslow's death? The legal cause? Was her suffocation a supervening cause, unrelated to Brackett's actions? Was there reasonable doubt as to whether the suffocation was related to Brackett's actions? Was Mrs. Winslow's age the cause of her death? Was the court adopting a but-for cause theory here? Is the brutality of the crime a factor in determining causation in this case? Should it be? Why? Why not?

Note Case   Kibbe and a companion met Stafford in a bar. They noticed Stafford had a lot of money and was drunk. When Stafford asked them for a ride, they agreed, having already decided to rob him. "The three men entered Kibbe's automobile and began the trip toward Canandaigua. Krall drove the car while Kibbe demanded that Stafford turn over any money he had. In the course of an exchange, Kibbe slapped Stafford several times, took his money, then compelled him to lower his trousers and to take off his shoes to be certain that Stafford had given up all his money; and when they were satisfied that Stafford had no more money on his person, the defendants forced Stafford to exit the Kibbe vehicle."

"As he was thrust from the car, Stafford fell onto the shoulder of the rural two-lane highway on which they had been traveling. His trousers were still down around his ankles, his shirt was rolled up towards his chest, he was shoeless and they had also been stripped of any outer clothing. Before the defendants pulled away, Kibbe placed Stafford's shoes and jacket on the shoulder of the highway. Although Stafford's eyeglasses were in Kibbe's vehicle, the defendants, either through inadvertence or perhaps by specific design, did not give them to Stafford before they drove away."

Michael W. Blake, a college student, was driving at a reasonable speed when he saw Stafford in the middle of the road with his hands in the air. Blake could not stop in time to avoid striking Stafford and killing him.

Who legally caused Stafford's death? The court said Kibbe and his companion. "The defendants do not dispute the fact that their conduct evinced a depraved indifference to human life which created a grave risk of death, but rather they argue that it was just as likely that Stafford would be miraculously rescued by a good samaritan. We cannot accept such an argument. There can be little doubt but that Stafford would have frozen to death in his state of undress had he remained on the shoulder of the road. The only alternative left to him was the highway, which in his condition, for one reason or another, clearly foreboded the probability of resulting death." *People v. Kibbe,* 35 N.Y.2d 407, 362 N.Y.S.2d 848, 321 N.E.2d 773 (1974)

A final causation problem arises when the result differs from what actors intend in purposeful and knowing conduct, expect in recklessness, and should expect in negligence. Chapter 5 discusses crimes in which the result is *less* than actors *intend,* such as in attempt. In cases where the actual harm *exceeds* what actors intend, expect, or should expect, criminal law generally does *not* hold defendants liable for these greater harms unless the harms are close in degree and kind to those intended. For example, a defendant who intends to beat a victim within an inch of her life, but does not want to kill her, has committed criminal homicide if the victim dies (see chapter 8). More difficult are cases where actual harm greatly exceeds intended harm. *Hyam v. Director of Public Prosecutions* addresses this problem.

CASE

Did She Intend to Kill or to Frighten?

Hyam v. Director of Public Prosecutions
2 All E.R. 43 (1974)

[Mrs. Hyam was convicted of murder. She appealed.]

FACTS
The facts are simple, and not in dispute. In the early hours of Saturday, 15th July 1972, the appellant set fire to a dwelling-house in Coventry by deliberately pouring about a half gallon of petrol through the letterbox and igniting it by means of a newspaper and a match. The house contained four persons, presumably asleep. They were a Mrs. Booth and her three children, a boy and the two young girls who were the subjects of the charges. Mrs. Booth and the boy escaped alive through a window. The two girls died as the result of asphyxia by the fumes generated by the fire. The appellant's motive (in the sense in which I shall use the word "motive") was jealousy of Mrs. Booth whom the appellant believed was likely to marry a Mr. Jones of whom the appellant herself was the discarded, or partly discarded, mistress. Her account of her actions, and her defence, was that she had started the fire only with the intention of frightening Mrs. Booth into leaving the neighbourhood, and that she did not intend to cause death or grievous bodily harm. The judge directed the jury:

> The prosecution must prove, beyond all reasonable doubt, that the accused intended to do serious bodily harm to Mrs. Booth, the mother of the deceased girls. If you are satis-

fied that when the accused set fire to the house she knew that it was highly probable that this would cause serious bodily harm then the prosecution will have established the necessary intent. It matters not if her motive was, as she says, to frighten Mrs. Booth.

OPINION
The judge explained that he had put brackets round the words "kill or" and "death or" in which it seems to be said that a rational man must be taken to intend the consequences of his acts. It is not a revival of the doctrine of constructive malice or the substitution of an objective for a subjective test of knowledge or intention. It is the man's actual state of knowledge and intent which, as in all other cases, determines his criminal responsibility.

It simply proclaims the moral truth that if a man, in full knowledge of the danger involved, and without lawful excuse, deliberately does that which exposes a victim to the risk of the probable grievous bodily harm (in the sense explained) or death, and the victim dies, the perpetrator of the crime is guilty of murder and not manslaughter to the same extent as if he had actually intended the consequence to follow, and irrespective of whether he wishes it. That is because the two types of intention are morally indistinguishable, although factually and logically distinct, and because it is therefore just that they should bear the same consequences to the perpetrator as they have the same consequences for the victim if death ensues.

This is not very far from the situation in this case. The jury appear to have taken this as a carefully premeditated case and that this was so can hardly be disputed, and, though it was disputed, the jury clearly rejected this view. The appellant had made her way to the house in a van in the early hours of the morning. She took with her a jerry can containing at least half a gallon of petrol. As she passed Mr. Jones's house she carefully made sure that he was in his own home and not with Mrs. Booth, because, as she said, she did not want to do Mr. Jones any harm.

She parked the van at a distance from Mrs. Booth's house, and when she got to the front door she carefully removed a milk bottle from the step in case she might knock it over and arouse somebody by the noise. And when she had started the fire she crept back to her van and made off home without arousing anyone or giving the alarm. Once it is conceded that she was actually and subjectively aware of the danger to the sleeping occupants of the house in what she did, and that was the point which the judge brought to the jury's attention, it must surely follow naturally that she did what she did with the intention of exposing them to the danger of death or really serious injury regardless of whether such consequences actually ensued or not.

Case Discussion

No problem arises about Mrs. Hyam's *mens rea*. She intended to frighten her victim. This intention was joined to an *actus reus*—setting the house on fire—to accomplish her purpose. The problem is that Mrs. Hyam intended only to frighten her victims, not to kill them. Therefore, she caused a harm greater than what she intended or expected. The court concluded that she can be held accountable for the greater harm, even though she did not intend it. The reasoning is that she acted purposely to create a risk that her victims might die or be seriously injured. Precisely, Mrs. Hyam's state of mind was purposeful in relation to the act of setting the house on fire and reckless with respect to her victims' deaths. She is therefore held accountable for the harmful consequences of the risk she recklessly created. Do you feel comfortable with making Mrs. Hyam a murderer when she meant only to frighten? Would you give her a punishment as severe as that given to a man who who wanted to kill his wife, said he had wanted to do it for eight years, and would do it again if he had the chance?

The established law in most jurisdictions is that conscious risk creators are accountable for the "natural and probable consequences" of their actions. Natural and probable consequences include killing a person other than the intended victim—as, for example, if I shoot at Jim, intending to kill him, but instead hit his friend Moira standing next to him. It does not include consequences that are accidental—as, for example, if I shoot at my wife, intending to kill her, but miss; and she is so distraught that she runs off to California, goes horseback riding to forget the horrible incident, is thrown off her horse, and dies when her head strikes a rock. In such cases, the harms are too remote to "justly" impose criminal liability. Note that the proximate cause standard also applies to the last example—striking the rock was the direct or efficient cause of death.

▼ GRADING OFFENSES

The seriousness of an offense rests on numerous considerations. First, and perhaps most serious, is the harm done. Harms to persons are generally considered most serious, followed by harms to habitation, property, public order, and public morals. Incomplete harms are less serious than completed ones (see chapter 5). Second, sometimes the act affects seriousness, such as in torture murder. Third, *mens rea* influences grading by suggesting justifying, excusing, and mitigating circumstances. For example, if I kill in self-defense, my intention to kill is justified; if I kill upon adequate provocation, I am guilty of manslaughter, a less serious criminal homicide than murder (see chapter 8). Finally, the level of *mens rea*—purposeful, knowing, reckless, and negligent—bears upon the determination of an offense's seriousness.

Purpose or specific intent is the most blameworthy, or "evil," mental state. Knowledge is next, followed in order by negligence and strict liability. Purposeful wrongdoing deserves more punishment than reckless harm, because reckless wrongdoers do not intend to harm their victims. Still less blameworthy are negligent wrongdoers, who do not consciously create risks that expose others to serious harm. Least blameworthy of all are those who harm others accidentally—that is, without regard to fault. Penalties account for these degrees of blameworthiness.

▼ *Summary* ▼

Every criminal code reflects the general principles of criminal liability; *actus reus, mens rea,* concurrence, causation, and resulting harm. The *actus reus* includes not only voluntary physical acts but also omissions and possession. The *mens rea* includes purpose, knowledge, recklessness, and negligence. Some crimes do not require a *mens rea;* they constitute criminal liability without fault—strict liability. Criminal conduct means that a *mens rea* prompted an *actus reus.* The principle that there is no criminal conduct without concurrence of *actus reus* and *mens rea* expresses this.

Criminal conduct sometimes constitutes a crime by itself—the harm is the conduct. In other crimes, conduct must cause a separate harm. The causal relation in crime is expressed both as factual causation, that is, "but for" or *sine qua non* causation, and as legal or proximate cause, the cause the law looks to in justifying criminal liability. Problems arise when the resulting harm exceeds what actors contemplated, expected, or should have expected. In those cases, actors are criminally liable for harms that exceed only slightly those contemplated; they are held accountable for harms that exceed in considerable degree those contemplated if punishment is "just." They are not criminally liable for harms distinct both in kind and degree from those intended or expected, or that occur too remote from the acts that led to the conduct or result.

▼ *Questions for Review and Discussion* ▼

1. Define *actus reus.* Should status ever be a ground of criminal liability? Possession? Failure to act? Explain why or why not.

2. Define the levels of culpability in criminal law. What is a proper standard for culpability in criminal law? Should negligent persons be punished? Should persons who accidentally harm be punished?

3. Explain the principle of concurrence. How does it relate to the term *criminal conduct?*

4. Define but-for and proximate cause. Why are they important in criminal law?

5. Under what circumstances should people be punished for harms that exceed what they intend, expect, or should expect?

6. To what extent should *mens rea* determine the seriousness of an offense.

▼ *Suggested Readings* ▼

1. George Fletcher, *Rethinking Criminal Law* (Boston: Little, Brown, 1978), pt. II. A thorough and thought-provoking discussion of the principles of criminal liability. Difficult in places.

2. Jerome Hall, *General Principles of Criminal Law,* 2d ed. (Indianapolis: Bobbs-Merrill, 1960), chap. 3–6, treats *mens rea.* Difficult but rewarding reading.

3. Hyman Gross, *A Theory of Criminal Justice* (New York: Oxford University Press, 1979), chap. 2, untangles knotty questions surrounding *actus reus.*

4. American Law Institute, *Model Penal Code and Commentaries* (Philadelphia: American Law Institute, 1985), pt. I. The best treatment of the general principles of criminal liability.

5. Rollin M. Perkins and Ronald N. Boyce, *Criminal Law,* 3d ed. (Mineola, N.Y.: Foundation Press, 1982), chap. 6 and 7. A straightforward analysis of *actus reus, mens rea,* and causation.

▼ *Notes* ▼

1. Oliver Wendell Homes, *The Common Law* (Boston: Little, Brown and Company, 1963), pp. 45–47.

2. Paul H. Robinson and Jane A. Grall, "Element Analysis in Defining Criminal Liability: The Model Criminal Code and Beyond," *Stanford Law Review* 35 (1983):681–762, esp. 691–705.

3. *Hales v. Petit,* 1 Plowd. 253, 259; 75 Eng. Rep. 387, 397 (cannot punish thoughts); Oliver Wendell Holmes, Jr. *The Common Law* (Boston: Little, Brown and Company, 1962), p. 45 (muscular contraction); George Fletcher, *Rethinking Criminal Law* (Boston: Little, Brown and Company, 1978), pp. 115–16 (manifest criminality).

4. Fletcher, *Rethinking Criminal Law,* p. 117.

5. Holmes, *Common Law,* pp. 46–47.

6. Samuel Butler, *Erewhon* (New York: Modern Library, 1927), pp. 104–111.

7. See Herbert Morris, *On Guilt and Innocence* (Los Angeles: University of California Press, 1976), chap. 1, "Punishing Thoughts."

8. Glanville Williams, *Criminal Law,* 2d ed. rev. (London: Stevens and Sons, 1961), p. 1–2.

9. Narrated in Norval Morris, "Somnambulistic Homicide: Ghosts, Spiders, and North Koreans," *Res Judicata* 5 (1951):29.

10. See Leo Katz, *Bad Acts and Guilty Minds* (Chicago: University of Chicago Press, 1987), chap. 2, for a provocative discussion of this and other cases like it.

11. Joseph Goldstein et al., *Criminal Law: Theory and Process* (New York: Free Press, 1974), p. 766.

12. Fletcher, *Rethinking Criminal Law,* pp. 421–22; *National Law Journal* (October 14, 1991), pp. 3, 38.

13. Wayne R. LaFave, *Criminal Law,* 2d ed. (St. Paul: West Publishing Co., 1986), p. 203.

14. Ibid., pp. 581–633.

15. Bibb Latane and John Darley, *The Unresponsive Bystander: Why Doesn't He Help?* (New York: Appleton-Crofts, 1970), pp. 1–2.

16. American Law Institute, *Model Penal Code and Commentaries,* vol. 1 (Philadelphia: American Law Institute, 1985), p. 24. See *Jenkins v. State,* 215 Md. 70, 137 A.2d 115 (1957), for the mere possession rule.

17. *Robinson v. California,* 370 U.S. 660 (1962); Fletcher, *Rethinking Criminal Law,* pp. 202–5.

18. Francis Bowes Sayre, "Mens Rea," *Harvard Law Review* 45 (1931–2):974.

19. Oliver Wendell Holmes, Jr., *The Common Law* (Boston: Little, Brown 1963), p. 7; American Law Institute, *Model Penal Code,* tentative draft no. 11 (1955).

20. Williams, *Criminal Law,* p. 1; quoted in Jerome Hall, *General Principles of Criminal Law,* 2d ed. (Indianapolis: Bobbs-Merrill, 1960), p. 153.

21. Quoted in Goldstein et al., *Criminal Law: Theory and Process.*

22. Wayne R. LaFave and Austin W. Scott, Jr., *Handbook on Criminal Law,* 2d ed. (St. Paul: West Publishing Co., 1972), pp. 201–2; Hall, *General Principles of Criminal Law,* pp. 142–44.

23. American Law Institute, *Model Penal Code and Commentaries,* pt I, p. 229.

24. *Haupt v. United States,* 330 U.S. 631, 67 S.Ct. 874, 91 L.Ed. 1145 (1947) (treason).

25. West's Revised Code Wash. Ann. 9A.08010(1)(b).

26. Michigan Statute 82; § 305(a) and (b).

27. *New York Times* (September 14, 1985).

28. Rollin M. Perkins and Ronald N. Boyce, *Criminal Law,* 3d ed. (Mineola, N.Y.: Foundation Press, 1982), pp. 896–907.

29. The Penal Code of California, § 20, *West's California Penal Codes,* 1988 compact ed. (St. Paul: West Publishing Company, 1988), p. 7.

30. Hall, *General Principles of Criminal Law,* pp. 185–90.

31. *Regina v. Cunningham,* 41 Crim.App.R. 155 (1957) (ripping out gas meter); *Regina v. Pembletonn,* 12 Cox Crim.Cas. 607 (1874) (throwing a rock); *Regina v. Faulkner,* 13 Cox Crim.Cas. 550 (1877).

32. LaFave and Scott, *Handbook on Criminal Law,* pp. 243–46.

33. Katz, *Bad Acts and Guilty Minds,* chap. 4.

34. Perkins and Boyce, *Criminal Law,* pp. 776–77.

35. *State v. Preslar,* 48 N.C. 421 (1856).

36. *State v. Casper,* 219 N.W.2d 226 (1974); see LaFave and Scott, *Criminal Law,* pp. 288–92, on intervening cause.

Chapter

Parties to Crime: The Doctrine of Complicity

▼ Chapter Outline ▼

I. Introduction
II. Parties to Crime
   A. *Actus Reus* of Parties before and during Crime
   B. *Mens Rea* of Parties before and during Crime
   C. Complicity following Crime
III. Vicarious Liability
   A. Vicarious Liability and Business Crime
   B. Vicarious Corporate Liability for Real Crime
   C. Vicarious Individual Liability for Corporate Crime
IV. Summary

1. The doctrine of complicity defines when one person may be criminally liable for another's conduct.

2. Parties before and during crime are liable for the principal crime; parties following crime are guilty of separate, lesser offenses.

3. The liability of accomplices and accessories depends on participation; vicarious liability depends on relationships.

4. Vicarious liability usually arises out of business relationships.

5. Vicarious liability may be either strict liability or based on culpable conduct.

6. Attributing responsibility to corporate officers is often difficult and sometimes impossible.

7. Businesses might be criminally responsible for harms they condoned or at least recklessly tolerated.

accessory—Following a crime, the party liable for separate, lesser offenses.

accomplices—Before and during a crime, the parties liable as principals.

alter ego **doctrine**—The principle that high corporate officers are the corporation's brain.

doctrine of complicity—The principle regarding parties to crime.

respondeat superior—The doctrine that employers are responsible for their employees' actions.

superior officer rule—The precept that only the highest corporate officers can incur criminal liability for a corporation.

vicarious liability—The principle regarding liability for another based on relationship.

▼ INTRODUCTION

The axioms, "Two hands are better than one," and "The sum is greater than its parts," express the positive side of teamwork, an ordinary phenomenon under ordinary circumstances. In criminal law, teamwork takes on a sinister character. Conspiracy, solicitation, gang rape, and partners in crime conjure up fears of group criminality, or teamwork under extraordinary circumstances. The **doctrine of complicity,** or parties to crime, establishes the conditions under which more than one person incurs liability before, during, and after committing crimes. As in most crimes, complicity requires criminal conduct in order to impose liability. Complicity, however, addresses the circumstances under which one person incurs liability for someone else's conduct. According to the doctrine of complicity, it is immaterial whether the defendant's own conduct, someone else's, or both together establish the elements of the crime charged. Those who join with others to commit crime share full and equal responsibility for the crime.

These problems arise in complicity: (1) What conduct does the doctrine include? (2) Whose conduct does the doctrine include? (3) What *mens rea* brings about the conduct of the others? Culpability depends both on the defendants' *mens rea* and conduct, and on the others' conduct brought about by defendants.[1]

▼ PARTIES TO CRIME

The common law recognized four parties to crime: (1) principals in the first degree—those who actually committed the crime; (2) principals in the second degree—aiders and abettors present when crimes are committed, such as lookouts, getaway drivers, and co-conspirators; (3) accessories before the fact—aiders and abettors *not* present when crimes are committed, such as one who provides the gun that someone else uses in a murder; and (4) accessories after the fact—individuals who give aid and comfort to per-

Elements of Complicity		
Complicity	**_Actus Reus_**	**_Mens Rea_**
Before and during Crime commission	*1.* aid *2.* incite *3.* abet *4.* encourage *5.* mere presence if legal duty to act	*1.* knowledge of principal's intent *2.* shared intent with principal *3.* intent to aid or encourage of crime
Following Crime	aid a person who actually committed felony	*1.* know that felony was committed *2.* specific intent to aid in hindering arrest, prosecution conviction, or punishment
Vicarious Liability	no action; relationship substitutes	no *mens rea;* usually strict liability

sons known to have committed crimes, such as those who harbor fugitives. The significance of these distinctions lay largely in the doctrine that only after principals were convicted could the government try accomplices. Hence, if principals were not convicted before the government brought accomplices to trial, common-law complicity shielded accomplices even in the face of certain proof of their guilt. The doctrine arose during a period in history when all felonies were capital offenses; it provided a way to ameliorate that harsh penalty. When the number of capital crimes diminished, the need to distinguish between principals and accessories dissipated.

Statutes in virtually all jurisdictions have removed the common law distinction by making **accomplices**—accessories before and during crime—principals. Most jurisdictions retain the common-law **accessory** after the fact for complicity following crime. Several states have adopted statutes similar to the Model Penal Code, § 2.06, reproduced here:

§ 2.06. Liability for Conduct of Another; Complicity.

1. A person is guilty of an offense if it is committed by his own conduct or by the conduct of another person for which he is legally accountable, or both.
2. A person is legally accountable for the conduct of another person when:
   a. acting with the kind of culpability that is sufficient for the commission of the offense, he causes an innocent or irresponsible person to engage in such conduct; or
   b. he is made accountable for the conduct of such other person by the Code or by the law defining the offense; or
   c. he is an accomplice of such other person in the commission of the offense.

3. A person is an accomplice of another person in the commission of an offense if:

    a. with the purpose of promoting or facilitating the commission of the offense, he

        i. solicits such other person to commit it, or

        ii. aids or agrees or attempts to aid such other person in planning or committing it, or

        iii. having a legal duty to prevent the commission of the offense, fails to make proper effort so to do; or

    b. his conduct is expressly declared by law to establish his complicity.

4. When causing a particular result is an element of an offense, an accomplice in the conduct causing such result is an accomplice in the commission of that offense if he acts with the kind of culpability, if any, with respect to that result that is sufficient for the commission of the offense.

5. A person who is legally incapable of committing a particular offense himself may be guilty thereof if it is committed by the conduct of another person for which he is legally accountable, unless such liability is inconsistent with the purpose of the provision establishing his incapacity.

6. Unless otherwise provided by the Code or by the law defining the offense, a person is not an accomplice in an offense committed by another person if:

    a. he is a victim of that offense; or

    b. the offense is so defined that his conduct is inevitably incident to its commission; or

    c. he terminates his complicity prior to the commission of the offense and

        i. wholly deprives it of effectiveness in the commission of the offense; or

        ii. gives timely warning to the law enforcement authorities or otherwise makes proper effort to prevent the commission of the offense.

7. An accomplice may be convicted on proof of the commission of the offense and of his complicity therein, though the person claimed to have committed the offense has not been prosecuted or convicted or has been convicted of a different offense or degree of offense or has an immunity to prosecution or conviction or has been convicted.

 Complicity requires that defendants

> in some sort associate [themselves] with the venture, that [t]he[y] participate in it as in something that [t]he[y] wish ... to bring about, that [t]he[y] seek by ... their action to make it succeed.[2]

The law of complicity, as represented in the statutes and case law, requires (1) an act contributing to the commission of a crime, (2) the *mens rea* to aid in the crime's execution, and (3) that someone actually commit the crime. Chapter 5 deals with teamwork that does not result in completed crimes—conspiracy and solicitation.[3]

Actus Reus *of Parties before and during Crime*

Although statutes have substantially altered the common-law categories of complicity, they have largely retained the words describing the common-law acts required to establish liability. "Aid" and "abet" appear frequently; others include "counsel, procure, hire, command, induce, advise," and "willfully cause." A widely accepted doctrine is that "aiding and abetting contemplates

Michigan would hold the same way!

some positive act in aid of the commission of the offense"; the "mere presence of a defendant at the scene of a crime is insufficient to establish guilt." Determining just how much action qualifies is difficult, however. The most common acts are providing guns, supplies, or other instruments of crime; serving as a lookout; driving a getaway car; sending the victim to the principal; or preventing warnings from reaching the victim.[4]

Where there is a duty to act, mere presence may suffice to satisfy the complicity *actus reus*. In *State v. Walden,* for example, a jury found Walden guilty as an accomplice to assault. Walden stood by and did nothing while her boyfriend beat her young son. On appeal, the court said that

> the trial court properly allowed the jury … to consider a verdict of guilty of assault … upon a theory of aiding and abetting, solely on the ground that the defendant was present when her child was brutally beaten.… A person who so aids or abets another in the commission of a crime is equally guilty with that other person as a principal.[5]

CASE

Was She an Accomplice to Murder?

State v. Ulvinen
313 N.W.2d 425 (Minn.1981)

Otis, Justice

Appellant was convicted of first degree murder pursuant to Minn.Stat. § 609.05, subd. 1 (1980), imposing criminal liability on one who "intentionally aids, advises, hires, counsels, or conspires with or otherwise procures" another to commit a crime. We reverse.

FACTS

Carol Hoffman, appellant's daughter-in-law, was murdered late on the evening of August 10th or the very early morning of August 11th by her husband, David Hoffman. She and David had spent an amicable evening together playing with their children, and when they went to bed David wanted to make love to his wife. However, when she refused him he lost his temper and began choking her. While he was choking her he began to believe he was "doing the right thing" and that to get "the evil out of her" he had to dismember her body.

After his wife was dead, David called down to the basement to wake his mother, asking her to come upstairs to sit on the living room couch. From there she would be able to see the kitchen, bathroom, and bedroom doors and could stop the older child if she awoke and tried to use the bathroom. Appellant didn't respond at first but after being called once, possibly twice more, she came upstairs to lie on the couch. In the meantime David had moved the body to the bathtub. Appellant was aware that while she was in the living room her son was dismembering the body but she turned her head away so that she could not see.

After dismembering the body and putting it in bags, Hoffman cleaned the bathroom, took the body to Weaver Lake and disposed of it. On returning home he told his mother to wash the cloth covers from the bathroom toilet and tank, which she did. David fabricated a story about Carol leaving the house the previous night after an argument, and Helen agreed to corroborate it. David phoned the police with a missing person report and during the ensuing searches and interviews with the police, he and his mother continued to tell the fabricated story.

On August 19, 1980, David confessed to the police that he had murdered his wife. In his statement he indicated that not only had his mother helped him cover up the crime but she had known of his intent to kill his wife that night. After hearing Hoffman's statement the police arrested appellant and questioned her with respect to her part in the cover up. Police typed up a two-page statement which she read and signed. The following day a detective questioned her further regarding events surrounding the crime, including her knowledge that it was planned.

Appellant's relationship with her daughter-in-law had been a strained one. She moved in with the Hoffmans on July 26, two weeks earlier to act as a live-in babysitter for their two children. Carol was unhappy about having her move in and told friends that she hated Helen, but she told both David and his mother that the could try the arrangement to see how it worked. On the morning of the murder Helen told her son that she was going to move out of the Hoffman residence because "Carol had been so nasty to me." In his statement to the police David reported the conversation that morning as follows:

> … Sunday morning I went downstairs and my mom was in the bedroom reading the newspaper and she had tears in her eyes, and she said in a very frustrated voice, "I've got to find another house" She said, "Carol don't want me here," and she said, "I probably shouldn't have moved in here." And I said then, "Don't let what Carol said hurt you. It's going to take a little more period of readjustment for her" Then I told mom that I've got to do it tonight so that there can be peace in this house.

Q. What did you tell your mom that you were going to have to do that night?
A. I told my mom I was going to have to put her to sleep.
Q. Dave, will you tell us exactly what you told your mother that morning, to the best of your recollection?
A. I said I'm going to have to choke her tonight and Ill have to dispose of her body so that it will never be found. That's the best of my knowledge.

Q. What did your mother say when you told her that?
A. She just—she looked at me with very sad eyes and just started to weep. I think she said something like "it will be for the best."

David spent the day fishing with a friend of his. When he got home that afternoon he had another conversation with his mother. She told him at that time about a phone conversation Carol had had in which she discussed taking the children and leaving home. David told the police that during the conversation with his mother that afternoon he told her "Mom, tonight's got to be the night."
Q. When you told your mother, "Tonight's got to be the night," did your mother understand that you were going to kill Carol later that evening?
A. She thought I was just kidding her about doing it. She didn't think I could….
Q. Why didn't your mother think that you could do it?
A. … Because for some time I had been telling her I was going to take Carol scuba diving and make it look like an accident.
Q. And she said?
A. And she always said, "Oh, you're just kidding me."…
Q. But your mother knew you were going to do it that night?
A. I think my mother sensed that I was really going to do it that night.
Q. Why do you think your mother sensed you were really going to do it that night?
A. Because when I came home and she told me what had happened at the house, and I told her, "Tonight's got to be the night," I think she said, again I'm not certain, that ["]it would be the best for the kids."

OPINION

… It is well-settled in this state that presence, companionship, and conduct before and after the offense are circumstances from which a person's participation in the criminal intent may be inferred. The evidence is undisputed that appellant was asleep when her son choked his wife. She took no active part in the dismembering of the body but came upstairs to intercept the children, should they awake, and prevent them from going into the bathroom.

She cooperated with her son by cleaning some items from the bathroom and corroborating David's story to prevent anyone from finding out about the murder. She is insulated by statute from guilt as an accomplice after-the-fact for such conduct because of her relation as a parent of the offender. See Minn.Stat. § 609.495, subd. 2 (1980). The jury might well have considered appellant's conduct in sitting by while her son dismembered his wife so shocking that it deserved punishment. Nonetheless, these subsequent actions do not succeed in transforming her behavior prior to the crime to active instigation and encouragement. Minn.Stat. § 609.05, subd. 1 (1980) implies a high level of activity on the part of an aider and abettor in the form of conduct that encourages another to act. Use of terms such as "aids," "advises," and "conspires" requires something more of a person than mere inaction to impose liability as a principal.

The evidence presented to the jury at best supports a finding that appellant passively acquiesced in her son's plan to kill his wife. The jury might have believed that David told his mother of his intent to kill his wife that night and that she neither actively discouraged him nor told anyone in time to prevent the murder. Her response that "it would be the best for the kids" or "it will be the best" was not, however, active encouragement or instigation. There is no evidence that her remark had any influence on her son's decision to kill his wife. Minn.Stat. § 609.05, subd. 1 (1980), imposes liability for actions which affect the principal, encouraging him to take a course of action which he might not otherwise have taken.

The state has not proved beyond a reasonable doubt that appellant was guilty of anything but passive approval. However morally reprehensible it may be to fail to warn someone of their impending death, our statutes do not make such an omission a criminal offense. We note that mere knowledge of a contemplated crime or failure to disclose such information without evidence of any further involvement in the crime does not make that person liable as a party to the crime under any state's statutes....

David told many people besides appellant of his intent to kill his wife but no one took him seriously. He told a co-worker, approximately three times a week that he was going to murder his wife, and confided two different plans for doing so. Another co-worker heard him tell his plan to cut Carol's air hose while she was scuba diving, making her death look accidental, but did not believe him. Two or three weeks before the murder, David told a friend of his that he and Carol were having problems and he expected Carol "to have an accident sometime." None of these people has a duty imposed by law, to warn the victim of impending danger, whatever their moral obligation may be....

[H]er conviction must be reversed.

Case Discussion

What were Mrs. Ulvinen's specific actions relevant to her liability? How much did she participate in the murder? Should she be guilty of some crime? Do you agree with the court that however morally reprehensible the crime, she nonetheless did not commit a crime? Why should she not be guilty of accessory after the fact? Why isn't her remark that "it would be for the best" sufficient to constitute the *actus reus?* Should it be? Explain.

Note Cases

1. Pace, his wife, and one child were in the front seat of their car driving from South Bend to LaParte, Indiana. Rootes and another of the Pace children sat in the back seat. Pace, after receiving his wife's permission, picked up Reppert, a hitchhiker. Later, Rootes pulled a knife on Reppert and took his wallet. Just before Reppert got out of the car, Rootes took Reppert's watch. Pace said nothing during the entire episode. Was he an accomplice to robbery? He was convicted, but on appeal, the supreme court said:

> [W]e have found no evidence ... which might demonstrate that the appellant aided and abetted in the alleged crime. While he was driving his car, nothing was said nor did he act in any manner to indicate his approval or countenance of the robbery. While there is evidence from which a jury might reasonably infer that he knew the crime was being committed, his situation was not one which would demonstrate a duty to oppose it. *State v. Pace,* 224 N.E.2d 312 (Ind.1967)

2. Mobley's boyfriend Fagan beat Mobley's young child, threw her in the air and let her drop on the concrete floor, burned her with cigarettes, and told her to run and pushed her over. These, and a series of other violent actions over a period of weeks, eventually led to the child's death. Mobley did not intervene in any of the actions Fagan took because, according to her, she was afraid Fagan would leave her. Was Mobley an accomplice to murder? The court said yes:

> It is true that mere presence of a person at the scene of a crime is insufficient to constitute him a principal therein, in the absence of anything in his conduct showing a design to encourage, incite, aid, abet or assist in the crime, the trier of the facts may consider failure of such person to oppose the commission of the crime in connection with other circumstances and conclude therefrom that he assented to the commission of the crime, lent his countenance and approval thereto and thereby aided and abetted it. This, it seems to us, is particularly true when the person who fails to interfere owes a duty to protect as a parent owes to a child. *Mobley v. State,* 85 N.E.2d 489 (Ind.1949)

3. Roberts' wife suffered from multiple sclerosis, which according to her doctor was incurable. She asked Roberts to get her some poison so she could kill herself. She could not do it herself because the disease had crippled her so she could no longer walk. Roberts complied with the request, placing the poison in a glass by her bed. She took the poison and died. Was Roberts an accomplice to murder? The court said yes.

> Where one person advises, aids, or abets another to commit suicide, and the other by reason thereof kills himself, and the adviser is present when he does so, he is guilty of murder as a principal.... It is said by counsel that suicide is no crime ... and that therefore there can be no accessories or principals ... in suicide. This is true. But the real criminal act charged here is not suicide, but the administering of poison.... We are of the opinion that, when defendant mixed the paris green with water and placed it within reach of his wife to enable her to put an end to her suffering by putting an end to her life, he was guilty of murder by means of poison within the meaning of the statute, even though she requested him to do so. By this act he deliberately placed within her reach the means of taking her own life, which she could have obtained in no other way by reason of her helpless condition. *People v. Roberts,* 178 N.W. 690 (Mich.1920)

Mens Rea *of Parties before and during Crime*

Complicity usually requires the intent or purpose to aid or abet third persons to commit crimes. Recklessness and negligence suffice when participants commit reasonably foreseeable crimes while committing the main crime. In *People v. Poplar,* for example, Poplar acted as a lookout for a breaking and entering. Poplar and the other participants were convicted of assault with intent to murder, on the ground that death during breaking and entering is reasonably foreseeable. In ruling so, the court reduced the *mens rea* to recklessness or even negligence in a crime of purpose—assault with *intent* to commit murder.[6]

CASE

Did He "Aid and Abet" the Sale of Marijuana?

State v. Gladstone
474 P.2d 274 (Wash.1970)

Hale, Justice

FACTS
... Douglas MacArthur Thompson, a 25-year-old student at the University of Puget Sound in Tacoma and an employee of the Internal Revenue Service of the United States, had done some investigative work for the government. From time to time, the Tacoma Police Department engaged him to investigate the use, possession and sale of narcotics, principally marijuana, among college students. When working for the Tacoma Police Department, he operated under the control and direction of the department's narcotics detail.

Thompson testified that Lieutenant Seymour and Detective Gallwas of the narcotics detail asked him to attempt a purchase of marijuana from Gladstone. During the evening of April 10, 1967—between 10 and 11 o'clock—the two officers and Thompson drove in a police car to the vicinity of defendant's apartment. Thompson went to Gladstone's door alone, beyond the hearing and out of the sight of the two officers.... He knocked at the door and Gladstone responded. Thompson asked Gladstone if he would sell him some marijuana.

Describing this incident, Thompson testified as follows: "Well, I asked—at the time Gladstone told me that he was—he did not have enough marijuana on hand to sell me any, but he did know an individual who had quite a sufficient quantity and that was very willing to sell and he named the individual as Robert Kent, or Bob Kent as he put it, and he gave me directions to the residence and he—due to the directions I asked him if, you know, if he could draw me a map and he did." When Thompson said he asked Gladstone to draw the map for him, he added, "I'm not sure whether he did give me the exact address or not, he told me where the residence was." He said that Gladstone then with pencil and paper sketched the location of Kent's place of residence.

Thompson had no prior knowledge of where Kent lived, and did not know if he might have marijuana or that he had ever possessed it. The two officers then took Thompson to Kent's residence where marijuana was purchased. The actual purchase was made by Thompson directly from Kent while Officer Gallwas and Lieutenant Seymour stayed in the police car. Kent was subsequently arrested and convicted of selling Thompson approximately 8 ounces of marijuana—the very sale which defendant here was convicted of aiding and abetting.

OPINION

A jury found defendant Bruce Gladstone guilty of aiding and abetting one Robert Kent in the unlawful sale of marijuana. Deferring imposition of sentence, the court placed defendant on probation. He appeals the order deferring sentencing contending that the evidence as a matter of law was insufficient to sustain a verdict of guilty. His point, we think, is well taken....

One who aids or abets another in the commission of a crime is guilty as a principal under RCW 9. 01. 030, which says: Every person concerned in the commission of a felony, gross misdemeanor or misdemeanor, whether he directly commits the act constituting the offense, or aids or abets in its commission, and whether present or absent; and every person who directly or indirectly counsels, encourages, hires, commands, induces or otherwise procures another to commit a felony, gross misdemeanor or misdemeanor, is a principal, and shall be proceeded against and punished as such.

The fact that the person aided, abetted, counseled, encouraged, hired, commanded, induced or procured, could not or did not entertain a criminal intent, shall not be a defense to any person aiding, abetting, counseling, encouraging, hiring, commanding, inducing or procuring him...."

Neither on direct examination nor under cross-examination did Thompson testify that he knew of any prior conduct, arrangements or communications between Gladstone and Kent from which it could be even remotely inferred that the defendant had any understanding, agreement, purpose, intention or design to participate or engage in or aid or abet any sale of marijuana by Kent.

Other than to obtain a simple map from Gladstone and to say that Gladstone told him Kent might have some marijuana available, Thompson did not even establish that Kent and the defendant were acquainted with each other. Testimony of the brief con-

versation and Gladstone's very crude drawing consisting of 8 penciled lines indicating where Kent lived constitute the whole proof of the aiding and abetting presented.

Except for the conversation between Gladstone and Thompson and the map, the state showed only that the officers and their informant, Thompson, went to Kent's residence, more than 3 or 4 blocks from where Gladstone lived, bought some marijuana from him and proved that it was the substance known scientifically as cannabis. Thus, at the close of its case in chief, the state had failed to show any connection or association whatever between Gladstone and Kent or even that they knew each other, and at that juncture a motion for dismissal would lie.

Defendant's proof did not aid the state's case either.... Gladstone took the stand and testified that he had been a student at the University of Puget Sound in Tacoma for 2 years and that he did not know the police informant, Douglas MacArthur Thompson, personally but had seen him on campus. Prior to the evening of April 10, 1967, he said, Thompson had never been in his home. As to Kent, the party whom he was accused of aiding and abetting, he said he had seen him between classes having coffee at the student union building, and perhaps had been in his company about 10 times altogether. He knew where Kent lived because once en route home in his car he had given Kent a lift from the student union building to the latter's house. On this singular occasion, Gladstone did not get out of the car. He said that he did not know that Kent used marijuana or kept it for sale to other people. Describing the incidents of April 10, 1967, when Thompson came to his door, Gladstone's version of the event differed somewhat from Thompson's. He testified that Thompson asked him to sell him some pot and Gladstone said, "No," and:

A. Then he asked me if I knew Rob Kent and I said yes.

Q. What did you tell him?

A. I said yes, I knew Rob Kent, and he asked he if I knew where Rob Kent lived and I said that I didn't know the address, nor did I know the street upon which he lived, but I told him that I could direct him there.

Q. And did he ask you to direct him?

A. Yes, I started to explain how to get there and he asked me if I would draw him a map.

Q. And did you do so?

A. Yes, I did.

They then had a conversation as to the location of a vacant grocery store above which was an apartment occupied by several college students, and as to the location of a house having the address of 1102 shown in the sketch. After that brief conversation, Thompson said, "Thank you," and left. Gladstone testified that he did not counsel, encourage, hire, command, induce or otherwise procure Robert Kent to make a sale of marijuana to Douglas Thompson—or do anything that would be their legal equivalent.

Thus, the state at the close of its case had not established prima facie that Gladstone, as charged, aided and abetted Kent in the sale of marijuana, and its position did not improve with the defendant's case....

One may become a principal through aiding and abetting another in the commission of a crime.... But to be a principal one must consciously share in a criminal act and participate in its accomplishment. Thus, even without prior agreement, arrangement or understanding, a bystander to a robbery could be guilty of aiding and abetting its commission if he came to the aid of a robber and knowingly assisted him in perpetrating the crime. But regardless of the *modus operandi* ... and whether present or away from the scene of it, there is no aiding and abetting unless one "in some sort associate himself with the venture, that he participate in it as in something that he wishes to bring about, that he seek by his action to make it succeed."

In the instant case, the record is totally devoid of any proof whatever that the defendant and Kent had any arrangement, agreement or understanding, or in any way conspired and confederated with each other concerning the sale of marijuana by Kent. There was no proof that they had talked about it with each other, directly or through others. Whatever information the defendant is shown by the record to have given the police informant, to the effect that Kent might sell him some marijuana, amounted at most to no more than a statement of opinion and possibly no more than campus gossip, rumor or innuendo. That the police ultimately bought marijuana from Kent would not, without more, operate to convert defendant's statement to the police, that Kent would or might sell marijuana, into an aiding, abetting, counseling or encouraging of Kent to make the sale....

It would be a dangerous precedent indeed to hold that mere communications to the effect that another might or probably would commit a criminal offense amount to an aiding and abetting of the offense should it ultimately be committed. There being no evidence whatever that the defendant ever communicated to Kent the idea that he would in any way aid him in the sale of any marijuana, or said anything to Kent to encourage or induce him or direct him to do so, or counseled Kent in the sale of marijuana, or did anything more than describe Kent to another person as an individual who might sell some marijuana, or would derive any benefit, consideration or reward from such a sale, there was no proof of an aiding and abetting, and the conviction should, therefore, be reversed as a matter of law. Remanded with directions to dismiss.

DISSENT

Hamilton, Justice (dissenting).

... As is apparent from its language, our statute does not require the presence at the scene of the crime of one aiding, abetting, counseling or inducing the commission of a crime. Neither does it require a community of intent, for by the last sentence it provides that absence of criminal intent on the part of the person aided, abetted or induced to commit the primary offense is no defense to the aider or abettor. The statutory language and the overt action it contemplates does, however, give rise to the requirement that the aider or abettor entertain a conscious intent, i.e., knowledge and intent that his action will instigate, induce, procure or encourage perpetration of the primary crime. *State v. Hinkley,* 52 Wash.2d 415, 325 P.2d 889 (1958).

The question to be resolved, then, in the instant case is whether the evidence sustains the jury's conclusion that the appellant entertain the requisite intent to render him culpable as an aider or abettor....;

Although the evidence in the case is conflicting, the jury was entitled to believe that on April 10, 1967, one Robert Kent sold marijuana to Douglas Thompson, who at the time was acting as an undercover agent for and in concert with officers of the Tacoma Police Department; that appellant Gladstone, Kent, and Thompson were students at the same school in Tacoma; that prior to the evening of April 10, 1967, when Thompson talked to appellant, Thompson and the Tacoma Police Department were unaware of Kent or his association with marijuana; that appellant knew Kent, whom he met and associated with on the campus of the school they respectively attended; that both appellant and Kent lived off campus; that appellant knew where Kent lived and on at least one occasion had driven him home; that at the time in question the Tacoma Police Department had information that appellant was supposed to be holding a supply of marijuana for sale; that Thompson, who was but slightly acquainted with appellant, approached appellant at his residence about 10:50 p.m. on April 10, 1967, and asked appellant to sell him some marijuana; that appellant then stated that he did not have enough marijuana on hand to sell but that he knew an individual who did have an ample supply and who was willing to sell some and named the individual as Robert

Kent; that upon request appellant orally gave Thompson directions to Kent's apartment and drew a map to aid Thompson in finding the address, utilizing as a reference point a building known to appellant to be a student rendezvous where drugs had been sold; that by using the map and oral directions Thompson and the police went to Kent's residence; that Thompson approached Kent and told him "Gladstone had sent me" whereupon Kent invited him to a room and sold him some marijuana for $30; and that Thompson and one of the police officers later returned to the Kent residence, after again visiting appellant, and made a second purchase of marijuana at which time Kent was arrested.

Based upon the foregoing circumstances and the inferences reasonably derivable therefrom, I am satisfied that the jury was fully warranted in concluding that appellant, when he affirmatively recommended Kent as a source and purveyor of marijuana, entertained the requisite conscious design and intent that his action would instigate, induce, procure or encourage perpetration of Kent's subsequent crime of selling marijuana to Thompson. Furthermore, insofar as an element of preconcert be concerned, certainly the readiness with which the passwords, "Gladstone had sent me," gained a stranger's late evening entree to Kent's domain and produced two illegal sales strongly suggests, if not conclusively establishes, the missing communal nexus which the majority belabors. Finally, the jury, with the witnesses before it, was in a far better position to evaluate the witnesses' candor, voice inflections, appearance, demeanor, attitude, and credibility than this court viewing naught but the cold record. I would sustain the jury's verdict and affirm the judgment.

McGovern, J., concurs.

Case Discussion   What specific actions of Gladstone's indicate his *mens rea?* How did the court define the *mens rea* requirement of complicity? How did the dissent define it differently? How would you define the *mens rea* in complicity? Did

Gladstone satisfy the requirement, according to your definition? Explain. Should the *mens rea* of complicity require that Gladstone intended to help Kent sell marijuana? That Gladstone knew that his information would lead to the sale of marijuana? Or simply that Gladstone's acts in fact aided in Kent's sale of marijuana?

1. In *Lewis et al. v. State,* 251 S.W.2d 490 (Ark.1952), Wren was driving his friend Lewis's car. En route from Atkins to Morrilton, they purchased twelve cans of beer and drank a considerable amount of beer and gin from 7 p.m. until immediately before colliding head on with another car. Occupants of both automobiles were seriously injured; and Mrs. Pounds, driver of the other car, died from her injuries three days later.

Was Lewis guilty of criminal homicide? The court said yes:

> If the owner of a dangerous instrumentality like an automobile knowingly puts that instrumentality in the immediate control of a careless and reckless driver, sits by his side, and permits him without protest so recklessly and negligently to operate the car as to cause the death of another, he is as much responsible as the man at the wheel.

2. Foster believed Bill had raped Foster's girlfriend. Foster beat Bill up. He handed his friend Otha a knife, telling him to keep Bill from leaving until Foster returned from getting his girlfriend to verify the rape. After Foster left, Otha got nervous and stabbed Bill, who died from the stab wounds. Was Foster an accomplice to negligent homicide? The court said yes, because even though Foster did not intend to kill Bill, he was negligent with respect to the death: he should have foreseen the consequences of leaving Otha, armed with the knife, to guard Bill. *State v. Foster,* 522 A.2d 277 (Conn.1987)

Complicity following Crime

The common law included accessories after the fact—complicity following the commission of crimes—within the scope of liability for the main offense. For example, one who gave a burglar a place to hide was an accessory after the fact, and as such was also guilty of burglary. Modern statutes impose liability for complicity following commission of the main crime, but the liability is for separate, less serious offenses, such as obstructing justice, interfering with prosecution, and aiding in escape.

Most statutes follow the common-law requirements for accessories after the fact: (1) that a third person had actually committed a felony; (2) that the accessory knew the other person had committed the felony; and (3) that the accessory personally aided the third person to hinder prosecution. Some statutes even preserve the term *accessory after the fact* in their classification scheme. The Supreme Court of Louisiana dealt with that state's accessory-after-the-fact statute in *State v. Chism.*

CASE

*Was He an Accessory
after the Fact?*

State v. Chism

436 So.2d 464 (La.1983)

*The defendant, Brian Chism, was convicted
by a judge of being an accessory after the
fact. Chism was sentenced to three years in
the parish prison, with two and one-half
years suspended. The defendant was placed
on supervised probation for two years. We
affirm his conviction. Justice Dennis gave the
opinion. Chief Justice Dixon gave a dissenting opinion.*

FACTS

On the evening of August 26, 1981 in
Shreveport, Tony Duke gave the defendant
Brian Chism, a ride in his automobile. Brian
Chism was impersonating a female, and
Duke was apparently unaware of Chism's
disguise. After a brief visit at a friend's
house the two stopped to pick up some
beer at the residence of Chism's grandmoth-
er. Chism's one-legged uncle, Ira Lloyd,
joined them, and the three continued on
their way, drinking as Duke drove the automobile. When Duke expressed a desire to
have sexual relations with Chism, Lloyd
announced that he wanted to find his ex-
wife Gloria for the same purpose. Shortly
after midnight, the trio arrived at the St.
Vincent Avenue Church of Christ and persuaded Gloria Lloyd to come outside. As Ira
Lloyd stood outside the car attempting to
persuade Gloria to come with them, Chism
and Duke hugged and kissed on the front
seat as Duke sat behind the steering wheel.

Gloria and Ira Lloyd got into an argument,
and Ira stabbed Gloria with a knife several
times in the stomach and once in the neck.
Gloria's shouts attracted the attention of two
neighbors, who unsuccessfully tried to prevent Ira from pushing Gloria into the front

seat of the car alongside Chism and Duke.
Ira Lloyd climbed into the front seat also,
and Duke drove off. One of the bystanders
testified that she could not be sure but she
thought she saw Brian's foot on the acceler-
ator as the car left.

Lloyd ordered Duke to drive to Willow
Point, near Cross Lake. When they arrived,
Chism and Duke, under Lloyd's direction,
removed Gloria from the vehicle and placed
her on some high grass on the roadway,
near a wood line. Ira was unable to help the
two because his wooden leg had come off.
Afterwards, as Lloyd requested, the two
drove off, leaving Gloria with him.

There was no evidence that Chism or
Duke protested, resisted or attempted to
avoid the actions which Lloyd ordered them
to take. Although Lloyd was armed with a
knife, there was no evidence that he threatened either of his companions with harm.

Duke proceeded to drop Chism off at a
friend's house, where he changed to male
clothing. He placed the blood-stained
women's clothes in a trash bin. Afterward,
Chism went with his mother to the police
station at 1:15 a.m. He gave the police a
complete statement, and took the officers to
the place where Gloria had been left with
Ira Lloyd. The police found Gloria's body in
some tall grass several feet from the spot.
An autopsy indicated that stab wounds had
caused her death. Chism's discarded clothing disappeared before the police arrived at
the trash bin.

OPINION

An accessory after the fact is any person,
who, after the commission of a felony, shall
harbor, conceal, or aid the offender, knowing or having reasonable ground to believe
that he has committed the felony, and with
the intent that he may avoid or escape from
arrest, trial, conviction, or punishment. La.
R.S. 14:25….

[A] person may be punished as an accessory after the fact if he aids an offender
personally, knowing or having reasonable
ground to believe that he has committed the
felony, and has a specific or general intent

that the offender will avoid or escape from arrest, trial, conviction, or punishment....

An accessory after the fact may be tried and convicted, notwithstanding the fact that the principal felon may not have been arrested, tried, convicted, or amenable to justice.... [I]t is essential to prove that a felony was committed and completed prior to the time the assistance was rendered the felon, although it is not also necessary that the felon already have been charged with the crime....

We must determine whether, after viewing the evidence in the light most favorable to the prosecution, any rational trier of fact could have found beyond a reasonable doubt that (a) a completed felony had been committed by Ira Lloyd before Brian Chism rendered him the assistance described below; (b) Chism knew or had reasonable grounds to know of the commission of the felony by Lloyd; and (c) Chism gave aid to Lloyd personally under circumstances that indicate either that he actively desired that the felon avoid or escape arrest, trial, conviction, or punishment or that he believed that one of these consequences was substantially certain to result from his assistance.

There was clearly enough evidence to justify the finding that a felony had been completed before any assistance was rendered to Lloyd by the defendant. The record vividly demonstrates that Lloyd fatally stabbed his ex-wife before she was transported to Willow Point and left in the high grass near the wood line. Thus, Lloyd committed the felonies of attempted murder, aggravated battery, and simple kidnapping, before Chism aided him in any way....

The evidence overwhelmingly indicates that Chism had reasonable grounds to believe that Lloyd had committed a felony before any assistance was rendered. In his confessions and his testimony Chism indicates that the victim was bleeding profusely when Lloyd pushed her into the vehicle, that she was limp and moaned as they drove to Willow Point, and that he knew Lloyd had inflicted her wounds with a knife....

The closest question presented is whether any reasonable trier of fact could have found beyond a reasonable doubt that Chism assisted Lloyd under circumstances that indicate that either Chism actively desired that Lloyd would avoid or escape arrest, trial, conviction, or punishment, or that Chism believed that one of these consequences was substantially certain to result from his assistance. After carefully reviewing the record, we conclude that the prosecution satisfied its burden of producing the required quantity of evidence....

(1) Chism did not protest or attempt to leave the car when his uncle, Lloyd shoved the mortally wounded victim inside; (2) he did not attempt to persuade Duke, his would-be lover, exit [sic] out the driver's side of the car and flee from his uncle, whom he knew to be one-legged and armed only with a knife; (3) he did not take any of these actions at any point during the considerable ride to Willow Point; (4) at their destination, he docilely complied with Lloyd's direction to remove the victim from the car and leave Lloyd with her, despite the fact that Lloyd made no threats and that his wooden leg had become detached; (5) after leaving Lloyd with the dying victim, he made no immediate effort to report the victim's whereabouts or to obtain emergency medical treatment for her; (6) before going home or reporting the victim's dire condition he went to a friend's house, changed clothing and discarded his own in a trash bin from which the police were unable to recover them as evidence; (7) he went home without reporting the victim's condition or location; (8) and he went to the police station to report the crime only after arriving home and discussing the matter with his mother....

Therefore, we affirm the defendant's conviction. We note, however, that the sentence imposed by the trial judge was illegal. The judge imposed a sentence of three years. He suspended two and one half of years [sic] of the term. The trial judge has no authority to suspend part of a sentence in a felony case. The correct sentence would have been a suspension of all three years of the term, with a six-month term as a condition of two years of probation....

DISSENT

I respectfully dissent from what appears to be a finding of guilt by association. The majority lists five instances of inaction, or failure to act, by defendant: (1) did not protest or leave the car; (2) did not attempt to persuade Duke to leave the car; (3) did neither (1) nor (2) on ride to Willow Point; (5) [sic] made no immediate effort to report crime or get aid for the victim; (7) failed to report victim's condition or location after changing clothes. The three instances of defendant's actions relied on by the majority for conviction were stated to be: (4) complying with Lloyd's direction to remove the victim from the car and leave the victim and Lloyd at Willow Point; (6) changing clothes and discarding bloody garments; and (8) discussing the matter with the defendant's mother before going to the police station to report the crime.

None of these actions or failures to act tended to prove defendant's intent, specifically or generally, to aid defendant avoid arrest, trial, conviction or punishment.

Case Discussion Was the crime completed at the time Chism aided Lloyd? What facts show this? Do you agree that Chism intended to help Lloyd avoid arrest, trial, conviction, or punishment? What does the dissent mean in saying that the ruling makes a person guilty of crime by association? Do you agree? In Louisiana, according to this ruling, is the *mens rea* for accessory after the fact purpose, knowledge, recklessness, or negligence? Explain.

▼ VICARIOUS LIABILITY

The doctrine of complicity applies to accomplices and accessories because they participate in crime. Complicity also encompasses vicarious liability. **Vicarious liability** bases liability on the relationship between the party who commits the crime and another party. Vicarious liability applies mainly to business relationships: employer-employee, manager-corporation, buyer-seller, producer-consumer, service provider-recipient. But it also applies to other situations, such as making the owner of a car liable for the driver's traffic violations, and holding parents liable for their minor children's crimes.

Vicarious liability, particularly when it involves large businesses, creates problems in criminal law. Pinpointing responsibility for corporate crime is especially difficult. Often, not one person but many participate in decisions that violate the law. This problem increases as corporate structures become more complex. The larger and more dispersed the corporation or business, the harder it is to attribute responsibility. A further, related issue is the difficulty of establishing *mens rea* in corporate crimes. A corporation cannot have a *mens rea* because it cannot think. To overcome this limitation, the criminal law makes corporations criminals by two methods: (1) strict liability eliminates the material element of *mens rea,* and (2) vicarious liability attributes the intent of managers and agents to the corporation. Although vicarious and strict liability work together to impose criminal liability, they are distinct doctrines: strict liability eliminates the *mens rea;* vicarious liability transfers the *actus reus.*[7]

Punishing corporate crime is also problematic. Most corporate crimes never enter the criminal justice system. Out-of-court arrangements lead to consent decrees, or agreements to settle matters between corporations and those complaining against them. When the government tries corporate crimes and obtains convictions, sentences often appear lenient and inadequate compared with penalties for street crimes. Courts can impose only fines, because corporations cannot go to jail. Furthermore, sending employers and managers to jail for the conduct of others raises constitutional problems. Some courts have ruled that imprisonment for vicarious liability violates the due process clause.

Even fines violate the due process clause when a noncriminal response to regulating business conduct suffices. Fines fall ultimately on stockholders, "most of whom, ordinarily had nothing to do with the offense and were powerless to prevent it." In addition, fines are ineffective if corporations consider them just another business expense. Finally, fines rarely deter officers or other agents who do not have to pay them; officers suffer no stigma if their organizations violate "mere regulations," not "real criminal laws." Quite the contrary. Some authorities believe officers risk prosecution and conviction for minor offenses in order to bring gains to their companies. By doing so, they receive their colleagues' approbation for "shrewd business."[8]

The general principles of criminal law apply to all crime, including corporate crime. However, corporate crime deserves special note for two reasons. First, some crimes are peculiar to business. Unlike most other crimes, the gains sought through corporate crime are neither individual nor personal. For example, corporate executives usually do not fix prices for their personal profit but rather to enhance the company's business position. Second, corporations do not ordinarily injure or cause disease or death because of personal vendettas and anger. They do so while their officers pursue company interests. Hence, corporate executives may not mean to injure workers or customers, but to make the company competitive they may cut corners in areas such as safety, thus potentially exposing employees and customers to serious injury or death. Robbers do not usually want to injure their victims either, but they are prepared to risk doing so in order to get the money they seek.[9]

> [W]e are talking about ... economic crime. We have tended in the past to call it property crime as distinguished from violent crime. And even there it is not easy to draw the line. If a surgeon knowingly commits unneeded surgery on a human being because he wants money, is that a less violent physical assault on an individual than to be mugged in the streets? I have to tell you that at a purely moral level I find it far more reprehensible.[10]

Vicarious Liability and Business Crime

Vicarious liability arises out of business relationships in some combination of the following circumstances: (1) where strict liability statutes or misdemeanors are involved; (2) where it is difficult to prove an employer's or corporate official's *legal* involvement; (3) where difficult burdens are put on prosecutors to obtain evidence to convict; (4) where widespread public harm is threatened by the prohibited conduct. Vicarious liability offends the notion of individual and personal guilt. The common law punished participants in crime. Corporate officers in high positions who either participated in, approved of, or consented to criminal conduct fall within the scope of common-law complicity. Corporations were not criminally liable under the common law; they could not form a *mens rea* because only "natural persons" think. The **alter ego doctrine**—that management was the corporation's "brain"—provided an exception to the common-law principle.[11]

The Wisconsin Supreme Court dealt with vicarious liability in *State v. Beaudry* .

CASE

Did She Unlawfully Remain Open for Business?

State v. Beaudry
365 N.W.2d 593 (Wis.1985)

Abrahamson, Justice
Janet Beaudry was fined $200 as agent of a corporation licensed to sell alcoholic beverages for violating the closing hours law.

FACTS

… Janet Beaudry's conviction grew out of events occurring during the early morning hours of February 9, 1983. At approximately 3:45 a.m., a deputy sheriff for the Sheboygan County Sheriff's Department drove past the Village Green Tavern. He stopped to investigate after noticing more lights than usual inside the building and also seeing two individuals seated inside. As he approached the tavern, he heard music, saw an individual standing behind the bar, and saw glasses on the bar. Upon finding the tavern door locked, the deputy sheriff knocked and was admitted by Mark Witkowski, the tavern manager.

The tavern manager and two men were the only persons inside the bar. All three were drinking. The deputy sheriff reported the incident to the Sheboygan County district attorney's office for a formal complaint.

At about noon on February 9, the tavern manager reported to Wallace Beaudry about the deputy's stop earlier that morning. After further investigation Wallace Beaudry discharged the tavern manager on February 11.

On March 2, 1983, the Sheboygan County Sheriff's Department served the defendant with a summons and a complaint charging her with the crime of keeping the tavern open after hours contrary to § 125.68(4)(c), Stats. and § 125.11(1), Stats. The tavern manager was not arrested or charged with an offense arising out of this incident.

The case was tried before a jury on May 20, 1983. At trial Janet Beaudry testified that she was not present at the tavern the morning of February 9. Wallace Beaudry testified that Janet Beaudry had delegated to him, as president of Sohn Manufacturing, the responsibilities of business administration associated with the Village Green Tavern; that he had hired Mark Witkowski as manager; that he had informed Witkowski that it was his duty to abide by the liquor laws; and that he never authorized Witkowski to remain open after 1:00 a.m., to throw a private party for his friends, or to give away liquor to friends.

Witkowski testified that he had served drinks after hours to two men. During cross-examination Witkowski confirmed that Wallace Beaudry had never authorized him to stay open after hours; that he had been instructed to close the tavern promptly at the legal closing time; that he knew it was illegal to serve liquor after 1:00 a.m. to anyone, including friends; that his two friends drank at the bar before 1:00 a.m. and had paid for those drinks; that he was having a good time with his friends before closing hours and wanted to continue partying and conversing with them after 1 a.m.; that after closing hours he was simply using the tavern to have a private party for two friends; that he did not charge his friends for any of the liquor they drank after 1:00 a.m.; and that by staying open he was trying to benefit not Wallace Beaudry but himself.

At the close of evidence, the jury was instructed that the law required the premises to be closed for all purposes between 1:00 a.m. and 8:00 a.m. and that if the jury found that there were patrons or customers on the premises after 1:00 a.m., it must find the premises open contrary to statute.

The jury was also instructed regarding Janet Beaudry's liability for the conduct of the tavern manager: As designated agent of the corporation, the defendant had full authority over the business and would be liable for the tavern manager's violation of the closing hour statute if he was acting within the scope of his employment. The instructions describe what activities are within the scope of employment and what are outside the scope of employment. Specifically, the jury was instructed as follows regarding the defendant's liability for the conduct of the tavern manager:

"It is also the law of the State of Wisconsin that violations of statutes regulating the sale of liquor do not require a showing of a willful or intentional act.

"It is a law that when a corporation is a licensee, the corporation vests in its agent, in this case Janet Beaudry, full control and authority over the premises and of the conduct of all business on the premises relative to alcohol beverages that the licensee could have exercised if it were a natural person.

"Under Wisconsin law if a person employs another to act for him [sic] in the conduct of his [sic] business, and such servant or agent violates the law, as in this case relating to open after hours, then the employer is guilty of that violation as if he [sic] had been present or had done the act himself [sic], if such act was within the scope of the employment of the servant or agent.

"It is no defense to prosecution under the statute that the employer was not upon the premises, did not know of the acts of his [sic] servant or agent, had not consented thereto, or even had expressly forbidden such act.

"A servant or agent is within the scope of his employment when he is performing work or rendering services he was hired to perform and render within the time and space limits of his authority and is actuated by a purpose in serving his employer in doing what he is doing. He is within the scope of his employment when he is performing work or rendering services in obedience to the express orders or directions of his master of doing that which is warranted within the terms of his express or implied authority, considering the nature of the services required, the instructions which he has received, and the circumstances under which his work is being done or the services are being rendered.

"A servant or agent is outside the scope of his employment when he deviates or steps aside from the prosecution of his master's business for the purpose of doing an act or rendering a service intended to accomplish an independent purpose of his own, or for some other reason or purpose not related to the business of his employer.

"Such deviation or stepping aside from his employer's business may be momentary and slight, measured in terms of time and space, but if it involves a change of mental attitude in serving his personal interests, or the interests of another instead of his employer's, then his conduct falls outside the scope of his employment.

"If you are satisfied beyond a reasonable doubt from the evidence in this case that Mark Witkowski, the employee of the registered agent, committed the acts charged in the complaint, that Mark Witkowski was the servant or agent of the defendant, and that the acts charged in the complaint were committed by him in the scope of his employment, then you should find the defendant guilty.

"If, however, you are not so satisfied, then you must find the defendant not guilty." Having been so instructed, the jury returned a verdict of guilty.

OPINION

... The state's prosecution of the defendant under the criminal laws rests on a theory of vicarious liability, that is **respondeat superior.** Under this theory of liability, the master (here the designated agent) is liable for the illegal conduct of the servant (here the tavern manager). Vicarious liability should be contrasted with liability for one's own acts as a party to a crime: that is, for directly committing the crime, for aiding and abetting the commission of a crime, or for being a party to a conspiracy to commit the crime. § 939.05, Stats.1981–82. It is apparently undisputed that the tavern manager violated the closing hour statute and could have been prosecuted as a party to the crime....

While the focus in this case is on the defendant's vicarious criminal liability, it is helpful to an understanding of vicarious liability to compare it with the doctrine of strict liability. Strict liability allows for criminal liability absent the element of *mens rea* found in the definition of most crimes.

Thus under strict liability the accused has engaged in the act or omission; the requirement of mental fault, *mens rea,* is eliminated. This court has construed violations of several statutes regulating the sale of alcoholic beverages which command that an act be done or omitted and which do not include words signifying scienter as imposing strict liability on the actor....

Vicarious liability, in contrast to strict liability, dispenses with the requirement of the *actus reus* and imputes the criminal act of one person to another....

[T]he defendant ... [argues] that due process requires blameworthy conduct on the part of the defendant as a prerequisite to criminal liability. Although the imposition of criminal liability for faultless conduct does not comport with the generally accepted premise of Anglo-American criminal justice that criminal liability is based on personal fault, this court and the United States Supreme Court have upheld statutes imposing criminal liability for some types of offenses without proof that the conduct was knowing or wilful or negligent.

The defendant's chief challenge to the constitutionality of the statute in issue in this case appears to be that the defendant could have received a jail sentence of up to 90 days for the violation. As the state points out, the defendant was fined $200, and the due process issue the defendant raises, whatever its validity, is not presented by the facts in this case. A decision by this court on the constitutionality of a jail term where the statute imposes vicarious liability would not affect the judgment of conviction in this case or the sentence imposed on this defendant. We therefore do not consider this issue.

We turn now to the question of whether the evidence supports the verdict that the tavern manager was acting within the scope of his employment. As we stated previously, the jury was instructed that the defendant is liable only for the acts of the tavern manager that were within the scope of his employment. Thus the defendant is not liable for all the acts of the tavern manager, only for those acts within the scope of employment. Neither the state nor the defense challenges this statement of the law limiting the designated agent's vicarious criminal liability. The scope of employment doctrine does not represent the only means of limiting the circumstances under which the acts of an employee may be imputed to the corporation or to a corporate officer for purposes of criminal liability....

The application of the standard of scope of employment limits liability to illegal conduct which occurred while the offending employee was engaged in some job-related activity and thus limits the accused's vicarious liability to conduct with which the accused has a factual connection and with which the accused has some responsible relation to the public danger envisaged by the legislature.

The defendant argues that … in this case the tavern manager went outside his scope of authority.

We agree with the conclusion reached by the court of appeals. The credibility of the bar manager's testimony was a matter for the jury. The bar manager's testimony which supports the defendant's position that the manager was acting outside the scope of employment was based on a statement the bar manager gave defendant's counsel the night before trial. The jury may not have believed this testimony which was favorable to the defendant. Considering that the conduct occurred on the employer's premises and began immediately after "closing time"; that the employee had access to the tavern after hours only by virtue of his role as an employee of the corporate licensee, which role vested him with the means to keep the tavern open; and that the defendant may anticipate that employees may be tempted to engage in such conduct; the jury could conclude that the tavern manager's conduct was sufficiently similar to the conduct authorized as to be within the scope of employment. The jury could view the tavern manager's conduct as more similar to that of an employee to whom the operation of the business had been entrusted and for whose conduct the defendant should be held criminally liable than to that of an interloper for whose conduct the defendant should not be held liable.

For the reasons set forth, we affirm the decision of the court of appeals affirming the conviction.

Decision of the court of appeals is affirmed.

DISSENT

Ceci, Justice (dissenting).

I respectfully dissent from the majority's conclusion that there is sufficient evidence to support the verdict in this case finding that Mark Witkowski, the tavern manager, was acting within the scope of his employment. In reviewing the evidence in the light most favorable to sustaining Janet Beaudry's conviction, I believe that the record is de-void of evidence to sustain the verdict. I would reverse the decision of the court of appeals which affirmed the defendant's conviction because I am convinced that, as a matter of law, no trier of fact, acting reasonably, could conclude beyond a reasonable doubt that Mark Witkowski was acting within the scope of his employment when he kept the Village Green tavern open after 1:00 a.m. in violation of § 125.68(4)(c), Stats.

We have previously held that a servant is not within the scope of his employment if (a) his acts were different in kind than those authorized by the master, (b) his acts were far beyond the authorized time or space limits, or (c) his acts were too little actuated by a purpose to serve the master. It is important to note that this test is set out in the disjunctive and not the conjunctive, and, thus, not all three elements must be satisfied before there can be a finding that the servant was outside the scope of his authority.

In conformance with this test, the jury was instructed that, "[a] servant or agent is within the scope of his employment when he is performing work or rendering services he was hired to perform and render within the time and space limits of his authority and is actuated by a purpose in serving his employer in doing what he is doing.…"

"A servant or agent is outside the scope of his employment when he deviates or steps aside from the prosecution of his master's business for the purpose of doing an act or rendering a service intended to accomplish an independent purpose of his own, or for some other reason or purpose not related to the business of his employer."…

I conclude that Mark Witkowski was not within the scope of employment when he kept the tavern open after 1:00 a.m. The first element of the test asks whether Witkowski's acts were different in kind than those authorized by the defendant. Witkowski stated that one of his duties as a manager included closing the tavern at one o'clock. He testified that Wallace Beaudry never authorized him to stay open after the legal closing time. In fact, he was specifically instructed to close promptly at the legal closing time. Additionally, Witkowski testified, "I knew that Wally would not want me to stay open after hours but I decided to do it anyway." Wally Beaudry also testified at the trial. He confirmed Witkowski's testimony by stating that one of Witkowski's duties was to follow all the liquor laws of this state and that he never authorized Witkowski to remain open after 1:00 a.m., throw a private party for his friends, or give away liquor.

A thorough review of the trial transcript reveals that this testimony of Witkowski and Wally Beaudry was in no way impeached by the state. The majority admits that this evidence is undisputed. This testimony was wrongly ignored by the majority. I conclude that Witkowski was not within his scope of employment, because his act of keeping the tavern open until 3:45 a.m. was not authorized by Mr. or Mrs. Beaudry.

The second element of the test ... asks whether Witkowski's acts were far beyond the authorized time or space limits. I conclude that Witkowski's acts were beyond the authorized time limit because, as stated above, there was testimony that Witkowski was not hired to stay open after hours, and, at the time the police arrived at the tavern, it was 3:45 a.m. Witkowski testified that he usually was done with his normal cleanup between 1:15 a.m. and 1:30 a.m. Over two hours passed between the time he should have locked up and left the tavern and the time the police arrived. Although there is no testimony to this fact, it can reasonably be inferred that Witkowski did not expect to get paid for these two hours when he was sitting at the bar and drinking with his friends. It is clear that Witkowski was no longer working at 3:45 a.m. and that his acts were far beyond the time limit authorized by Janet or Wally Beaudry.

The third and final factor to be considered is whether Witkowski's acts were too little actuated by a purpose to serve the defendant. Not only the direct testimony of Witkowski, but also the circumstantial evidence, provide support for the finding that Witkowski's acts were in no way intended to further the defendant's business, but were

motivated solely for his own enjoyment and convenience.

Witkowski testified that after the other patrons left the Village Green tavern, he was not performing any work duties, but was entertaining his "real good friends." Witkowski stated, "I was not trying to benefit Wallace Beaudry by staying open after hours. I was simply using Wally's tavern to have a private party for my two friends. By staying open for my two friends I was not trying to benefit Wallace Beaudry in any way, rather I was trying to benefit myself by continuing the conversation I had started with my friends."

The undisputed circumstantial evidence also bears out the fact that Witkowski's acts were not serving the purpose of the defendant. Deputy Sheriff Kenneth Van Ess testified that he arrived at the tavern at 3:45 a.m. Loud music was coming from within the tavern. The door was locked to outside patrons. Witkowski and Pethan were sitting at the bar, and Dickman, a nonemployee, was standing behind the bar. Dickman later testified that he went behind the bar to get another bottle of liquor. There were glasses and a bottle of liquor sitting on the bar. Van Ess testified that it was quite apparent that all three men had been drinking. Witkowski was not performing any cleanup or maintenance duties. Finally, Witkowski, Dickman, and Pethan all testified that Witkowski had been charging Dickman and Pethan for drinks before 1:00 a.m. Witkowski testified that he did not charge his friends for drinks after 1:00 a.m. This statement is also confirmed by the testimony of Dickman. Ken Pethan testified that he does not remember if he had anything to drink after 1:00 a.m.

Based on this testimony, I conclude that Witkowski was not acting within the scope of his authority, because his acts were in no way intended to serve the defendant. The fact that Witkowski gave his employer's liquor to his friends without charge after 1:00 a.m., when he knew it was illegal and contrary to his authority as a manager of the tavern to stay open after closing hours, strongly supports the conclusion that

Witkowski did not intend to further the defendant's business, but was acting solely for his own enjoyment and convenience.

Unfortunately, the majority fails to consider these factors in making its determination....

For the above-stated reasons, I dissent.

Case Discussion

What circumstances does the court conclude justify imposing vicarious liability on Janet Beaudry? How do you justify criminal liability when there is neither *actus reus* nor *mens rea*? Do you believe that punishing Janet Beaudry violates the due process clause? If she were put in jail, would you answer differently? Was the majority or dissent correct in its conclusion regarding Witkowski's acting within the scope of his employment? Explain.

Note Cases

1. New Hampshire makes parents vicariously liable for offenses committed by their minor children. Two fathers were convicted because their minor sons drove snowmobiles on a public road in violation of a New Hampshire statute. According to the New Hampshire Supreme Court:

> [W]e have no hesitancy in holding that any attempt to impose ... [vicarious] liability on parents simply because they occupy the status of parents, without more, offends the due process clause of our State constitution. Parenthood lies at the very foundation of our civilization. The continuance of the human race is entirely dependent upon it.... Considering the nature of parenthood, we are convinced that the status of parenthood cannot be made a crime.... Even if the parent has been as careful as anyone could be, even if the parent has forbidden the conduct, and even if the parent is justifiably unaware of the activities of the child, criminal liability is still imposed under the wording of the present statute. *State v. Akers,* 400 A.2d38 (N.H.1979)

2. Nolan was convicted of over a dozen parking violations and fined $20. Would Nolan have to pay the fine even if the violations occurred when someone else was driving his car? The court said yes. *Iowa City v. Nolan,* 239 N.W.2d 102 (Iowa1976)

Vicarious Corporate Liability for Real Crime

Vicarious corporate liability most often arises in connection with strict liability for misdemeanors, but is by no means limited to minor offenses. The criminal law also imposes vicarious criminal liability on corporations for real, or true, crimes. Several states have adopted corporate criminal liability statutes.

These statutes have several features in common: (1) They impose liability for all crimes, although the most commonly prosecuted crimes are involuntary manslaughter and property offenses. (2) Officials or agents high in the corporate structure must authorize, commit, request, or "recklessly tolerate" the conduct that constitutes the crime. This is called the **superior officer rule.** (3) Officers or agents must act for the corporation's benefit, not for their own personal gain. (4) Officers must act within the scope of their authority. Corporations can commit any crimes under these conditions.

Most statutes restrict corporate liability to the conduct of officers and agents who are sufficiently high in the corporate hierarchy that their actions reflect corporate policy. This limitation originated in the **alter ego doctrine.** Only leading officers, such as (but not only) presidents—who constitute the corporation's brain—can impose vicarious corporate criminal liability. The *alter ego* doctrine stems from the common-law rule that corporations cannot commit crimes because they do not possess minds. The doctrine also accords with *mens rea*, culpability, and personal and individual responsibility; corporations are blameworthy when the officers' mental states and the corporate structure correspond. Therefore, statutes adopting the *alter ego* doctrine impose corporate vicarious liability for the actions of a firm's president and general manager, but not for the actions of either a large plant's supervisor or a small branch's manager.[12]

Vicarious Individual Liability for Corporate Crime

Under most modern statutes, individuals who act for the corporation's benefit are as liable for that conduct as they would be if they were acting in their own behalf for their own private gain.

CASE

Did the Corporation President Commit the Crime?

United States v. Park
421 U.S. 658, 95 S.Ct. 1903, 44 L.Ed.2d 489 (1975)

The president of Acme Markets, Inc., was charged with and convicted of five counts of violating the Federal Food, Drug, and Cosmetic Act[13] because food in the corporation's warehouses was exposed to rodent contamination. The act provides for up to a $1,000 fine or not more than one year of imprisonment or both. Park was fined $250, $50 on each count. He appealed. Chief Justice Burger delivered the opinion, in which justices Douglas, Brennan, White, Blackmun, and Rehnquist joined. Justice Stewart filed a dissenting opinion in which justices Marshall and Powell joined.

FACTS
In April 1970 the Food and Drug Administration (FDA) advised respondent by letter of insanitary conditions in Acme's Philadelphia warehouse. In 1971 the FDA found that similar conditions existed in the firm's Baltimore warehouse. An FDA consumer safety officer testified concerning evidence of rodent infestation and other insanitary conditions discovered during a 12-day inspection of the Baltimore warehouse in November and December 1971. The witness testified with respect to the inspection of the basement of the "old building" in the warehouse complex:

We found extensive evidence of rodent infestation in the form of rat and mouse pellets throughout the entire perimeter area and along the wall. We also found that the doors leading to the basement area from the rail siding had openings at the bottom or openings beneath part of the door that came down at the bottom large enough to admit rodent entry. There were also roden[t] pellets found on a number of different packages of boxes of various items stored in the basement, and looking at this document, I see there were also broken windows along the rail siding.

On the first floor of the "old building," the inspectors found:

Thirty mouse pellets on the floor along walls and on the ledge in the hanging meat room. There were at least twenty mouse pellets beside bales of lime Jello and one of the bales had a chewed rodent hole in the product. He also related that a second inspection of the warehouse had been conducted in March 1972. On that occasion the inspectors found that there had been improvement in the sanitary conditions, but that "there was still evidence of rodent activity in the building and in the warehouses and we found some rodent-contaminated lots of food items."

The Government also presented testimony by the Chief of Compliance of the FDA's Baltimore office, who informed respondent by letter of the conditions at the Baltimore warehouse after the first inspection. The letter, dated January 27, 1972, included the following:

We note with much concern that the old and new warehouse areas used for food storage were actively and extensively inhabited by live rodents. Of even more concern was the observation that such reprehensible conditions obviously existed for a prolonged period of time without any detection, or were completely ignored. We trust this letter will serve to direct your attention to the seriousness of the problem and formally advise you of the urgent need to initiate whatever measures are necessary to prevent recurrence and ensure compliance with the law.

There was testimony by Acme's Baltimore division vice president, who had responded to the letter on behalf of Acme and respondent and who described the steps taken to remedy the insanitary conditions discovered by both inspections. The Government's final witness, Acme's vice president for legal affairs and assistant secretary, identified respondent as the president and chief executive officer of the company and read a bylaw prescribing the duties of the chief executive officer. The bylaw provided in pertinent part:

The Chairman of the board of directors or the president shall be the chief executive officer of the company as the board of directors may from time to time determine. He shall, subject to the board of directors, have general and active supervision of the affairs, business, offices and employees of the company.

He shall, from time to time, in his discretion or at the order of the board, report the operations and affairs of the company. He shall also perform such other duties and have such other powers as may be assigned to him from time to time by the board of directors.

He testified that respondent functioned by delegating "normal operating duties," including sanitation, but that he retained "certain things, which are the big, broad, principles of the operation of the company," and had "the responsibility of seeing that they all work together."

At the close of the Government's case in chief, respondent moved for a judgment of acquittal on the ground that "the evidence in chief has shown that Mr. Park is not personally concerned in this Food and Drug violation." The trial judge denied the motion. Respondent was the only defense witness. He testified that, although all of Acme's employees were in a sense under his general direction, the company had an "organizational structure for responsibilities for certain functions" according to which different phases of its operation were "assigned to individuals who, in turn, have staff and departments under them." He identified those individuals responsible for sanitation, and related that upon receipt of the January 1972 FDA letter, he had conferred with the vice president for legal affairs, who in-formed him that the Baltimore division vice president "was investigating the situation immediately and would be taking corrective action and would be preparing a summary of the corrective action to reply to the letter." Respondent stated that he did not "believe there was anything [he] could have done more constructively than what [he] found was being done."

On cross-examination, respondent conceded that providing sanitary conditions for food offered for sale to the public was something that he was "responsible for in the entire operation of the company," and he stated that it was one of many phases of the company that he assigned to "dependable subordinates." Respondent was asked about and, over the objections of his counsel, admitted receiving, the April 1970 letter addressed to him from the FDA regarding insanitary conditions at Acme's Philadelphia warehouse. The April 1970 letter informed respondent of the following "objectionable conditions" in Acme's Philadelphia warehouse:

> *1.* Potential rodent entry ways were noted via ill fitting doors and door in irrepair at Southwest corner of warehouse; at dock at old salvage room and at receiving and shipping doors which were observed to be open most of the time.
> *2.* Rodent nesting, rodent excreta pellets, rodent stained bale bagging and rodent gnawed holes were noted among bales of flour stored in warehouse.
> *3.* Potential rodent harborage was noted in discarded paper, rope, sawdust and other debris piled in corner of shipping and receiving dock near bakery and warehouse doors. Rodent excreta pellets were observed among bags of sawdust (or wood shavings).

He acknowledged that, with the exception of the division vice president, the same individuals had responsibility for sanitation in both Baltimore and Philadelphia. Finally, in response to questions concerning the Philadelphia and Baltimore incidents, respondent admitted that the Baltimore problem indicated the system for handling sanitation "wasn't working perfectly" and that as Acme's chief executive officer he was responsible for "any result which occurs in our company."

At the close of the evidence, respondent's renewed motion for a judgment of acquittal was denied. The relevant portion of the trial judge's instructions to the jury challenged by respondent ... [include]:

> In order to find the Defendant guilty on any count of the Information, you must find beyond a reasonable doubt on each count.

Thirdly, that John R. Park held a position of authority in the operation of the business of Acme Markets, Incorporated.

However, you need not concern yourselves with the first two elements of the case. The main issue for your determination is only with the third element, whether the Defendant held a position of authority and responsibility in the business of Acme Markets.

The statute makes individuals, as well as corporations, liable for violations. An individual is liable if it is clear, beyond a reasonable doubt, that the elements of the adulteration of the food as to travel in interstate commerce are present. As I have instructed you in this case, they are, and that the individual had a responsible relation to the situation, even though he may not have participated personally.

The individual is or could be liable under the statute, even if he did not consciously do wrong. However, the fact that the Defendant is pres[id]ent and is a chief executive officer of the Acme Markets does not require a finding of guilt. Though, he need not have personally participated in the situation, he must have had a responsible relationship to the issue. The issue is, in this case, whether the Defendant, John R. Park, by virtue of his position in the company, had a position of authority and responsibility in the situation out of which these charges arose. Respondent's counsel objected to the instructions on the ground that they failed ... to define "responsible relationship." The trial judge overruled the objection. The jury found respondent guilty on all counts of the information, and he was subsequently sentenced to pay a fine of $50 on each count.[14]

The Court of Appeals reversed the conviction and remanded for a new trial. That court viewed the Government as arguing "that the conviction may be predicated solely upon a showing that [respondent] was the President of the offending corporation," and it stated that as "a general proposition, some act of commission or omission is an essential element of every crime."... The Court of Appeals concluded that the trial judge's instructions "might well have left the jury with the erroneous impression that Park could be found guilty in the absence of 'wrongful action' on his part," and that proof to his element was required by due process.

OPINION

... [T]hose corporate agents vested with the responsibility, and power commensurate with that responsibility, to devise whatever measures are necessary to ensure compliance with the [Federal Food, Drug, and Cosmetic] Act [of 1938] bear a "responsible relationship" to, or have a "responsible share" in, violations.

[I]n providing sanctions which reach and touch the individuals who execute the corporate mission the Act imposes not only a positive duty to seek out and remedy violations when they occur but also, and primarily, a duty to implement measures that will insure that violations will not occur. The requirements of foresight and vigilance imposed on responsible corporate agents are beyond question demanding, and perhaps onerous, but they are no more stringent than the public has a right to expect of those who voluntarily assume positions of authority in business enterprises whose services and products affect the health and well-being of the public that supports them.

Cases under the Federal Food and Drug Act reflected the view both that knowledge or intent were not required to be proved in prosecutions under its criminal provisions, and that responsible corporate agents could be subjected to the liability thereby imposed. Moreover, the principle had been recognized that a corporate agent, through whose act, default, or omission the corporation committed a crime, was himself guilty individually of that crime. The principle had been applied whether or not the crime required "consciousness of wrongdoing," and it had been applied not only to those corporate agents who themselves committed the criminal act, but also to those who by virtue of their managerial positions or other

similar relation to the actor could be deemed responsible for its commission.

In the latter class of cases, the liability of managerial officers did not depend on their knowledge of, or personal participation in, the act made criminal by the statute. Rather, where the statute under which they were prosecuted dispensed with "consciousness of wrongdoing," all omission or failure to act was deemed a sufficient basis for a responsible corporate agent's liability. It was enough in such cases that, by virtue of the relationship he bore to the corporation, the agent had the power to prevent the act complained of.

Thus, the Court has reaffirmed the proposition that "the public interest in the purity of its food is so great as to warrant the imposition of the highest standard of care on distributors." In order to make "distributors of food the strictest censors of their merchandise," the Act punishes "neglect where the law requires care, or inaction where it imposes a duty." "The accused, if he does not will the violation, usually is in a position to prevent it with no more care than society might reasonably expect and no more exertion than it might reasonably exact from one who assumed his responsibilities."

Turning to the jury charge in this case, it is of course arguable that isolated parts can be read as intimating that a finding of guilt could be predicated solely on respondent's corporate position. But this is not the way we review jury instructions, because "a single instruction to a jury may not be judged in artificial isolation, but must be viewed in the context of the overall charge."

Reading the entire charge satisfies us that the jury's attention as adequately focused on the issue of respondent's authority with respect to the conditions that formed the basis of the alleged violations. Viewed as a whole, the charge did not permit the jury to find guilt solely on the basis of respondent's position in the corporation; rather, it fairly advised the jury that to find guilt it must find respondent "had a responsible relation to the situation," and "by virtue of his position had authority and responsibility" to deal with the situation. The situation referred to could only be "food held in unsanitary conditions in a warehouse with the result that it consisted, in part, of filth or may have been contaminated with filth."

[The evidence showed that] respondent was on notice that he could not rely on his system of delegation to subordinates to prevent or correct insanitary conditions at Acme's warehouses, and that he must have been aware of the deficiencies of this system before the Baltimore violations were discovered. The evidence was therefore relevant since it served to rebut respondent's defense that he had justifiably relied upon subordinates to handle sanitation matters.

Affirmed.

Case Discussion

The Park case tries to resolve the very difficult issue of just how far individual vicarious liability for corporate crime extends, particularly when the officer does not intend to commit crimes and did not act directly to violate the law. Park was the corporation president and was generally responsible for the corporation's operation. But was he responsible for keeping rats out of the corporation's warehouses? Did the court base Park's individual liability merely on his position in the company or on something he did or failed to do? In other words, is this a status offense, or is it liability based on conduct? If liability is based on conduct and not on status, was Park reckless or negligent with respect to the rats in the warehouse? Or was he strictly liable for the contamination? If keeping foods pure is so important, why did the trial court fine Park only $250? And why did he appeal his case all the way to the United States Supreme Court? Why was so much made of a $250 fine?

▼ *Summary* ▼

Several persons may participate before, during, and after committing crimes. The doctrine of complicity defines the extent to which criminal liability attaches to these parties to crime. The common-law doctrine of complicity recognized four categories of participants: (1) principals in the first degree, (2) principals in the second degree, (3) accessories before the fact, and (4) accessories after the fact. Modern statutes have merged complicity before and during crime into one category—accomplices—while retaining the category of accessory after the fact. Accomplices are equally liable for the principal crime; accessories after the fact are liable for separate, lesser offenses.

Accomplice and accessory liability rest upon *participation*. The doctrine of complicity also includes liability based on *relationships* without participation. Vicarious liability applies to those who have not participated but whose relationship with actors justifies criminal sanction. Business relationships—employer-employee, principal-agent, and corporation-management—most commonly give rise to vicarious criminal liability. However, states have occasionally imposed vicarious liability on parents for minor children and on owners of cars for those who drive them. Vicarious liability may be strict, in which case the vicariously liable party lacks both *actus reus* and *mens rea*. Penalties for vicarious strict liability are limited to fines.

Vicarious liability also extends to crimes requiring a *mens rea,* in which case the actor's conduct is imputed to the vicariously liable party. In real crimes, the law requires culpability. To convict, the prosecution must prove several elements, including the following: (1) the acts are done for the company's benefit, not for personal profit; (2) the acts are within the scope of the actor's authority; and (3) the acts are attibutable to officers high in the organization. Culpability might vary from purposeful to recklessness and even negligence, covering everything from participation, approval, and encouragement to "recklessly tolerating." Once these conditions are satisfied, business enterprises can—at least in theory—be prosecuted for any crime, including murder. Hence, high officers can be criminally liable for, and can make their corporations criminally liable for, criminal conduct that benefits the business enterprises they head.

▼ Questions for Review and Discussion ▼

1. Define complicity. Distinguish between common-law and statutory complicity.

2. Distinguish accomplices from accessories under modern law. Should accomplices receive harsher punishment than accessories? Defend your answer.

3. How do accomplices, accessories, and vicariously liable parties differ from each other?

4. What is vicarious strict liability? Give the arguments in favor of and against it.

5. In what sense are corporate officers a corporation's brain?

6. Who in the corporate structure should be punished for corporate crimes?

7. What *mens rea* should business crime require? Should it be the same for all crimes committed for the company's benefit?

▼ Suggested Readings ▼

1. George P. Fletcher, *Rethinking Criminal Law* (Boston: Little, Brown, 1978), pp. 131–205, 218–32. This work contains provocative discussions about complicity. Professor Fletcher clearly defines the complicity in considerable detail. He also assesses participation in crime in ways that provoke considerable thought about the role of those terms in criminal law.

2. American Law Institute, *Model Penal Code and Commentaries,* vol. 1 (Philadelphia: American Law Institute, 1985), pt. 1, pp. 295–348. A detailed analysis of all elements in complicity and vicarious liability, especially of corporations, as well as arguments why these should be included in criminal law and to what extent participants should be criminally liable. This is an advanced discussion written for experts in the field but is well worth the effort to read and consider its points.

3. Rollin M. Perkins and Ronald N. Boyce, *Criminal Law,* 3d ed. (Mineola, N.Y.: Foundation Press, 1982), pp. 718–20, 911–22. The authors discuss vicarious liability and corporate crime in some detail. They also provide a brief history of how these arose.

4. John Monahan, Raymond W. Novaco, and Gilbert Geis, "Corporate Violence: Research Strategies for Community Psychology," in *Challenges to the Criminal Justice System,* ed. Theodore R. Sarbin and Daniel Adelson (New York: Human Sciences Press, 1979), pp. 117–41. An excellent, clearly written, and easy-to-understand discussion of corporate violence. It defines and describes corporate violence, and includes a thorough bibliography for those who wish to read further.

▼ *Notes* ▼

1. American Law Institute, *Model Penal Code and Commentaries* (Philadelphia: American Law Institute, 1985), pp. 299–301.

2. United States v. Peoni, 100 F.2d 401 (2d. Cir. 1938).

3. United States v. Greer, 467 F.2d 1064 (7th Cir. 1972).

4. Model Penal Code, tentative draft no. 1, p. 43 (1953); *State v. Spillman,* 105 Ariz. 523, 468 P.2d 376 (1970); Wayne LaFave and Arthur Scott, *Criminal Law* (St. Paul: West Publishing Co., 1972), p. 504.

5. 306 N.C. 466, 293 S.E.2d 780 (1982).

6. 20 Mich. App. 132, 173 N.W.2d 732 (1969).

7. Brian Fisse, "Sanctions against Corporations: Economic Efficiency or Legal Efficacy?" in Groves and Newman, *Punishment and Privilege,* pp. 23–54.

8. Commonwealth v. Koczwara, 397 Pa. 575, 155 A.2d 825 (1959); *Davis v. Peachtree,* 251 Ga. 219, 304 S.E.2d 701 (1983).

9. Marshall B. Clinard and Richard Quinney, *Criminal Behavior Systems,* 2d ed. (Cincinnati: Anderson, 1986), chap. 7–8.

10. U.S. Congress, House Subcommittee on the Judiciary, *Hearings before the Subcommittee on White Collar Crime,* 95th Cong., 2d sess., June 21, July 12, and December 1, 1978 (Washington, D.C.: U.S. Government Printing Office, 1979).

11. Commonwealth v. Koczwara, 397 Pa. 575, 155 A.2d 825, 827 (1959).

12. American Law Institute, *Model Penal Code and Commentaries,* vol. 1, pt. 1, pp. 335–41.

13. § 402 of the act, 21 U.S.C.; § 342, provides in pertinent part: "A food shall be deemed to be adulterated (a) (3) if it consists in whole or in part of any filthy, putrid, or decomposed substance, or if it is otherwise unfit for food; or (4) if it has been prepared, packed or held under insanitary conditions whereby it may have become contaminated with filth, or whereby it may have been rendered injurious to health." § 301 of the act, 21 U.S.C. § 331, provides in pertinent part: "The following acts and the causing thereof are prohibited: (k) The alteration, mutilation, destruction, obliteration, or removal of the whole or any part of the labeling of, or the doing of any other act with respect to, a food, drug, device, or cosmetic, if such act is done while such article is held for sale (whether or not the first sale) after shipment in interstate commerce and results in such article being adulterated or misbranded."

14. § 303(a) and (b) of the act, 21 U.S.C. §§ 333(a) and (b), provide:

> (a) Any person who violates a provision of § 331 of this title shall be imprisoned for not more than one year or fined not more than $1,000, or both.
> (b) Notwithstanding the provisions of subsection (a) of this section, if any person commits such a violation after a conviction of him under this section has become final, or commits such a violation with the intent to defraud or mislead, such person shall be imprisoned for not more than three years or fined not more than $10,000, or both.

Chapter
5

Uncompleted Crimes: Attempt, Solicitation, and Conspiracy

▼ *Chapter Outline* ▼

I. Introduction

II. Attempt
   A. Rationale of Attempt Law
   B. Material Elements in Attempt
   C. Attempt *Mens Rea*
   D. Attempt *Actus Reus*
   E. Legal and Factual Impossibility
   F. Renunciation
   G. Summary of Attempt

III. Conspiracy
   A. Material Elements in Conspiracy
   B. Conspiracy *Actus Reus*
   C. Conspiracy *Mens Rea*
   D. The Objective of Conspiracy
   E. Parties to Conspiracy
   F. Summary of Conspiracy

IV. Solicitation

V. Summary

1. The doctrine of inchoate offenses imposes criminal liability on those who intend to commit crimes and take some steps toward completing the crimes.

2. The principal inchoate crimes are attempt, conspiracy, and solicitation.

3. Attempts to commit crimes stand closest, conspiracies are further removed, and solicitations are most remote from completed crimes.

4. The inchoate offenses require the highest culpability—specific intent—to offset the corresponding absence of harm.

5. According to attempt doctrine, those bent on committing crimes should not benefit from a fortuity that interrupts their purpose.

6. Attempt requires a specific intent to commit a crime, steps to commit the crime, and ordinarily, a failure to complete the commission.

7. Voluntary abandonment sometimes removes criminal liability for attempt.

8. Legal impossibility is a defense to attempt.

9. Factual impossibility is not a defense to attempt.

10. Conspiracy requires an agreement or combination entered into for the specific purpose of committing an unlawful act or of committing a lawful act by unlawful means.

11. Solicitation requires the specific intent to induce another to commit a crime accompanied by action urging the other person to commit the crime.

▼ *Chapter Key Terms* ▼

equivocality approach—The theory that attempt *actus reus* requires an act that can have no other purpose than the commission of a crime.

extraneous factor—A condition beyond the attempter's control.

factual impossibility—The defense that facts make it impossible to complete a crime.

inchoate crimes—Offenses based on crimes not yet completed.

legal impossibility—The defense that what the actor attempted was not a crime.

Model Penal Code standard—The precept that attempt *actus reus*

requires substantial steps that strongly corroborate the actor's purpose.

physical proximity doctrine—The principle that the number of remaining acts in attempt determines attempt *actus reus*.

probable desistance approach—Whether the act in attempt would naturally lead to the commission of the crime.

Wharton rule—The principle that more than two parties must conspire to commit crimes that naturally involve at least two parties.

M.C.L.A
750.92

▼ INTRODUCTION

Criminal law punishes not only completed crimes but also conduct that requires further action to result in crime. Reckless endangerment (such as reckless driving), possession (see chapter 3), burglary (see chapter 10), and driving while intoxicated (chapter 12) are crimes even though they require further actions to culminate in intended conduct or harm. Reckless driving, or driving while intoxicated are crimes even if the driver injures no one; possessing a bomb may be a crime even though it does no harm until the bomb explodes; and burglary consists of breaking and entering with the *intent* to commit a crime. The doctrine of **inchoate crimes** applies specifically to three crimes: attempt, conspiracy, and solicitation. According to the doctrine, it is a separate offense to attempt, conspire to commit, or solicit another person to commit a crime. Each inchoate offense has its own features, but they share in common a criminal purpose combined with some action short of fulfilling that purpose. Incomplete criminal conduct poses a dilemma: whether to punish someone who has harmed no one or to set free someone determined to commit a crime. The criminal law resolves the dilemma by imposing lesser penalties for inchoate offenses than for completed harms that have been attempted, conspired, or solicited.[1]

▼ ATTEMPT

Failure is, although unwelcome, an ordinary phenomenon. Criminal attempt is about failure under extraordinary circumstances: shooting at someone and missing the target; holding up a 7-Eleven and discovering no money in the cash register; reaching for a CD to put under your coat and having a store detective catch you. The place of attempt in criminal law has plagued lawmakers, judges, and philosophers for centuries. In *Laws,* Plato wrote that one who

> has a purpose and intention to slay another and he [merely] wounds him should be regarded as a murderer.[2]

But, he added, the law should punish such wounding less than it would murder. In the thirteenth century, the great English jurist Bracton disagreed: "For what harm did the attempt cause, since the injury took no effect?" By the next century, English judges were applying what became a famous common-law maxim: "The will shall be taken for the deed." Justice Shardlowe held:

> One who is taken in the act of robbery or burglary, even though he does not carry it out, will be hanged.[3]

Common-law attempt meant more than the mere intention to harm: "The thoughts of man shall not be tried, for the devil himself knoweth not the thought of man." The early cases required that both substantial acts and harm accompany the intent. The two leading cases involved a servant who, after cutting his master's throat, fled with the latter's goods, and a wife's lover who attacked and seriously injured her husband, leaving him for dead. The servant and the lover were punished for attempted murder; both had taken substantial steps toward completing the crime and had substantially harmed their victims.[4]

By the sixteenth century, criminal attempt began to resemble its modern counterpart. Responding to dangers threatening peace and safety in a society known for its hot, short tempers and its violent, quarrelsome tendencies, the English Court of Star Chamber punished wide-ranging potential harms, hoping to nip violence in the bud. Typical cases included "lying in wait," threats, challenges, and even "words tending to challenge." Local records are replete with efforts to punish incipient violence.[5]

By the early seventeenth century, an attempt doctrine was emerging. Stressing a need to prevent serious harms in dueling, Francis Bacon maintained that "all the acts of preparation should be punished." He then went on to argue for adopting the following criminal attempt principle:

> I take it to be a ground infallible: that wheresoever an offense is capital, or matter of felony, though it be not acted, there the combination or acting tending to the offense is punishable.... Nay, inceptions and preparations in inferior crimes, that are not capital have likewise been condemned.[6]

As this brief historical sketch shows, the law has punished incomplete crimes since the sixteenth century, albeit at first without a clear attempt doctrine. Since the seventeenth century, a formal attempt doctrine has governed attempt cases. Not until the late eighteenth century, however, did the English courts adopt a general inchoate offense doctrine. In *Rex v. Scofield,* a servant put a lighted candle in his master's house, intending to burn the house down. The house did not burn, but the servant suffered punishment for attempt nevertheless. The court held:

The intent may make an act, innocent in itself, criminal; nor is the completion of an act, criminal in itself, necessary to constitute criminality.[7]

By the nineteenth century, common-law attempt was well defined:

[A]ll attempts whatever to commit indictable offenses, whether felonies or misdemeanors, and whether, if misdemeanors they are so by statute or at common law, are misdemeanors, unless by some special statutory enactment they are subjected to special punishment.[8]

Some jurisdictions retain the common law of attempt today. According to one recent case, "the common law is still alive and well in Maryland," and the common law of attempt, the Maryland Supreme Court held, "still prospers on these shores."[9]

Rationale of Attempt Law

Two rationales underlie criminal attempt doctrine. One focuses on *actus reus,* the objective dimension to criminal liability, justifying the punishment of attempts because it controls dangerous *conduct*. The other focuses on *mens rea,* the subjective element, justifying punishment because it controls dangerous *persons*. Jurisdictions adopting the dangerous conduct rationale focus on how close the actor came to completing the crime. The dangerous person rationale aims as curbing persons determined to commit crimes. It concentrates not on how close actors came to completing their plans, but on how fully actors have developed their criminal designs. Both rationales measure dangerousness according to actions: the dangerous conduct rationale does so to determine proximity to completion, the dangerous person rationale to gauge developed design.[10]

Material Elements in Attempt

Common-law attempt consisted of an intent to carry out an act or bring about certain consequences that amounted to a crime, coupled with an act beyond mere preparation, in furtherance of that intent.[11]

The material elements of attempt include (1) an intent (or purpose) to commit a crime, (2) some overt act or acts in pursuance of the intention, and in most jurisdictions, (3) a failure to consummate the crime. Some jurisdictions make criminal an actor's attempts to commit any crime; others restrict the crimes that actors can criminally attempt to commit, either by eliminating specific categories or by listing specific crimes.[12]

Material Elements in Attempt		
Actus Reus	**Mens Rea**	**Result**
1. all but the last act, or *2.* substantial steps beyond preparation	specific intent	failure to complete crime in most jurisdictions

Attempt **Mens Rea**

Attempt is a crime of purpose; it requires specific intent. There are no reckless, negligent, or strict liability attempts. However, knowledge, recklessness, or negligence concerning material circumstances can support attempt. For example, if I try to kill someone whom I should know is an FBI agent, I have attempted to kill a law enforcement officer, even though I have been only negligent concerning the material circumstance that the intended victim was an FBI agent.

According to one authority:

> To attempt something ... necessarily means to seek to do it, to make a deliberate effort in that direction. Intent is inherent in the notion of attempt; it is the essence of the crime. An attempt without intent is unthinkable; it cannot be.[13]

Holmes, in his classic treatise on the common law, criticized this view:

> Acts should be judged by their tendency, under the known circumstances, not by the actual intent which accompanies them. It may be true that in the region of attempts, as elsewhere, the law began with cases of actual intent, as these cases were the most obvious ones. But it cannot stop with them, unless it attaches more importance to the etymological meaning of the word *attempt* than to the general principles of punishment.[14]

Despite Holmes's view, specific intent remains central to the crime of attempt.

CASE

Did He Intend to Rob the Convenience Store?

People v. **Kimball**

311 N.W.2d 343 (Mich.App.1981)

Maher, Judge

"Defendant was charged with and convicted of attempted unarmed robbery, M.C.L. § 750.530; M.S.A. § 28.798, M.C.L. § 750.92; M.S.A. § 28.287, at a bench trial conducted in early August of 1979. He was sentenced to a prison term of from 3 to 5 years and appeals by leave granted. There is really very little dispute as to what happened on May 21, 1979, at the Alpine Party Store near Suttons Bay, Michigan. Instead, the dispute at trial centered on whether what took place

amounted to a criminal offense or merely a bad joke."

FACTS

It appears that on the day in question the defendant went to the home of a friend, Sandra Storey, where he proceeded to consume a large amount of vodka mixed with orange juice. Defendant was still suffering from insect stings acquired the previous day so he also took a pill called "Eskaleth 300," containing 300 milligrams of Lithium, which Storey had given him. After about an hour, the pair each mixed a half-gallon container of their favorite drinks (vodka and orange juice, in the defendant's case), and set off down the road in Storey's '74 MGB roadster.

At approximately 8:15 or 8:30 in the evening, defendant (who was driving) pulled into the parking lot of the Alpine Party Store. Although he apparently did not tell Storey why he pulled in, defendant testified that the reason for the stop was to buy a pack of cigarettes. Concerning events inside the store, testimony was presented by Susan Stanchfield, the clerk and sole employee present at the time. She testified that defendant came in and began talking to and whistling at the Doberman Pinscher guard dog on duty at the time. She gave him a "dirty look," because she didn't want him playing with the dog. Defendant then approached the cash register, where Stanchfield was stationed, and demanded money.

Stanchfield testified that she thought the defendant was joking, and told him so, until he demanded money again in a "firmer tone."

STANCHFIELD: "By his tone I knew he meant business; that he wanted the money."

PROSECUTION: "You felt he was serious?

STANCHFIELD: "I knew he was serious."

Stanchfield then began fumbling with the one dollar bills until defendant directed her to the "big bills." Stanchfield testified that as she was separating the checks from the twenty dollar bills defendant said "I won't do it to you; you're good looking and I won't do it to you this time, but if you're here next time, it won't matter."

A woman then came in (Storey) who put a hand on defendant's shoulder and another on his stomach and directed him out of the store. Stanchfield testified that she called after the defendant, saying that she would not call the police if he would "swear never to show your face around here again." To this defendant is alleged to have responded: "You could only get me on attempted anyway." Stanchfield then directed a customer to get the license plate number on defendant's car while she phoned the owner of the store.

Defendant also testified concerning events inside the store. He stated that the first thing he noticed when he walked in the door was the Doberman Pinscher. When he whistled the dog came to him and started licking his hand. Defendant testified that while he was petting the dog Stanchfield said "[w]atch out for the dog; he's trained to protect the premises."

DEFENDANT: "Well, as soon as she told me that the dog was a watchdog and a guard-dog [sic], I just walked up in front of the cash register and said to Sue (Stanchfield) I said, 'I want your money.'

"I was really loaded and it just seemed to me like it was kind of a cliché because of the fact that they've got this big bad watchdog there that's supposed to watch the place and there I was just petting it, and it was kind of an open door to carry it a little further and say hey, I want all your money because this dog isn't going to protect you. It just kind of happened all at once."

"She said I can't quote it, but something to the effect that if this is just a joke, it's a bad joke, and I said, 'Just give me your big bills.'

"Then she started fumbling in the drawer, and before she pulled any money out of the drawer I don't know whether she went to the ones or the twenties I said as soon as she went toward the drawer to actually give me the money, I said, 'Hey, I'm just kidding,' and something to the effect that you're too good-looking to take your money.

"[A]nd she said, 'Well, if you leave right now and don't ever come back, I won't call the police,' and I said, 'Okay, okay,' and I started to back up.

"[A]nd Sandy (Storey) I mean I don't know if I was stumbling back or stepping back, but I know she grabbed me, my arm, and said, 'Let's go,' and we turned around and left, and that was it."

Both Stanchfield and the defendant testified that there were other people in the store during the time that defendant was in the store, but the testimony of these people revealed that they did not hear what was said between Stanchfield and the defendant.

Storey testified that she remained in the car while defendant went into the store but that after waiting a reasonable time she went inside to see what was happening. As she approached the defendant she heard Stanchfield say "just promise you will never do that again and I won't take your license number." She then took defendant's arm, turned around, gave Stanchfield an "apologetic smile," and took defendant back to the car. Once in the car, defendant told Storey what had happened in the store, saying "but I told her (Stanchfield) I was only kidding." Defendant and Storey then drove to a shopping center where defendant was subsequently arrested.

OPINION

The general attempt statute, under which defendant was prosecuted, provides in part as follows: "Any person who shall attempt to commit an offense prohibited by law, and in such attempt shall do any act towards the commission of such offense, but shall fail in the perpetration, or shall be intercepted or prevented in the execution of the same, when no express provision is made by law for the punishment of such attempt, shall be punished...."

The elements of an attempt are (1) the specific intent to commit the crime attempt-

ed and (2) an overt act going beyond mere preparation towards the commission of the crime. Considering the second element first, it is clear that in the instant case defendant committed sufficient overt acts. As the trial court noted, there was evidence on every element of an unarmed robbery except for the actual taking of money. From the evidence presented, including the evidence of defendant's intoxication, the question of whether defendant undertook these acts with the specific intent to commit an unarmed robbery is a much closer question. After hearing all the evidence, however, the trial court found that defendant possessed the requisite intent and we do not believe that finding was clearly erroneous.

Reversed on other grounds.

Case Discussion If you were a juror and heard the testimony of Kimball and Stanchfield, who would you believe? Has the prosecution proved the *mens rea* beyond a reasonable doubt? What in the testimony of each specifically bears on Kimball's *mens rea?* Did he have the specific intent to rob the store? Is the answer as clear as the court believes? Why? Why not?

Note Cases *1.* Thacker shot a gun through a tent, intending to "shoot the light out." The shot passed through the tent. People were inside the tent at the time Thacker fired the shot. A bullet hit the bed, barely missing the heads of a woman and her baby who were lying on the bed. Did Thacker attempt to murder them? The Virginia supreme court said no, because Thacker lacked the specific intent to kill. He intended to put the light out, not to kill the woman and her baby. *Thacker v. Commonwealth,* 114 S.E. 504 (Va.1922)

2. Robert and his mother were visiting Johnnie Shields' apartment. Robert got drunk and fell, breaking a table. Some time after Robert and his mother returned to their apartment (which was next door to Johnnie Shields'), Johnnie appeared at Robert's door with a gun, threatening to kill him. Robert and his mother fled the apartment; Johnnie chased them. Outside, Robert's mother stood in front of Robert to shield him. Johnnie told her to step aside or he "would blow her brains out." After a scuffle over possession of the gun, Johnnie fired, wounding her. Did he attempt to murder her? The trial court instructed the jury that they could find Johnnie guilty of murder if they believed that he intended to kill *or cause great bodily harm.* The jury found him guilty. The Illinois Supreme Court reversed, holding that attempted murder required the specific intent to kill and did not include the alternative intent to cause great bodily harm. *People v. Shields,* 377 N.E.2d 28 (1978)

Attempt Actus Reus

Criminal attempt does not require completed crime, but most agree that mere preparation does not constitute criminal attempt. Hence, if I sit in my armchair at home, plotting to buy a gun and kill my enemy, but before leaving my chair I decide against it, I am committing no crime. Attempt law must determine at which point on the spectrum between mere intention and ultimate harm a crime has taken place.[15]

Attempt law requires action or steps beyond preparation to constitute attempt, but jurisdictions vary in distinguishing preparation and attempt. Some states require "some steps." At the other extreme, a few states demand "all but the last act." Most states, along with the Model Penal Code, require "substantial steps" toward completing the crime. Under all three tests, if I stand over my enemy on the verge of pulling the trigger, I am attempting murder. Most jurisdictions require considerably less. But how much less? If I leave my house only to buy a handgun to do the job, I am merely preparing to murder my enemy. Courts distinguish mere preparation from criminal attempt according to: (1) the **physical proximity doctrine,** (2) the **probable desistance approach,** (3) the **equivocality approach,** and (4) the **Model Penal Code standard.**

Physical proximity emphasizes time, space, and the number of necessary acts—the acts remaining to complete the crime. The easiest point to justify criminal liability is when the attempter has taken all but the last act necessary to commit the crime. This was the test the court used in *Commonwealth v. Peaslee* to reverse an attempted arson case; the court reversed Peaslee's conviction because Peaslee, "the would-be criminal," had not "done his last act." This rule is easy to apply but it insulates much dangerous conduct from criminal liability. Physical proximity looks to dangerous conduct, not dangerous actors; according to the physical proximity doctrine, the criminal law punishes conduct when it reaches a "dangerous proximity to success." Great importance, therefore, attaches to how close the actor's conduct is to the intended crime. The physical proximity doctrine does not answer "how close is close enough for attempt liability."[16]

The probable desistance approach considers whether an act in the ordinary course of events would lead to the commission of the crime but for some timely interference. Acts must pass the point where ordinary law-abiding citizens would think better of what they are about to do, and desist from going further. The equivocality approach distinguishes preparation from attempt *actus reus* when the act can have no other purpose than committing the crime intended.

The Model Penal Code approach requires "substantial steps" to corroborate intent. In contrast to the proximity doctrines, the code focuses on neutralizing dangerous persons. Key phrases of the code include "substantial step in a course of conduct planned to culminate in his [the actor's] commission of the crime" and "strongly corroborative of the actor's criminal purpose." Substantial steps corroborate the *mens rea*. In other words, the code requires sufficient steps toward completing the crime, not because such steps show that harms are about to occur but to prove that attempters intend to commit crimes. "Substantial steps" defines attempt *actus reus* vaguely.

The drafters of the code argue that the provision definitely improves the proximity doctrines in the following respects: (1) It emphasizes already completed conduct, not what remains to do in order to complete the crime. (2) It reduces *mens rea* difficulties. (3) It removes "very remote preparatory acts" from criminal liability. (4) It brings persons whose behavior manifests dangerousness within the ambit of criminal law. (5) It illustrates actions that amount to substantial steps, such as lying in wait, searching and following, enticing, reconnoitering, entering unlawfully, possessing incriminating materials, and soliciting innocent agents.[17]

According to drafters of the code, lying in wait and searching and following satisfy *actus reus.* Many jurisdictions, however, consider these actions mere preparation. In *People v. Rizzo,* for example, the court ruled that searching for a victim to rob was preparation. Some states, such as Louisiana, consider lying in wait, or searching and following, attempts only if they occur while actors are armed.

Borrowing from indecent liberties statutes, which make it a crime to lure minors into cars or houses for sex, the Model Penal Code makes enticement an *actus reus.* In defending their position, the drafters note that enticement demonstrates a firm purpose to commit a crime; hence, enticers are sufficiently dangerous to deserve punishment.[18]

The code includes reconnoitering—popularly called "casing a joint"—within the scope of attempted *actus reus,* because "scouting the scene of a contemplated crime" sufficiently demonstrates a firm criminal purpose. Unlawful intruders also demonstrate their criminal purpose. Including unlawful entry within attempt relieves burglary from pressures to cover more than it rationally ought to (see chapter 10). The unlawful entry provision particularly helps two types of cases: entries to commit sexual abuse and entries to commit larceny. In one case, two defendants entered a car intending to steal it, but they got out when the owner returned. The court ruled that the defendants had not attempted to steal the car. Under the Model Penal Code provision, however, they committed unlawful entry for a criminal purpose.[19]

Under existing law, collecting, possessing, or preparing materials used to commit crimes is preparation, not attempt. Hence, courts have found that buying a gun to murder someone, making a bomb to blow up a house, and collecting tools for a burglary are preparations, not attempts. Many jurisdictions, however, make it a crime to possess designated items and substances such as burglary tools, illegal drugs, drug paraphernalia, and concealed weapons. The Model Penal Code provision makes such possessions criminal only if they strongly corroborate a purpose to commit a crime. The drafters of the code concluded that people who carry weapons and burglary tools with the clear intent to commit crimes are dangerous enough to punish.[20]

The Model Penal Code also includes bringing weapons, equipment, and other materials to the scene of a crime, and intending to commit crimes with them. Examples are bringing guns to a robbery, explosives to an arson, a ladder to a burglary. The code posits that such "bringing" constitutes a substantial step, not mere preparation, in committing a crime. The drafters contend that actors demonstrate a firm purpose to commit crimes if materials are so plainly instrumentalities that their possession constitutes a sufficient, substantial step toward completing the crime. A potential robber who takes a gun to a bank clearly falls within its scope; a would-be forger who takes a fountain pen into a bank does not. Acquiring these items alone does not suffice; attempters who bring them to the contemplated crime scene are sufficiently dangerous to punish.[21]

Preparation is not criminal attempt, but some jurisdictions make specified preparations separate, less serious, inchoate offenses. In Nevada, for example, preparing to commit arson is a crime. In some jurisdictions it is a crime to prepare to manufacture illegal liquor. These statutes balance the degree of threatening behavior and the dangerousness of persons against the remoteness in time and place of the intended harm.[22]

CASE

Did He Take Substantial Steps toward Robbing the Bank?

Young v. State
303 Md. 298, 493 A.2d 352 (1985)

Orth, Judge

Young was convicted of attempted armed robbery and sentenced to 20 years in prison. He appealed.

FACTS

… Several banks … had been held up…. In the early afternoon of 26 November 1982 the police … observed Young driving an automobile in such a manner as to give rise to a reasonable belief that he was casing several banks. They followed him in his reconnoitering. At one point when he left his car to enter a store, he was seen to clip a scanner onto his belt. The scanner later proved to contain an operable crystal number frequency that would receive Prince George's County uniform patrol transmissions. At that time Young was dressed in a brown waist-length jacket and wore sunglasses.

Around 2:00 p.m. Young came to rest at the rear of the Fort Washington branch of the First National Bank of Southern Maryland. Shortly before, he had driven past the front of the Bank and had parked in the rear of it for a brief time. He got out of his car and walked hurriedly beside the Bank toward the front door. He was still wearing the brown waist-length jacket and sunglass-

es, but he had added a blue knit stocking cap pulled down to the top of the sunglasses, white gloves and a black eye-patch. His jacket collar was turned up. His right hand was in his jacket pocket and his left hand was in front of his face. As one of the police officers observing him put it, he was sort of "duck[ing] his head."

It was shortly after 2:00 p.m. and the Bank had just closed. Through the windows of his office the Bank Manager saw Young walking on the "landscape" by the side of the Bank toward the front door. Young had his right hand in his jacket pocket and tried to open the front door with his left hand. When he realized that the door was locked and the Bank was closed, he retraced his steps, running past the windows with his left hand covering his face. The Bank Manager had an employee call the police.

Young ran back to his car, yanked open the door, got in, and put the car in drive "all in one movement almost," and drove away. The police stopped the car and ordered Young to get out. Young was in the process of removing his jacket…. The butt of what proved to be a loaded .22 caliber revolver was sticking out of the right pocket of his jacket. On the front seat of the car were a pair of white surgical gloves, a black-eye patch, a blue knit stocking cap, and a pair of sunglasses. Young told the police that his name was Morris P. Cunningham. As Young was being taken from the scene, he asked "how much time you could get for attempted robbery."

OPINION

The determination of the overt act which is beyond mere preparation in furtherance of the commission of the intended crime is a most significant aspect of criminal attempts. If an attempt is to be a culpable offense serving as the basis for the furtherance of the important societal interests of crime prevention and the correction of those persons who have sufficiently manifested their dangerousness, the police must be able to ascertain with reasonable assurance when it is proper for them to intervene. It is not enough to say merely that there must be "some overt act beyond mere preparation in furtherance of the crime" as the general definition puts it.

It is true that this definition is in line with the observation of Justice Holmes that

> [i]ntent to commit a crime is not itself criminal. There is no law against a man's intending to commit a murder the day after tomorrow. The law deals only with conduct. An attempt is an overt act. O. Holmes, The Common Law 65 (1923)....

What act will suffice to show that an attempt itself has reached the stage of a completed crime has persistently troubled the courts. They have applied a number of approaches in order to determine when preparation for the commission of a crime has ceased and the actual attempt to commit it has begun. It is at the point when preparation has been completed and perpetration of the intended crime has started that a criminal attempt has been committed and culpability for that misdemeanor attaches....

[Here the court defines the proximity, probable desistance, the equivocality, and Model Penal Code approaches.]

We believe that the preferable approach is one bottomed on the "substantial step" test as is that of Model Penal Code. We think that using a "substantial step" as the criterion in determining whether an overt act is more than mere preparation to commit a crime is clearer, sounder, more practical and easier to apply to the multitude of differing fact situations which may occur....

We are by no means alone in the belief that an approach based on the substantial step is superior. This belief was shared by the Commission which drafted a proposed criminal code for this State following the Model Penal Code approach with respect to criminal attempts. Courts in eight of the federal circuits and courts or legislatures in 23 states also share This belief.... [Here the court adopts and reproduces the Model Penal Code provision, except for] the elimination of failure as a necessary element....

When the facts and circumstances of [this] ... case are considered in the light of the overt act standard which we have adopted, it is perfectly clear that the evidence was sufficient to prove that Young attempted the crime of armed robbery as charged. As we have seen, the police did not arrive on the scene after the fact. They had the advantage of having Young under observation for some time before his apprehension. They watched his preparations. They were with him when he reconnoitered or cased the banks. His observations of the banks were in a manner not usual for law-abiding individuals and were under circumstances that warranted alarm for the safety of persons or property.

Young manifestly endeavored to conceal his presence by parking behind the Bank which he had apparently selected to rob. He distinguished himself with an eyepatch and made an identification of him difficult by turning up his jacket collar and by donning sunglasses and a knit cap which he pulled down over his forehead. He put on rubber surgical gloves. Clipped on his belt was a scanner with a police band frequency. Except for the scanner, which he had placed on his belt while casing the Bank, all this was done immediately before he left his car and approached the door of the Bank.

As he walked towards the Bank he partially hid his face behind his left hand and ducked his head. He kept his right hand in the pocket of his jacket in which, as subsequent events established, he was carrying, concealed, a loaded handgun, for which he had no lawful use or right to transport. He walked to the front door of the Bank and tried to enter the premises.

When he discovered that the door was locked, he ran back to his car, again partially concealing his face with his left hand. He got in his car and immediately drove away. He removed the knit hat, sunglasses, eyepatch and gloves, and placed the scanner over the sun visor of the car. When apprehended, he was trying to take off his jacket. His question as to how much time he could get for attempted bank robbery was not without significance.

It is clear that the evidence which showed Young's conduct leading to his apprehension established that he performed the necessary overt act towards the commission of armed robbery, which was more than mere preparation. Even if we assume that all of Young's conduct before he approached the door of the Bank was mere preparation, on the evidence, the jury could properly find as a fact that when Young tried to open the bank door to enter the premises, that act constituted a "substantial step" toward the commission of the intended crime. It was strongly corroborative of his criminal intention.

One of the reasons why the substantial step approach has received such widespread favor is because it usually enables the police to intervene at an earlier stage than do the other approaches. In this case, however, the requisite overt act came near the end of the line. Indeed, it would qualify as the necessary act under any of the approaches—the proximity approach, the probable desistance approach or the equivocality approach. It clearly met the requirements of the substantial step approach.

Since Young, as a matter of fact, could be found by the jury to have performed an overt act which was more than mere preparation, and was a substantial step towards the commission of the intended crime of armed robbery, it follows as a matter of law that he committed the offense of criminal attempt.

We think that the evidence adduced showed directly, or circumstantially, or supported a rational inference of, the facts to be proved from which the jury could fairly be convinced, beyond a reasonable doubt, of Young's guilt of attempted armed robbery as charged. Therefore, the evidence was sufficient in law to sustain the conviction. We so hold. Judgments of the Court of Special Appeals affirmed; costs to be paid by appellant.

Case Discussion   Identify the relevant facts in the case to determine *actus reus*. What four tests does the court outline to determine whether they constitute the *actus reus* of attempted armed robbery? What reasons does the court give for adopting the Model Penal Code standard? Do you agree that it is the best test of attempt *actus reus?* If you were deciding this case, what test would you adopt? According to your test, did Young attempt an armed robbery? At what point did preparation become attempt? Defend your position.

Note Cases   1. On 21 September 1976, at Dallas State Correctional Institution, a guard discovered that the bars of the window in Gilliam's cell had been cut and were being held in place by sticks and paper. The condition of the bars was such that they could be removed manually at will. The same guard observed that a shelf hook was missing from its place in the cell. A subsequent search revealed visegrips concealed inside appellant's mattress, and two knotted extension cords attached to a hook were found in a box of clothing. At trial, evidence showed that the hook had been fashioned from the missing shelf hook. The visegrips were capable of cutting barbed wire of the type located along the top of the fence that was the sole barrier between appellant's cell window and the perimeter of the prison compound. Inspection of the cell immediately before it was assigned to Gilliam as its sole occupant had disclosed bars intact and the shelf hooks in place.

Did Gilliam commit the crime of attempted escape? The court said yes, because Gilliam had taken substantial steps by not only gathering the tools for his escape but also sawing through the bars. According to the court, the substantial step test

> broadens the scope of attempt liability by concentrating on the acts the defendant has done and does not ... focus on the acts remaining to be done before actual commission of the crime. *Commonwealth v. Gilliam,* 273 Pa. Super. 586, 417 A.2d 1203 (1980)

2. In *People v. Rizzo,* Rizzo and his cohorts were driving through Boston looking for a payroll clerk they intended to rob. While Rizzo and his cohorts were still looking for their victim, the police apprehended and arrested them. They were tried for attempted robbery but were acquitted because "they had not found or reached the presence of the person they intended to rob." The New York Court of Appeals held:

> [M]any acts in the way of preparation are too remote to constitute the crime of attempt. The line has been drawn between those acts which are remote and those which are proximate and near to the consummation. The law must be practical, and therefore considers those acts only as tending to the commission of the crime which are so near to its accomplishment that in all reasonable probability the crime itself would have been committed but for timely interference. The cases which have been before the courts express this idea in different language, but the idea remains the same. The act or acts must come or advance very near to the accomplishment of the intended crime. *People v. Rizzo,* 158 N.E. 888 (N.Y.App.1927)

3. Peaslee had constructed and arranged combustibles in a building he owned in such a way that they were ready to be lighted, and if lighted would have set fire to the building and its contents. He got within a quarter of a mile of the building, but his would-be accomplice refused to light the fire. Did Peaslee attempt to commit arson? According to the court, he did not:

> A mere collection and preparation of materials in a room, for the purpose of setting fire to them, unaccompanied by any present intent to set the fire, would be too remote and not all but "the last act" necessary to complete the crime. *Commonwealth v. Peaslee,* 59 N.E. 55 (Mass.1901)

Legal and Factual Impossibility

Suppose a man sneaks an old book past customs, believing the law requires him to pay a duty. In fact, however, the law exempts antiques from custom duty. Has he committed a crime by attempting to evade customs? Suppose a woman stabs her enemy while she believes he is asleep, not knowing that the victim died of a heart attack two hours before. Has she committed

the law does not prohibit what they did

attempted murder? The man in the first hypothetical case represents an example of legal impossibility. **Legal impossibility** means that actors have done all they intend to do, and yet the law does not prohibit what they did. The man intended to commit a crime and did everything he believed constituted that crime. Yet his act could not amount to a crime because the jurisdiction did not make such conduct criminal.

The woman in the second hypothetical case represents an example of factual impossibility. **Factual impossibility** exists when the actor intends to commit a crime but some fact—**extraneous factor**—prevents its completion. The woman intended to commit murder. She did all she could to commit it; if the facts were different (if her victim had been alive), she would have committed murder.

Legal impossibility requires a different law to make the conduct criminal; factual impossibility requires different facts to complete the crime. In most jurisdictions, legal impossibility is a defense to criminal attempt; factual impossibility is not. The principal reason for the difference is that to convict for conduct that the law does not prohibit, no matter what the actor's intentions, violates the principle of legality—no crime without a law, no punishment without a law. (Chapter 2.) Factual impossibility, on the other hand, would permit luck to determine criminal liability. A person who is determined to engage in conduct or cause harm prohibited by the criminal law, and who acts on that determination, should not escape liability and punishment because of luck.[23]

CASE

Was the Unloaded Gun a "Stroke of Luck?"

State v. Damms
9 Wis. 2d 183, 100 N.W.2d 592 (1960)

Currie, Justice

The defendant Ralph Damms was charged ... with the offense of attempt to commit murder in the first degree contrary to §§ 940.01 and 939.32, Stats. The jury found the defendant guilty as charged, and the defendant was sentenced to imprisonment in the state prison at Waupun for a term of not more than ten years. The defendant has appealed from the judgment of conviction entered.

FACTS
... The alleged crime occurred near Menomonee Falls in Waukesha county. Prior to [the attempt] ... Marjory Damms, wife of the defendant, had instituted an action for divorce against him and the parties lived apart. She was thirty-nine years and he thirty-three years of age. Marjory Damms was also estranged from her mother, Mrs. Laura Grant. That morning, a little before eight o'clock, Damms drove his automobile to the vicinity in Milwaukee where he knew Mrs. Damms would take the bus to go to work. He saw her walking along the sidewalk, stopped, and induced her to enter the car by falsely stating that Mrs. Grant was ill and dying. They drove to Mrs. Grant's home. Mrs. Damms then discovered that her mother was up and about and not seriously ill. Nevertheless, the two Damms remained there nearly two hours conversing and drinking coffee. Apparently it was the intention of Damms to induce a reconciliation between mother and daughter, hoping it would result in one between himself and his wife, but not much progress was achieved in such direction.

At the conclusion of the conversation Mrs. Damms expressed the wish to phone for a taxi-cab to take her to work. Damms insisted on her getting into his car, and said he would drive her to work. They again entered his car but instead of driving south towards her place of employment, he drove in the opposite direction. Some conversation was had in which he stated that it was possible for a person to die quickly and not be able to make amends for anything done in the past, and referred to the possibility of "judgment day" occurring suddenly. Mrs. Damms' testimony as to what then took place is as follows:

"When he was telling me about this being judgment day, he pulled a cardboard box from under the seat of the car and brought it up to the seat and opened it up and took a gun out of a paper bag. [He] aimed it at my side and he said, 'This is to show you I'm not kidding.' I tried to quiet him down. He said he wasn't fooling. I said if it was just a matter of my saying to my mother that everything was all right, we could go back and I would tell her that."

They did return to Mrs. Grant's home and Mrs. Damms went inside and Damms stayed outside. In a few minutes he went inside and asked Mrs. Damms to leave with him. Mrs. Grant requested that they leave quietly so as not to attract the attention of the neighbors. They again got into the car and this time drove out on Highway 41 towards Menomonee Falls. Damms stated to Mrs. Damms that he was taking her "up North" for a few days, the apparent purpose of which was to effect a reconciliation between them. As they approached a roadside restaurant, he asked her if she would like something to eat. She replied that she wasn't hungry but would drink some coffee. Damms then drove the car off the highway beside the restaurant and parked it with the front facing, and in close proximity to, the restaurant wall.

Damms then asked Mrs. Damms how much money she had with her and she said "a couple of dollars." He then requested to see her checkbook and she refused to give it to him. A quarrel ensued between them. Mrs. Damms opened the car door and started to run around the restaurant building screaming, "Help!"

Damms pursued her with the pistol in his hand. Mrs. Damms' cries for help attracted the attention of the persons inside the restaurant, including two officers of the State Traffic Patrol who were eating their lunch. One officer rushed out of the front door and the other the rear door. In the meantime, Mrs. Damms had run nearly around three sides of the building.

In seeking to avoid colliding with a child, who was in her path, she turned, slipped and fell. Damms crouched down, held the pistol at her head, and pulled the trigger, but nothing happened. He then exclaimed, "It won't fire. It won't fire." Damms testified that at the time he pulled the trigger the gun was pointing down at the ground and not at Mrs. Damms' head. However, the two traffic patrol officers both testified that Damms had the gun pointed directly at her head when he pulled the trigger.

The officers placed Damms under arrest. They found that the pistol was unloaded. The clip holding the cartridges, which clip is inserted in the butt of the gun to load it, they found in the cardboard box in Damms' car together with a box of cartridges.

That afternoon, Damms was questioned by a deputy sheriff at the Waukesha county jail, and a clerk in the sheriff's office typed out the questions and Damms' answers as they were given. Damms later read over such typed statement of questions and answers, but refused to sign it. In such statement Damms stated that he thought the gun was loaded at the time of the alleged attempt to murder. Both the deputy sheriff and the undersheriff testified that Damms had stated to them that he thought the gun was loaded. On the other hand, Damms testified at the trial that he knew at the time of the alleged attempt that the pistol was not loaded.

OPINION

The two questions raised on this appeal are:

1. Did the fact, that it was impossible for the accused to have committed the act of murder because the gun was unloaded, preclude his conviction of the offense of attempt to commit murder?

2. Assuming that the foregoing question is answered in the negative, does the evidence establish the guilt of the accused beyond a reasonable doubt?

§ 939.32(2), Stats., provides as follows:

"An attempt to commit a crime requires that the actor have an intent to perform acts and attain a result which, if accomplished, would constitute such crime and that he does acts toward the commission of the crime which demonstrate unequivocally, under all the circumstances, that he formed that intent and would commit the crime except for the intervention of another person or some other extraneous factor."

The issue with respect to the first ... question boils down to whether the impossibility of accomplishment due to the gun being unloaded falls within the statutory words, "except for the intervention of ... some other extraneous factor." We conclude that it does.

Prior to the adoption of the new criminal code by the 1955 legislature the criminal statutes of this state had separate sections making it an offense to assault with intent to do great bodily harm, to murder, to rob, and to rape, etc. The new code did away with these separate sections by creating § 939.32, Stats., covering all attempts to commit a battery or felony, and making the maximum penalty not to exceed one-half the penalty imposed for the completed crime, except that, if the penalty for a completed crime is life imprisonment, the maximum penalty for the attempt is thirty years imprisonment.

In an article in 1956 Wisconsin Law Review, 350, 364, by assistant attorney general Platz, who was one of the authors of the new criminal code, explaining such code, he points out that "attempt" is defined therein in a more intelligible fashion than by using such tests as "beyond mere preparation," "locus poenitentiae" (the place at which the actor may repent and withdraw), or "dangerous proximity to success." Quoting the author

> Emphasis upon the dangerous propensities of the actor as shown by his conduct, rather than upon how close he came to succeeding, is

more appropriate to the purposes of the criminal law to protect society and reform offenders or render them temporarily harmless.

Robert H. Skilton, in an article entitled, "The Requisite Act in a Criminal Attempt (1937)," advances the view, that impossibility to cause death because of the attempt to fire a defective weapon at a person, does not prevent the conviction of the actor of the crime of attempted murder:

> [If] the defendant does not know that the gun he fires at B is defective, he is guilty of an attempt to kill B, even though his actions under the circumstances given never come near to killing B.... The possibility of the success of the defendant's enterprise need only be an apparent possibility to the defendant, and not an actual possibility.

In *State v. Mitchell,* 1908, 139 Iowa 455, 116 N.W. 808, 810, the defendant was convicted of assault with intent to do great bodily injury, and, on appeal, complained among other things that the charge in the indictment was insufficient, because it failed to allege that the gun in question was loaded. In sustaining the conviction, the Iowa court held in part as follows:

> The specific objection made is that there is no allegation that the gun was loaded; but how could the defendant have intended to shoot the person assaulted unless the gun which he held in his hands, was, in fact, or, as he believed, so loaded as that it could be fired? If he believed that it was loaded and intended to fire it at the person assaulted, he was guilty of an assault with intent to commit great bodily injury, although in fact and contrary to his belief it was not loaded. The indictment was sufficient, therefore, in charging an intent to do great bodily injury by shooting the person assailed with a gun, although it was not specifically alleged that the gun was in fact loaded.

The facts in *Mullen v. State,* 1871, 45 Ala. 43, were that the accused pointed a loaded gun at another and pulled the trigger three times, but the gun would not fire because of the absence of a percussion cap. The defendant was convicted of attempt to murder. On appeal, the court upheld a charge to the jury that the absence of the cap would not avail the defendant if he supposed it was on the gun, but the jury must be satisfied beyond all reasonable doubt that the defendant did not know there was no cap on the gun. In its opinion the court quoted from Bishop's *Criminal Law* to the effect that in order to be guilty of the offense of an attempt to commit a felony, such as murder, assuming the necessary intent to exist, the act must have some adaptation to accomplish the result intended, but the adaptation need only be apparent, not perfect. The conviction was reversed on other grounds not here material.

A case contra to *State v. Mitchell,* and *Mullen v. State,* supra, is *State v. Swails,* 1857, 8 Ind. 524. In the *Swails* case the accused was indicted for shooting at a person with intent to commit murder. The gun which was fired was loaded with powder and a light cotton wad, but no shot or ball. The court upheld a charge that the accused could not be convicted of the crime of the indictment if the life of the person fired upon was not at all endangered, or put in jeopardy by the act of the accused. In its opinion the court declared: "To constitute an assault, the intent and the present ability to execute, must be conjoined. Thus, in this case, there was the intent, but not the power."

However, the efficacy of the Swails case as a precedent is virtually destroyed by the later Indiana case of *Kunkle v. State,* 1869, 32 Ind. 220, 230, in which it was stated: "But if the case *[State v. Swails]* is to be understood as laying down the broad proposition, that to constitute an assault, or an assault and battery, with intent to commit a felony, the intent and the present ability to execute must necessarily be conjoined, it does not command our assent or approval. The case does not seem to have been very carefully considered, and no authority is referred to in support of the proposition." In addition to the authorities hereinbefore cited, it is stated in two recent works on criminal law that pointing an unloaded firearm at another and

pulling the trigger is an attempt if the actor believes the gun to be loaded.

Sound public policy would seem to support the majority view that impossibility not apparent to the actor should not absolve him from the offense of attempt to commit the crime he intended. An unequivocal act accompanied by intent should be sufficient to constitute a criminal attempt. Insofar as the actor knows, he has done everything necessary to insure the commission of the crime intended, and he should not escape punishment because of the fortuitous circumstance that by reason of some fact unknown to him it was impossible to effectuate the intended result.

Counsel for Damms advance the contention that the legislative history of § 939.32, Stats., demonstrates that the legislature intended that such section should not be construed so as to make one guilty of the offense of attempt to commit a crime, if the attending circumstances were such as to render it impossible for the actor to have committed the crime intended.

The new criminal code was adopted in tentative form by ch. 623, Laws of 1953. By the provision of § 282 of such chapter, this tentative code was not to take effect until the 1955 legislature had completed final action on the bills to be offered by the legislative council on the recommendation of the criminal code advisory committee for amending such code. Such chapter also provided for the creation of such advisory committee. The section covering attempts in such 1953 tentative criminal code was numbered § 339.32, and contained three subsections, Sub. (3) thereof read as follows:

"It is not a defense to a prosecution under this section that, because of a mistake of fact or law other than criminal law, which does not negative the actor's intent to commit the crime, it would have been impossible for him to commit the crime attempted." At a meeting of the Criminal Code Advisory Committee held on June 18, 1955, sub. (2) of such § 339.32 was amended to greatly simplify its language and have the same wording as it now appears in § 939.32(2), Stats. Immediately following such amendment, a further amendment was adopted by this committee striking sub. (3) of such § 339.32. It is this last action upon which counsel relies to establish the legislative intent contended for.

However, we do not deem that this demonstrates an unequivocal legislative intent that impossibility should always be a defense in a prosecution for an attempt. This is because there are other plausible explanations as to why the committee may have voted to strike sub. (3) of such § 339.32. One is that the committee may have thought that under the revision made in the language of sub. (2), the provision of sub. (3) was no longer necessary. Another is that the committee may have been motivated by the idea that the legal effect of impossibility be better left to the development of the common law rather than incorporating it in the code.

It is our considered judgment that the fact that the gun was unloaded when Damms pointed it at his wife's head and pulled the trigger, did not absolve him of the offense charged, if he actually thought at the time that it was loaded.

We do not believe that the further contention raised in behalf of the accused, that the evidence does not establish his guilt of the crime charged beyond a reasonable doubt, requires extensive consideration on our part.

The jury undoubtedly believed the testimony of the deputy sheriff and undersheriff that Damms told them on the day of the act that he thought the gun was loaded. This is also substantiated by the written statement constituting a transcript of his answers given in his interrogation at the county jail on the same day. The gun itself, which is an exhibit in the record, is the strongest piece of evidence in favor of Damms' present contention that he at all times knew the gun was unloaded. Practically the entire bottom end of the butt of the pistol is open. Such opening is caused by the absence of the clip into which the cartridges must be inserted in order to load the pistol. This readily demonstrates to anyone looking at the gun that it could not be loaded.

Because the unloaded gun with this large opening in the butt was an exhibit which went to the jury room, we must assume that the jury examined the gun and duly considered it in arriving at their verdict.

We are not prepared to hold that the jury could not come to the reasonable conclusion that, because of Damms' condition of excitement when he grabbed the gun and pursued his wife, he so grasped it as not to see the opening in the end of the butt which would have unmistakably informed him that the gun was unloaded. Having so concluded, they could rightfully disregard Damms' testimony given at the trial that he knew the pistol was unloaded. Judgment affirmed.

Martin, C. J., not participating.

DISSENT

Dietrich, Justice (dissenting).

I disagree with the majority opinion in respect to their interpretations and conclusions of § 939.32(2), Stats. The issue raised on this appeal: Could the defendant be convicted of murder, under § 939.32(2), Stats., when it was impossible for the defendant to have caused the death of anyone because the gun or pistol involved was unloaded?

§ 939.32(2), Stats., provides: "An attempt to commit a crime requires that the actor have an intent to perform acts and attain a result which, if accomplished, would constitute such crime and that he does acts toward the commission of the crime which demonstrate unequivocally, under all the circumstances, that he formed that intent and would commit the crime except for the intervention of another person or some other extraneous factor."

In view of the statute, the question arising under § 939.32(2), is whether the impossibility of accomplishment due to the pistol being unloaded falls with the statutory words "except for the intervention of … some other extraneous factor."

In interpreting the statute we must look to the ordinary meaning of words. Webster's *New International Dictionary* defines "extraneous" as not belonging to or dependent upon a thing, … originated or coming from without.

The plain distinct meaning of the statute is: A person must form an intent to commit a particular crime and this intent must be coupled with sufficient preparation on his part and with overt acts from which it can be determined clearly, surely and absolutely the crime would be committed except for the intervention of some independent thing or something originating or coming from some one or something over which the actor has no control.

As an example,—if the defendant actor had formed an intent to kill someone, had in his possession a loaded pistol, pulled the trigger while his intended victim was within range and the pistol did not fire because the bullet or cartridge in the chamber was defective or because someone unknown to the actor had removed the cartridges or bullets or because of any other thing happening which happening or thing was beyond the control of the actor, the actor could be guilty under § 339.32(2), Stats.

But when as in the present case (as disclosed by the testimony) the defendant had never loaded the pistol, although having ample opportunity to do so, then he had never completed performance of the act essential to kill someone, through the means of pulling the trigger of the pistol. This act, of loading the pistol, or using a loaded pistol, was dependent on the defendant himself. It was in no way an extraneous factor since by definition an extraneous factor is one which originates or comes from without.

Under the majority opinion the interpretations of the statute are if a person points an unloaded gun (pistol) at someone, knowing it to be unloaded and pulls the trigger, he can be found guilty of an attempt to commit murder. This type of reasoning I cannot agree with.

He could be guilty of some offense, but not attempt to commit murder. If a person uses a pistol as a bludgeon and had struck someone, but was prevented from killing his victim because he (the actor) suffered a heart attack at that moment, the illness would be an extraneous factor within the statute and the actor could be found guilty

of attempt to commit murder, provided the necessary intent was proved.

In this case, there is no doubt that the pistol was not loaded. The defendant testified that it had never been loaded or fired. The following steps must be taken before the weapon would be capable of killing....

The pistol is State's evidence exhibit 'B'.

Type of Pistol: 32 semi automatic
Assembly of Pistol

    A. Pistol grip or butt hand grasp
    B. Barrel
    C. Slide
    D. Trigger housing.

Mechanism

    A. To load pistol requires pulling of slide operating around barrel toward holder or operator of pistol.
    B. After pulling slide to rear, safety latch is pushed into place by operator of pistol to hold pistol in position for loading.
    C. A spring lock is located at one side of opening of magazine located at the bottom grip or butt of gun.
    D. This spring is pulled back and the clip is inserted into magazine or bottom of pistol and closes the bottom of the grip or butt of the pistol.
    E. The recoil or release of the safety latch on the slide loads the chamber of the pistol and it is now ready to fire or be used as a pistol.

The law judges intent objectively. It is impossible to peer into a man's mind particularly long after the act has been committed. Viewing objectively the physical salient facts, it was the defendant who put the gun, clip and cartridges under the car seat. It was he, same defendant, who took the pistol out of the box without taking clip or cartridges. It is plain he told the truth, he knew the gun would not fire, nobody else knew that so well. In fact his exclamation was "It won't fire. It won't fire."

The real intent showed up objectively in those calm moments while driving around the county with his wife for two hours, making two visits with her at her mother's home, and drinking coffee at the home. He could have loaded the pistol while staying on the outside at his mother-in-law's home on his second trip, if he intended to use the pistol to kill, but he did not do this required act.

The majority states: "The gun itself, which is an exhibit in the record, is the strongest piece of evidence in favor of Damms' present contention that he at all times knew the gun was unloaded. Practically the entire bottom end of the butt of the pistol is open.... This readily demonstrates to anyone looking at the gun that it could not be loaded." They are so correct.

The defendant had the pistol in his hand several times before chasing his wife at the restaurant and it was his pistol. He, no doubt, had examined the pistol at various times during his period of ownership— unless he was devoid of all sense of touch and feeling in his hands and fingers it would be impossible for him not to be aware or know that the pistol was unloaded.

He could feel the hole in the bottom of the butt, and this on at least two separate occasions for he handled the pistol by taking it out of the box and showing it to his wife before he took her back to her mother's home the second time, and prior to chasing her at the restaurant.

Objective evidence here raises reasonable doubt of intent to attempt murder. It nega-

tives intent to kill. The defendant would have loaded the pistol had he intended to kill or murder or used it as a bludgeon....

The Assistant Attorney General contends and states in his brief: "In the instant case, the failure of the attempt was due to lack of bullets in the gun but a loaded magazine was in the car. If defendant had not been prevented by the intervention of the two police officers, or possibly someone else, or conceivably by the flight of his wife from the scene, he could have returned to the car, loaded the gun, and killed her. Under all the circumstances the jury were justified in concluding that that is what he would have done, but for the intervention."

If that conclusion is correct, and juries are allowed to convict persons based on speculation of what might have been done, we will have seriously and maybe permanently, curtailed the basic rights of our citizenry to be tried only on the basis of proven facts. I cannot agree with his contention or conclusion. The total inadequacy of the means (in this case the unloaded gun or pistol) in the manner intended to commit the overt act of murder, precludes a finding of guilty of the crime charged under § 939.32(2), Stats.

Case Discussion

Does it matter whether or not the gun was loaded? Hasn't Damms done everything possible to commit the terrible crime of murdering his wife? What if Damms subconsciously "forgot" to load the gun because he meant only to frighten his wife? Such speculation depends on a belief in Freudian psychology. But assuming that Damms forgot, was the unloaded gun then an extraneous factor, or within Damms' control? Is the Wisconsin rule punishing attempts at about half the amount for completed crimes a good idea? Some states punish attempts at the same level on the ground that when a person intends to commit a crime and only a fortuity prevents its commission, that person deserves punishment equal to the person whom a fortuity did not prevent. Should criminal law consider only intent in determining the seriousness of an offense? What else should it take into account?

Distinguishing between factual and legal impossibility creates enormous difficulties for courts. In *United States v. Thomas,* the court reviewed and applied the tests of legal and factual impossibility in the law of attempt.

CASE

Was the Rape Legally Impossible?

United States v. Thomas
32 CMR 278 (1962)

Kilday, Judge

... Thomas and McClellan, were tried in common by general court-martial. Separate charges against the pair alleged the offenses of conspiracy to commit rape, rape, and lewd and lascivious conduct.... Each was acquitted of rape, but the court-martial found them guilty of attempted rape.... Both received identical sentences to dishonorable discharge, confinement at hard labor for three years, forfeiture of all pay and allowances for a like period, and reduction to the grade of airman recruit.

Thereafter, the findings and sentences adjudged by the trial court were approved by the officer exercising general court-martial jurisdiction. The board of review, however, set aside the findings of guilty of attempted rape and conspiracy as to both accused. It approved a modified finding of lewd and lascivious conduct as to each and reassessed the punishment, reducing the sentences of the pair to bad-conduct discharge, confinement at hard labor for five months, total forfeitures, and reduction. The case is before this Court on the following question ...

Was the Board of Review correct in setting aside, with respect to both accused, the findings of guilty of Charge I, attempted rape?...

FACTS

The evidence adduced at the trial presents a sordid and revolting picture which need not be discussed in detail other than as necessary to decide the certified issues. In brief, both these young accused—Thomas being twenty years of age, and McClellan only nineteen, at the time of the instant offenses—started their fateful evening on a "bar hopping" spree. They were accompanied by an eighteen-year-old companion, Abruzzese, who, like both accused, held the grade of airman in the Navy. The latter was a co-actor in these offenses, but was granted immunity from prosecution for his criminality in the incidents, and testified as a witness for the Government.

After several stops the trio entered a tavern known as "Taylor's Place" where McClellan began dancing with a girl. Almost at once she collapsed in McClellan's arms. Thereafter, he, with his two companions, volunteered to take her home. They placed the apparently unconscious female in McClellan's car and left. Abruzzese was seated beside McClellan, who drove; Thomas was in the left rear seat next to the girl. Before they had proceeded very far McClellan, in frank, expressive language, suggested that this was a good chance for sexual intercourse as apparently this woman was just drunk and would never know the difference. Each of the three subsequently did or attempted to consummate this act and then started their return to town. The three became concerned as the woman had not regained consciousness.

In the meantime they dropped Abruzzese off at the USO. The accused, unable to find the female's home and becoming more concerned about her condition, stopped at a service station seeking help. The attendant called the police who, upon arriving at the service station, examined the girl and determined she was dead. An ambulance was called and she was taken to a hospital for further examination. An autopsy, later performed, revealed that she apparently died of "acute interstitial myocarditis." In general terms this is a weakening of the heart muscles with edema and inflammation which occurs more in young people without its presence being suspected. It was the general undisputed opinion that her death probably occurred at the time she collapsed on the dance floor at Taylor's Place or very shortly thereafter. Apparently, in deaths of this type, rigor mortis does not usually begin for some time and as a result the accused were unaware of the fact she was dead.

OPINION

... [N]o factual dispute exists as to the death of the female involved and the cause thereof. It is clear, as that appellate body concluded, the victim was dead at the time she was removed from the tavern or relatively shortly thereafter, and the prosecution adduced no convincing evidence that she was alive at the time the offenses were committed. Indeed, on the merits trial counsel argued there could be no question but that the accused were guilty of attempted rape, "because the evidence shows that they would be guilty of rape if it wasn't for the fact that the government failed in its proof, perhaps, that she was alive at the time of the intercourse." Neither—at least as we need be concerned, since we deal here only with convictions for ... attempt, and not with the substantive offense of rape itself—can there be any real controversy regarding the acts done by Abruzzese and the two accused....

Text writers have covered the subject extensively....

In practically all of the foregoing articles and texts, the specific question involved in this case—impossibility of completion of the substantive crime—is discussed at very considerable length. The two reasons for "impossibility" are treated in this connection: (1) If the intended act is not criminal, there can be no criminal liability for an attempt to commit the act. This is sometimes described as a "legal impossibility." (2) If the intended substantive crime is impossible of accomplishment because of some physical impossibility unknown to the accused, the elements of a criminal attempt are present. This is sometimes described as "impossibility in fact."

The authorities seem to be in fair accord that (1), above, is not punishable as an attempt. There is some considerable conflict of authority as to whether (2), above, is punishable as an attempt, but the preponderance seems to be that such instances do constitute attempts. What is abundantly clear, however, is that it is most difficult to classify any particular state of facts as positively coming within one of these categories to the exclusion of the other....

The lack of logic between some of the holdings, ... the inherent difficulty in assigning a given set of facts to a proper classification; the criticism of existing positions in this area; and, most importantly, the denial of true and substantial justice by these artificial holdings have led, quite naturally, to proposals for reform in the civilian legal concepts of criminal attempts. In addition to a progressive and modern view now evident in some judicial decisions and writings, The American Law Institute ... in *Tentative Draft No. 10* of the Model Penal Code ... stated: "... It should suffice, therefore, to indicate at this stage what we deem to be the major results of the draft. They are: (a) to extend the criminality of attempts by sweeping aside the defense of impossibility (including the distinction between so-called factual and legal impossibility) and by drawing the line between attempt and non-criminal preparation further away from the final act; the crime becomes essentially one of criminal purpose implemented by an overt act strongly corroborative of such purpose...."

After having given this entire question a great deal more than casual attention and study, we are forced to the conclusion that the law of attempts in military jurisprudence has tended toward the advanced and modern position, which position will be achieved for civilian jurisprudence if The American Law Institute is completely successful in its advocacy of this portion of the Model Penal Code.

Because of the legal acumen of the law officer of this general court-martial, the trial was conducted in accordance with this approach. We conclude that his instructions to the court-martial with reference to the offense of rape, the lesser included offenses thereto, including attempt to rape, and conspiracy, furnished correct advice on impossibility insofar as the same is affected by the death of the victim.

In its effort to follow civilian authorities into the intricacies and artificial distinctions they draw in the field of criminal attempts, however, the board of review fell into error. And, it is error of serious proportions which, if affirmed, would lead military jurisprudence into the morass of confusion as to criminal attempts in which civilian jurisprudence finds itself immobilized, and from which heroic efforts are being made to extricate it....

We hold, therefore ... that in this instance the fact that the female, upon whom these detestable acts were performed, was already dead at the time of their commission, is no bar to conviction for attempted rape....

[W]e hold that the law officer did not err in the instructions given to the court-martial in connection with attempted rape and conspiracy to commit rape.

It is clear from this record, by the findings of the court-martial and the facts as sustained by the board of review, that each of these appellants was guilty of each element necessary to the crime of attempted rape. That is, each of the appellants did:

1. A certain overt act.
2. The act was done with the specific intent to commit the offense of rape; that is, each intended to have sexual intercourse with a female, not his wife, by force and without her consent.
3. The act amounted to more than mere preparation.
4. It apparently tended to effect the commission of the intended offense, even though
5. The intended offense failed of completion because, unknown to either appellant and as a matter beyond their control, their victim was already dead....

All the elements of ... attempted rape ... are present and were returned by the members of the court-martial under correct standards set out in the law officer's instructions. The board of review, therefore, erred in holding to the contrary.

The certified issues are answered in the negative, and the decision of the board of review is reversed. This case is returned to The Judge Advocate General of the Navy for action not inconsistent with this opinion.

DISSENT

Ferguson, Judge:

... I am inclined to attribute [the difficulty in analyzing the defense of impossibility in criminal attempts] ... to a growing tendency on the part of legal theoreticians to attach more importance to the evilness of a man's intent than to his acts—a belief, if you will, that the law should punish sinful thoughts if accompanied by any sort of antisocial conduct which evidences the design to execute forbidden acts. When certain courts adopt such broad penal theories and others reject them, the result is the legal morass to which my brothers refer.

The path which they have found out of this bog of theory, speculation, and learned dissertations is indeed tempting, for it eliminates any need to concern ourselves with the close and intricate question where accused's actions fall within the area of legal impossibility. But I cannot in good conscience agree with a position which adopts a completely novel approach to the law of criminal attempts without the slightest indication that such was the intent of Congress in passing Uniform Code of Military Justice, Article 80, 10 USC § 880.

The mentioned statute provides pertinently:

An act, done with specific intent to commit an offense under this chapter, amounting to more than mere preparation and tending, even though failing, to effect its commission, is an attempt to commit that offense....

[W]e have heretofore implied that the victim must be alive in order for the accused to be found guilty of rape. As it is, therefore, an utter impossibility for the consummated offense of rape to be committed upon the body of a dead person, may the accused who commits all the acts necessary to such offense upon a dead body, with the requisite *mens rea,* be convicted of an attempt to rape?

[Here the justice reviewed most of the leading cases on legal impossibility, concluding that they overwhelmingly permit the defense of legal impossibility.]

The barrier to consummation of the crime charged here is not factual but legal. Indeed, accused did everything they set out to do, but they admittedly could not commit the actual crime of rape because their victim was dead and thus outside the protection of the law appertaining to that offense. Because the objective of their loathsome attentions was no longer subject to being raped, it seems to me that there cannot be any liability for an attempt, for ... a legal rather than a factual impediment existed to the offense's consummation....

"It is not an attempt when every act intended by the accused [sexual intercourse with a woman in fact dead] could be completed without committing an offense [rape], even though the accused may at the time believe he is committing an offense [rape]."

Finally, I believe that the position which my brothers take unnecessarily emphasizes the accused's mental frame of reference at the expense of what they actually did. The common law concept that danger to society lay chiefly in action rather than in thought has much to commend it, based as it is upon centuries of experiential development....

When ... it is found that such acts, albeit legally incapable of consummation, are also punishable as attempted rape, I believe we so widen the thrust of Code ... that we permit punishment to be predicated upon one's plans quite without regard to whether they may legally be completed....

Case Discussion   Can you tell the difference between legal and factual impossibility? Why should the law reject the defense of factual but not legal impossibility? Why does the defense accept the defense of legal impossibility? Should the law recognize the defense of legal impossibility? If you were deciding this case, would the defendants be guilty of attempted rape? Explain why it does, or does not, make a difference that the victim was dead.

Renunciation

If an ~~extraneous~~ *outside* factor interrupts an attempt to commit a crime, the law does not permit the interruption to benefit the attempter. If the attempter decides not to complete the crime, the renunciation sometimes benefits the actor. If I am about to steal a watch from a department store and a house detective stops me just as I am reaching for the watch, the detective's appearance is an extraneous factor, a preventive force outside myself that the law does not allow to benefit me. If, on the other hand, just as I am about to pick up the watch, I am overcome with pangs of conscience and put it back, my voluntary actions constitute the force that interrupts the crime. Such purity does not prompt all renunciations. Suppose a woman spits out a pill to cause abortion because it tastes awful, or a robber does not go through with a robbery because the amount of money is too small to bother with. These last are renunciations but not morally inspired.

Some argue that the law should encourage renunciation by rewarding those who renounce their criminal plans in progress, no matter what their motives for doing so. Others contend that only those whose moral standards prompt the abandonment should benefit from renunciation. They argue that renunciation should not benefit those whom material considerations motivate because such persons remain dangerous and need "neutralizing." Still others maintain that a "simple change of heart is

[handwritten margin note: Changes his mind before he gets into fx.]

insufficient for expiation and that a punishment to balance the scales of justice ... is deserved." About half the states have statutes permitting the defense of voluntary renunciation, sometimes called abandonment. No state has legislated against the defense, leaving it to the courts to determine whether to allow it or not. Courts in nine states have rejected the defense. One of the most cited cases involving the defense of voluntary renunciation is *Le Barron v. State.*[24]

CASE

Did He Voluntarily Renounce His Intent to Rape?

Le Barron v. State
32 Wis.2d 294, 145 N.W.2d 79 (1966)

[Le Barron was convicted of attempted rape and sentenced to not more than fifteen years in prison. He appealed. Chief Justice Currie delivered the opinion.]

FACTS

On March 3, 1965 at 6:55 p.m., the complaining witness, Jodean Randen, a housewife, was walking home across a fairly well-traveled railroad bridge in Eau Claire. She is a slight woman whose normal weight is 95 to 100 pounds. As she approached the opposite side of the bridge she passed a man who was walking in the opposite direction. The man turned and followed her, grabbed her arm and demanded her purse. She surrendered her purse and at the command of the man began walking away as fast as she could. Upon discovering that the purse was empty, he caught up with her again, grabbed her arm and told her that if she did not scream he would not hurt her. He then led her—willingly, she testified, so as to avoid being hurt by him—to the end of the bridge. While walking he shoved her head down and warned her not to look up or do anything and he would not hurt her.

On the other side of the bridge along the railroad tracks there is a coal shack. As they approached the coal shack he grabbed her, put one hand over her mouth, and an arm around her shoulder and told her not to

scream or he would kill her. At this time Mrs. Randen thought he had a knife in his hand. He then forced her into the shack and up against the wall. As she struggled for her breath he said, "You know what else I want," unzipped his pants and started pulling up her skirt. She finally succeeded in removing his hand from her mouth, and after reassuring him that she would not scream, told him she was pregnant and pleaded with him to desist or he would hurt her baby. He then felt her stomach and took her over to the door of the shack, where in the better light he was able to ascertain that, under her coat, she was wearing maternity clothes. He thereafter let her alone and left after warning her not to scream or call the police, or he would kill her.

OPINION

The material portions of the controlling statutes provide: § 944.01(1), Stats. "Any male who has sexual intercourse with a female he knows is not his wife, by force and against her will, may be imprisoned not more than 30 years."

§ 939.32(2), Stats. "An attempt to commit a crime requires that the actor have an intent to perform acts and attain a result which, if accomplished, would constitute such crime and that he does acts toward the commission of the crime which demonstrate unequivocally, under all the circumstances, that he formed that intent and would commit the crime except for the intervention of another person or some other extraneous factor."

The two statutory requirements of intent and overt acts which must concur in order to have attempt to rape are as follows: (1) The male must have the intent to act so as to have intercourse with the female by overcoming or preventing her utmost resistance by physical violence, or overcoming her will to resist by the use of threats of imminent physical violence likely to cause great bodily harm; (2) the male must act toward the commission of the rape by overt acts which demonstrate unequivocally, under all the circumstances, that he formed the intent to rape and would have committed the rape except for the intervention of another person or some other extraneous factor.

The thrust of defendant's argument, that the evidence was not sufficient to convict him of the crime of attempted rape, is twofold: first, defendant desisted from his endeavor to have sexual intercourse with complainant before he had an opportunity to form an intent to accomplish such intercourse by force and against her will; and, second, the factor which caused him to desist, viz., the pregnancy of complainant, was intrinsic and not an "extraneous factor" within the meaning of § 939.32(2), Stats.

It is difficult to consider the factor of intent apart from that of overt acts since the sole evidence of intent in attempted rape cases is almost always confined to the overt acts of the accused, and intent must be inferred therefrom. In fact, the express wording of § 939.32(2), Stats. recognizes that this is so.

We consider defendant's overt acts, which support a reasonable inference that he intended to have sexual intercourse with complainant by force and against her will, to be these: (1) He threatened complainant that he would kill her if she refused to cooperate with him; (2) he forced complainant into the shack and against the wall; and (3) he stated, "You know what else I want," unzipped his pants, and started pulling up her skirt. The jury had the right to assume that defendant had the requisite physical strength and weapon (the supposed knife) to carry out the threat over any resistance of complainant.

We conclude that a jury could infer beyond a reasonable doubt from these overt acts of defendant that he intended to have sexual intercourse with defendant by force and against her will. The fact, that he

desisted from his attempt to have sexual intercourse as a result of the plea of complainant that she was pregnant, would permit of the opposite inference. However, such desistance did not compel the drawing of such inference nor compel, as a matter of law, the raising of a reasonable doubt to a finding that defendant had previously intended to carry through with having intercourse by force and against complainant's will.

Defendant relies strongly on *Oakley v. State* where this court held that defendant Oakley's acts were so equivocal as to prevent a finding of intent beyond a reasonable doubt to have sexual intercourse by force and against the will of the complainant. The evidence in the case disclosed neither physical violence nor threat of physical violence up to the time Oakley desisted from his attempt to have sexual intercourse with the complainant. He did put his arm around her and attempted to kiss her while entreating her to have intercourse, and also attempted to put his hand in her blouse and to lift up her skirt but did not attempt to renew this endeavor when she brushed his hand away. Thus the facts in Oakley are readily distinguishable from those of the case at bar.

To argue that the two cases are analogous because, in the one instance the accused desisted because the complainant was menstruating and in the other because of pregnancy, is an oversimplification. Such an argument overlooks the radical difference in the nature of the overt acts relied upon to prove intent.

The argument, that the pregnancy of the instant complainant which caused defendant's desistance does not qualify as an "extraneous factor" within the meaning of § 939.32, Stats., is in conflict with our holding in *State v. Damms*. There we upheld a conviction of attempt to commit murder where the accused pulled the trigger of an unloaded pistol intending to kill his estranged wife thinking the pistol was loaded. It was held that the impossibility of accomplishment due to the gun being unloaded fell within the statutory words, "except for the intervention of some other extraneous factor." Particularly significant is this statement in the opinion:

> An unequivocal act accompanied by intent should be sufficient to constitute a criminal attempt. Insofar as the actor knows, he has done everything necessary to insure the com-

mission of the crime intended, and he should not escape punishment because of the fortuitous circumstance that by reason of some fact unknown to him it was impossible to effectuate the intended result.

Affirmed.

Case Discussion

Le Barron demonstrates how difficult it can be to apply the renunciation doctrine. Did Le Barron desist because he believed it was morally wrong to rape a pregnant woman, or did the pregnancy simply repel him sexually? Should his reason make a difference? Is Le Barron equally dangerous, whichever reason led to interrupting the rape? Do you agree that Le Barron's victim's pregnancy was an extraneous factor? The court said a jury could conclude either that it was, or that Le Barron voluntarily renounced his intention to rape because the victim was pregnant. If you were a juror, how would you have voted on the pregnancy question?

Note Cases

1. Wiley had wedged a large pinch bar between the door and jamb of a real estate office, trying to pry open the door in the early morning hours. A police officer testified that he surprised Wiley in the act of prying open the door. Wiley testified that he intended to break into the office and had actually begun to do so, but that "I had only hit the door with [the pinch bar] twice … and … I just got scared and I abandoned the idea of breaking in the place." Was he guilty of attempting to enter the real estate office? The court said yes, rejecting Wiley's defense of voluntary abandonment.

> [I]f one who has intended to attempt to commit a crime freely and voluntarily abandons the idea before it has progressed beyond mere preparation, he has not committed the crime of attempt; but … a voluntary abandonment of an attempt which has proceeded beyond mere preparation into an overt act or acts in furtherance of the commission of the attempt does not expiate the guilt of, or forbid punishment for, the crime already committed. *Wiley v. State,* 207 A.2d 478 (Md.1965)

2. [F]ollowing a fight with a friend outside a bar where the two had been drinking.… [Johnson] walked a mile to his house, retrieved his .22 rifle and ten cartridges, walked back to the bar, and crawled under a pickup truck across the street to wait for the friend.… [Johnson] testified that he, at first, intended to shoot the friend to "pay him back" for the beating he had received in their earlier altercation. When the owner of the pickup arrived,… [Johnson] obtained his keys, instructed him to sit in the pickup, and gave him one or more bottles of beer.… [Johnson] then crawled back under the pickup to resume his wait for his friend. The police were alerted by a passerby and arrested … [Johnson] before his friend emerged from the bar. There was also testimony that while he was lying under the pickup truck,… [Johnson] sobered up somewhat and began to think through his predicament. He testified that he changed his mind and removed the shells from the rifle, placing them in his pocket. By that time there were two persons in the pickup truck, and he began a discussion with them, telling them his name and address and inviting them to his residence to have a party.

The three of them were still there drinking and conversing when the police arrived, at which time the rifle was found to be unloaded and the shells were still in ... [Johnsons] pocket.

The trial court refused Johnson's request for an instruction on the question of abandonment. The appellate court reversed, holding that sufficient evidence existed to instruct the jury on the question of voluntary renunciation. *People v. Johnson,* 750 P.2d 72 (Colo.1987)

3. [W]hile his wife was away on a trip,... [Staples], a mathematician, under an assumed name, rented an office on the second floor of a building in Hollywood which was over the mezzanine of a bank. Directly below the mezzanine was the vault of the bank.... [Staples] was aware of the layout of the building, specifically of the relation of the office he rented to the bank vault.... [Staples] paid rent for the period from October 23 to November 23. The landlord had 10 days before commencement of the rental period within which to finish some interior repairs and painting. During this prerental period ... [Staples] brought into the office certain equipment. This included drilling tools, two acetylene gas tanks, a blow torch, a blanket, and a linoleum rug. The landlord observed these items when he came in from time to time to see how the repair work was progressing.... [Staples] learned from a custodian that no one was in the building on Saturdays. On Saturday, October 14,... [Staples] drilled two groups of holes into the floor of the office above the mezzanine room. He stopped drilling before the holes went through the floor. He came back to the office several times thinking he might slowly drill down, covering the holes with the linoleum rug. At some point in time he installed a hasp lock on a closet, and planned to, or did, place his tools in it. However, he left the closet keys on the premises. Around the end of November, apparently after November 23, the landlord notified the police and turned the tools and equipment over to them.... [Staples] did not pay any more rent. It is not clear when he last entered the office, but it could have been after November 23, and even after the landlord had removed the equipment. On February 22, 1968, the police arrested ... [Staples].

After receiving advice as to his constitutional rights,... [Staples] voluntarily made an oral statement: "Saturday, the 14th ... I drilled some small holes in the floor of the room. Because of tiredness, fear, and the implications of what I was doing, I stopped and went to sleep. At this point I think my motives began to change. The actual (sic) commencement of my plan made me begin to realize that even if I were to succeed, a fugitive life of living off of stolen money would not give the enjoyment of the life of a mathematician however humble a job I might have. I still had not given up my plan however. I felt I had made a certain investment of time, money, effort and a certain psychological (sic) commitment to the concept. I came back several times thinking I might store the tools in the closet and slowly drill down (covering the hole with a rug of linoleum square.) As time went on (after two weeks or so), my wife came back and my life as bank robber seemed more and more absurd."

Did Staples voluntarily renounce his attempt to commit burglary? A jury found Staples guilty of attempted burglary and the appellate court affirmed the conviction. It held that although the police did not directly intercept Staples, he knew that the landlord had turned the tools over to the police and had resumed control over the office. This, the court held, was equivalent to a direct interception. In other words, an extraneous factor prevented the burglary, not Staples' change of heart. *People v. Staples,* 85 Cal.Rptr. 589 (Cal.1970)

━━━━━⟫●⟪━━━━━

Summary of Attempt

Attempt requires a purpose to commit a crime combined with some steps toward completing that crime. Several difficult issues surround attempt law. First, conflicting rationales support criminal attempt. Some justify it on the ground that it controls dangerous persons; others maintain that it aims to prevent crime. Second, dispute arises over how many acts toward completion constitute attempt. Generally, this requires distinguishing between preparation and attempt. Third, difficulties surround legal and factual impossibility. Is it attempt if it was impossible to complete the crime? Most jurisdictions say no to legal impossibility but yes to factual impossibility. Factual impossibilities are generally referred to as extraneous factors. Finally, renunciation creates problems: Should it matter if a person bent on criminal conduct has a change of heart and desists from committing the crime? If the answer is yes, does it matter whether moral or nonmoral considerations prompted the change?

▼ CONSPIRACY

As a general rule, the more remote from completion, the less justifiable is punishment for crimes. In this respect preparation, attempt, conspiracy, and solicitation stand on a continuum, with attempt closest to and solicitation farthest from actual commission of the crime. Conspiracy "strikes against the special danger incident to group activity, facilitating prosecution of the group, and yielding a basis for imposing added penalties when combination is involved."[25]

Material Elements in Conspiracy

At common law, conspiracy is a combination between two or more persons formed for the purpose of doing either an unlawful act or a lawful act by an unlawful means. In words famous in conspiracy law, Justice Oliver Wendell Holmes defined conspiracy as "a partnership in criminal purpose." Holme's

Elements of Conspiracy			
Offense	***Actus Reus***	***Mens Rea***	**Result**
Conspiracy	*1.* agreement or in some jurisdictions *2.* agreement plus some act in furtherance of its purpse	specific intent or purpose to *1.* commit an unlawful act, or *2.* commit a lawful act by unlawful means	none beyond making the agreement or the act in furthering it

broad definition needs some refinement, but it captures the basic idea of conspiracy. A conspiracy is (1) an agreement or combination (Holmes's partnership") (2) for the purpose of attaining (3) an unlawful (Holmes's "criminal") objective, or a lawful objective by unlawful means.

Conspiracy Actus Reus

Conspiracy *actus reus* requires an agreement but not a formal signed contract; unwritten understandings suffice. That makes sense since conspirators rarely put their agreement in writing. Some courts hold that agreement includes "aid," even when given without another party's consent. In one case, a judge learned that someone planned to kill one of the judge's enemies. The judge wanted the plan to succeed, so he intercepted a letter warning the intended victim of the plan. The court held that the judge committed conspiracy to commit murder because he aided the other conspirators, even though he had nothing to do with them.

Defining agreement imprecisely can lead to abuses. In one famous trial, the government tried Dr. Benjamin Spock for conspiracy to avoid the draft law. Videotapes showed several hundred spectators clapping while Dr. Spock urged young men to resist the draft during the Vietnam War. According to the prosecutor, any person seen clapping on videotape was a coconspirator. By virtue of their encouragement, according to the prosecutor, these people were aiding Dr. Spock, hence agreeing to violate the draft law.[26]

In most jurisdictions, the agreement alone constitutes the conspiracy *actus reus*. Some jurisdictions, however, require action beyond the agreement. They differ as to how much action in addition to the agreement the criminal design requires. Some specify "some act"; in others "any act" suffices. One jurisdiction demands that conspirators "go forth for the purpose of committing" the prohibited act. The federal statute requires an "act to effect the object of the conspiracy."[27]

CASE

Did They Agree to Distribute Heroin?

United States v. Brown
776 F.2d 397 (2d.Cir.1985)

[A jury convicted Brown and Valentine (a fugitive) of conspiring to distribute heroin. Circuit judge Friendly delivered the opinion.]

FACTS
[William Grimball, a New York City undercover police officer, purchased a "joint" of "D" ($40 worth of heroin) in Harlem.] Officer Grimball was the government's principal witness. He testified that in the evening of October 9, 1984, he approached Gregory Valentine on the corner of 115th Street and Eighth Avenue and asked him for a joint of "D." Valentine asked Grimball whom he knew around the street. Grimball asked if Valentine knew Scott. He did not. Brown "came up" and Valentine said, "He wants to buy a joint, but I don't know him." Brown looked at Grimball and said, "He looks okay to me." Valentine then said, "Okay. But I am going to leave it somewhere and you [Grimball] can pick it up." Brown interjected, "You don't have to do that. Just go and get it for him. He looks all right to me." After looking at Grimball, Brown said, "He looks all right to me" and "I will wait right here."

Valentine then said, "Okay. Come on with me around to the hotel." Grimball followed him to 300 West 116th Street, where Valentine instructed him, "Sit on the black car and give me a few minutes to go up and get it." Valentine requested and received $40, which had been prerecorded, and then said, "You are going to take care of me for doing this for you, throw some dollars my way?" to which Grimball responded, "Yeah."

Valentine then entered the hotel and shortly returned. The two went back to 115th Street and Eighth Avenue, where Valentine placed a cigarette box on the hood of a blue car. Grimball picked up the cigarette box and found a glassine envelope containing white powder, stipulated to be heroin. Grimball placed $5 of the prerecorded buy money in the cigarette box, which he replaced on the hood. Valentine picked up the box and removed the $5. Grimball returned to his car and made a radio transmission to the backup field team that "the buy had went down" and informed them of the locations of the persons involved. Brown and Valentine were arrested. Valentine was found to possess two glassine envelopes of heroin and the $5 of prerecorded money. Brown was in possession of $31 of his own money; no drugs or contraband were found on him. The $40 of marked buy money was not recovered, and no arrests were made at the hotel.

[At the trial Grimball testified that] the typical drug buy in the Harlem area involved two to five people. As a result of frequent police sweeps, Harlem drug dealers were becoming so cautious that they employed people who act as steerers and the steerer's responsibility is basically to determine whether or not you are actually an addict or a user of heroin and they are also used to screen you to see if there is any possibility of you being a cop looking for a bulge or some indication that would give them that you are not actually an addict. And a lot of the responsibility relies [sic] on them to determine whether or not the drug buy is going to go down or not.

Officer Grimball ... then ... testif[ied] that based on his experience as an undercover agent he would describe the role that Ronald Brown played in the transaction as that of a steerer. When asked why, he testified ... "Because I believe that if it wasn't for his approval, the buy would not have gone down."

OPINION

... Since the jury convicted on ... conspiracy ... the evidence must permit a reasonable juror to be convinced beyond a reasonable doubt not simply that Brown had aided and abetted the drug sale but that he had agreed to do so....

A review of the evidence convinces us that it was sufficient.... Although Brown's mere presence at the scene of the crime and his knowledge that a crime was being committed would not have been sufficient to establish Brown's knowing participation in the conspiracy, the proof went considerably beyond that. Brown was not simply standing around while the exchanges between Officer Grimball and Valentine occurred. He came on the scene shortly after these began and Valentine immediately explained the situation to him. Brown then conferred his seal of approval on Grimball, a most unlikely event unless there was an established relationship between Brown and Valentine. Finally, Brown took upon himself the serious responsibility of telling Valentine to desist from his plan to reduce the risks by not handing the heroin directly to Grimball. A rational mind could take this as bespeaking the existence of an agreement whereby Brown was to have the authority to command, or at least to persuade. Brown's remark, "Just go ahead and get it for him," permits inferences that Brown knew where the heroin was to be gotten, that he knew that Valentine knew this, and that Brown and Valentine had engaged in such a transaction before....

When we add to the inferences that can be reasonably drawn from the facts to which Grimball testified ... his testimony about the use of steerers in street sales of narcotics ... we conclude that the Government offered sufficient evidence ... for a reasonable juror to be satisfied beyond a reasonable doubt not only that Brown had acted as a steerer but that he had agreed to do so. Affirmed.

DISSENT

While it is true that this is another $40 narcotics case, it is also a conspiracy case.... An agreement—a "continuous and conscious union of wills upon a common undertaking ... [was not proved here] unless an inference that Brown agreed to act as a "steerer" can be drawn from the fact that he said to Valentine (three times) that Grimball "looks okay [all right] to me," as well as "[j]ust go and get it for him.".... It could not be drawn from Brown's possession, constructive or otherwise, of narcotics or narcotics paraphernalia, his sharing in the proceeds of the street sale, his conversations with others, or even some hearsay evidence as to his "prior arrangements" with Valentine or an "established working relationship" with Brown and Valentine.... [I]ndeed, Brown was apprehended after leaving the area of the crime with only thirty-one of his own dollars in his pocket, and no drugs or other contraband. He did not even stay around for another Valentine sale....

I cannot believe there is proof of conspiracy, or Brown's membership in it, beyond a reasonable doubt....

This case may be unique. It ... supports Justice Jackson's reference to the history of the law of conspiracy as exemplifying, in Cardozo's phrase, the "tendency of a principle to expand itself to the limits of its logic...." If today we uphold a conspiracy to sell narcotics on the street, on this kind of evidence, what conspiracies might we approve tomorrow. The majority opinion will come back to haunt us, I fear.... Accordingly, I dissent.

Case Discussion What specific facts point to an agreement in the case? Do they convince you beyond a reasonable doubt that Brown and Valentine had a "continuous and conscious union of wills upon a common undertaking?" Is the dissent right that this case pushes conspiracy law to "the limits of its logic"? Why do you think the prosecution chose to charge Brown with conspiracy instead of with aiding and abetting? (Review relevant sections in chapter 4.) If the police had found evidence of possession (see chapter 3) or the marked money, would they have charged Brown with conspiracy? Should they have done so?

Conspiracy Mens Rea

Statutes and courts frequently define conspiracy *mens rea* vaguely. Common-law and modern statutes traditionally have not mentioned conspiracy *mens rea*, leaving courts to define it. The courts in turn have taken imprecise, widely divergent, and often inconsistent approaches to the *mens rea* problem. According to former Supreme Court Justice Robert Jackson, "The modern crime of conspiracy is so vague that it almost defies definition."[28]

Authorities frequently call conspiracy a specific intent crime. But what does that mean? Does it mean that conspiracy involves intent to enter a criminal agreement or combination? Or must conspiracy also include an intent to attain a particular criminal objective, or at least to use a specific criminal means to attain the objective? For example, if two men agree to burn down a building, they have conspired to commit arson. However, if they do not intend to hurt anyone, do they also conspire to commit murder? Surely not, if the conspiracy *mens rea* requires an intent to attain a particular criminal objective. The example demonstrates the importance of distinguishing between the intent to make agreements or combinations and the intent to attain a particular criminal objective. If the objective is to commit a specific crime, it must satisfy that crime's *mens rea*. Hence, conspiring to take another's property is not conspiring to commit larceny unless the conspirators intended to permanently deprive the owner of possession (see larceny in chapter 11).

Courts further complicate *mens rea* by not clarifying whether they require purpose. Consider cases involving suppliers of goods and services, such as doctors who order from drug supply companies in order to use or sell drugs illegally. At what point do suppliers become coconspirators, even though they have not agreed specifically to supply drugs for illegal distribution? Must prosecutors prove that suppliers entered an agreement or combination intending specifically to further buyers' criminal purposes? Most courts require such proof, even though it is difficult to obtain, because conspirators rarely subject their purposes to written contracts. Purpose must therefore be inferred from circumstances surrounding the combination, such as sales quantities, the continuity of the supplier-recipient relationship, the seller's initiative, a failure to keep records, and the relationship's clandestine nature.[29]

Some argue that knowing, or conscious, wrongdoing ought to satisfy the conspiracy *mens rea*. However, in *People v. Lauria,* the court refused to substitute knowledge for purpose.

CASE

Did He Conspire to run a "Call Girl" Service?

People v. Lauria
59 Cal.Rptr. 628 (Cal.1967)

Fleming, Associate Justice

FACTS
In an investigation of call-girl activity police focused their attention on three prostitutes actively plying their trade on call, each of whom was using Lauria's telephone answering service, presumably for business purposes.

On January 8, 1965, Stella Weeks, a police-woman, signed up for telephone service with Lauria's answering service. Mrs. Weeks,

in the course of her conversation with Lauria's office manager, hinted broadly that she was a prostitute concerned with the secrecy of her activities and their concealment from the police. She was assured that the operation of the service was discreet and "about as safe as you can get." It was arranged that Mrs. Weeks need not leave her address with the answering service, but could pick up her calls and pay her bills in person.

On February 11, Mrs. Weeks talked to Lauria on the telephone and told him her business was modelling and she had been referred to the answering service by Terry, one of the three prostitutes under investigation. She complained that because of the operation of the service she had lost two valuable customers, referred to as tricks. Lauria defended his service and said that her friends had probably lied to her about having left calls for her. But he did not respond to Mrs. Weeks' hints that she needed customers in order to make money, other than to invite her to his house for a personal visit in order to get better acquainted. In the course of his talk he said "his business was taking messages."

On February 15, Mrs. Weeks talked on the telephone to Lauria's office manager and again complained of two lost calls, which she described as a $50 and a $100 trick. On investigation the office manager could find nothing wrong, but she said she would alert the switchboard operators about slip-ups on calls.

On April 1 Lauria and the three prostitutes were arrested. Lauria complained to the police that this attention was undeserved, stating that Hollywood Call Board had 60 to 70 prostitutes on its board while his own service had only 9 or 10, that he kept separate records for known or suspected prostitutes for the convenience of himself and the police. When asked if his records were available to police who might come to the office to investigate call girls, Lauria replied that they were whenever the police had a specific name.

However, his service didn't "arbitrarily tell the police about prostitutes on our board. As long as they pay their bills we tolerate them." In a subsequent voluntary appearance before the Grand Jury Lauria testified he had always cooperated with the police. But he admitted he knew some of his customers were prostitutes, and he knew Terry was a prostitute because he had personally used her services, and he knew she was paying for 500 calls per month.

Lauria and the three prostitutes were indicted for conspiracy to commit prostitution, and nine overt acts were specified. Subsequently the trial court set aside the indictment as having been brought without reasonable or probable cause. (Pen.Code, § 995.) The *People* have appealed, claiming that a sufficient showing of an unlawful agreement to further prostitution was made.

OPINION

To establish agreement, the *People* need show no more than a tacit, mutual understanding between coconspirators to accomplish an unlawful act. Here the *People*

attempted to establish a conspiracy by showing that Lauria, well aware that his codefendants were prostitutes who received business calls from customers through his telephone answering service, continued to furnish them with such service. This approach attempts to equate knowledge of another's criminal activity with conspiracy to further such criminal activity, and poses the question of the criminal responsibility of a furnisher of goods or services who knows his product is being used to assist the operation of an illegal business. Under what circumstances does a supplier become a part of a conspiracy to further an illegal enterprise by furnishing goods or services which he knows are to be used by the buyer for criminal purposes?

Proof of knowledge is ordinarily a question of fact and requires no extended discussion in the present case. The knowledge of the supplier was sufficiently established when Lauria admitted he knew some of his customers were prostitutes and admitted he knew that Terry, an active subscriber to his service, was a prostitute. In the face of these admissions he could scarcely claim to have relied on the normal assumption an operator of a business or service is entitled to make, that his customers are behaving themselves in the eyes of the law. Because Lauria knew in fact that some of his customers were prostitutes, it is a legitimate inference he knew they were subscribing to his answering service for illegal business purposes and were using his service to make assignations for prostitution. On this record we think the prosecution is entitled to claim positive knowledge by Lauria of the use of his service to facilitate the business of prostitution.

The more perplexing issue in the case is the sufficiency of proof of intent to further the criminal enterprise. The element of intent may be proved either by direct evidence, or by evidence of circumstances from which an intent to further a criminal enterprise by supplying lawful goods or services may be inferred. Direct evidence of participation, such as advice from the supplier of legal goods or services to the user of those goods or services on their use for illegal purposes ... provides the simplest case. When the intent to further and promote the criminal enterprise comes from the lips of the supplier himself, ambiguities of inference from circumstances need not trouble us. But in cases where direct proof of complicity is lacking, intent to further the conspiracy must be derived from the sale itself and its surrounding circumstances in order to establish the supplier's express or tacit agreement to join the conspiracy.

In the case at bench the prosecution argues that since Lauria knew his customers were using his service for illegal purposes but nevertheless continued to furnish it to them, he must have intended to assist them in carrying out their illegal activities. Thus through a union of knowledge and intent he became a participant in a criminal conspiracy. Essentially, the People argue that knowledge alone of the continuing use of his telephone facilities for criminal purposes provided a sufficient basis from which his intent to participate in those criminal activities could be inferred. In examining precedents in this field we find that sometimes, but not always, the criminal intent of the supplier may be inferred from his knowledge of the unlawful use made of the product he supplies. [Here the court conducted an exhaustive examination of precedents.] ...

From this analysis of precedent we deduce the following rule: the intent of a supplier who knows of the criminal use to which his supplies are put to participate in the criminal activity connected with the use of his supplies may be established by (1) direct evidence that he intends to participate, or (2) through an inference that he intends to participate based on, (a) his special interest in the activity, or (b) the aggravated nature of the crime itself.

When we review Lauria's activities in the light of this analysis, we find no proof that Lauria took any direct action to further, encourage, or direct the call-girl activities of his codefendants and we find an absence of circumstances from which his special interest in their activities could be inferred. Neither excessive charges for standardized services, nor the furnishing of services without a legitimate use, nor an unusual quantity of business with call girls, are present. The offense which he is charged with furthering is a misdemeanor, a category of crime which has never been made a required subject of positive disclosure to public authority. Under these circumstances, although proof of Lauria's knowledge of the criminal activities of his patrons was sufficient to charge him with that fact, there was insufficient evidence that he intended to further their criminal activities, and hence insufficient proof of his participation in a criminal conspiracy with his codefendants to further prostitution. Since the conspiracy centered around the activities of Lauria's telephone answering service, the charges against his codefendants likewise fail for want of proof.

In absolving Lauria of complicity in a criminal conspiracy we do not wish to imply that the public authorities are without remedies to combat modern manifestations of the world's oldest profession. Licensing of telephone answering services under the police power, together with the revocation of licenses for the toleration of prostitution, is a possible civil remedy. The furnishing of telephone answering service in aid of prostitution could be made a crime. (Cf. Pen.Code, § 316, which makes it a misdemeanor to let an apartment with knowledge of its use for prostitution.) Other solutions will doubtless occur to vigilant public authorities if the problem of call-girl activity needs further suppression. The order is affirmed.

Case Discussion Of what exactly did the agreement in this case consist? What is the precise point of the court's distinguishing between knowledge and purpose? In what circumstances can courts infer intent from knowledge in conspiracy cases? Do you agree that the law has better, or at least other, ways to deal with prostitution than convicting Lauria? Which of the alternatives, if any, that the court suggests would you adopt?

—————⟫•⟪—————

The Objective of the Conspiracy

What objectives constitute conspiratorial agreements and combinations? In some states—Texas and Arkansas, for example—only combinations or agreements to commit felonies constitute conspiracies. Several other states—such as Colorado, Arizona, and Hawaii—include both felonies and misdemeanors. Still other states follow the broad, common-law definition, making it a crime to enter into any conspiracies, agreements, or combinations to "accomplish any unlawful object by lawful means," or "any lawful object by unlawful means," or any "unlawful object by unlawful means." Courts have even extended "unlawful" to embrace civil wrongs. For example, an agreement to interfere unfairly with trade is not a crime in most states, but it may be against the law. An agreement to engage in unfair trade practices has an unlawful, if not criminal, objective and is considered a conspiracy.

Some conspiracy statutes reach still further. In Alabama, for instance, conspiracy not only applies to agreements and combinations to accomplish criminal and other unlawful objectives, it also encompasses "any act injurious to public health, morals, trade, and commerce." Agreements and combinations falling within this sweeping phrase are almost limitless in number. Examples include combinations to commit fornication, to interfere with social intercourse at a picnic, and to use another person's car without permission.[30]

Reformers have urged courts to declare the most sweeping statutes void for vagueness. In *State v. Musser,* the state of Utah prosecuted Mormons for urging the practice of polygamy. The Utah Supreme Court ruled that the "public morals" provision in Utah's conspiracy statute was unconstitutionally vague. Most efforts have failed, however. Courts have actually expanded the federal conspiracy to defraud provision in the United States Code to encompass "virtually any impairment of the Government's operating efficiency." The United States Supreme Court remarked that these broad statutes

> would seem to be warrant for conviction for agreement to do almost any act which a judge and jury might find at the moment contrary to his or its notions of what was good for health, morals, trade, commerce, justice or order.[31]

Another path toward reform is to draft narrower conspiracy statutes. The Model Penal Code, for example, includes only agreements or combinations with "criminal objectives." Several states have followed suit. Connecticut, Georgia, Illinois, and others now include only agreements or combinations made to pursue criminal objectives.

Parties to Conspiracy

At common law and in most jurisdictions today, a conspiracy requires two or more parties to the agreement. The criminal law punishes conspiracies in

[Handwritten margin note: two or more people. Object by unlawful or lawful means either or could occur to make this happen.]

part because group offenses threaten more danger than offenses committed by individuals. Thus, some have argued that when unlawful combinations do not have an element of added danger they are not conspiracies unless they involve more than the number of parties required to commit the completed crime. According to **Wharton's rule** (named after a nineteenth-century criminal law commentator), in a crime that requires two or more persons (such as bigamy, bribery, incest, and gambling) the state must prove that three or more persons agreed to commit the offense. For example, a police officer who agreed not to arrest a person in exchange for money did not conspire to obstruct justice, because bribery itself requires at least two persons—the offerer and receiver. Had two police officers agreed to take the money, then conspiracy would have occurred because three parties (the two officers and the briber) agreed to commit the crime.[32]

Some jurisdictions have abolished the Wharton rule on the ground that whether or not the object offense required more than one party, the danger the actor poses to society justifies making the effort criminal. The Model Penal Code adopts this unilateral approach to liability for conspiracy. The New Jersey Supreme Court took this approach in *State v. Lavary.*[33]

CASE

Did She Conspire to Commit Atrocious Assault and Battery?

State v. Lavary
377 A.2d 1255 (1977)

After her conviction of conspiracy to commit atrocious assault and battery and to commit mayhem upon a policeman, defendant sought postconviction relief. The Superior Court, Law Division, Arnone, J. S. C., held, inter alia, that defendant could be convicted of conspiracy even though the person with whom she allegedly conspired was actually himself an undercover police officer. Motion to dismiss indictment or grant judgment notwithstanding the verdict denied.
Arnone, J. S. C.

FACTS
Defendant brings this motion seeking a number of different postconviction remedies. She seeks (1) the merger of the three counts of the indictment; (2) a new trial pursuant to R. 3:20–1, or (3) dismissal of the indictment. [The excerpt here deals only with the conspiracy.]

Briefly, the evidence indicated that defendant had gone to Maryland at the request of New Jersey law enforcement authorities for whom she had been working as an informant from time to time. The purpose of the trip was to ascertain if defendant could provide evidence against her former husband who was suspected of involvement in a murder.

While there she met a woman named Billie, a prior acquaintance from New Jersey. In the course of renewing their acquaintance defendant represented to Billie that the major irritation in her life was a Lt. Halliday of the Middletown Tp. Police Dept. She indicated to Billie that Lt. Halliday was constantly harassing her and was the source of all her major problems. She also stated to Billie that she was looking for someone who could "get" Lt. Halliday. Billie, who was an informant for the Maryland State Police, told defendant that she might know such a person. Billie subsequently told the Maryland State Police of the conversation.

When the Maryland State Police learned that the intended victim was a New Jersey police officer, they resolved to have one of their undercover agents, Lt. Mazzone, introduced by Billie to defendant as the "hit man" defendant was seeking.

A number of telephone conversations ensued, beginning December 19, 1975. These conversations were taped by Lt. Mazzone. The gist of the conversations was that Lt. Mazzone would be paid a sum of money plus expenses to severely beat Lt. Halliday.

Defendant was subsequently indicted and convicted on three counts of an indictment charging conspiracy with an "undercover agent with the Maryland State Police" (Lt. Mazzone). Two counts charged conspiracy to commit atrocious assault and battery; one charged conspiracy to commit mayhem. Defendant and the undercover agent of the Maryland State Police were the only individuals named in the indictment.

... [T]he jury had available for its consideration the following conversations and statements by defendant:

MAZZONE: Well, how much you got to pay for the present?

LAVARY: Well, you see, that's not too much of a problem, cause what I want done, I waited many years for. I mean if it's a whole lot then I have to wait a little bit, but, I don't know, I need an idea about how much it would cost. I don't know if she explained it, I don't want a permanent Christmas present, did she explain that to you?

MAZZONE: No, why don't you give me a rundown?

LAVARY: Well, I just rather it be put out of commission but around to realize it, you know what I mean, cause to me that's so much more appropriate. The other way it's done, it's over with, and you know, use it up and it's all gone. Once you use something, it's forgotten, but I'd like this one to kind of linger on for years and years, and years, so he'll always remember who gave it to him.

MAZZONE: That ain't bad. Understand the Dude's a cop or wears some kind of uniform.

LAVARY: Yea.

MAZZONE: That makes it extra special.

LAVARY: Yes. They immediately start right here, but there's been so many other people

that, they could bat their head against the wall for the next 20 years with just a list; it's been a long time comin [sic]. I never had it done before because it was always right here, I mean they knew, I came into a lot of money once before, and that's when I planned to give him his last present, but I couldn't because they watched me like a hawk for almost a year, and it was just no good, now things have lightened up for over a year.

LAVARY: I'll meet him on the turnpike, that's not far from my house any way. You don't know how much I appreciate this Billie, cause, I've been waiting a long time, biting my tongue, biding my time, all fall directly in my head, and I feel the time is quite appropriate now, specially being you know, I got such good backing right now.

MAZZONE: You want him crippled?

LAVARY: I just want him maimed for the rest of his life. Every time he looks at his twisted (expletive) self he'll know somebody who hated him wanted it.

MAZZONE: You want him maimed for the rest of his life. What do you mean, legs, arms, eyes, what?

LAVARY: Just about everything, I just wanted him (expletive) up.

MAZZONE: Who you talking it over with?

LAVARY: My old man.

MAZZONE: He's ok with just the maiming?

LAVARY: I don't want him dead.

MAZZONE: No, I mean the old man.

LAVARY: Well it's me who wanted it, he kind of wanted me to forget it for a while because they picked me up once since then, you know, he's afraid of a little heat coming back on me, but I don't care....

[On other grounds,] defendant's motion for a new trial is denied.

Defendant's final argument which she advances on this motion is for dismissal of the indictment ... or a judgment of acquittal....

OPINION

The question presented by defendant's argument is whether a defendant may be convicted of conspiracy when the conspiracy is between two persons, one of whom is defendant and the other an undercover agent for a law enforcement agency who only pretends to participate in the conspiracy for the purpose of obtaining evidence against the defendant.

The gist of the offense of conspiracy lies not in the doing of the act, nor in effecting the purpose for which the conspiracy is formed, nor in attempting to accomplish that purpose, but in the forming of the scheme or agreement between the parties. It is the unlawful purpose upon which they agreed which makes a conspiracy punishable once any overt act is committed in furtherance of it. This is so because such unions are vested with a potentiality for evil that renders the plans criminal in themselves and punishable as such if acts are done to effect their object.

The legislative intent underlying the statute is founded upon the plain fact that a conspiracy is an evil apart from the substantive offense, and at times even a greater evil, for the conspiracy may lead to other substantive offenses of a like sort and perhaps to habitual practices....

[D]efendant was found guilty of conspiring with an undercover agent of the Maryland State Police. She now seeks to assert as a complete defense the fact that since her coconspirator could not be guilty of committing the crime, neither could she. She argues that since Lt. Mazzone did not intend to agree, it is irrelevant that she did intend to agree, since a conspiracy requires a common intent in the minds of both conspirators.

Closer examination of defendant's position reveals that its basis is "factual impossibility." She argues that Lt. Mazzone's status as an undercover police officer makes a conspiracy an impossibility since the facts reveal that Lt. Mazzone only pretended to enter the conspiracy and that their mistake as to his actual intent is sufficient to vitiate the conspiracy.

In this case defendant's intent to have bodily harm inflicted upon Lt. Halliday is clear; believing Lt. Mazzone to intend the same result, she did all that was in her power to bring about the criminal result she desired. The fact that Lt. Mazzone was an undercover agent does not diminish the criminal quality of defendant's intent. The consequence which defendant intended was a result which, if successful, would have been a crime. The fact that Lt. Mazzone was an undercover agent should in no way negate defendant's clearly manifested intent to commit a criminal act. It should be immaterial to her guilt that the person with whom he is alleged to have conspired might have a complete defense in that he did not have the prerequisite intent....

This court holds that when the consequences sought by defendant are unlawful, it is no defense to a charge of conspiracy that she could not reach her goal because of circumstances unknown to her, or that the person with whom she conspired has not been or cannot be convicted....

To hold otherwise here would mock justice, interfere with the interest of society in repressing crime, and lead to absurd results. The court finds that a unilateral approach to the crime of conspiracy is appropriate and fully justified in New Jersey....

The court finds this interpretation ... consistent with the increased danger and social harm inherent in the crime of conspiracy. The "intricacies and artificial distinctions" urged by defendant thwart rather than serve substantial justice and are hereby rejected.

For the above reasons, the motion to dismiss the indictment or grant judgment notwithstanding the verdict is denied.

Case Discussion   What reasons does the court give for rejecting the Wharton rule and adopting the "unilateral" approach? Do you think Lavary is equally blameworthy and dangerous whether or not the undercover police officer only pretended to enter the agreement? Why? Is it fair to punish someone for an agreement that never results in injury to anyone? Why? Why not?

The relationships of parties to conspiracies can get intricate, particularly when they involve large operations. Most of these large-scale conspiracies fall into two major patterns, "wheel" and "chain" conspiracies. In wheel conspiracies, one or more defendants participate in every transaction. These participants constitute the hub of the wheel conspiracy. Others participate in only one transaction; they are the spokes in the wheel. Chain conspiracies usually involve the distribution of some commodity, such as illegal drugs. In chain conspiracies, participants at one end of the chain may know nothing of each other, but every participant handles the same commodity at different points in its distribution, such as manufacture, distribution, and selling. In *U.S. v. Bruno,* for example, smugglers brought narcotics into New York, middlemen purchased the narcotics, and two groups of retailers (one operating in New York and the other in Louisiana) bought narcotics from middlemen.

Failure to convict one party does not prevent conviction of the other party or parties to the combination or conspiracy. Typically, statutes similar to the Illinois Criminal Code provide:

> It shall not be a defense to conspiracy that the person or persons with whom the accused is alleged to have conspired
>
> *1.* Has not been prosecuted or convicted, or
> *2.* Has been convicted of a different offense, or
> *3.* Is not amenable to justice, or
> *4.* Has been acquitted, or
> *5.* Lacked the capacity to commit an offense.[34]

CASE

Were They Partners in Crime?

Williams v. State
274 Ind. 94, 409 N.E.2d 571 (1980)

[Carl and Diane Williams were convicted of conspiracy to commit murder. Carl Williams was sentenced to thirty years in prison. Diane Williams was sentenced to twenty years in prison. She appealed. Justice Pivarnik delivered the opinion.]

FACTS
[The Indiana Criminal Code] codifies the offense of conspiracy. That section provides:]

Conspiracy.— (a) A person conspires to commit a felony when, with intent to commit the felony, he agrees with another person to commit the felony. A conspiracy to commit a felony is a felony of the same class as the underlying felony. However, a conspiracy to commit murder is a class A felony. (b) The state must allege and prove that either the person or the person with whom he agreed performed an overt act in furtherance of the agreement.

In early January, 1978, Hammond police officer James Lawson was working as an undercover agent for the Drug Enforcement Administration branch of the United States Department of Justice. During the course of his work for the federal government, he came in contact with Dr. Carl N. Williams and Diane Kendrick Williams, the defendants in this case. On January 5, Lawson was in the Williams' home in Gary, Indiana, discussing certain other matters not related to the present case. Dr. Williams and appellant both engaged in conversation with Lawson. Late in the afternoon, appellant began reading that day's edition of the Gary

Post-Tribune. The January 5 edition of the Post-Tribune carried an article on page one under the by-line of Alan Doyle. This article related how the Williams had been charged in connection with an automobile theft. Appellant Diane Williams brought the story to the attention of Dr. Williams and Officer Lawson. Dr. and Mrs. Williams became very angry over the contents of the article. Appellant explained the general content of the story to Lawson, and he remarked, "It sounds like they are really trying to get you." Dr. Williams explained that his family had been involved in politics and that Gary was a "dog town."

When Diane Williams asked what they were going to do about the article, Dr. Williams stated that he wanted "something" done about it. Lawson's suggestion that they talk to their attorneys and pursue legal remedies was rejected out of hand by both Dr. Williams and appellant. Diane Williams stated that lawyers were of no help, and Dr. Williams said he was tired of dealing with lawyers. Both remained very angry over the article, and appellant again asked what they were going to do about Doyle and his article. Dr. Williams then stated that he wanted Doyle "shut up."

Dr. Williams then asked Lawson if he could "undertake an extra service." Lawson asked what he was referring to, and Dr. Williams repeated that he wanted Doyle "shut up." When Lawson asked him exactly what he meant by "shutting someone up," the doctor said he wanted to stop what he called "this malicious slander." Lawson remarked that breaking somebody's legs and arms wouldn't necessarily shut them up, and appellant Diane Williams agreed. Dr. Williams asked Lawson again if he would "perform an extra service." He stated that he wanted Alan Doyle killed, and he asked Lawson if he knew someone who would do the job. Lawson said he could put them in touch with someone who would, but that whoever he contacted would want to know "specifics" about the intended victim, such as his appearance, his place of employment, and what kind of car he drove. Dr. Williams said he would go to the newspaper office to

learn this information, but appellant Diane Williams counselled against such an idea, saying it would connect Dr. Williams too closely with what was going to happen.

Lawson and Dr. Williams left the room to pick up a two-way police radio Williams possessed, because he thought it would be helpful in their plans. A short time later, they returned to the room where Diane was sitting. Lawson reiterated his feeling that the people he contacted to perform the killing would need to know who Doyle is, where he worked, and the kind of car he drove. Appellant Diane Williams volunteered to obtain this information.

The next day, Lawson returned to the Williams home with Michael Bolin, another undercover police officer. Lawson identified Bolin to Dr. Williams as the person who would perform the killing for them. Bolin demanded one thousand dollars for his services, half to be paid at that time, and the remainder after the job was completed. Dr. Williams then paid five hundred dollars to Bolin. Appellant Diane Williams was not present during this conversation.

On January 12, 1978, Lawson and Bolin went back to the Williams residence. After a brief conversation, Lawson, Bolin and Dr. Williams went for a drive in the agents' car. At their request, Dr. Williams directed them to the location of the Post-Tribune offices in Gary. During the course of the conversation in the car, Dr. Williams stated on two occasions that appellant Diane Williams knew of and concurred in their plan to kill Alan Doyle.

OPINION

Thus, in this case, the prosecution must have proved that Diane Williams had the intent to commit murder; that she agreed with another person to commit murder; and that some overt act was performed in furtherance of that agreement. The requisite intent, of course, may be inferred from the acts committed and the circumstances surrounding the case.

We think there was substantial evidence from which the jury could have found beyond a reasonable doubt that Diane

Williams had the intent to kill Alan Doyle, and that she had an intelligent understanding with Dr. Williams and Lawson that the killing would be done. Clearly, Dr. Williams committed several overt acts in pursuance of this agreement and plan. Thus, the evidence is sufficient to support the jury's finding that appellant Diane Williams conspired to commit murder.

Case Discussion Did Diane Williams conspire to commit murder? What was the agreement? The act in furthering it? The criminal purpose? Do you think the penalty is excessive? Is Diane Williams as guilty as her husband, Dr. Williams? Why is he punished more severely?

Summary of Conspiracy

Conspiracy is further removed from completed crimes than are both attempt and preparation. Conspiracy law is based on the rationale that it not only prevents dangerous persons from completing their evil plans but also strikes at a second evil, combinations for wrongful purposes, a serious social problem in itself. Conspiracy's material elements are simply stated—conspiracy is an agreement or combination intended to achieve an illegal objective—but are applied according to widely varied interpretation and meaning.

The often vague definitions of the material elements in conspiracy offer considerable opportunity for prosecutorial and judicial discretion. At times, this discretion borders on abuse, leading to charges that conspiracy law is unjust. First, a general criticism is that conspiracy law punishes conduct far remote from actual crime. Second, labor organizations, civil liberties groups, and large corporations charge that conspiracy is a weapon against their legitimate interests of collective bargaining and strikes, dissent from accepted points of view and public policies, and profit making. Critics say that when prosecutors do not have enough evidence to convict for the crime itself, they turn as a last hope to conspiracy. Conspiracy's vague definitions greatly enhance the chance for a guilty verdict.

Not often mentioned, but extremely important, is that intense media attention to conspiracy trials can lead to abuse. This happened in the conspiracy trials of Dr. Benjamin Spock and the Chicago Eight, and in other conspiracy trials involving radical politics during the 1960s. It also occurred in the Watergate conspiracy trials involving President Nixon's associates during the 1970s, and in the alleged conspiracies surrounding the sale of arms to Iran for hostages and the subsequent alleged diversion of funds during the 1980s.

Several states have made efforts to overcome these criticisms by defining conspiracy elements more narrowly. Agreement or combination are no longer so vague as they once were. The Model Penal Code requires acts in furtherance of agreement, and several states are following that lead. Those states have refined *mens rea* to include only purposeful conduct, that is, a specific intent to carry out the objective of the agreement or combination. Knowledge, recklessness, and negligence are increasingly attacked as insufficient culpability for an offense as remote from completion as conspiracy.

Furthermore, most recent legislation restricts conspiratorial objectives to criminal ends. Phrases like "unlawful objects," lawful objects by unlawful means," and "objectives harmful to public health, morals, trade, and commerce" are increasingly regarded as too broad and, therefore, unacceptable.

On the other hand, the Racketeer Influenced and Corrupt Organizations Act (RICO) demonstrates the continued vitality of conspiracy law. RICO is based on the need for effective means to meet the threat posed by organized crime. It imposes enhanced penalties for

> all types of organized criminal behavior, that is, enterprise criminality—from simple political to sophisticated white collar schemes to traditional Mafia-type endeavors.[35]

Racketeering activity includes any act chargeable under state and federal law, including murder, kidnapping, bribery, drug dealing, gambling, theft, extortion, and securities fraud. Among other things, the statute prohibits using income from a "pattern of racketeering activity" to acquire an interest in or establish an enterprise affecting interstate commerce; conducting an enterprise through a pattern of racketeering; or conspiring to violate these provisions.[36]

RICO's drafters intended the statute to "break the back of organized crime." The racketeers they had in mind were

> loansharks, drug kingpins, prostitution overlords, and casino operators who hired murderers and arsonists to enforce and extort—you know, the designated bad guys who presumably did not deserve the rights of due process that should protect all of us.

Now however, aggressive prosecutors use RICO against white-collar crime. Rudolf Giuliani, for example, caused Drexel Burnham Lambert to plead guilty to several counts of securities violations in order to avoid RICO prosecution, which would not only result in harsher legal penalties but also attach the label of racketeer to white-collar criminals.[37]

▼ SOLICITATION

Most remote from its underlying substantive crime is solicitation. At common law—and under most modern statutes—solicitation is a command, urging, or request to a third person to commit a crime. Suppose I want to murder my wife but am afraid to do it. If I ask a friend and he kills her, then we are both murderers. If he tries to kill her and fails because his gun is defective, then he has committed attempted murder. If he agrees to kill her and buys the gun but gets no further, then we have conspired to commit murder. But simply soliciting or urging another to commit murder is also a crime. Hence, if I ask my friend to commit murder and offer him money to do it, even if he rejects the offer, I have committed the crime called solicitation to commit murder.

Opinion differs as to whether solicitation to commit a crime presents a sufficient social danger to constitute a crime. On one side, it is argued that solicitation is not dangerous because an independent moral agent (the person solicited) stands between solicitors and their criminal objectives.

Furthermore, by soliciting others to commit crimes, solicitors demonstrate their reluctance to commit crimes themselves. On the other side, advocates argue that solicitation creates the special danger inherent in group participation in crime; in this sense, solicitation is an attempt to conspire. In addition, solicitors manifest masterful and intelligent manipulation of their underlings. According to the commentary of the Model Penal Code,"[t]here should be no doubt on this issue. Purposeful solicitation presents dangers calling for preventive intervention and is sufficiently indicative of a disposition towards criminal activity to call for liability."[38]

Elements of Solicitation			
Offense	***Actus Reus***	***Mens Rea***	**Result**
Solicitation	words of inducement to commit a crime	specific intent or purpose to induce someone to commit a crime	no substantive crime need result

Words constitute the *actus reus* in solicitation, but the law imprecisely prescribes what words qualify. Courts generally agree that statements simply favoring or approving crime do not constitute solicitation. Hence, someone who merely says "I think it would be great if someone killed that terrorist" has not solicited murder. Courts demand some sort of inducement. Statutes or judicial decisions have deemed sufficient a statement that does any of the following: advises, commands, counsels, encourages, entices, entreats, importunes, incites, induces, instigates, procures, requests, solicits, and urges. Uttering the proper inducement accompanied by the required *mens rea* constitutes solicitation. In other words, criminal solicitation consists of the effort to engage another in crime, whether or not the inducement ever ripens into a completed crime. The law considers that those who urge others to commit crimes are sufficiently dangerous to punish.[39]

Must the solicitor address the words to particular individuals? Some say yes, but courts have ruled that public exhortations to audiences suffice. One speaker who was convicted urged his audience from a public platform to commit murder and robbery. It is also solicitation to put an inducement in writing and send it through the mail, even if the part solicited never receives the letter. Soliciting is a crime even if the solicitor does not personally communicate the inducement, and despite the inducement's failure to reach its object. Hence, if I send a letter to my hoped-for collaborator, offering her $30,000 to kill my enemy, I have solicited murder even if the letter gets lost in the mail. The danger of a criminal solicitor does not depend on the inducement's reaching its object; a solicitor bent on engaging another in crime will simply try again.[40]

Some statutes restrict the objective in solicitation to felonies, in some cases to violent felonies. In other jurisdictions, it is a crime to solicit another to commit any crime, whether felony, misdemeanor, or violation.

Furthermore, solicitation need not include an inducement to commit a crime. For example, suppose a robber urges a friend to borrow money and lend it to the robber for a plane ticket to escape from the jurisdiction. The robber has solicited escape, or aiding and abetting a robbery. Although borrowing money is not a crime, and lending money to a robber is not by itself a crime, both escape and aiding and abetting robbers are crimes. One who urges another to commit those crimes has committed the crime of solicitation.

Solicitation *mens rea* requires purpose or specific intent. The words in a solicitation must convey the author's intention to induce another to commit the substantive offense. If I urge my friend who works in an expensive jewelry shop to take a gold chain for me, I have solicited larceny. If, on the other hand, I ask another friend who works in a clothing shop to get a coat for me to use for the evening, and I plan to return the coat the next morning before anyone knows it is missing, I have not solicited larceny because I do not intend to steal the coat, only to use it for the night (see larceny in chapter 11).

A problem arises when law enforcement officers solicit in order to determine whether someone is disposed to commit a crime. For example, police decoys who try to get suspected prostitutes to offer sex for money have not solicited criminally under present law, because the decoys' motive is not dangerous. It is maintained (not without objection) that the decoys' motives are nobly addressed to upholding the law, hardly a dangerous propensity. Similarly, narcotics police or street decoys hoping to catch muggers are working to prevent and control crime, not to foster crime, according to supporters. Others argue that decoys encourage innocent people to commit crimes. Although law enforcement officers acting properly in the course of their duties may not be guilty of solicitation, their too-energetic encouragement may constitute entrapment (see chapter 7).

CASE

Did He Solicit His Wife's Murder?

State v. Furr
292 N.C. 711, 235 S.E.2d 193 (1977)

[Furr was convicted of three counts of soliciting to commit his wife's murder. He was sentenced to three consecutive eight- to ten-year prison terms for each murder. He appealed. Justice Exum gave the opinion.]

FACTS

The defendant and his wife had been married about 21 years and had four children when they separated in 1973. After the separation, Furr moved his real estate office from their home to a nearby location near the square in Locust, North Carolina. His wife, Earlene, continued to live at the house on Willow Drive and Furr moved into Western Hills Mobile Home Park. The couple's relationship was apparently quite volatile and Furr exhibited increasing hostility towards Earlene after the separation.

In April, 1973, Earlene filed a civil action against defendant resulting in a judgment against him in October, 1973. A year later, on his wife's motion, defendant was adjudged to be in contempt and was committed to jail. While in Stanly County jail, Furr met Raymond Clontz and Donald Owens, and related his marital problems to them, especially his concern over the property dispute. He was released from jail on December 6, 1974, upon payment of $13,623.00.

After his release, Furr approached Clontz and Owens, drove them by Earlene's home and explained how to get into the house. He offered Owens $3,000.00 to kill Earlene and offered to give Clontz a lot which the latter wanted to store cars on if Clontz would do the job. Neither man accepted the offer.

In October, 1974, defendant asked "Buck" Baker if he knew a "hit man." At the time Furr was angry because Earlene had disposed of some racing equipment. Furr also approached Donald Eugene Huneycutt on several occasions to ask whether Huneycutt knew a "hit man." In the initial encounters, Furr wanted Johny Jhue Laney killed because Laney had murdered his own wife, Doris, who was defendant's girl friend. By early 1975, however, Furr's plans extended as well to Earlene and her attorney, Charles Brown. Huneycutt told him killing women and lawyers would create "too much heat," but defendant responded that he could stand the heat and had his mother for an alibi.

Defendant also asked George Arnold Black, Jr., to kill Earlene, and drove him by the house in the fall of 1974. Like the others, Black declined the offer.

OPINION

Solicitation of another to commit a felony is a crime in North Carolina, even though the solicitation is of no effect and the crime solicited is never committed. The gravamen of the offense of soliciting lies in counseling, enticing or inducing another to commit a crime.

Defendant argues that the evidence shows only that defendant requested that Huneycutt find someone else to murder each of the three intended victims, and not that Huneycutt himself commit the crime. "Under no authority," says defendant, "is that a criminal offense." Accepting for the moment defendant's argument that defendant solicited Huneycutt only to find another "hit man," we hold that such a request constitutes the crime of solicitation to commit a felony in North Carolina. In W. LaFave and A. Scott, *Criminal Law,* 419

(1972) it is observed that "[i]n the usual solicitation case, it is the solicitor's intention that the criminal result be directly brought about by the person he has solicited; that is, it is his intention that the crime be committed and that the other commit it as a principal in the first degree, as where A asks B to kill C. However, it would seem sufficient that A requested B to get involved in the scheme to kill C in any way which would establish B's complicity in the killing of C were that to occur. Thus it would be criminal for one person to solicit another to in turn solicit a third party, to solicit another to join a conspiracy, or to solicit another to aid and abet the commission of a crime."

Defendant further contends that there was no evidence to support three indictments alleging solicitation of Raymond Clontz to murder Earlene Furr. There is no merit to these contentions in two of the counts. Indictment Number 76–CR–700 alleges that Clontz was solicited in January to murder Furr's wife. The evidence is that during that month, shortly after both men were released from jail where defendant had been quite talkative about his marital problems, Clontz and Furr met to discuss a lot which Clontz wished to purchase. Furr said he wanted $3,000.00 for the lot and Clontz agreed to take it. Then, as Clontz related at trial Furr told him not to be so hasty, that "he would make some arrangements about the payment for the lot in another way; that he wanted me to do a job for him." Clontz told Furr that he "knew what he was talking about, but that [he] wasn't interested in it." Defendant then told him he had to go to court with his wife in a few weeks and "that he had to have something done before court time or he was going to be in serious trouble. He said his wife was already getting $250.000 a week from him, and she had possession of the house, and had his property tied up and that he had to have something done." In the context, we find no other reasonable interpretation of defendant's words on this occasion than that he was requesting Clontz to kill his wife.

Affirmed.

Case Discussion   Can you identify Furr's *mens rea,* his *actus reus,* and the resulting harm? Do you think the prosecution proved them beyond a reasonable doubt? Solicitation is aimed at controlling dangerous persons. Is Furr a dangerous social problem who should be punished whether or not his inducements ever came to fruition? Do you think eight to ten years' imprisonment is too little, too much, or just about enough punishment for what he did? Why or why not?

▼ *Summary* ▼

Attempt, conspiracy, and solicitation aim primarily to prevent crime and control dangerous persons. Clear commitment to crime, measured by intent and conduct, sufficiently indicates a person's dangerousness. Persons who demonstrate their determination to commit crimes deserve punishment and justify making even some incomplete crimes punishable. If extraneous factors interrupt or frustrate completion—such as when police officers or others arrive at the scene—that fortuity should not permit would-be criminals to escape punishment. However, if perpetrators voluntarily renounce their efforts because their consciences compel them, some argue that the law should excuse them because they are no longer dangerous. Because the dangerousness of the actor, not the actuality of harm, justifies making inchoate harms criminal, most agree that it does not matter whether it was impossible to complete the harm intended. It is enough that the crime could have been committed if circumstances were as the perpetrator reasonably believed they would be.

The justification for imposing criminal liability in inchoate crimes rests, therefore, not only on the danger of potential conduct but also on the danger of individuals. When dangerousness (and not harmful result) is the criterion for punishment, it is always possible to erroneously predict who is dangerous. Available research strongly suggests that high risks of error attend any such predictions, especially when those predictions are directed toward violent behavior. This finding has led some to argue that criminal law should never punish potential harm, only past conduct.

▼ *Questions for Review and Discussion* ▼

1. What is the difference between preparation and attempt?

2. What kinds of agreement should conspiracy encompass?

3. What two reasons support making conspiracies crimes?

4. Should renunciation of criminal intent be a defense to inchoate offenses? Explain.

5. Why are inchoate offenses crimes? Should they be?

6. What is the act in attempt? In conspiracy? In solicitation?

7. What is the *mens rea* in attempt? In conspiracy? In solicitation?

8. What is the objective in attempt? In conspiracy? In solicitation?

9. Should it be a crime to attempt to commit any offense, or only felonies? To conspire to commit any crime, or only felonies? To solicit any crime, or only felonies?

▼ Suggested Readings ▼

1. Jerome Hall, *General Principles of Criminal Law,* 2d ed. (Indianapolis: Bobbs-Merrill, 1960), chap. 15. An excellent survey of attempt law. Hall includes a good history of attempt and the theoretical justifications for it, and discusses some proper limits to be placed on it.

2. George P. Fletcher, *Rethinking Criminal Law* (Boston: Little, Brown, 1978), pp. 131–205, 218–32. Contains provocative discussions about the inchoate offenses. Professor Fletcher clearly defines the terms in considerable detail. He also assesses the inchoate crimes and participation in crime in ways that provoke considerable thought about the roles of those terms in criminal law.

3. Jessica Mitford, *The Trial of Dr. Spock* (New York: Knopf, 1969). An excellent narrative, written for the general public. It reveals much about conspiracy within the context of a real case that attracted enormous publicity.

4. American Law Institute, *Model Penal Code and Commentaries,* vol. 1 (Philadelphia: American Law Institute, 1985), pt. 1, pp. 295–328. A detailed analysis of all elements in complicity, as well as arguments for why complicity should be included in criminal law and to what extent participants should be criminally liable. This is an advanced discussion written for experts in the field but is well worth the effort to read and consider its points. In vol. 2, pt. 1, the inchoate offenses are treated similarly.

▼ Notes ▼

1. Rollin M. Perkins and Ronald N. Boyce, *Criminal Law,* 3d ed. (Mineola, N.Y.: Foundation Press, 1982), pp. 611–58, 700–14; American Law Institute, *Model Penal Code and Commentaries,* vol. 2 (Philadelphia: American Law Institute, 1985), pp. 293–98.

2. George P. Fletcher, *Rethinking Criminal Law,* (Boston: Little, Brown, 1978), p. 131; Plato, *The Laws,* trans. Trevor J. Saunders (Middlesex, England: Penguin Books, 1975), pp. 397–98; Jerome Hall, *General Principles of Criminal Law,* 2d ed. (Indianapolis: Bobbs-Merrill, 1960), pp. 560–64.

3. Quoted in Hall, *General Principles of Criminal Law,* p. 560.

4. Ibid.

5. Geoffrey R. Elton, *The Tudor Constitution* (Cambridge, Eng.: Cambridge University Press, 1972), pp. 170–71.

6. Joel Samaha, *Law and Order in Historical Perspective* (New York: Academic Press, 1974); Joel Samaha, "The Recognizance in Elizabethan Law Enforcement," *American Journal of Legal History* 25 (1981):189–204.

7. Cald. 397 (1784).

8. Sir James F. Stephen, *A History of the Criminal Law of England,* reprint (New York: Burt Franklin, 1973), p. 224.

9. Justice Moylan in *Gray v. State,* 403 A.2d 853 (Md.1979).

10. Arnold N. Enker, "*Mens Rea* and Criminal Attempt," *American Bar Foundation Research Journal* (1977): 845.

11. Wayne R. LaFave and Austin W. Scott, Jr., *Criminal Law,* (St. Paul: West Publishing Co., 1972), p. 423.

12. U.S. v. Mandujano, 499 F.2d 370, 374 (5th Cir. 1974); *Young v. State,* 493 A.2d 352 (Md.1985) (failure not an element); see also Perkins and Boyce, *Criminal Law,* 612–17.

13. Enker, "*Mens Rea* and Criminal Attempt," p. 847.

14. Oliver Wendell Holmes, Jr., *The Common Law* (Boston: Little Brown, 1963), pp. 54–55.

15. United States v. Mandujano, 499 F.2d 370, 375–76 (5th Cir. 1974) (more than intention required).

16. Commonwealth v. Peaslee, 59 N.E. 55 (1901); Fletcher, *Rethinking Criminal Law,* pp. 139–40; American Law Institute, *Model Penal Code and Commentaries,* 2:321–22.

17. American Law Institute, *Model Penal Code and Commentaries,* 2:329–31.

18. Ibid.

19. Bradley v. Ward, N.Z.L.R. 471 (1955).

20. American Law Institute, *Model Penal Code and Commentaries,* 2:337–46.

21. Ibid.

22. Nev.Rev.Stat. § 205.055; American Law Institute, *Model Penal Code and Commentaries,* 2:354–55.

23. Fernand N. Dutile and Harold F. Moore, "Mistake and Impossibility: Arranging a Marriage between Two Difficult Partners," *Northwestern University Law Review* 74 (1979):166, 181 ff.

24. American Law Institute, *Model Penal Code and Commentaries,* 2:356–62; Daniel G. Moriarty, "Extending the Defense of Renunciation," *Temple Law Review* 62(1989):1.

25. Model Penal Code and Commentaries, p. 387.

26. Jessica Mitford, *The Trial of Dr. Spock* (New York: Knopf, 1969), pp. 70–71.

27. Fletcher, *Rethinking Criminal Law,* pp. 218, 223, 225; Kentucky Rev. Stat. 427.110 (1958).

28. Concurring in *Krulewich v. United States,* 336 U.S. 440, 445–46, 69 S.Ct. 716, 719–20, 93 L.Ed. 790 (1949).

29. Direct Sales Co. v. United States, 319 U.S.703 (1943).

30. Ala.Gen.tat. 54–197 (1958); *Baker v. Commonwealth,* 204 Ky. 420, 264 S.W. 1069 (1924); *State v. Ameker,* 53 S.E. 484 (1906); *State v. Davis,* 229 S.E. 811 (1911).

31. 118 Utah 537, 223 P.2d 193 (1950); 18 U.S.C.A.; st 371 (1976); *Musser v. Utah,* 333 U.S. 95, 97, 68 S.Ct. 397, 92 L.Ed.562 (1948).

32. *People v. Davis,* 408 Mich. 255, 290 N.W.2d 366 (1980).

33. *Model Penal Code,* § 5.03.

34. *Illinois Criminal Law and Procedure* (St. Paul: West Publishing Co., 1988), chap. 38, § 8–4.

35. Blakely and Gettings, "Racketeer Influenced and Corrupt Organizations (RICO): Basic Concepts—Criminal and Civil Remedies," *Temple Law Quarterly* 53 (1980):1013–14.

36. 18 U.S.C.A. § 1961 et seq.

37. William Safire, "The End of RICO," *The New York Times,* (January 30, 1989), p. 19.

38. American Law Institute, *Model Penal Code and Commentaries,* 2:365–66.

39. LaFave and Scott, *Criminal Law,* p. 419.

40. *State v. Schleifer,* 99 Conn. 432 121 A. 805 (1923).

Chapter

6

Defenses to Criminal Liability: Justifications

▼ *Chapter Outline* ▼

   I. Introduction
  II. Self-Defense
      A. Elements of Self-Defense
      B. The Retreat Doctrine
  III. Defense of Others
  IV. General Principle of Necessity
   V. Execution of Public Duties
  VI. Resisting Unlawful Arrest
  VII. Defense of Homes and Property
 VIII. Consent
  IX. Summary

▼ *Chapter Main Points* ▼

1. Defenses to criminal liability are either justifications or excuses.

2. In justifications, defendants admit responsibility but maintain that under the circumstances what they did was right.

3. In excuses, defendants admit what they did was wrong but maintain that under the circumstances they were not responsible.

4. Self-defense justifies using force or threats of force to ward off attacks from individuals who it is reasonable to believe threaten imminent death or serious bodily harm.

5. Self-defense justifies protection from immediate harm; neither retaliation nor preemptive strikes for a future threat suffice.

6. Necessity justifies otherwise criminal conduct (a lesser evil) when it avoids a greater imminent evil.

7. Law enforcement officers may use force, including deadly force, when it is reasonable to enforce the criminal law.

8. Citizens may, in a few jurisdictions, use force (but not deadly force) to defend against an unlawful arrest.

9. Owners may use reasonable force, including deadly force, to defend their property.

10. Voluntary, knowing consent may justify minor assaults.

▼ *Chapter Key Terms* ▼

affirmative defense—A defense in which the defendant bears the burden of production.

burden of persuasion—The responsibility to convince the fact finder of the truth of the assertion.

burden of production—The responsibility to introduce initial evidence to support a claim.

burden of proof—The responsibility to produce the evidence to persuade the fact finder.

castle exception—Defenders have no need to retreat when attacked at home.

defenses—Justifications and excuses to criminal liability.

excuses—Wrongdoing without criminal responsibility.

imperfect defense—Defense reducing but not eliminating criminal liability.

justifications—Otherwise criminal conduct right under the circumstances.

mitigating circumstances—Facts that reduce but do not eliminate culpability.

motive—The reason why a defendant commits a crime.

objective test—External measure or reasonableness of belief.

perfect defense—A defense that leads to acquittal.

subjective test—An internal or honest belief test.

▼ INTRODUCTION

In all criminal cases, the government has the **burden of proof.** It must prove all the elements—*actus reus, mens rea,* and, where relevant, causation and resulting harm—beyond a reasonable doubt. The **defenses** allow defendants to avoid criminal liability even when the government has met its burden and proved all the elements beyond a reasonable doubt. Defenses arise in three main ways. First, someone else committed the crime, in which case defendants have the defense of alibi. For example, a defendant who proves he was with his girlfriend in San Francisco at the time robbers took the money from a 7-Eleven in Los Angeles has an alibi. Second, a material element may be missing; here, failure to establish the element provides the defense. For example, suppose a defendant shows that a partner consented to sexual intercourse in a charge of rape. The case lacks a material element in rape; sexual penetration without consent (see chapter 9). Finally, the general defenses of justification and excuse can lead to acquittal. In **justifications,** the subject of this chapter, defendants admit responsibility for crimes, but argue that, under the circumstances, what they did was right. In **excuses,** the subject of chapter 7, defendants admit that what they did was wrong but argue that, under the circumstances, they were not responsible for what they did.[1]

Justification permits certain circumstances to justify (make right) otherwise criminal conduct and causing of criminal harms. Justified behavior precludes punishment because the conduct lacks blameworthiness. For example, it is wrong to blame—hence, to punish—one who kills another in self-defense. Similarly, it is unjust to punish those not responsible for their conduct or its results. If I am so mentally diseased that I think I am squeezing a lemon when, in fact, I am choking my wife, my conduct is wrong but my insanity excuses my responsibility for the wrong[2] (see chapter 7).

The defenses require defendants to bear some burden in presenting evidence to support an **affirmative defense.** An affirmative defense admits the crime charged but "seeks to justify, excuse, or mitigate the defendant's conduct." In all jurisdictions, defendants bear the **burden of production,** that is, "the defendant is obliged to start matters off by putting in some evidence in support" of the defense. "We can assume that those who commit crimes are sane, sober, conscious, and acting freely. It makes sense, therefore, to make defendants responsible for injecting these extraordinary circumstances into the proceedings." The amount of evidence required "is not great; some credible evidence" suffices. Once defendants meet the burden of production by introducing some evidence of justification or excuse, they may or may not have the further **burden of persuasion;** that is, the responsibility to prove justification or excuse. Typically, jurisdictions require defendants to prove their defenses by a preponderance of the evidence, that is, by proving that more evidence than not supports justification or excuse. Occasionally, jurisdictions require that once the defendant meets the burden of persuasion, the burden shifts to the prosecution to prove beyond a reasonable doubt that the defendant did not have the defense.[3]

Perfect defenses, such as self-defense successfully pleaded, lead to outright acquittal. On the other hand, even if successfully pleaded, insanity ordinarily does not set defendants free, at least not automatically. Frequently, special insanity hearings following insanity verdicts result in defendants being sent to maximum-security hospitals until they regain their sanity. Often, defendants never regain their sanity; they remain committed for life to maximum-security hospitals. (Chapter 7.)

Sometimes evidence that does not lead to a perfect defense results in conviction for a lesser charge, such as when provocation reduces murder to manslaughter. This **imperfect defense** can mean the difference between death or life imprisonment for murder, and ten to twenty years for manslaughter (see chapter 8).

Even when defenses do not lead to acquittal or to conviction for lesser crimes, they may still influence punishment. Evidence that does not amount to a perfect or imperfect defense might still demonstrate **mitigating circumstances**, or facts that convince judges or juries that defendants do not deserve the maximum penalty for the crimes they committed. For example, if a state authorized the death penalty for first-degree murder, a murderer who killed without legal provocation might still get life imprisonment instead of the death penalty. Although words, however provocative, do not amount to legal provocation that reduces murder to manslaughter, they are a mitigating circumstance that might reduce capital punishment to life imprisonment. Hence, if a black person killed someone in an outburst of rage brought about by the victim's relentless taunting with the racist epithet "nigger," the taunting might mitigate the death penalty (see chapter 8).

Motive also influences punishment, or even conviction itself in some cases. **Motive** refers to the reason why individuals commit crimes. You should distinguish it from *mens rea,* which refers to intention. *Mens rea* reveals whether defendants acted or caused a result purposely, knowingly, recklessly, or negligently. Suppose a burglar purposely breaks into and enters a house with the intent to steal food because she is hungry. Hunger is the motive; breaking and entering with the intent to steal food is the *mens rea*. Mercy killing also illustrates both *mens rea* and motive: the mercy killer kills on purpose in order to ease the victim's suffering. The law does not recognize motive in most instances; *mens rea* suffices. However, motive might aid in proving *mens rea:* knowing that defendant killed to end the victim's suffering helps prove purpose and knowledge.

The motive of mercy might also affect conviction and punishment. A jury might refuse to convict a mercy killer even though the *mens rea* clearly exists—the premeditated, purposeful causing of another's death. Or, a judge might reduce the sentence to a minimum, and corrections officials might parole the mercy killer at the earliest possible date. For example, seventy-eight-year-old Oscar Carlson, who could no longer endure his wife's suffering from advanced Alzheimer's disease, shot and killed his wife. On his first day in prison, Carlson said, "I know it's better for me to sit here in prison than for Agnes to sit up there in the home like she was." A barrage of negative publicity surrounded his sentence to prison, generating considerable sympathy for the elderly murderer and leading to his early release. Mitigating circumstances are extraordinarily important in criminal law, especially because American judges have wide sentencing discretion.[4]

▼ SELF-DEFENSE

Several justifications—self-defense, defense of others, law enforcement, and sometimes defense of home and property—define what circumstances justify the use of force. Self-defense refers to using or threatening to use force against another in order to repel an unprovoked attack. At common law, self-defense was defined as follows:

> A man may repel force by force in the defense of his person, habitation, or property, against one or many who manifestly intend and endeavor, by violence or surprise, to commit a known felony on either. In such a case he is not obliged to retreat, but may pursue his adversary until he find himself out of danger; and if, in a conflict between them, he happen to kill, such killing is justifiable. The right of self-defense in cases of this kind is founded on the law of nature; and is not, nor can be, superseded by any law of society.... To make homicide excusable on the ground of self-defense, the danger must be actual and urgent.[5]

Self-defense rests on the notion that those subjected to unprovoked attacks may use force to do for themselves what the law cannot, at the moment, do for them. Self-defense does not include preemptive strikes, or attacks based on the prediction that an assailant will use force some time in the future. Nor does it include retaliation, or the use of force to "pay back" an assailant for an attack. The law allows private citizens to use force only for *protection* when *necessary* against *imminent* attack. Citizens must use

[handwritten margin notes:] Use force against another important attacks. What the law can not do for them. ☆ imminent attack

other means to protect against future attacks, and only the state can punish past attacks.[6]

CASE

Did He Shoot in Self-Defense?

People v. Goetz
68 N.Y.2d 96, 506 N.Y.S.2d 18, 497 N.E.2d 41 (1986)

Chief Justice Watchler delivered the opinion.

A Grand Jury has indicted defendant on attempted murder, assault, and other charges for having shot and wounded four youths on a New York City subway train after one or two of the youths approached him and asked for $5. The lower courts, concluding that the prosecutor's charge to the Grand Jury on the defense of justification was erroneous, have dismissed the attempted murder, assault, and weapons possessions charges. We now reverse and reinstate all counts of the indictment.

FACTS

The precise circumstances of the incident giving rise to the charges against defendant are disputed, and ultimately it will be for a trial jury to determine what occurred. We feel it necessary, however, to provide some factual background to properly frame legal issues before us....

On Saturday afternoon, December 22, 1984, Troy Canty, Darryl Cabey, James Ramseur, and Barry Allen boarded an IRT express subway train in The Bronx and headed south toward lower Manhattan. The four youths rode together in the rear portion of the seventh car of the train. Two of the four, Ramseur and Cabey, had screw drivers inside their coats, which they said were to be used to break into the coin boxes of video machines.

Defendant Bernhard Goetz boarded this subway train at 14th Street in Manhattan and sat down on a bench towards the rear section of the same car occupied by the four youths. Goetz was carrying an unlicensed .38 caliber pistol loaded with five rounds of ammunition in a waistband holster. The train left the 14th Street station and headed towards Chambers Street.

It appears from the evidence before the Grand Jury that Canty approached Goetz, possibly with Allen beside him, and stated "give me five dollars." Neither Canty nor any of the other youths displayed a weapon. Goetz responded by standing up, pulling out his handgun and firing four shots in rapid succession. The first shot hit Canty in the chest; the second struck Allen in the back; the third went through Ramseur's arm and into his left side; the fourth was fired at Cabey, who apparently was then standing in the corner of the car, but missed, deflecting instead off of a wall of the conductor's cab. After Goetz briefly surveyed the scene around him, he fired another shot at Cabey, who was then sitting on the end bench of the car. The bullet entered the rear of Cabey's side and severed his spinal cord.

All but two of the passengers fled the car when, or immediately after, the shots were fired. The conductor, who had been in the next car, heard the shots and instructed the motorman to radio for emergency assistance. The conductor then went into the car where the shooting occurred and saw Goetz sitting on a bench, the injured youths lying on the floor or slumped against a seat, and two women who had apparently taken cover, also lying on the floor. Goetz told the conductor that the four youths had tried to rob him.

While the conductor was aiding the youths, Goetz headed towards the front of the car. The train had stopped just before the Chambers Street station and Goetz went between two of the cars, jumped onto the tracks, and fled. Police and ambulance crews arrived at the scene shortly thereafter. Ramseur and Canty, initially listed in critical condition, have fully recovered. Cabey remains paralyzed, and has suffered some degree of brain damage.

On December 31, 1984, Goetz surrendered to police in Concord, New Hampshire.... Later that day, after receiving *Miranda* warnings, he made two lengthy statements, both of which were tape recorded with his permission. In his statements, which are substantially similar, Goetz admitted that he had been illegally carrying a handgun in New York City for three years. He stated that he had first purchased a gun in 1981 after he had been injured in a mugging. Goetz also revealed that twice between 1981 and 1984 he had successfully warded off assailants simply by displaying the pistol.

According to Goetz's statement, the first contact he had with the four youths came when Canty, sitting or lying on the bench across from him, asked "how are you," to which he replied "fine." Shortly thereafter, Canty, followed by one of the other youths, walked over to the defendant and stood to his left, while the other two youths remained to his right, in the corner of the subway car. Canty then said "give me five dollars." Goetz stated that he knew from the smile on Canty's face that they wanted to "play with me." Although he was certain that none of the youths had a gun, he had a fear, based on prior experiences, of being "maimed."

Goetz then established "a pattern of fire," deciding specifically to fire from left to right. His stated intention at that point was to "murder [the four youths], to hurt them, to make them suffer as much as possible." When Canty again requested money, Goetz stood up, drew his weapon, and began firing, aiming for the center of the body of each of the four. Goetz recalled that the first two he shot "tried to run through the crowd [but] they had nowhere to run." Goetz then turned to his right to "go after the other two." One of these two "tried to run through the wall of the train, but ... he had nowhere to go." The other youth (Cabey) "tried pre-

tending that he wasn't with [the others]" by standing still, holding on to one of the subway hand straps, and not looking at Goetz. Goetz nonetheless fired his fourth shot at him. He then ran back to the first two youths to make sure they had been "taken care of." Seeing that they had both been shot, he spun back to check on the other two. Goetz noticed that the youth who had been standing still was now sitting on a bench and seemed unhurt. As Goetz told the police, "I said '[y]ou seem to be all right, here's another,'" and he fired the shot which severed Cabey's spinal cord. Goetz added that "if I was a little more under self-control ... I would have put the barrel against his forehead and fired." He also admitted that "if I had had more [bullets], I would have shot them again, and again, and again."

After waiving extradition, Goetz was brought back to New York and arraigned on a felony complaint charging him with attempted murder and criminal possession of a weapon. The matter was presented to a Grand Jury in January 1985, with the prosecutor seeking an indictment for attempted murder, assault, reckless endangerment, and criminal possession of a weapon.... [T]he Grand Jury indicted defendant on one count of criminal possession of a weapon in the third degree for possessing the gun used in the subway shootings, and two counts of criminal possession of a weapon in the fourth degree.... It dismissed, however, the attempted murder and other charges stemming from the shootings themselves.

Several weeks after the Grand Jury's action, the People, asserting that they had newly available evidence, moved for an order authorizing them to resubmit the dismissed charges to a second Grand Jury....

... [T]he second Grand Jury filed a 10-count indictment, containing four charges of attempted murder, four charges of assault in the first degree, one charge of reckless endangerment in the first degree, and one charge of criminal possession of a weapon in the second degree....

On October 14, 1985, Goetz moved to dismiss the charges contained in the second indictment alleging, among other things, that the evidence before the second Grand Jury was not legally sufficient to establish the offenses charged and that the prosecutor's instructions to that Grand Jury on the defense of justification were erroneous and prejudicial to the defendant so as to render its proceedings defective.

On November 25, 1985, while the motion to dismiss was pending before Criminal Term, a column appeared in the *New York Daily News* containing an interview which the columnist had conducted with Darryl Cabey the previous day in Cabey's hospital room. The columnist claimed that Cabey had told him in this interview that the other three youths had all approached Goetz with the intention of robbing him....

... The court, after inspection of the Grand Jury minutes, ... held ... that the prosecutor, in a supplemental charge elaborating upon the justification defense, had erroneously introduced an objective element into this defense by instructing the grand jurors to consider whether Goetz's conduct was that of a "reasonable man in [Goetz's] situation." The court ... concluded that the statutory test for whether the use of deadly force is justified to protect a person should be wholly subjective, focusing entirely on the defendant's state of mind when he used such force. It concluded that dismissal was required for this error because the justification issue was at the heart of the case....

On appeal by the People, a divided Appellate Division affirmed Criminal Term's dismissal of the charges....

Justice Asch, in a dissenting opinion in which Justice Wallach concurred, disagreed with both bases for dismissal relied upon by Criminal Term. On the justification question, he opined that the statute requires consideration of both the defendant's subjective beliefs and whether a reasonable person in defendant's situation would have had such beliefs.... Justice Wallach stressed that the plurality's adoption of a purely subjective test effectively eliminated any reasonableness requirement contained in the statute.

Justice Asch granted the People leave to appeal to this court.

OPINION

Penal Law article 35 recognizes the defense of justification, which "permits the use of force under certain circumstances."... Penal Law § 35.15 (1) sets forth the general principles governing all such uses of force: "[a] person may ... use physical force upon another person when and to the extent he *reasonably believes* such to be necessary to defend himself or a third person from what he *reasonably believes* to be the use or imminent use of unlawful physical force by such other person." [Emphasis added.]

§ 35.15 (2) ... "A person may not use deadly physical force upon another person under circumstances specified in subdivision one unless (a) He *reasonably believes* that such other person is using or about to use deadly physical force ... or (b) He *reasonably believes* that such other person is committing or attempting to commit a kidnapping, forcible rape, forcible sodomy or robbery." [Emphasis added.]

Thus, consistent with most justification provisions, Penal Law § 35.15 permits the use of deadly physical force only where requirements as to triggering conditions and the necessity of a particular response are met. As to the triggering of conditions, the statute requires that the actor "reasonably believes" that another person either is using or about to use deadly physical force or is committing or attempting to commit one of certain enumerated felonies, including robbery. As to the need for the use of deadly physical forces as a response, the statute requires that the actor "reasonably believes" that such force is necessary to avert the perceived threat.

Because the evidence before the second Grand Jury included statements by Goetz that he acted to protect himself from being maimed or to avert robbery, the prosecutor correctly chose to charge the justification defense.... The prosecutor properly instructed the grand jurors to consider whether the use of deadly physical force was justified to prevent, either serious physical injury or a robbery, and, in doing so, to separately analyze the defense with respect to each of the charges....

When the prosecutor had completed his charge, one of the grand jurors asked for clarification of the term "reasonably believes." The prosecutor responded by instructing the grand jurors that they were to consider the circumstances of the incident and determine "whether the defendant's conduct was that of a reasonable man in the defendant's situation." It is this response by the prosecutor—and specifically his use of "a reasonable man"—which is the basis for the dismissal of the charges by the lower courts. As expressed repeatedly in the Appellate Division's plurality opinion, because § 35.15 uses the term *he* reasonably believes," the appropriate test, according to that court, is whether a defendant's beliefs and reactions were "reasonable to *him*." Under that reading of the statute, a jury which believed a defendant's testimony that he felt that his own actions were warranted and were reasonable would have to acquit him, regardless of what anyone else in defendant's situation might have concluded. Such an interpretation defies the ordinary meaning and significance of the term "reasonably" in a statute, and misconstrues the clear intent of the Legislature, in enacting § 35.15, to retain an objective element as part of any provision authorizing the use of deadly physical force....

We cannot lightly impute to the Legislature an intent to fundamentally alter the principles of justification to allow the perpetrator of a serious crime to go free simply because the person believed his actions were reasonable and necessary to prevent some perceived harm. To completely exonerate such an individual, no matter how aberrational or bizarre his thought patterns, would allow citizens to set their own standards for the permissible use of force. It would also allow a legally competent defendant suffering from delusions to kill or perform acts of violence with impunity, contrary to fundamental principles of justice and criminal law.

We can only conclude that the Legislature retained a reasonableness requirement to avoid giving a license for such actions. The plurality's interpretation, as the dissenters ... recognized, excises the impact of the word "reasonably."...

Accordingly, the order of the Appellate Division should be reversed, and the dismissed counts of the indictment reinstated.

Case Discussion

New York tried Goetz for attempted murder and assault. The jury acquitted him of both charges. The jury said Goetz "was justified in shooting the four men with a silver-plated .38-caliber revolver he purchased in Florida." They did convict him of illegal possession of a firearm, for which the court sentenced Goetz to one year in jail. Following the sentencing, Goetz told the court that "[t]his case is really more about the deterioration of society than it is about me.... Well, I don't believe that's the case.... I believe society needs to be protected from criminals."[a]

Criminal law professor George Fletcher followed the trial closely. Following the acquittal, he commented that

> [t]he facts of the Goetz case were relatively clear, but the primary fight was over the moral interpretation of the facts.... I am not in the slightest bit convinced that the four young men were about to mug Goetz. If he had said, "Listen buddy, I wish I had $5, but I don't," and walked to the other side of the car the chances are 60–40 nothing would have happened. Street-wise kids like that are more attuned to the costs of their behavior than Goetz was.[b]

a. *New York Times* (January 14, 1989), p. 9.
b. Quoted in *New York Times* (January 23, 1989), p. 14; see also Professor Fletcher's book on the Goetz trial, *A Crime of Self-Defense: Bernhard Goetz and the Law on Trial* (New York: Free Press, 1988).

If Professor Fletcher is right, was Goetz justified in shooting? Under what circumstances can people use deadly force, according to the New York statutes cited in the opinion? Do you agree with those circumstances? Would you add more? Remove some? Which ones? Why? Were Goetz's shots a preemptive strike? Retaliation? Necessary for self-protection? Explain.

Elements of Self-Defense

Using force for self-protection does not always qualify as self-defense under the law. Self-defense justifies the use of force only (1) against unprovoked attacks (ones that the defender did not encourage, invite, or cause); (2) when victims honestly and reasonably believe their assailants will kill or seriously injure them; (3) when victims honestly and reasonably believe they must kill or seriously injure their attackers in order to repel the attack; (4) against imminent attacks, that is, those that will occur immediately, (5) with the intent to defend, not to prevent a future attack.

Those who provoke attacks cannot later claim they were defending themselves. However, if attackers completely withdraw from fights they start, they can forcibly defend themselves against a subsequent attack by their initial victims. Thus, a man who attacked another with a knife was acquitted on self-defense even though he provoked the attack. After attacking a much larger man with the knife, he realized he had taken on too much. He retreated in an effort to escape, but to no avail. The larger man, now thoroughly aroused, pursued him relentlessly. Unable to escape, the smaller man finally stood his ground and, in the process, stabbed his attacker to death. He was acquitted on self-defense because the jury was satisfied that he "withdrew in good faith," and had not merely retreated in order to regain enough strength to resume the attack. The court dealt with self-defense to provoked attacks in *Townshend v. Commonwealth*.[7]

CASE

Did the Defendant Kill in Self-Defense?

Townshend v. Commonwealth
474 S.W.2d 352 (Ky.1971)

Vance, Commissioner

FACTS
The appellant was convicted of the offense of voluntary manslaughter and sentenced to confinement for a term of twenty-one years. The sole question presented on this appeal is whether the evidence conclusively established that the shooting was done in self-defense. The appellant contends that he was entitled to a directed verdict and that the evidence did not support the verdict but both contentions are grounded in the claim that the evidence conclusively established that the shooting was done in self-defense.

... On the day of the shooting the appellant and some of his friends were rabbit hunting near the farm of the deceased. Their automobiles were parked on the side of a public road near decedent's home. After the day's hunting was over and while the hunters were standing in the road attempting to get their dogs in their respective cars, they were fired upon with a shotgun from the direction of decedent's home. Some of the buckshot struck appellant but did not injure him.

Appellant placed his shotgun inside his motor vehicle without unloading it and started home. The roadway passed directly in front of decedent's house and as appellant approached the house, the decedent was in his front yard talking to another man whose car was parked on the roadside.

Appellant brought his car to a halt and inquired why decedent had fired upon him. Decedent denied firing the shotgun whereupon the appellant called him a "God-Damned-Liar."

Decedent then whirled around and started toward appellant, bending forward in a crouching manner. At some point in time the appellant got outside his car and left the door open.

As the decedent advanced upon him, appellant repeatedly told him not to come any closer. He backed up to his car, reached inside and obtained his shotgun and told decedent if he came any closer he would have to shoot him. Decedent continued to advance toward appellant with his hand inside his shirt front and appellant testified that he thought he saw an object resembling a pistol in decedent's hand. Appellant shot decedent and then struck him in the head with the butt of the shotgun. No weapon was discovered on the body of the decedent.

OPINION

… Although all the witnesses were in agreement that the decedent was advancing upon the appellant at the time of the shooting, there was evidence from which a reasonable inference could have been drawn that appellant intended to and did provoke the difficulty with the deceased.

Whether the appellant harbored ill feelings toward the deceased by reason of the previous shooting incident; whether appellant placed his shotgun in his car without unloading it was simply because he forgot to unload it or because he intended to use it further, and whether appellant at the scene of the shooting could have gotten into his automobile and driven away as easily as he could have returned to the automobile to get his shotgun and shoot deceased are matters which the jury might properly consider as bearing upon motive, intent and appellant's belief in the necessity of shooting decedent to avoid danger to himself. The fact that appellant stopped in front of decedent's home and got out of his car when he could have driven on by; and the fact that he called the decedent a "God-Damned-Liar" were circumstances from which the jury could have believed the appellant attempted to provoke the incident.

One who by his words and acts provokes and brings about a fight cannot claim self defense. The law does not allow a man to create a bad or dangerous situation and then fight his way out.

The evidence in this case did not conclusively establish that the shooting was done in self defense and that issue was therefore properly submitted to the jury.

The judgment is affirmed.

All concur.

Case Discussion

Exactly what evidence exists here to show that Townshend provoked the attack? Why should the law deny Townshend defense in this case? Because he provoked the attack? Or because one of the other elements outlined above were missing? Which ones?

[handwritten notes in margin:]
Michigan law
① defendant can not be aggressor
② grievous bodily injury
③ no retreat open
only safety is repelling the attack

———— ❦ ————

Self-defense includes more than killing an assailant who threatens to kill. Less-than-deadly attacks authorize resort to less-than-deadly responses. Thus, self-defense applies in all crimes against persons: homicide, rape, other assaults, and battery. Threats to persons constitute the common element in all these crimes. Self-defense also applies to defending property, but with limits.

Only attacks in progress, or on the verge of taking place, justify the use of force. Thus, after a street gang member threw a brick at a cabdriver from the far side of an intersection, the driver justifiably shot into the gang because, despite their distance, they could have killed the driver at any moment.[8]

Some maintain that present danger suffices, and that self-defense does not require immediate or imminent danger. For example, if an assailant leaves a scene to get reinforcements in order to continue an attack with a better advantage, the victim is not in immediate danger because the attack is not on the verge of happening. Nevertheless, some argue, the present danger justifies using force. The Model Penal Code permits using force to repel present but not imminent danger. A few states, such as Delaware, Hawaii, New Jersey, Nebraska, and Pennsylvania, have followed the Model Penal Code, substituting present for imminent danger. Most states, however, retain the immediate or imminent danger requirement.[9]

How does the law determine immediate or present danger of attack? Must defenders face actual danger? Or is it enough that there are reasonable grounds to believe danger exists? Or is the honest belief that danger exists enough, even if in fact no danger exists and believing so is not reasonable?

Most jurisdictions adopt an **objective test;** they permit force only if under the circumstances actors reasonably believed the use of force was necessary. In some states, such as Illinois, Connecticut, and Wisconsin, statutes spell this out specifically. In states where statutes do not prescribe a test—**subjective test** (honest belief), objective test (reasonable belief), or combination (honest and reasonable belief)—courts imply a reasonableness test. Before Illinois legislated an objective test, for example, the Illinois Supreme Court ruled that a man who turned and immediately shot an unknown attacker who struck him in the head from behind "was not under a reasonable apprehension of death or great bodily harm."[10]

Occasionally, courts adopt a combined objective-subjective test. In *Beard v. United States,* Beard killed an attacker who threatened to assault him. The court ruled that Beard must have had "reasonable grounds to believe, and in good faith believed" he had to use force to protect against great bodily harm.

The reasonableness test and the objective-subjective test create *mens rea* problems. Defendants who, like Beard, make honest but unreasonable mistakes about danger—that is, reckless or negligent mistakes—cannot claim self-defense.[11]

Glanville Williams, a respected British criminal law scholar, strongly objects to the reasonableness test:

> The criminal law of negligence works best when it gives effect to the large number of rules of prudence which are commonly observed though not directly incorporated into the law. Such rules include the rule against pulling out on a blind corner, the rule against carrying a gun in such a way that it is pointing at another person, the rule against deliberately pointing a gun at another person, even in play, and so on. These rules are not part either of enacted or of common law, but as customary standards of behavior they become binding via the law of negligence. Are there any similar rules of behavior applicable when a person acts in self defense or in making an arrest? It must be recollected that the injury he inflicts on the other is in itself intentional, so that the usual rules of prudence in respect to the handling of

weapons are not in question. The only question is whether the defendant was negligent in arriving at the conclusion that the use of the force in question was called for. It is hard to imagine what rules of prudence could normally serve in this situation. Either the defendant is capable of drawing the inferences that a reasonable man would draw or he is not. If he is not, and he is a peace officer, his tendency to make miscalculations would certainly justify his dismissal from the police force. But there is no obvious case for the intervention of the criminal courts.[12]

Despite criticism, few states have removed the reasonableness requirement. Tennessee is one that has. In *Frazier v. State,* a hemophiliac assaulted Frazier. Frazier struck a moderate blow to defend himself. The hemophiliac bled to death from Frazier's moderate blow. The court stated the self-defense requirement as follows: "If the defendant honestly fears himself to be in danger of life or great bodily harm from the circumstances as they appear to him, and he acts under that fear to kill his assailant, it is justifiable homicide."[13]

Defenders may not use excessive force. They may use only the amount of force they honestly and reasonably believe necessary to repel an attack. If someone slaps my face, I cannot shoot my assailant to death. Defenders may use only nondeadly force to repel a nondeadly attack; they may use deadly force only to prevent death or grievous bodily harm. It is always reasonable to use nondeadly force to repel deadly force. Threatened force is justified to stave off threatened physical injury and is reasonable to stop attacks in progress, whether deadly or not. However ominous, threats by themselves do not justify using force. For example, a prisoner threatened another prisoner with sodomy if the prisoner did not immediately pay back a loan. The prisoner stabbed his would-be sodomizer. The court held that mere threats do not justify preventive assaults.[14]

CASE

Was She in Imminent Danger of Death or Serious Bodily Harm?

State v. Stewart
763 P.2d 572 (Kan.1988)

Lockett, Justice

FACTS
... Following an annulment from her first husband and two subsequent divorces in which she was the petitioner, Peggy Stewart married Mike Stewart in 1974. Evidence at trial disclosed a long history of abuse by Mike against Peggy and her two daughters from one of her prior marriages. Laura, one of Peggy's daughters, testified that early in the marriage Mike hit and kicked Peggy, and that after the first year of the marriage Peggy exhibited signs of severe psychological problems. Subsequently, Peggy was hospitalized and diagnosed as having symptoms of paranoid schizophrenia; she responded to treatment and was soon released. It appeared to Laura, however, that Mike was encouraging Peggy to take more than her prescribed dosage of medication.

In 1977, two social workers informed Peggy that they had received reports that Mike was taking indecent liberties with her daughters. Because the social workers did not want Mike to be left alone with the girls, Peggy quit her job. In 1978, Mike began to taunt Peggy by stating that Carla, her 12-year-old daughter, was "more of a wife" to him than Peggy.

Later, Carla was placed in a detention center, and Mike forbade Peggy and Laura to visit her. When Mike finally allowed Carla to return home in the middle of summer, he forced her to sleep in an un-air conditioned room with the windows nailed shut, to wear a heavy flannel nightgown, and to cover herself with heavy blankets. Mike would then wake Carla at 5:30 a.m. and force her to do all the housework. Peggy and Laura were not allowed to help Carla or speak to her.

When Peggy confronted Mike and demanded that the situation cease, Mike responded by holding a shotgun to Peggy's head and threatening to kill her. Mike once kicked Peggy so violently in the chest and ribs that she required hospitalization. Finally, when Mike ordered Peggy to kill and bury Carla, she filed for divorce. Peggy's attorney in the divorce action testified in the murder trial that Peggy was afraid for both her and her children's lives.

One night, in a fit of anger, Mike threw Carla out of the house. Carla, who was not yet in her teens, was forced out of the home with no money, no coat, and no place to go. When the family heard that Carla was in Colorado, Mike refused to allow Peggy to contact or even talk about Carla. Mike's intimidation of Peggy continued to escalate. One morning, Laura found her mother hiding on the school bus, terrified and begging the driver to take her to a neighbor's home. That Christmas, Mike threw the turkey dinner to the floor, chased Peggy outside, grabbed her by the hair, rubbed her face in the dirt, and then kicked and beat her.

After Laura moved away, Peggy's life became even more isolated. Once, when Peggy was working at a cafe, Mike came in and ran all the customers off with a gun because he wanted Peggy to go home and have sex with him right that minute. He abused both drugs and alcohol, and amused himself by terrifying Peggy, once waking her from a sound sleep by beating her with a baseball bat. He shot one of Peggy's pet cats, and then held the gun against her head and threatened to pull the trigger. Peggy told friends that Mike would hold a shotgun to her head and threaten to blow if off, and indicated that one day he would probably do it.

In May 1986, Peggy left Mike and ran away to Laura's home in Oklahoma. It was the first time Peggy had left Mike without telling him. Because Peggy was suicidal, Laura had her admitted to a hospital. There, she was diagnosed as having toxic psychosis as a result of an overdose of her medication. On May 30, 1986, Mike called to say he was coming to get her. Peggy agreed to return to Kansas. Peggy told a nurse she felt like she wanted to shoot her husband. At trial, she testified that she decided to return with Mike because she was not able to get the medical help she needed in Oklahoma.

When Mike arrived at the hospital, he told the staff that he "needed his housekeeper." The hospital released Peggy to Mike's care, and he immediately drove her back to Kansas. Mike told Peggy that all her problems were in her head and he would be the one to tell her what was good for her, not the doctors. Peggy testified that Mike threatened to kill her if she ever ran away again. As soon as they arrived at the house, Mike forced Peggy into the house and forced her to have oral sex several times.

The next morning, Peggy discovered a loaded .357 magnum. She testified she was afraid of the gun. She hid the gun under the mattress of the bed in a spare room. Later that morning, as she cleaned house, Mike kept making remarks that she should not bother because she would not be there long, or that she should not bother with her things because she could not take them with her. She testified she was afraid Mike was going to kill her.

Mike's parents visited Mike and Peggy that afternoon. Mike's father testified that Peggy and Mike were affectionate with each other during the visit. Later, after Mike's parents had left, Mike forced Peggy to perform oral sex. After watching television, Mike and Peggy went to bed at 8:00 p.m.

As Mike slept, Peggy thought about suicide and heard voices in her head repeating over and over, "kill or be killed." At this time, there were two vehicles in the driveway and Peggy had access to the car keys. About 10:00 p.m. Peggy went to the spare bedroom and removed the gun from under the mattress, walked back to her bedroom, and killed her husband while he slept. She then ran to the home of a neighbor, who called the police.

When the police questioned Peggy regarding the events leading up to the shooting, Peggy stated that things had not gone quite right that day, and that when she got the chance she hid the gun under the mattress. She stated that she shot Mike to "get this over with, this misery and this torment." When asked why she got the gun out, Peggy stated to the police:

"I'm not sure exactly what … led up to it … and my head started playing games with me and I got to thinking about things and I said I didn't want to be by myself again…. I got the gun out because there had been remarks made about me being out there alone. It was as if Mike was going to do something again like had been done before. He had gotten me down here from McPherson one time and he went and told them that I had done something and he had me put out of the house and was taking everything I had. And it was like he was going to pull the same thing over again."

Two expert witnesses testified during the trial. The expert for the defense, psychologist Marilyn Hutchinson, diagnosed Peggy as suffering from "battered woman syndrome," or post-traumatic stress syndrome. Dr. Hutchinson testified that Mike was preparing to escalate the violence in retaliation for Peggy's running away. She testified that loaded guns, veiled threats, and increased sexual demands are indicators of the escalation of the cycle. Dr. Hutchinson believed Peggy had a repressed knowledge that she was in a "really grave lethal situation."

The State's expert, psychiatrist Herbert Modlin, neither subscribed to a belief in the battered woman syndrome nor to a theory of learned helplessness as an explanation for why women do not leave an abusive relationship. Dr. Modlin testified that abuse such as repeated forced oral sex would not be trauma sufficient to trigger a post-traumatic stress disorder. He also believed

Peggy was erroneously diagnosed as suffering from toxic psychosis. He stated that Peggy was unable to escape the abuse because she suffered from schizophrenia, rather than the battered woman syndrome.

At defense counsel's request, the trial judge gave an instruction on self-defense to the jury. The jury found Peggy not guilty [first-degree murder. Upon a special appeals procedure, the state appealed, arguing that the trial judge erred in his self-defense instruction.]

OPINION

… K.S.A. 21–3211 … provides: "A person is justified in the use of force against an aggressor when and to the extent it appears to him and he reasonably believes that such conduct is necessary to defend himself or another against such aggressor's imminent use of unlawful force."

The traditional concept of self-defense has posited one-time conflicts between persons of somewhat equal size and strength. When the defendant claiming self-defense is a victim of long-term domestic violence, such as a battered spouse, such traditional concepts may not apply. Because of the prior history of abuse, and the difference in strength and size between the abused and the abuser, the accused in such cases may choose to defend during a momentary lull in the abuse, rather than during a conflict. However, in order to warrant the giving of a self-defense instruction, the facts of the case must still show that the spouse was in imminent danger close to the time of killing.

A person is justified in using force against an aggressor when it appears to that person and he or she reasonably believes such force to be necessary. A reasonable belief implies both an honest belief and the existence of facts which would persuade a reasonable person to that belief. A self defense instruction must be given if there is any evidence to support a claim of self-defense, even if that evidence consists solely of the defendant's testimony.

Where self-defense is asserted, evidence of the deceased's long-term cruelty and violence towards the defendant is admissible. In cases involving battered spouses, expert evidence of the battered woman syndrome is relevant to a determination of the reasonableness of the defendant's perception of danger....

In order to instruct a jury on self-defense, there must be some showing of an imminent threat or a confrontational circumstance involving an overt act by an aggressor. There is no exception to this requirement where the defendant has suffered long-term domestic abuse and the victim is the abuser. In such cases, the issue is not whether the defendant believes homicide is the solution to past or future problems with the batterer, but rather whether circumstances surrounding the killing were sufficient to create a reasonable belief in the defendant that the use of deadly force was necessary.... Here ... there is an absence of imminent danger to defendant:

Peggy told a nurse at the Oklahoma hospital of her desire to kill Mike. She later voluntarily agreed to return home with Mike when he telephoned her. She stated that after leaving the hospital Mike threatened to kill her if she left him again. Peggy showed no inclination to leave. In fact, immediately after the shooting, Peggy told the police that she was upset because she thought Mike would leave her. Prior to the shooting, Peggy hid the loaded gun. The cars were in the driveway and Peggy had access to the car keys. After being abused, Peggy went to bed with Mike at 8 p.m. Peggy lay there for two hours, then retrieved the gun from where she had hidden it and shot Mike while he slept.

Under these facts, the giving of the self-defense instruction was erroneous. Under such circumstances, a battered woman cannot reasonably fear imminent life-threatening danger from her sleeping spouse. We note that other courts have held that the sole fact that the victim was asleep does not preclude a self-defense instruction. In *State v. Norman*, 89 N.C.App. 384, 366 S.E.2d 586 (1988), cited by defendant, the defendant's evidence disclosed a long history of abuse. Each time defendant attempted to escape, her husband found and beat her. On the day of the shooting, the husband beat defendant continually throughout the day, and threatened either to cut her throat, kill her, or cut off her breast. In the afternoon, defendant shot her husband while he napped.

The North Carolina Court of Appeals held it was reversible error to fail to instruct on self-defense. The court found that, although decedent was napping at the time defendant shot him, defendant's unlawful act was closely related in time to an assault and threat of death by decedent against defendant and that the decedent's nap was "but a momentary hiatus in a continuous reign of terror."

There is no doubt that the North Carolina court determined that the sleeping husband was an evil man who deserved the justice he received from his battered wife. Here, similar comparable and compelling facts exist. But, as one court has stated: "To permit capital punishment to be imposed upon the subjective conclusion of the [abused] individual that prior acts and conduct of the deceased justified the killing would amount to a leap into the abyss of anarchy." *Jahnke v. State*, 682 P.2d 991, 997 (Wyo.1984).

Finally, our legislature has not provided for capital punishment for even the most heinous crimes. We must, therefore, hold that when a battered woman kills her sleeping spouse when there is no imminent danger, the killing is not reasonably necessary and a self-defense instruction may not be given. To hold otherwise in this case would in effect allow the execution of the abuser for past or future acts and conduct.

One additional issue must be addressed. In its amicus curiae brief, the Kansas County and District Attorney Association contends the instruction given by the trial court improperly modified the law of self-defense to be more generous to one suffering from the battered woman syndrome than to any other defendant relying on self-defense. We agree....

The appeal is sustained.

DISSENT

Prager, C.J., dissents.

Herd, Justice, dissenting:

... It is evident ... appellee met her burden of showing some competent evidence that she acted in self-defense, thus making her defense a jury question. She testified she acted in fear for her life, and Dr. Hutchinson corroborated this testimony. The evidence of Mike's past abuse, the escalation of violence, his threat of killing her should she attempt to leave him, and Dr. Hutchinson's testimony that appellee was indeed in a "lethal situation" more than met the minimal standard of "any evidence" to allow an instruction to be given to the jury.

The evidence showed Mike had a "Dr. Jekyll and Mr. Hyde" personality. He was usually very friendly and ingratiating when non-family persons were around, but was belligerent and domineering to family members. He had a violent temper and would blow up without reason. Mike was cruel to his two stepdaughters, Carla and Laura, as well as to the appellee. He took pride in hurting them or anything they held dear, such as their pets. Mike's violence toward appellee and her daughters caused appellee to have emotional problems with symptoms of paranoid schizophrenia. He would overdose appellee on her medication and then cut her off it altogether. Mike's cruelty would culminate in an outburst of violence, and then he would suddenly become very loving and considerate. This was very confusing to appellee. She lived in constant dread of the next outburst....

It is a jury question to determine if the battered woman who kills her husband as he sleeps fears he will find and kill her if she leaves, as is usually claimed. Under such circumstances the battered woman is not under actual physical attack when she kills but such attack is imminent, and as a result she believes her life is in imminent danger. She may kill during the tension-building stage when the abuse is apparently not as severe as it sometimes has been, but nevertheless has escalated so that she is afraid the acute stage to come will be fatal to her. She only acts on such fear if she has some survival instinct remaining after the husband-induced "learned helplessness."...

The majority claims permitting a jury to consider self-defense under these facts would permit anarchy. This underestimates the jury's ability to recognize an invalid claim of self-defense. Although this is a case of first impression where an appeal by the State has been allowed, there have been several similar cases in which the defendant appealed on other grounds. In each of these cases where a battered woman killed the sleeping batterer, a self-defense instruction has been given when requested by the defendant....

The majority bases its opinion on its conclusion appellee was not in imminent danger, usurping the right of the jury to make that determination of fact. The majority believes a person could not be in imminent danger from an aggressor merely because the aggressor dropped off to sleep. This is a fallacious conclusion. For instance, picture a hostage situation where the armed guard inadvertently drops off to sleep and the hostage grabs his gun and shoots him. The majority opinion would preclude the use of self-defense in such a case....

I would deny this appeal.

Case Discussion

How does the court define imminent? Can battered women ever be in imminent danger when their husbands are sleeping? Should we have a special battered women's defense of justification? Or should we expand the definition of *imminent,* or change the requirement from imminent to present, or continuing danger? Why does the court talk about putting the power of capital punishment into the hands of battered wives?

Consider the following comment:

> [R]etaliation, as opposed to defense, is a common problem in cases arising from wife battering and domestic violence. The injured wife waits for the first

possibility of striking against a distracted or unarmed husband. The man may even be asleep when the wife finally reacts. Retaliation is the standard case of "taking the law into your own hands." There is no way, under the law, to justify killing a wife batterer or a rapist in retaliation or revenge, however much sympathy there may be for the wife wreaking retaliation. Private citizens cannot act as judge and jury toward each other. They have no authority to pass judgment and to punish each other for past wrongs.

Do you agree? Was Peggy's act one of self-defense, a preemptive strike, or retaliation?

The Retreat Doctrine

What if escape is open to those who are attacked? Must they retreat? Or can they stand their ground? Different values underlie each of these alternatives. The retreat rule places a premium on human life, and discourages inflicting bodily injury and death except as a last resort. A different rule permitting victims to stand their ground against unwarranted attacks rests on the idea that retreat forces innocent people to take a cowardly or humiliating position. This idea is captured by the phrase used to describe the rule: the **true man doctrine.** Most jurisdictions require retreat if retreat does not unreasonably risk the retreater's life.[15]

Jurisdictions requiring retreat have carved out a major exception to the retreat doctrine, sometimes called the **castle exception.** According to the castle exception to the retreat doctrine, when attacked in their homes, defenders may stand their ground and use deadly force to repel an unprovoked attack, if the unprovoked attack reasonably threatens life or serious bodily injury. A problem arises over just what "home" means. Does it include the entryway? The sidewalk in front of the house? Does it extend to the property line? What if a person lives in a car, a hotel room, or under a bridge? Similarly, does it include businesses? The court, in *State v. Quarles,* dealt with the castle exception when both the attacker and victim live in the same house.

CASE

Did He Have to Retreat from His Own Home?

State v. Quarles
504 A.2d 473 (R.I.1986)

Kelleher, Justice
Ronald Quarles (Quarles), indicted for murder in the second degree, was convicted by a Providence County jury of manslaughter in the slaying of Lorraine Pinto (Pinto), his cohabitant. After his postverdict motion for a new trial was denied, a fourteen-year sentence was imposed. On appeal Quarles claims that the trial justice committed prejudicial error in refusing to instruct the jury that he was not obligated to retreat before resorting to the use of deadly force in his own defense.

FACTS
Quarles's version of what happened on the evening of October 4, 1983, follows. After

eating dinner at home with Pinto, Quarles went to a union meeting, planning to meet Pinto at a local barroom after the meeting ended. Upon entering the bar, Quarles saw Pinto talking with a man he did not recognize. At first he felt angry because he thought Pinto was "trying to sneak around behind my back" with another man, but his anger quickly subsided.

As the night wore on, Quarles and Pinto drank and shot some pool. Several arguments erupted over Pinto's refusals to go home with Quarles; finally he walked back to their common residence in Newport. About ten minutes later Pinto walked into the house and informed Quarles that he had one week to find another place to live. Quarles agreed to leave in a week and went upstairs to their bedroom and began to undress. Pinto followed him upstairs and started to choke him. He punched her in order to get her to release him. Infuriated, she told him to get out "tonight." Quarles caller her a "tramp" and indicated that he would not put up with her antics any longer. Pinto went downstairs into the kitchen.

After Quarles dressed, he followed her downstairs. When he entered the kitchen, Pinto swung a nine-inch kitchen knife at him. He stepped back and wrestled the knife out of her hands. Quarles conceded that at this point he could have left the house with the knife under his control. But Pinto suddenly grabbed his arm and struggled with him in an attempt to regain control over the knife.

During the ensuing affray, in the early morning hours of October 5, Pinto was fatally stabbed by Quarles. Quarles claims that the stabbing occurred when Pinto grabbed his arm and drew the knife toward herself. When he withdrew the knife and saw blood on it, he realized that there had been a stabbing. He insists that Pinto's wound was self-inflicted.

The trial justice instructed the jury on second-degree murder, on manslaughter, and on the defense theories of accident and self-defense. His instruction on the issue of self-defense follows:

"[A] person who reasonably believes that he's in imminent danger of harm at the hands of another may defend himself. He does not have to wait for the first blow to land. However, if such person strikes first, he may only use such force as is reasonably necessary for his own protection. The permissible degree of force used in self-defense depends on that which is necessary under all the circumstances to prevent an impending injury.

"In a case such as this it is the burden of the State to prove beyond a reasonable doubt that the defendant was not acting in self-defense. If it is not proved, this element, beyond a reasonable doubt, then you must find the defendant not guilty.

"The test of whether or not the defendant acted in self-defense is not whether the fact finder, you, the jury, believe the force used was necessary, but whether the defendant, under the circumstances he experienced at the time in question, reasonably believed that the force used by him was necessary to prevent eminent harm."

The trial justice refused to instruct the jury that Quarles was not obligated to attempt retreat prior to resorting to the use of deadly force.

The defendant submitted the following instruction concerning this issue:

"REQUEST NO. 31 If the defendant had reasonable grounds to believe and actually did believe that he was in imminent danger of death or serious bodily harm and that deadly force was necessary to repel such danger, he is not required to retreat or to consider whether he can retreat safely. He was entitled to stand his ground and use such force as was reasonably necessary under the circumstances to save his life or protect himself from serious bodily harm. *Beard v. United States,* 158 U.S. 550, 563, 15 S.Ct. 962, 967 [39 L.Ed. 1086] (1895)."

OPINION

Quarles objected to the omission of his requested instruction and now contends that the failure to instruct the jury in accordance with his request was reversible error requiring a new trial. We disagree.

The law concerning self-defense in Rhode Island permits persons who believe that they are in imminent peril of bodily harm to use such nondeadly force as is reasonably necessary in the circumstances to protect themselves. Before resorting to the use of deadly force, the person attacked must attempt retreat if he or she is consciously aware of an open, safe, and available avenue of escape. The only exception in Rhode Island to the obligation to attempt retreat was created by statute. It exempts an individual from the duty to retreat and permits the use of deadly force by an owner, tenant, or occupier of premises against any person engaged in the commission of an unlawful breaking and entering or burglary.

Quarles attempts to persuade us to create a new exception to the retreat requirement by adopting the common-law castle doctrine. He asserts that this "universally recognized" doctrine exempts the person assailed from the obligation of attempting retreat when the attack occurs in the defendant's dwelling. Quarles contends that the castle doctrine, which embodies the notion that a person's authority is paramount in his own home and need not be compromised in the face of an unlawful attack, should be adhered to even when, as in the instant case, the assailant is a cohabitant.

We have grave doubts that Quarles's reliance on the theory of self-defense was relevant once he had wrested the deadly weapon from his assailant, especially since he insists the wound inflicted was accidental. However, because the issue of retreat that Quarles attempted to raise is one that will undoubtedly be raised again, we believe that we should make our position clear.

We are of the opinion that a person assailed in his or her own residence by a co-occupant is not entitled under the guise of self-defense to employ deadly force and kill his or her assailant. The person attacked is obligated to attempt to retreat if he or she is aware of a safe and available avenue of retreat.

In *State v. Guillemet,*—R.I. at—, 430 A.2d at 1069 n.2, we noted that a majority of jurisdictions have recognized an exception to the requirement of retreat when the attack occurs in the occupant's home. This exception prevails without regard to whether the assailant's status is that of an intruder or a co-occupant.

However, several jurisdictions that have adopted the castle doctrine have held that it has no application to cases between two persons entitled to occupy the same dwelling....

In *Commonwealth v. Shaffer,* 367 Mass. 508, 326 N.E.2d 880 (1975), the defendant, convicted of manslaughter in the shooting of her cohabitant, claimed the trial justice erred in failing to instruct the jury that she was not obligated to attempt retreat from her assailant in her own home. The Supreme Judicial Court dismissed her appeal and adhered to its "long-established rule that the right to use deadly force by way of self-defense is not available to one threatened until he has availed himself of all reasonable and proper means in the circumstances to avoid combat...." We are aware that the Massachusetts Legislature altered the holding in *Shaffer* as it applies to unlawful intruders.

We find the rationale of *Shaffer* persuasive in that it affords due recognition to the value of human life while recognizing that the right of self-defense is born of necessity and should terminate when the necessity is no more.

Consequently, we are of the belief that even in the so-called co-occupant situation, no justification exists for departing from our long-established rule that when a person "is attacked by another under such circumstances as to lead him to apprehend peril to his life, or great bodily harm, he may kill his assailant, provided he cannot otherwise protect himself, as by retreating from danger, by warding off the attack by a weapon not deadly, by disabling his adversary without killing him, or in any other way preserving his own life and person...."

Thus, the obligation to attempt retreat exists where one is assaulted in his or her own living quarters by his or her co-occupant. Therefore, the trial justice did not err in refusing to instruct the jury in the manner requested by Quarles. Accordingly, Quarles's appeal is denied and dismissed, and the judgment appealed from is affirmed.

**Case
Discussion**   What is the rationale for the castle exception? Do you agree with it? Should anyone have to retreat in the face of an attack? Why? Why not? What reasons does the Rhode Island court give for rejecting the castle exception? Do you agree with them? Why?

Note Case   Leon Cooper and his brother, Robert Parker, lived with their mother, Alice Cooper. In the early part of August 1981, Parker unexpectedly left home for ten days. Early on the morning of August 12, he returned. He did not tell his mother or brother where he had been.

Parker stayed home for much of the day. Mrs. Cooper returned from work in the evening, and Cooper returned from his job shortly afterward. Cooper was carrying a pistol when he returned. The three were sitting in Mrs. Cooper's small living room when the two brothers began to quarrel after Cooper asked Parker where he had been during the past ten days.

Suddenly the quarrel escalated, and the two brothers found themselves standing in the middle of the living room, shouting at each other. Parker hit Cooper in the head with a small radio; Mrs. Cooper ran upstairs to call for help. She then heard a "pop." She went downstairs and saw Parker lying on the floor. Cooper said "I have shot my brother," and "Mama, I am so sorry. I mean—" Cooper later told the police that he had just shot his brother, that his brother was hitting him with the radio and "I couldn't take it anymore and I just shot him."

Was Cooper entitled to the castle exception? In affirming the conviction, the court held:

> [A]ll co-occupants, even those unrelated by blood or marriage, have a heightened obligation to treat each other with a degree of tolerance and respect. That obligation does not evaporate when one co-occupant disregards it and attacks another. We are satisfied, moreover, that an instruction that embraces the middle ground approach appropriately permits the jury to consider the truly relevant question, i.e., whether a defendant, "if he safely could have avoided further encounter by stepping back or walking away, was actually or apparently in imminent danger of bodily harm." We hold that evidence that the defendant was attacked in his home by a co-occupant did not entitle him to an instruction that he had no duty whatsoever to retreat. The trial court did not err in refusing to give a castle doctrine instruction under the circumstances of this case. *Cooper v. United States,* 512 A.2d 1002 (D.C.1986)

▼ DEFENSE OF OTHERS

Historically, self-defense meant protecting both the individuals attacked and their immediate families. Although several jurisdictions still require a special relationship, the trend is definitely away from such a prescription. Several states that retain it have relaxed its meaning to include lovers and friends. Many states have abandoned the special relationship requirement altogether. They either write a special provision for defending others, which is the same as that for defending oneself, or they modify their self-defense statutes to read "himself or third persons."[16]

Whatever the limits, the defense-of-others defense requires that the "other" have the right to defend him or herself in order for the defender to claim the defense. Therefore, where abortion rights protesters argued that they had the right to prevent abortions by violating the law because they were defending the right of unborn children to live, the court rejected the defense:

> The "defense of others" specifically limits the use of force or violence in protection of others to situations where the person attacked would have been justified in using such force or violence to protect himself. In view of *Roe* [v. Wade] ... and the provisions of the Louisiana abortion statute, defense of others as justification for the defendants' otherwise criminal conduct is not available in these cases. Since abortion is legal in Louisiana, the defendants had no legal right to protect the unborn by means not even available to the unborn themselves.[17]

▼ GENERAL PRINCIPLE OF NECESSITY

Some argue that creating special defenses for every situation prevents designing a rational criminal code. They maintain that a defense governed by a principle of necessity makes more sense. The general principle of necessity includes self-defense, as well as other justifications, because it encompasses not only crimes against persons—homicide, rape, and assault—but also most other crimes. Correctly choosing a lesser of two evils constitutes the essence of the necessity principle. The Model Penal Code has adopted a necessity provision that takes these elements into account. When actors believe conduct is necessary to avoid a greater evil, they are justified in causing a lesser evil:

§ 3.02. Justification Generally: Choice of Evils.

1. Conduct that the actor believes to be necessary to avoid a harm or evil to himself or to another is justifiable, provided that:
    a. the harm or evil sought to be avoided by such conduct is greater than that sought to be prevented by the law defining the offense charged; and
    b. neither the Code nor other law defining the offense provides exceptions or defenses dealing with the specific situation involved; and
    c. a legislative purpose to exclude the justification claimed does not otherwise plainly appear.
2. When the actor was reckless or negligent in bringing about the situation requiring a choice of harms or evils or in appraising the necessity for his conduct, the justification afforded by this Section is unavailable in a prosecution for any offense for which recklessness or negligence, as the case may be, suffices to establish culpability.

Some states, such as Illinois, New York, and Texas, have enacted necessity defense statutes that follow to some extent the Model Penal Code provision.[18]

Self-defense illustrates how the necessity principle works. Self-defense involves a series of discrete, if not always articulated, analytical steps. First, the law identifies two conflicting values and their opposite "evils": the values sanctioning the crime that would be committed if self-defense were not available (the assailant's life), and the value protected by violating the law (the defender's life). The law ranks the defender's life higher than the assailant's. If defenders must choose between protecting their own lives and their assailants', the necessity principle guarantees that those who defend themselves will not suffer criminal punishment for choosing correctly. In other words, self-defense protects those who, out of necessity, choose to cause a lesser evil (injuring or killing their assailants) rather than submit to a greater one (losing their own lives or suffering injury themselves).

The analytical steps in self-defense permit a straightforward application of the necessity principles. Other justifications, however, give rise to greater complexity. Until recently, most jurisdictions did not formulate a general necessity principle. Since the Model Penal Code articulated a general principle of necessity, twenty-one states have done so. The Model Penal Code's provision extends the necessity principle beyond self-defense to include (1) destroying property to prevent spreading fire; (2) violating a speed limit to get a dying person to a hospital; (3) throwing cargo overboard to save a sinking vessel and its crew; (4) dispensing drugs without a prescription in an emergency; and (5) breaking and entering a mountain cabin to avoid freezing to death. In all these instances, life, safety, and health are values superior to the strict property interests that actors violate to protect these superior interests.[19]

CASE

Did She Choose to Avoid the Lesser Evil?

State v. O'Brien
784 S.W.2d 187 (Mo.1989)

Joseph J. Simeone, Senior Judge

Appellant, Ann L. O'Brien, was charged by information with the offense of trespass in the first degree for trespassing on the premises of the Reproductive Health Services located in the City of St. Louis.... [The court denied O'Brien claim of justification by necessity.] The court found the appellant guilty of trespass in the first degree and sentenced her [to 75 days in a medium security prison]. On August 17, 1988, appellant filed a motion contending ... the court erred in overruling her motion to offer evidence in justification.

On September 16, 1988, the court ... set aside the sentence of August 5, and, after overruling appellant's motion for new trial, *resentenced appellant to 75 days without probation from which she appeals.*

FACTS
The police reports containing the stipulated facts upon which the cause was submitted show that on July 3, 1987, appellant, together with several other persons, came into the waiting room of Reproductive Health Services and were "asked" by Delores Wrzesniewski "if they had an appointment." Witness Wrzesniewski stated to the officers that the "subjects refused to answer her and that they also refused to leave the waiting room." The witness advised the individuals that "if they did not leave she would call the police." The police reports show that officers received a radio call to proceed to the premises "in regards to a disturbance," and proceeded to the scene. "An investigation revealed eight subjects were creating a disturbance at that location."

Witness Wrzesniewski stated that the individuals "disrupted the business activities" and "also disturbed several of their customers." Another witness at the premises corroborated the statements of witness

Wrzesniewski. The officers reported that they observed appellant, and others, "standing inside the waiting room of Reproductive Health Services making several verbal comments against abortion." They observed several persons inside the waiting room with their legs interlocked and their hands handcuffed together. The officers took appellant and others into custody. These proceedings followed.

OPINION

On this appeal, appellant contends that the trial court erred in ... denying her motion to admit evidence of the defense of justification because her acts were within the meaning of "acts of necessity" as defined by § 563.026, R.S.Mo.1986, since such evidence would have demonstrated that her actions were reasonably calculated to save human lives which were in immediate danger of being destroyed....

... The defense of necessity has its roots deep in the common law. It is an affirmative defense which is expressed in terms of choice of evils. It has been said that when the "pressure of circumstances presents one with a choice of evils, the law prefers that a person avoid the greater evil by bringing about the lesser evil." Thus, conduct which would otherwise be a crime is, under unusual and imminent circumstances, the lesser of two evils and no offense.

Traditionally, the harm to be avoided had to be caused by physical forces of nature, rather than from human beings, but this requirement apparently has been somewhat relaxed so that the defense may encompass harms caused by human beings. The defense is based on social policy which recognizes that individuals should at times be free from legal restraints in order to avoid certain imminent harms. But the defense has very narrow limits. Under the common law, the defense must be one of absolute and uncontrollable necessity and this must be established beyond a reasonable doubt....

There are certain essential requirements for the defense of necessity ...: (1) the defendant is faced with a clear and imminent danger, not one which is debatable or speculative; (2) the defendant can reasonably expect that his action will be effective as the direct cause of abating the danger; (3) there is no legal alternative which will be effective in abating the danger; and (4) the legislature has not acted to preclude the defense by a clear and deliberate choice regarding the values at issue.

"... Under any definition of [the necessity defense] one principle remains constant: if there was a reasonable legal alternative to violating the law 'a chance both to refuse to do the criminal act and also to avoid the threatened harm,' the defense will fail...." "Those who wish to protest in an unlawful manner frequently are impatient with less visible and more time consuming alternatives. Their impatience does not constitute the 'necessity' that the defense of necessity requires.... A defendant's failure to resort to the political process precludes the assertion of the necessity...."

Since abortion remains a constitutionally protected right, the defense of necessity must be viewed in that context. Viewed in that setting every court which has considered the defense of necessity has for various reasons, rejected it when asserted in trespass-abortion proceedings....

[T]he defense of necessity asserted here cannot be utilized when the harm sought to be avoided [abortion] remains a constitutionally protected activity and the harm incurred [trespass] is in violation of the law....

Our conclusion is ... supported by general policy considerations. A resort to the defense of necessity in this context would lead to incongruous results: If abortion trespassers are given license to disrupt the activities of abortion clinics and refuse to desist upon being requested to vacate the premises ... the continuing battle between those who abhor abortion and those who believe it is a private moral decision could well be joined in physical confrontations into which the police and the courts would be rendered unable to intervene....

[T]he enduring clashes of beliefs in this fractious dispute must be resolved not by physical confrontations at the front line, but rather through the legislative and judicial framework created for the very purpose of undertaking the sometimes formidable tasks of choosing between extreme positions and competing values.

In short, if necessity were a valid defense at a time when abortion is a constitutionally protected right, the result would be an endless physical and, perhaps, violent impasse. Based upon the foregoing, we hold (1) the defense of necessity as presently interpreted in this and other jurisdictions is not a defense to a charge of trespass in the con-

text where appellant seeks to halt abortions, and (2) the findings of the Missouri General Assembly that life begins at conception as construed in light of the present law declared by the Supreme Court of the United States, and in light of the language of the preamble that the rights of the unborn are subject to the Constitution, do not vary the holding that necessity is not a defense to a charge of trespass in the abortion context....

Judgment affirmed.

Case Discussion

What are the two evils here? Or, was there only one? How did the court formulate the evils? How do you rank the evils here? Does the court say that fetal lives are not as important as property rights? Or does the court say that fetal life did not require trespass to preserve it? Did O'Brien honestly believe that she had to commit trespass to protect fetal lives? Was her belief reasonable? Was this act one of civil disobedience? Do you agree that to allow the defense of necessity here will lead to "physical confrontations?" Will denying the defense reduce such confrontations? Why? Why not? Is the court overstepping its authority in denying the defense here?

Note Case

The prosecution proved beyond a reasonable doubt by the use of radar readings that Dover was driving eighty miles per hour in a fifty-five-mile-per-hour zone. However, the court also found that the defendant, who is a lawyer, was not guilty on the grounds that his speeding violation was justified because he was late for a court hearing in Denver as a result of a late hearing in Summit County, Colorado.

A Colorado statute, § 42–4–1001(8)(a) provides:

The conduct of a driver of a vehicle which would otherwise constitute a violation of this section is justifiable and not unlawful when:

a. It is necessary as an emergency measure to avoid an imminent public or private injury which is about to occur by reason of a situation occasioned or developed through no conduct of said driver and which is of sufficient gravity that, according to ordinary standards of intelligence and morality, the desirability and urgency of avoiding the injury clearly outweigh the desirability of avoiding the consequences sought to be prevented by this section.

The Colorado supreme court reversed. It held: "In this case, the defendant did not meet the foundational requirements of § 42–4–1001(8)(a). He merely testified that he was driving to Denver for a 'court matter' and that he was late because of the length of a hearing in Summit County. No other evidence as to the existence of emergency as a justification for speeding was presented. The defendant did not present evidence as to the type or extent of the injury that he would suffer if he did not violate § 42–4–1001(1). He also failed to establish that he did not cause the situation or that his injuries would outweigh the consequences of his conduct. The record does not include evidence to establish a sufficient foundation to invoke the emergency justification defense provided by § 42–4–1001(8)(a). Since the defendant did not lay a proper foundation as to the existence of the defense, the prosecution was not required to prove beyond a reasonable doubt that the defendant was not justified in violating § 42–4–1001(1). § 18–1–407(2). The county court erred by finding the defendant not guilty because the defendant's speeding was justified because of an emergency. § 42–4–1001(8)(a). Accordingly, we reverse the district court and disapprove the ruling of the county court." *People v. Dover,* 790 P.2d 834 (Colo.1990)

The defense of necessity appears periodically in English and American history. The great thirteenth-century jurist Bracton declared that what "is not otherwise lawful, necessity makes lawful." Other famous commentators, such as Sir Francis Bacon, Sir Edward Coke, and Sir Matthew Hale in the sixteenth and seventeenth centuries, concurred with Bracton's judgment. The influential seventeenth-century judge Hobart expressed the argument this way: "All laws admit certain cases of just excuse, when they are offended in letter, and where the offender is under necessity, either of compulsion or inconvenience."[20]

Early cases record defendants successfully pleading necessity. The most common example in older cases is destroying a house to stop fires from spreading. As early as 1499, jurors could leave a trial without a judge's permission for good cause—to avoid injury from a melee that broke out. In 1500, a prisoner successfully defended against a prison break because he was trying to avoid a fire that burned down the jail. In 1912, a man was acquitted who burned a strip of heather to prevent a fire from spreading.[21]

Perhaps the most famous case to deal with the defense of necessity was *The Queen v. Dudley and Stephens.* Dudley and Stephens, two adults with families, and Brooks, a youth of eighteen without family responsibilities, were lost in a lifeboat on the high seas without food or water, except for two cans of turnips and a turtle they caught in the sea on the fourth day. After twenty days (the last eight without food), perhaps a thousand miles from land and with virtually no hope of rescue, Dudley and Stephens—after failing to secure Brooks's agreement to cast lots—told Brooks that if no rescue vessel appeared by the next day, they were going to kill him for food. They explained to Brooks that his life was the most expendable, because Dudley and Stephens had family responsibilities whereas Brooks did not. The following day, no vessel appeared. After saying a prayer for him, Dudley and Stephens killed Brooks, who was too weak to resist. They survived on his flesh and blood for four days, when they were finally rescued. Dudley and Stephens were prosecuted, convicted, and sentenced to death for murder. They appealed, pleading the defense of necessity.

> Lord Coleridge, in this famous passage, rejected the defense: [T]he temptation to act ... here was not what the law ever called necessity. Nor is this to be regretted. Though law and morality are not the same, and many things may be immoral which are not necessarily illegal, yet the absolute divorce of law from morality would be of fatal consequence; and such divorce would follow if the temptation to murder in this case were to be held by law an absolute defense of it. It is not so....
>
> To preserve one's life is generally speaking a duty, but it may be the plainest and the highest duty to sacrifice it. War is full of instances in which it

is a man's duty not to live, but to die. The duty, in case of shipwreck, of a captain to his crew, of the crew to the passengers, of soldiers to women and children ...; these duties impose on men the moral necessity, not of the preservation, but of the sacrifice of their lives for others.... It is not correct, therefore, to say that there is any absolute or unqualified necessity to preserve one's own life....

It is not needful to point out the awful danger of admitting the principle contended for. Who is to be the judge of this sort of necessity? By what measure of the comparative value of lives to be measured? Is it to be strength, or intellect, or what? It is plain that the principle leaves to him who is to profit by it to determine the necessity which will justify him in deliberately taking another's life to save his own. In this case, the weakest, the youngest, the most unresisting, was chosen. Was it more necessary to kill him than one of the grown men? The answer must be "No"—

"So spake the Fiend, and with necessity,
The tyrant's plea, executed his devilish deeds.
It is not suggested that in this particular case, the deeds were "devilish," but it is quite plain that such a principle once admitted might be made the legal cloak for unbridled passion and atrocious crime.

Lord Coleridge sentenced them to death, but expressed the hope that Queen Victoria would pardon them. The queen commuted their sentence to six months in prison.[22]

As a practical matter, the necessity defense creates problems. Most legislatures write statutes—and most lawyers and judges think—in terms of specific defenses for particular crimes. For example, they regard self-defense as a particular defense against homicide, not as a subdivision of the necessity principle. Furthermore, the necessity principle has strong critics. Nineteenth-century historian and judge Sir James F. Stephen believed the necessity defense to be so vague that judges could interpret it to mean anything they wanted. In the same vein, Glanville Williams, a modern criminal law professor, writes: "It is just possible to imagine cases in which the expediency of breaking the law is so overwhelmingly great that people may be justified in breaking it, but these cases cannot be defined beforehand."[23]

Defining necessity is a major problem and therefore an obstacle to stating clearly how to apply it in real cases. The Model Penal Code provision attempts to deal with this problem by the choice-of-evils concept. The code does not leave the ranking decision to individuals who claim its protection; legislatures, or judges and juries at trial, must rank the evils in advance. Once actors have made the "right" choice, the code either frees them entirely from criminal liability or considers the right choice a mitigating circumstance.

The great French novel, *Les Miserables,* dealt with a compelling problem: whether it was right for a father to steal a loaf of bread to feed his starving children. That problem is not always fiction, as *State v. Celli* makes clear. Because it requires balancing values, the necessity defense creates both ethical and social dilemmas. In *Celli,* the conflict was between life and property, between breaking and entering or freezing to death. The natural thing to do in the situation is just what the defendants did.

Sharp disagreement has always existed over stealing to avert hunger. Conflicting comments abound throughout Anglo-American law regarding "economic necessity." In *Maxims,* Francis Bacon asserted that stealing food to satisfy present hunger was not larceny. In *Leviathan,* written later in the seventeenth century, Thomas Hobbes was more cautious, asserting that hungry people could take food during great famine if they could not get it either with money or through charity. In *Pleas of the Crown,* Hawkins claimed that necessity was not a defense if hunger was due to the defendants' own unthriftiness. Late in the seventeenth century, Sir Matthew Hale stated the law as it is today; he rejected the defense altogether, because (1) the poor are already adequately cared for, (2) "[m]en's properties would be under a strange insecurity, being laid open to other men's necessities, whereof no man can possibly judge, but the party himself," and (3) pardons can resolve economic necessity cases. Blackstone adopted the same rule and reasoning in the eighteenth century, and American law imported it from him. The doctrine has prevailed since then in both America and England.[24]

Blackstone and Hale have not persuaded everyone. Professor Glanville Williams assesses it this way:

> Although Hale and Blackstone settled the rule that economic necessity is no defense, their arguments were not impressive. The Crown's power of pardon really means the discretion of a politician who happens to be Home Secretary, and its existence is hardly a valid justification for what may otherwise be thought to be imperfect law. It is not a sincere argument to say that no one can judge the extremity of want, especially when the argument goes on to say that the Home Secretary can judge it. In fact, Blackstone's opinion would have the logical result of ruling out the whole defense of necessity in criminal law, including the defenses of self-defense and duress; yet Blackstone himself admitted them. The argument based upon the existence of the poor law has a much stronger foundation; but English social history does not suggest that the scale occurred after Blackstone's day, in the troubled years following the Napoleonic wars, when public assistance was kept at only just above starvation level, notwithstanding the desperate straits of the working classes and the growing wealth of farmers and landlords. It became clear at that time that no trust could be placed in the executive to look with sympathetic eye upon the defense of economic necessity. On the contrary, the hunger riots and machine breaking that inevitably followed from the mass misery were vindictively suppressed. If the judges of this period had had the courage to recognize famine as an excuse for stealing, they might have helped to bring the Government to a realization of the need for adequate public relief.
>
> Whatever the defects of the poor law in the past, it can hardly be doubted that the only satisfactory solution of the problem of economic necessity is through the provision of social services that prevent the question arising. Otherwise an impossible conflict is created between humanitarianism and social exigencies. No society, capitalist or communist, can tolerate a state of affairs in which the poorest are allowed to help themselves. The law must set its face against anarchy, but it can morally do so only on condition of itself making provision for the relief of extreme need.[25]

CASE

Is Economic Necessity a Defense?

State v. Moe
24 P.2d 638 (Wash.1933)

Blake, Justice
The defendants were convicted of the crimes of grand larceny and riot.

FACTS

In the afternoon of September 3, 1932, a large number of unemployed people, among whom were the appellants, gathered together and marched to the Red Cross commissary in the city of Anacortes. Their purpose was to make a demonstration in support of a demand for a greater allowance of flour than had theretofore been made by the relief committee. Not finding the chairman of the committee at the commissary, they dispatched a messenger for him. On being informed that the chairman could not leave his place of business, they then marched to his office.

All of the appellants were present during these movements, and they were present in the office of the chairman when the written demand was presented. The appellant Anderson, in fact, presented the demand, and seems to have been the principal spokesman for the people at the meeting in the chairman's office. The chairman advised them that it was impossible to comply with the demand, whereupon some one asked if that was final. Being informed that it was, several persons in the crowd said, in substance: "Very well, we'll get it." Up to this point the assemblage had been peaceable and lawful.

The crowd then left the chairman's office, and a large number of them (variously estimated from forty to seventy-five) proceeded to the Skaggs store, which they entered. Many of them helped themselves to groceries, which they took away without paying for them. The appellants were in the store during all of the time the groceries were being taken. There is ample positive evidence of the ... active participation [of Moe, Trafton, and Wollertz] in the offenses. The evidence is conflicting, but we can concern ourselves only as to whether there was sufficient evidence to take the case to the jury on both counts. In considering the evidence, it must be borne in mind that, when several people are engaged in perpetrating a crime, each is responsible for the acts of the others done in furtherance of the common purpose. So, as here, where a larceny is committed by a number of people by force and violence, all who participate are chargeable with the offenses of larceny and riot. This, even though some take the property without outward manifestations of force and violence, and others manifest force and violence, but take no property.

Measured by these rules, we find evidence that Wollertz left the store carrying groceries for which he did not pay. We find evidence that Moe and Trafton, by threat of physical violence, compelled the manager of the store to unlock and open the door, which he had closed and locked after the rioters entered. This evidence of larceny by Wollertz and of force and violence threatened by Moe and Trafton was sufficient to take the case to the jury on both counts as to all of them.

Contention is made that there was not sufficient evidence that the value of the groceries taken was in excess of $25. This contention is addressed rather to the weight and credibility of the evidence in that respect than to the absence of such proof. At least two witnesses, the manager of the store and one of his clerks, testified directly that, in the aggregate, more than $25 worth of groceries were taken by the rioters. This was sufficient to make a case of grand larceny for the jury.

Appellants offered to prove the conditions of poverty and want among he unemployed of Anacortes and Skagit county on and prior to September 3d. This proof was offered for the purpose of showing a motive and justification for the raid on the Skaggs store and to show that the raid was spontaneous and not premeditated.

OPINION

Economic necessity has never been accepted as a defense to a criminal charge. The reason is that, were it ever countenanced, it would leave to the individual the right to take the law into his own hands. In larceny cases economic necessity is frequently invoked in mitigation of punishment, but has never been recognized as a defense.

Nor is it available as a defense to the charge of riot. The fact that a riot is spontaneous makes it none the less premeditated. Premeditation may, and frequently does, arise on the instant. A lawful assembly may turn into a riotous one in a moment of time over trivial incident or substantial provocation. When it does, those participating are guilty of riot, and neither the cause of the riot nor their reason for participation in it can be interposed as a defense. The causes, great or small, are available to the participants only in mitigation of punishment. The court did not err in rejecting the offer of proof....

It is next contended that the prosecuting attorney was guilty of prejudicial misconduct, in his closing argument to the jury, by referring to appellants as radicals and communists. The court immediately instructed the jury to disregard the remark. However, we do not regard the remark as misconduct in the light of the facts developed and the arguments made by the appellants themselves.

During the examinations of jurors on voir dire, appellants referred to themselves as militant members of labor organizations, and brought out the fact that two of their number were members of the Communist Party. One of the appellants, in his argument to the jury, said: "The groceries were taken, of course, but remember this, there is a higher law that says that a person holds his responsibility to himself first. There is a law of self-preservation, and how can you expect a man to go against the most fundamental

urges—the most prominent is the quest for food. Even the cave man in days gone by must have food."

The remarks of the prosecutor, now complained of, were made in the course of an argument in answer to the tenets appellants themselves made of record, namely, that, acting under economic necessity, they had the right to disregard and violate the laws of the state. The full context of the prosecutor's argument in this respect was as follows: "It is not a question with these people here as to whether a crime was committed. Mr. Moe has admitted to you that a crime was committed, so have the rest of them, but they say to you 'There is a higher law' than the laws of the United States and the state of Washington and we are going to obey that higher law. Has the time come in this country and in our county when the laws of the United States and the laws of the state of Washington are to be ignored by a small group of radicals, and the country turned over to communism?"....

The judgments are affirmed as to appellants Moe, Trafton, and Wollertz.

Case Discussion

Why did the court reject the defense of economic necessity? Was it for legal or political reasons? What were the evils balanced here? Which is greater? Was the danger from the greater evil imminent? Did the defendants have alternatives?

Note Case

On a cold winter day, Celli and his friend left Deadwood, South Dakota, hoping to hitchhike to Newcastle, Wyoming, to look for work. The weather turned colder, they were afraid of frostbite, and there was no place of business open for them to get warm. Their feet were so stiff from the cold that it was difficult for them to walk. They entered the only structure around, a cabin, breaking the lock on the front door. "Celli immediately crawled into a bed to warm up, and defendant Brooks attempted to light a fire in the fireplace. They rummaged through drawers to look for matches, which they finally located and started a fire. Finally defendant Celli emerged from the bedroom, took off his wet moccasins, socks and coat, placed them near the fire, and sat down to warm himself. After warming up somewhat they checked the kitchen for edible food. That morning they had shared a can of beans, but had not eaten since. All they found was dry macaroni, which they could not cook because there was no water.

"A neighbor noticed the smoke from the fireplace and notified the police. When the police entered the cabin, both defendants were warming themselves in front of the fireplace. The defendants were searched, but nothing belonging to the cabin owners was found. Do they have the defense of necessity? The trial court convicted them of fourth-degree burglary. The appellate court reversed on other grounds. *State v. Celli,* 263 N.W.2d 145 (S.D.1978)

———►▶◀◄———

▼ EXECUTION OF PUBLIC DUTIES

Public executioners throw switches to electrocute condemned murderers; soldiers shoot and kill wartime enemies; police officers use force to make arrests or to take citizens' property pursuant to search warrants. In all these examples, individuals' lives, liberty, and property are intentionally taken away. Yet, none of these examples is a crime. Why? Because all the actors were doing their jobs, and the deprivations they caused were justified because they were carried out as public duties.

These examples illustrate the justification called execution of public duty. The defense is at least as old as the sixteenth century, as its common-law definition illustrates: "A public officer is justified in using reasonable force against the person of another, or in taking his property, when he acts pursuant to a valid law, court order, or process, requiring or authorizing him so to act."[26]

The values underlying the execution-of-public-duty defense are clear: Once the state legitimately formulates laws, citizens must obey them; the law takes precedence over citizens' property, their liberty, and even their lives. Therefore, the value in enforcing the law ranks higher than individual property, liberty, and life.

The public duty defense arouses most controversy over the power of the police to kill suspects. A furious debate has raged over whether, and under what circumstances, the police may lawfully kill fleeing suspects. Some say the defense should cover officers who "need" to kill in order to make arrests. Others insist that only protecting officers' or other innocent people's lives justifies killing—that police have only the defense of self-defense belonging to private citizens. Still others believe that officers cannot shoot at fleeing suspects if doing so endangers innocent lives.

At one time, state laws authorized police officers to kill when necessary to effect felony arrests, including property crimes. Recently, however, the Supreme Court has restricted the constitutionality of police use of deadly force under the Fourth Amendment search and seizure clause (see *Tennessee v. Garner,* excerpted later in this section). Furthermore, police departments have established rules that prescribe in detail when officers can use force, including deadly force, in arresting suspects.[27]

The argument favoring the police power to kill in order to arrest fleeing suspects is based not only on protecting lives but also on maintaining respect for law enforcement authority. One commentator said:

> I am convinced that only through truly effective power of arrest can law be satisfactorily enforced. Obviously until violators are brought before the courts the law's sanctions cannot be applied to them. But effectiveness in making arrests requires more than merely pitting the footwork of policemen against that of suspected criminals. An English director of public prosecutions once explained to me that the English police had no need to carry pistols because (1) no English criminal would think of killing a police officer, and (2) even if

a suspected offender should outrun an officer in the labyrinth of London he could be found eventually in Liverpool or Birmingham. As the director put it, if a man offends in his own district everyone knows him, if he goes somewhere else everyone notices him.

[Without such power, he continued] we say to the criminal, "You are foolish. No matter what you have done you are foolish if you submit to arrest. The officer dare not take the risk of shooting at you. If you can outrun him, if you are faster than he is, you are free, and God bless you." I feel entirely unwilling to give that benediction to the modern criminal.[28]

The value of general obedience to the law rests on the reasonable assumption that life, liberty, and property mean little without order. The power to kill in order to take an arrest is therefore grounded not only on the value of life but also on the need for law observance in general. On the other hand, critics contend that the police power to kill creates social problems. More than twenty years ago, during the troubled 1960s, the United States attorney general, Ramsey Clarke, commented:

In these dog days of 1968, we have heard much loose talk of shooting looters. This talk must stop. The need is to train adequate numbers of police to prevent riots and looting altogether. Where prevention fails, looters must be arrested not shot. The first need in a civil disorder is to restore order. To say that when the looting starts, the shooting starts means either that shooting is preferable to arrest, or that there are [sic] not enough police protection, or the unpredictable nature of a disorder makes arrest impossible. Other techniques—including the use of tear gas—may be necessary. The use of deadly force is neither necessary, effective nor tolerable.

Far from being effective, shooting looters divides, angers, embitters, drives to violence. It creates the very problems its advocates claim is their purpose to avoid. Persons under the influence of alcohol killed 25,000 Americans in automobile accidents in 1967. Fewer than 250 people have died in all riots since 1964. Looters, as such, killed no one. Why not shoot drunken drivers? What is it that causes some to call for shooting looters when no one is heard to suggest the same treatment for a far deadlier and less controllable crime?

Is the purpose to protect property? Bank embezzlers steal ten times more money each year than bank robbers. Should we shoot embezzlers? What do the police themselves believe? It is the police to whom some would say, pull the trigger when looters are fleeing—perhaps dozens of looters fleeing toward a crowd; women, children; some making trouble, some committing crime, some trying to talk sense to a mob, to cool it.[29]

CASE

Did He Use Reasonable Force to Execute the Arrest?

Tennessee v. Garner
471 U.S. 1, 105 S.Ct. 1694, 85 L.Ed.2d 1 (1985)

[Justice White delivered the opinion, joined by Justices Brennan, Marshall, Blackmun, Powell, and Stevens. Justice O'Connor filed a dissenting opinion, joined by Chief Justice Burger and Justice Rehnquist.]

FACTS

At about 10:45 p.m. on October 3, 1974, Memphis Police Officers Elton Hymon and Leslie Wright were dispatched to answer a "prowler inside call." Upon arriving at the scene they saw a woman standing on her porch gesturing toward the adjacent house. She told them she had heard glass breaking and that "they" or "someone" was breaking in next door. While Wright radioed the dispatcher to say that they were on the scene, Hymon went behind the house. He heard a door slam and saw someone run across the back yard. The fleeing suspect, who was appellee-respondent's descendent, Edward Garner, stopped at a 6-feet-high chain link fence at the edge of the yard. With the aid of a flashlight, Hymon was able to see Garner's face and hands. He saw no sign of a weapon, and, though not certain, was "reasonably sure" and "figured" that Garner was unarmed. He thought Garner was 17 or 18 years old and about 5'5" or 5'7" tall. While Garner was crouched at the base of the fence, Hymon called out "police, halt" and took a few steps toward him. Garner began to climb over the fence. Convinced that if Garner made it over the fence he would elude capture, Hymon shot him. The bullet hit Garner in the back of the head. Garner was taken by ambulance to a hospital, where he died on the operating table. Ten dollars and a purse taken from the house were found on his body.

In using deadly force to prevent escape, Hymon was acting under the authority of a Tennessee statute and pursuant to Police Department policy. The statute provides that "[i]f, after notice of the intention to arrest the defendant, he either flee or forcibly resist, the officer may use all the necessary means to effect the arrest." Tenn. Code Ann. § 40–7–108 (1982). The Department policy was slightly more restrictive than the statute, but still allowed the use of deadly force in cases of burglary. The incident was reviewed by the Memphis Police Firearm's Review Board and presented to a grand jury. Neither took any action.

Garner's father then brought this action in the Federal District Court for the Western District of Tennessee, seeking damages under 42 U.S.C. § 1983 for asserted violations of Garner's constitutional rights. The complaint alleged that the shooting violated the Fourth, Fifth, Sixth, Eighth, and Fourteenth Amendments of the United States Constitution. It named as defendants Officer Hymon, the Police Department, its Director, and the Mayor and city of Memphis. After a 3-day bench trial, the District Court entered judgment for all defendants. It dismissed the claims against the Mayor and the Director for lack of evidence. It then concluded that Hymon's actions were authorized by the Tennessee statute, which in turn was constitutional. Hymon had employed the only reasonable and practicable means of preventing Garner's escape. Garner had "reck-lessly and heedlessly attempted to vault over the fence to escape, thereby assuming the risk of being fired upon."

The District Court ... found that the statute, and Hymon's actions, were constitutional. The Court of Appeals reversed and remanded....

OPINION

... Whenever an officer restrains the freedom of a person to walk away, he has seized that person.... [T]here can be no question that apprehension by the use of deadly force is a seizure subject to the reasonableness requirement of the Fourth Amendment.

A police officer may arrest a person if he has probable cause to believe that person committed a crime. Petitioners and appellant argue that if this requirement is satisfied the Fourth Amendment has nothing to say about how that seizure is made. This submission ignores the many cases in which this Court, by balancing the extent of the intrusion against the need for it, has examined the reasonableness of the manner in which a search or seizure is conducted....

The use of deadly force to prevent the escape of all felony suspects, whatever the circumstances, is constitutionally unreasonable. It is not better that all felony suspects die than that they escape. Where the suspect poses no immediate threat to the officer and no threat to others, the harm resulting from failing to apprehend him does not justify the use of deadly force to do so. It is no doubt unfortunate when a suspect who is in sight escapes, but the fact the police arrive a little late or are a little slower afoot does not always justify killing the suspect. A police officer may not seize an unarmed, nondangerous suspect by shooting him dead. The Tennessee statute is unconstitutional insofar as it authorizes the use of deadly force against such fleeing suspects....

Officer Hymon could not reasonably have believed that Garner—young, slight, and unarmed—posed any threat. Indeed, Hymon never attempted to justify his actions on any basis other than the need to prevent escape.... [T]he fact that Garner was a suspected burglar could not, without regard to the other circumstances, automatically justify the use of deadly force. Hymon did not have probable cause to believe that Garner, whom he correctly believed to be unarmed, posed any physical danger to himself or to others.

DISSENT

For purposes of Fourth Amendment analysis, I agree with the Court that Officer Hymon "seized" Garner by shooting him. Whether that seizure was reasonable and therefore permitted by the Fourth Amendment requires a careful balancing of the important public interest in crime prevention and detection and the nature and quality of the intrusion upon legitimate interests of the individual. In striking this balance here, it is crucial to acknowledge that police use of deadly force to apprehend a fleeing criminal suspect falls within the "rubric of police conduct ... necessarily [involving] swift action predicated upon the on-the-spot observations of the officer on the beat."...

The public interest involved in the use of deadly force as a last resort to apprehend a fleeing burglary suspect relates primarily to the serious nature of the crime. Household burglaries represent not only the illegal entry into a person's home, but also "pos[e] a real risk of serious harm to others." According to recent Department of Justice statistics, "[t]hree-fifths of all rapes in the home, three-fifths of all home robberies, and about a third of home aggravated and simple assaults are committed by burglars."...

Against the strong public interests justifying the conduct at issue here must be weighed the individual interests implicated in the use of deadly force by police officers. The majority declares that "[t]he suspect's fundamental interest in his own life need not be elaborated upon." This blithe assertion hardly provides an adequate substitute for the majority's failure to acknowledge the distinctive manner in which the suspect's interest in his life is even exposed to risk. For purposes of this case, we must recall that the police officer, in the course of investigating a nighttime burglary, had reasonable cause to arrest the suspect and ordered him to halt. The officer's use of force resulted because the suspected burglar refused to heed this command and the officer reasonably believed that there was no means short of firing his weapon to apprehend the suspect.... "[T]he policeman's hands should not be tied merely because of the possibility that the suspect will fail to cooperate with legitimate actions by law enforcement personnel."...

Case Discussion Should the Fourth Amendment prohibit the use of deadly force to arrest property felons? Is residential burglary simply a property crime? Do you agree with the majority or dissent? Explain. Will this rule embolden criminals? Defend your answer.

▼ RESISTING UNLAWFUL ARREST

A problem related to the execution of public duty arises when citizens use force to resist arrests. Jurisdictions differ over how much force citizens may use to resist unlawful arrests. They range across this spectrum:

1. Citizens cannot use force against even a plainclothes officer whom they know or believe is an officer.
2. Citizens can never use force against a known police officer.
3. Citizens can use nondeadly force against police officers.
4. If citizens use deadly force against officers, resisting unlawful arrest may reduce the charge from criminal homicide to a lesser degree of homicide.

Two policies underlie restricting citizens' use of force against police officers. These are (1) to encourage obedience to police, and (2) to encourage preferable remedies to force, such as civil lawsuits against the police, their departments, or the governmental units they serve.

Arguments favoring citizens' use of force to resist unlawful arrests are based on two major premises. First, citizens in a free society need not submit passively to detention when the government unlawfully deprives them of liberty. Under such circumstances, the use of force is crucial to a free society. Second, illegal arrests cause even the most restrained people to lose control, at least to the extent that they feel outraged at the arrest. Realistically therefore, citizens will resist arrests they believe are unlawful. Legislatures and courts have never accepted these arguments. The Maine Supreme Court addressed a citizen's use of force to resist arrest in *Maine v. Austin*.

CASE

Can You Use Force to Resist an Unlawful Arrest?

Maine v. Austin
381 A.2d 652 (Me.1978)

[Chief Justice McKusick delivered the opinion.]

FACTS

At approximately 1 a.m. on July 11, 1976, Officer John Bernard, Jr., police chief of the Town of Mexico, and Officer Gregory Gallant of the Mexico Police Department, stationed themselves in a marked police cruiser opposite the MGM lounge on Main Street in Mexico, for the purpose of investigating repeated citizen complaints of loud noises from persons leaving the MGM

around closing time. The officers observed several patrons come out of the MGM, some congregating in small groups on the sidewalk. Although some persons in the crowd were using loud language, the officers took no action until Chief Bernard heard someone shout an obscene name. As the same person repeated the phrase twice more, Chief Bernard singled out the defendant as the speaker and observed that he appeared to be directing his speech to a group of some five persons who were standing in an area between the MGM and an adjacent restaurant. As Chief Bernard watched, Austin crossed the street and started a conversation with one John Porello, who was seated in his parked car about 50 feet from the passenger side of the police cruiser. Chief Bernard, who was sitting in the seat with the window down, then heard Austin repeat the obscenity. Austin then put his arm up over the top of Porello's vehicle and, pointing his hand directly at the cruiser, called out another obscene name. Chief Bernard immediately got out of the cruiser and went over to Austin. When asked whether "he would clean up his mouth" and told by Chief Bernard that he did not appreciate Austin's name-calling, Austin replied that he had not called the Chief the obscene name. Chief Bernard, at that moment, advised Austin that he was under arrest for disorderly conduct.

Officer Gallant, who by that time had joined the others at the Porello car, assisted Chief Bernard, who was unsuccessfully attempting to put Austin in handcuffs, by picking Austin up around his waist from the rear and physically carrying him to the cruiser. There, the officers succeeded in handcuffing him, but in the process of placing him in the back seat of the cruiser, Austin kicked out at Officer Gallant, striking him in the thigh. On the ride to the police station, Austin continued to be unruly, positioning himself over the back of the front seat "screaming obscenities and threats." At one point, when Chief Bernard attempted to push him back down into the rear seat, Austin fell back and with his foot struck Chief Bernard in the area of his left ear, neck, and jaw. At the station, Austin was charged with disorderly conduct and two counts of assault [and was convicted. He appealed.]

OPINION

The thrust of the defendant's arguments on appeal concerns his asserted right to resist an illegal arrest with force. Prior to the effective date of the Criminal Code, May 1, 1976, Maine followed the prevailing common law rule that

> [a]n illegal arrest is an assault and battery. The person so attempted to be restrained of his liberty has the same right, and only the same right, to use force in defending himself as he would have in repelling any other assault and battery. *State v. Robinson,* 72 A.2d 260, 262 (1950).

Reading the provisions of the Criminal Code as a whole shows, however, that Robinson no longer states the law of Maine.

We thus read the Criminal Code as an integrated whole declaring the entire law

relating to criminal responsibility for violence during an attempted arrest. In general, under [§ 107 of] the code a person being arrested must not respond violently. On the other hand, a police officer is given by the code substantial leeway in using nondeadly force in making an arrest—namely, that amount he reasonably believes necessary to make the arrest—provided he does not know the arrest is illegal. § 108 gives the arrested person a right of self-defense against unlawful or excessive force used by the police officer; but if he reacts violently to nondeadly force applied by the police, he takes his chances on being able later to show the officer was not justified under § 107.

The legislature has thus cast the advantage on the side of law enforcement officers, leaving the person arrested in most cases to pursue his rights, not through violent self-help, but through prompt hearing before a magistrate with prompt consideration for release on bail or personal recognizance. At the same time, the police should exercise their code-granted prerogatives with restraint, with police departments using administrative discipline to assure that individual officers in fact use no more force than necessary to effect arrests. Violence breeds violence, whoever starts it.

The defendant has assigned as error the presiding justice's refusal to grant the following jury instruction:

That when a person is illegally arrested, he is privileged to use such force as is reasonably necessary and calculated, in view of the totality of the circumstances, to resist and deter the unlawful apprehension and detention by the party effecting the arrest.

The requested instruction was obviously derived from the rule of *State v. Robinson,* which no longer is the law. The requested instruction was properly denied. The presiding justice's charge correctly stated the principles of law relevant to the defendant's defense of justification.

We have examined the defendant's remaining claims of error, and finding none with merit, the entry must be: Appeal denied. Judgments affirmed.

Case Discussion   Self-defense does not mean defense only against death or bodily injury. It also includes defending personal liberty. Resisting unlawful arrests is a good, but controversial, example. Can citizens ever use force against the police, and if so, how much force can they use? *Maine v. Austin* answers these questions, at least as far as concerns Maine's law on the matter. Note the competing interests present in permitting citizens to use force against unlawful arrests.

▼ DEFENSE OF HOMES AND PROPERTY

Ranking values is a complicated business, as shown by the foregoing discussion concerning executing the public duty to make arrests. Similarly complex values lie under the justification to defend property. From the early days of the common law, force, including deadly force, was justified in protecting homes:

> If any person attempts ... to break open a house in the nighttime (which extends also to an attempt to burn it) and shall be killed in such attempt, the slayer shall be acquitted and discharged. This reaches not to ... the breaking open of any house in the daytime, unless it carries with it an attempt of robbery.[30]

Nearly all states authorize the use of force to protect homes; some states go further and adopt provisions authorizing the use of force to protect property. Texas, for example, has enacted the following statute:

§ 9.42 Deadly Force to Protect Property
A person is justified in using deadly force against another to protect land or tangible, movable property:

1. if he would be justified in using force against the other under § 9.41 of this code; and
2. when and to the degree he reasonably believes the deadly force is immediately necessary:
    A. to prevent the other's imminent commission of arson, burglary, robbery, aggravated robbery, theft during the nighttime, or criminal mischief during the nighttime; or
    B. to prevent the other who is fleeing immediately after committing burglary, robbery, aggravated robbery, or theft during the nighttime from escaping with the property; and
3. he reasonably believes that:
    A. the land or property cannot be protected or recovered by any other means; or
    B. the use of force other than deadly force to protect or recover the land or property would expose the actor or another to a substantial risk of death or serious bodily injury.

CASE

Did He Lawfully Use Deadly Force to Protect His Home?

Bishop v. State

356 S.E.2d 503 (Georgia 1987)

Gregory, Justice

Robert C. Bishop was convicted of malice murder and sentenced to life imprisonment. We affirm.

FACTS

Bishop lived in a trailer park in Coweta County. Because he was concerned about past break-ins to his trailer, he erected a spring gun or trap gun. He positioned a Mauser 8mm high-powered rifle on two chairs with the barrel pointed in the direction of the trailer's front door. A string attached to the door knob ran over the back of one of the chairs and was connected to the trigger.

Bishop went to work on the night of February 13, 1986 with the spring gun in place. Later, James Freeman, an acquaintance of Bishop, attempted to enter the front door of the trailer. The rifle discharged and hit the metal molding at the foot of the door. Freeman was hit by either a ricocheting bullet fragment or a piece of flying metal. Neighbors heard the shot and found Freeman lying wounded in Bishop's driveway. The neighbors said the trailer was dark, but that Bishop's car was in the driveway.

Freeman was taken to a Newnan hospital. The doctor on duty found the projectile had glanced off Freeman's right thigh and fractured his forearm. Freeman was transferred to an Atlanta hospital, where doctors performed tissue and vascular transplants on the arm using grafts from Freeman's left leg. Freeman was released from the hospital two weeks later. The following night, on February 27, 1986, he died. The pathologist performing the autopsy said Freeman died of a pulmonary embolism or blood clot.

Bishop was tried by a jury and found guilty of malice murder.

OPINION

… Bishop … contends erecting the spring gun was not unlawful in his case because the killing of Freeman was justified. He cites OCGA § 16–3–23, which provides:

> A person is justified in threatening or using force against another when and to the extent that he reasonably believes that such a threat or force is necessary to prevent or terminate such other's unlawful entry into or attack upon a habitation; however, he is justified in the use of force which is intended or likely to cause death or great bodily harm only if: … (2) He reasonably believes that the entry is made or attempted for the purpose of committing a felony therein and such force is necessary to prevent the commission of the felony.

Apparently Bishop's trailer had been broken into on several occasions. According to Bishop, the evidence indicates Freeman was burglarizing the trailer when he was shot, although the State disputes this. Bishop argues had he been at home in the darkened trailer and Freeman attempted to enter unannounced he could have reasonably believed a felony was being committed upon his habitation and been justified in using deadly force pursuant to § 16–3–23.

The weakness in Bishop's argument is that he was working and not at home when the spring gun activated. Bishop contends the traditional rule observed in other jurisdictions is that a person is not justified in taking a life indirectly with a mechanical device unless he would have been justified had he been personally present and taken the life with his own hand.

We decline Bishop's invitation to adopt such a rule in these circumstances. § 16–3–23 justifies the use of deadly force to protect a habitation only when the inhabitant "reasonably believes" the entry is made for the purpose of committing a felony.

We find that under these circumstances, however, it was impossible for Bishop to form a reasonable belief in light of his absence from the trailer. Allowing persons, at their own risk, to employ deadly mechanical devices imperils the lives of children, firemen and policemen acting within the scope of their employment, and others.

Where the actor is present, there is always a possibility he will realize that deadly force is not necessary, but deadly mechanical devices are without mercy or discretion.... It seems clear that the use of such devices should not be encouraged. Moreover, whatever may be thought in torts, the foregoing rule setting forth an exception to liability for death or injuries inflicted by such devices "is inappropriate in penal law for it is obvious it does not prescribe a workable standard of conduct; liability depends upon fortuitous results." [Model Penal Code]

We have reviewed all the evidence ... and find in the light most favorable to the jury's verdict that a rational trier of fact could have found Bishop guilty beyond a reasonable doubt.

Judgment affirmed.

DISSENT

Smith, Justice, dissenting.

"Every man's home is his castle." This statement all of us have heard since childhood. This case involves the extent to which a man may use deadly force to protect that "castle."

In the venerable case *Collins v. Rennison,* 1 Sayer 138 (K.B.1754), an English court described the allowable extent by employing the phrase "moliter manus imposuit." The use of this phrase indicated that a person should gently push a nonfelonious intruder out the door. Blackstone, in advocating a tougher response to intrusions into the home, noted that all felonies were punishable by death. He advocated sanction of the use of deadly force to prevent an intruder from entering a home to commit a felony....

Since the early cases, the courts and legislatures in this country have in the absence of complete prohibition, drawn a line between spring guns used in the home and spring guns used elsewhere. Some cases have stated that spring guns could be used to protect dwelling places when the owner could have used deadly force had he been present. Others like the majority opinion here, flatly forbid the use of spring guns.

From the broad range of standards dealing with spring guns and criminal law, I would select the rule that views as justified a homicide committed by spring gun at night in the home of the defendant when the defendant can establish under the totality of the circumstances that he possessed a reasonable expectation that someone would be breaking into his home to commit a felony and that the victim was, indeed, breaking into his home to commit a felony. To do this, we simply should look to the intent of the defendant at the time that he sets the spring gun, setting the chain of events leading to the death in motion, rather than to the time at which the victim is shot. Viewed in this manner, OCGA § 16–3–23 would justify a homicide such as the one involved in this case. I would reverse.

Case Discussion What rule does the court adopt in the use of force to protect homes? Why does it reject the use of spring guns? What facts bear on the question of justification here? Does the dissent have the better of the argument in maintaining that the law should accept the use of spring guns? If it does, was it justified here?

Note Case In 1986 Colorado enacted a "make my day law" for the protection of homes. § 18–1–704.5, 8B, C.R.S. (1986) provides:

> *1.* The general assembly hereby recognizes that the citizens of Colorado have a right to expect absolute safety within their own homes.

2. ... [A]ny occupant of a dwelling is justified in using any degree of physical force, including deadly physical force, against another person when that other person has made an unlawful entry into the dwelling, and when the occupant has a reasonable belief that such other person has committed a crime in the dwelling in addition to the uninvited entry, or is committing or intends to commit a crime against a person or property in addition to the uninvited entry, and when the occupant reasonably believes that such other person might use any physical force, however slight, against any occupant.

3. Any occupant of a dwelling using physical force, including deadly force, in accordance with the provisions in subsection (2) of this section shall be immune from criminal prosecution for the use of such force.

4. Any occupant of a dwelling using physical force, including deadly physical force, in accordance with the provisions of subsection (2) of this section shall be immune from any civil liability for injuries or death resulting from the use of such force.

When neighbors pounded on David and Pam Guenther's door, and Pam Guenther went outside the door and got into a struggle with one of the neighbors, David Guenther shot and killed two neighbors outside the front door with four shots from a Smith and Wesson .357 Magnum six-inch revolver. Did David Guenther use lawful force to protect his home? The court held:

> In accordance with the explicit terms of the statute, we hold that § 18–1–704.5 provides the home occupant with immunity from prosecution only for force used against one who has made an unlawful entry into the dwelling, and that this immunity does not extend to force used against non-entrants. *People v. Guenther*, 740 P.2d 971 (Colo.1987)

▼ CONSENT

The consent defense constitutes a special defense to some crimes. In theft, for example, taking property without the owner's consent is central to the crime. In rape, too, consent eliminates the *mens rea*—the intent is to have sexual penetration without consent. Furthermore, the same act may be criminal in one situation and appropriate in another. Grabbing another forcibly around the ankles and bringing him or her abruptly to the ground is assault if it happens between strangers on the street, but it generates thunderous approval from fans supporting the defensive team if it takes place on the playing field during the Super Bowl. A surgeon commits neither assault and battery by cutting into a patient's body nor murder if the patient dies. Furthermore, consent constitutes either the general defense of justification or excuse. Consent justifies conduct or results when they were right under the circumstances.[31]

Consent gives rise to two critical issues: (1) To what crimes can victims consent? For example, can you consent to your own murder? (2) What constitutes legal consent? For example, can a four-year-old child legally consent to sexual penetration? In all jurisdictions, consent constitutes a defense to crime if it negates a material element (such as consent to sexual penetration). In most jurisdictions, consent constitutes a justification or excuse only when conduct causes only minor injuries, such as in some assault and battery. Courts tend to recognize the defense only when (1) no serious injury results, such as with a slap in the face that requires no medical treatment; (2) society widely accepts the risk of injury, such as in ice hockey, football, soccer, and boxing; and (3) the defendant's conduct has a beneficial result, such as with a doctor who performs surgery.[32]

"Victims" must legally consent to the conduct or its result for their consent to constitute a defense. Parties must consent voluntarily; that is, consent must result from their own free will without compulsion or duress. The person consenting must be competent to do so; youth, intoxication, or mental abnormality might disable the consent. Consent by fraud or deceit renders the consent ineffective. Finally, forgiveness after defendants have committed crimes does not constitute consent. (See chapter 9 for consent in sex offenses.)

CASE

Was Her Consent a Justification?

State v. Brown
143 N.J. Super. 571, 364 A.2d 27 (1976)

Bachman, J.S.C.

In a prosecution for atrocious assault and battery, defendant asserted that the victim had consented to his physical assault. The Superior Court, Law Division, Bachman, J.S.C., held that a battery cannot be consented to by a victim. Judgment accordingly.

Pursuant to R.2:5—1, this opinion is to serve as amplification of this court's ruling on the issue of consent of the victim to the alleged atrocious assault and battery (N.J.S.A. 2A:90—1). Specifically, defendant contends that he is not guilty of the alleged atrocious assault and battery because he and Mrs. Brown, the victim, had an understanding to the effect that if she consumed any alcoholic beverages (and/or became intoxicated), he would punish her by physically assaulting her.

FACTS
The testimony revealed that the victim was an alcoholic. On the day of the alleged crime she indulged in some spirits, apparently to Mr. Brown's dissatisfaction. As per their agreement, defendant sought to punish Mrs. Brown by severely beating her with his hands and other objects.

OPINION
This court was able to find only two early cases in this State dealing with the consent defense in criminal assault cases. Though they are somewhat inferentially and analogously enlightening, they are not entirely dispositive of the question of consent in this case, for they, like many cases (including those in this and other jurisdictions that have held consent to be a defense in a prosecution for criminal assault) involve sexual assaults of one kind or another.

Some courts have allowed the defense of consent in civil suits, while denying it in criminal prosecutions for battery. According to these courts, there are two different interests at stake.

While criminal law is designed to protect the interests of society as a whole, the civil law is concerned with enforcing the rights of each individual within the society. So, while the consent of the victim may relieve defendant of liability in tort, this same consent has been held irrelevant in a criminal prosecution, where there is more at stake than a victim's rights.

Because of the dearth of authority in New Jersey, it will be useful to examine the manner in which other jurisdictions have resolved the issue of consent to criminal assaults. Several of these courts have ruled on the issue of consent in criminal assault cases that did not have sexual overtones but did involve actual batteries. These courts have almost invariably taken the position that since the offense in question involved a breach of the public peace as well as an invasion of the victim's physical security, the victim's consent would not be recognized as a defense, especially where the battery is a substantial or severe one.

It was very early held to be a crime to cut off the hand of a person at his request and with his full consent. Wright's Case (Leicester Assizes 1604). Professor Beale explained that

> Homicide, mayhem and battery may be committed, though the individual injured consented to the injury. The reason for this is clear: The public has an interest in the personal safety of its citizens and is injured where the safety of any individual is threatened, whether by himself or another. (Beale, "Consent in the Criminal Law," 8 Harv.L.Rev. 317, 324 (1895)).

Atrocious assault and battery is a crime in this State, as it is in others. As noted by the court in *Martin v. Commonwealth,* 184 Va. 1009, 37 S.E.2d 43 (Sup.Ct.App.1946),

> Invitations and consent to the perpetration of a crime do not constitute defenses.... If the doing of a particular act is a crime regardless of the consent of anyone, consent is obviously no excuse.... The right to life and security is not only sacred in the estimation of the common law, but it is inalienable....

The reasoning and public interest that is of concern and served by this rule is that of peace, health and good order. An individual or victim cannot consent to a wrong that is committed against the public peace. The state, not the victim, punishes a person for fighting or inflicting assaults.... There are three parties involved in criminal assaults, one being the state, which for its own good does not suffer the others to deal on a basis of contract with the public. It has been stat-

ed, and perhaps rightly so, that the only true consent to a criminal act is that of the community.

This is so because these acts (the physical assaults by defendant upon Mrs. Brown), even if done in private, have an impingement (whether direct or indirect) upon the community at large in that the very doing of them may tend to encourage their repetition and so to undermine public morals....

There are a few situations in which the consent of the victim (actual or implied) is a defense. These situations usually involve ordinary physical contact or blows incident to sports such as football, boxing, or wrestling. *People v. Samuels,* 250 Cal.App.2d 501, 58 Cal.Rptr. 439 (D.Ct.App.1967), Cert. den. Sub nom. *Samuels v. California,* 390 U.S. 1024, 88 S.Ct. 1404, 20 L.Ed.2d.

But this is expected and understood by the participants. The state cannot later be heard to charge a participant with criminal assault upon another participant if the injury complained of resulted from activity that is reasonably within the rules and purview of the sports activity. However this is not to be confused with sports activities that are not sanctioned by the state. Thus, street fighting which is disorderly and mischievous on many obvious grounds (even if for a purse and consented to), and encounters of that kind which tend to and have the specific objective of causing bodily harm, serve no useful purpose, but rather tend to breach the peace and thus are unlawful.

No one is justified in striking another, except it be in self-defense, and similarly whenever two persons go out to strike each other and do so, each is guilty of an assault. It is no matter who strikes the first blow, for the law proscribes such striking.

... [I]t is a matter of common knowledge that a normal person in full possession of his or her mental faculties does not freely and seriously consent to the use upon his or herself of force likely to produce great bodily harm. Those persons that do freely consent to such force and bodily injury no doubt require the enforcement of the very laws that were enacted to protect them and other humans. A general principle of law is that a person cannot contract out of protective legislation passed for his other benefit.... The laws of this State and others that have dealt with the question are simply and unequivocally clear that the defense of consent cannot be available to a defendant charged with any type of physical assault that causes appreciable injury. If the law were otherwise, it would not be conducive to a peaceful, orderly and healthy society....

This court concludes that, as a matter of law, no one has the right to beat another even though that person may ask for it. Assault and battery cannot be consented to by a victim, for the State makes it unlawful and is not a party to any such agreement between the victim and perpetrator. To allow an otherwise criminal act to go unpunished because of the victim's consent would not only threaten the security of our society but also might tend to detract from the force of the moral principles underlying the criminal law....

Thus, for the reasons given, the State has an interest in protecting those persons who invite, consent to and permit others to assault and batter them. Not to enforce these laws which are geared to protect such people would seriously threaten the dignity, peace, health and security of our society.

Case Discussion   The court ruled that consent to assault is no defense because victims cannot contract away their interests, especially when it involves a state interest as well. Do you agree? Doesn't the state also have an interest in curing drunkenness? Why should the law intervene where citizens agree to what otherwise would be crimes? Is Mrs. Brown really an assault victim? What rule would you make for this case?

Note Case   Fransua and the victim were in a bar in Albuquerque. Fransua had apparently been drinking heavily that day and the previous day. Some time around 3:00 p.m., after an argument, Fransua told the victim that if Fransua had a gun, he would shoot the victim. The victim then left the bar, went to his own automobile, removed a loaded pistol from the automobile, and returned to the bar. he came up to Fransua, laid the pistol on the bar, and made the following remark: "There is the gun. If you want to shoot me, go ahead." Fransua picked up the pistol, put the barrel next to the victim's head and pulled the trigger, wounding him seriously.

Was Fransua guilty of aggravated battery or was the victim's consent a justification? The court said consent was not a defense.

> It is generally conceded that a state enacts criminal statutes making certain violent acts crimes for at least two reasons: One reason is to protect the persons of its citizens; the second, however, is to prevent a breach of the public peace. While we entertain little sympathy for either the victim's absurd actions or the defendant's equally unjustified act of pulling the trigger, we will not permit the defense of consent to be raised in such cases. Whether or not the victims of crimes have so little regard for their own safety as to request injury, the public has a stronger and overriding interest in preventing and prohibiting acts such as these. We hold that consent is not a defense to the crime of aggravated battery, irrespective of whether the victim invites the act and consents to the battery. *State v. Fransua,* 85 N.M. 173, 510 P.2d 106, 58 A.L.R.3d 656 (App.Ct.1973).

▼ *Summary* ▼

This chapter confronted defendants who denied criminal liability because they were justified. They assumed full responsibility for their actions but maintained that special circumstances justified, or made right, their conduct or its result. They were confronted with a dilemma: choosing between two evils. They killed or injured persons, or violated property, to avoid an imminent or present greater evil, or because they were performing a public duty, defending their rights against government invasion, or carrying out an agreement with the consent of the "victim."

Theoretically, these evils—and the greater ones defended against—apply the general principle of necessity to specific crimes. Practically, however, neither legislators, judges, prosecutors, nor defense attorneys think in such broad, theoretical terms. Rather, they look at specific defenses to particular crimes. Hence, self-defense means defending against homicide charges or, less frequently, rape and assault. Other defenses, such as executing public duties and protecting property, also occur in this light. Necessity appears as a special defense, not a general principle, applying to cases such as where freezing people break into deserted cabins to keep warm.

Viewed in this practical light, the distinction between justification (responsible action that is right under the circumstances) and excuse (wrongful action for which perpetrators are not responsible) is not important. Nevertheless, justification does differ from excuse, even though both bring about the same practical result: acquittal, reduced charges, or punishments. The distinction makes sense of the "laundry list" of offenses usually presented in cases and criminal codes.

Finally, distinguishing between justification and excuse is not always easy. In consent, defendants may have meant to do what they did, but since their victims consented, what they did was right under the circumstances. Of, even if what defendants did was wrong, their victims are responsible because they consented to it.[33]

▼ *Questions for Review and Discussion* ▼

1. Distinguish between justification and excuse. What is the practical difference?

2. Define and discuss the elements of self-defense. Why is the imminence requirement important in spousal abuse cases?

3. Distinguish between the "all-American" and retreat doctrines. What is the castle exception: What are the rationales for the all-American, the retreat doctrine, and the castle exception?

4. Should there be a general principle of necessity? How should it be formulated? Explain.

5. To what extent, and under what circumstances, may force be used to protect property?

6. Should there be a defense of economic necessity? How should it be formulated?

7. When is it justifiable for public officers to use force?

8. When is it justifiable for a private citizen to use force against a law enforcement officer?

9. Should consent of the victim ever be a defense to crime? Under what circumstances? Why? Why not?

▼ *Suggested Readings* ▼

1. George Fletcher, "Justification, in *Encyclopedia of Crime and Justice,* vol. 3, ed. Sanford H. Kadish (New York: Free Press, 1983), pp. 941–46. An excellent introduction to the theory of justification in criminal law. Professor Fletcher describes and assesses the scope and criteria for justification, balancing evils and the imminent risk requirement.

2. American Law Institute, *Model Penal Code and Commentaries,* vol. 2 (Philadelphia: American Law Institute, 1985), pp. 8–22. The most complete discussion of the principle of necessity by the foremost authorities on the subject. Although written primarily for lawyers, it is worth the serious student's effort.

3. George F. Dix, "Self-Defense," in *Encyclopedia of Crime and Justice,* vol. 3, pp. 946–53, is a good general discussion of self-defense. Professor Dix covers the main elements in the defense, the defense by battered wives who attack their husbands, the retreat doctrine, the defense of others, and the use of force to resist arrest.

4. Rollin M. Perkins and Ronald N. Boyce, *Criminal Law,* 3d ed. (Mineola, N.Y.: Foundation Press, 1982), pp. 1074–92. The authors thoroughly discuss the consent defense in criminal law. Both the legal effect of consent and the crimes to which consent is a defense are described, and arguments both for and against consent are appraised, as is the law as it stands in several jurisdictions.

▼ *Notes* ▼

1. George Fletcher, *Rethinking Criminal Law* (Boston: Little, Brown, 1978), chap. 10; Rollin M. Perkins and Ronald N. Boyce, *Criminal Law,* 3d ed. (Mineola, N.Y.: Foundation Press, 1982), chap. 8–10; Thomas Morawetz, "Reconstructing the Criminal Defenses: The Significance of Justification," *Journal of Criminal Law and Criminology* 77(1986):277.

2. American Law Institute, *Model Penal Code and Commentaries,* vol. 2 (Philadelphia: American Law Institute, 1985), pt. I, 3.

3. See Arnold H. Loewy, *Criminal Law* (St. Paul: West Publishing Co., 1987), pp. 192–204, for a brief introduction to the topics of burdens and amount of proof. Also, more thorough discussion appears in Wayne R. LaFave and Austin W. Scott,

Criminal Law, 2d ed. (St. Paul: West Publishing Company, 1986), pp. 51–56; *People v. Dover,* 790 P.2d 834 (Colo.1990).

4. Perkins and Boyce, *Criminal Law,* pp. 926–32; Jerome Hall, *General Principles of Criminal Law,* 2d ed. (Indianapolis: Bobbs-Merrill, 1960), pp. 86–88, 97–102; Carol Byrne, "Was Mercy in This Killing?" *Minneapolis Star and Tribune* (May 1, 1988), p. 1A; Carol Byrne, "An Old Man Starts a New Life—In Prison," *Minneapolis Star and Tribune* (June 5, 1988), p. 1A.

5. Francis Wharton, *A Treatise on the Criminal Law of the United States* (Philadelphia: Kay and Brother, 1861), § 1020.

6. American Law Institute, *Model Penal Code and Commentaries,* vol. 2, pt. I, pp. 30–61; George P. Fletcher, *A Crime of Self-Defense: Bernhard Goetz and the Law on Trial* (New York: Free Press, 1988), pp. 18–27.

7. *State v. Goode,* 195 S.W. 1006 (Mo.1917); Perkins and Boyce, *Criminal Law,* pp. 1128–29.

8. *People v. Williams,* 56 Ill.App.2d 159, 205 N.E.2d 749 (1965).

9. American Law Institute, *Model Penal Code and Commentaries,* art. 3.04.

10. *People v. Johnson,* 2 Ill.2d 165, 117 N.E.2d 91 (1954).

11. 158 U.S. 550, 15 S.Ct. 962, 39 L.Ed. 1086 (1894); American Law Institute, *Model Penal Code and Commentaries,* vol. 3, pt. I, pp. 35–37.

12. Quoted in *Model Penal Code,* tentative draft no. 8 (Philadelphia: American Law Institute, 1958), pp. 79–80.

13. 117 Tenn. 430 (1907).

14. *State v. Schroeder,* 199 Neb. 822, 261 N.W.2d 759 (1978).

15. *State v. Kennamore,* 604 S.W.2d 856 (Tenn.1980).

16. Ibid.

17. *State v. Aguillard,* 567 So.2d 674 (La.1990).

18. For a general introduction to the topic, see Edward Arnolds and Norman Garland, "The Defense of Necessity in Criminal Law: Right to Choose the Lesser Evil," *Journal of Criminal Law and Criminology* 65 (1974):291-93; see American Law Institute, *Model Penal Code and Commentaries,* vol. 2, pt. I, pp. 8–22, for a summary of this position.

19. American Law Institute, *Model Penal Code and Commentaries,* vol. 1, pt. I, 18.

20. Quoted in Glanville Williams, *Criminal Law,* 2d ed. rev. (London: Stevens and Sons, 1961), p. 725.

21. Hall, *General Principles of Criminal Law,* pp. 425 ff.

22. *The Queen v. Dudley and Stephens,* 14 Q.B.D. 273 (1884).

23. American Law Institute, *Model Penal Code and Commentaries,* vol. 3, pt. I, 18; Williams, *Criminal Law,* p. 724.

24. *The Queen v. Dudley and Stephens,* 14 Q.B.D. 273 (1884).

25. Williams, *Criminal Law,* pp. 735–36.

26. Wayne R. LaFave and Austin W. Scott, *Criminal Law,* p. 389.

27. *Mattis v. Schnarr,* 547 F.2d 1007 (8th Cir. 1976); Catherine H. Milton et al., *Police Use of Deadly Force* (Washington, D.C.: The Police Foundation, 1977), contains a detailed discussion. See also Lawrence O'Donnell, Jr., *Deadly Force* (New York: Morrow, 1983), for a spirited attack on deadly force.

28. Quoted in American Law Institute, *Model Penal Code,* tentative draft no. 8, pp. 60–62.

29. Address delivered to National College of State Trial Judges, Chapel Hill, North Carolina, August 15, 1968. Quoted in Sanford Kadish and Manfred Paulson,

Criminal Law and Its Processes, 3d ed. rev. (Boston: Little, Brown, 1975), pp. 541–42.

30. Sir William Blackstone, *Commentaries on the Laws of England* (New York: Garland, 1978), pt. IV, p. 180.

31. Perkins and Boyce, *Criminal Law,* pp. 1154–60.

32. Richard L. Binder, "The Consent Defense: Sports, Violence, and the Criminal Law," *The American Criminal Law Review* 13 (1975):235–48.

33. American Law Institute, *Model Penal Code and Commentaries,* vol. 2, pt. I, pp. 1–5.

Chapter 7

Defenses to Criminal Liability: Excuses

▼ Chapter Outline ▼

   I. Introduction
  II. Duress
 III. Intoxication
 IV. Mistake
  V. Age
 VI. Entrapment
VII. Insanity
     A. Right-Wrong Test
     B. Irresistible Impulse Test
     C. Substantial Capacity Test
     D. Burden of Proof
VIII. Diminished Capacity
 IX. Syndromes
  X. Summary

1. In excuse, defendants admit they did wrong but argue that under special circumstances they were not responsible.

2. The main excuses are duress, intoxication, mistake, age entrapment, insanity, diminished capacity, and syndromes.

3. Duress excuses some crimes when defendants are in immediate danger of death or serious harm.

4. Voluntary intoxication never excuses; involuntary intoxication excuses if it impairs specific intent.

5. Age, either old or young, may excuse if it impairs *mens rea*.

6. Mistakes of law never excuse; honest and reasonable mistakes of fact sometimes excuse; legal and factual mistakes are sometimes difficult to distinguish.

7. Entrapment excuses if the government induces an otherwise law-abiding citizen to commit a crime he or she would not have committed.

8. Insanity is a legal concept; mental illness is a medical condition.

9. A mental disease or defect excuses criminal liability when it impairs *mens rea*.

10. Various tests of insanity focus on reason and will.

11. Insanity is an affirmative defense.

12. Diminished capacity reduces but does not remove responsibility when mental disease or defect less than insanity impairs *mens rea*.

> ▼ *Chapter Key Terms* ▼

diminished capacity—Mental capacity less than "normal" but more than insane.

Durham rule,* or *product test—An insanity test to determine whether a crime was a product of mental disease or defect.

irresistible impulse—Impairment of the will that makes it impossible to control the impulse to do wrong.

***M'Naghten* rule, or right-wrong test**—A defense pleading insanity due to mental disease or defect that impairs the capacity to distinguish right from wrong.

substantial capacity test—Insanity due to mental disease or defect impairing the substantial capacity either to appreciate the wrongfulness of conduct or to conform behavior to the law.

▼ INTRODUCTION

For defendants, most excuses and justifications provide the same opportunity: to avoid criminal liability. Theoretically, however, the two defenses differ. Defendants who plead justification accept responsibility, but claim that under the circumstances what they did was right. Those who plead excuse admit what they did was wrong but deny that they were responsible under the circumstances. The most common excuses include duress, intoxication, mistake, age, entrapment, insanity, diminished capacity and responsibility, and various syndromes.

▼ DURESS

Professor Hyman Gross admirably states the problem of duress:

> Sometimes people are forced to do what they do. When what they are forced to do is wrong it seems that the compulsion ought to count in their favor. After all, we say, such a person wasn't free to do otherwise—he couldn't help himself, not really. No claim to avoid blame appeals more urgently to our moral intuitions, yet none presents more problems of detail. There are times, after all, when we ought to stand firm and run the risk of harm to ourselves instead of taking a way out that means harm to others. In such a situation we must expect to pay the price if we cause harm when we prefer ourselves, for then the harm is our fault even though we did not mean it and deeply regret it.[1]

At common law, duress consisted of

> threats or menaces, which induce a fear of death or other bodily harm, and which take away for that reason the guilt of many crimes and misdemeanors;

at least before a human tribunal. But then that fear, which compels a man to do an unwarrantable action, ought to be just and well grounded... [However,] though a man be violently assaulted, and hath no other possible means of escaping death, but by killing an innocent person; this fear and force shall not acquit him of murder; for he ought rather to die himself, than escape by the murder of an innocent.[2]

The defense of duress presents four major issues: (1) What crimes does duress excuse? (2) What constitutes duress? (3) How close to committing the crime must coercion take place? (4) Is an honest belief in threat sufficient, or must the belief by reasonable? In some states, duress excuses all crimes except murder; in others, duress excuses only minor crimes. Some jurisdictions require that only the fear of instant death amounts to sufficient coercion; others accept an imminent fear of death or serious bodily harm.[3]

Theorists and scholars disagree over what ought to constitute duress. English jurist Sir James F. Stephen argued that duress should never be a defense to criminal liability because "it is at the moment when temptation is strongest that the law should speak most clearly and emphatically to the contrary." Stephen conceded that judges might mitigate sentences if offenders committed crimes under duress. Borrowing from necessity, American theorist Jerome Hall maintained that coercion should excuse only minor crimes committed under the threat of death. Professor Glanville Williams argued that duress should excuse because the law has no effect on defendants' choices when defendants are "in thrall to some power," such as duress.[4]

As for the kind of threat required to invoke the defense, states differ. Some permit only threats to kill: With a loaded gun at another's head, a robber says, "If you do not take that purse from her, I'll pull this trigger!" Other states accept threats to do serious bodily harm: "If you don't steal that car for me, I'll break your arms!" Threats to property—such as a threat to smash a car if another does not steal a stereo—do not constitute duress. Neither do threats to reputation: "If you don't smoke this marijuana, I'll tell your boss you have AIDS." In some states, threats to harm others, such as to kill a mother, son, or lover, do not constitute duress.[5]

The immediacy of the threat is important in most jurisdictions, but the degree varies from state to state. In Minnesota, for example, only threats of "instant death" qualify. Most states are somewhat less restrictive, accepting immediate or imminent threats. Disagreement arises over what constitutes an immediate threat. For example, a man threatened to stab a woman if she did not lie in court to give him an alibi. The man who threatened her sat in the courtroom while she committed the perjury. The trial court ruled that he did not threaten her with an immediate threat because he could not stab her at that moment. The appellate court disagreed:

> In the present case the threats of Farrell were likely to be no less compelling, because their execution could not be effected in the court room, if they could be carried out in the streets of Salford the same night. Insofar, therefore, as the [trial judge] ruled the threats were not sufficiently present and immediate to support the duress we think that he was in error.[6]

Jurisdictions also differ over whether to measure threats objectively or subjectively. Some states accept the subjective, honest belief; others demand reasonable belief and honest belief. A few states speak of actual compulsion. Finally, courts do not always distinguish clearly between duress and necessity, recognizing a difficult-to-draw line between justification and excuse in duress. The Kansas Supreme Court dealt with some of these problems in *State v. Riedl.*[7]

CASE

Was He Compelled to Commit the Crime?

State v. Riedl
807 P.2d 697 (Kansas 1991)

Gernon, Judge

FACTS

Riedl and a friend went to a bar and drank beer for approximately two hours. When they left the bar, they were confronted by three people in the parking lot standing near Riedl's vehicle. One of the three shouted a threat to Riedl. Riedl testified he reached for his keys, was punched by one of the three, ran for his car, got in, and started the vehicle. Riedl concedes he hit another car while attempting to get away. Traveling toward the direction of his home, Riedl's speed attracted the attention of Officers Costello and Bowman some five miles from the site of the confrontation.

Riedl contends that the fact that he had had two friends killed in bar fights and that he had worked in a hospital contributed to his state of mind and his "compulsion" to act as he did.

The trial court found Riedl guilty of driving at a speed greater than prudent and of fleeing or attempting to elude a police officer. Riedl appeals.... The trial court ... ruled, as a matter of law, that the compulsion defense was not available to the offenses with which he was charged....

OPINION

... Riedl's challenge to the trial court's ruling that, as a matter of law, the compulsion defense was not available to the offenses with which he is charged is one of first impression in Kansas. The precise question is whether compulsion is a legally recognizable defense to an absolute liability traffic offense.

K.S.A. 21–3209 provides:

"(1) A person is not guilty of a crime other than murder or voluntary manslaughter by reason of conduct which he performs under the compulsion or threat of the imminent infliction of death or great bodily harm, if he reasonably believes that death or great bodily harm will be inflicted upon him or upon his spouse, parent, child, brother or sister if he does not perform such conduct.

"(2) The defense provided by this section is not available to one who willfully or wantonly places himself in a situation in which it is probable that he will be subjected to compulsion or threat."

In the case before us, our threshold question is whether the defense of compulsion is available to a defendant charged with [a strict liability] ... offense. We conclude that it is.... When enacting K.S.A. 21–3209, the legislature created specific exceptions: the compulsion defense is not applicable to charges of murder or voluntary manslaughter. The legislature could easily create an additional exception for strict liability traffic offenses if it so desired....

We conclude that Kansas case law supports a conclusion that the compulsion defense is applicable to this type of offense....

The case law from other jurisdictions overwhelmingly supports the conclusion that the compulsion defense, or similar defenses, should be deemed applicable to traffic offenses which do not require proof of criminal intent....

Once we accept the availability of the compulsion defense to absolute liability traffic offenses, we must examine the record carefully to determine whether there was sufficient evidence to invoke the compulsion defense.

The Kansas Supreme Court recently stated in *State v. Hunter,* 241 Kan. 629, Syl. P 10, 740 P.2d 559: "In order to constitute the DEFENSE of compulsion, the coercion or DURESS must be present, imminent, and impending, and of such a nature as to induce a well-grounded APPREHENSION of DEATH or serious bodily INJURY if the act is not done. The doctrine of coercion or duress cannot be invoked as an excuse by one who had a reasonable opportunity to avoid doing the act without undue exposure to death or serious bodily harm. In addition, the compulsion must be continuous and there must be no reasonable opportunity to escape the compulsion without committing the crime."

In *People v. Pena,* 197 Cal.Rptr. 264, the elements of the duress defense were listed as:

1. the act charged as criminal must have been done to prevent a significant evil;
2. there must have been no adequate alternative to the commission of the act;
3. the harm caused by the act must not be disproportionate to the harm avoided;
4. the accused must entertain a good faith belief that his act was necessary to prevent the greater harm;
5. such belief must be objectively reasonable under all the circumstances; and
6. the accused must not have substantially contributed to the creation of the emergency.

At trial, Riedl did not argue that the compulsion defense was applicable to the charges of refusing to submit to a preliminary breath test and failure to stop at a stop sign. In addition, we conclude that the evidence was insufficient to establish the compulsion defense with respect to the charge of driving while under the influence of alcohol or drugs. The evidence fails to demonstrate that the compulsion was "continuous." Riedl himself testified, "When I left out of there, I thought there was a possibility that the guys in the parking lot would chase us."

There is no evidence to indicate that Riedl was, in fact, followed. Riedl drove his vehicle for approximately five miles without stopping or otherwise seeking assistance. This lack of a continuous threat is fatal to any attempt to assert the compulsion defense.

The distance traveled and the time involved provided Riedl with ample opportunity to withdraw from the criminal activity and seek aid.

The difficulty in this case is in the consideration of the charge of leaving the scene of an accident. Riedl testified he was between the entrance to the bar and his car when the confrontation began. Understandably, the trial court made no factual findings concerning the elements or requirements of the compulsion defense. Our reading of the record leads us to conclude that the evidence is uncertain as to whether Riedl had a reasonable opportunity to escape. Absent this evidence, we are required to reverse the conviction for leaving the scene of an accident and remand the case for further factual findings by the trial court.

The trial court erred in concluding that the compulsion defense was not applicable as a matter of law to absolute liability traffic offenses. However, the record clearly indicates that Riedl's evidence does not support the defense in so far as driving while under the influence of alcohol or drugs. Our appellate courts have often stated that we will affirm a trial court's decision that is correct even though it may be based on an incorrect reason. "[W]here the trial court reaches the correct result based upon the wrong reason, this court will affirm the trial court."

The conviction for leaving the scene of an accident is reversed and remanded for further factual findings. Affirmed in part, reversed in part, and remanded.

Case Discussion

Is this a case of justification or excuse? Does the court clearly distinguish compulsion or duress from choice of evils or necessity? Can you distinguish them clearly? How would you formulate duress as a justification? As an excuse? What are the core elements of duress, according to the court? What were the relevant facts to determining whether Riedl had the defense? Why does the court believe he had the defense with respect to leaving the scene of an accident, but not to driving while intoxicated? Do you agree?

One variation, or extension, to duress is superior orders. The United States Court of Military Appeals considered this problem in a famous case following the Vietnam War, *United States v. Calley.*

CASE

Do Superior Orders Constitute Duress?

United States v. Calley
46 C.M.R. 1131 (1975)

[Calley was convicted of murder. He appealed.]

FACTS

[D]uring midmorning on 16 March 1968 a large number of unresisting Vietnamese were placed in a ditch on the eastern side of My Lai and summarily executed by American soldiers.

[PFC] Meadlo gave the most graphic and damning evidence. He had wandered back into the village alone after the trail incident. Eventually, he met his fire team leader, Specialist Four Grzesik. They took seven or eight Vietnamese to what he labeled a "ravine," where Lieutenant Calley, Sledge, and Dursi and a few other Americans were located with what he estimated as seventy-five to a hundred Vietnamese. Meadlo remembered also that Lieutenant Calley told him, "We got another job to do, Meadlo," and that the appellant started shoving people into the ravine and shooting them. Meadlo, in contrast to Dursi, followed the directions of his leader and himself fired into the people at the bottom of the "ravine." Meadlo then drifted away from the area but he doesn't remember where.

Specialist Four Grzesik found PFC Meadlo, crying and distraught, sitting on a small dike on the eastern edge of the village. He and Meadlo moved through the village, and came to the ditch, in which Grzesik thought were thirty-five to fifty dead bodies. Lieutenant Calley walked past and ordered Grzesik to take his fire team back into the village and help the following platoon in their search. He also remembered that Calley asked him to "finish them off," but he refused.

Specialist Four Turner saw Lieutenant Calley for the first time that day as Turner walked out of the village near the ditch. Meadlo and a few other soldiers were also present. Turner passed within fifteen feet of the area, looked into the ditch and saw a pile of approximately twenty bodies covered with blood. He also saw Lieutenant Calley and Meadlo firing from a distance of five feet into another group of people who were kneeling and squatting in the ditch. Turner recalled he then went north of the ditch about seventy yards, where he joined with Conti at a perimeter position. He remained there for over an hour, watching the ditch. Several more groups of Vietnamese were brought to it, never to get beyond or out of it. In all he thought he observed about ninety or a hundred people brought to the ditch and slaughtered there by Lieutenant Calley and his subordinates.

OPINION

There is no dispute as to the fact of killings by and at the instance of appellant at a ditch on the eastern edge of My Lai.

Of the several bases for his argument that he committed no murder at My Lai because he was void of mens rea, appellant emphasized most of all that he acted in obedience to orders....

An order of the type appellant says he received is illegal. Its illegality is apparent upon even cursory evaluation by a man of ordinary sense and understanding.

[Calley argues] essentially that obedience to orders is a defense which strikes at mens rea; therefore in logic an obedient subordinate should be acquitted so long as he did not personally know of the order's illegality. [We] [do] not agree with the argument. Heed must be given not only to subjective innocence-through-ignorance in the soldier, but to the consequences for his victims. Also, barbarism tends to invite reprisal to the detriment of our own force or disrepute which interferes with the achievement of war aims, even though the barbaric acts were preceded by orders for their commission. Casting the defense of obedience to orders solely in subjective terms of mens rea would operate practically to abrogate those objective restraints which are essential to functioning rules of war. The court members, after being given correct standards, properly rejected any defense of obedience to orders.

We find no impediment to the findings that appellant acted with murderous mens rea, including premeditation. The aggregate of all his contentions against the existence of murderous mens rea is no more absolving than a bare claim that he did not suspect he did any wrong act until after the operation, and indeed is not convinced of it yet. This is no excuse in law.

Affirmed.

Case Discussion

Lieutenant Calley's defense was that he was obeying the orders of his superior officer, Captain Medina. Because he was not free to disobey the orders, Calley maintained, he was not responsible for the My Lai massacre. He was therefore coerced into killing. Rejecting Calley's defense, the court ruled that every person must accept responsibility for killing. No one who obeys the order to kill can transfer that responsibility. Despite the need for military discipline, which is admittedly great, the court held that officers must disobey clearly illegal orders, particularly when they lead to death.

The Nazi war criminals tried to use the same defense after World War II. In the famous Nuremberg trials, German officers attempted to defend Nazi atrocities against the Jews, claiming they were merely obeying their commanders' orders and were not criminally responsible for the people they killed. Their defenses were rejected for reasons similar to those in *Calley*.

An attempt was made to extend the defense of duress to brainwashing, which came to public view several years ago in the robbery trial of heiress Patty Hearst. A self-styled revolutionary group, the Symbionese Liberation Army (SLA), kidnapped Hearst and confined her for months. During that time, she and her abductors robbed a bank. Hearst's defense against the bank robbery charge was that her captors pressured her for months, breaking down and overcoming her will. She had no mind of her own left, their beliefs became her beliefs, and thus her actions were their actions. Therefore, she was not responsible for what she did.

The court denied the defense, but its logic is clear. The Model Penal Code reporters say that the Model Penal Code's duress provision includes brainwashing by implication because it includes coercion, which means breaking down a person's will.[8]

The Puerto Rico Statute provides specifically for brainwashing:

> Whoever acts compelled by intimidation or violence shall not be held liable [and] [t]he concept of violence also includes the use of hypnotic means, narcotic substances, depressant or stimulant drugs, or other means or substances.[9]

Three reasons support the duress defense. First, those forced to commit a crime did not act voluntarily; hence, there is no *actus reus* unless actors intentionally, recklessly, or negligently put themselves in a position where others could coerce them. Second, subjection to another's will removes *mens rea*. Third, as a practical matter, the criminal law cannot force people to act irrationally against their own self-interest. Under enough pressure, people will save their own lives even if it means hurting someone else. The limits to duress, on the other hand, are supposed to encourage resistance to pressure to commit crimes.

▼ INTOXICATION

Professor George Fletcher summarizes the problem of conflicting principles in the excuse of intoxication:

> The issue of intoxication is buffeted between two conflicting principles.... There has to be some accommodation between (1) the principle that if someone gets drunk, he is liable for the violent consequences, and (2) the principle that liability and punishment should be graded in proportion to actual culpability.[10]

The common-law approach focused on the first principle:

> As to artificial, voluntarily contracted madness, by drunkenness or intoxication, which, depriving men of their reason, puts them in a temporary frenzy; our law looks upon this as an aggravation of the offense, rather than as an excuse for any criminal misbehavior.[11]

The effect of intoxication on criminal liability differs according to whether the intoxication was voluntary or involuntary. Involuntary intoxication excuses criminal liability. Modern law follows the common law with respect to voluntary intoxication: it never constitutes a total defense. However, it sometimes negatives *mens rea* in crimes of specific intent by reducing the degree of those crimes to lesser degree, such as first-degree to second-degree murder. Jurisdictions define voluntary and involuntary intoxication differently, as the common law and representative statutes demonstrate.

Involuntary intoxication includes cases where defendants do not know they are taking intoxicants, or know but do so under duress. In one case, a man took what his friend told him were "breath perfumer" pills; in fact, they were cocaine tablets. While under their influence, he killed someone. The court allowed the defense of intoxication.[12]

Only extreme duress qualifies as involuntary intoxication. One author concluded that "a person would need to be bound hand and foot and the liquor literally poured down his throat, or ... would have to be threatened with immediate serious injury."[13]

In one case, an eighteen-year-old youth was traveling with an older man across the desert. The man insisted that the youth drink some whisky with him. When the youth declined, the man became abusive. The youth, fearing the man would put him out of the car in the middle of the desert without any money, drank the whisky, became intoxicated, and killed the man. The court rejected the involuntary intoxication by duress excuse because the man had not compelled the youth "to drink against his will and consent."[14]

Some physiological abnormalities lead to involuntary intoxication. Owing to these abnormalities, intoxicating substances cause defendants to act in ways they cannot control. In one case:

> A twenty-year-old man, living alone with his mother, stabbed her to death with a kitchen knife, inflicting many wounds on her body. In the five days preceding the murder he had worked hard and had had but irregular meals. Also, there had been some quarreling with his mother over money. On the morning of the day of the murder he struck her, a very unusual act, for which he apologized. He ate poorly on that day. He had his last carbohydrate meal at noon. Between 9 and 10:30 p.m. he drank four pints of mild ale. At 11 p.m. there was again a quarrel with his mother over money and she pushed him out of her room. At this moment he suddenly felt thirsty, went to the kitchen to get a bottle opener, saw a knife, and then "something came over" him: "I was like a homicidal maniac." He stabbed his mother to death.... There is a gap in his memory for seven hours following the crime. The next day, he gave himself up to the police....
>
> After the patient's arrest, his family physician notified the defense that two years prior to the crime a sugar tolerance curve had shown a tendency to hypoglycemia.... [A] number of tests ... showed that the prisoner was definitely suffering from hypoglycemia.... [H]is blood at the time of the crime must have been below 100 mgm and ... his brain at that time was functioning abnormally; ... his judgment was impaired at the time.[15]

Some maintain that denying the excuse of intoxication—whether involuntary or voluntary—results in punishing involuntary acts. Others say that those who are intoxicated cannot form the requisite *mens rea*. Supporters argue that those who voluntarily get intoxicated to a point where they are likely to reduce or eliminate normal control should and must take the consequences stemming from their lost control. Those who voluntarily induced their intoxicated state should not then escape criminal liability simply because they either acted involuntarily or could not form the requisite intent.[16]

Voluntary intoxication, although not a defense, may negate a material element in the crime. It may impair the capacity to form either the purpose or the knowledge required to prove particular crimes. Hence, in crimes requiring purpose and knowledge, sufficient intoxication might negative *mens rea*. For example, a heavily intoxicated person may not have the capacity to premeditate a homicide, or intoxication may have prevented premeditation in fact. Both cases lack a material element in first-degree murder: premeditation. However, intoxication may not have impaired the capacity to form, or to have in fact formed, the *mens rea* for manslaughter. Generally, intoxication may disprove purpose or knowledge, but not recklessness or negligence.[17]

Intoxication might also prove that defendants were unable to commit the requisite act in the crime charged. Hence, a man so intoxicated he could not get an erection could not commit rape, because performing the requisite act was impossible. This should not be taken to mean that defendants who voluntarily induce intoxication act involuntarily. Their voluntary act in drinking establishes voluntariness, even though when committing the crime charged they were "overwhelmed or overpowered by alcohol to the point of losing [their] ... faculties or sensibilities." (Chapter 3.) The court dealt with intoxication, and its impact on *mens rea* and criminal liability, in *State v. Stasio*.[18]

CASE

Does Intoxication Excuse Criminal Liability?

State v. Stasio
78 N.J. 467, 396 A.2d 1129 (1979)

[Stasio appealed from conviction for assault with intent to rob and assault while armed with a dangerous knife, for which he was sentenced to three to five years and one to two years, respectively. Justice Schreiber delivered the opinion.]

FACTS

Robert Colburn had frequented the Silver Moon Tavern not only for its alcoholic wares but also to engage in pool. On October 7, Colburn arrived at the Tavern about 11:00 a.m. and started to play pool. Sometime before noon the defendant joined him. They stayed together until about 3:00 p.m. when the defendant left the bar. Though the defendant had been drinking during this period, in Colburn's opinion the defendant was not intoxicated upon his departure. Neither the defendant's speech nor his mannerisms indicated drunkenness.

Peter Klimek arrived at the Tavern shortly before 5:00 p.m. and assumed his shift at tending bar. There were about eight customers present when, at approximately 5:40 p.m., the defendant entered and walked in a normal manner to the bathroom. Shortly thereafter he returned to the front door, looked around outside and approached the bar. He demanded that Klimek give him some money. Upon refusal, he threatened Klimek. The defendant went behind the bar toward Klimek and insisted that Klimek give him $80 from the cash register. When Klimek persisted in his refusal, the defendant pulled out a knife. Klimek grabbed the defendant's right hand and Colburn, who had jumped on top of the bar, seized the defendant's hair and pushed his head toward the bar. The defendant then dropped the knife.

Almost immediately thereafter Police Officer Rowan arrived and placed the defendant in custody.

[Stasio's defense was that he "was so intoxicated he could not form intent to rob."]

OPINION

It is generally agreed that a defendant will not be relieved of criminal responsibility because he was under the influence of intoxicants or drugs voluntarily taken. This principle rests upon public policy, demanding that he who seeks the influence of liquor or narcotics should not be insulated from criminal liability because that influence impaired his judgment or his control. The required element of badness can be found in the intentional use of the stimulant or depressant.

[I]f a person casts off the restraints of reason and consciousness by a voluntary act, no wrong is done to him if he is held accountable for any crime which he may commit in that condition. Society is entitled to this protection.

Purpose or knowledge has been made a component of many offenses so that voluntary intoxication will be an available defense in those situations. Thus, voluntary intoxication may be a defense to aggravated assaults consisting of attempts to cause bodily injury to another with a deadly weapon. Intoxication could exonerate those otherwise guilty of burglaries and criminal trespass. It would be an available defense to arson....

Our holding today does not mean that voluntary intoxication is always irrelevant in criminal proceedings. Evidence of intoxication may be introduced to demonstrate that premeditation and deliberation have not been proven so that a second degree murder cannot be raised to first degree murder or to show that the intoxication led to a fixed state of insanity. Intoxication may be shown to prove that a defendant never participated in a crime. Thus it might be proven that a defendant was in such a drunken stupor and unconscious state that he was not a part of a robbery. His mental faculties may be so prostrated as to preclude the commission of the criminal act. Under some circumstances intoxication may be relevant to demonstrate mistake. However, in the absence of any basis for the defense, a trial court should not in its charge introduce that element. A trial court, of course, may consider intoxication as a mitigating circumstance when sentencing a defendant.

Affirmed.

DISSENT

Today's holding by the majority stands logic on its head. This Court and the Legislature have long adhered to the view that criminal sanctions will not be imposed upon a defendant unless there exists a "concurrence of an evil-meaning mind with an evil-doing hand." The policies underlying this proposition are clear. A person who intentionally commits a bad act is more culpable than one who engages in the same conduct without any evil design. The intentional wrongdoer is also more likely to repeat his offense, and hence constitutes a greater threat to societal repose. A sufficiently intoxicated defendant is thus subject to less severe sanctions not because the law "excuses" his conduct but because the circumstances surrounding his acts have been deemed by the Legislature to be less deserving of punishment.

It strains reason to hold that a defendant may be found guilty of a crime whose definition includes a requisite mental state when the defendant actually failed to possess that state of mind. Indeed, this is the precise teaching of cases allowing the intoxication defense in first-degree murder prosecutions. To sustain a first-degree murder conviction, the State must prove that the homicide was premeditated, willful, and deliberate. If the accused, due to intoxication, did not in fact possess these mental attributes, he can be convicted of at most second-degree murder.

That offense, however, can be sustained on a mere showing of recklessness, and the necessary recklessness can be found in the act of becoming intoxicated.

Just as the lack of premeditation, willfulness, or deliberation precludes a conviction for first-degree murder, so should the lack of intent to rob or steal be a defense to assault and battery with intent to rob, or breaking and entering with intent to steal. The principle is the same in both situations. If voluntary intoxication negates an element of the offense, the defendant has not engaged in the conduct proscribed by the criminal statute, and hence should not be subject to the sanctions imposed by that statute.

**Case
Discussion**
Stasio points up the disagreement over whether intoxication ought to excuse criminal liability. The majority follows most jurisdictions, ruling that ordinarily it does not. However, as the court notes, if intoxication impairs the capacity to form specific intent in crimes such as first-degree murder, which requires premeditation, then raising a reasonable doubt concerning *mens rea* is relevant. The dissent makes this latter point even more strongly, arguing that Stasio may well have been so drunk he could not form the intent to rob. The jury should have been allowed to decide that, according to the dissent. Furthermore, the excuse is not related to the harm caused by intoxicated persons. It has only to do with their culpability. They cannot form the intent to commit the crime with which they are charged. In this case, Stasio could not be guilty of an assault with intent to rob, because he was too drunk to form that intent. Do you agree with the majority or with the dissent? Does your answer depend on the harm Stasio caused, or on his capacity to form the intent to rob?

Intoxication might result from chronic alcoholism, increasingly regarded as a disease among experts. If alcoholism is a disease and intoxication a symptom, then punishing an intoxicated alcoholic is in effect punishing an illness, a status, or a condition, which, according to *Robinson v. California,* is cruel and unusual punishment (see discussion in chapter 3). In *Powell v. Texas* (excerpted in chapter 2), the United States Supreme Court rejected Powell's defense that his alcoholism excused him from liability for "being drunk in public." The Court ruled that Powell's conviction for appearing on the street drunk was not for his alcoholism, but rather for his voluntary act—going outdoors while he was drunk—and offending public decency while he was out there. Even if alcoholism is a disease and Powell suffered from it, the Court reasoned, he could refrain from exhibiting its offensive symptom, drunkenness, in public. His failure to do so was a proper ground for criminal liability; therefore, punishing him did not violate the Eighth Amendment prohibition against cruel and unusual punishment.[19]

Alcohol is the most widely used intoxicant, but it is not the only one qualifying defendants to claim the intoxication excuse. The Model Penal Code and most states define intoxication to include disturbing mental and physical capacities by introducing "substances" into the body. *State v. Hall* illustrates this point. Hall's friend gave him a pill containing LSD (lysergic acid diethylamide). Hall did not know this; he knew only that, as his friend assured him, it was only a "little sunshine" to make him feel "groovy." A car picked up the hitchhiking Hall. At that time, the drug caused Hall to hallucinate that the driver was a rabid dog. Under this sad delusion, he shot and killed the driver. The court recognized no legal distinction between the voluntary use of alcohol and the voluntary use of other intoxicants in determining criminal responsibility.[20]

▼ MISTAKE

"Ignorance of the law is no excuse," nearly everyone knows; most do not know that this doctrine is no longer hard and fast, if it ever was. Ignorance of fact, on the other hand, has always excused criminal responsibility under some circumstances.

Mistake of fact excuses criminal liability when it negates a material element in the crime. For example, if I take from a restaurant coatroom a coat that I believe is mine, I have not stolen the coat because I do not have the requisite *mens rea:* to deprive the owner of his or her property. The actor's mistake must be "honest" and "reasonable"; hence, the proper way to state the defense is that an honest and reasonable mistake of fact excuses criminal responsibility. For example, if I take the coat because it is where I left mine an hour ago, it is the same color and size as mine, and no other coat hanging there resembles it, I have honestly and reasonably mistaken the coat for mine. (For a full discussion of mistake of fact in statutory rape, see chapter 9.)

Mistake of law does not ordinarily excuse criminal responsibility, for several reasons grounded in public policy. First, the state must determine what constitutes crime; individuals cannot define crimes for themselves. Second, the doctrine supposedly encourages citizens to know the law. Finally, nearly everyone could shield themselves behind the claim, since most people do not know the specifics of criminal statutes and court decisions interpreting them. Hence, the law presumes that everyone knows the law.[21]

Oliver Wendell Holmes says the *a material element of the crime itself* true explanation of the rule is the same as that which accounts for the law's indifference to a man's particular temperament, faculties, and so forth. Public policy sacrifices the individual to the general good. It is desirable that the burden of all should be equal, but it is still more desirable to put an end to robbery and murder. It is no doubt true that there are many cases in which the criminal could not have known that he was breaking the law, but to admit the excuse at all would be to encourage ignorance where the law-maker has determined to make men know and obey, and justice to the individual is rightly outweighed by the larger interests on the other side of the scales.[22]

Ignorance of the law, following reasonable efforts to learn it, sometimes excuses criminal liability. For example, a defendant carried on a lottery, relying on a statute that a state supreme court later ruled unconstitutional. The defendant's honest and reasonable belief that the lottery was lawful was an excuse, even though the supreme court later ruled that the lottery was unconstitutional. Furthermore, relying on an attorney's advice does not constitute an excuse to criminal liability. Hence, if I ask my lawyer if it is lawful to put a sign in my front yard and she tells me yes, and later the government prosecutes me for violating an ordinance prohibiting signs in residential areas, I have no defense of mistake. If I had instead asked the prosecutor, I might have an excuse; some states permit reliance on such officials, others do not.[23]

The distinction between law and fact, although important legally, is not easy to draw in practice. In *People v. Snyder,* the court addresses the defense of mistake, and the problem in determining whether the defendant mistook the law or a fact.

CASE

*Did Her Mistake
Excuse Her?*

People v. Snyder

186 Cal.Rptr. 485 (Cal.1982)

Richardson, Justice

Defendant Neva B. Snyder appeals from a judgment convicting her of possession of a concealable firearm by a convicted felon (Pen.Code, § 12021), based upon her 1973 conviction for sale of marijuana, a felony (former Health & Saf.Code, § 11531). Defendant contends that the trial court erred in excluding evidence of her mistaken belief that her prior conviction was only a misdemeanor. We will conclude that defendant's asserted mistake regarding her legal status as a convicted felon did not constitute a defense to the firearm possession charge. Accordingly, we will affirm the judgment.

FACTS

At trial, defendant offered to prove the following facts supporting her theory of mistake: The marijuana possession charge resulted from a plea bargain not involving a jail or prison sentence. At the time the bargain was struck, defendant's attorney advised her that she was pleading guilty to a misdemeanor. Believing that she was not a felon, defendant thereafter had registered to vote, and had voted. On one prior occasion, police officers found a gun in her home but, after determining that it was registered to her husband, the officers filed no charges against defendant.

The trial court refused to admit any evidence of defendant's mistaken belief that her prior conviction was a misdemeanor and that she was not a felon. The court also rejected proposed instructions requiring proof of defendant's prior knowledge of her felony conviction as an element of the offense charged.

OPINION

Penal Code § 12021, subdivision (a), provides: "Any person who has been convicted of a felony under the laws of the ... State of California ... who owns or has in his possession or under his custody or control any pistol, revolver, or other firearm capable of being concealed upon the person is guilty of a public offense...."

The elements of the offense proscribed by § 12021 are conviction of a felony and ownership, possession, custody or control of a firearm capable of being concealed on the person. No specific criminal intent is required, and a general intent to commit the proscribed act is sufficient to sustain a conviction. With respect to the elements of possession or custody, it has been held that knowledge is an element of the offense.

Does § 12021 also require knowledge of one's legal status as a convicted felon? No case has so held. Penal Code § 26 provides that a person is incapable of committing a crime if he acted under a "mistake of fact" which disproves criminal intent. In this regard, the cases have distinguished between mistakes of fact and mistakes of law. As we stated in an early case:

"It is an emphatic postulate of both civil and penal law that ignorance of a law is no excuse for a violation thereof. Of course it is based on a fiction, because no man can know all the law, but it is a maxim which the law itself does not permit any one to gainsay....

"The rule rests on public necessity; the welfare of society and the safety of the state depend upon its enforcement. If a person accused of a crime could shield himself behind the defense that he was ignorant of the law which he violated, immunity from punishment would in most cases result."

Accordingly, lack of actual knowledge of the provisions of Penal Code § 12021 is irrelevant; the crucial question is whether the defendant was aware that he was engaging in the conduct proscribed by that section.

In the present case, defendant was presumed to know that it is unlawful for a convicted felon to possess a concealable firearm. (Pen.Code, § 12021.) She was also charged with knowledge that the offense of which she was convicted (former Health & Saf. Code, § 11531) was, as a matter of law, a felony. That section had prescribed a state prison term of from five years to life, and the express statutory definition of a "felony" is "a crime which is punishable with death or by imprisonment in the state prison." (Pen.Code, § 17, subd. (a).)

Thus, regardless of what she reasonably believed, or what her attorney may have told her, defendant was deemed to know under the law that she was a convicted felon forbidden to possess concealable firearms. Her asserted mistake regarding her correct legal status was a mistake of law, not fact. It does not constitute a defense to § 12021....

We conclude that the trial court properly excluded evidence of defendant's asserted mistake regarding her status as a convicted felon.

The judgment is affirmed.

DISSENT

Broussard, Justice, dissenting. I dissent.

The two elements of a violation of Penal Code § 12021 are felony status and possession of a concealable firearm. While no specific criminal intent is required, a general criminal intent should be required as to both elements in accordance with long-settled rules of statutory interpretation, and an honest and reasonable mistake as to either element of the offense, however induced, should negate the requisite general criminal intent. Defendant's testimony if believed would have established an honest and reasonable mistaken belief that her prior offense was not a felony but a misdemeanor, and it was prejudicial error to refuse to admit the evidence and to refuse instructions on the mistake doctrine...

During a lawful search of defendant and her husband's home in 1979, officers found one loaded handgun and two other handguns which were partially disassembled. In 1973 she had been convicted upon a guilty plea of sale of marijuana, a felony.

Defendant sought to testify that she believed that her marijuana possession conviction

had been for a misdemeanor rather than a felony. She offered to testify that she had not been sentenced to jail or prison but was on probation for two years, that her attorney told her at the time of the plea bargain that she was pleading guilty to a misdemeanor, and that believing she was not a felon she had since registered to vote and voted. She also offered to testify that on a prior occasion, officers found a pistol in her home but that after determining the gun was registered to her husband, no charges were filed for possession of the gun. Other charges were filed but dismissed.

Her husband had also been convicted in 1973 of the same marijuana charge. The trial court refused to admit the evidence of defendant's mistaken belief that the prior conviction was a misdemeanor and that she was not a felon.

The court also rejected offered instructions to require knowledge of a prior felony conviction as an element of the offense, and to define "knowingly," to explain the effect of ignorance or mistake of fact disproving criminal intent. The instructions, if given, would have required the jury to find that defendant knew she was a felon as an element of the crime....

Penal Code § 12021, subdivision (a) provides: "Any person who has been convicted of a felony under the laws of the ... State of California ... who owns or has in his possession or under his custody or control any pistol, revolver, or other firearm capable of being concealed upon the person is guilty of a public offense...."

At common law an honest and reasonable belief in circumstances which, if true, would make the defendant's conduct innocent was held to be a good defense. The concept of mens rea, the guilty mind, expresses the principle that it is not conduct alone but conduct accompanied by certain mental states which concerns, or should concern, the law....

The elements of the offense proscribed by § 12021 are conviction of a felony and ownership, possession, custody or control of a firearm capable of being concealed on the person. While no specific criminal intent is required, a general intent to commit the proscribed act is necessary. As to the element of possession or custody, it has been held that knowledge is an element of the offense....

To hold otherwise is contrary to the settled California rule that a mens rea requirement is an "invariable" element of every crime unless excluded expressly or by necessary implication. Having established the rule, we must assume the Legislature is aware of it and acting in accordance with it, and the absence of any provision to establish strict liability must be read as reflecting legislative intent to require wrongful intent....

In determining whether a defendant's mistaken belief disproves criminal intent pursuant to Penal Code § 26, the courts have drawn a distinction between mistakes of fact and mistakes of law. Criminal intent is the intent to do the prohibited act, not the intent to violate the law. "It is an emphatic postulate of both civil and penal law that ignorance of a law is no excuse for a violation thereof. Of course it is based on a fiction, because no man can know all the law, but it is a maxim which the law itself does not permit any one to gainsay.... The rule rests on public necessity; the welfare of society and the safety of the state depend upon its enforcement. If a person accused of a crime could shield himself behind the defense that he was ignorant of the law which he violated, immunity from punishment would in most cases result." Accordingly, lack of knowledge of the pro-

visions of Penal Code § 12021 is irrelevant; the crucial question is whether the defendant was aware that he was engaging in the conduct proscribed by that section....

I am perplexed by the majority's apparent limitation of the mistake doctrine to would-be "moral leper[s]." The more heinous the crime the more reason to limit defenses, and the majority's suggested limitation appears to turn the usual relationship between law and morality upside down. Had the trial court in the instant case admitted the offered evidence and given the requested instruction, the jury could properly have concluded that defendant had a reasonable and good faith belief that her conviction was not a felony conviction. She was granted probation without jail or prison sentence.

Her attorney had advised her that the offense was a misdemeanor (It has been held that advice of counsel that prohibited conduct is lawful is not a defense because it would place the advice of counsel above the law.) and there were additional circumstances reflecting a good faith belief. Counsel's advice in the instant case is relevant to establish good faith; it does not in and of itself establish a defense.

The errors in excluding the offered evidence and refusing the offered instructions denied defendant the right to have the jury determine substantial issues material to her guilt and require reversal of the conviction. I would reverse the judgment.

Case Discussion   Does the majority or dissent make clear what distinguishes mistakes of fact from mistakes of law? Should it make any difference? What arguments does the majority give for rejecting evidence of mistake in the case? Why does the dissent reject them? Should the defendant's reliance on her attorney's statements excuse her from liability? Why? Why not? Does the dissent have a point in stressing that "moral lepers" have a better chance at the defense than misdemeanants? Explain.

▼ AGE

A four-year-old boy stabs his two-year-old sister in a murderous rage. Is this a criminal assault? What if the boy is eight? or twelve? or sixteen? or eighteen? At the other end of the age spectrum, what if he is eighty-five? At how early an age are people liable for criminal conduct? And when, if ever, has someone become too old for criminal responsibility? Age—both old and young—does affect criminal liability, sometimes to excuse it, sometimes to mitigate it, and sometimes even to aggravate it.

Ever since the early days of the English common law, immaturity has excused criminal liability. A rigid but sensible scheme for administering the defense was developed at least by the sixteenth century. The irrebuttable presumption was that no one under age seven had the mental capacity to commit crimes. That meant juries had to conclude that children under seven could not form *mens rea,* no matter what the evidence in particular cases might show to the contrary. Everyone over fourteen was presumed conclusively to have the mental capacity to form *mens rea.* For those between the ages of seven and fourteen, the law presumed incapacity. The presumption, however, was rebuttable, meaning that evidence that capacity in fact existed could set aside the presumption. The presumption was strong at age seven but gradually weakened until it disappeared at age fourteen.

About half the states initially adopted the common-law approach, but altered the specific ages within it. Some excluded the juvenile court from proceeding when juveniles committed serious crimes, such as those carrying the death penalty or life imprisonment. Recently, guided by the Model Penal Code, states have increasingly integrated the age of criminal responsibility with the jurisdiction of the juvenile courts. Some grant the juvenile court exclusive jurisdiction up to a particular age, usually between fifteen and sixteen. Then, from sixteen to eighteen (although occasionally up to twenty-one), juvenile court judges can transfer, or certify, cases to adult criminal courts. The number of cases certified has increased with the public recognition that youths commit serious felonies.[24]

CASE

Too Young to Murder?

People v. Wolff
61 Cal.2d 795, 40 Cal.Rptr. 271, 394 P.2d 959 (1964)

[Wolff was convicted of first-degree murder for killing his mother. He was sentenced to life imprisonment. Wolff was fifteen years old when the crime occurred.]

Schauer, Justice

FACTS

In the year preceeding the commission of the crime defendant "spent a lot of time thinking about sex." He made a list of the names and addresses of seven girls in his community whom he did not know personally but whom he planned to anesthetize by ether and then either rape or photograph nude. One night about three weeks before the murder he took a container of ether and attempted to enter the home of one of these girls through the chimney, but he became wedged in and had to be rescued. In the ensuing weeks defendant apparently delib-

erated on ways and means of accomplishing his objective and decided that he would have to bring the girls to his house to achieve his sexual purposes, and that it would therefore be necessary to get his mother (and possibly his brother) out of the way first.

The attack on defendant's mother took place on Monday, May 15, 1961. On the preceding Friday or Saturday defendant obtained an axe handle from the family garage and hid it under the mattress of his bed. At about 10 p.m. on Sunday he took the axe handle from its hiding place and approached his mother from behind, raising the weapon to strike her. She sensed his presence and asked him what he was doing; he answered that "it was nothing," and returned to his room and hid the handle under his mattress again. The following morning defendant arose and put the customary signal (a magazine) in the front window to inform his father that he had not overslept. Defendant ate the breakfast that his mother prepared, then went to his room and obtained the axe handle from under the mattress.

He returned to the kitchen, approached his mother from behind and struck her on the back of the head. She turned around screaming and he struck her several more blows. They fell to the floor, fighting. She called out her neighbor's name and defendant began choking her. She bit him on the hand and crawled away. He got up to turn off the water running in the sink, and she fled through the dining room. He gave chase, caught her in the front room, and choked her to death with his hands. Defendant then took off his shirt and hung it by the fire, washed the blood off his face and hands, read a few lines from a Bible or prayer book lying upon the dining room table, and walked down to the police station to turn himself in. Defendant told the desk officer, "I have something I wish to report. I just killed my mother with an axe handle." The officer testified that defendant spoke in a quiet voice and that "His conversation was quite coherent in what he was saying and he answered everything I asked him right to a T."

OPINION

Defendant's counsel repeatedly characterizes as "bizarre" defendant's plan to rape or photograph nude the seven girls on his list. Certainly in common parlance it may be termed "bizarre;" likewise to a mature person of good morals, it would appear highly unreasonable. But many a youth has committed—or planned—acts which were bizarre and unreasonable. This defendant was immature and lacked experience and judgment in sexual matters.

[D]efendant was questioned by Officers Stenberg and Hamilton shortly after he came to the police station and voluntarily announced that he had just killed his mother. The interrogation was transcribed and shown to defendant; he changed the wording of a few of his answers, then affixed his signature and the date on each page. When asked by Officer Hamilton why he had turned himself in, defendant replied, "Well, for the act I had just committed." Defendant then related the events leading up to and culminating in the murder, describing his conduct in the detail set forth hereinabove. With respect to the issue of his state of mind at the time of the crime, the following language is both relevant and material: When asked how long he had thought of killing his mother, defendant replied, "I can't be clear on that. About a week ago, I would suppose, the very beginning of the thoughts. First I thought of giving her the ether. Then Thursday and Friday I thought of it again.

Q: Of killing your mother?

A: "Not of killing. Well, yes, I think so. Then Saturday and Sunday the same." After stating that he struck her the first blow on the back of the head, defendant was asked:

Q: Did you consider at the time that this one blow would render her unconscious, or kill her?

A: I wasn't sure. I was hoping it would render her unconscious.

Q: Was it your thought at this time to kill her?

A: I am not sure of that. Probably kill her, I think. Defendant described the struggle in which he and his mother fell to the floor, and was asked:

Q: Then what happened.

A: She moved over by the stove, and she just laid still. She was breathing, breathing heavily. I said "I shouldn't be doing this"— not those exact words, but something to that effect, and laid down beside her, because we were on the floor.

Q: Were you tired?

A: Yes

After defendant had choked her to death he said, "God loves you, He loves me, He loves my dad, and I love you and my dad. It is a circle, sort of, and it is horrible you have done all that good and then I come along and destroy it."

Detective Stenberg thereafter interrupted Officer Hamilton's interrogation, and asked the following questions:

Q: (Det. W. R. Stenberg) You knew the wrongfulness of killing your mother?

A: I did. I was thinking of it. I was aware of it.

Q: You were aware of the wrongfulness. Also had you thought what might happen to you?

A: That is a question. No.

Q: Your thought has been in your mind for three weeks of killing her?

A: Yes, or of just knocking her out.

Q: Well, didn't you feel you would be prosecuted for the wrongfulness of this act?

A: I was aware of it, but not thinking of it.

Officer Hamilton asked:

Q: Can you give a reason or purpose for this act of killing your mother? Have you thought out why you wanted to hurt her?

A: There is a reason why we didn't get along. There is also the reason of sexual intercourse with one of these other girls, and I had to get her out of the way.

Q: Did you think you had to get her out of the way permanently?

A: I sort of figured it would have to be that way, but I am not quite sure.

Thus, contrary to the misunderstanding of counsel and amicus curiae, Officer

Stenberg's question ("You knew the wrongfulness of killing your mother?") related unequivocally to defendant's knowledge at the time of the commission of the murder; and defendant's equally unequivocal answer ("I did. I was thinking of it. I was aware of it.") related to the same period of time. This admission, coupled with defendant's uncontradicted course of conduct and other statements set forth hereinabove, constitutes substantial evidence from which the jury could find defendant legally sane at the time of the matricide.

Certainly in the case now at bench the defendant had ample time for any normal person to maturely and appreciatively reflect upon his contemplated act and to arrive at a cold, deliberated and premeditated conclusion. He did this in a sense—and apparently to the full extent of which he was capable. But, indisputably on the record, this defendant was not and is not a fully normal or mature, mentally well person. He knew the difference between right and wrong; he knew that the intended act was wrong and nevertheless carried it out. But the extent of his understanding, reflection upon it and its consequences, with realization of the enormity of the evil, appears to have been materially as relevant to appraising the quantum of his moral turpitude and depravity vague and detached. We think that ... the use by the legislature of "wilful, deliberate, and premeditated" in conjunction indicates its intent to require as an essential element of first degree murder ... substantially more reflection; i.e., more understanding and comprehension of the character of the act than the mere amount of thought necessary to form the intention to kill.... Dividing intentional homicides into murder and voluntary manslaughter was a recognition of the infirmity of human nature. Again dividing the offense of murder into two degrees is a further recognition of that infirmity and of difference in the quantum of personal turpitude of the offenders....

Upon the facts, upon the law, and for all of the reasons hereinabove stated we are satisfied that the evidence fails to support the finding that the murder by this defendant, in the circumstances of his undisputed mental illness, was of the first degree, but that it amply sustains conviction of second degree murder.

The fact that we reduce the degree of the penal judgment from first to second degree murder is not to be understood as suggesting that this defendant's confinement should be in an institution maintaining any lower degree of security than for persons convicted of murder in the first degree. To the contrary, we approve of the trial court's recommendation that defendant be placed in a hospital for the criminally insane of a high security character....

[T]he judgment is modified by reducing the crime to murder in the second degree and, as so modified, is affirmed. The cause is remanded to the trial court with directions to arraign and pronounce judgment on defendant in accordance with foregoing ruling.

Case Discussion

Do you agree that Wolff was too immature to premeditate his mother's murder? Would you treat him just as you would an adult? Would you sentence him to death if capital punishment was legal for adults? Would you remove him altogether from the adult criminal justice system? Would you convict him but send him to a juvenile institution? Or would you do what the court did: convict him, but of the lesser crime, second-degree murder, and place him in a high-security hospital for the criminally insane? For how long?

Following this decision, the California legislature modified its first-degree murder statute to include the following:

> § 189 ... To prove the killing was "deliberate and premeditated," it shall not be necessary to prove the defendant maturely and meaningfully reflected upon the gravity of his or her act.[25]

Why did the legislature enact such a provision? What effect does it have on the court's ruling in *Wolff?*

Youth does not always excuse criminal responsibility, or mitigate the punishment; sometimes it aggravates conduct. For example, seventeen-year-old Muñoz was convicted of possessing a switchblade under a New York City ordinance that prohibited youths under twenty-one from carrying such knives. Had Muñoz been over twenty-one, what he did would not have been a crime.[26]

CASE

Too Old to Commit Crimes?

Old Age as Criminal Defense[27]

[A prosecutor related the following tragedy.]

You have this married couple, married for over 50 years, living in a retirement home. The guy sends his wife out for bagels and while the wife can still get around she forgets and brings back onion rolls. Not a capital offense, right? Anyway, the guy goes berserk and he axes his wife; he kills the poor woman with a Boy Scout-type axe! What do we do now? Set a high bail? Prosecute? Get a conviction and send the fellow to prison? You tell me! We did nothing. The media dropped it quickly and, I hope, that's it.

**Case
Discussion**
Which alternatives available to the prosecutor would you choose? What about an old age defense? In *Regina v. Kemp,* a respectable old man, who had never been in trouble, beat his wife. The old man, Kemp, suffered from arteriosclerosis, or hardening of the arteries, a disease that affects mental capacity. The condition caused him to assault his wife. Although the court did not permit his old age to excuse him, the judges did permit his arteriosclerosis to prove he was insane. The jury found Kemp not guilty but insane.[28]

▼ ENTRAPMENT

Law enforcement officers who lead citizens to commit crimes provide those citizens with the excuse called entrapment. Entrapment does not justify crime; it excuses crime because the law enforcement officer "manufactured" the crime. Entrapment also excuses criminal liability in order to deter police from encouraging crime; it allows the "criminal" to go free because the police abused their power. Police encouragement of crime breeds public resentment toward law and undermines the law's effectiveness. The verdict acquitting John DeLorean of drug charges illustrates this public resentment. Jurors said the FBI went too far in trying to prove DeLorean guilty. Although DeLorean was, in their estimation, clearly guilty, the jurors acquitted him to show the FBI that it should use less offensive methods to catch criminals.[29]

Entrapment does not excuse the most serious crimes, such as murder and rape. Until recently, the government used decoys and other undercover tactics mainly against consensual crimes, such as narcotics, prostitution, and gambling. Increasingly, the government has come to rely on similar tactics against street muggers and white-collar criminals, such as in the ABSCAM cases (involving members of Congress) and "greylord" (involving Chicago judges). Furthermore, not everybody can legally entrap. Paid, full-time law enforcement officers can entrap. So can paid informants, private detectives, and other "civilians" working for the government. Private persons who induce others to commit crime cannot entrap.[30]

Some state courts prohibit defendants from taking inconsistent positions by denying that they committed the crime charged and pleading the defense of entrapment. For example, a defendant cannot deny buying crack by claiming that she was in another city when an undercover agent testified she bought the heroin from him, and then claims that the officer entrapped her by pressuring her into buying it. The United States Supreme Court, however, has ruled that defendants can deny guilt and then plead entrapment under federal criminal law. The reason for the rule prohibiting inconsistent positions rests in part on the logic that without crime there can be no entrapment.[31]

Jurisdictions vary as to what constitutes entrapment. According to the traditional, or subjective, entrapment test, entrapment required the officer to instigate the crime; that is, to create or manufacture the intent to commit a crime in the mind of one who was not otherwise disposed to commit it. Entrapment, therefore, depends on what stimulated the specific defendant

to commit the crime; if the stimulus came from the government, then the law excuses the defendant. The subjective standard assumes that the legislature did not intend to make criminals out of people whom the police (or other government agents) induced to commit crimes.

The subjective test requires more than the government merely providing the defendant with the opportunity to commit a crime. For example, if I am walking down the street looking for a drunk to roll and I find a decoy with $100 sticking out of her pocket and take it, the decoy did not entrap me. I was predisposed to commit the crime; the decoy only provided me with the opportunity to commit it. On the other hand, suppose I am in a drug treatment center where for months I have tried to control my addiction to heroin. An undercover agent begs me to get him some heroin. At first I refuse, but after repeated pressure in which he appeals to my sympathy for his desperate need for it, I finally get some for him. The agent entrapped me because I did not want to deal in heroin; he instigated the crime.[32]

Some courts have adopted an objective test to determine entrapment. The objective test finds entrapment whenever law enforcement activity would cause a reasonable person who is not so predisposed to commit a crime. The objective standard focuses on the government's actions, not the defendant's. The test asks: Would a reasonable person have responded to the officer's action by committing the crime? The primary objective of the standard is to discourage government misconduct, not to protect "innocent" defendants. Under the objective test, entrapment is not an excuse, but a mechanism to control government abuse of power. Therefore, in theory the objective test for entrapment falls into a separate category. However, for practical purposes, it appears here.[33]

CASE

Are Police Decoys Illegal Traps?

Cruz v. State
465 So.2d 516 (Fla.1985)

[Cruz was convicted of grand theft. He appealed.]
    Ehrlich, Justice

FACTS

Tampa police undertook a decoy operation in a high-crime area. An officer posed as an inebriated indigent, smelling of alcohol and pretending to drink wine from a bottle. The officer leaned against a building near an alleyway, his face to the wall. Plainly displayed from a rear pants pocket was $150 in currency, paper-clipped together. Defendant Cruz and a woman happened upon the scene as passersby sometime after 10 p.m. Cruz approached the decoy officer, may have attempted to say something to him, then continued on his way. Ten to fifteen minutes later, the defendant and his companion returned to the scene and Cruz took the money from the decoy's pocket without harming him in any way. Officers then arrested Cruz as he walked from the scene. The decoy situation did not involve the same modus operandi as any of the unsolved crimes which had occurred in the area. Police were not seeking a particular individual, nor were they aware of any prior criminal acts by the defendant.

OPINION

The entrapment defense arises from a recognition that sometimes police activity will

induce an otherwise innocent individual to commit the criminal act the police activity seeks to produce.

In articulating [the entrapment doctrine], our Court has adopted two standards respecting entrapment. The traditional or subjective standard defines entrapment as law enforcement conduct which implants in the mind of an innocent person the disposition to commit the alleged crime, and hence induces its commission. Under this traditional formulation, the defense of entrapment is limited to those defendants who were not predisposed to commit the crime induced by government actions.

In recent years, however, this Court has fashioned a second, independent standard for assessing entrapment. It recognizes that when official conduct inducing crime is so egregious as to impugn the integrity of a court that permits a conviction, the predisposition of the defendant becomes irrelevant.

[A]s the part played by the State in the criminal activity increases, the importance of the factor of defendant's criminal intent decreases, until finally a point may be reached where the methods [employed] by the state to obtain a conviction cannot be countenanced, even though a defendant's predisposition is shown. Whether the police activity has overstepped the bounds of permissible conduct is a question to be decided by the trial court rather than the jury.

To guide the trial courts, we propound the following threshold test of an entrapment defense: Entrapment has not occurred as a matter of law where police activity (1) has as its end the interruption of a specific ongoing criminal activity; and (2) utilizes means reasonably tailored to apprehend those involved in the ongoing criminal activity.

The first prong of this test addresses the problem of police "virtue testing," that is, police activity seeking to prosecute crime where no such crime exists but for the police activity engendering the crime. "Society is at war with the criminal classes." Police must fight this war, not engage in the manufacture of new hostilities.

The second prong of the threshold test addresses the problem of inappropriate techniques. Considerations in deciding whether police activity is permissible under this prong include whether a government agent "includes or encourages another person to engage in conduct constituting such offense by either: (a) making knowingly false representations designed to induce the belief that such conduct is not prohibited; or (b) employing methods of persuasion or inducement which create a substantial risk that such an offense will be committed by persons other than those who are ready to commit it." Model Penal Code § 2.13 (1962).

Applying this test to the case before us, we find that the drunken bum decoy operation fails. In Cruz's motion to dismiss, one of the undisputed facts was that "none of the unsolved crimes occurring [sic] near this location involved the same modus operandi as the simulated situation created by the officers." The record thus implies police were apparently attempting to interrupt some kind of ongoing criminal activity. However, the record does not show what specific activity was targeted. This lack of focus is sufficient for the scenario to fail the first prong of the test. However, even if the police were seeking to catch persons who had been "rolling" drunks in the area, the criminal scenario here, with $150 (paper-clipped to ensure more than $100 was taken, making the offense a felony) enticingly protruding from the back pocket of a person seemingly incapable of noticing its removal, carries with it the "substantial risk that such an offense will be committed by persons other than those who are ready to commit it." Model Penal Code § 2.13. This sufficiently addresses the proper recognition that entrapment has occurred where "the decoy simply provided the opportunity to commit a crime to anyone who succumbed to the lure of the bait." This test also recognizes, that the considerations inherent in our threshold test are not properly addressed in the context of the predisposition element of the second, subjective test.

For reasons discussed, we hold that the police activity in the instant case constituted entrapment as a matter of law under the threshold test adopted here. Accordingly, we quash the district court decision.

It is so ordered.

Case Discussion

Notice that the court adopts both the objective test (whether reasonable persons would be enticed by the police decoy tactic used) and the subjective test (whether Cruz himself was enticed into doing something he would otherwise not do). Most courts do not use both tests; they use one or the other. States are divided on the question. Some use the subjective test; others use the objective test. Which do you prefer? Or would you do as this court did: adopt a threshold objective test, which if passed, then goes to a subjective test?

▼ **INSANITY**

*Legal Concept
Mental & does
not
Criminal liability*

The insanity defense commands great public and scholarly attention. However, defendants rarely plead insanity because they have too much to lose and too little to gain if they succeed. Contrary to widely held beliefs, and unlike all other defenses discussed up to this point, a successful insanity plea does not lead to automatic freedom. The verdict is "not guilty by reason of insanity." Because defendants were insane when they committed the crime, they do not automatically or immediately walk out of the courtroom following the verdict. Instead, special proceedings take place in which the court decides whether they still require custody for their own and society's safety. In other words, successful insanity pleas bestow upon the government the authority to incarcerate without conviction. Persons found not guilty by reason of insanity rarely go free immediately; some never do. Courts nearly always commit them to maximum-security hospitals, institutions virtually indistinguishable from prisons. Not surprisingly, then, only a few defendants resort to the insanity plea. The few who do plead insanity—nearly all charged with capital crimes or crimes subject to life imprisonment—rarely succeed.[34]

Insanity excuses criminal liability because it impairs *mens rea.* Punishing insane persons does not serve the major objectives of criminal law. If defendants were so mentally diseased that they could not form *mens rea,* then they are not blameworthy and retribution is out of order. Neither would it deter either the defendant or other mentally ill people who cannot form *mens rea.* Also, the government can invoke its civil commitment authority to incapacitate and treat mentally ill persons without calling upon the criminal law to control them.

Insanity is a legal concept, not a medical term. What psychiatry calls mental illness may or may not conform to the law's definition of insanity. Mental illness, alone does not prove insanity, and only insanity excuses criminal responsibility. Psychiatrists testify in courts to aid fact finders in determining whether defendants are legally insane, not to prove they are mentally ill. The verdict "guilty but mentally ill" makes this point clear. In that verdict, used in some jurisdictions, the jury can find that defendants were not insane but were mentally ill when they committed crimes. These defendants receive criminal sentences and go to prison, but they may require, and are supposed to receive, treatment for their mental illness while in prison.[35]

Jurisdictions determine insanity according to two primary tests: (1) the right-wrong test and (2) the substantial capacity test. Both require looking at defendants' mental capacity, but they differ in what they emphasize about that capacity. The right-wrong test focuses on the intellect, or cognition—what defendants know. The substantial capacity test focuses not only on knowledge, but also on the emotional dimension to understanding—defendants' appreciation of what they did. Freud expressed this distinction in his phrase, "there is knowing, and there is *knowing!*" A child knows intellectually that stealing is wrong but does not fully appreciate, or feel, its significance. The substantial capacity test also stresses volition, or defendants' will to control their actions. Defendants may know that what they are doing is wrong but lack the will to control their actions.

Right-Wrong Test

The **M'Naghten rule,** or **right-wrong test,** focuses narrowly on defendants' intellectual capacity to know what they are doing and to distinguish right from wrong. In *Rex v. Porter,* the judge explains the right-wrong test in these instructions to the jury:

> I wish to draw your attention to some general considerations affecting the question of insanity in the criminal law in the hope that by so doing you may be helped to grasp what the law prescribes. The purpose of the law in punishing people is to prevent others from committing a like crime or crimes. Its prime purpose is to deter people from committing offenses. It may be that there is an element of retribution in the criminal law, so that when people have committed offenses the law considers that they merit punishment, but its prime purpose is to preserve society from the depredations of dangerous and vicious people.
>
> Now, it is perfectly useless for the law to attempt, by threatening punishment, to deter people from committing crimes if their mental condition is such that they cannot be in the least influenced by the possibility or probability of subsequent punishment; if they cannot understand what they are doing or cannot understand the ground upon which the law proceeds.
>
> The law is not directed, as medical science is, to curing mental infirmities. The criminal law is not directed, as the civil law of lunacy is, to the care and custody of people of weak mind whose personal property may be in jeopardy through someone else taking a hand in the conduct of their affairs and their lives. This is quite a different thing from the question, what utility there is in the punishment of people who, at a moment, would commit acts which, if done when they were in sane minds, would be crimes.
>
> What is the utility of punishing people if they be beyond the control of the law for reasons of mental health? In considering that, it will not perhaps, if you have ever reflected upon the matter, have escaped your attention that a great number of people who come into a Criminal Court are abnormal. They would not be there if they were the normal type of average everyday people. Many of them are very peculiar in their dispositions and peculiarly tempered. That is markedly the case in sexual offences. Nevertheless, they are mentally

quite able to appreciate what they are doing and quite able to appreciate the threatened punishment of the law and the wrongness of their acts, and they are held in check by the prospect of punishment. It would be very absurd if the law were to withdraw that check on the ground that they were somewhat different from their fellow creatures in mental make-up or texture at the very moment when the check is most needed.

You will therefore see that the law, in laying down a standard of mental disorder sufficient to justify a jury in finding a prisoner not guilty on the ground of insanity at the moment of offence, is addressing itself to a somewhat difficult task. It is attempting to define what are the classes of people who should not be punished although they have done actual things which in others would amount to crime. It is quite a different object to that which the medical profession has in view or other departments of the law have in view of defining insanity for the purpose of the custody of the person's property, capacity to make a will, and the like.[36]

The right-wrong test, although it has deep historical antecedents, derived its present form from the famous English *M'Naghten* case. In 1843, Daniel M'Naghten suffered the paranoid delusion that the prime minister, Sir Robert Peel, had masterminded a conspiracy to kill M'Naghten. M'Naghten shot at Peel in delusional self-defense, but killed Peel's secretary, Edward Drummond, by mistake. Following his trial for murder, the jury returned a verdict of not guilty by reason of insanity. On appeal, England's highest court, the House of Lords, formulated the right-wrong test, or M'Naghten rule. According to the rule, the court designed a two-pronged insanity test: (1) the defendant must suffer from a *disease* or defect of the mind, and (2) the disease or defect must cause the defendant either to not know the nature and quality of the criminal act or to know that the act was wrong.[37]

The right-wrong test, as the House of Lords formulated it, creates several difficulties. First, what mental diseases or defects does the "disease of the mind" include? All formulations include severe psychoses, such as the paranoia from which M'Naghten himself suffered, and schizophrenia. Virtually all also include severe mental retardation affecting cognition. They exclude neuroses and/or personality disorders, particularly psychopathic and sociopathic personalities—those who engage in repeated criminal or antisocial conduct.[38]

The word "knowing" also creates problems. Most statutes and decisions say it means pure intellectual awareness: cognition. Others include more than intellectual awareness, which nearly everyone possesses. They bring within the compass of knowing the ability to understand or appreciate, meaning to grasp an act's true significance. Hence, some courts add to cognition or intellectual awareness an emotional, affective, or feeling dimension. Some jurisdictions do not define the term, leaving it to juries to define it by applying it to the facts of specific cases.

The following example captures the meaning of not knowing the "nature and quality of the act," as *M'Naghten* defined that phrase: If a man believes he is squeezing lemons when in fact he is strangling his wife, he clearly does not know the nature and quality of his act. Some hold that the phrase means knowing right from wrong. A few go further, contending that it refers to more than knowing the nature of the physical act. One court, for example, required "true insight" into the act's consequences. This does not mean that defendants must believe the act is wrong. M'Naghten himself knew that he was killing, but he thought the killing was justified.

The word "wrong" itself has created problems in the definition of the right-wrong test. Some jurisdictions require that defendants did not know their conduct was legally wrong; others interpret "wrong" to mean that defendants did not know their conduct was morally wrong. Consider the person who kills another person under the insane delusion that his subsequent conviction and execution for the murder will save the human race. The person knew that killing was legally, but not morally, wrong. If "wrong" means "legal," the person is guilty; if it means "moral," he is insane. Some jurisdictions adopt an objective test to determine moral wrongfulness: Do defendants lack the capacity to know that their conduct violated the prevailing moral standard of the community? Others adopt a subjective test: Do defendants know the conduct was wrong by their own moral standards?[39]

CASE

*Too Insane to
Be Guilty?*

State v. Crenshaw

98 Wn.2d 789, 659 P.2d 488 (1983)

[Crenshaw was convicted of first-degree murder. He appealed. Justice Brachtenbach delivered the opinion.]

FACTS

While defendant and his wife were on their honeymoon in Canada, petitioner was deported as a result of his participation in a brawl. He secured a motel room in Blaine, Washington and waited for his wife to join him. When she arrived 2 days later, he immediately thought she had been unfaithful—he sensed "it wasn't the same Karen. She'd been with someone else."

Petitioner did not mention his suspicions to his wife, instead he took her to the motel room and beat her unconscious. He then went to a nearby store, stole a knife, and returned to stab his wife 24 times, inflicting a fatal wound. He left again, drove to a nearby farm where he had been employed and borrowed an ax. Upon returning to the

motel room, he decapitated his wife with such force that the ax marks cut into the concrete floor under the carpet and splattered blood throughout the room.

Petitioner then proceeded to conceal his actions. He placed the body in a blanket, the head in a pillowcase and put both in his wife's car. Next, he went to a service station, borrowed a bucket and sponge, and cleaned the room of blood and fingerprints. Before leaving, petitioner also spoke with the motel manager about a phone bill, then chatted with him for awhile over a beer.

When Crenshaw left the motel he drove to a remote area 25 miles away where he hid the two parts of the body in thick brush. He then fled, driving to the Hoquiam area, about 200 miles from the scene of the crime. There he picked up two hitchhikers, told them of his crime, and enlisted their aid in disposing of his wife's car in a river. The hitchhikers contacted the police and Crenshaw was apprehended shortly thereafter. He voluntarily confessed to the crime.

The defense of not guilty by reason of insanity was a major issue at trial. Crenshaw testified that he followed the Moscovite religious faith, and that it would be improper for a Moscovite not to kill his wife if she committed adultery. Crenshaw also has a history of mental problems, for which he has been hospitalized in the past. The jury, however, rejected petitioner's insanity defense, and found him guilty of murder in the first degree.

OPINION

The insanity defense is not available to all who are mentally deficient or deranged; legal insanity has a different meaning and a different purpose than the concept of medical insanity. A verdict of not guilty by reason of insanity completely absolves a defendant of any criminal responsibility. Therefore, "the defense is available only to those persons who have lost contact with reality so completely that they are beyond any of the influences of the criminal law."

Petitioner assigned error to insanity defense instruction 10 which reads:

> Insanity existing at the time of the commission of the act charged is a defense.
>
> For a defendant to be found not guilty by reason of insanity you must find that, as a result of mental disease or defect, the defendant's mind was affected to such an extent that the defendant was unable to perceive the nature and quality of the acts with which the defendant is charged or was unable to tell right from wrong with reference to the particular acts with which defendant is charged.
>
> What is meant by the terms "right and wrong" refers to knowledge of a person at the time of committing an act that he was acting contrary to the law.

Petitioner contends ... that the trial court erred in defining "right and wrong" as legal right and wrong rather than in the moral sense.

First, in discussing the term "moral" wrong, it is important to note that it is society's morals, and not the individual's morals, that are the standard for judging moral wrong under *M'Naghten*. If wrong meant moral wrong judged by the individual's own conscience, this would seriously undermine the criminal law, for it would allow one who violated the law to be excused from criminal responsibility solely because, in his own conscience, his act was not morally wrong.

This principle was emphasized by Justice Cardozo: The anarchist is not at liberty to break the law because he reasons that all government is wrong. The devotee of a religious cult that enjoins polygamy or human sacrifice as a duty is not thereby relieved from responsibility before the law.

There is evidence on the record that Crenshaw knew his actions were wrong according to society's standards, as well as legally wrong. Dr. Belden testified:

> I think Mr. Crenshaw is quite aware on one level that he is in conflict with the law *and with people*. However, this is not something that he personally invests his emotions in. [Italics ours.]

We conclude that Crenshaw knew his acts were morally wrong from society's viewpoint and also knew his acts were illegal. His personal belief that it was his duty to kill his wife for her alleged infidelity cannot serve to exculpate him from legal responsibility for his acts.

We also find that, under any definition of wrong, Crenshaw did not qualify for the insanity defense under *M'Naghten;* therefore, any alleged error in that definition must be viewed as harmless.

Here, any error is harmless for two alternate reasons. First, Crenshaw failed to prove an essential element of the defense because he did not prove his alleged delusions stemmed from a mental defect; second, he did not prove by a preponderance of the evidence that he was legally insane at the time of the crime.

In addition to an incapacity to know right from wrong, *M'Naghten* requires that such incapacity stem from a mental disease or defect. RCW 9A.12.010. Assuming, arguendo, that Crenshaw did not know right from wrong, he failed to prove that a mental defect was the cause of this inability.

Petitioner's insanity argument is premised on the following facts: (1) he is a Moscovite and Moscovites believe it is their duty to assassinate an unfaithful spouse; (2) he "knew," without asking, that his wife had been unfaithful when he met her in Blaine and this was equivalent to an insane delusion; and (3) at other times in his life, he had been diagnosed as a paranoid personality and had been committed to mental institutions. A conscientious application of the *M'Naghten* rule demonstrates, however, that these factors do not afford petitioner the sanctuary of the insanity defense.

To begin, petitioner's Moscovite beliefs are irrelevant to the insanity defense, because they are not insane delusions. Some notion of morality, unrelated to a mental illness, which disagrees with the law and mores of our society is not an insane delusion.

Nor was petitioner's belief that his wife was unfaithful an insane delusion. Dr. Trowbridge, a psychiatrist, explained:

> A man suspects his wife of being unfaithful. Certainly such suspicions are not necessarily delusional, even if they're ill based. Just because he suspected his wife of being unfaithful doesn't mean that he was crazy.
>
> Certainly when a man kills his wife he doesn't do it in a rational way. No one ever does that rationally. But that is not to suggest that every time a man kills his wife he was *[sic]* insane.

Finally, evidence of prior commitments to mental institutions is not proof that one was legally insane at the time the criminal act was committed.

Those who are commonly regarded as "odd" or "unsound" or even "deranged" would not normally qualify [for the insanity defense]. Many, if not most, mentally ill persons presently being treated in the mental institutions of this state who are there under the test of "likelihood of serious harm to the person detained or to others," would not meet the *M'Naghten* test, if charged with a crime.

Thus, petitioner does not establish the necessary connection between his criminal acts and his psychological problems to qualify for the insanity defense.

In addition, the preponderance of the evidence weighs against finding Crenshaw legally insane. All of the psychological experts, save one, testified that defendant was not insane at the time of the murder. The only doctor who concluded defendant

(petitioner) was legally insane, Dr. Hunger, was a psychologist who had not examined petitioner for a year and a half.

Given the various qualifications of the experts, the time they spent with the petitioner, and the proximity in time of their examinations to the murder, the testimony does not establish by a preponderance of the evidence that petitioner was legally insane at the time of the murder.

Furthermore, in addition to the expert testimony, there was lay testimony that petitioner appeared rational at the time of the killing. After cleaning the motel room, Crenshaw resolved a phone bill dispute with the manager, then shared a beer with him without arousing any suspicion in the manager's mind. Also, the woman who gave him the ax testified as to his behavior the day before the murder:

> Well, he seemed very normal or I certainly wouldn't have handed him an ax or a hoe. He was polite, he done his work. He didn't, I wasn't afraid of him or anything. I mean we were just out there working and I certainly wouldn't have handed him an ax or anything like that if I would have thought that there was anything even remotely peculiar about him.

And, with specific reference to the time when petitioner borrowed the ax to decapitate his wife:

Q: Did he seem rational to you?
A: Oh, yes, he was very nice.
Q: Did he seem coherent when he spoke to you?
A: Oh, yes.
Q: Did he appear to be sane to you then?
A: Yes.

Thus, at the same time that he was embroiled in the act of murdering his wife, he was rational, coherent, and sane in his dealings with others.

Finally, evidence of petitioner's calculated execution of the crime and his sophisticated attempts to avert discovery support a finding of sanity. Crenshaw performed the murder methodically, leaving the motel room twice to acquire the knife and ax necessary to perform the deed. Then, after the killing he scrubbed the motel room to clean up the blood and remove his fingerprints. Next, he drove 25 miles to hide the body in thick brush in a remote area. Finally, he drove several hundred miles and ditched the car in a river.

Such attempts to hide evidence of a crime manifest an awareness that the act was legally wrong. Moreover, petitioner testified that he did these things because he "didn't want to get caught."

To summarize thus far, we find no error in instruction 10 for the following reasons: (1) As we interpret the *M'Naghten* case, it was not improper for the trial court to instruct with reference to the law of the land, under the facts of this case; (2) because the concept of moral wrong refers to the mores of society and not to the individual's morals, "moral" wrong is synonymous with "legal" wrong with a serious crime such as this one, therefore, instructing in terms of legal wrong did not alter the meaning of the *M'Naghten* rule; (3) any error was harmless because (a) Crenshaw did not show that at the time of the crime his mind was affected as a result of a mental disease or defect and without this essential element the insanity defense was not available to him, and (b) an overwhelming preponderance of the evidence supports the finding that Crenshaw was not legally insane when he killed his wife. We thus conclude that the additional statement in instruction 10 was not improper, or, at the very least, that it was harmless error.

Affirmed.

Case Discussion

Do you agree that moral wrong and legal wrong are the same? Should the test be whether Crenshaw knew he was breaking the law or that he knew it was wrong in the general sense? What would you do with Crenshaw? Do you think it is possible to be objective about Crenshaw's insanity? Or does the brutal way he killed his wife make you want to call him a criminal, no matter what his state of mind? Do you see how this can create serious problems with the insanity defense?

The right-wrong test has generated protracted argument. Critics mainly contend that modern developments in both law and psychiatry have rendered the test obsolete. This criticism loomed large during the 1950s, when many social reformers relied on Freudian psychology to cure a wide spectrum of individual and social ills. *Durham v. Unites States* reflects psychiatry's influence on criminal law generally and on the insanity defense particularly. With regard to the right-wrong test, the court said:

> The science of psychiatry now recognizes that a man is an integrated personality and that reason, which is only one element in that personality, is not the sole determinant of his conduct. The right-wrong test, which considers knowledge or reason alone, is therefore an inadequate guide to mental responsibility for criminal behavior.[40]

Borrowing from a New Hampshire rule formulated in 1871 and still in effect in that state, the *Durham* court formulated a broad insanity definition reflecting the influence of psychiatry. According to the **Durham rule,** or **product test,** acts that are the product of mental disease or defect excuse criminal liability. The court aimed to broaden the concept of insanity beyond the purely intellectual knowledge in the right-wrong test to deeper areas of cognition and will. Only New Hampshire (where the test originated), the federal court of appeals for the District of Columbia (which decided *Durham*), and Maine ever adopted the product test. The federal court and Maine have since abandoned the test, leaving it in effect only in New Hampshire.[41]

M'Naghten's defenders contend that the product test misses the point of legal insanity. They maintain that the right-wrong test should not substitute mental illness for insanity. Rather, it is an instrument to determine which mental states ought to relieve persons of criminal responsibility. Two articulate defenders put it this way:

> It is always necessary to start any discussion of *M'Naghten* by stressing that the case does not state a test of psychosis or mental illness. Rather, it lists conditions under which those who are mentally diseased will be relieved from criminal responsibility. Thus, criticism of *M'Naghten* based on the proposition that the case is premised on an outdated view of mental disease is inappropriate. The case can only be criticized justly if it is based on an outdated view of the mental conditions that ought to preclude application of criminal sanction.[42]

Other critics contend that the *M'Naghten* rule focuses too narrowly on intellectual knowledge of right and wrong in cognition, neglecting the deeper emotional components necessary to full appreciation of conduct. Furthermore, considering only cognition excludes volition—whether defendants can control their behavior even though they fully appreciate, both intellectually and emotionally, that they are acting wrongfully. These critics say that criminal law acts inappropriately if it excuses only those who do not know or appreciate what they are doing while punishing those who cannot stop themselves from doing what they know is wrong. We can neither blame nor deter those who cannot conform their conduct to what the law requires. The law of civil commitment can protect society from them and treat them without resorting to criminal sanctions.

M'Naghten's supporters contend that the law should presume everyone has some control because operating on that assumption deters more potential offenders. Therefore, the insanity defense ought to include only those who (1) did not know what they were doing or (2) did know what they were doing but did not know it was wrong, assuming that the second group can choose right if they know what right is.

Irresistible Impulse Test

Several jurisdictions have supplemented the right-wrong test with the irresistible impulse test in an effort to deal with the volition problem. **Irresistible impulse** requires

> a verdict of not guilty by reason of insanity if it is found that the defendant has a mental disease which kept him from controlling his conduct. Such a verdict is called for even if the defendant knew what he was doing and that it was wrong.[43]

Although the irresistible impulse test predates *M'Naghten* (it goes back to at least 1834 in England), the leading American case was decided in 1877.

In *Parsons v. State,* the court held that when defendants plead insanity, juries should determine the following:

> *1.* At the time of the crime was the defendant afflicted with "a disease of the mind?"
> *2.* If so, did the defendant know right from wrong with respect to the act charged? If not, the law excuses the defendant.
> *3.* If the defendant did have such knowledge the law will still excuse the defendant if two conditions concur:
> > a. if mental disease caused the defendant to so far lose the power to choose between right and wrong and to avoid doing the alleged act that the disease destroyed the defendant's free will, and
> > b. if the mental disease was the sole cause of the act.[44]

Despite broadening the right-wrong defense, critics maintain that the irresistible impulse supplement still restricts the insanity defense too much. It includes only impulsive acts, ignoring mental disease "characterized by brooding and reflection." Defenders deny this. Courts do not tell juries that they must limit their findings to sudden and unplanned impulses; juries can consider any evidence showing that defendants lack control owing to mental disease. Critics also claim that the irresistible requirement implies that defendants must lack control totally. In practice, however, juries do acquit defendants who have some control; rarely do juries demand an utter lack of control.

Other critics claim that irresistible impulse includes too much. By permitting people who lack control to escape criminal liability, the test unduly curtails the deterrent purposes of criminal law. For example, the jury acquitted John Hinckley, Jr., on the grounds that Hinckley was insane when he attempted to assassinate former president Ronald Reagan in order to gain the attention of actress Jodie Foster. Shortly after Hinckley's trial, Harvard criminal law professor Charles Nesson wrote:

> [T]o many Mr. Hinckley seems like a kid who had a rough life and who lacked the moral fiber to deal with it. This is not to deny that Mr. Hinckley is crazy but to recognize that there is a capacity for craziness in all of us. Lots of people have tough lives, many tougher than Mr. Hinckley's, and manage to cope. The Hinckley verdict let those people down. For anyone who experiences life as a struggle to act responsibly in the face of various temptations to let go, the Hinckley verdict is demoralizing, an example of someone who let himself go and who has been exonerated because of it.[45]

Defenders claim that empirical research has not demonstrated the effectiveness of deterrence; hence, the law should not base the insanity defense on it. Finally, opponents who are disillusioned with the rehabilitative ideal argue that the state should not engage in hopeless efforts to treat and cure the mentally diseased (see chapter 2 on deterrence).

Despite its defenders, several jurisdictions have recently rejected irresistible impulse on the ground that juries cannot accurately distinguish between irresistible and merely unresisted impulses. Unresisted impulses should not excuse criminal conduct. The federal statute abolishing irresistible impulse in federal cases provides as follows:[46]

> It is an affirmative defense to a prosecution under any Federal statute that, at the time of the commission of the acts constituting the offense, the defendant, as a result of a severe mental disease or defect, was unable to

appreciate the nature and quality or the wrongfulness of his acts. Mental disease or defect does not otherwise constitute a defense.[47]

Substantial Capacity Test

The right-wrong test, either supplemented by the irresistible impulse or not, was the rule in most states until the 1960s, after which the Model Penal Code's **substantial capacity test** became the majority rule. During the 1970s, and in the 1980s following John Hinckley's trial, the pure right-wrong test (unencumbered by the emotional component of understanding, irresistible impulse, or both) has enjoyed a resurgence.[48]

The Model Penal Code provision resulted from efforts to remove objections to both the *M'Naghten* rule and the irresistible impulse test while preserving the legal nature of both tests. It emphasizes the qualities in insanity that affect culpability: the intellectual (cognitive) and emotional (affective) components of understanding, and will (volition).

The Model Penal Code requires that defendants lack "substantial," not total, mental capacity. Both the right-wrong and irresistible impulse test are ambiguous on this point, leading some to maintain that both require total lack of knowledge and control. Hence, persons who know right and wrong minimally and whose will to resist is slightly intact are insane according to the code provision.

> A person is not responsible for criminal conduct if at the time of such conduct as a result of mental disease or defect he lacks substantial capacity either to appreciate the criminality [wrongfulness] of his conduct or to conform his conduct to the requirements of law.[49]

The use of "appreciate" instead of "know" makes clear that mere intellectual awareness does not constitute culpability. The code includes affective or emotional components of understanding. The phrase "conform conduct" removes the requirement of a "sudden" lack of control. In other words, the code provision eliminates the suggestion that losing control means losing it on the spur of the moment, as the irresistible impulse test unfortunately implies. The code's definition of "mental disease or defect" excludes psychopathic personalities, habitual criminals, and antisocial personalities from the defense.

Until the recent return to right-wrong, the substantial capacity test had replaced right-wrong as the majority rule. The history of the insanity defense in California illustrates the original adoption of the *M'Naghten* rule, then the Model Penal Code substantial capacity test, and then a return to right-wrong by an initiative that the electorate approved in 1982. *People v. Skinner* raised the issue of whether the insanity test approved by the electorate reverted to an even stricter test of insanity, the wild beast test in effect before 1850. In 1724, Judge Tracy instructed an English jury in *Rex v. Arnold:*

> If a man be deprived of his reason and consequently of his intention he cannot be guilty.... [I]t is not every kind of frantic humour ... that points him out to be such a madman as is to be exempted from punishment: it must be a man that is totally deprived of his understanding and memory, and doth not know what he is doing, no more than infant, than a brute, or a wild beast, such a one is never the object of any punishment.[50]

CASE

Was He Insane?

People v. Skinner

39 Cal.3d 765, 217 Cal.Rptr. 685, 704 P.2d
752 (1985)

*[Skinner was convicted of second-degree
murder, being determined legally sane, and
he appealed. The California Supreme Court
reversed, finding Skinner not guilty by reason of insanity, without further hearing on
the sanity issue.]*
   Groddin, Justice

FACTS

... Defendant strangled his wife while he
was on a day pass from the Camarillo State
Hospital at which he was a patient. [Psychi-
atric testimony included] the opinion ... that
defendant suffered from either classical
paranoic schizophrenia, or schizo-affective
illness with significant paranoid features. A
delusional product of this illness was a
belief held by the defendant that the marriage vow "till death do us part" bestows on
a marital partner a God-given right to kill
the other partner who has violated or was
inclined to violate the marital vows, and that
because the vows reflect the direct wishes of
God, the killing is with complete moral and
criminal impunity. The act is not wrongful
because it is sanctified by the will and desire
of God....

OPINION

For over a century prior to the decision in
People v. Drew, (1978), California courts
framed this state's definition of insanity, as a
defense in criminal cases, upon the two-
pronged test adopted by the House of Lords
in *M'Naghten's* Case ... [owing to mental
disease or defect, defendant (1) did not
know the nature and quality of the act he
was doing or (2) if he did know it, he did

not know that it was wrong]. Over the years
the *M'Naghten* test became subject to considerable criticism and was abandoned in a
number of jurisdictions. In Drew this court
followed suit, adopting the test for mental
incapacity proposed by the American Law
Institute....

In June 1982 the California electorate
adopted an initiative measure ... which ...
for the first time established a statutory definition of insanity.... It is apparent from the
language of § 25(b) that it was designed to
eliminate the Drew test and to reinstate the
prongs of the *M'Naghten* test. However, the
section uses the conjunctive "and" instead of
the disjunctive "or" to connect the two
prongs. Read literally, therefore, § 25(b)
would do more than reinstate the *M'Naghten*
test. It would strip the insanity defense from
an accused who, by reason of mental disease, is incapable of knowing that the act he
was doing was wrong. That is, in fact, the
interpretation adopted by the trial court in
this case....

The judge stated that under the Drew test
of legal insanity defendant would qualify as
insane, and also found that "under the right-
wrong prong of § 25(b), the defendant
would qualify as legally insane; but under
the other prong, he clearly does not." Concluding that by the use of the conjunctive
"and" in § 25(b), the electorate demonstrated
an intent to establish a stricter test of insanity than the *M'Naghten* test, and to "virtually
eliminate" insanity as a defense, the judge
found that defendant had not established
that he was legally insane....

In this context we must determine whether
the trial court's conclusion ... was correct,
and if not, whether the court's finding that
defendant met the "right-wrong" aspect of the
test requires reversal....

For more than a century after ... the
M'Naghten test [was adopted in this state],
although sometimes stated in the conjunctive, [it] was in fact applied so as to permit a
finding of insanity if either prong of the test
was satisfied.... [T]he insanity defense
reflects a fundamental legal principle common to the jurisprudence of this country and

to the common law of England that criminal sanctions are imposed only on persons who act with wrongful intent in the commission of a malum in se offense. Since 1850 the disjunctive *M'Naghten* test of insanity has been accepted as the rule by which the minimum cognitive function which constitutes wrongful intent will be measured in this state. As such it is itself among the fundamental principles of our criminal law. Had it been the intent of the drafters ... or of the electorate which adopted it both to abrogate the more expansive ALI-Drew test and to abandon that prior fundamental principle of culpability for crime, we would anticipate that this intent would be expressed in some more obvious manner than the substitution of a single conjunctive in a lengthy initiative provision....

Applying § 25(b) as a conjunctive test of insanity would erase that fundamental principle. It would return the law to that which preceded *M'Naghten,* a test known variously as the "wild beast test" and as the "good and evil" test under which an accused could be found insane only if he was "totally deprived of his understanding and memory, and doth not know what he is doing, no more than an infant, than a brute, or a wild beast...." We find nothing in the language ... [of the initiative], or in any other source from which the intent of the electorate may be divined which indicates that such a fundamental, far-reaching change in the law of insanity as that was intended....

We conclude ... that § 25(b) reinstated the *M'Naghten* test as it was applied in California prior to Drew as the test of legal insanity in criminal prosecutions in this state....

The judgment is reversed and the superior court is directed to enter a judgment of not guilty by reason of insanity....

DISSENT
Byrd, Chief Justice

In June of 1982, the voters adopted a ballot measure which radically altered the test for criminal insanity in this state.... I cannot ignore the fact that they adopted language which unambiguously requires the accused to demonstrate that "he or she was incapable of knowing or understanding the nature and quality of his or her act *and* of distinguishing right from wrong at the time of the commission of the offense." [Emphasis added.] There is nothing in the statute ... or in the ballot arguments that implies that the electorate intended "and" to be "or." However unwise that choice, it is not within this court's power to ignore the expression of popular will and rewrite the statute.

Since appellant failed to establish his insanity under the test enunciated in Penal Code § 25, subdivision (b), I cannot join the decision of my brethren.

Case Discussion Did the electorate make its position clear by using "and" rather than "or," as Chief Justice Byrd argued in her dissent? Or is the majority right in arguing that the electorate should have made the statute clearer? How could the statute be more precise? Do you think the court violated the electorate's intent by interpreting the provision to mean "or"? Now that you have had the chance to consider right-wrong, irresistible impulse, substantial capacity, and the California statutory initiative, what definition do you favor? Explain.

Burden of Proof

Insanity not only poses definition problems but also gives rise to difficulties in application. Authorities disagree and critics hotly debate who must prove insanity, and how convincingly. The burden-of-proof question received public attention, and generated hostility among both the public and criminal justice professionals when the jury acquitted John Hinckley, Jr. Federal law required that the government prove Hinckley's sanity beyond a reasonable doubt. Thus, if Hinckley's lawyers could raise a doubt in jurors' minds about his sanity, the jury had to acquit. Even though the jury may have thought Hinckley was insane, if they were not convinced beyond a reasonable doubt that he was, then they had to acquit. That is what happened. They thought he was insane but had their doubts, so they acquitted.

The result was not only criticism but also swift legislative action. In the Comprehensive Crime Control Act of 1984, the burden of proof was shifted from the government proving sanity beyond a reasonable doubt to defendants having to prove they were insane by clear and convincing evidence.[51]

The Model Penal Code rejects this standard, and so do most states. The Model Penal Code adopts the standard of affirmative defenses. Sanity and responsibility are presumed unless the defense offers some evidence to show that defendants are insane. Once the sanity presumption is overcome by some evidence, then under the Model Penal Code provision, prosecutors must prove the defendants sane beyond a reasonable doubt. Prosecutors need not prove sanity, however, unless defendants raise the issue. Insanity is also an affirmative defense under the new federal rule.

Some jurisdictions require proof beyond a reasonable doubt. Others accept proof by a preponderance of the evidence. There is a trend in favor of shifting the burden to defendants and making that burden heavier. This is both because Hinckley's trial generated antagonism toward the insanity defense and owing to growing hostility toward rules that the public believes coddle criminals.[52]

The insanity defense has only one purpose in criminal law. No matter how advanced psychiatry becomes, no matter who must prove it and by how much, the insanity defense is primarily a legal, not a medical question: Has a mental disease or defect, however defined, sufficiently altered defendants' mental states to excuse their crimes? The United States Supreme Court grappled with several of these complex problems in *Jones v. United States.*

CASE

Was the Commitment Unconstitutional?

Jones v. United States
103 S.Ct. 3043 (1983)

Justice Powell delivered the opinion of the Court.

The question presented is whether petitioner, who was committed to a mental hospital

upon being acquitted of a criminal offense by reason of insanity, must be released because he has been hospitalized for a period longer than he might have served in prison had he been convicted.

In the District of Columbia a criminal defendant may be acquitted by reason of insanity if his insanity is "affirmatively established by a preponderance of the evidence." D.C.Code § 24–301(j) (1981). If he successfully invokes the insanity defense, he is committed to a mental hospital. § 24–301(d)(1). The statute provides several ways of obtaining release. Within 50 days of commitment the acquittee is entitled to a judicial hearing to determine his eligibility for release, which he has the burden of proving by a preponderance of the evidence that he is no longer mentally ill or dangerous. § 24–301(d)(2). If he fails to meet this burden at the 50-day hearing, the committed acquittee subsequently may be released, with court approval, upon certification of his recovery by the hospital chief of service. § 24–301(e). Alternatively, the acquittee is entitled to a judicial hearing every six months at which he may establish by a preponderance of the evidence that he is entitled to release. § 24–301(k).

Independent of its provision for the commitment of insanity acquittees, the District of Columbia also has adopted a civil-commitment procedure, under which an individual may be committed upon clear and convincing proof by the Government that he is mentally ill and likely to injure himself or others. § 21–545(b). The individual may demand a jury in the civil-commitment proceeding. § 21–544. Once committed, a patient may be released at any time upon certification of recovery by the hospital chief of service. §§ 21–546, 21–548. Alternatively, the patient is entitled after the first 90 days, and subsequently at 6-month intervals, to request a judicial hearing at which he may gain his release by proving by a preponderance of the evidence that he is no longer mentally ill or dangerous. §§ 21–546, 21–547; see Dixon v. Jacobs, 138 U.S.App.D.C. 319, 328, 427 F.2d 589, 598 (1970).

FACTS

On September 19, 1975, petitioner was arrested for attempting to steal a jacket from a department store. The next day he was arraigned in the District of Columbia Superior Court on a charge of attempted petit larceny, a misdemeanor punishable by a maximum prison sentence of one year. §§ 22–103, 22–2202. The court ordered petitioner committed to St. Elizabeths, a public hospital for the mentally ill, for a determination of his competency to stand trial. [§ 24–301(a) authorizes the court to "order

the accused committed to the District of Columbia General Hospital or other mental hospital designated by the court, for such reasonable period as the court may determine for examination and observation and for care and treatment if such is necessary by the psychiatric staff of said hospital."]

On March 2, 1976, a hospital psychologist submitted a report to the court stating that petitioner was competent to stand trial, that petitioner suffered from "Schizophrenia, paranoid type," and that petitioner's alleged offense was "the product of his mental disease." The court ruled that petitioner was competent to stand trial. Petitioner subsequently decided to plead not guilty by reason of insanity. The Government did not contest the plea, and it entered into a stipulation of facts with petitioner. On March 12, 1976, the Superior Court found petitioner not guilty by reason of insanity and committed him to St. Elizabeths pursuant to § 24–301(d)(1).

On May 25, 1976, the court held the 50-day hearing required by § 24–301(d)(2)(A). A psychologist from St. Elizabeths testified on behalf of the Government that, in the opinion of the staff, petitioner continued to suffer from paranoid schizophrenia and that "because his illness is still quite active, he is still a danger to himself and to others." Petitioner's counsel conducted a brief cross-examination, and presented no evidence. [COURT'S NOTE: "Petitioner's counsel seemed concerned primarily about obtaining a transfer for petitioner to a less restrictive wing of the hospital."]

The court then found that "the defendant-patient is mentally ill and as a result of his mental illness, at this time, he constitutes a danger to himself or others." Petitioner was returned to St. Elizabeths. Petitioner obtained new counsel and, following some procedural confusion, a second release hearing was held on February 22, 1977.

By that date petitioner had been hospitalized for more than one year, the maximum period he could have spent in prison if he had been convicted. On that basis he demanded that he be released unconditionally or recommitted pursuant to the civil-commitment standards in § 21–545(b), including a jury trial and proof by clear and convincing evidence of his mental illness and dangerousness. The Superior Court denied petitioner's request for a civil-commitment hearing, reaffirmed the findings made at the May 25, 1976, hearing, and continued petitioner's commitment to St. Elizabeths. [COURT'S NOTE: "A subsequent motion for unconditional release under § 301(k) was denied in March of 1977. Three months later, however, [petitioner] was granted conditional release on terms recommended by St. Elizabeths' staff, allowing daytime and overnight visits into the community. He was also admitted into the civil division of the hospital, though as a result of disruptive behavior, he was retransferred to the forensic division."]

Petitioner appealed to the District of Columbia Court of Appeals. A panel of the court affirmed the Superior Court, 396 A.2d 183 (1978), but then granted rehearing and reversed, 411 A.2d 624 (1980). Finally, the court heard the case en banc and affirmed the judgment of the Superior Court. 432 A.2d 364 (1981). The Court of Appeals rejected the argument "that the length of the prison sentence [petitioner] might have received determines when he is entitled to release or civil commitment under Title 24 of the D.C.Code." It then held that the various statutory differences between civil commitment and commitment of insanity acquittees were justified under the equal protection component of the Fifth Amendment. [We granted certiorari, and now affirm.]

OPINION

... We turn first to the question whether the finding of insanity at the criminal trial is sufficiently probative of mental illness and dangerousness to justify commitment. A verdict of not guilty by reason of insanity establishes two facts: (i) the defendant committed an act that constitutes a criminal offense, and (ii) he committed the act because of mental illness. Congress has

determined that these findings constitute an adequate basis for hospitalizing the acquittee as a dangerous and mentally ill person. See H.R.Rep. No. 91–907, supra, at 74 (expressing fear that "dangerous criminals, particularly psychopaths, [may] win acquittals of serious criminal charges on grounds of insanity" and yet "escape hospital commitment"); S.Rep. No. 1170, 84th Cong., 1st Sess. 13 (1955) ("Where [the] accused has pleaded insanity as a defense to a crime, and the jury has found that the defendant was, in fact, insane at the time the crime was committed, it is just and reasonable in the Committee's opinion that the insanity, once established, should be presumed to continue and that the accused should automatically be confined for treatment until it can be shown that he has recovered"). We cannot say that it was unreasonable and therefore unconstitutional for Congress to make this determination.

The fact that a person has been found, beyond a reasonable doubt, to have committed a criminal act certainly indicates dangerousness. Indeed, this concrete evidence generally may be at least as persuasive as any predictions about dangerousness that might be made in a civil-commitment proceeding. We do not agree with petitioner's suggestion that the requisite dangerousness is not established by proof that a person committed a non-violent crime against property.

This Court never has held that "violence," however that term might be defined, is a prerequisite for a constitutional commitment. [COURT NOTE: "See *Overholser v. O'Beirne,* 112 App.D.C. 267, 302 F.2d 852, 861 (1961) ([T]o describe the theft of watches and jewelry as 'non-dangerous' is to confuse danger with violence. Larceny is usually less violent than murder or assault, but in terms of public policy the purpose of the statute is the same as to both.)

It also may be noted that crimes of theft frequently may result in violence from the efforts of the criminal to escape or the victim to protect property or the police to apprehend the fleeing criminal. The relative 'dangerousness' of a particular individual, of course, should be a consideration at the release hearings."] ...

Nor can we say that it was unreasonable for Congress to determine that the insanity acquittal supports an inference of continuing mental illness. It comports with common sense to conclude that someone whose mental illness was sufficient to lead him to commit a criminal act is likely to remain ill and in need of treatment....

Petitioner next contends that his indefinite commitment is unconstitutional because the proof of his insanity was based only on a preponderance of the evidence, as compared to Addington's civil-commitment requirement of proof by clear and convincing evidence. In equating these situations, petitioner ignores important differences between the class of potential civil-commitment candidates and the class of insanity acquittees that justify differing standards of proof. The Addington Court expressed particular concern that members of the public could be confined on the basis of "some abnormal behavior which might be perceived by some as symptomatic of a mental or emotional disorder, but which is in fact within a range of conduct that is generally acceptable." 441 U.S., at 426–427, 99 S.Ct., at 1809–1810. See also *O'Connor v. Donaldson,* 422 U.S., at 575, 95 S.Ct., at 2493. In view of this concern, the Court deemed it inappropriate to ask the individual "to share equally with society the risk of error."

But since automatic commitment under § 24–301(d)(1) follows only if the acquittee himself advances insanity as a defense and proves that his criminal act was a product of his mental illness, there is good reason for diminished concern as to the risk of error. More important, the proof that he committed a criminal act as a result of mental illness eliminates the risk that he is being committed for mere "idiosyncratic behavior," *Addington,* 441 U.S., at 427, 99 S.Ct., at 1810. A criminal act by definition is not "within a range of conduct that is generally acceptable."

We therefore conclude that concerns critical to our decision in Addington are diminished or absent in the case of insanity acquittees. Accordingly, there is no reason for adopting the same standard of proof in both cases. "[D]ue process is flexible and calls for such procedural protections as the particular situation demands." The preponderance of the evidence standard comports with due process for commitment of insanity acquittees.

The remaining question is whether petitioner nonetheless is entitled to his release because he has been hospitalized for a period longer than he could have been incarcerated if convicted. The Due Process Clause "requires that the nature and duration of commitment bear some reasonable relation to the purpose for which the individual is committed." The purpose of commitment following an insanity acquittal, like that of civil commitment, is to treat the individual's mental illness and protect him and society from his potential dangerousness. The committed acquittee is entitled to release when he has recovered his sanity or is no longer dangerous. And because it is impossible to predict how long it will take for any given individual to recover—or indeed whether he ever will recover—Congress has chosen, as it has with respect to civil commitment, to leave the length of commitment indeterminate, subject to periodic review of the patient's suitability for release.

In light of the congressional purposes underlying commitment of insanity acquittees, we think petitioner clearly errs in contending that an acquittee's hypothetical maximum sentence provides the constitutional limit for his commitment. A particular sentence of incarceration is chosen to reflect society's view of the proper response to commission of a particular criminal offense, based on a variety of considerations such as retribution, deterrence, and rehabilitation. The State may punish a person convicted of a crime even if satisfied that he is unlikely to commit further crimes. Different considerations underlie commitment of an insanity acquittee. As he was not convicted, he may not be punished. His confinement rests on his continuing illness and dangerousness. Thus, under the District of Columbia statute, no matter how serious the act committed by the acquittee, he may be released within 50 days of his acquittal if he has recovered. In contrast, one who committed a less serious act may be confined for a longer period if he remains ill and dangerous....

We hold that when a criminal defendant establishes by a preponderance of the evidence that he is not guilty of a crime by reason of insanity, the Constitution permits the Government, on the basis of the insanity judgment, to confine him to a mental institution until such time as he has regained his sanity or is no longer a danger to himself or society. This holding accords with the widely and reasonably held view that insanity acquittees constitute a special class that should be treated differently from other candidates for commitment.

[COURT'S NOTE: "A recent survey of commitment statutes reported that 14 jurisdictions provide automatic commitment for at least some insanity acquittees, while many other States have a variety of special methods of committing insanity acquittees. Nineteen States commit insanity acquittees under the same procedures used for civil commitment. It appears that only one State has enacted into law petitioner's suggested requirement that a committed insanity acquittee be released following expiration of his hypothetical maximum criminal sentence."]

We have observed before that "[w]hen Congress undertakes to act in areas fraught with medical and scientific uncertainties, legislative options must be especially broad and courts should be cautious not to rewrite legislation.... This admonition has particular force in the context of legislative efforts to deal with the special problems raised by the insanity defense. The judgment of the District of Columbia Court of Appeals is Affirmed.

DISSENT

Justice Brennan, with whom Justice Marshall and Justice Blackmun join, dissenting.

... [Determining the standards for com-

treating those who may be mentally ill and dangerous; the difficulty of proving or disproving mental illness and dangerousness in court; and the massive intrusion on individual liberty that involuntary psychiatric hospitalization entails....

A "not guilty by reason of insanity" verdict is backward-looking, focusing on one moment in the past, while commitment requires a judgment as to the present and future. In some jurisdictions, most notably in federal criminal trials, an acquittal by reason of insanity may mean only that a jury found a reasonable doubt as to a defendant's sanity and as to the casual relationship between his mental condition and his crime. As we recognized in *Addington,* "the subtleties and nuances of psychiatric diagnosis render certainties virtually beyond reach in most situations." The question is not whether "government may not act in the face of this uncertainty;" everyone would agree that it can. Rather, the question is whether—in light of the uncertainty about the relationship between petitioner's crime, his present dangerousness, and his present mental condition—the Government can force him for the rest of his life "to share equally with society the risk of error."

Is is worth examining what is known about the possibility of predicting dangerousness from any set of facts. Although a substantial body of research suggests that a consistent pattern of violent behavior may, from a purely statistical standpoint, indicate a certain likelihood of further violence in the future, mere statistical validity is far from perfect for purposes of predicting which individuals will be dangerous. Commentators and researchers have long acknowledged that even the best attempts to identify dangerous individuals on the basis of specified facts have been inaccurate roughly two-thirds of the time, almost always on the side of over-prediction. On a clinical basis, mental health professionals can diagnose past or present mental condition with some confidence, but strong institutional

especially when the consequence of a finding of dangerousness is that an obviously mentally ill patient will remain within their control.

Research is practically nonexistent on the relationship of non-violent criminal behavior, such as petitioner's attempt to shoplift, to future dangerousness. We do not even know whether it is even statistically valid as a predictor of similar non-violent behavior, much less of behavior posing more serious risks to self and others.

Even if an insanity acquittee remains mentally ill, so long as he has not repeated the same act since his offense the passage of time diminishes the likelihood that he will repeat it. Furthermore, the frequency of prior violent behavior is an important element in any attempt to predict future violence. Finally, it cannot be gainsaid that some crimes are more indicative of dangerousness than others.... [A] State may consider non-violent misdemeanors "dangerous," but there is room for doubt whether a single attempt to shoplift and a sting of brutal murders are equally accurate and equally permanent predictors of dangerousness. As for mental illness, certainly some conditions that satisfy the "mental disease" element of the insanity defense do not persist for an extended period—thus the traditional inclusion of "temporary insanity" within the insanity defense....

Justice Stevens, dissenting.

The character of the conduct that causes a person to be incarcerated in an institution is relevant to the length of his permissible detention. In my opinion, a plea of not guilty by reason of insanity, like a plea of guilty, may provide a sufficient basis for confinement for the period fixed by the legislature as punishment for the acknowledged conduct, provided of course that the acquittee is given a fair opportunity to prove that he has recovered from his illness. But surely if he is to be confined for a longer period, the State must shoulder the burden of proving by clear and convincing evidence that such additional confinement is appropriate. As Justice Brennan demonstrates, that result is dictated by our prior cases. What Justice Powell has written lends support to the view that the initial confinement of the acquittee is permissible, but provides no support for the conclusion that he has the burden of proving his entitlement to freedom after he has served the maximum sentence authorized by law. I respectfully dissent because I believe this shoplifter was presumptively entitled to his freedom after he had been incarcerated for a period of one year.

Case Discussion Who should have to prove insanity, the prosecution or the defense? How high should the burden of persuasion be? Proof beyond a reasonable doubt? A preponderance of the evidence? Clear and convincing evidence? Should Jones have to stay in the hospital after the term that he would have served in prison? Why? For how long? Is he dangerous? Do you agree with Judge Burger's explanation of why Jones was dangerous?

▼ DIMINISHED CAPACITY

Some defendants suffer from mental diseases or defects that do not affect their mental capacity sufficiently to make them insane. They may still have a defense, if the mental disease or defect impairs their capacity to form *mens rea*. Theoretically, this defense ought to apply to all crimes requiring *mens rea*, if impaired mental capacity raises a reasonable doubt about *mens rea*. In practice, however, jurisdictions severely restrict the use of **diminished capacity**.

Some jurisdictions prohibit all evidence of mental impairment short of insanity; defendants are either sane or insane. California, in the wake of hostility to mental impairment excuses, recently enacted the following provision to replace its diminished capacity provision:

> The defense of diminished capacity is hereby abolished. In a criminal action ... evidence concerning an accused person's intoxication, mental illness, disease, or defect shall not be admissible to show or negate capacity to form the particular purpose, intent, motive, malice aforethought, knowledge, or other mental state required for the commission of the crime charged.... Notwithstanding the foregoing, evidence of diminished capacity or of a mental disorder may be considered by the court at the time of sentencing or other disposition or commitment.[53]

At the other extreme, the Model Penal Code provision admits evidence of impaired mental capacity to negative the *mens rea* in all crimes. For example, if some mental disease or defect not sufficient to constitute insanity causes a defendant to believe property she took belonged to her, the belief caused by the impairment would negative the specific intent to take "another's property" that larceny *mens rea* requires.

The few jurisdictions that permit evidence of diminished capacity take a middle ground. They restrict its use to crimes of more than one degree that require specific intent, almost always murder. A defendant in these jurisdictions can introduce evidence that a mental disease or defect negatives the capacity to form the specific intent to premeditate a homicide, but not the general intent to kill. Hence, the defendant could not commit first-degree murder requiring premeditation, but could commit second-degree murder requiring the general intent to kill. Some states go further, permitting mental impairment to reduce murder to manslaughter if a mental disease or defect generated the required heat of passion in manslaughter[54] (see chapter 8 on homicide).

CASE

Does Diminished Capacity Constitute a Defense?

State v. Gallegos
628 P.2d 999 (Colo. 1981)

[Gallegos was convicted of second-degree murder. He appealed.]
   Quinn, Justice

FACTS

The defendant, Leroy Joe Gallegos, was charged with murder in the first degree after deliberation. The charge arose out of the shooting death of the defendant's wife on December 19, 1977. The prosecution's evidence established that the defendant and his wife were living apart and on the night of the homicide he visited her about a possible reconciliation. After a prolonged argument during which she accused him of incompetence and sexual inadequacy he shot her five times with a pistol.

The defense presented opinion evidence from two psychiatrists and a psychologist that the defendant was afflicted with minimal brain dysfunction and an associated explosive personality disorder with paranoid features. Minimal brain dysfunction was described as a biochemical imbalance in the brain that prevents a person from maintaining control over his bodily functions and emotional impulses, especially in situations of stress. The expert witnesses expressed the opinion that the defendant's condition rendered him incapable of forming the specific intent to kill at the time of the shooting of his wife. The defendant offered no testimony specifically addressing his capacity to act "knowingly" at the time of the homicide, although some of the expert testimony described the shooting as beyond the defendant's control. The trial court submitted the case to the jury on the charge of first-degree murder after deliberation and on the lesser offenses of murder in the second degree and manslaughter upon sudden heat of passion. The jury was instructed that the requisite culpability for first-degree murder and manslaughter was the specific intent to cause the death of another, and that the culpable mental state for second-degree murder was knowingly causing the death of another. The instructions on the affirmative defense of impaired mental condition were as follows:

Instruction No. 13

The evidence presented in this case has raised the issue of the affirmative defense of impaired mental condition. The prosecution, therefore, has the burden of proving to your satisfaction beyond a reasonable doubt the guilt of the defendant as to that issue as well as all of the elements of the crime charged. If, after consideration of the evidence concerning the affirmative defense, along with all the other evidence, you are not convinced beyond a reasonable doubt of the guilt of the defendant then you must return a verdict of not guilty.

Instruction No. 14

It is an affirmative defense to the crime of murder in the first degree and manslaughter that the defendant, due to an impaired mental condition, did not have the capacity to form the specific intent required by the offense.

OPINION

Under the Colorado Criminal Code issues relating to lack of responsibility are affirmative defenses. One may be relieved of criminal responsibility on the grounds of insufficient age, insanity, impaired mental condition, or intoxication.

The statutory categorization of a matter as an affirmative defense has consequences for the prosecution's burden of proof. Under the Colorado Criminal Code once the issue of an affirmative defense is raised, the prosecution must prove the guilt of the defendant beyond a reasonable doubt as to that issue as well as all other elements of the offense.

Second-degree murder is defined as causing "the death of a person knowingly." By statute, offenses with the culpability requirement of "knowingly" are deemed to be general, rather than specific, intent crimes. § 18–3–102(2), C.R.S. 1973 (1978 Repl. Vol. 8) states that "[d]iminished responsibility due to lack of mental capacity is not a defense to murder in the second degree." A diminished responsibility attributable to a lack of mental capacity is the statutory equivalent of the affirmative defense of impaired mental condition in § 18–1–803, C.R.S.1973 (1978 Repl. Vol. 8), which provides:

Evidence of an impaired mental condition though not legal insanity may be offered in a proper case as bearing upon the capacity of the accused to form the specific intent if such an intent is an element of the offense charged.

Thus, § 18–3–103(2) merely makes explicit with respect to second-degree murder what already is implicit in § 18–1–803: the affirmative defense of diminished responsibility due to impaired mental condition is not an affirmative defense to the general intent crime of second-degree murder.

The record before us establishes that the defendant's psychiatric and psychological experts testified without restriction to the defendant's mental status. Each witness expressed the opinion that at the time of the shooting the defendant was incapable not only of forming an intent to kill but also of exercising any control over his actions. One psychiatrist described the shooting as "an act based on a chemical brain disorder" rather than "a wilful, voluntary act." When this opinion evidence was admitted, the trial court did not caution the jury to consider it in relation to the specific intent crimes of first-degree murder and manslaughter only. One must conclude, therefore, that it was admitted and consid- ered as to all offenses, including second-degree murder.

Jury's guilty verdict reinstated.

Case Discussion   Should Gallegos's brain dysfunction and the chemical imbalance resulting from it reduce his liability? If so, is it right to reduce the sentence to only second-degree murder? Do you agree that it is possible to intend something, but not as much, when you are somewhat incapacitated? Or do you believe the rule should be that either you intended to kill or you did not? In other words, do you believe that "sort of" intending something is not possible? The difficulty in applying the rule and the objections raised to deciding who is "sort of" responsible have led California to abolish its diminished capacity defense.

▼ **SYNDROMES**

Recently, a range of "syndromes" affecting mental states have led to novel defenses in criminal law. The most bizarre of these include the policeman's, love fear, chronic brain, and holocaust syndromes.

When former San Francisco city official Dan White was tried for killing fellow official Harvey Milk and Mayor George Moscone, the defense introduced the junk food syndrome, popularly called the Twinkie defense. White's lawyer argued that junk food diminished White's mental faculties. One psychiatrist testified as follows concerning White's frequent depressions:

> During these spells he'd become quite withdrawn, quite lethargic. He would retreat to his room. Wouldn't come to the door. Wouldn't answer the phone. And during these periods he found that he could not cope with people. Any confrontations would cause him to kind of become argumentative. Whenever he felt things were not going right he would abandon his usual program of exercise and good nutrition and start gorging himself on junk foods. Twinkies, Coca Cola.
>
> Mr. White had always been something of an athlete, priding himself on being physically fit. But when something would go wrong he'd hit the high sugar stuff. He'd hit the chocolate and the more he consumed the worse he'd feel, and he'd respond to his ever-growing depression by consuming even more junk food. The more junk food he consumed, the worse he'd feel. The worse he'd feel, the more he'd gorge himself.

The defense argued that these depressions, which junk food aggravated, sufficiently diminished White's capacity to reduce his responsibility. The jury returned a verdict of manslaughter, and White was sentenced to a relatively short prison term. Recently, he was released from prison and committed suicide. No one has ventured to blame his suicide on junk food.

During the White case, much public comment—most of it negative—was directed at the Twinkie defense. Despite that derision, substantial evidence exists to suggest that white sugar does indeed diminish capacity.

Whether or not it does so to sufficiently reduce responsibility is a highly controversial and far-from-settled question.[55]

Three additional syndromes suggest more widespread and serious use to excuse criminal conduct. The battered spouse syndrome has appeared in self-defense (see chapter 6). The premenstrual syndrome and posttraumatic stress syndrome are discussed here.

A New York case raised the possibility that premenstrual stress (PMS) syndrome excuses criminal liability. Shirley Santos called the police, telling them, "My little girl is sick." The medical team in the hospital emergency room diagnosed the welts on the girl's legs and blood in her urine as the results of child abuse. The police arrested Santos, who explained, "I don't remember what happened…. I would never hurt my baby … I just got my period." At a preliminary hearing, Santos asserted PMS as a complete defense to assault and endangering the welfare of a child, both felonies. She admitted beating her child but argued that she had blacked out owing to PMS, hence could not have formed the intent to assault or endanger her child's welfare. After lengthy plea bargaining, the prosecutor dropped the felony charges and Santos pleaded guilty to the misdemeanor of harassment. Santos received no sentence, not even probation or a fine, even though her daughter spent two weeks in the hospital from the injuries. The plea bargaining prevented a legal test of the PMS defense in this case. Nevertheless, the judge's leniency suggests that PMS affected the outcome informally.

Three difficulties stand in the way of proving the PMS defense: (1) Defendants must prove that PMS is a disease; little medical research exists to demonstrate that it is. (2) The defendant must suffer from PMS; rarely do medical records document the disease. (3) The PMS must cause the mental impairment that excuses the conduct; too much skepticism still surrounds PMS to expect ready acceptance that it excuses criminal conduct.[56]

The years since the Vietnam War have revealed that combat soldiers suffered more lasting and serious casualties than physical injury. The war took a heavy emotional and mental toll on the veterans. The effects have created what some call a "mental health crisis which has had a dramatic impact on the incidence of major crime." Medical research has established a complex relationship between the stress of the combat tour in guerilla type, as opposed to conventional, warfare and later antisocial conduct. At the same time, lawyers have begun to consider the effect the Vietnam Vet syndrome has on criminal responsibility.

CASE

Did Vietnam Vet Syndrome Excuse His Crime?[57]

A man had been charged with assaulting a group of police officers who had been sum-

moned to investigate a call that a man (the defendant) was wandering about in a park late at night. The police reports indicated that when the officers arrived in the park they could hear someone thrashing about in the wooded area. While attempting to follow the sounds they were suddenly confronted by the defendant who was carrying a large log as if it were a rifle. The officers reported that the man did not respond to their orders and seemed to be in a drunken and incoherent rage. The man charged toward the officers, wounded two of them, and was finally subdued and arrested.

A series of discussions with the defendant revealed that he was a Vietnam combat veteran who had a post-military history of job-related difficulties and marital discord. His wife related that he had begun within the last few years to suffer from periods of depression which were usually punctuated by episodes of excessive drinking, explosive violence, and recurrent nightmares. He had apparently been in the midst of such a period on the date of the incident and had spent a few hours drinking in a bar just prior to stopping in the park on his way home. When asked why he had stopped in the park, he responded that he was unsure but thought that he had needed some fresh air to "clear his head." He professed to have no recollection of the attack on the police and attributed it to his drunken condition.

The extensive medical investigation disclosed that the defendant was, at the time of the incident, engulfed in a delusional flashback in which he genuinely believed he was once again in the jungles of Vietnam and perceived the police officers to be enemy soldiers who were experiencing an incident in which his patrol had been ambushed and a friend killed. As a result of this information, the medical experts were able to testify that although it was clear that he "knew the nature and quality of his acts" in the sense that he knew he was attacking someone, it was equally clear that he "did not know that those acts were wrong" since, in his mind, he was not attacking police officers but was attacking enemy soldiers. The defendant was accordingly found to be not guilty by reason of insanity. [The defendant was hospitalized shortly after his arrest for two months, then was released but continued out-patient therapy until the trial.] On the basis of his response to this treatment, the court ... conclude[d] that the defendant no longer constituted a danger and could therefore be placed on probation, with a condition that he continue his therapy.

Case Discussion   Would you recommend that your state allow the Vietnam Vet defense? Why? If you did allow the defense, should this vet fall under it? Is he too dangerous to be free? Do you think probation with treatment properly serves the aims of the criminal law? Why? Why not? What disposition in this case do you recommend?

▼ Summary ▼

The general defenses to criminal liability rest on two rationales. In justification, defendants admit responsibility but maintain that under the circumstances they did the right thing. Self-defense is the primary justification, but a general defense called necessity also exists in most jurisdictions. In excuse, defendants admit they did the wrong thing but deny responsibility under the circumstances. The main excuses are duress, intoxication, mistake, age, entrapment, insanity, diminished capacity, and syndromes. The line between justification is not clearly drawn, and some defenses fall outside the principles altogether, such as entrapment based on the objective theory of controlling government misconduct.

Whatever their theoretical underpinning, most defenses have the same practical effect—acquittal. But not always. Defenses can also work to reduce the degree of an offense or to reduce the offense to a lesser, related offense. In some cases, defenses offer an opportunity to lighten a penalty attached to a particular crime because of mitigating circumstances. Finally, the insanity defense can lead to confinement in a mental hospital rather than incarceration. Whatever their specific consequences, the general defenses to criminal liability are based on the idea that the special circumstances of necessity, human frailty, and human imperfection ought to lessen the harshness of the criminal law. In this sense, the defenses are companions to the general principles of criminal liability outlined in chapter 3. The principles of liability, justification, and excuse work together to ensure that criminal law works fairly and according to well-defined principles, so that the state does not punish persons if circumstances surrounding otherwise criminal conduct justify or excuse that conduct.

▼ *Questions for Review and Discussion* ▼

1. What are the main elements in duress? The main problems? How would you define duress? Explain why.

2. Should superior orders ever be a defense to crime? Should brainwashing? Duress? Why or why not?

3. Why does the law distinguish between voluntary and involuntary intoxication? Under what circumstances, if any, should intoxication be a defense to crime?

4. When, if ever, should age be an excuse for criminal liability?

5. Explain the two theories of entrapment. Which is not based on excuse? What is a proper limit to the defense of entrapment?

6. Define the major tests of insanity. Which one do you favor? Would you abolish the insanity defense? Why?

7. What are the major levels of proof required to prove insanity? Who should have the burden of proof in insanity? Explain.

8. If you were writing a criminal code, would you include a partial defense called diminished capacity? If so, how would you justify such a defense? If you would not permit it, what reasons would you give for denying it?

▼ *Suggested Readings* ▼

1. Telford Taylor, *Nuremberg and Vietnam: An American Tragedy* (New York: Quadrangle, 1970). Discusses the superior orders defense as Taylor tells the stories of the Nuremberg trials and the Calley case. This is an interesting book, written for the general public.

2. David G. Bromley and James T. Richardson, *The Brainwashing/ Deprogramming Controversy: Sociological, Psychological, Legal, and*

Historical Perspectives (New York: Edwin Mellen Press, 1983). Discusses brainwashing from a multidisciplinary perspective, covering many topics relevant to the defense of brainwashing.

3. Peter Meyer, *The Yale Murder* (New York: Empire Books, 1982). A compelling narrative relating the "fatal romance" of Yale student Richard Herrin and Bonnie Garland. Meyer gives a detailed account of the trial, the insanity plea, the jury deliberations, and the verdict. This is an excellent journalistic account revealing much about the insanity plea and written for the general reader.

4. Joseph Livermore and Paul Meehl, "The Virtues of M'Naghten," *Minnesota Law Review* 51 (1967):800. A well argued, articulate defense of the right-wrong test. Although intended for specialists, it is well worth the novice's efforts.

5. Mike Weiss, *Double Play: The San Francisco City Hall Killings* (Reading, Mass.: Addison-Wesley, 1984). A detailed account of former San Francisco city supervisor Dan White's shooting of Mayor George Moscone and fellow supervisor Harvey Milk in San Francisco City Hall, and of the trial that followed. Weiss gives an excellent description of the diminished capacity defense, which came to be called the Twinkie defense because it was based on the argument that White's excessive use of junk food, particularly those containing white sugar, led to his erratic behavior.

▼ *Notes* ▼

1. Hyman Gross, *A Theory of Criminal Justice* (New York: Oxford University Press, 1978), p. 276.

2. William Blackstone, *Commentaries on the Laws of England* (New York: Garland Publishing, 1978), pt. IV, p. 30.

3. American Law Institute, *Model Penal Code and Commentaries,* vol. 1 (Philadelphia: American Law Institute, 1985), pt. I, pp. 368–80.

4. Jerome Hall, *General Principles of Criminal Law,* 2d ed. (Indianapolis: Bobbs-Merrill, 1960), pp. 437–44; Glanville Williams, *Criminal Law: The General Part,* 2d ed. rev. (London: Stevens and Sons, 1961), pp. 765–66; American Law Institute, *Model Penal Code and Commentaries,* vol. 1, pt. I, pp. 372–73.

5. American Law Institute, *Model Penal Code and Commentaries,* vol. 1, pt. I, pp. 380–81.

6. *Regina v. Hudson,* 2 All E.R. 244 (1971).

7. Hyman Gross, *Theory of Criminal Justice,* pp. 276–292; Wayne R. LaFave and Austin W. Scott, Jr., *Criminal Law* (St. Paul: West Publishing Co., 1972), pp. 434–439; George Fletcher, *Rethinking Criminal Law* (Boston: Little, Brown and Co., 1978), pp. 429–435.

8. American Law Institute, *Model Penal Code and Commentaries,* vol. 1, pt. I, 376.

9. P. R. tit. 33, 3098.

10. Fletcher, *Rethinking Criminal Law,* p. 846.

11. Blackstone, *Commentaries,* pt. IV, pp. 25–26.

12. *People v. Penman,* 271 Ill. 82, 110 N.E. 894 (1915).

13. Hall, *General Principles of Criminal Law,* p. 540.

14. Burrows v. State, 38 Ariz. 99, 297 P. 1029 (1931).

15. Podolsky, "The Chemical Brew of Criminal Behavior," *Journal of Criminal Law, Criminology, and Police Science* 45 (1955):676–77.

16. American Law Institute, *Model Penal Code and Commentaries,* vol. 1, pt. I, pp. 350–66, surveys most of these arguments.

17. State v. Hall, 214 N.W.2d 205 (Iowa 1974).

18. Powell v. Texas, 392 U.S. 514, 88 S.Ct. 2145, 20 L.Ed.2d 1254 (1968); American Law Institute, *Model Penal Code and Commentaries,* vol. 1, pt. I, p. 353; *Commonwealth v. Reiff,* 489 Pa. 12, 413 A.2d 672 (1980).

19. 392 U.S. 514, 88 S.Ct. 2145, 20 L.Ed.2d 1254 (1968).

20. 214 N.W.2d 205 (Iowa 1974).

21. Rollin M. Perkins and Ronald N. Boyce, *Criminal Law,* 3d ed. (Mineola, N.Y.: Foundation Press, 1982), p. 1030.

22. Oliver Wendell Holmes, Jr., *The Common Law* (Boston: Little, Brown, and Company, 1963), p. 41.

23. Brent v. State, 43 Ala. 297 (1869) (lottery); *Ostrosky v. State,* 704 P.2d 786 (Alaska App. 1985) (game laws); *Hopkins v. State,* 193 Md. 489, 69 A.2d 456 (1949) (sign).

24. American Law Institute, *Model Penal Code and Commentaries,* vol. 1, pt. I, pp. 273–79.

25. West's California Penal Code (St. Paul: West Publishing Company, 1988), p. 53.

26. People v. Munoz, 22 Misc.2d 1078, 200 N.Y.S.2d 957 (1960).

27. Taken from Fred Cohen, *Criminal Law Bulletin* 21 (1985):9.

28. Regina v. Kemp, 3 All E.R. 249 (1956).

29. "Feds Run into an Entrapment Backlash," *New York Times* (August 19, 1984), p. 2.

30. See American Law Institute, *Model Penal Code and Commentaries,* vol. 1, pt. I, pp. 406–20, for a full discussion of entrapment and its status in today's criminal law.

31. State v. Nilsen, 134 Ariz. 433, 657 P.2d 419 (1983) (defendant cannot deny guilt and plead entrapment); *Mathews v. United States,* U.S. 109 S.Ct. 162, 102 L.Ed.2d 132 (1988).

32. Sherman v. United States, 356 U.S. 369, 78 S.Ct. 819, 2 L.Ed.2d 848 (1958).

33. People v. Barraza, 23 Cal.3d 675, 153 Cal.Rptr. 459, 591 P.2d 947 (1979).

34. American Law Institute, *Model Penal Code and Commentaries,* vol. 1, pt. I, pp. 182–83.

35. Mich. Stat. Ann. § 28.1059(1).

36. 55 Comm. L.R. 182, 186–188 (1933).

37. M'Naghten's Case, 8 Eng.Rep. 718 (1843).

38. Herbert M. Fingarette, *The Meaning of Criminal Insanity* (Berkeley: University of California, 1972), contains a full treatment of the subject. A good introduction is Abraham S. Goldstein, "Insanity," in *Encyclopedia of Crime and Justice,* ed. Sanford Kadish (New York: Free Press, 1983), pp. 735–42; American Law Institute, *Model Penal Code and Commentaries,* vol. 1, pt. I, pp. 174–76.

39. People v. Schmidt, 110 N.E. 949 (1915).

40. 214 F.2d 862 (D.C.Cir.1954).

41. 18 U.S.C.A § 17 adopted the right-wrong test; *United States v. Brawner,* 471 F.2d 969 (D.C.Cir.1972) rejected the *Durham* rule for that circuit; adopted by Maine Rev.

Stat. Ann. tit. 15, § 102 (1964), superseded by Maine Rev. Stat. Ann. tit. 17–A, § 58 adopting the substantial capacity test.

42. Joseph Livermore and Paul Meehl, "The Virtues of M'Naghten," *Minnesota Law Review* 51 (1967):800.

43. LaFave and Scott, *Criminal Law,* p. 283.

44. 2 So. 854 (Ala.1877).

45. "A Needed Verdict: Guilty but Insane," *New York Times* (July 1, 1982), p. 29.

46. See Slovenko, "The Insanity Defense in the Wake of the Hinckley Trial," *Rutgers Law Journal* 14 (1983):373.

47. 18 U.S.C.A § 17.

48. Robert F. Schopp, "Returning to M'Naghten to Avoid Moral Mistakes: One Step Forward, or Two Steps Backward for the Insanity Defense?" *Arizona Law Review* 30 (1988):135.

49. Model Penal Code, § 4.01(1).

50. *Rex v. Arnold,* 16 Howell State Trials, pp. 695, 764–765 (Eng.1724), quoted in Perkins and Boyce, *Criminal Law,* p. 951.

51. *Federal Criminal Code and Rules* (St. Paul: West Publishing Co., 1988), § 17(b).

52. American Law Institute, *Model Penal Code and Commentaries,* vol. 2, pt. I, p. 226.

53. *California Penal Code,* § 25 (b); (c).

54. *People v. Colavecchio,* 11 A.D.2d 161, 202 N.Y.S.2d 119 (1960) (mental disease negatives the specific intent to take another's property).

55. Mike Weiss, *Double Play: The San Francisco City Hall Killings* (Reading, Mass.: Addison-Wesley, 1984), pp. 349–50.

56. "Not Guilty Because of PMS?" *Newsweek* (November 8, 1982), p. 111; "Premenstrual Syndrome: A Criminal Defense," *Notre Dame Law Review* 59 (1983), pp. 263–69.

57. "In Defense of the Defenders: The Vietnam Vet Syndrome," John R. Ford, *Criminal Law Bulletin* 19 (1983), pp. 434–43.

Chapter

Crimes Against Persons I: Criminal Homicide

▼ *Chapter Outline* ▼

I. Introduction
II. Criminal Homicide *Actus Reus*
   A. The Beginning of Life
   B. The End of Life
III. Causing Another's Death
IV. Criminal Homicide *Mens Rea*
V. Types and Degrees of Criminal Homicide
   A. First-Degree Murder
   B. Felony Murder
   C. Second-Degree Murder
   D. Corporate Murder
   E. Summary of Murder
   F. Manslaughter
      1. Voluntary Manslaughter
      2. Involuntary Manslaughter
   G. Negligent Homicide
VI. Summary

▼ *Chapter Main Points* ▼

1. The criminal homicide *actus reus* requires taking the life of another human being.

2. Determining when life begins and ends for the purposes of criminal homicide raises difficult policy and legal questions.

3. The law divides criminal homicide into several categories of murder and manslaughter, grading them according to *mens rea, actus reus,* and special circumstances.

4. The murder *mens rea* includes not only the intent to kill but also the intent to seriously injure, to commit certain felonies, and to resist lawful arrests.

5. Voluntary manslaughter is an intentional killing that takes human frailty into account when adequate provocation leads to killing in the sudden heat of passion, without adequate time for the passions to cool.

6. Involuntary manslaughter is reckless killing.

7. Vehicular homicide, a separate offense, requires gross negligence *mens rea* in most jurisdictions.

Chapter Key Terms

deliberate—Referring to an act committed with a cool, reflecting mind.

felony murder—A death occurring in the course of committing a serious felony other than homicide.

malice aforethought—The common-law murder *mens rea*.

misdemeanor-manslaughter rule—If death occurs during the

commission of a misdemeanor, the death is an involuntary manslaughter.

paramour rule—The principle that a husband discovering his wife in an adulterous act is adequate provocation.

premeditated—Planned in advance.

year and a day rule—No act occurring more than one year and one day before death is a cause of death.

▼ INTRODUCTION

Homicide—killing another human being—took three forms at common law: (1) justifiable homicides, such as self-defense and police use of deadly force; (2) excusable homicides, such as those caused by accident or insanity; and (3) criminal homicides, or all homicides that were neither justified nor excused—murder and manslaughter. Criminal homicides include an *actus reus* (some act that results in death) and a *mens rea* (purpose, knowledge, recklessness, or negligence), concurring to cause the harm of death. In other words, the elements of homicide require applying the general principles of criminal liability, as well as the excuses and justifications that eliminate or reduce that liability. Because the excuses are general to most crimes and the principal justification relating to homicide (self-defense) was discussed fully in chapter 6, they are not repeated here.

Criminal homicide *actus reus*—taking another's life—requires deciding the thorny moral questions of when life begins and ends, and whether particularly atrocious acts aggravate the offense. Criminal homicide refines *mens rea* to its highest point in criminal law; it encompasses purposeful, knowing, reckless, and negligent killings. Furthermore, premeditation and deliberation aggravate, and sudden heat of passion upon adequate provocation mitigates, purposeful killings. Capital murder takes into account a range of circumstances in addition to *mens rea* that can aggravate first-degree murder into a crime mandating either the death penalty or life imprisonment.[1]

Criminal homicides constitute the most serious, but by no means the only, crimes against persons. Other crimes against the person include criminal sexual conduct; a wide range of other attacks on the person, such as nonsexual assaults and batteries; and crimes against free movement, such as kidnapping and false imprisonment. These other crimes, which far outnumber criminal homicide, are discussed in chapter 9.

Elements of Criminal Homicide			
Actus Reus	*Mens Rea*	Causation	Result
killing another live human being	purposely, or knowingly, or recklessly, or negligently causing either death or serious bodily harm	acts set in motion that contribute sufficiently to death	death

▼ CRIMINAL HOMICIDE *ACTUS REUS*

The criminal homicide *actus reus* requires taking another's life. Defining life at its extremes creates major problems in the law of criminal homicide: When does life begin? When does it end? Increasingly, courts have interpreted, and legislatures are interpreting, the beginning of life to include fetuses. Some statutes say that life begins at conception; others include only "viable fetuses," such as those twenty-eight weeks past conception. Still other jurisdictions follow the common-law definition, "born alive."[2]

The Beginning of Life

Fetal death statutes have generated heated debate over whether abortion is criminal homicide. However, fetal death statutes and abortion differ fundamentally. Whatever personal values concern abortion, the procedure involves terminating pregnancies *with* the mother's consent. Fetal death statutes address killing fetuses *without* the mother's consent outside normal medical means. Many who oppose making abortion murder support fetal death statutes directed toward third persons who, without the mothers' consent, injure or kill fetuses. Furthermore, after *Roe v. Wade,* in which the Supreme Court upheld mothers' right to terminate pregnancies under some conditions, equating abortion with criminal homicide violated the constitution.[3]

In Minnesota, two groups in the legislature vied to enact different statutes. One group hoped to make fetal death equivalent to homicide. Another, trying to separate fetal death from abortion, drafted a bill to punish people who injure or kill fetuses while committing other crimes. The impetus for passing this version stemmed from two types of cases: when perpetrators injure or kill fetuses in the course of either (1) assaulting pregnant women or (2) killing or injuring pregnant women in automobile crashes. In the end, Minnesota opted for the following definition: "the unborn offspring of a human being conceived but not yet born," except in the case of legal abortions.

Defining the beginning of life is neither a medical nor a legal problem. Such a definition relies more on religious, moral, and ethical values than on technical legal rules and medical science. Public policy requires that legislators determine when life in its earliest—and latest—stages is sufficiently valuable that taking it constitutes criminal homicide. No amount of medical knowledge or skill in the techniques of law can answer these questions. One art student captured the dilemma in a poster. Under a drawing of a just-fertilized egg in a happy, laughing fourteen-year-old girl is a caption that reads: "Which life is worth more?" The Minnesota statute did not resolve this dilemma, as its opinion and dissents make clear in *State v. Merrill*.[4]

CASE

Did He Kill an "Unborn Child"?

State v. Merrill
450 N.W.2d 318 (Minn.1990).

Heard, considered, and decided by the court en banc.
Simonett, Justice
  Defendant has been indicted for first- and second-degree murder of Gail Anderson and also for first- and second-degree murder of her "unborn child." The trial court denied defendant's motion to dismiss the charges....

FACTS
On November 13, 1988, Gail Anderson died from gunshot wounds allegedly inflicted by the defendant. An autopsy revealed Ms. Anderson was pregnant with a 27- or 28-day-old embryo. The coroner's office concluded that there was no abnormality which would have caused a miscarriage, and that death of the embryo resulted from the death of Ms. Anderson. At this stage of development, a 28-day-old embryo is 4- to 5-millimeters long and, through the umbilical cord, completely dependent on its mother. The Anderson embryo was not viable. Up to the eighth week of development, it appears that an "unborn child" is referred to as an embryo; thereafter it is called a fetus. The evidence indicates that medical science generally considers a fetus viable at 28 weeks following conception although some fetuses as young as 20 or 21 weeks have survived.

The record is unclear in this case whether either Ms. Anderson or defendant Merrill knew she was pregnant at the time she was assaulted. Defendant was indicted for the death of Anderson's "unborn child" under two statutes entitled, respectively, "Murder of an Unborn Child in the First Degree" and "Murder of an Unborn Child in the Second Degree."

These two statutes, enacted by the legislature in 1986, follow precisely the language of our murder statutes, except that "unborn child" is substituted for "human being" and "person." The term "unborn child" is defined as "the unborn offspring of a human being conceived, but not yet born." Minn.Stat. § 609.266(a) (1988).

[COURT NOTE: "Minn.Stat. § 609.2661 (1988), provides in part: Whoever does any of the following is guilty of murder of an unborn child in the first degree and must be sentenced to imprisonment for life: (1) causes the death of an unborn child with premeditation and with intent to effect the death of the unborn child or of another;...

Minn.Stat. § 609.2662 (1988), provides in part: Whoever does either of the following is guilty of murder of an unborn child in the second degree and may be sentenced to imprisonment for not more than 40 years: (1) causes the death of an unborn child with intent to effect the death of that unborn child or another, but without premeditation;..."]

OPINION
This legislative approach to a fetal homicide statute is most unusual and raises the constitutional questions certified to us. Of the 17 states that have codified a crime of murder of an unborn, 13 create criminal liability only if the fetus is "viable" or "quick." Additionally, two noncode states have

expanded their definition of common law homicide to include viable fetuses [Massachusetts and South Carolina]. Arizona and Indiana impose criminal liability for causing the death of a fetus at any stage, as does Minnesota, but the statutory penalty provided upon conviction is far less severe. Ariz.Rev.Stat.Ann. § 13–1103(A)(5) (1989) (5-year sentence); Ind.Code Ann. § 35–42–1–6 (Burns 1985) (2-year sentence).

Before discussing the Minnesota statutes, three preliminary observations must be made. First, to challenge successfully the constitutional validity of a statute, the challenger bears the very heavy burden of demonstrating beyond a reasonable doubt that the statute is unconstitutional.

Second, there are no common-law crimes in this state. Minnesota is a code state," i.e., the legislature has exclusive province to define by statute what acts constitute a crime. *State v. Soto,* 378 N.W.2d 625, 627 (Minn.1985).

And, third, the role of the judiciary is limited to deciding whether a statute is constitutional, not whether it is wise or prudent legislation. We do not sit as legislators with a veto vote, but as judges deciding whether the legislation, presumably constitutional, is so.

I.

Defendant first contends that the unborn child homicide statutes violate the Equal Protection Clause. Defendant premises his argument on *Roe v. Wade,* 410 U.S. 113, 93 S.Ct. 705, 35 L.Ed.2d 147 (1973), which, he says, holds that a nonviable fetus is not a person. He then argues that the unborn child criminal statutes have impermissibly "adopted a classification equating viable fetuses and nonviable embryos with a person."...

The state's interest in protecting the "potentiality of human life" includes protection of the unborn child, whether an embryo or a nonviable or viable fetus, and it protects, too, the woman's interest in her unborn child and her right to decide whether it shall be carried in utero. The interest of a criminal assailant in terminating a woman's pregnancy does not outweigh the woman's right to continue the pregnancy. In this context, the viability of the fetus is "simply immaterial" to an equal protection challenge to the feticide statute.

We conclude that sections 609.2661(1) and 609.2662(1) do not violate the Fourteenth Amendment by failing to distinguish between a viable and a nonviable fetus.

II.

A more difficult issue, as the trial court noted, is whether the unborn child criminal statutes are so vague as to violate the Due Process Clause of the Fourteenth Amendment. Defendant claims the statutes are unconstitutionally vague because they fail to give fair warning of the prohibited conduct and because they encourage arbitrary and discriminatory enforcement....

A.

Defendant first contends that the statutes fail to give fair warning to a potential violator. Defendant argues it is unfair to impose on the murderer of a woman an additional penalty for murder of her unborn child when neither the assailant nor the pregnant woman may have been aware of the pregnancy....

In this case, defendant seems to be arguing that an intent to kill the mother is not transferable to the fetus because the harm to the mother and the harm to the fetus are not the same. We think, however, the harm is substantially similar. The possibility that a female homicide victim of childbearing age may be pregnant is a possibility that an assaulter may not safely exclude. We conclude, therefore, that the statutes provide the requisite fair warning.

B.

Defendant next contends that the unborn child criminal statutes are fatally vague because they do not define the phrase "causes the death of an unborn child." As a result, defendant argues, the statutes invite or permit arbitrary and discriminatory enforcement. Defendant argues that the statute leaves uncertain when "death" occurs, or, for that matter, when "life" begins....

Some background is necessary to put the issue in its proper perspective. In 1985 this court, in *State v. Soto,* 378 N.W.2d 625 (Minn.1985), held that when the legislature referred to the death of a "human being" in the homicide statutes, the term "human being" was being used in its well-established common-law sense of a person born alive. Consequently, we held that the homicide statutes did not apply to the death of an 8-month-old fetus yet unborn. The legislature was free, of course, if it wished to do so, to create a crime to cover feticide. Traditionally, the crime of feticide imposed criminal liability for the death of a "viable" fetus, that is, a fetus at that stage of development which permits it to live outside the mother's womb, or a fetus that has "quickened," that is, which moves within the mother's womb.

Apparently in response to *Soto,* the legislature has enacted criminal statutes to cover feticide. In so doing, it has enacted very unusual statutes which go beyond traditional feticide, both in expanding the definition of a fetus and in the severity of the penalty imposed. The statutes in question impose the criminal penalty for murder on whoever causes the death of "the unborn offspring of a human being conceived, but not yet born." Whatever one might think of the wisdom of this legislation, and notwithstanding the difficulty of proof involved, we do not think it can be said the offense is vaguely defined. An embryo or nonviable fetus when it is within the mother's womb is "the unborn offspring of a human being."

Defendant argues, however, that to cause the death of an embryo, the embryo must first be living; if death is the termination of life, something which is not alive cannot experience death. In short, defendant argues that causing the death of a 27-day-old embryo raises the perplexing question of when "life" begins, as well as the question of when "death" occurs.

The difficulty with this argument, however, is that the statutes do not raise the issue of when life as a human person begins or ends. The state must prove only that the implanted embryo or the fetus in the mother's womb was living, that it had life, and that it has life

no longer. To have life, as that term is commonly understood, means to have the property of all living things to grow, to become. It is not necessary to prove, nor does the statute require, that the living organism in the womb in its embryonic or fetal state be considered a person or a human being. People are free to differ or abstain on the profound philosophical and moral questions of whether an embryo is a human being, or on whether or at what stage the embryo or fetus is ensouled or acquires "personhood." These questions are entirely irrelevant to criminal liability under the statute. Criminal liability here requires only that the genetically human embryo be a living organism that is growing into a human being. Death occurs when the embryo is no longer living, when it ceases to have the properties of life.

Defendant wishes to argue that causing the death of a living embryo or nonviable fetus in the mother's womb should not be made a crime. This is an argument, however, that must be addressed to the legislature. Our role in the judicial branch is limited solely to whether the legislature has defined a crime within constitutional parameters. Indeed, in this case, our role is further limited to answering only the two specific questions certified to us for a ruling. We answer both questions no.
✍ Certified questions answered.

DISSENT

Wahl and Keith, JJ., dissent. Kelley, Justice (concurring in part, dissenting in part):

… It cannot be gainsaid that few topics today compel as fierce public debate and evoke the passionate convictions of as many of our citizens as does the issue of when "life" in a fetus begins. In view of the stridency of that debate, it appears conceivable, perhaps even predictable, that two juries having the same evidence could arrive at the same factual conclusions, but due to divergent and strongly held beliefs arrived at a dissimilar legal result.

By way of example, in the case before us, one jury sharing a common viewpoint of when life commences could find the defendant guilty of fetal murder, whereas another whose members share the view that life was nonexistent in a 26 to 28-day-old embryo, could exonerate the appellant.

The likelihood of discriminatory enforcement is further enhanced when the discretionary charging function possessed by a grand jury is considered. The decision to charge must be concurred in by only a majority of the panel. Thus, the decision to charge or not may well pivot on the personal philosophical and moral tenets of a majority of the potential panel—a majority whose beliefs may vary from grand jury panel to grand jury panel…. I think the proper forum for defining life's onset and its cessation in these feticide statutes is the legislature….

Wahl, Justice (dissenting).

The trial court … noted that "the Minnesota crimes against unborn children statutes represent the most sweeping legislative attempt in the country to criminalize actions of third parties which harm fetuses and embryos."…

Defendant is charged with murder of an unborn child in the first degree carrying a sentence of life imprisonment, Minn.Stat. § 609.2661(1), and murder of an unborn child in the second degree, carrying a sentence of imprisonment for not more than 40 years, Minn.Stat. § 609.2662(1). These statutes track, respectively, the language and sentences of murder in the first degree, Minn.Stat. § 609.185(1) (1988), and murder in the second degree, Minn.Stat. § 609.19(1) (1988), with one exception. In both §§ 609.2661(1) and 609.2662(1), the actor, to be guilty of murder and to be sentenced for murder, must cause the death, not of a human being, but of an unborn child. An unborn child is the unborn offspring of a human being conceived, but not yet born. Minn.Stat. § 609.266(a) (1988). Thus an

unborn child can be a fertilized egg, an embryo, a nonviable fetus or a viable fetus.

The law with regard to murder is clear. Murder is the "unlawful killing of a human being by another…." Black's Law Dictionary 918 (5th ed. 1979). The term murder implies a felonious homicide, which is the wrongful killing of a human being. A nonviable fetus is not a human being, nor is an embryo a human being, nor is a fertilized egg a human being. None has attained the capability of independent human life. Each has the potentiality of human life. In this potential human life the state has an important and legitimate interest—an interest which becomes compelling at viability. Only at viability does the fetus have the "capability of meaningful life outside the mother's womb."…

The underlying rationale of *[Roe v.] Wade* … is that until viability is reached, human life in the legal sense has not come into existence. Implicit in *Wade* is the conclusion that as a matter of constitutional law the destruction of a non-viable fetus is not a taking of human life. It follows that such destruction cannot constitute murder or other form of homicide, whether committed by a mother, a father (as here), or a third person….

The fundamental right involved in the case before us as far as defendant is concerned is his liberty. He is charged with two counts of murder of a woman who was 26 to 28 days pregnant at the time of her death. For the death of the 28-day embryo he is further charged with murder of an unborn child in the first degree and murder of an unborn child in the second degree for which he may be sentenced to life imprisonment and 40 years. The state does not have a compelling interest in this potential human life until the fetus becomes viable….

Case Discussion

What objections did the defendant make to the unborn child homicide statutes? How does the majority answer these objections? Why does the dissent disagree with the majority? Isn't the statute perfectly clear—that life begins at conception? Why does it therefore give the court so much difficulty? Do you agree that the penalties should be the same for killing embryos? Fetuses? Born babies? Adults? Why? Why not? Who should resolve these questions? Legislatures? Courts? Public opinion polls? Doctors? Lawyers? Priests, ministers, and rabbis?[5]

The End of Life

Determining when life ends has become increasingly complex as organ transplants and sophisticated artificial life support mechanisms maintain some vital life signs. To kill a dying person, to accelerate a person's death, or to kill a "worthless" person are clearly homicide under current law. Under these general rules, a doctor who with requisite *mens rea* kills another person by removing a vital organ too soon has committed criminal homicide. Anyone who kills another by purposely disconnecting a respirator has also committed criminal homicide.[6]

Historically, "alive" meant breathing and having a heartbeat. Recently, the new concept of brain death has gained prominence, with implications not only for medicine and morals but also for criminal law. If artificial supports alone maintain breathing and heartbeat while brain waves remain minimal or flat, brain death has occurred. The Uniform Brain Death Act provides that an individual who has suffered irreversible cessation of all brain functions, including those of the brain stem, is dead.[7]

More difficult are cases involving individuals with brain functions sufficient to sustain breathing and heartbeat but nothing more, such as patients in a deep coma who have suffered serious injury. They may breathe and their hearts may beat, even without artificial support, but they are not alive for criminal law purposes. Troubling cases arise where medical specialists have described deep coma patients as "vegetables," but the patients regain consciousness and live for a considerable time afterwards. A Minneapolis police officer was shot and written off for dead after more than a year of deep coma, but then regained consciousness and lived several years. Reports of other such cases appear from time to time.

CASE

Were They "Dead"?

People v. Eulo
482 N.Y.S.2d 436 (N.Y. 1984)

Cooke, Chief Judge
People v. Eulo

FACTS

On the evening of July 19, 1981, defendant and his girlfriend attended a volunteer firemen's fair in Kings Park, Suffolk County. Not long after they arrived, the two began to argue, reportedly because defendant was jealous over one of her former suitors, whom they had seen at the fair. The argument continued through the evening; it became particularly heated as the two sat in defendant's pick-up truck, parked in front of the home of the girlfriend's parents. Around midnight, defendant shot her in the head with his unregistered handgun.

The victim was rushed by ambulance to the emergency room of St. John's Hospital. A gunshot wound to the left temple causing extreme hemorrhaging was apparent. A tube was placed in her windpipe to enable artificial respiration and intravenous medication was applied to stabilize her blood pressure.

Shortly before 2:00 a.m., the victim was examined by a neurosurgeon, who undertook various tests to evaluate damage done to the brain. Painful stimuli were applied and yielded no reaction. Various reflexes were tested and, again, there was no response. A further test determined that the victim was incapable of spontaneously maintaining respiration. An electroencephalogram

(EEG) resulted in "flat," or "isoelectric," readings indicating no activity in the part of the brain tested.

Over the next two days, the victim's breathing was maintained solely by a mechanical respirator. Her heartbeat was sustained and regulated through medication. Faced with what was believed to be an imminent cessation of these two bodily functions notwithstanding the artificial maintenance, the victim's parents consented to the use of certain of her organs for transplantation.

On the afternoon of July 23, a second neurosurgeon was called in to evaluate whether the victim's brain continued to function in any manner. A repetition of all of the previously conducted tests led to the same diagnosis: the victim's entire brain had irreversibly ceased to function. This diagnosis was reviewed and confirmed by the Deputy Medical Examiner for Suffolk County and another physician.

The victim was pronounced dead at 2:20 p.m. on July 23, although at that time she was still attached to a respirator and her heart was still beating. Her body was taken to a surgical room where her kidneys, spleen, and lymph nodes were removed. The mechanical respirator was then disconnected, and her breathing immediately stopped, followed shortly by a cessation of the heartbeat.

Defendant was indicted for second degree murder. After a jury trial, he was convicted of manslaughter. The Appellate Division, 97 A.D.2d 682, 467 N.Y.S.2d 464, unanimously affirmed the conviction, without opinion.

People v. Bonilla

FACTS

At approximately 10:30 p.m. on February 6, 1979, a New York City police officer found a man lying faceup on a Brooklyn street with a bullet wound to the head. The officer transported the victim in his patrol car to the Brookdale Hospital, where he was placed in an intensive care unit. Shortly after arriving at the hospital, the victim became comatose and was unable to breathe spontaneously.

He was placed on a respirator and medication was administered to maintain his blood pressure.

The next morning, the victim was examined by a neurologist. Due to the nature of the wound, routine tests were applied to determine the level, if any, of the victim's brain functions. The doctor found no reflex reactions and no response to painful stimuli. The mechanical respirator was disconnected to test for spontaneous breathing. There was none, and the respirator was reapplied. An EEG indicated an absence of activity in the part of the brain tested. In the physician's opinion, the bullet wound had caused the victim's entire brain to cease functioning.

The following day, the tests were repeated and the same diagnosis was reached. The victim's mother had been informed of her son's condition and had consented to a transfer of his kidneys and spleen. Death was pronounced following the second battery of tests and, commencing at 9:25 p.m., the victim's kidneys and spleen were removed for transplantation. The respirator was then disconnected, and the victim's breathing and heartbeat stopped.

An investigation led to defendant's arrest. While in police custody, defendant admitted to the shooting. He was indicted for second degree murder and criminal possession of a weapon. A jury convicted him of the weapons count and of first degree manslaughter. The conviction was affirmed by a divided Appellate Division.

OPINION

... Death has been conceptualized by the law as, simply, the absence of life: "Death is the opposite of life; it is the termination of life." But, while erecting death as a critical milepost in a person's legal life, the law has had little occasion to consider the precise point at which a person ceases to live. Ordinarily, the precise time of death has no legal significance....

Within the past two decades, machines that artificially maintain cardiorespiratory functions have come into widespread use. This technical accomplishment has called into question the universal applicability of the traditional legal and medical criteria for determining when a person has died.

These criteria were cast into flux as the medical community gained a better understanding of human physiology. It is widely understood that the human brain may be anatomically divided, generally, into three parts: the cerebrum, the cerebellum, and the brain stem. The cerebrum, known also as the "higher brain," is deemed largely to control cognitive functions such as thought, memory, and consciousness. The cerebellum primarily controls motor coordination. The brain stem, or "lower brain," which itself has three parts known as the midbrain, pons, and medulla, controls reflexive or spontaneous functions such as breathing, swallowing, and "sleep-wake" cycles.

In addition to injuries that directly and immediately destroy brain tissue, certain physical traumas may indirectly result in a complete and irreversible cessation of the brain's functions. For example, a direct trauma to the head can cause great swelling of the brain tissue, which, in turn, will stem the flow of blood to the brain. A respiratory arrest will similarly cut off the supply of oxygen to the blood and, hence, the brain. Within a relatively short period after being deprived of oxygen, the brain will irreversibly stop functioning. With the suffocation of the higher brain all cognitive powers are lost and a cessation of lower brain functions will ultimately end all spontaneous bodily functions.

Notwithstanding a total irreversible loss of the entire brain's functioning, contemporary medical techniques can maintain, for a limited period, the operation of the heart and the lungs. Respirators or ventilators can substitute for the lower brain's failure to maintain breathing. This artificial respiration, when combined with a chemical regimen, can support the continued operation of the heart. This is so because, unlike respiration, the physical contracting or "beating" of the heart occurs independently of impulses from the brain: so long as blood containing oxygen circulates to the heart, it may continue to beat and medication can take over the

lower brain's limited role in regulating the rate and force of the heartbeat.

It became clear in medical practice that the traditional "vital signs"—breathing and heartbeat—are not independent indicia of life, but are, instead, part of an integration of functions in which the brain is dominant. As a result, the medical community began to consider the cessation of brain activity as a measure of death.

The movement in law towards recognizing cessation of brain functions as criteria for death followed this medical trend. The immediate motive for adopting this position was to ease and make more efficient the transfer of donated organs. Organ transfers, to be successful, require a "viable, intact organ." Once all of a person's vital functions have ceased, transferable organs swiftly deteriorate and lose their transplant value. The technical ability to artificially maintain respiration and heartbeat after the entire brain has ceased to function was sought to be applied in cases of organ transplant to preserve the viability of donated organs....

Professional and quasi-governmental groups (including the American Bar Association, the American Medical Association, the President's Commission for the Study of Ethical Problems in Medicine and Biomedical and Behavioral Research, and the National Conference of Commissioners on Uniform State Laws) have jointly indorsed a single standard that includes both cardiorespiratory and brain-based criteria.

The recommended standard provides: "An individual who has sustained either (1) irreversible cessation of circulatory and respiratory functions, or (2) irreversible cessation of all functions of the entire brain, including the brain stem, is dead. A determination of death must be made in accordance with accepted medical standards."

In New York, the term "death," although used in many statutes, has not been expressly defined by the Legislature. This raises the question of how this court may construe these expressions of the term "death" in the absence of clarification by the Legislature. When the Legislature has failed to assign definition to a statutory term, the courts will generally construe that term according to "its ordinary and accepted meaning as it was understood at the time."...

We hold that a recognition of brain-based criteria for determining death is not unfaithful to prior judicial definitions of "death," as presumptively adopted in the many statutes using that term. Close examination of the common-law conception of death and the traditional criteria used to determine when death has occurred leads inexorably to this conclusion.

Courts have not engaged in a metaphysical analysis of when life should be deemed to have passed from a person's body, leaving him or her dead. Rather, they have conceptualized death as the absence of life, unqualified and undefined. On a practical level, this broad conception of death as "the opposite of life" was substantially narrowed through recognition of the cardiorespiratory criteria for determining when death occurs. Under these criteria, the loci of life are the heart and the lungs: where there is no breath or heartbeat, there is no life. Cessation manifests death.

Considering death to have occurred when there is an irreversible and complete cessation of the functioning of the entire brain, including the brain stem, is consistent with the common-law conception of death (see *Commonwealth v. Golston,* 373 Mass. 249, 254, 366 N.E.2d 744). Ordinarily, death will be determined according to the traditional criteria of irreversible cardiorespiratory repose. When, however, the respiratory and circulatory functions are maintained by mechanical means, their significance, as signs of life, is at best ambiguous. Under such circumstances, death may nevertheless be deemed to occur when, according to accepted medical practice, it is determined that the entire brain's function has irreversibly ceased....

[I]n each case, the order of the Appellate Division should be affirmed.... Order affirmed.

Case Discussion

What facts indicate death in the cases? What facts indicate the victims were still alive? What determines death, according to the court's criteria? How would you define death for purposes of the law of homicide? Is putting another in a deep coma murder? The underlying idea in brain death is that insufficient activity exists to appreciate life. Do you agree? What about killing other people in somewhat similar circumstances? What about persons who are born so retarded or so seriously brain damaged that they cannot ever hope to perform life's most basic tasks? Are they "live" human beings? What about psychotics so deep in paranoia that they have no lucid intervals? Are such tragic persons "alive" in a meaningful sense? How would you define death for homicide purposes?

As was true for defining when life begins, defining death need not be fastened to traditional legal doctrine or medical practice. Definitions that satisfy the purposes of criminal law should rather depend on the underlying values that homicide statutes are meant to preserve. Resolving definition problems, therefore, requires policymakers and legislators to grapple with how to determine what worth they ultimately attribute to continuing life for the critically and hopelessly injured, the gravely mentally ill, and other victims of advanced disease and life's vicissitudes.

▼ CAUSING ANOTHER'S DEATH

The material element, causing another's death, occasionally creates difficulties. Some killers never touch their victims but still cause their deaths. For example, if I invite my blind enemy to step over a precipice he cannot see, and he dies, I have caused his death. If I expose my helpless child to freezing temperatures, I have killed him or her. Such bizarre examples rarely occur.[8]

More commonly, death stems from several causes. In some cases, victims do not die immediately after brutal attacks. One man beaten almost to death was taken to a hospital where, in a delirious state, he pulled life support plugs and died. Another victim was so stunned from a beating that he stumbled in front of a speeding car and was killed. Factual cause exists in these killings because the assailants set in motion chains of events that ended in the victims' deaths. Whether the assailants legally caused their victims' deaths depends on whether it is fair, just, and expedient to impose liability for criminal homicide. (See chapter 3). In *Commonwealth v. Golston,* the court ruled that even if a doctor's negligence contributed to the victim's death, Golston's brutal attack with a baseball bat constituted sufficient evidence for the jury to find Golston's actions the legal cause of death.[9]

The ancient **year-and-a-day rule,** still followed in some states today, mandates that no act occurring more than one year and one day before death constitutes the legal cause of death for purposes of the law of criminal homicide. According to the year-and-a-day rule, the law conclusively presumes that death was due to "natural causes," not the defendant's acts. The rigid common-law formulation of this rule does not conform to modern medical realities. The case of *State v. Minster* deals with this problem.

Abolished in Michigan we in the felony

CASE

What Caused the Death?

State v. Minster
486 A.2d 1197 (Md.1985)

Couch, Judge

   The issue here is whether we should abrogate the common law rule of "a year and a day," which bars a prosecution for murder when the victim dies more than a year and a day after being injured. Inasmuch as we believe this issue is more appropriately addressed by the legislature, we shall not abrogate the common law rule. Accordingly, we affirm the trial court's dismissal of the indictment filed against the appellee, Larry Edmund Minster.

FACTS

The facts in this case are undisputed. On July 8, 1982, Minster shot the victim, Cheryl Dodgson, in the neck. As a result of the shooting, Ms. Dodgson became a quadriplegic. Minster was charged in Prince George's County Circuit Court with attempted first degree murder, assault with intent to murder, assault and battery and use of a handgun in a crime of violence. He was brought to trial in April of 1983.

Minster was convicted of attempted first degree murder and the use of a handgun in a crime of violence. He was sentenced to 20 years imprisonment for attempted murder and received a 10 year concurrent sentence for the handgun violation. The Court of Special Appeals affirmed his conviction in an unreported per curiam opinion.

On October 3, 1983, Ms. Dodgson died from injuries the State contends resulted directly from Minster's actions on July 8, 1982 one year and eighty-seven days before the victim's death. One month after Ms. Dodgson's death, Minster was indicted for first degree murder. The Circuit Court for Prince George's County dismissed the indictment because the death of Ms. Dodgson occurred more than a year and a day after the shooting. Judge Johnson [the trial judge] noted that *State v. Brown,* 21 Md.App. 91, 318 A.2d 257 (1974), which held that the year and a day rule was valid in Maryland, barred the indictment. The State appealed the dismissal to the Court of Special Appeals. We granted certiorari prior to consideration by the Court of Special Appeals in order to address an issue of public importance.

OPINION

The State's issue is simply stated: should the prosecution of Minster for the murder of Cheryl Dodgson be barred by the year and a day rule. It argues that the common law rule is now archaic and, in light of medical advances in life-saving techniques, there is no sound reason for retaining the rule today. Minster argues that there are legitimate justifications for the rule's continued application; moreover, because of the number of alternatives available to replace the year and a day rule, a change in the rule should be left to the legislature.

In *Brown,* this identical issue came before the Court of Special Appeals.... The Court held that the rule was part of our common law and, although no Maryland case had previously addressed the issue, the rule was "in full force and effect in Maryland." In addition, "if change is to be made in the rule it should be by the General Assembly because expression and weighing of divergent views, consideration of potential effect, and suggestion of adequate safeguards, are better suited to the legislative forum." We are in accordance with this view.

We agree with Minster that there are a number of sound justifications for retaining this rule. As Chief Judge Orth stated in *Brown,* "[a]bolition of the rule may well result in imbalance between the adequate protection of society and justice for the individual accused, and there would remain a need for some form of limitation on causation."

Justice Musmanno, who dissented from the judicial abrogation of the rule in *Commonwealth v. Ladd,* 402 Pa. 164, 166 A.2d 501 (1960), stated this concern more fully:

> Dorothy Pierce, the alleged victim, died of pneumonia. It is possible, of course, that her weakened condition, due to the alleged hurt received thirteen months before, made her more susceptible to the attack of pneumonia. On the other hand, there is the likely possibility that the pneumonia had no possible connection with the injury allegedly inflicted by the defendant.
>
> Suppose that the pneumonia occurred two years after the physical injury, would it still be proper to charge the defendant with murder? If a murder charge can be brought two years after a blow has been struck, will there ever be a time when the Court may declare that the bridge between the blow and death has now been irreparably broken? May the Commonwealth indict a man for murder when the death occurs ten years after the blow has fallen? Twenty years? Thirty years? One may search the majority opinion through every paragraph, sentence, clause, phrase and comma, and find no answer to this very serious question. The majority is content to open a Pandora's box of interrogation and let it remain unclosed, to the torment and possible persecution of every person who may have at one time or another injured another. I don't doubt that an "expert" of some kind can be found to testify that a slap in the face was the cause of a death fifteen years later.
>
> If there is one thing which the criminal law must be, if it is to be recognized as just, it must be specific and definitive.

We are reminded of the oft-cited explanation for the rule's existence: "[I]f he die[d] after that time [of a year and a day], it cannot be discerned, as the law presumes, whether he died of the stroke or poison, etc. or of a natural death; and in the case of life, the rule of law ought to be certain." 3 Coke, *Institutes of the Laws of England* at 52 (1797)

In addition, a person charged with attempted first degree murder (as was the case here) can be sentenced to life imprisonment. Moreover, a sentencing judge may always consider the seriousness of the injury to, or the subsequent death of, the victim. The only additional conceivable punishment a first degree murder conviction entails is the death penalty.

We do not believe this distinction is a sufficient reason to rescind a common law rule which has existed for over seven hundred years.

[COURT NOTE: "The rule has been traced back to the Statutes of Gloucester (1278) in the reign of King Edward I.]

Assuming, arguendo, that we abrogate this rule, with what do we replace it? In *People v. Stevenson,* 416 Mich. 383, 331 N.W.2d 143 (1982), the court addressed the identical issue we address today. Five alternatives to the rule were offered to that court:

1. The Court could retain the year and a day rule.
2. The Court could modify the rule by extending the span of time, for example, to three years and a day. California Penal Code § 194.
3. The Court could extend the rule to any length of time it chooses, perhaps two years, five years, or ten years.
4. The Court could change the rule from an irrebuttable presumption to a rebuttable one, but with a higher burden of proof. Cf., *Serafin v. Serafin,* 401 Mich. 629, 258 N.W.2d 461 (1977), requiring clear and convincing evidence.
5. Finally, the Court could simply abolish the rule entirely, leaving the issue of causation to the jury in light of the facts and arguments in each particular case.

Similarly, in *State v. Young,* 77 N.J. 245, 390 A.2d 556 (1978), the justices were split between three alternatives: four justices favoring abrogation, two justices favoring retention, and one justice favoring a compromise "three years and a day" rule. In fact, two jurisdictions, California and Washington, have enacted a three year and a day rule.

Thus we find there is a great difference of opinion surrounding the appropriate length of the period after which prosecution is barred and some doubt whether the rule should exist at all. Consequently, we believe it is the legislature which should mandate any change in the rule, if indeed any change is appropriate in Maryland. The legislature may hold hearings on this matter; they can listen to the testimony of medical experts; and they may determine the viability of this rule in modern times.

We also observe that if there is any discernible trend towards abrogation of the year and a day rule, the trend is towards abrogation by act of the legislature, not the judiciary. Of the thirteen jurisdictions which had enacted the year and a day rule by statute in 1941, only four jurisdictions retain the rule today. In addition, in two jurisdictions (New York and Oregon) the judiciary has held that the legislature abrogated the rule by failing to include it in the comprehensive revision of the state's Criminal Code. Thus, in eleven jurisdictions the rule has been abrogated by legislative action or omission. In contrast, judicial abrogation has occurred in only five jurisdictions.

[COURT NOTE: "The statistical breakdown of the above analysis is as follows:

A. Jurisdictions legislatively retaining the rule—California, Idaho, Nevada and South Carolina (reckless manslaughter by vehicle).
B. Jurisdictions legislatively abrogating the rule—Arizona, Arkansas, Colorado, Delaware, Illinois, Montana, North Dakota, Texas and Utah.
C. Jurisdictions judicially abrogating the rule—Massachusetts, Michigan, New Jersey, Ohio and Pennsylvania."]

We recognize the cogency of the State's argument concerning medical advances in life-saving techniques, and we are aware that other courts have been persuaded by this argument. Yet recent decisions have affirmed the viability of the year and a day rule, and, by our count, the rule remains extant in twenty six states.

In sum, we uphold the application of the year and a day rule in Maryland. Accordingly, we affirm the trial court's dismissal of the indictment. Judgment affirmed; costs to be paid by appellant.

**Case
Discussion**   What reasons does the court give for maintaining the year-and-a-day rule? Do they make sense in the 1990s? Why or why not? Why does the court believe that if Maryland wishes to change the year-and-a-day rule, the legislature should make the change? Do you agree? Is it important that this rule has existed for more than seven hundred years? Does its longevity argue in favor of keeping this rule or rejecting it?

▼ CRIMINAL HOMICIDE *MENS REA*

*1) murder
2) Manslaughter*

Mens rea largely, but not wholly, accounts for grading criminal homicides. In fact, criminal homicide law refines *mens rea* more than in any other crime. The culpability levels comprised in the general principal of *mens rea*—purposeful, knowing, reckless, and negligent—apply with particular reference to criminal homicide. Most of the time, but not always, criminal homicide law grades purposeful killings most serious and negligent killings least serious.

Criminal homicide divides intentional killings into several categories. The law treats premeditated murder (first-degree murder) more seriously than purposeful killing without deliberation (second-degree murder), which it treats more seriously than sudden killing with adequate provocation (voluntary manslaughter). Furthermore, some surrounding circumstances can aggravate—and others mitigate—purposeful, reckless, and negligent homicides. Deaths that occur in the course of committing other felonies, such as armed robbery, constitute first-degree murder in some states even when the killer's *mens rea* was reckless or even negligent with respect to the death. The mental element combined with special material surrounding circumstances provides the basis for grading criminal homicide.

▼ TYPES AND DEGREES OF CRIMINAL HOMICIDE

Criminal law divides homicide into two major kinds: murder and manslaughter. These in turn are subdivided into several categories. Nearly all distinctions among these categories depend on the killer's mental state. The discussion that follows treats homicide as an organized whole, but simplified compared with actual homicide law, which is filled with many special homicide statutes enacted over time to meet special situations arising as society became more complex. Special statutes govern deaths resulting from operating machinery in a negligent manner, leaving vicious animals at large, overloading passenger vessels, and driving or practicing as a doctor while drunk.[10]

First-Degree Murder

At common law, murder occurs

> [w]hen a man of sound memory and of the age of discretion unlawfully kills any reasonable creature in being, and under the King's peace, with malice

aforethought, either express or implied by the law, the death taking place within a year and a day.[11]

In the sixteenth century when Lord Coke defined murder, malice aforethought may have referred to purposeful killings planned well in advance, such as when someone lay in wait to kill, or poisoned an enemy. In modern times it refers to several states of mind, as well as to causing death during the course of some specified felonies whether or not the felon premeditated the killing.

Malice aforethought includes the intent to do all the following:

* Kill
* Do serious bodily harm
* Commit specified serious felonies
* Create a greater than reckless risk of death or serious bodily harm, acting with such disregard for human life that the action evidences an "abandoned and depraved heart," such as by shooting into a crowd of people
* Resist arrest by force

This broad scope has rendered the term "malice aforethought" almost meaningless; hence, most statutes and cases have refined the murder *mens rea* to make it more practical to apply to the situations just listed.

The common law did not recognize degrees of murder; all criminal homicides were capital felonies. Pennsylvania departed from the common law in 1794, enacting the first statute that divided murder into degrees. The Pennsylvania statute provided that

> all murder, which shall be perpetrated by means of poison, lying in wait, or by any other kind of wilful, deliberate or premeditated killing, or which shall be committed in the perpetration, or attempt to perpetrate any arson, rape, robbery or burglary shall be deemed murder in the first degree; and all other kinds of murder shall be deemed murder in the second degree.[12]

Pennsylvania created first-degree murder in order to confine the death penalty (at the time prescribed for all common-law murders) to particularly heinous murders. Most states followed the practice of calling first-degree murder capital murder. As states abolished the death penalty, first-degree murder became a life imprisonment felony.

Elements of Murder			
Actus Reus	*Mens Rea*	**Causation**	**Result**
1. killing another live human being *2.* atrocious, cruel or heinous killing	*1.* premeditated deliberate or *2.* intent to commit some felonies	acts that concur with *mens rea* to set in motion a chain of events that sufficiently lead to death	death

Capital murder has recently attracted attention in view of the constitutionality of the death penalty. The Supreme Court has ruled that states with a mandatory death penalty are not constitutional unless courts take into account specified aggravating and mitigating circumstances, adjudicated and decided according to strict procedural safeguards. As a result, most states that prescribe the death penalty for murder now have statutes outlining the aggravating and mitigating circumstances that qualify convicted murderers for the death penalty.[13]

The most common first-degree murders are premeditated, purposeful, and deliberate killings. **Premeditated** means "planned in advance. **Deliberate** means done with a cool, reflecting mind. A person who kills in a towering rage is not a deliberate killer; neither, in some cases, is an intoxicated person too drunk to act with cool reflection. Two other first-degree murders, felony murder and heinous murder, do not require proof of purpose, deliberation, and premeditation.[14]

Courts variously define premeditation. Some require substantial time to formulate a well-laid plan to kill. According to one court:

> A verdict of murder in the first degree ... [on a theory of willful, deliberate, and premeditated killing] is proper only if the slayer killed "as a result of careful thought and weighing of considerations; as a *deliberate* judgment or plan; carried on coolly and steadily, according to a *preconceived* design.[15]

Other courts virtually eliminate the element of advanced planning by holding that premeditation includes killing instantly after forming the intent. One judge said that a defendant premeditated when the intent to kill arose "at the very moment the fatal shot was fired." Some require sufficient maturity or mental health (or both) to appreciate fully what it means to plan to kill in advance of doing so. The Idaho Supreme Court dealt with deliberate, premeditated murder in the capital murder case of *State v. Snowden*.[16]

CASE

Did He "Premeditate" the Killing?

State v. Snowden
79 Idaho 266, 313 P.2d 706 (1957)

[Snowden was found guilty of first-degree murder and sentenced to death. He appealed. Justice McQuade delivered the opinion.]

FACTS

Defendant Snowden had been playing pool and drinking in a Boise pool room early in the evening. With a companion, one Carrier, he visited a club near Boise, then went to nearby Garden City. There the two men visited a number of bars, and defendant had several drinks. Their last stop was the HiHo Club.

Witnesses related that while defendant was in the HiHo Club he met and talked to Cora Lucyle Dean. The defendant himself said he hadn't been acquainted with Mrs. Dean prior to that time, but he had "seen her in a couple of the joints up town." He danced with Mrs. Dean while at the HiHo Club. Upon departing from the tavern, the two left together.

In statements to police officers, that were admitted in evidence, defendant Snowden said after they left the club Mrs. Dean wanted him to find a cab and take her back to

Boise, and he refused because he didn't feel he should pay her fare. After some words, he related:

> [S]he got mad at me so I got pretty hot and I don't know whether I back handed her there or not. And, we got calmed down and decided to walk across to the gas station and call a cab.

They crossed the street, and began arguing again. Defendant said: "She swung and at the same time she kneed me again. I blew my top."

Defendant said he pushed the woman over beside a pickup truck which was standing near a business building. There he pulled his knife—a pocket knife with a two-inch blade—and cut her throat.

The body, which was found the next morning, was viciously and sadistically cut and mutilated. An autopsy surgeon testified the voice box had been cut, and that this would have prevented the victim from making any intelligible outcry. There were other wounds inflicted while she was still alive—one in her neck, one in her abdomen, two in the face, and two on the back of the neck. The second neck wound severed the spinal cord and caused death. There were other wounds all over her body, and her clothing had been cut away. The nipple of the right breast was missing. There was no evidence of a sexual attack on the victim; however, some of the lacerations were around the breasts and vagina of the deceased. A blood test showed Mrs. Dean was intoxicated at the time of her death.

Defendant took the dead woman's wallet. He hailed a passing motorist and rode back to Boise with him. There he went to a bowling alley and changed clothes. He dropped his knife into a sewer, and threw the wallet away. Then he went to his hotel and cleaned up again. He put the clothes he had worn that evening into a trash barrel.

OPINION

By statute, murder is defined as the unlawful killing of a human being with malice aforethought. Degrees of murder are defined by statute as follows:

All murder which is perpetrated by means of poison, or lying in wait, torture, or by any other kind of wilful, deliberate and premeditated killing, or which is committed in the perpetration of, or attempt to perpetrate arson, rape, robbery, burglary, kidnapping or mayhem, is murder of the first degree. All other murders are of the second degree.

The defendant admitted taking the life of the deceased. The principal argument of the defendant pertaining to … [premeditation] is that the defendant did not have sufficient time to develop a desire to take the life of the deceased, but rather this action was instantaneous and a normal reaction to the physical injury which she had dealt him.

There need be no appreciable space of time between the intention to kill and the act of killing. They may be as instantaneous as successive thoughts of the mind. It is only necessary that the act of killing be preceded by a concurrence of will, deliberation, and premeditation on the part of the slayer, and, if such is the case, the killing is murder in the first degree.

In the present case, the trial court had no other alternative than to find the defendant guilty of willful, deliberate, and premeditated killing with malice aforethought in view of the defendant's acts in deliberately opening up a pocket knife, next cutting the victim's throat, and then hacking and cutting until he had killed Cora Lucyle Dean and expended himself. The full purpose and design of defendant's conduct was to take the life of the deceased....

[Snowden objected to the imposition of the death penalty. Idaho provides the following punishment for murder:]

Every person guilty of murder in the first degree shall suffer death or be punished by imprisonment in the state prison for life, and the jury may decide which punishment shall be inflicted....

The trial court could have imposed life imprisonment, or, as in the instant case, sentenced the defendant to death. It is abuse of discretion we are dealing with, and in particular the alleged abuse of discretion in prescribing the punishment for murder in the first degree as committed by the defendant. To choose between the punishments of life imprisonment and death there must be some distinction between one homicide and another. This case exemplifies an abandoned and malignant heart and sadistic mind, bent upon taking human life. It is our considered conclusion, from all the facts and circumstances, the imposition of the death sentence was not an abuse of discretion by the trial court. The judgment is affirmed.

Case Discussion

The *Snowden* court had no difficulty finding that Snowden premeditated Dean's death. In fact, in a part of the opinion not included here, the court approved the trial judge's death sentence over life imprisonment because Snowden clearly premeditated Dean's murder. Do you agree? If you were defining premeditation in a criminal statute, would you say it is sufficient that the deed followed instantly upon the intention? What practical meaning does premeditation have according to that definition? Do you think the court used premeditation as an "excuse" to make it possible to sentence Snowden to death for the especially brutal way he murdered Dean? (When you read about second-degree murder, rethink how you defined premeditation in first-degree murder.) As for the sentence, do you find any mitigating circumstances, such as Snowden's intoxication, Dean's provocation, and Snowden's quick response to Dean's provocation?

Not everyone agrees that premeditated killings constitute the worst murders. According to James F. Stephen, a nineteenth-century English judge and criminal law reformer:

> As much cruelty, as much indifference to the life of others, a disposition at least as dangerous to society, probably even more dangerous, is shown by sudden as by premeditated murders. The following cases appear to me to set this in a clear light. A, passing along the road, sees a boy sitting on a bridge over a deep river and, out of mere wanton barbarity, pushes him into it and so drowns him. A man makes advances to a girl who repels him. He deliberately but instantly cuts her throat. A man civilly asked to pay a just debt pretends to get the money, loads a rifle and blows out his creditor's brains. In none of these cases is there premeditation unless the word is used in a sense as unnatural as "aforethought" in "malice aforethought," but each represents even more diabolical cruelty and ferocity than that which is involved in murders premeditated in the natural sense of the word.[17]

The British Home Office's remarks to the Royal Commission on Capital Punishment observed that

> [a]mong the worst murders are some which are not premeditated, such as murders committed in connection with rape, or murders committed by criminals who are interrupted in some felonious enterprise and use violence without premeditation, but with a reckless disregard of the consequences to human life. There are also many murders where the killing is clearly intentional, unlawful and unaccompanied by any mitigating circumstances, but where there is no evidence to show whether there was or was not premeditation. For the foregoing reasons, we deem ourselves constrained to reject the determinants of first degree murder suggested by existing law. The question then is whether it is possible to construct a more satisfactory delineation of the class

of murders to which the capital sanction ought to be confined insofar as it is used at all.[18]

Atrocious murder constitutes another kind of first-degree murder in some jurisdictions. In atrocious murder, the killer not only means to kill but also does it in an especially brutal manner. Atrocious murder usually appears as an aggravating circumstance that qualifies a murderer for the death penalty or life imprisonment without parole. The court considered the "heinous" or "atrocious" aggravating circumstance in *Smith v. State*.

CASE

Was the Murder Atrocious?

Smith v. State
727 P.2d 1366 (Okla.1986)

Bussey, Judge: The appellant, Lois Nadean Smith, was convicted in the District Court of Sequoyah County, of Murder in the First Degree for which she received a sentence of death.

FACTS

The evidence shows that the appellant, her son Greg, and Teresa Baker picked up Cindy Baillee at a Tahlequah motel early on the morning of July 4, 1982. Baillee had been Greg's girlfriend, but allegedly had made threats to have him killed. As the group drove away from the motel, appellant confronted Ms. Baillee with rumors that she had arranged for Greg's murder. When Ms. Baillee denied making any threats or arrangements, appellant choked the victim and stabbed her in the throat with a knife found in the victim's purse. The car traveled to the home of Jim Smith, the appellant's ex-husband and Greg's father in Gans, Oklahoma. Present at the house were Smith and his wife Robyn. She left shortly after the group arrived.

While at the Smith house, appellant forced Ms. Baillee to sit in a recliner chair. She then threatened to kill Ms. Baillee, and taunted her with a pistol. Finally, appellant fired a shot into the recliner, near Ms. Baillee's head. She then fired a series of shots at Ms. Baillee, and the wounded victim fell to the floor. As Greg Smith reloaded the pistol, appellant laughed while jumping on the victim's neck. Appellant took the pistol from Greg and fired four more bullets into the body. A subsequent autopsy showed Ms. Baillee had been shot five times in the chest, twice in the head, and once in the back. Five of these gunshot wounds were fatal. The knife wound was also potentially fatal.

An expert in blood splatter analysis testified blood stains on the blouse worn by appellant proved circumstantially that she had fired the fatal shots. Evidence also was presented by the State that appellant directed her companions to dispose of some evidence and arranged an alibi story for them. Appellant testified on her own behalf that Teresa Baker actually shot and killed Ms. Baillee. She claimed Ms. Baker killed the victim because of jealousy over Greg.

OPINION

... We find that the aggravating circumstance of "heinous, atrocious, or cruel" is ... supported. The victim was first choked, then stabbed in the throat, then taken to a house where she continued to beg for her life while the appellant tormented her with a revolver by shooting it into the chair in which the victim sat, and by alternately pointing it at her head and stomach until the first bullet wounds were inflicted. When the victim fell to the floor, the appellant jumped on her neck until the reloaded pistol was handed back to the appellant who discharged all six rounds into the helpless victim.... The judgment and sentence is affirmed.

**Case
Discussion**

What facts amounted to atrocious and heinous, according to the court? What about the facts makes them atrocious? That they were planned? That she got pleasure from them? That they were brutal? That they had no motive? That they were totally unprovoked? What penalty would you attach to this crime? Why? Does it deserve the most severe punishment the law allows? Why?

Note Cases

1. "About 2 p.m. on Sunday, August 24, 1975, the victim, a white man thirty-four years old, came out of a store in Dorchester and walked toward his car. The defendant, a black man of eighteen, tiptoed behind him and hit him on the head with a baseball bat. The defendant then went into a building, changed his clothes, and crossed the street to the store, where he worked. When asked why he had hit the man, he said 'For kicks.'" The victim later died. Was this atrocious murder, qualifying Golston for the death penalty? According to the court, it was.

> [T]here was evidence of great and unusual violence in the blow, which caused a four-inch cut on the side of the skull.... [T]here was also evidence that after he was struck the victim fell to the street, and that five minutes later he tried to get up, staggered to his feet and fell again to the ground. He was breathing very hard and a neighbor wiped vomit from his nose and mouth. Later, according to the testimony, the defendant said he did it, "For kicks."
>
> There is no requirement that the defendant know that his act was extremely atrocious or cruel, and no requirement of deliberate premeditation. A murder may be committed with extreme atrocity or cruelty even though death results from a single blow. Indifference to the victim's pain, as well as actual knowledge of it and taking pleasure in it, is cruelty; and extreme cruelty is only a higher degree of cruelty. *Commonwealth v. Golston,* 373 Mass. 249, 366 N.E.2d 744 (1977).

2. On February 15, 1982, defendant was seen by witnesses carrying a knife in the waistband of his pants. Subsequently, he told a witness that he was going to a gay bar to "roll a fag." Defendant was later seen at a predominantly gay bar with John Pope, the victim. The two of them then left the bar in Pope's gold Camaro. Several hours later, Pope's roommate returned home and found the house unlocked, the lights on, the stereo on loud, and blood on the bed. The sheriff was contacted. Upon arrival, the deputy sheriff found Pope on the bathroom floor in a pool of blood with multiple stab wounds. Defendant was found and arrested on April 18, 1982. Defendant was tried and found guilty of first-degree murder. In accordance with the jury's advisory recommendation, the trial judge imposed the death sentence. The defendant argued that this was not a particularly heinous or atrocious killing. The court said:

> We disagree with the defendant. The evidence presented at trial shows that the victim received eleven stab wounds, some of which were inflicted in the bedroom and some inflicted in the bathroom. The medical examiner's testimony revealed that the victim lived some few minutes before dying. *State v. Duest,* 462 So.2d 446 (Fla.1985)

Felony Murder

In most jurisdictions, deaths that occur during the commission, or attempted commission, of specified felonies constitute another form of murder: **felony murder,** in most states second-degree murder. The felonies underlying felony murder include arson, rape, robbery, burglary, kidnapping, mayhem, and sexual molestation of a child.

Elements of Felony Murder			
Actus Reus	**Mens Rea**	**Causation**	**Result**
killing another live human being while committing designated felonies	intent to commit the underlying or predicate felony	acts that substantially lead to death	death

Felony murder does not require the intent to kill or inflict serious bodily harm. In fact, most felony murderers do not intend to kill their victims. Frequently, they recklessly or negligently kill their victims. The underlying felonies constitute the reckless or negligent state of mind. For example, if a robber's gun fires during the robbery and kills a 7-Eleven clerk, even if the robber does not intend to kill, the robbery constitutes sufficient recklessness (or negligence) to constitute first-degree felony murder. Similarly, if a man forcibly rapes a child, not intending to kill, but the child dies, the rape amounts to recklessness sufficient to constitute first-degree felony murder. Some felony murder statutes impose strict liability for deaths occurring during the commission of some felonies. In other words, even accidental killings during felonies constitute felony murder.

The felony murder doctrine aims to accomplish several policy goals. First, the rule might deter would-be felons from committing crimes because of the added threat of a murder conviction, perhaps even first-degree capital murder. Second, the rule might curtail the use of violence during the commission of felonies. Research has not demonstrated that the rule accomplishes either of these goals. Finally, the rule also embodies the idea that people who commit felonies, creating high risks, should take the most serious possible consequences for their actions.

Owing to skepticism about the effectiveness of the policy goals the doctrine is supposed to achieve, four states—Ohio, Hawaii, Michigan, and Kentucky—have abolished felony murder. Other states have placed restrictions on felony murder. Some courts require that death resulting from the underlying felony was foreseeable. Some courts readily find foreseeability in the facts of a particular case. In *State v. Noren,* for example, Noren struck a drunken man three times in the head in the course of robbing him. The blows rendered the victim unconscious, and he died from asphyxiation. The court found that striking an intoxicated victim involves a foreseeable risk of causing death. Similarly, in *State v. McKeiver,* McKeiver robbed a bar. During the robbery, a woman suffered a fatal heart attack. The court upheld McKeiver's conviction for felony murder, finding that the woman died "as a result of fear and apprehension during defendant's commission of a robbery."[19]

Problems arise when someone other than the felon causes a death. The third person who actually kills might be the victim, police officers, or even a co-felon. Some states exclude from the felony murder rule deaths caused by third persons. For example, a resisting victim who shot and killed one of two burglars relieved the other burglar from felony murder liability. Similarly, it was not felony murder when a cab driver and police officer shot at two men attempting to rob the driver, killing one of the would-be robbers. Other states include within the scope of felony murder deaths caused by resisting victims. Where a victim of felonious assault returned fire and killed one assailant, a co-felon of the deceased was convicted of felony murder.[20]

Only deaths occurring during "dangerous" felonies constitute felony murder. For example, the California Supreme Court held that a chiropractor was not guilty of felony murder when he fraudulently treated cancer with chiropractic and the patient died. The court ruled that fraud was not a "dangerous" felony.[21]

The Kansas Supreme Court dealt with the meaning of felonies endangering life in *State v. Wesson.*

CASE

*Is Selling Crack
Inherently Dangerous?*

State v. Wesson
802 P.2d 574 (Kan.1990)

Abbott, Justice: This is a direct appeal by the defendant, Kurt Donnell Wesson, from his convictions of felony murder (K.S.A.1989 Supp. 21–3401) and of attempted sale of crack cocaine (K.S.A.1989 Supp. 65–4127a). Wesson contends that the sale, or attempted sale, of crack cocaine cannot be the underlying felony to support a charge of felony murder....

FACTS
Early in the morning of June 11, 1989, a Kansas City, Kansas, police officer noticed a vehicle on a sidewalk that had run into a light pole. The tires were spinning and smoking, the windshield was cracked, and the left window was broken out. Inside the vehicle the officer found Cletis Crowley slumped against the steering wheel. The officer tore open Crowley's shirt and found stab wounds on Crowley's upper chest and arms. Crowley died a short time later from one of the stab wounds, which had penetrated his heart. An autopsy revealed that Crowley had been stabbed eight times by a single-edged instrument.

Crowley had in his possession a pipe with traces of cocaine in it. Because there was little broken glass on the ground where the car had come to rest, the officers surmised that an altercation had taken place elsewhere. They backtracked to 13th and Wood, an area where drug sales are common, and discovered newly broken auto glass on the ground and two wooden knife handle halves. Lab tests showed that the glass found at 13th and Wood was consistent with the glass from Crowley's car.

Officers arrested Kurt Wesson at 13th and Wood later that day. A lock-blade knife was recovered from his pocket with the wooden handles missing. A subsequent analysis showed that the knife handles found at the scene were originally attached to Wesson's knife. After arrest, Wesson told the police that he was trying to sell cocaine to Crowley. He told police that there were two people in the car and that the driver reached out and grabbed the cocaine and drove away. He told the officers that as the car turned the corner, it looked like the driver was fighting with the passenger. He said he chased the car, it stopped and the passenger jumped out, and he noticed the driver had blood on his chest.

He said he broke the half open window, reached in, and retrieved his cocaine. The car then drove away.

At trial, Wesson denied making the preceding statement to officers. Wesson testified that he was selling fake crack made out of soap, wax, and baking soda. He testified that when he showed a sample to Crowley, Crowley took the sample, rolled up the car window trapping Wesson's arm and the sample inside and started driving. He testified that he eventually broke the window and escaped. He testified that an acquaintance, Philip White, had given him the knife to dispose of and that he did not know who stabbed Crowley.

Officers questioned two witnesses, Philip White and Kenneth Williams, both acquaintances of Wesson. At the preliminary hearing, they testified that they were at 13th and Wood early on the 11th. They saw Wesson with the upper half of his body inside the driver's side of Crowley's car, being dragged along.

They both testified they ran after the car to try and help Wesson.

Both witnesses saw Wesson hitting Crowley. White testified he saw a knife in Wesson's hand. Both witnesses testified the car drove off after Wesson was freed. After Wesson was freed from the vehicle, White, Williams, and Wesson went to White's apartment. Both observed a knife and cuts on

Wesson's hand. Both testified that Wesson admitted he stabbed Crowley. At trial, the State was unable to procure White's and Williams' attendance, and the court ultimately found them unavailable and allowed their testimony at the preliminary hearing to be introduced. The jury found Wesson guilty and he appeals.

OPINION

… The trial court found in part:

> Mere possession of crack is not an inherently dangerous crime, but I am of the opinion … that the sale or attempted sale of crack is an inherently dangerous felony. I don't care if we view the crime in the abstract or if we view it in reality. In reality, we know that the sale or attempted sale of dangerous drugs, narcotics, is a dangerous occupation.
>
> We see—as courts, every day where people are injured and killed during the sale or attempted sale of narcotic drugs.… We know that people who sell and who buy drugs are dangerous and sometimes violent individuals, that considerable money can be present during drug transactions.… So whether we view it in reality or in the abstract, I am of the opinion that the sale or attempted sale of a controlled substance, and especially cocaine or hard drugs, is an inherently dangerous crime.

On appeal, Wesson renews this argument that attempted sale of narcotics (or sale of narcotics) is not inherently dangerous.

In Kansas, unlike most states, felony murder is classified as first-degree murder. Most states set out specific felonies (for example, rape, robbery, burglary, and aggravated arson) as underlying felonies sufficient for first-degree murder and then make all other felony murders second degree. The purpose of the felony-murder rule is to supply the elements of premeditation and intent that are otherwise required to establish first-degree murder. Consequently, only felonies which are inherently dangerous are held to support felony murder. That the crime must be inherently dangerous has been the rule in Kansas for many years. In *State v. Hoang,* the court said:

To support a conviction for felony murder, all that is required is to prove that a felony was being committed, which felony was inherently dangerous to human life, and that the homicide which followed was a direct result of the commission of that felony....

[T]he underlying felony in a felony-murder case must be a forcible felony, one inherently danger to human life.

K.S.A. 21–3110(8) provides that forcible felonies include "treason, murder, voluntary manslaughter, rape, robbery, burglary, arson, kidnapping, aggravated battery, aggravated sodomy and any other felony which involves the use or threat of physical force or violence against any person."...

In determining whether a crime is inherently dangerous, the majority of states examine the circumstances of the particular incident and determine whether the way that the particular crime was committed was inherently dangerous. This previously was the law in Kansas. See *State v. Goodseal,* 220 Kan. 487, 553 P.2d 279 (1976), and *State v. Moffitt,* 199 Kan. 514, 431 P.2d 879 (1967); both overruled by *State v. Underwood,* 228 Kan. 294, 615 P.2d 153 (1980).

In *State v. Goodseal,* the court considered and expressly rejected the minority/California rule that the underlying felony is viewed only in the abstract in determining whether it is inherently dangerous. *Goodseal,* 220 Kan. at 493, 553 P.2d 279. However, in *State v. Underwood,* 228 Kan. at 306, 615 P.2d 153, this court, in a 4 to 3 vote, held that the circumstances of the commission of the felony are not to be examined—the underlying felony is to be analyzed only in the abstract. *Goodseal* and *Moffitt* were overruled.

This rule—that the underlying felony is examined in the abstract—has been stated in subsequent cases, but not always strictly followed. In *State v. Lashley,* 233 Kan. 620, 664 P.2d 1358 (1983), the court held that felony theft, by obtaining or exerting unauthorized control over property, is an inherently dangerous felony. This court added: "[W]e wish to emphasize that theft may be the underlying felony in a charge of felony murder only in cases where the discovery of the thief during the course of the theft results in the death of a person."

Other cases, which apply the abstract analysis, are instructive in this case. In *Underwood,* this court held that unlawful possession of a firearm by a felon could not support felony murder, reasoning:

> The possession of the firearm when viewed in the abstract is not inherently dangerous to human life. This is true because it seems unlikely that mere possession, which has been defined as dominion and control over an object, and not its use, could be undertaken in so dangerous a manner that the prohibited possession would result in murder in the first degree ... It appears quite impossible to find an intent in this collateral felony encompassing malice, deliberation and premeditation so as to transfer these elements to the homicide and relieve the prosecution from proof of the same.

The possession or sale (attempted or actual) of cocaine is like the unlawful possession of a weapon. There is nothing inherently violent or forcible in the sale of crack cocaine. The State attempts to distinguish ... *Underwood* on the basis that [it] involved status crimes—it is the status of the person and mere possession which determine the illegality. The State argues that drug sales, on the other hand, are active crimes and that the nature of the "seedy" locations where the sales take place and the fact that most sales are for cash and large amounts of money may be present, and combine to "create a reckless disregard of consequences and fuel that opportunity for confrontation that the Court requires."

The State's argument fails for several reasons. The intent being transferred or presumed is not recklessness—it is premeditation, malice, etc. The determinative factor of *Brantley* and *Underwood* was not that the crimes therein were status crimes, but that there was no active violence as a part of the crimes; no threat of violence against the persons present. The violence accompanying drug sales is coincidental rather than necessarily inherent.

... [T]his state has a history of requiring that the question of whether a felony is inherently dangerous to human life must be determined when considered in the abstract only. We are not urged in this case that the rule be changed.

The legislature has been aware of this rule for many years and has not seen fit to change either the felony-murder statute or the definition of a "forcible felony." We invite the legislature to consider adopting a more specific first-degree felony-murder statute and a second-degree felony-murder statute.

Viewing a "sale" of a narcotic in the abstract does not mean we use the definition of a sale contained in the Uniform Commercial Code or consider sales of legitimate items by legitimate merchants in the ordinary course of their business. What it does mean is that we consider all sales of crack cocaine and not confine ourselves to the facts of this particular sale. A sale under the Uniform Controlled Substances Act has a broader meaning than "sale" usually has. In addition to "sale's" usual meaning, it includes a gift or any offer to make a gift, a barter, or an exchange, and it is not necessary that the prohibited substance be the property of the defendant or be in his or her physical possession. Simply put, we consider only the question whether the sale of

crack cocaine, when viewed in the abstract, is inherently dangerous.

The record in this case is devoid of any evidence concerning whether the sale of crack cocaine is inherently dangerous. We are not unmindful of the cost to society of the use of illicit drugs and the cost in human tragedy. The legislature has recognized this problem and has consistently sought to control the problem with stiffer penalties and mandatory sentences. That, however, does not make the sale, when viewed in the abstract, inherently dangerous.

The sale, when viewed in the abstract, takes place literally everywhere in our society and with alarming frequency. On occasions isolated sales turn violent. We can only surmise from limited knowledge of the total number of sales alleged to take place in our society that violence is only involved in an extremely small percentage of the sales of illicit drugs. We cannot say that a sale of crack cocaine, when viewed in the abstract, is inherently dangerous. See *People v. Williams,* 63 Cal.2d 452, 47 Cal.Rptr. 7, 406 P.2d 647 (1965) (conspiracy to possess a prohibited drug was not inherently dangerous when the attempted purchaser stabbed the dealer to death). Thus, the conviction for felony murder must be reversed and remanded to the trial court for retrial....

Case Discussion What test did the Kansas court adopt to determine if the felony of selling crack cocaine is inherently dangerous to life? Did Wesson intend to kill the victim? Do we know? Should it matter? Do you think that anyone who dies during a crack deal is murdered? Did Wesson murder his victim? Was it first or second degree? Explain. Should dealing crack substitute for the intent to kill? What if he had merely possessed the crack instead of trying to sell it and someone got killed? Is he guilty of felony murder, since possessing crack cocaine is a felony? Should the court have distinguished between possessing and dealing crack? Why?

Note Cases *1.* Cline, Smith, and Bragg got together to "do drugs." Cline had illegally obtained phenobarbital tablets and the three shared them. Bragg seemed unable to get high on them, so he asked for more, which Cline readily supplied. Later in the evening, after taking a total of 52 tablets, Bragg lapsed into unconsciousness. A few days later, Bragg died from a central nervous system depression caused by barbiturate intoxication. The state of California prosecuted Cline for felony murder, and he was convicted. Cline maintained that the underlying felony—illegal use of narcotics—was not inherently dangerous to human life.

On appeal, the California Supreme Court held:

> A homicide that is a direct causal result of the commission of a felony inherently dangerous to human life (other than the six felonies enumerated in Pen.Code, § 189) constitutes at least second degree murder. However, there can be no deterrent where the felony is not inherently dangerous, since the potential felon will not anticipate that any injury or death might arise solely from the fact that he will commit the felony.... The crucial issue that must be resolved in this appeal is, as pointed out by both parties, whether the felony of furnishing a restricted dangerous drug in violation of § 11912 of the Health and Safety Code is inherently dangerous to human life.
>
> The trial judge found that defendant's act in furnishing a restricted dangerous drug to the deceased in violation of law was inherently dangerous to human life. His finding in this respect is amply supported by the evidence. It was the uncontroverted testimony of the pathologist that the consumption of phenobarbital in unknown strength was dangerous to human life. There was clear evidence that within a period of one-half hour this drug was consumed in considerable quantity by Bragg in defendant's presence and with his knowledge. Even defendant admitted that the deceased consumed 15 of these pills within one-half hour. It is also significant that the Legislature has defined this type of drug as "dangerous." (Health & Saf.Code, § 11901.) *People v. Cline,* 75 Cal.Rptr. 459 (1969)

2. Lee Swatsenbarg had been diagnosed by the family physician as suffering from terminal leukemia. Unable to accept impending death, the 24-year-old Swatsenbarg unsuccessfully sought treatment from a variety of traditional medical sources. He and his wife then began to participate in Bible study, hoping that through faith Lee might be cured. Finally, on the advice of a mutual acquaintance who had heard of defendant's ostensible successes in healing others, Lee turned to defendant for treatment.

During the first meeting between Lee and defendant, the latter described his method of curing cancer. This method included consumption of a unique "lemonade," exposure to colored lights, and a brand of vigorous massage administered by defendant. Defendant remarked that he had successfully treated "thousands" of people, including a number of physicians. He suggested the Swatsenbargs purchase a copy of his book, *Healing for the Age of Enlightenment.* If after reading the book Lee wished to begin defendant's unorthodox treatment, defendant would commence caring for Lee immediately. During the thirty days designated for the treatment, Lee would have to avoid contact with his physician.

Lee read the book, submitted to the conditions delineated by defendant, and placed himself under defendant's care. Defendant instructed Lee to drink the lemonade, salt water, and herb tea, but consume nothing more for the ensuing thirty days. At defendant's behest, the Swatsenbargs bought a lamp equipped with some colored plastic sheets, to bathe Lee in various tints of light. Defendant also agreed to massage Lee from time to time, for an additional fee per session.

Rather than improve, within two weeks Lee's condition began rapidly to deteriorate. He developed a fever, and was growing progressively weaker. Defendant counseled Lee that all was proceeding according to plan, and convinced the young man to postpone a bone marrow test urged by his doctor. During the next week Lee became increasingly ill. He was experiencing severe pain in several areas, including his abdomen, and vomiting frequently.

Defendant administered "deep" abdominal massages on two successive days, each time telling Lee he would soon recuperate. Lee did not recover as defendant expected, however, and the patient began to suffer from convulsions and excruciating pain. He vomited with increasing frequency. Despite defendant's constant attempts at reassurance, the Swatsenbargs began to panic when Lee convulsed for a third time after the latest abdominal massage.

Three and half weeks into the treatment, the couple spent the night at defendant's house, where Lee died of a massive hemorrhage of the mesentery in the abdomen. The evidence presented at trial strongly suggested the hemorrhage was the direct result of the massages performed by defendant.

Did the defendant commit a felony murder? In deciding that he did not, the California Supreme Court noted:

> the few times we have found an underlying felony inherently dangerous (so that it would support a conviction of felony murder), the offense has been tinged with malevolence totally absent from the facts of this case. *People v. Burroughs,* 678 P.2d 894 (Cal.1984)

Second-Degree Murder

Second-degree murder, a catchall, includes all criminal homicides that are neither first-degree murder nor manslaughter. A good way to think of murder is to consider the "ordinary" murder second degree. Some circumstances, outlined under first-degree murder, aggravate murder to first degree. Other circumstances, outlined under manslaughter later in this chapter, reduce murder to manslaughter.

Elements of Second-Degree Murder			
Actus Reus	**Mens Rea**	**Causation**	**Result**
killing another live human being	*1.* intent without premeditation to kill or inflict serious bodily harm, or *2.* intent to commit underlying or predicate felony.	set in motion acts sufficiently related to cause death	death

The court dealt with the *mens rea* of second-degree murder in *People v. Thomas.*

Catch-all of criminal suicides

CASE

Did He Intend to Kill?

People v. Thomas
85 Mich. App. 618, 272 N.W.2d 157 (1978)

[Thomas was convicted of second-degree murder. He appealed. Presiding judge D. E. Holbrook, Jr., delivered the opinion.]

FACTS

The victim, a 19-year-old male "catatonic schizophrenic," was at the time of his death a resident of Oak Haven, a religious practical training school. When it appeared he was not properly responding to ordinary treatment, defendant, the work coordinator at Oak Haven, obtained permission from the victim's parents to discipline him if such seemed necessary. Thereafter defendant, together with another supervisor at Oak Haven, took decedent to the edge of the campus, whereupon decedent's pants were taken down, following which he was spanked with a rubber hose. Such disciplinary session lasted approximately 15 to 30 minutes. During a portion thereof decedent's hands were tied behind his back for failure to cooperate.

Following the disciplinary session aforesaid, defendant testified that the young man improved for awhile but then commenced to backslide. Defendant again received permission from decedent's parents to subject him to further discipline. On September 30, 1976, defendant again took decedent to the approximate same location, removed his pants, bound his hands behind him with a rope looped over a tree limb and proceeded to beat him with a doubled-over rubber hose. This beating lasted approximately 45 minutes to an hour. While the evidence conflicted, it appears that the victim was struck between 30 to 100 times. The beating resulted in severe bruises ranging from the victim's waist to his feet. Decedent's room-

mate testified that decedent had open bleeding sores on his thighs. On the date of death, which was nine days after the beating, decedent's legs were immobile. At no time did defendant obtain medical attention for the victim.

Defendant admitted he had exercised poor judgment, after seeing the bruises, in continuing the discipline. He further testified that in the two days following the discipline, decedent seemed to be suffering from the flu, but by Sunday was up and walking and was in apparent good health until one week following the beating, when decedent became sick with nausea and an upset stomach. These symptoms continued for two days, when decedent died.

As a result of the autopsy, one Dr. Clark testified that the bruises were the result of a trauma and that decedent was in a state of continuous traumatization because he was trying to walk on his injured legs. Dr. Clark testified that decedent's legs were swollen to possibly twice their normal size. He further testified that the actual cause of death was acute pulmonary edema, resulting from the aspiration of stomach contents. Said aspiration caused a laryngeal spasm, causing decedent to suffocate on his own vomit. Although pulmonary edema was the direct cause of death, Dr. Clark testified that said condition usually had some underlying cause and that, while there were literally hundreds of potential underlying causes, it was his opinion that in the instant case the underlying cause was the trauma to decedent's legs. In explaining how the trauma ultimately led to the pulmonary edema, Dr. Clark testified that the trauma to the legs produced "crush syndrome" or "blast trauma," also known as "tubular necrosis." "Crush syndrome" is a condition caused when a part of the body has been compressed for a long period of time and then released. In such cases, there is a tremendous amount of tissue damage to the body part that has been crushed. When the compression is relieved, the tissues begin to return to their normal position, but due to the compression, gaps appear between the layers of tissues, and these areas fill up with blood and other body fluids, causing swelling. In the present case, Dr. Clark estimated that about 10–15% of decedent's entire body fluids were contained in the legs, adding an additional ten pounds in weight to the normal weight of the legs and swelling them to twice their normal size. This extra blood and body fluid decreased the amount of blood available for circulation in the rest of the body and would cause the person to become weak, faint and pass out if he attempted to sit up or do other activities. Decedent was sitting up when he died. It was Dr. Clark's opinion that the causal connection between the trauma and death was more than medically probable and that it was "medically likely." He further testified he could say with a reasonable degree of medical certainty that the trauma to the legs was the cause of death.

OPINION

Appellant claims that the prosecution failed to establish the malice element of second-degree murder. We disagree. Malice or intent to kill may be inferred from the acts of the defendant. In *People v. Morrin,* then Judge, now Justice Levin, stated that the intent to kill may be implied where the actor actually intends to inflict great bodily harm or the natural tendency of his behavior is to cause death or great bodily harm. In the instant case defendant's savage and brutal beating of the decedent is amply sufficient to establish malice. He clearly intended to beat the victim and the natural tendency of defendant's behavior was to cause great bodily harm.

Death was medically likely to have been caused by the beating through a chain of natural effects and causes unchanged by human action. Pulmonary edema resulted and the victim choked to death on his own vomit. Sufficient evidence of causal relationship was established by the prosecution. No reversible error occurred.

Affirmed.

Case Discussion

The court in *Thomas* ruled that Thomas had the requisite *mens rea* for second-degree murder because he intended to "inflict great bodily harm" on the deceased. The reason it is murder even though Thomas did not intend to kill is plain: Intending to beat someone within an inch of his or her life is not different enough from intending to beat someone to death to grade the two crimes differently. Do you agree that it is murder if Thomas intended only to beat the deceased severely? What is Thomas's *mens rea* with respect to the death: purposeful, reckless, negligent? Does this case mean that reckless homicide is murder?

What if a man, intending merely to unload his gun, shoots into the air, and bullets penetrate an airplane passing overhead, killing a passenger? Here, an intent neither to kill nor even to harm accompanied the death. Can this be murder? According to what used to be called depraved-heart murder and what is now called reckless murder, the answer is yes. Defendants who create high risks that people will either die or suffer serious injury and know they are creating those risks are considered sufficiently culpable to be punished for criminal homicide. Suppose the man shooting the gun had said aloud: "I know I might hit this plane and kill someone. Of course, I don't want to hurt or kill anyone. I hope I don't, but I'm going to clear the gun anyway." He thus created the risk of death purposely or at least consciously or knowingly. If death results from such a conscious risk creation, holding the risk creator criminally liable is considered reasonable. Whether the crime is murder, however, is open to debate.

To some analysts, careful adherence to *mens rea* suggests that too great a distance separates purposely or knowingly creating a risk to life from actually intending to kill. Intent to kill, they contend, is the only proper murder *mens rea*. Despite these objections, depraved heart killing constitutes murder in most jurisdictions, although only in the second degree.

In addition to murders that result from intent to do serious bodily harm and depraved-heart murders, some felony murders constitute second-degree murders. Several jurisdictions distinguish between two types of felony murders. First degree is reserved for murders committed during the most dangerous felonies: rape, armed robbery, and arson. Killings resulting from some abortions and from felonies that are considered less life threatening, including aggravated assault and felonious drunken driving, are made second-degree murder. Courts have rejected the notion that an accidental death during a forcibly resisted lawful arrest constitutes second-degree murder.[22]

Corporate Murder

Several recent cases have raised the question of whether corporations can commit murder. Prosecutors have charged several corporations with criminal homicide, even murder in a few cases.

Three young women were killed on an Indiana highway when their Ford Pinto exploded after being struck from behind. The explosion followed several other similar incidents that led to grisly deaths. Evidence was published revealing that perhaps Ford knew the Pinto gas tanks were not safe but took the risk that they would not explode and injure or kill anyone. Following the three young women's deaths, Indiana indicted Ford Motor Company for reckless homicide, charging that Ford had recklessly authorized, approved, designed, and manufactured the Pinto and allowed the car to remain in use with defectively designed fuel tanks. These tanks, the indictment charged, killed the three young women in Indiana. For a number of reasons not related directly to whether corporations can commit murder, the case was later dismissed.[23]

In 1986, Autumn Hills Convalescent Centers, a corporation that operates nursing homes, went on trial under charges that it had murdered an eighty-seven-year-old woman by neglect. David Marks, a Texas assistant attorney general, said, "From the first day until her last breath, she was unattended to and allowed to lie day and night in her own urine and waste." The case attracted attention because charges were made that as many as sixty elderly people had died from substandard care at the Autumn Hills nursing home near Galveston, Texas. The indictment charged that the company had failed to provide nutrients, fluids, and incontinent care for Mrs. Breed and neglected to turn and reposition her regularly to combat bedsores. One prosecution witness testified that Mrs. Breed's bed was wet constantly and the staff seldom cleaned her. The corporation defended against the charges, claiming that Mrs. Breed had died from colon cancer, not improper care.[24]

The Model Penal Code and most comparable state criminal codes apply to criminal homicide as they do to other crimes committed for the corporation's benefit. Specifically, both corporations and high corporate officers acting within the scope of their authority for a corporation's benefit can commit murder. Practically speaking, however, prosecutors rarely charge corporations of their officers with criminal homicide, and convictions rarely, if ever, follow when they do.

The reluctance to prosecute corporations for murder or for any homicide requiring intent has to do with the hesitation to view corporations as persons. Although theoretically the law clearly makes that possible, in practice prosecutors and courts have drawn the line at involuntary manslaughter, a crime whose *mens rea* is negligence and occasionally recklessness. As for corporate executives, the reluctance to prosecute stems from vicarious liability and the questions it raises about culpability (see chapter 4). It has been difficult to attribute deaths linked with corporate benefit to corporate officers who were in charge generally but did not order or authorize a killing, did not know about it, or even did not want it to happen.

A third, and practical, reason why so few corporations or their officers face murder charges is that prosecutors cannot link particular officers with the deaths. Therefore, they cannot prove guilt beyond a reasonable doubt—the standard required in criminal cases. This is particularly true where organizations are complex and authority is diffused among so many officers and their subordinates that blaming any one or a few might not be feasible. Although signs indicate that this is changing, the cases brought to date are noteworthy mainly because they are exceptions to the general rule that corporations and their officers are rarely, if ever, charged with or found guilty of any criminal homicide except involuntary manslaughter.

Only in egregious cases that receive strong public attention, such as the Pinto and nursing home cases mentioned earlier, do prosecutors risk acquittal by trying corporations and their officers for criminal homicide. In these cases, prosecutors do not hope to win the case in traditional terms, meaning to secure convictions. Business law professor William J. Maakestad says:

> At this point, success of this type of corporate criminal prosecution is defined by establishing the legitimacy of the case. If you can get the case to trial, you have really achieved success.[25]

CASE

Did They "Murder" Their Employee?

Three Executives Convicted of Murder for Unsafe Workplace Conditions[26]

On 14 June 1985, Steven J. O'Neill, former president of Film Recovery Systems, Charles Kirschbaum, the plant supervisor, and Daniel Rodriguez, the plant foreman, were convicted of murder. They face prison sentences ranging from twenty to forty years.

The prosecution arose when Stefan Golab, a fifty-nine-year-old Polish immigrant, died from what the coroner declared was cyanide poisoning. Golab worked at the Film Recovery Systems plant, which used cyanide to extract silver from old films. The poisoning occurred from breathing hydrogen cyanide fumes present in the plant. The prosecution argued that the defendants knew about the fumes and did nothing about them. Workers testified that the stench from the fumes was often so bad they had to rush outside the plant to vomit.

The prosecution argued further that many employees did not speak or read English, so they could not read warnings and were not told the bubbling vats from which the cyanide fumes emanated were dangerous.

The defense argued that after federal and state regulatory agencies had inspected the plant, they never told the defendants that they were doing anything wrong. Their case was built mainly on the argument that the defendants were not aware they had created the risk that led to Golab's death. "There has been nobody who ever came forward to say, 'Fellas, this plant is not being operated acceptably,'" said one defense attorney. Ronald J. P. Banks, Cook County Circuit Court judge, ruled:

> The conditions under which workers performed their duties "were totally unsafe" and the executives "were totally knowledgeable" of the plant's hazardous conditions.

In a trial without a jury, Judge Banks found all three defendants guilty.

Case Discussion

According to Judge Banks's ruling, the defendants consciously created a risk that Golab might die from cyanide poisoning but did nothing about it. Is this murder or manslaughter? If you were deciding the case, what crime would you call it if the defendants are telling the truth? If the prosecution's version is the truth? Do you see why vicarious liability is a difficult ground upon which to rest a criminal homicide conviction?

Following the conviction, Attorney Richard M. Daley said the verdicts meant that employers who knowingly expose their workers to dangerous conditions leading to injury or even death can be held criminally responsible for the results of their actions.

Ralph Nader, consumer advocate lawyer, said:

> The public is pretty upset with dangerously defective products, bribery, toxic waste, and job hazards. The polls all show it. The verdict today will encourage other prosecutors and judges to take more seriously the need to have the criminal law catch up with corporate crime.

Professor John Coffee, Columbia University Law School, said, "When you threaten the principal adequately, he will monitor the behavior of his agent."

A California deputy district attorney put it more bluntly: "A person facing a jail sentence is the best deterrent against wrongdoing."

Joseph E. Hadley, Jr., a corporate lawyer who specializes in health and safety issues, said the decision would not send shock waves through the corporate community:

> I don't think corporate America should be viewed as in the ballpark with these folks. This was a highly unusual situation, but now people see that where the egregious situation occurs, there could be a criminal remedy.

Robert Stephenson, a lawyer defending another corporation, said, "I don't believe these statutes [murder and aggravated battery] were ever meant to be used in this way."

Utah's governor Scott M. Matheson refused to extradite Michael T. McKay, a former Film Recovery vice-president then living in Utah, because he was an "exemplary citizen who should not be subjected to the sensational charges in Illinois."

Which of the preceding statements best describes what you think is proper policy regarding corporate executive murder prosecutions?

Summary of Murder

Murder includes all killings committed with malice. Legal malice does not mean hate or spite as those terms are commonly used. Rather, it embraces several mental states, including a purpose to kill, an intent to do serious bodily harm, a depraved heart, and the intent to commit a serious felony.

Murder is divided into degrees. First-degree murder includes (1) purposeful, premeditated, and deliberate killing; (2) atrocious or cruel murder; and sometimes (3) felony murder. Second-degree murder is a catchall category including all criminal homicides that constitute neither first-degree murder nor manslaughter. The principal second-degree murders include (1) murders not premeditated or deliberate; (2) killings resulting from the intent to inflict great bodily injury; (3) some felony murders; and, in a few states, (4) murders that occur while resisting lawful arrest.

Manslaughter

Manslaughter, another catchall, includes all homicides that are neither justified nor excused at one extreme, nor murder at the other. The criminal law divides manslaughter into two categories: voluntary and involuntary. A third type of manslaughter—negligent homicide—includes many fatal automobile accidents. At common law, manslaughter meant

> the unlawful killing of another, without malice either express or implied ... either voluntarily, upon a sudden heat; or involuntarily, but in the commission of some unlawful act.[27]

Elements of Manslaughter

Actus Reus	Mens Rea	Causation	Result
killing another live human being	1. purpose or intent to kill or inflict serious bodily harm in the sudden heat of passion upon adequate provocation, or 2. reckless, or 3. negligent	acts set in motion chain of events sufficiently related to causing death	death

Voluntary Manslaughter   Voluntary manslaughter, another catchall, includes all homicides that are neither murder, involuntary manslaughter, negligent homicide, justifiable, nor excusable. Several circumstances reduce murder to voluntary manslaughter. An intentional killing in the unreasonable belief that self-defense required use of deadly force, sometimes called imperfect self-defense (chapter 6), can reduce murder to voluntary manslaughter even if it is not justified enough to constitute self-defense.

> A person is guilty of voluntary manslaughter, if, in taking another's life, he believes that he is in danger of losing his own life or suffering great bodily harm but his belief is unreasonable.[28]

Voluntary manslaughters require provocation. While the criminal law aims to bridle passions and build self-control, it does not ignore the frailty of human nature. Hence, an intentional killing, while still a crime, might fall into a lower grade than murder. In other words, the law does not reward individuals who give in to their rages by freeing those individuals; it reduces murder to manslaughter under carefully defined conditions under the provocation rule, including killings that occur

☐ With provocation the law deems adequate
☐ In a "sudden heat of passion"
☐ Without time for passions reasonably to cool
☐ Where a causal connection links the provocation, the passion, and the fatal act[29]

The law recognizes only some provocations, called adequate provocation. Everyone who flies into a rage and suddenly kill someone has not committed voluntary manslaughter instead of murder. The main provocations the law regards as adequate to reduce murder to manslaughter include mutual combat or quarrel, battery, assault, trespass, some informational words, and adultery.

The law recognizes mutual fights as provocations sufficient to reduce murder to manslaughter only if the fight is serious; scuffles do not qualify. The fight must generate a sudden passion without reasonable time to cool off before the killing. And, the fight, passion, and death must have causal links.

The law also recognizes some batteries, but not all offensive touching (chapter 9), as adequate provocation. Pistol whipping on the head, striking hard with fists in the face, and "staggering" body blows constitute adequate provocation. Slight slaps do not qualify.

Assault, where the assailant establishes no body contact, is sometimes adequate provocation. In one case, a man shot at the defendant and missed him. The defendant was so enraged that as the assailant ran away, he shot him in the back. The initial assault, although not enough to qualify the defendant's action as self-defense, was regarded sufficiently provocative to reduce murder to manslaughter.[30]

Insulting gestures are not adequate provocation, at least not on their own. If, however, they indicate an intent to attack with deadly force, they constitute adequate provocation. Thus, using a well-known obscene gesture is not adequate provocation, but waving a gun around in a threatening manner can be.

[handwritten in margin: Words or insults, gestures from are not [illegible] provocation [illegible]]

Some trespasses are sufficient provocation to reduce murder to manslaughter. A common statement is that trespasses are adequate provocation only if trespassers invade slayers' home and put them in danger.[31]

The case of *State v. Watson* examined whether certain informational words provide adequate provocation.

CASE

Are Words Adequate Provocation?

State v. Watson

287 N.C. 147, 214 S.E.2d 85 (1975)

[Watson was convicted of second-degree murder and was sentenced to life imprisonment. He appealed, arguing that he was legally provoked. Justice Copeland delivered the opinion.]

FACTS

At the time of this incident, defendant, a black, was twenty-years-old. He was serving a twenty-five year prison sentence on judgment imposed at the October, 1972, Session of Rockingham County Superior Court upon his plea of guilty to second-degree murder. The decedent Samples, was white. Neither Samples' age nor the basis for his incarceration appears from the record.

The defendant was called "Duck" by his fellow prisoners in I-Dorm. Samples, the decedent, was known as "Pee Wee." Although Samples was referred to as "Pee Wee," there appeared to be no relation between this nickname and his physical size. In fact, he was a strong man who worked out daily with weights.

The "hearsay" among the residents of I-Dorm was to the effect that Watson and Samples were "swapping-out." "Swapping-out" is a prison term that means two inmates are engaging in homosexual practices. Generally, prisoners that are "swapping-out" try to hide the practice from their fellow inmates. In particular, they try to hide it

from any "home-boys" that may be in their particular unit. A "home-boy," in the prison vernacular, is a fellow inmate from one's own hometown or community. One of the State's witnesses, Johnny Lee Wilson, a resident of I-Dorm on the date of the offense, was Samples' "home-boy."

It appears that Watson and Samples had been "swapping-out" for several months. Approximately a month or so prior to the date of the killing, Watson and Samples had engaged in a "scuffle" while working in the prison kitchen. This appears to have been nothing more than a fist-fight. Samples was the winner. Although it is by no means clear from the record, it appears that this "scuffle" arose out of Samples' suspicion that Watson had been "swapping-out" with another prisoner.

At approximately 4:30 p.m. on the afternoon of the killing, Johnny Lee Wilson, Samples' "home-boy," saw Watson and Samples sitting together on a bunk in the back of I-Dorm. At this time, "they were close talking, they were close." Apparently, assuming that they were about to "swap-out," and not wanting to embarrass Samples, Wilson quickly turned around and left the dorm.

Shortly before the lights were to be dimmed (10:00 p.m.), Watson and Samples began to argue. After several minutes, Watson got up and walked across the aisle, a distance of approximately seven feet, to his bunk. Samples subsequently followed him and renewed the dispute. At this time, both parties were seated on Watson's bottom bunk. During the course of the renewed argument, Samples was verbally abusing Watson and challenging him to fight. At one point, he said: "Nigger, nigger, you're just like the rest of them." He also told Watson that he was too scared to fight him and that all he was going to do was tremble and stay in his bunk. Finally, Samples made several derogatory and obscene references to Watson's mother. The prisoners refer to this as "shooting the dove." Generally, when a prisoner "shoots the dove," he expects the other party to fight. At this point, Watson told Johnny Lee Wilson, whose bunk was nearby on Watson's side of the room: "You better get your home-boy straightened out before I f—— him up." Responding to this statement, Samples said: "Why don't you f—— me up if that's what you want to do. All you're gonna do is tremble, nigger."

As Samples was making the above quoted statement, he was walking over to Wilson's bunk. Samples borrowed a cigarette from Wilson and then proceeded to his own bed. He got up in his bunk (top) and was more or less half sitting up with his back propped up against the wall. At this point, he renewed the argument with Watson, who was still in his bottom bunk on the opposite side of the room. He called Watson a "nigger" and "a black mother f——." While this was going on, Watson, without saying a word, either walked or ran across the aisle between the two rows of bunks and violently and repeatedly stabbed Samples with a kitchen-type paring knife. According to the State's witnesses, this occurred approximately two (2) to ten (10) minutes after Samples had left Watson's bed.

After summarizing the evidence, and prior to fully instructing on first-degree murder, the court stated: "[L]et me say here, that mere words will not form a justification or excuse for a crime of this sort."

In instructing the jury on voluntary manslaughter, the court stated: "[T]he defendant must satisfy you that this passion was produced by acts of Samples which the law regards as adequate provocation. This may consist of anything which has a natural tendency to produce such passion in a person of average mind and disposition. However, words and gestures alone, where no assault is made or threatened, regardless of how insulting or inflammatory those words or gestures may be, does not constitute ade-

quate provocation for the taking of a human life."

OPINION

[After reviewing several other decisions, the court wrote:]

These decisions establish the following rules as to the legal effect of abusive language: (1) Mere words, however abusive, are never sufficient legal provocation to mitigate a homicide to a lesser degree; and (2) A defendant, prosecuted for a homicide in a difficulty that he has provoked by the use of language "calculated and intended" to bring on the encounter, cannot maintain the position of perfect self-defense unless, at a time prior to the killing, he withdrew from the encounter within the meaning of the law. These two rules are logically consistent and demonstrate that abusive language will not serve as a legally sufficient provocation for a homicide in this State.

These well-settled rules are clearly controlling in the instant case. Hence, if defendant had provoked an assault by the deceased through the use of abusive language and had thereafter killed the deceased, then it would have been for the jury to determine if the language used by defendant, given the relationship of the parties, the circumstances surrounding the verbal assertions, etc., was "calculated and intended" to bring on the assault. If the jury had found this to be the case, then defendant would not have had the benefit of the doctrine of perfect self-defense, even though the deceased instigated the actual physical attack. But, here there was no evidence that defendant killed the deceased in self-defense. In fact, all of the evidence tends to show that the fatal attack was brought on by the continued verbal abuses directed toward defendant by the deceased. Under these circumstances, there was no basis for a jury determination of whether any of the words were "calculated and intended" to bring on the difficulty.

At this point, we note that in those few jurisdictions that permit abusive language to mitigate the degree of homicide, the majority hold that the words are only deemed sufficient to negate premeditation, thereby reducing the degree of homicide from first to second. Most of these courts reason that since the deceased had made no attempt to endanger the life of the accused, the action of the latter in meeting the insulting remarks with sufficient force (deadly or otherwise) to cause the death of the former, was beyond the bounds of sufficient retaliation to constitute sufficient provocation to reduce the homicide to manslaughter. See Annot., 2 A.L.R.3d 1292, 1308–10 (1965). Although we expressly decline to adopt this minority view, we note that the jury in the instant case apparently applied the same reasoning and found defendant guilty of second-degree murder. Thus, even if the minority rule applied in this State, defendant would not be entitled to a new trial as a result of the instructions here given.

Defendant contends that the trial court committed prejudicial error in charging the jury as follows:

Now, ladies and gentlemen of the jury, this case is to be tried by you under the laws of the State of North Carolina, and not upon the rules and regulations and customs and unwritten code that exists within the walls of the North Carolina Department of Correction. I can't charge you on that law because I don't know that law. I think I know this one, and this is the law that you are trying this case under.

Defendant argues that this instruction "tends to discount as a matter of law all of the factual information" that the jury was "entitled to consider, not as law, but as a part of the factual background situation within which the incident took place." We find nothing in the charge to support such an inference. During the course of the trial, several of the State's witnesses (either present or former prison inmates) testified about a "prison code," i.e., a set of unwritten rules developed by the prisoners themselves. For example, one of the State's witnesses made the following statements on cross-examination:

> In the prison system, if Watson had not fought after Samples had called him nigger, nigger, and talked about his mother, I guess, you know, everybody else probably would be jugging at him. What I mean by "jugging at him," I mean, messing with him, you know. Taking advantage of the fact that he won't stand up for himself. It is important that you stand up for yourself in the system because if you don't, somebody might get you down in the shower, you know. You might get dead-ended. It means if you don't take up for yourself, everybody picks on you.

Apparently, standing up for oneself was a vital part of this so-called "prison code." In this context, the import of the above instruction was clearly to inform the jurors that the case—like all other criminal cases tried in the North Carolina General Courts of Justice—had to be tried under the laws of this State and not upon any unwritten prisoners' code that existed within the walls of North Carolina's prisons. It is certainly not error for a trial judge to so instruct a jury. Furthermore, it appears that defendant's conduct even constituted a violation of the prisoners' code. We refer to the following redirect testimony of the same witness previously quoted above: "Standing up for yourself in the prison system would not necessarily include using a knife. He could have run over there and fought with bare fists, that would have been standing up for himself."

Defendant's contention under this assignment is without merit. Therefore, it is overruled. Affirmed.

Case Discussion The *Watson* court states flatly that words are never adequate provocation to reduce murder to manslaughter, although they may be adequate to reduce murder from first to second degree. Do you think this is a good rule for this case? Especially, is it good when the prison code called on Watson to stand up for himself or be mistreated in the future? In fact, if the unwritten prison code does call for him to stand up for himself, was it the words or fears for his personal safety that provoked him? If you were the judge, would you have interpreted the provocation rule differently? Why or why not?

Some jurisdictions have replaced specific lists of adequate provocations, taking the view that the law does not require a "specific type of provocation." According to the court in *People v. Berry:*

> In the present condition of our law *it is left to the jurors* to say whether the facts and circumstances in evidence are sufficient to lead them to believe that the defendant did, or to create a reasonable doubt in their minds as to whether or not he did, commit his offense under the heat of passion.[32]

Is this a better rule? If so, how would you as a juror apply it in this case?

<hr />

According to the common law, a man who caught his wife in the act of adultery had adequate provocation to kill: "there could be no greater provocation than this." Many cases have held that it is voluntary manslaughter for a husband to kill his wife, her paramour, or both in the first heat of passion following the sight of adultery. For a short time, statutes went beyond the common-law rule and called paramour killings justified homicide. Historically, the **paramour rule** did not apply to both spouses; the common law made it available only to husbands. Furthermore, the common law and statutes have restricted the rule to cases where spouse are caught in adulterous acts; the rule has not covered spouses who reacted upon learning about adultery after it occurred.[33]

CASE

Did She Adequately Provoke Him?

Commonwealth v. Schnopps
383 Mass. 178, 417 N.E.2d 1213 (1981)

[Schnopps was convicted of first-degree murder. He appealed. Justice Abrams delivered the opinion.]

FACTS
On October 13, 1979, Marilyn R. Schnopps was fatally shot by her estranged husband, George A. Schnopps. A jury convicted Schnopps of murder in the first degree, and he was sentenced to the mandatory term of life imprisonment. Schnopps claims that the trial judge erred by refusing to instruct the

jury on voluntary manslaughter. We agree. We reverse and order a new trial.

Schnopps testified that his wife had left him three weeks prior to the slaying. He claims that he first became aware of problems in his fourteen-year marriage at a point about six months before the slaying. According to the defendant, on that occasion he took his wife to a club to dance, and she spent the evening dancing with a coworker. On arriving home, the defendant and his wife argued over her conduct. She told him that she no longer loved him and that she wanted a divorce. Schnopps became very upset. He admitted that he took out his shotgun during the course of this argument, but he denied that he intended to use it.

During the next few months, Schnopps argued frequently with his wife. The defendant accused her of seeing another man, but she steadfastly denied the accusations. On more than one occasion Schnopps threatened his wife with physical harm. He testified he never intended to hurt his wife but only wanted to scare her so that she would end the relationship with her coworker.

One day in September, 1979, the defendant became aware that the suspected boy friend used a "signal" in telephoning Schnopps' wife. Schnopps used the signal, and his wife answered the phone with "Hi, Lover." She hung up immediately when she recognized Schnopps' voice. That afternoon she did not return home. Later that evening, she informed Schnopps by telephone that she had moved to her mother's house and that she had the children with her. She told Schnopps she would not return to their home. Thereafter she "froze [him] out," and would not talk to him. During this period, the defendant spoke with a lawyer about a divorce and was told that he had a good chance of getting custody of the children, due to his wife's "desertion and adultery."

On the day of the killing, Schnopps had asked his wife to come to their home and talk over their marital difficulties. Schnopps told his wife that he wanted his children at home, and that he wanted the family to remain intact. Schnopps cried during the conversation, and begged his wife to let the children live with him and to keep their family together. His wife replied, "No, I am going to court, you are going to give me all the furniture, you are going to have to get the Hell out of here, you won't have nothing." Then, pointing to her crotch, she said, "You will never touch this again, because I have got something bigger and better for it."

On hearing those words, Schnopps claims that his mind went blank, and that he went "berserk." He went to a cabinet and got out a pistol he had bought and loaded the day before, and he shot his wife and himself. When he "started coming to" as a result of the pain she asked him to summon help. The victim was pronounced dead at the scene, and the defendant was arrested and taken to the hospital for treatment of his wound.

OPINION

The issue raised by Schnopps' appeal is whether in these circumstances the judge was required to instruct the jury on voluntary manslaughter. Instructions on voluntary manslaughter must be given if there is evidence of provocation deemed adequate in law to cause the accused to lose his self control in the heat of passion, and if the killing followed the provocation before sufficient time had elapsed for the accused's temper to cool. A verdict of voluntary manslaughter requires the trier of fact to conclude that there is a causal connection between the provocation, the heat of passion, and the killing.

Schnopps argues that "[t]he existence of sufficient provocation is not foreclosed absolutely because a defendant learns of a fact from oral statements rather than from personal observation," and that a sudden admission of adultery is equivalent to a discovery of the act itself, and is sufficient evidence of provocation.

Schnopps asserts that his wife's statements constituted a "peculiarly immediate and intense offense to a spouse's sensitivities." He concedes that the words at issue are indicative of past as well as present adultery. Schnopps claims, however, that his wife's admission of adultery was made for the first time on the day of the killing, and hence the evidence of provocation was sufficient to trigger jury consideration of voluntary manslaughter as a possible verdict.

Reversed and remanded for new trial on manslaughter issue.

Case Discussion The paramour rule was adopted to cover cases where husbands found their wives in bed with other men. The provocation was the sight itself. Thus, the passion was immediately connected to the adulterous act. If you were a juror, could you in good conscience say that Schnopps was adequately provoked? If so, was it the adultery that provoked him or the provocative words his wife used to describe her adulterous relationship? Do you think the prohibition against provocative words makes sense? If you were writing a manslaughter law, how would you treat cases like *Schnopps?*

Adequate provocation means reasonable provocation. But reasonable to whom? Reasonableness can mean reasonable in the statistical sense; that is, how would the majority of people react under similar circumstances? Or, it can mean reasonable in a normative sense; that is, how should the person react under the circumstances, or how does the law expect people to react in these circumstances?

Sometimes defendants in special circumstances argue that the standard should be whether the circumstances would have provoked a reasonable person in their special category. In *People v. Washington,* Merle Francis Washington shot his homosexual partner following a lover's quarrel, brought on by the victim Owen Wilson Brady's unfaithfulness. The court instructed the jury on provocation as follows:

> [T]he jury was instructed that to reduce the homicide from murder to manslaughter upon the ground of sudden quarrel or heat of passion, the conduct must be tested by the ordinarily reasonable man test. Defendant argues without precedent that to so instruct was error because, "Homosexuals are not at present a curiosity or a rare commodity. They are a distinct third sexual class between that of male and female, are present in almost every field of endeavor, and are fast achieving a guarded recognition not formerly accorded them. The heat of their passions in dealing with one another should not be tested by standards applicable to the average man or the average woman, since they are aberrant hybrids, with an obvious diminished capacity.
>
> Defendant submits that since the evidence disclosed that he was acting as a servient homosexual during the period of his relationship with the victim, that his heat of passion should have been tested, either by a standard applicable to a female, or a standard applicable to the average homosexual, and that it was prejudicial error to instruct the jury to determine his heat of passion defense by standards applicable to the average male."
>
> We do not agree:
>
> In the present condition of our law it is left to the jurors to say whether or not the facts and circumstances in evidence are sufficient to lead them to believe that the defendant did, or to create a reasonable doubt in their minds as to whether or not he did, commit his offense under a heat of passion. The jury is further to be admonished and advised by the court that this heat of passion must be such a passion as would naturally be aroused in the mind of an ordinarily reasonable person under the given facts and circumstances, and that, consequently, no defendant may set up his own standard of conduct and justify or excuse himself because in fact his passions were aroused, unless further the jury believe that the facts and circumstances were sufficient to arouse the passions of the ordinarily reasonable man. Thus no man of extremely violent passion could so justify or excuse himself if the exciting cause be not adequate, nor could an excessively cowardly man justify himself unless the circumstances were such as to arouse the fears of the ordinarily courageous man. Still further, while the conduct of the defendant is to be measured by that of the ordinarily reasonable man placed in identical circumstances, the jury is properly to be told that the exciting cause must be such as would naturally tend to arouse the passion of the ordinarily reasonable man.[34]

Voluntary manslaughter requires not only adequate or reasonable provocation but also actual provocation. The provocation must, in fact, provoke the defendant. The provocation rule contains both objective and subjective dimensions. The provocations that the law recognizes as adequate constitute the objective side of provocation; that these provocations in fact provoke the defendant constitute the subjective side.

At common law, and in most modern statutes, voluntary manslaughter requires killing in the "sudden heat of passion" with no "cooling off" period. The actual time between provocation and killing, whether seconds, hours, or even days, depends upon the facts of the individual case. Courts usually apply an objective test: Would a reasonable person under the same circumstances have had time to cool off? If defendants had reasonable time for their murderous rages to subside, the law views their killings as murders even if the provocations were adequate to reduce those killings to manslaughter had they taken place immediately following the provocations.

Using the same objective test, the time for cooling off may be considerable. In one case, a man's wife told him her father had raped her. The court ruled that the husband's passion had not reasonably cooled even after he walked all night to his father-in-law's house and killed him the next day! The court said the heinous combination of incest and rape was sufficient to keep a reasonable person in a murderous rage for at least several days.[35]

To prove voluntary manslaughter, the prosecution must prove a causal link between the provocation, passion, and killing. It is not voluntary manslaughter if I intend to kill an enemy, and, just as I am about to execute my intent, I find him in bed with my wife and use that as my excuse to kill. The provocation must cause the passion that leads to the killing.

Voluntary manslaughter, then, consists of the following material elements: (1) intentional or purposeful killing that (2) occurs in a sudden heat of passion (3) without time to cool off and that is (4) caused by (5) reasonable and actual provocation.

Involuntary Manslaughter   Involuntary manslaughter is criminal homicide in which the killers did not intend to cause death. In involuntary manslaughters, deaths result from either reckless or negligent legal acts, or during illegal conduct. The last case, called the **misdemeanor manslaughter rule,** is the counterpart to the felony murder doctrine. According to this rule, if death occurs during the commission of a misdemeanor, the misdemeanant has committed involuntary manslaughter. Courts vary as to the kinds of unlawful acts that qualify under the misdemeanor manslaughter doctrine. Most include breaches of public order, injuries to persons or property, and outrages against public decency and morals. Examples include nonfelonious assault, carrying a concealed weapon, driving illegally, and dispensing drugs.

CASE

*Did He Commit
Involuntary
Manslaughter?*

Commonwealth v. Feinberg
253 A.2d 636 (Pa.1969)

Jones, Justice

FACTS
Appellant Max Feinberg owned and operated a cigar store in the skid-row section of Philadelphia. One of the products he sold was Sterno, a jelly-like substance composed primarily of methanol and ethanol and designed for cooking and heating purposes.

Sterno was manufactured and sold in two types of containers, one for home use and one for industrial use. Before September, 1963, both types of Sterno contained approximately 3.75% methanol, or wood alcohol, and 71% ethanol, or grain alcohol; of the two types of alcohols, methanol is far more toxic if consumed internally. Beginning in September of 1963, the Sterno company began manufacturing a new type of industrial Sterno which was 54% methanol. The cans containing the new industrial Sterno were identical to the cans containing the old industrial Sterno except in one crucial aspect: on the lids of the new 54% methanol Sterno were imprinted the words "Institutional Sterno. Danger. Poison. For use only as a Fuel. Not for consumer use. For industrial and commercial use. Not for home use." A skull and crossbones were also lithographed on the lid. The carton in which the new Sterno cans were packaged and shipped did not indicate that the contents differed in any respect from the old industrial Sterno.

According to its records, Sterno Corporation sent only one shipment of the new Sterno to the Philadelphia area; that shipment went to the Richter Paper Company and was received on December 17, 1963. Charles Richter, president of the firm, testified that his company, in turn, made only one sale of the new industrial Sterno, and that was to appellant. Richter testified that his records indicated that appellant received the Sterno on December 21 and, since Richter had not opened any of the cartons, he was unaware that he was selling appellant a new type of industrial Sterno. On December 27, Richter received a call from appellant informing him that the cartons contained a new type of Sterno and that appellant wished to return the portion of his order that he had not sold. The unused cartons were picked up by Richter's deliveryman the next day.

Meanwhile, between December 21 and December 28, appellant had sold approximately 400 cans of the new industrial Sterno. Between December 23 and December 30, thirty-one persons died in the skid-row area as a result of methanol poisoning. In many of the cases the source of the methanol was traced to the new industrial Sterno. Since appellant was the only retail outlet of this type of Sterno in Philadelphia, he was arrested and indicted on thirty-one counts charging involuntary manslaughter.... Appellant was convicted on seventeen counts of involuntary manslaughter....

OPINION

... The ... issue in this case is whether appellant is guilty of involuntary manslaughter in each or any of the four appeals presently before us. The Penal Code defines involuntary manslaughter as a death "happening in consequence of an unlawful act, or the doing of a lawful act in an unlawful way."...

[COURT NOTE: "We express no opinion as to whether appellant violated the Pennsylvania Liquor Code in selling Sterno for drinking purposes. At least two courts have held that the manufacture of moonshine, which violates liquor control laws, is merely *malum prohibitum* and that if a death results from drinking the moonshine, the violation of the liquor code is insufficient to justify a conviction for misdemeanor manslaughter."]

When a death results from the doing of an act lawful in itself but done in an unlawful manner, in order to sustain a conviction for manslaughter the Commonwealth must present evidence to prove that the defendant acted in a rash or reckless manner. The conduct of the defendant resulting in the death must be such a departure from the behavior of an ordinary and prudent man as to evidence a disregard of human life or an indifference to the consequences. Furthermore, there must be a direct causal relationship between the defendant's act and the deceased's death.

We have searched in vain for cases from this Commonwealth involving factual situations similar to the one now before us. We have, however, found four cases from other jurisdictions which are on point. In the leading case, *Thiede v. State,* 106 Neb. 48, 182 N.W. 570 (1921), the defendant gave the deceased moonshine containing methanol, the drinking of which resulted in his death. While noting that the defendant had violated the state prohibition laws, the court refused to rest the manslaughter conviction on this statutory violation, holding that the manufacturing and distribution of moonshine was merely malum prohibitum and not malum per se. The court continued, "We cannot go so far as to say that (dispensing moonshine), prompted perhaps by the spirit of good-fellowship, though prohibited by law, could ever, by any resulting consequence, be converted into the crime of manslaughter; But, where the liquor by reason of its extreme potency or poisonous ingredients, is dangerous to use as an intoxicating beverage, where the drinking of it is capable of producing direct physical injury, other than as an ordinary intoxicant, and of perhaps endangering life itself, the case is different, and the question of negligence enters; for, if the party furnishing the liquor knows, or was apprised of such facts that he should have known, of the danger, there then appears from his act a recklessness which is indifferent to results. Such recklessness in the furnishing of intoxicating liquors, in violation of law, may constitute such an unlawful act as, if it results in causing death, will constitute manslaughter."

We conclude, after studying the record, that appellant fits within the blackletter rule laid down in *Thiede* and that the Commonwealth has made out all the elements necessary to warrant a conviction for involuntary manslaughter. First, the record establishes that appellant sold the Sterno with the knowledge that at least some of his customers would extract the alcohol for drinking purposes. Witnesses for the Commonwealth testified that when they purchased the Sterno from appellant, they would merely say "make one" or hold up fingers to indicate how many cans they wanted; one witness testified that appellant referred to the Sterno as shoe polish and on one occasion shouted to him on the street asking how he and his wife were making out with their shoe polish; finally, the witnesses testified that appellant asked them to conceal the Sterno under their coats when leaving his store. Such conduct does not square with the conclusion that appellant was merely selling the Sterno for cooking and heating purposes. Second, appellant was aware, or should have been aware, that the Sterno he was selling was toxic if consumed.

The new industrial Sterno was clearly marked as being poisonous. Even the regular Sterno is marked "Caution. Flammable. For Use only as a Fuel" and if consumed internally may have serious consequences. Furthermore, when appellant was informed about the first deaths from methanol poisoning, he told the boy who worked in his shop to tell any police who came around that there was no Sterno in the store. Appellant also told the police that he had never purchased any Sterno from the Richter Paper Company. This evidence indicates to us that appellant was aware that he was selling the Sterno for an illicit purpose....

"Defendant contends that the drinking of liquor, by deceased was his voluntary act and served as an intervening cause, breaking the causal connection between the giving of the liquor by defendant and the resulting death. The drinking of the liquor, on consequence of defendant's act, was, however, what the defendant contemplated. Deceased, it is true, may have been negligent in drinking, but, where the defendant was negligent, then the contributory negligence of the deceased will be no defense in a criminal action."

Appellant next criticizes the following sentence in Judge Montgomery's opinion: "In the light of the Recognized weaknesses of the purchasers of the product, and appellant's greater concern for profit than with the results of his actions, he was grossly negligent and demonstrated a wanton and reckless disregard for the welfare of those whom he might reasonably have expected to use the product for drinking purposes." Appellant argues that the Superior Court is here imposing an inequitable burden on sellers of Sterno by requiring them to recognize the "weaknesses" of their customers. Appellant has exaggerated the import of this sentence. The Superior Court was not imposing a duty on all sellers of Sterno to determine how their customers will use the product. The Court was merely saying that if a seller of Sterno is aware that the purchaser is an alcoholic and will use Sterno as a source of alcohol, then the seller is grossly negligent and wantonly reckless in selling Sterno to him. We do not think this imposes an intolerable burden on sellers of Sterno....

Orders affirmed.

CONCURRING OPINION

Roberts, Justice (concurring).

Although I join in the opinion of the Court, I believe it is necessary to emphasize the controlling considerations which support the Court's holding that this case is an appropriate one for criminal sanctions. There can be little question that the record before us not only supports the findings of the court below but leads to the almost unalterable conclusion that appellant knew (or should have known) of the toxic nature of the product he was selling and knew of the exact use to which the Sterno would be put. Appellant was dealing with a product

which when taken internally clearly was a dangerous instrumentality. By selling it to the persons to whom he sold it, knowing that they would use it in a way that was certain to cause serious harm to themselves, appellant exhibited the indifference to and reckless disregard for human life that is the classic element of the involuntary manslaughter offense....

In my view, it is crucial that this record presents no question whether appellant investigated—or was obligated to investigate—the use to which his customers would put the product. It is clear that appellant knew that the skid-row alcoholics to whom he dispensed the Sterno would extract the alcohol for drinking purposes. As the majority correctly points out, our decision and the decisions below did not impose "a duty on all sellers of Sterno to determine how their customers will use the product. The Court was merely saying that if a seller of Sterno is aware that the purchaser is an alcoholic and will use Sterno as a source of alcohol, then the seller is grossly negligent and wantonly reckless selling Sterno to him."

Case Discussion   What definition does the court give for involuntary manslaughter? Is the *mens rea* negligence? Recklessness? Gross negligence? Or something else? What are the relevant facts in the case to determine whether Feinberg was guilty of involuntary manslaughter? If you were deciding the case, how would you define the *mens rea?* Do the facts support a conviction, according to your definition? Do you think the facts might support a *mens rea* more culpable than either negligence or recklessness, such as knowing or even purpose? What facts might support such a conclusion?

Note Case   Dr. Youngkin wrote a prescription for 3-grain size tablets of Tuinal (twice the normal dosage of the barbiturate) for one of his patients, seventeen-year-old Barbara Fedder. She died of an overdose of Tuinal and the state charged and convicted Dr. Youngkin of involuntary manslaughter. The indictment charged that Fedder died as a "direct result of the reckless and grossly negligent manner in which he [Dr. Youngkin] prescribed the drug Tuinal." One pharmacist testified that

> the decedent came into his store on one occasion, about a month before her death, in such a dazed and stuporous condition that she had to hold onto the cash register to maintain her balance. Leery of selling the decedent a prescription that would enhance her stuporous state, the pharmacist telephoned appellant, described to him Ms. Fedder's condition, and queried whether it was advisable to fill the prescription in those circumstances. Appellant's response to the pharmacist was "fill the damn thing."

In upholding the conviction, the court held:

> Our review of the evidence leads us to the conclusion that there was sufficient
> evidence to prove each element of involuntary manslaughter. The evidence
> indicates that appellant prescribed Tuinal to the decedent in quantities and
> frequencies termed irresponsible and totally inappropriate in the circum-
> stances. The frequency with which the prescriptions were written should have
> suggested that the decedent was abusing Tuinal. Moreover, this fact was
> specifically brought to appellant's attention by a pharmacist who called appel-
> lant alarmed over the decedent's physical condition. However, appellant
> chose to ignore these indications of abuse and continued to prescribe the
> drug to decedent. In these circumstances the record supports and justifies the
> jury's conclusion that appellant consciously disregarded a substantial and
> unjustifiable risk, which disregard involved a gross deviation from the stan-
> dard of conduct a reasonable person would have observed. *Commonwealth v.
> Youngkin*, 285 Pa. Super. 417, 427 A.2d 1356 (1981)

Negligent Homicide

Involuntary manslaughter also includes criminally negligent homicides, that
is, unintentional killings in which actors should have known they were creating substantial and unjustified risks of death by conduct that grossly
deviated from ordinary care. The common law did not recognize these
involuntary manslaughters. However, statutes have brought within the scope
of criminal law a variety of deaths caused by criminal negligence, including
negligently using firearms, handling explosives, allowing vicious animals to
run free, practicing medicine, and operating trains, planes, and ships.

[margin note:] Shown have known

The most common negligent homicide involves negligent driving. Most
states require gross negligence to convict drivers in fatal accidents.
However, a few states have reduced the culpability to something less than
gross negligence in special vehicular homicide statutes. One court held that

> [b]y the enactment of this [vehicular homicide] statute, the Legislature obvious-
> ly intended to create a lesser offense than involuntary manslaughter ... where
> the negligent killing was caused by the operation of a vehicle.... Therefore,
> this statute was intended to apply only to cases where the negligence is of a
> lesser degree than gross negligence.[36]

Under this scheme, if drivers' reckless or grossly negligent driving causes death, they have committed involuntary manslaughter. If the death
resulted from less than gross negligence, the driver has committed negligent, or vehicular, homicide.

In effect, then, three degrees of negligence govern liability: (1) gross
negligence for involuntary homicide, (2) something less than gross negligence for vehicular homicide, and (3) ordinary carelessness for civil liability
in wrongful death actions. A fine line separates gross negligence and recklessness; courts and numerous statutes use the distinction nonetheless. Fact

finders, whether juries or judges, apply the definition or standard to particular facts before them. Hence, although criminal recklessness, gross and lesser criminal negligence, and ordinary negligence are difficult to quantify, they nonetheless determine how to grade conduct resulting in death.

According to one court, gross negligence .

> means with very great negligence or without even scant care. Stated another way, it means failure to perform a duty in disregard of the consequences as affecting life or property of another.... Therefore, gross negligence requires no conscious and intentional action which the defendant knows or should know creates an unreasonable risk of harm to others. It is substantially higher in magnitude than ordinary or reasonable care, but it falls short of an intentional wrong.[37]

The reason for this complex grading in vehicular homicide has to do with the reluctance of juries to convict drivers in fatal car accidents of manslaughter. They do so more willingly in vehicular homicide, with its milder penalties and reduced stigma. In line with this thinking, some states have included vehicular homicide in their motor vehicle or traffic codes, rather than placing it in the criminal code sections.[38]

Neither legislatures, courts, nor juries extend the same leniency to fatal accidents involving drunken drivers. Thirteen states have, in fact, found defendants in vehicular homicides guilty of murder. In *State v. Rasinski,* the Minnesota Supreme Court dealt with the *mens rea* problem and the proper sentence in vehicular homicide where Miller was driving while intoxicated.[39]

CASE

Was He Guilty of Vehicular Homicide?

State v. Rasinski
464 N.W.2d 517 (Minn.1991)

Huspeni, Judge. Appellant Gerald Charles Rasinski challenges his conviction and sentence for two counts of Criminal Vehicular Operation resulting in death. He assigns a number of errors including evidentiary rulings, sufficiency of the evidence, the sentence of the court, and the court's denial of his demand to execute his stayed sentence. We affirm as modified.

FACTS

Early on the morning of July 4, 1989, appellant's van collided with a vehicle driven by Brett Callan while traveling eastbound on Highway 8 in Chisago County. Mr. Callan and his passenger, Wayne Faris, were killed in the accident. At the time of the collision, appellant's vehicle was traveling eastbound in the westbound lane of traffic. Earlier on the evening of July 3, 1989, appellant finished work at 8:30 p.m., and purchased a case of beer in an Elk River liquor store. After placing the beer in a cooler in the back of his van, appellant drove to Lake Orono where he testified he drank two beers, which were provided by others already at the lake. He ate nothing while at the lake, left at approximately 10:30 p.m., and headed to Anoka.

On the way to Anoka, appellant stopped to ask his friend, Randy Steen, whether he would like to go to a party. Steen agreed and he, together with two other friends, followed appellant home and joined him in the van. While appellant drove to the party, the passengers drank beer. Appellant admits having a third beer when the van stopped at a friend's home.

After resuming the journey and failing to locate the party in Blaine, appellant asked the passengers whether they wanted to go to Wisconsin to go fishing. The men initially agreed, but Steen changed his mind and asked to return to his car. Appellant stopped at a convenience store and consumed another beer while waiting for his friends to purchase "some munchies." Appellant returned to Elk River, dropped off the passengers and headed back toward Wisconsin at approximately midnight. According to appellant's testimony, he drank four beers between 8:30 p.m. and midnight without eating anything.

Appellant provided the following verbatim account of the accident:

A. I remember seeing lights in front of me.
Q. Where?
A. In my lane in front of me up ahead.
Q. What did you do then?
A. I moved to the right, but there were headlights in front of me in the right, and then there was a car sliding sideways coming in front of me and I slammed on my brakes.
Q. Where were you when you slammed on your brakes?
A. I was in the other lane.
Q. Which lane?
A. The right lane.
Q. The right lane or the left lane?
A. The right lane.
Q. That would be your own lane?
A. I was in the west lane.
Q. Westbound lane?
A. Yeah.
Q. What were you over there for?
A. I was trying to avoid a car coming at me in my lane.

Officers at the scene testified that appellant had a strong odor of alcohol on his breath and red and watery eyes. At the hospital, following the reading of the implied consent advisory, appellant's blood was drawn. The hospital tested the blood and determined that it had a blood alcohol content of .16; the Bureau of Criminal Apprehension found a blood alcohol content of .13.

Shortly after the accident, Steen gave a statement to the police in which he stated that appellant told him he may have fallen asleep at the wheel. On cross-examination at trial, however, he testified he could not remember exactly what appellant said.

The highway patrol created a video re-enactment of the accident using sketches and measurements made by Trooper Hurd. Trooper Scott McAllen directed the production of the videotape. The short tape has two sections: the first section shows vehicles colliding at 55 m.p.h.; the second section shows the accident in slow motion. Testimony at trial showed that the vehicles were not traveling faster than the posted speed limit....

Before imposing sentence, the court reviewed the presentence investigation report and victim impact statements, heard the statement of Keith Davis, a licensed clinical social worker called by appellant regarding appellant's alcohol problem, and listened to statements made by each member of the two victims' families.

The court then imposed two consecutive eighteen month sentences. The court stayed the sentences and placed the defendant on probation for ten years (five years for each count sentenced). The court imposed numerous conditions of probation including 24 months in the county jail, no use of a motor vehicle, a psychological and alcohol evaluation, and writing a letter of apology to the victims' families. The district court denied appellant's motion to execute his sentence.

OPINION

Was the evidence sufficient to convict appellant of CRIMINAL VEHICULAR OPERATION resulting in death?

... In order for the jury to convict the defendant of CRIMINAL VEHICULAR OPERATION resulting in death, it must find that the defendant operated a motor vehicle:

1. in a grossly negligent manner;
2. in a negligent manner while under the influence of alcohol, a controlled substance, or any combination of those elements; or

3. in a negligent manner while having an alcohol concentration of .10 or more. Minn.Stat. § 609.21, subd. 1 (1988)

Thus, in order for the jury to convict under either subsection 2 or 3, the state had the burden of proving both intoxication and negligence. In this case, appellant argues that the mere fact that his vehicle was traveling eastbound in the westbound lane is insufficient to establish negligence and that he swerved into the westbound lane to avoid an oncoming vehicle in his lane. However, the record does not provide any evidence supporting appellant's claim of an oncoming vehicle. The physical evidence gathered at the accident scene and the opinions developed based on the evidence show that appellant was traveling in the wrong lane before impact.

The accident reconstructionist testified that the victims' vehicle took evasive action first. Furthermore, appellant presented no physical evidence of the alleged sudden swerve from the eastbound into the westbound lane. Steen testified that he warned appellant not to go to Wisconsin, that appellant told him after the accident that he might have fallen asleep at the wheel, and that appellant was drinking while driving. Other testimony showed that a recently opened can of beer was found in the front seat of the van along with a number of empty cans scattered in the rear of the van. We conclude that the jury had ample evidence of negligence upon which to conclude that appellant was guilty of CRIMINAL VEHICULAR OPERATION....

Appellant ... challenges four conditions imposed by the court: (1) a psychological evaluation; (2) no possession or use of a motor vehicle; (3) random chemical testing; and (4) the requirement that appellant read and understand the materials submitted by the victims' families and write an appropriate letter of apology.

The restriction on owning or operating a motor vehicle and random chemical testing are reasonable under the facts of this case. Appellant's decision to drink and drive

result in the death of two persons. The restrictions imposed by these two probationary requirements help assure that appellant will not drive while under the influence of alcohol. We similarly find the psychological examination to be within the court's discretion, because it will assist appellant in identifying the reasons for his repeated involvement in drinking and driving episodes, and for his excessive reliance on alcohol.

Although we sanction the court's requirement that appellant read the victim impact materials and write a letter of apology, we cannot adopt the subjective conditions that appellant understand what he has read and write an appropriate letter of apology. The trial court's conditions of probation are modified to this limited extent....

The ... record contains ample evidence to support the conviction, appellant's sentence and probation are warranted and appellant is not entitled to demand execution of his stayed sentence.

Affirmed as modified.

DISSENT

Davies, Judge (dissenting).

I respectfully dissent as to the term of probation requiring appellant to serve more than a year in a county jail and as to forced imposition of probation when appellant has requested execution of sentence....

I.

[B]y making probationary jail time consecutive, the trial court has sentenced the appellant to spend 20 months in the Chisago County jail, without benefit of Department of Corrections programs.

Not surprisingly, appellant asks relief from his "probation." He asks that he be turned over to the Department of Corrections to serve a 24-month sentence, as would be required if his sentence is executed and he earns the standard good time credit. I believe appellant should be turned over to the Department of Corrections pursuant to Minn.Stat. § 609.105, even if he remains under probation.

II.

Appellant also argues that he has a right to reject probation altogether, by choosing execution of his sentence.... Probation is an act of "grace and clemency." Black's Law Dictionary 1082 (5th ed. 1979). Forced probation contradicts this fundamental idea. Probation is perverted when used over the offender's protest and as a device to extend authority over the offender's life for years beyond the period of permitted incarceration. I think appellant correctly identifies his probation as a more onerous penalty, rather than as an act of "grace and clemency."

Since *State v. Randolph,* 316 N.W.2d 508 (Minn.1982), the Minnesota Supreme Court and this court have consistently allowed offenders to demand execution of their sentences. Randolph and all subsequent supreme court and appellate court cases on requests for execution of sentence have concluded by holding that, if the defendant insists upon execution of the sentence, the request should be granted.

The right of execution is not an abstract right, but one predicated upon the idea that a probationary sentence ought not be "more onerous" than any nonprobation sentence. As Randolph pointed out, "the presumptive sentence is the most onerous sentence that should be imposed absent aggravating factors constituting grounds for departure." 316 N.W.2d at 510. The supreme court stated further that: If the presumptive sentence is probation but the trial court attaches conditions of probation that make the probationary sentence more onerous in reality than a prison sentence, then the trial court, in effect, has not followed the Sentencing Guidelines. Id.

The majority here holds that the probationary sentence is "not more onerous than the executed sentence." That is not how it is perceived by the appellant. Who is in a better position than the offender to decide whether probation is "more onerous" than the executed sentence? In making its own determination of onerousness, the majority here makes a first ad hoc evaluation, and starts down the road to a system of judicial review of probationary sentences. Many more cases will follow if this is the road taken. I am unwilling to have this new burden imposed on this court and on the Minnesota Supreme Court. Therefore, I would continue to allow the defendant to reject a "probationary" sentence. I would reaffirm a defendant's right to demand execution of sentence in all cases where the defendant perceives the conditions of probation to be more onerous than execution of sentence.

Furthermore, I believe the majority misjudges onerousness, if judging onerousness is what the appellate courts are now to do. The test ought not be relative length of incarceration alone, although that is the test applied by the majority. If the supreme court had intended length of jail time to be the exclusive test, it should and would have used the word "longer." It must have had in mind a more complex idea because it used a more complex term: "onerous." Here the appellant wants to trade seven years of highly restrictive probation for four months of additional incarceration. That is a rational choice, measured on a scale of intrusiveness, or embarrassment, or economic cost. *Randolph,* 316 N.W.2d at 510, in dictum, said forced probation might be justified "when the public interest is served." The majority here relies on that dictum, which has never before been followed, as a basis for forced probation.

We have here a case of creative sentencing. Creativity to serve "the public interest" is admirable, but "probation" sentences, if unconstrained, could destroy the system of proportionality we seek through guidelines and judicial review of sentencing. Creativity, therefore, must be on the side of "grace and clemency" to be permissible. Otherwise, probation is turned into a device for ratcheting up the penalty.

Furthermore, I believe the majority misjudges what terms of probation serve "the public interest." Nothing in the record suggests that ten years of restrictive probation will help the appellant defeat his alcoholism. Experience teaches that the end to an individual's drunk driving comes when recovery from alcoholism begins. To deprive appellant for a decade of an essential economic tool, the power to own and drive a car, seems ill designed to help him remake his life free of alcohol. I would reject this probationary sentence as not in "the public interest."

Rasinski has not yet served the jail time imposed as a condition of probation and, if

he had done so, there would still be some four months of additional time which could be served if probation were revoked. He should be able to substitute those four months in the custody of the Department of Corrections for seven additional years of probation. His request for execution of his sentence should be honored.

Case Discussion

What is the *mens rea* required for vehicular homicide? Negligence? Recklessness? Gross negligence? What facts were relevant to determining whether Miller had the requisite *mens rea?* What part did intoxication play in the determination of his *mens rea?* What objections does the dissent have to the sentence? Does he have a point? How would you grade the offense of killing someone while you are driving drunk? Should Miller get to choose between probation and incarceration? Why? Why not?

Note Cases

1. David Fleming drove his car on Virginia's George Washington Memorial Parkway between 70 and 100 mph in a 45-mph zone. At times he crossed the median of the divided highway to avoid police officers pursuing him and drove around the traffic coming in the opposite direction. Eventually he lost control of his vehicle, striking head on a car travelling in the opposite direction, killing the occupant. At the time of the collision he was travelling between 70 mph and 80 mph in a 30-mph zone. Police dragged Fleming from the wreckage of his car. At the hospital, his blood alcohol level was 0.315! In affirming Fleming's conviction for murder—not manslaughter—the court held:

> Malice aforethought ... is the distinguishing characteristic which, when present, makes a homicide murder rather than manslaughter. Whether malice is present or absent must be inferred by the jury from the whole facts and circumstances surrounding the killing. Proof of the existence of malice does not require a showing that the accused harbored hatred or ill will against the victim or others. Neither does it require proof of an intent to kill or injure. Malice may be established by evidence of conduct which is "reckless and wanton and a gross deviation from a reasonable standard of care, of such a nature that a jury is warranted in inferring that defendant was aware of a serious risk of death or serious bodily harm." To support a conviction for murder, the government need only have proved that defendant intended to operate his car in the manner in which he did with a heart that was without regard for the life and safety of others.
>
> We conclude that the evidence regarding defendant's conduct was adequate to sustain a finding by the jury that defendant acted with malice aforethought....
>
> The difference between malice, which will support conviction for murder, and gross negligence, which will permit conviction only for manslaughter, is one of degree rather than kind. In the vast majority of vehicular homicides, the accused has not exhibited such wanton and reckless disregard for human

life as to indicate the presence of malice on his part. In the present case, however, the facts show a deviation from established standards of regard for life and the safety of others that is markedly different in degree from that found in most vehicular homicides. In the average drunk driving homicide, there is no proof that the driver has acted while intoxicated with the purpose of wantonly and intentionally putting the lives of others in danger. Rather, his driving abilities were so impaired that he recklessly put others in danger simply by being on the road and attempting to do the things that any driver would do. In the present case, however, danger did not arise only by defendant's determining to drive while drunk. Rather, in addition to being intoxicated while driving, defendant drove in a manner that could be taken to indicate depraved disregard of human life, particularly in light of the fact that because he was drunk his reckless behavior was all the more dangerous. *U.S. v. Fleming,* 739 F.2d 945 (4th Cir. 1984)

2. Miller's semi tractor trailer collided with a vehicle, killing the driver and her two passengers. The roads were dry and in good condition; no drivers were drinking. An inspection of the truck, however, revealed defective brakes and failure by Miller to conduct regular brake checks of his truck, as federal regulations and state law required. A grand jury indicted Miller with vehicular homicide. A trial judge dismissed the indictment because of insufficient evidence of "gross negligence." The trial court found:

> The only conduct pointed to is Defendant's failure to inspect his brakes as required by Statute and Regulation which would have, presumably, revealed 50 percent braking capacity. Based upon the above principles of law the court finds that there is insufficient evidence to establish the offenses charged.... Because the court has determined that the evidence does not rise to the level necessary to support a charge of gross negligence against Defendant,... the Indictment against Defendant [is] dismissed.

On appeal, the Minnesota Supreme Court affirmed the dismissal:

> Gross negligence is substantially and appreciably higher in magnitude than ordinary negligence. It is materially more want of care than constitutes simple inadvertence. It is an act or omission respecting legal duty of an aggravated character as distinguished from a mere failure to exercise ordinary care.... But it is something less than the willful, wanton and reckless conduct which renders a defendant who has injured another liable to the latter even though guilty of contributory negligence, or which renders a defendant in rightful possession of real estate liable to a trespasser whom he has injured. *State v. Miller,* 471 N.W.2d 380 (Minn.1991)

▼ *Summary* ▼

The following outline summarizes the complicated and intricate elements in criminal homicide.

I. Criminal homicide is divided into two main categories: murder and manslaughter.

II. Murder requires taking another's life with malice aforethought.

    A. The precise points at which life begins and ends for purposes of criminal homicide are difficult to determine.

    B. Malice aforethought includes five distinct mental states—the specific intent or purpose to do one of the following:

        1. Kill another person

        2. Seriously injure another person

        3. Forcibly resist a lawful arrest

        4. Commit specified dangerous felonies

        5. Create a higher than criminally reckless risk of death or serious bodily injury

    C. Murder is divided into two primary degrees.

        1. First-degree murder

            a. Premeditated, deliberate killings

            b. Killings that take place while committing some dangerous felonies

            c. Particularly brutal or cruel murders

        2. Second-degree murder

            a. Killings resulting from the intent to do serious bodily injury

            b. Killings resulting from the resisting of lawful arrest

            c. Killings taking place during the commission of less serious felonies

III. Manslaughter is either voluntary or involuntary.

    A. Voluntary manslaughter is the intentional killing of another in the following circumstances:

        1. Under provocation, where such provocation

            a. is actual and adequate

            b. occurs in the heat of passion

            c. occurs before an adequate cooling off period

        2. Where defendants believe they acted in self-defense but where it was unreasonable to do so

    B. Involuntary manslaughter is the killing of another person unintentionally, either

        1. recklessly or

        2. with gross criminal negligence

        3. while committing certain misdemeanors

    C. Negligent homicide is causing death by negligence that is less than gross but more than careless and sufficient to sustain civil tort liability. It is ordinarily limited to fatal car accidents.

▼ *Questions for Review and Discussion* ▼

1. For purposes of the law of criminal homicide, when does life begin and end?

2. Why is *mens rea* so important in the law of criminal homicide?

3. Should there be such a thing as felony murder? Why? If so, what degree of murder should it be?

4. What distinguishes first- from second-degree murder?

5. What is the difference between murder and manslaughter?

6. What are the elements of voluntary manslaughter? What is the rationale in grading voluntary manslaughter as a less serious offense than murder?

7. What are the elements of involuntary manslaughter?

8. What is the difference between involuntary manslaughter and vehicular homicide?

▼ Suggested Readings ▼

1. Rollin M. Perkins and Ronald N. Boyce, *Criminal Law,* 3d ed. (Mineola, N.Y.: Foundation Press, 1982), pp. 46–151. Thoroughly covers criminal homicide, using many cases and examples to illustrate the complicated elements in criminal homicide. In addition, Perkins and Boyce discuss new developments in the law, including the Model Penal Code approach to negligent homicide.

2. George Fletcher, *Rethinking Criminal Law* (Boston: Little, Brown, 1978), chap. 4 and 5. Professor Fletcher takes a critical look at criminal homicide, stressing the uniqueness of homicide as a crime because of its irreversibility. He goes into the philosophical underpinnings of homicide law. These chapters enhance much of what Fletcher says in this text about various homicides, including the *mens rea* and circumstances surrounding them.

3. American Law Institute, *Model Penal Code and Commentaries,* vol. 1 (Philadelphia: American Law Institute, 1980), pt. II, pp. 1–90. This volume develops the Model Penal Code's restruction of homicide law, doing away with degrees and replacing them with three classifications: murder, manslaughter, and negligent homicide. It is a thorough, thought-provoking discussion, well worth the serious student's efforts.

▼ Notes ▼

1. Rollin M. Perkins and Ronald N. Boyce, *Criminal Law,* 3d ed. (Mineola, N.Y.: Foundation Press, 1982), pp. 46–150.

2. Ibid., pp. 49–53.

3. 410 U.S. 113, 93 S.Ct. 705, 35 L.Ed.2d 147 (1973); American Law Institute, *Model Penal Code and Commentaries,* vol. 1 (Philadelphia: American Law Institute, 1980), pt. II, pp. 11–13, maintains that abortion and fetal death statutes should be kept distinct.

4. I am grateful to Randall Rogers, the poster's creator, for this idea.

5. Minnesota Statutes Annotated § 609.266(a).

6. Quoted in *State v. Fierro,* 124 Ariz. 182, 603 P.2d 74, 77–78 (1979); Perkins and Boyce, *Criminal Law,* pp. 48–49.

7. American Law Institute, *Model Penal Code and Commentaries,* vol. 1, pt. II, pp. 10–11, discusses this and summarizes recent legislation on the subject.

8. Perkins and Boyce, *Criminal Law,* pp. 822–24.

9. 366 N.E.2d 744 (Mass.1977)

10. American Law Institute, *Model Penal Code and Commentaries,* vol. 1, pt. II, pp. 6–7.

11. Quoted in American Law Institute, *Model Penal Code and Commentaries,* vol. 1, pt. 11, p. 14.

12. Pa. Laws of 1794, ch. 257, §§ 1,2 (1794); Herbert Wechsler and Jerome Michael discuss this development thoroughly in "A Rationale of the Law of Homicide I," *Columbia Law Review* 37(1937):703–17.

13. *Gregg v. Georgia,* 428 U.S. 153, 96 S.Ct. 2909, 49 L.Ed.2d 859 (1976); *Proffitt v. Florida,* 428 U.S. 242, 96 S.Ct. 2960, 49 L.Ed.2d 913 (1976); *Woodson v. North Carolina,* 428 U.S. 280, 96 S.Ct. 2978, 49 L.Ed.2d 944 (1976).

14. *Goodman v. State,* 573 P.2d 400 (Wyo.1977); Perkins and Boyce, *Criminal Law,* pp. 131–34.

15. Quoted in *People v. Anderson,* 70 Cal.2d 15, 73 Cal.Rptr. 550, 447 P.2d 942 (1968).

16. *State v. Hall,* 54 Nev. 213, 13 P.2d 624 (1932) (intent formed when shot fired); *People v. Wolff,* 61 Cal.2d 795, 40 Cal.Rptr. 271, 394 P.2d 959 (1964) (immaturity).

17. Sir James F. Stephens, *History of the Criminal Law* (New York: Burt Franklin, 1973), p. 94.

18. "Minutes of Evidence," *Report* 12, pp. 174–75.

19. 125 Wis.2d 204, 371 N.W.2d 381 (1985); 89 N.J. Super. 52, 213 A.2d 320 (1965).

20. *State v. Crane,* 247 Ga. 779, 279 S.E.2d 695 (1981) (victim shooting burglar); *Campbell v. State,* 293 Md. 438, 444 A.2d 1034 (1982) (victim cab driver and police officer); *State v. O'Dell,* 684 S.W.2d 453 (Mo.App.1984) (victim of felonious assault).

21. *People v. Phillips,* 64 Cal.2d 574, 51 Cal.Rptr. 225, 414 P.2d 353 (1966).

22. *State v. Weisengoff,* 85 W.Va. 271, 101 S.E. 450 (1919) (accidental death); Jerome Hall, "The Substantive Law of Crimes—1187–1936," *Harvard Law Review* 50 (1937):616, 642.

23. Francis T. Cullen, William J. Maakestad, and Gray Cavender, *Corporate Crime under Attack: The Ford Pinto Case and Beyond* (Cincinnati: Anderson Publishing Company, 1987).

24. "Texas Nursing Home on Trial in Death," *New York Times* (October 1, 1985); and (March 18, 1986), p. 11.

25. "Business and the Law, *New York Times* (March 5, 1985), p. 30; and (May 19, 1985).

26. *New York Times* (June 14, 1985), pp. 1, 9.

27. Sir William Blackstone, *Commentaries* (University of Chicago Press, 1979), IV:191.

28. *People v. Davis,* 33 Ill.App.3d 105, 337 N.E.2d 256 (1975); also *State v. Grant,* 418 A.2d 154 (Me.1980); but to the contrary see *State v. Tuzon,* 118 Ariz. 205, 575 P.2d 1231 (1978).

29. Perkins and Boyce, *Criminal Law,* p. 85.

30. *Beasley v. State,* 64 Miss. 518, 8 So. 234 (1886).

31. Perkins and Boyce, *Criminal Law,* pp. 95–96.

32. People v. Berry, 556 P.2d 777 (Cal.1976).

33. *Manning's Case,* 83 Eng. Rep. 112 (1793); *Palmore v. State,* 283 Ala. 501, 218 So.2d 830 (1969) (husband killed wife); *Dabney v. State,* 21 So. 211 (Ala.1897) (husband killed both wife and paramour).

34. *People v. Washington,* 130 Cal.Rptr. 96 (1976).

35. *State v. Flory,* 40 Wyo. 184, 276 P. 458 (1929).

36. *People v. Campbell,* 237 Mich. 424, 212 N.W. 97 (1927).

37. *State v. Miller,* 471 N.W.2d 380 (Minn.1991).

38. Perkins and Boyce, *Criminal Law,* pp. 116–18.

39. James B. Jacobs, *Drunk Driving* (Chicago: University of Chicago Press, 1989), p. 86.

Chapter

Crimes against Persons II: Criminal Sexual Conduct, and Others

▼ *Chapter Outline* ▼

I. Introduction
II. Criminal Sexual Conduct
   A. History of Rape
   B. The *Actus Reus* of Rape
   C. The *Mens Rea* of Rape
   D. Statutory Rape
   E. Criminal Sexual Conduct with Children
   F. Marital Rape Exception
   G. Criminal Sexual Conduct Statutes
   H. Grading Rape
   I. Summary of Rape and Criminal Sexual Conduct
III. Battery
   A. The *Actus Reus* of Battery
   B. The *Mens Rea* of Battery
   C. The Harm in Battery
IV. Assault
V. False Imprisonment
VI. Kidnapping
VII. Summary

1. Sex offenses cover a broad spectrum, including everything from violent assaults to nonviolent private sex between consenting adults.

2. Rape is both a violent crime and a sexual violation.

3. Criminal sexual conduct statutes have expanded traditional rape law, making sexual violations, no matter what their nature, gender-neutral crimes.

4. Violence is not always required in rape and related offenses; immaturity and other conditions sometimes substitute for it.

5. Battery is the crime of offensive physical contact.

6. Assault is either an attempted battery or a threatened battery.

7. Injury and the use of weapons aggravate simple battery and assault.

8. False imprisonment is the misdemeanor of illegal detention against the victim's will.

9. Kidnapping is the use of force or fear of force to move or keep in secret another person beyond the reach of help from the law or friends.

▼ *Chapter Key Terms* ▼

assault—An attempt to commit a battery, or intentionally putting another in fear.

battery—Offensive bodily contact.

carnal knowledge—Sexual intercourse.

constructive force—A substitute for actual force in rape cases.

criminal sexual conduct—A gender-neutral offense making both sexual penetrations and contacts crimes.

marital rape exception—The rule that husbands cannot rape their wives.

reasonable resistance standard—Women must use the amount of force required by the totality of the circumstances surrounding sexual assault.

statutory rape—Carnal knowledge of a person under the age of consent whether or not accomplished by force.

utmost resistance standard—Rape victims must use all the physical strength they have to prevent penetration.

▼ INTRODUCTION

Crimes against persons include more than conduct causing death; they also encompass a range of conduct that injures, invades personal sexual integrity, and frightens and exploits youth and children. Criminal conduct against persons includes violence and coercion, threats, putting others in fear, deception, and taking advantage of positions of trust and authority to exploit others. It includes both sexual and nonsexual dimensions.

Although they share much with other crimes against persons, sex offenses are treated by the law and society as especially serious. Sexual violation may, but need not, include physical injury; it violates intimacy in a way that physical injury does not. Even offensive sexual touching, such as pinching buttocks and so on, bear this special violation. Rape stands only slightly below murder in both public recognition and law as the most serious crime against a person. The public and the law regard offensive sexual contacts short of rapes as more serious than other offensive touching found in the law of battery. An unwanted erotic caress can offend more than an insulting spit in the face.[1]

▼ CRIMINAL SEXUAL CONDUCT

Historically, the principal sex offenses were rape and sodomy. Modern statutes have added conduct that extends beyond the forced heterosexual penetration and consensual homosexual conduct included in common-law rape and sodomy. Modern **criminal sexual conduct** embraces a wide range of nonconsensual penetrations, contacts, and other abuses not restricted to violence. Until recently, public attention and the criminal justice response focused on rape by strangers: the classic case of a man who jumps

▼ Table 9.1 ▼
Criminal Victimizations, 1990

	Number	Rate
Personal Crimes	18,984	93.4
All crimes	34,404	
Crimes of violence	6,009	29.6
Completed	2,422	11.9
Attempted	3,587	17.6
Rape	130	0.6
Robbery	1,150	5.7
Completed	801	3.9
with injury	286	1.4
without injury	514	2.5
Attempted	349	1.7
with injury	110	0.5
without injury	239	1.2
Assault	4,729	23.3
Aggravated	1,601	7.9
with injury	627	7.9
attempted with weapon	974	4.8
Simple	3,128	15.4
with injury	931	4.6
attempted without weapon	2,197	10.8

SOURCE: *Criminal Victimization in the United States 1990*, Bureau of Justice Statistics, United States Justice Department, Washington D.C., October 1991.

from the shadows and attacks a defenseless woman on a dark street at night. Another type of rape, long held in secret, has come to public attention and has brought changes in both the law of rape and the criminal justice response to it: cases of men who rape the women they know. The overwhelming number of rapes occur within relationships, involving men who rape their employees, their dates, their fellow workers, and their wives. In one survey, according to the women interviewed who do not report rapes to the police, more than eighty percent were raped by men they knew! In three separate surveys of college women, one in five reported being "physically forced" to have sexual intercourse by their dates.[2]

History of Rape

Rape, an ancient crime, in Anglo-Saxon England was punishable by death. At common law, rape was the **carnal knowledge** (sexual intercourse) by a man with a woman not his wife, forcibly and without her consent. These elements of common-law rape limited it to these conditions: (1) only men could rape, not minors or women; (2) rape included only vaginal intercourse, not anal intercourse or fellatio; (3) men could rape only women, not other men or boys; (4) men could not rape their wives—the marital rape exception; (5) rape required force, it was a crime of violence; and (6) rape had to occur against the woman's will, or without her consent, unless she was a minor or otherwise incompetent.[3]

The common law required high standards of proof because, as Lord Hale noted in the seventeenth century, it must be remembered, that it is an accusation to make, hard to be proved, and harder to be defended by the party accused, though innocent.... [T]he heinousness of the offence many times transporting the judge and jury with so much indignation, that they are overhastily carried to the conviction of the person accused thereof, by the confident testimony of sometimes false and malicious witnesses.[4]

The common law allowed the victim to testify, leaving the jury to determine her credibility. Credibility depended on the victim's "good fame," meaning chastity (although Blackstone in the eighteenth century said men could rape prostitutes), promptly reporting the rape, and the corroboration of witnesses other than the victim. On the other hand, Blackstone warned, if the victim

be of evil fame, and stand unsupported by others; if she concealed the injury for any considerable time after she had opportunity to complain; if the place where the fact was alleged to be committed, was where it was possible she might have been heard, and she made no outcry: these and the like circumstances carry a strong, but not conclusive, presumption that her testimony is false or feigned.[5]

From the seventeenth century to the 1970s, the law concentrated on the element of consent in rape cases. Women had to show by resistance that they did not consent:

[V]oluntary submission by the woman, while she has power to resist, no matter how reluctantly yielded, removes from the act an essential element of the crime of rape ... if the carnal knowledge was with the consent of the woman, no matter how tardily given, or how much force had theretofore been employed, it is not rape.[6]

The requirement that women show their nonconsent by resistance is peculiar to the law of rape. In other crimes, passive acceptance does not constitute consent. Robbery requires taking another's property by force or threat of force, yet the law of robbery does not require victims to resist in order to prove the material element of force. Entering a house because the door was unlocked is still trespass; the owner does not have to prove she did not consent to the entry. In criminal procedure, defendants' passive acceptance of violations of their rights does not constitute consent to violations. The law requires positive proof that the government obtained suspects' and defendants' consent, not that defendants merely acquiesced. For example, suspects do not waive their right to remain silent by failing to object to illegal questioning by the police; the police must warn suspects that they have a right to remain silent, and then suspects have to specifically waive the right.[7]

The amount of resistance required to prove lack of consent changed over time. From the nineteenth century until the 1950s, the **utmost resistance standard** prevailed; it required that women use all the power at their command to physically resist. In *Brown v. State,* the victim, a sixteen-year-old virgin, testified that her neighbor grabbed her, tripped her to the ground, and forced himself on her.

I tried as hard as I could to get away. I was trying all the time to get away just as hard as I could. I was trying to get up; I pulled at the grass; I screamed as hard as I could, and he told me to shut up, and I didn't, and then he held his hand on my mouth until I was almost strangled.

The jury convicted the neighbor of rape. On appeal, the Supreme Court reversed because the victim had not adequately demonstrated that she did not consent.

Not only must there be entire absence of mental consent or assent, but there must be the most vehement exercise of every physical means or faculty within the woman's power to resist the penetration of her person, and this must be shown to persist until the offense is consummated.[8]

In another case, the Nebraska Supreme Court put the matter even more strongly:

[T]he general rule is that a mentally competent woman must in good faith resist to the utmost with the most vehement exercise of every physical means or faculty naturally within her power to prevent carnal knowledge, and she must persist in such resistance as long as she has the power to do so until the offense is consummated.[9]

The law did not require physical resistance in all cases. Intercourse with women who were incapacitated by intoxication, mental deficiency, or insanity was rape regardless of force or consent. Sexual penetration obtained by fraud did not constitute rape. Only fraud as to the nature of the act constituted rape. For example, if a doctor told a woman he needed to insert an instrument into her vagina for treatment, but in fact was engaging in intercourse, the law did not recognize her consent. On the other hand, if a woman consented to sexual intercourse because a doctor convinced her that it was good for her health, the law recognized this consent because the woman was defrauded only as to the benefits, not as to the act of sexual intercourse. Finally, sexual intercourse with a minor who consented and did not resist constituted rape.[10]

By the 1950s, courts began replacing the utmost resistance test with a **reasonable resistance standard;** it measured resistance by the amount required by the totality of the circumstances in individual cases. For example, the Virginia Supreme Court ruled that a

woman is not required to resist to the utmost of her physical strength if she reasonably believes that resistance would be useless and result in serious bodily injury.[11]

The Illinois Appeals Court dealt with the problem of consent and reasonable resistance in *People v. Borak.*

CASE

Did Dr. Borak Use Force against His Patient's Will?

People v. Borak
13 Ill.App.3d 815, 301 N.E.2d 1 (1973)

[Dr. Borak was convicted of rape and sodomy and was sentenced to two concurrent eight-year prison terms. He appealed. Justice Seidenfeld delivered the opinion.]

FACTS

The prosecutrix, a married woman 18 years of age at the time of the acts in question, testified that defendant, a doctor, conducted gynecological examinations on her on two occasions. During the examinations, she laid on an examining table, unclothed from the waist down, with her hips at the end of the table and her feet in stirrups about a foot higher than the table and a foot out from it on either side. She had never before been examined internally.

She testified that during the first examination, conducted on September 22, 1970, defendant asked extremely personal questions about the details of her sexual relationship with her husband, and conducted intimate manipulations of her body for which he gave medical explanations. Defendant breathed heavily, but was not flushed. Defendant ceased his manipulations when she told him they were hurting her. After leaving, prosecutrix did not tell anyone what took place at this examination.

During the second examination, conducted two days after the first, defendant again asked personal questions and manipulated her body. Prosecutrix did not wear a brassiere to this examination. While manipulating his finger in her vagina, defendant asked, "Why don't you come?" "Why don't you come with your husband?" Prosecutrix noticed that he was breathing heavy and was flushed. She said she couldn't get off the table because he was standing right there, and she didn't ask him to let her up because she was scared and thought he was sexually stimulated. She closed her eyes, as instructed, and felt defendant's tongue on her vaginal area. She got up on her elbows, but laid back down and closed her eyes when defendant told her to in a voice that was not loud or soft, but "(k)ind of commanding." About thirty seconds later, she felt his organ enter hers, at which time she sat up quickly and got dressed. After a brief conversation about what she owed defendant, she left. On arriving home, she related the incident to her husband, and the police were called.

Prosecutrix testified that she was not tied down or restrained while on the examining table, and could remove her feet from the stirrups. She also stated that defendant had no weapon and never threatened her or used force against her, and that she never cried out for help or used force against defendant.

OPINION

The difficult questions before us are whether the act of intercourse was performed "by force and against her will," as required to sustain a rape conviction (Ill.Rev.Stat. 1969, ch. 38, par. 11–1(a)).

The general rules as to the degree of force required under our rape statute are [:] ... that the degree of force exerted by the defendant and the amount of resistance on the part of the complaining witness are matters that depend on the facts of the particular case; that resistance is not necessary under circumstances where resistance would be futile and would endanger the life of the female as where the assailant is armed with a deadly weapon, and that proof of physical force is unnecessary if the prosecuting witness was paralyzed by fear or overcome by superior strength of her attacker; that it is, however, fundamental that there must be evidence to show that the act was committed by force and against the will of the female, and if she has the use of her faculties and physical powers, the evidence must show such resistance as will demonstrate that the act was against her will.

In the case before us, due to the nature of the examination being conducted, defendant was allegedly able to accomplish the acts by surprise, and the necessity for force, as the term is generally used in rape and deviate sexual assault cases, was negated. The question then becomes whether some theory of implied or statutory force can be employed.

It would indeed be a reproach upon our statute if a physician, under the pretense that it was necessary for a woman patient to submit to examination of her sexual organs in order to assist him in the diagnosis of her ailment, and under the pretense that it was necessary for her to expose her person and to assume a position which, at the same time, incidently afforded ready opportunity for sexual attack, could safely take advantage of her position and make an unexpected and uninvited sexual invasion of her person. If, under such circumstances, a physician takes such an unconscionable advantage of the woman's position, and, to her complete surprise, and without the slightest ground to assume that he has her consent, violates the trust and confidence imposed in him and perverts her position and his opportunity into an uninvited and cowardly attempt to gratify his lust, the force merely incident to penetration should be deemed sufficient force within the meaning of our rape statute.

In the case before us, even if the prosecutrix realized that defendant's questions were improper, this would not in itself indicate what was to follow. While defendant's appearance indicated to prosecutrix that he was sexually aroused, he had not performed any actions which she knew to be improper, and prosecutrix was not put on notice that defendant would perform an overt, deviate act upon her body. Defendant's act of deviate sexual conduct was, "through surprise," with prosecutrix being "utterly unaware of

his intention in that regard." Prosecutrix was therefore incapable of consenting to the act, and "statutory" force was present.

However, the contrary is true as to the act of intercourse. When defendant put his mouth on prosecutrix's organ, she became aware of his intentions, and nothing he did thereafter could come as a surprise. It then became her duty, under the previously stated general rules of force applicable to rape cases to use resistance to prevent further acts. Yet she failed to object and followed defendant's instruction to lay back down and close her eyes. While prosecutrix points to her testimony that the instruction was given in a commanding voice, and that she was scared because of his appearance, the evidence does not show that she was restrained in any way, or that defendant used any actual force or threat of force upon her. We cannot conclude that prosecutrix was paralyzed by fear or overcome by defendant's superior strength. Her failure to resist when it was within her power to do so amounts to consent, and removes from the act an essential element of the crime of rape. We therefore reverse defendant's rape conviction.

Case Discussion

Unlike the night prowler rapist who violently attacks a young woman on a lonely street despite her utmost resistance, Dr. Borak approached his victim while she was in his office undergoing a gynecological examination. Dr. Borak did not use actual physical force to have sexual intercourse with his patient. Did he use force? Do you think his patient was "paralyzed with fear?" Even if she was not, do you think Dr. Borak's special relationship with her removed the need to resist? Do you agree with the court that his patient consented to sexual intercourse? If someone picked up my wallet from a restaurant table and I did not resist, does this mean the person who took the wallet did not steal it? How would you treat force as an element in rape? Would you add patients who tend to do what doctors tell them to the list of conditions under which victims effectively cannot consent?

During the 1970s and 1980s, major reforms took place in the substantive law of rape, and several changes took place in the procedural law of rape. Many states no longer required corroboration to prove rape. Most states had enacted rape shield statutes, which prohibited the wholesale exposure of women's sexual pasts. Many states have relaxed the requirement that prohibits prosecution unless women promptly report rapes. A few states have abolished the marital exception.

States have also made substantive changes. Some have addressed the fundamental problem of the element of consent and its relationship to force. Recently enacted criminal sexual conduct statutes have shifted the emphasis from the victims' consent by failure to resist to the force rapists use to effect penetration. The Pennsylvania Superior Court found that the common-law emphasis on lack of consent had

> worked to the unfair disadvantage of the woman who, when threatened with violence, chose quite rationally to submit to her assailant's advances rather than risk death or serious bodily injury.[12]

The Model Penal Code eliminated consent as an element in rape because of its "disproportionate emphasis upon objective manifestations by the woman." However, the drafters of the code recognized the complex relationship between force and consent. Unlike the acts in all other criminal assaults, in ordinary circumstances the victim may desire the physical act in rape—sexual intercourse:

> This unique feature of the offense necessitates the drawing of a line between forcible rape on the one hand and reluctant submission on the other, between true aggression and desired intimacy. The difficulty in drawing this line is compounded by the fact that there will often be no witness to the event other than the participants and that their perceptions may change over time. The trial may turn as much on an assessment of the motives of the victim as of the actor.[13]

These statutes have also expanded the definition of criminal sexual conduct to include all sexual penetrations: vaginal, anal, and oral. Sexual contact now constitutes a lesser degree of criminal sexual conduct. Statutes have also made criminal sexual conduct gender-neutral; men can rape men or women, and women can rape men or women. The trend seems definitely toward including a wide range of gender-neutral sexual penetrations and contacts within the scope of criminal sexual conduct.[14]

Elements of Rape		
Actus Reus	**Mens Rea**	**Material Circumstances**
sexual penetration by male penis of a woman's vagina accomplished by some force	intent to sexually penetrate	1. nonconsent of victim 2. injury 3. age of victim 4. use of weapon 5. accomplices

The Actus Reus *of Rape*

The rape *actus reus* requires sexual penetration plus some force beyond that required to effect penetration. From the earliest days of the common law, rape did not require full sexual intercourse to emission. The common-law phrase "penetration however slight" describes the modern requirement. For example, the defendant "put[ting his] fingers between folds of skin over her vagina, but not insert[ing] his fingers ..." satisfies the penetration requirement.[15]

The amount of force required varies according to the circumstances of particular cases.

The Model Penal Code focuses on the "objective manifestations of aggression by the actor." Force that "compels" the victim to "submit" constitutes the rape *actus reus*. Threats of "imminent death, serious bodily injury, extreme pain or kidnapping, to be inflicted on anyone" and the infliction of serious bodily harm aggravate the offense to first-degree rape.

The rape *actus reus* does not require actual force when threats secure the submission. Hence, **constructive force,** consisting of threats to kill, seriously injure, or kidnap either the victim or another, substitutes for the actual use of force. Finally, the *actus reus* requires neither force nor threat where actors obtain consent fraudulently, or when a minor, a mentally deficient, or an insane person consents. In these cases, the act of penetration itself suffices.

The court in *People v. Evans* dealt with the difficult problem of whether Evans forced or seduced his victim.

CASE

Did He Seduce or Rape Her?

People v. Evans
379 N.Y.S.2d 912 (N.Y.1975)

Edward J. Greenfield, Justice

The question presented in this case is whether the sexual conquest by a predatory male of a resisting female constitutes rape or seduction. In making the distinction, we must deal with patterns of behavior which have been exhibited by aggressive males towards gentle or timid or submissive females, the broad outlines of which have been similar for hundreds or maybe thousands of years, but the particulars of which vary markedly in individual cases. It is a fact, I suppose, that since before the dawn of history men with clubs have grabbed women, willing or unwilling, by the hair, to have their way with them. Techniques have become more varied and more subtle with the years.

As we have become more civilized, we have come to condemn the more overt, aggressive and outrageous behavior of some men towards women and we have labelled it "rape." We have attempted to control or deter it by providing for extremely heavy sentences, second to and, in some jurisdictions, equalled by the penalties set by the law for murder.

At the same time we have recognized that there are some patterns of aggression or aggressive male sexual behavior toward females which do not deserve such extreme penalties, in which the male objective may be achieved through charm or guile or protestations of love, promises or deceit.

Where force is not employed to overcome reluctance, and where consent, however reluctant initially, can be spelled out, this we label "seduction," which society may condone, even as it disapproves.

There is some conduct which comes close to the line between rape and seduction. This is such a case. Since a jury has been waived, this Court is called upon to scrutinize the conduct involved and to draw the line

*between the legally permissible and the
impermissible and to determine on which
side of the line this conduct falls.*

*Rape is defined in our Penal Law,
§ 130.35, subdivision 1, as follows:*

*A male is guilty of rape in the first degree when
he engages in sexual intercourse with a
female: 1. By forcible compulsion.*

*Rape can also be premised upon other
conditions which would indicate the incapacity of a female to give consent either in
actuality or as a matter of law. We are concerned here with the first subdivision, sexual
intercourse by forcible compulsion. That is
the essence of the crime.*

*Forcible compulsion is defined in § 130.00
subdivision 8, of the Penal Law as "physical
force that overcomes earnest resistance; or a
threat, express or implied, that places a person in fear of immediate death or serious
physical injury to himself or another person,
or in fear that he or another person will
immediately be kidnapped."*

*Rape, though it sometimes may be abetted
by other females, appears to be exclusively a
proscribed activity for males. Seduction, on
the other hand, may be freely indulged in by
both sexes. It involves allurement, enticement,
or persuasion, to overcome initial unwillingness or resistance. Its ends may be achieved
by fair means or foul, but seduction eschews
the crudities of force and threats. In which
category does defendant's conduct fall? In
answering that inquiry, and based upon the
testimony in this case, the Court first makes
the following findings of fact.*

FACTS

The defendant, a bachelor of approximately
thirty-seven years of age, aptly described in
the testimony as "glib," on July 15, 1974 met
an incoming plane at LaGuardia Airport,
from which disembarked Lucy Elizabeth
Peterson, of Charlotte, North Carolina, a
twenty-year-old petite, attractive second-year
student at Wellesley College, an unworldly
girl, evidently unacquainted with New York
City and the sophisticated city ways, a girl
who proved to be, as indicated by the testi-

mony, incredibly gullible, trusting and naive.
The testimony indicates that the defendant
struck up a conversation with her, posing as
a psychologist doing a magazine article and
using a name that was not his, inducing
Miss Peterson to answer questions for an
interview.

The evidence further shows that the
defendant invited Miss Peterson to accompany him by automobile to Manhattan, her
destination being Grand Central Station.
They were accompanied in the automobile
by other persons, some of whom were
introduced by the defendant as colleagues
on a professional basis. But it appears that a
funny thing happened on the way to the station. There were numerous detours before
Beth Peterson ever found her way to Grand
Central Station. First, they were taken to an
apartment on the east side. Some of the
party were left there.

Then the evidence indicates that this
defendant and a girl named Bridget took
Miss Peterson to an establishment called
Maxwell's Plum, which the defendant
explained was for the purpose of conducting a sociological experiment in which he
would observe her reactions and the reactions of males towards her in the setting of a
singles bar. After several hours there, in
which Miss Peterson evidently was still
under the belief that her stopping for a
drink at Maxwell's Plum was part of this
psychological and sociological experiment,
she was persuaded to accompany the defendant to the west side, upon the defendant's
explanation that he was there going to pick
up his automobile and drive her to Grand
Central Station.

Instead of going to the automobile, she
was induced to come up to an apartment on
the fourteenth floor, which the defendant
explained was used as one of his five offices
or apartments throughout the city; and Miss
Peterson, still believing that the defendant
was in fact what he purported to be, went
up and accompanied him there. That apartment, Apartment 14–D, at 1 Lincoln Plaza,
was in truth and in fact the apartment of
one Heinz Patzak, who ran the Austrian

National Tourist Bureau and who at that time was in Austria. Mr. Patzak has testified that he never had given approval or permission for the defendant to enter, use or occupy that apartment.

Miss Peterson came to the apartment and her questions as to the existence of photographs of children, a crib, stuffed animals and toys, were readily explained away by the defendant as being connected with his treatment of patients as a psychologist, the explanation of the crib and the toys being that they were used for the purposes of primal therapy to enable his patients to associate with their childhood years more readily. In the apartment the psychological interviewing continued, the defendant having explained to Miss Peterson that he was searching for the missing link between the "girl-woman" and the "woman-girl." Miss Peterson, who was then working in a psychiatric branch of New York Hospital, Cornell Medical School, in White Plains, and who had some training in psychology, believed that all of this legitimately related to a psychological research project which the defendant was conducting.

During the course of the interview in the apartment the defendant probed Miss Peterson's life and she had, during the course of their conversation together, made a revelation of her prior intimacies and her feelings, and her experiences with respect to various people. In the apartment she was asked to participate in an adjective word game, applying five adjectives to certain designated persons, including herself and the defendant.

She had been there for one to two hours when the defendant made his move and pulled her on to the opened sofa-bed in the living room of that apartment and attempted to disrobe her. She resisted that, and she claims that as articles of clothing were attempted to be removed she would pull them back on and ultimately she was able to ward off these advances and to get herself dressed again. At that point, the defendant's tactics, according to her testimony, appeared to have changed.

First, he informed her of his disappointment that she had failed the test, that this was all part of his psychological experiment, that, in fact, this was a way in which he was trying to reach her innermost consciousness, one of the ways in which that could be done. Then, after expressing disappointment in the failure of this psychological experiment, he took steps to cause doubt and fear to arise in the mind of Miss Peterson. He said, "Look where you are. You are in the apartment of a strange man. How do you know that I am really who I say I am? How do you know that I am really a psychologist?" Then, he went on and said, "I could kill you. I could rape you. I could hurt you physically."

Miss Peterson testified that at that point she became extremely frightened, that she realized, indeed, how vulnerable she was. The defendant did not strike her, did not beat her, he exhibited no weapons at the time, but he made the statement, "I could kill you; I could rape you."

Then there was yelling and screaming, further to intimidate the defendant, and then an abrupt switch in which the defendant attempted to play on the sympathy of Miss Peterson by telling her a story about his lost love, how Miss Peterson had reminded him of her, and the hurt that he had sustained when she had driven her car off a cliff. Obviously, Miss Peterson's sympathy was engaged, and at that time acting instinctively, she took a step forward and reached out for him and put her hand on his shoulders, and then he grabbed her and said, "You're mine, you are mine." There thereupon followed an act of sexual intercourse, an act of oral-genital contact; a half-hour later a second act of sexual intercourse, and then, before she left, about seven o'clock that morning, an additional act. The sexual intercourse appears to be corroborated by the findings of the laboratory confirmation of seminal fluid on the underclothing which she had worn at the time.

The testimony indicates that during these various sexual acts Miss Peterson, in fact, offered little resistance. She said that she was pinned down by the defendant's body weight, but in some manner all her clothing was removed, all his clothing was removed, and the acts took place. There was no torn clothing, there were no scratches, there were no bruises. Finally, at approximately 7 a.m. Miss Peterson dressed and left the apartment. She says that the defendant acknowledged to her that he was aware that it had been against her will, but he nevertheless gave her three telephone numbers. Miss Peterson then returned to White Plains, where later that day she recited some of the events to a fellow-worker, and then to a roommate.

Ultimately she reported the facts to the New York City Police and to the Westchester County Sheriff's office, resulting in her being taken to New York City by personnel from the Westchester County Sheriff's office where, at the Gulf & Western Building at Columbus Circle they saw the defendant emerging from an elevator. Despite her identification of him at that time the defendant initially denied that his name was Marty, that he knew Miss Peterson, or that he had had any involvement with her in any way. After he had been placed under arrest in a coffee shop of the Mayflower Hotel, and they had proceeded to the building at No. 1 Lincoln Plaza, the defendant began to make partial admissions as to his identity, his occupation of Apartment 14–D at No. 1 Lincoln Plaza, his knowledge of Miss Peterson and ultimately the fact that he had had sexual intercourse with her, which he claimed was consensual and a matter of mutual enjoyment. He further told the police officers that the whole psychology bit was a "game that he played with girls' heads."

The testimony further indicates that after he had been placed under arrest, and while he was in custody, he escaped from the police car in which he had been placed, and that Detective Kelleher chased him in and around the streets and up 15 flights of a building, where he ultimately located Evans on a water tower. The explanation given to Detective Magnusson was that he was looking for a lawyer.

OPINION

Those being the facts, the Court arrives at the following conclusions: The Court finds that the testimony of Beth Peterson was essentially credible testimony. The Court finds from the story which she has narrated that the defendant was a person who was crafty, scheming, manipulative, and ever ready with explanations.

From the testimony which has been given there are some factors which tend to point toward guilt and some towards innocence. As factors indicating guilt are the assumption of the false identity by the defendant, his not giving his true name, his denial to the police when first confronted of what his name was, and his denial of any knowledge of Miss Peterson, which denials he ultimately retracted. Then, of course, there is the evidence about flight which is always evidence that can be considered as evincing some consciousness of guilt.

On the other hand, there are some factors pointing to innocence on the part of the defendant, and a lack of criminal culpability on his part. The fact that Miss Peterson had no bruises or scratches, no torn clothing, that she had been allowed to proceed from the apartment without any further threats or concealment as to location. The fact that she was given phone numbers by the defendant which made it relatively easy to trace his location and whereabouts; the fact that he attempted to call her on several occasions after she had left the apartment; and the fact that he had continued in his prior haunts at the Gulf & Western Building and at No. 1 Lincoln Plaza. From all this, the Court concludes that the defendant inveigled Miss Peterson, deceived her, put her on, and took advantage of her.

The question is whether having had sexual intercourse by the same means described constitutes rape in the first degree. The essential element of rape in the first degree is forcible compulsion. The prevailing view in this country is that there can be no rape which is achieved by fraud, or trick, or stratagem. Provided there is actual consent, the nature of the act being understood, it is not rape, absent a statute, no matter how despicable the fraud, even if a woman has intercourse with a man impersonating her husband; or if a fraudulent ceremony leads her to believe she is legally married to a man, (contra if an explicit statute to that effect exists, or even if a doctor persuades her that sexual intercourse is necessary for her treatment and return to good health. "Fraud cannot be allowed to supply the place of the force which the statute makes mandatory...."

It is clear from the evidence in this case that Beth Peterson was intimidated; that she was confused; that she had been drowned in a torrent of words and perhaps was terrified. But it is likewise clear from the evidence that the defendant did not resort to actual physical force. There was "no act of violence, no struggle, no outcry, and no attempt to restrain or confine the person ... which constitute the usual ... and essential evidence of rape....

The restraint which was imposed upon Miss Peterson was a restraint imposed by his body weight, which would be the normal situation in which any sexual contact would be achieved. Miss Peterson manifested little or no resistance....

A woman is not obligated to resist to the uttermost under all circumstances, when her will to resist has been paralyzed by fear and by threats. That is why the law recognizes the existence of a threat as being the equivalent of the use of actual force....

So the question here is not so much the use of force, but whether threats uttered by the defendant had paralyzed her capacity to resist and had, in fact, undermined her will. Now, what was it the defendant said? He said, "Look where you are. You are in the apartment of a strong man. How do you know that I really am who I say I am? How do you know that I am really a psychologist? I could kill you. I could rape you. I could hurt you physically." Those words, as uttered, are susceptible to two possible and diverse interpretations. The first would be in essence that—you had better do what I say, for you are helpless and I have the power to use ultimate force should you resist. That clearly would be a threat which would induce fear and overcome resistance. The second possible meaning of those words is, in effect, that—you are a foolish girl. You are in the apartment of a strange man. You put yourself in the hands of a stranger, and you are vulnerable and defenseless. The possibility would exist of physical harm to you were you being confronted by someone other than the person who uttered this statement....

[T]his being a criminal trial, it is basic that the criminal intent of the defendant must be shown beyond a reasonable doubt. It is his intent when he acts, his intent when he speaks, which must therefore be controlling. And so, if he utters words which are taken as a threat by the person who hears them, but are not intended as a threat by the person who utters them, there would be no basis for finding the necessary criminal intent to establish culpability under the law. So where a statement is ambiguous, where the words and the acts which purport to constitute force or threats are susceptible of diverse interpretations, which may be consistent with either guilt or innocence, the Court, as the trier of the facts, cannot say beyond a reasonable doubt that the guilt of the defendant has been established with respect to the crime of rape. The words which were uttered both as to what the defendant could do, "I could kill you. I could rape you." and subsequent words that he was going to do to the complainant what his lost love had done to him—the Court finds are ambiguous.

They were not accompanied by violence. They were not accompanied by a demonstration of the intention to carry out the threats. There was no beating. There was no weapon displayed. There was a statement as to a possibility, a statement of vulnerability. The Court finds it cannot conclude that there was the utterance of a threat of such a nature as to enable the Court to find the defendant guilty of the crime of rape in the first degree beyond a reasonable doubt. Since the Court, therefore, can find neither forcible compulsion nor threat beyond a reasonable doubt, the defendant is found not guilty on the charges of rape, sodomy and unlawful imprisonment.

Now, acquittal on these charges does not imply that the Court condones the conduct of the defendant. The testimony in the case reveals that the defendant was a predator, and that naive and gullible girls like Beth Peterson were his natural prey. He posed. He lied. He pretended and he deceived. He used confidences which were innocently bestowed as leverage to effect his will. He used psychological techniques to achieve vulnerability and sympathy, and the erosion of resistance. A young and inexperienced girl like Beth Peterson was then unable to withstand the practiced onslaught of the defendant. The defendant apparently got his kicks through the exercise of these techniques. He apparently spurned the readily available women, the acquiescent women, like Bridget, who was living in the same apartment. To him, the game was worth more than the prize. He boasted to the police that this was a game he played with girls' heads. The Court finds his conduct, if not criminal, to be reprehensible. It was conquest by con job. Truly, therefore, this defendant may be called "The Abominable Snowman."

So bachelors, and other men on the make, fear not. It is still not illegal to feed a girl a line, to continue the attempt, not to take no for a final answer, at least not the first time. But there comes a point at which one must desist. It is not criminal conduct for a male to make promises that will not be kept, to indulge in exaggeration and hyperbole, or to assure any trusting female that,

as in the ancient fairy tale, the ugly frog is really the handsome prince. Every man is free, under the law, to be a gentleman or a cad. But take heed. Violence, force and threats are totally out of bounds. Their employment will transform a heel into a criminal.

While the Court must conclude that the defendant's conduct towards Miss Peterson cannot be adjudged criminal so as to subject him to the penalty of imprisonment for up to twenty-five years, the Court finds, on the undisputed facts, that defendant did enter Apartment 14–D, at No. 1 Lincoln Plaza, the dwelling of Heinz Patzak and his family, illegally and without permission or authority. There being no proof that the illegal entry was for the purpose of committing a crime, the defendant is found not guilty of the charge of burglary in the second degree. But he is found guilty of the lesser included offense of criminal trespass in the second degree, pursuant to § 140.15 of the Penal Law, under Indictment No. 3861 of 1974. Further, the evidence clearly establishes that the defendant, after having been arrested for a felony, escaped from the custody of the police officers, and he is found guilty of the crime of escape in the second degree, under § 205.10 of the Penal Law.

It may be ironic that the defendant, having been acquitted of the charges for which he was arrested, is found guilty of attempting to flee from the possibilities of having to face up to the charge. But the facts are clear, and whatever consequences flow from that fact will flow. The defendant fancied himself to be terribly clever, but, as frequently happens with terribly clever men, he made a rather stupid mistake.

Case Discussion   What facts indicate the use of force? What facts indicate seduction? Can you separate them, as the judge thinks you can? If you were deciding this case, would you say it was rape? Why? Do you think this man's approach to this woman, even if it was not force, is still rape? Why? How do you draw the line between rape and seduction? Do you agree with the judge's conclusion that this man's conduct was reprehensible, but not rape?

Note Case   Pat, the twenty-one-year-old prosecuting witness, went to a bar with a friend to "have a few drinks." She met Eddie Rusk. They struck up a conversation, learning that they were both separated from their spouses, and that they both had children. Pat eventually told Eddie she had to leave because it was a week night and she had to get up early with her baby. Rusk asked Pat for a ride home. She agreed, but told him, "I'm just giving you a ride home, you know, as a friend, not anything to be, you know, thought of other than a ride." He said, "Oh, o.k." When they got to his building, in a part of town she did not know, he asked her to come up to his apartment. She declined. He asked again. She declined again. He reached over, turned off the key, removed the key from the ignition, got out of the car, walked around to Pat's side, and said, "Now, will you come up?" Pat, frightened, went up to the apartment. After sitting for a few minutes, Rusk excused himself and went into the bathroom. He returned about five minutes later. He sat beside her and turned off the light. She asked if she could go. He said he wanted her to stay. He asked her to get on the bed with him, and pulled her by the arms onto the bed and began to undress her. She took off her pants when he asked her to. She removed his pants, because "he asked me to do it." Pat explained what happened next:

> I was still begging him to please let, you know, let me leave. I said, "you can get a lot of other girls down there, for what you want," and he just kept saying, "no"; and then I was really scared, because I can't describe, you know, what was said. It was more the look in his eyes; and I said, at that point—I didn't know what to say; and I said, "If I do what you want, will you let me go without killing me?" Because I didn't know, at that point, what he was going to do; and I started to cry; and when I did, he put his hands on my throat, and started lightly to choke me; and I said, "If I do what you want, will you let me go?" And he said, yes, and at the same time, I proceeded to do what he wanted me to.
>
> Pat testified that Rusk made her perform oral sex and then vaginal intercourse.

Did Eddie rape Pat? The rape statute in the state required intercourse "by force or threat of force against the will and without consent." On appeal, in affirming Eddie Rusk's rape conviction, the appellate court wrote:

> [I]t is readily apparent to us that the trier of fact could rationally find that the elements of force and nonconsent had been established and that Rusk was guilty of the offense beyond a reasonable doubt. Of course, it was for the jury to observe the witnesses and their demeanor, and to judge their credibility and weigh their testimony. Quite obviously, the jury ... believed Pat's testimony....
>
> Just where persuasion ends and force begins in cases like the present is essentially a factual issue, to be resolved in light of the controlling legal precepts. That threats of force need not be made in any particular manner in order to put a person in fear of bodily harm is well established. Indeed, conduct, rather than words, may convey threat.... *State v. Rusk*, 424 A.2d 720 (1981)

The Mens Rea of Rape

The *actus reus* in forcible rape implies that the defendant intends to effect sexual penetration by force or threat. In *Regina v. Morgan,* a widely publicized English case, four companions were drinking in a bar. When they failed to "find some women," Morgan invited the other three to come home with him to have sexual intercourse with his wife. Morgan told the others not to worry if she struggled because she was "kinky"; the struggle "turned [her] on." The trial court convicted the men and the intermediate appellate court upheld the conviction. The House of Lords, England's highest appeal court, overturned the conviction because the defendants lacked the *mens rea*. Rape requires the specific intent to have sexual intercourse by force and without consent. Since the men believed Morgan's wife wanted the struggle, they could not have formed that intent.[17]

Regina v. Morgan generated a storm of debate. Although England has adhered to the specific intent requirement, American statutes and decisions barely mention intent, except in attempted rape where intent is the essence of the crime. Where courts face the intent question, they vary in their response. The Maine Supreme Judicial Court ruled that forcible rape is a strict liability crime:

> [C]ertain crimes are defined to expressly include a culpable state of mind and others are not. The more forceful or egregious sexual conduct, including rape compelled by force, is defined without reference to the actor's state of mind. The legislature, by carefully defining the sex offenses in the criminal code, and by making no reference to a culpable mental state for rape, clearly indicated that rape compelled by force or threat requires no culpable state of mind.[18]

Other courts have adopted a reckless or negligent standard with regard to the sexual penetration, saying that rapists must be either aware that they are risking coerced sexual intercourse or should know that their victims have not consented. Against the argument that rape constitutes a crime too serious with penalties too harsh for the law to impose liability for reckless or negligent rape, law professor Susan Estrich responds:

> If inaccuracy or indifference to consent is "the best that this man can do" because he lacks the capacity to act reasonably, then it might well be unjust and ineffective to punish him for it.... More common is the case of the man who could have done better but did not; heard her refusal or saw her tears, but decided to ignore them. The man who has the inherent capacity to act reasonably but fails to has, through that failure, made a blameworthy choice for which he can justly be punished. The law has long punished unreasonable action which leads to the loss of human life as manslaughter—a lesser crime than murder, but a crime nonetheless.... The injury of sexual violation is sufficiently great, the need to provide that additional incentive pressing enough, to justify negligence liability for rape as for killing.[19]

In some cases, the defendant may not even intend a sexual assault, and yet satisfy the criminal sexual conduct *mens rea*. In *State v. Bonds,* Bonds got into an altercation with another tenant in his rooming house. When she confronted him, Bonds grabbed the nipple of his victim's left breast "intending to hurt her, not to violate her sexually." In upholding his conviction the court held that the intent to injure by contacting victims' intimate parts satisfies the criminal sexual conduct *mens rea.*[20]

Statutory Rape

No longer in MICH

Statutory rape, or carnal knowledge of a woman under the age of consent, requires neither force in the *actus reus* nor *mens rea*. Immaturity substitutes for force in all jurisdictions. A few states, such as California and Alaska, however, permit the defense of reasonable mistake of age, if a man reasonably believes his victim is over the age of consent. California initiated the defense of honest mistake in *People v. Hernandez.*

CASE

Is Reasonable Belief She Was Eighteen a Defense to Statutory Rape?

People v. Hernandez
39 Cal.Rptr. 361 (Cal.1964)

Peek, Justice

FACTS
The undisputed facts show that the defendant and the prosecuting witness were not married and had been companions for several months prior to January 3, 1961 the date of the commission of the alleged offense. Upon that date the prosecutrix was 17 years and 9 months of age and voluntarily engaged in an act of sexual intercourse with defendant.

OPINION
The sole contention raised on appeal is that the trial court erred in refusing to permit defendant to present evidence going to his guilt for the purposes of showing that he had in good faith a reasonable belief that the prosecutrix was 18 years or more of age.... [D]efendant relies upon Penal Code, § 20, which provides that "there must exist a union, or joint operation of act and intent, or criminal negligence" to constitute the commission of a crime. He further relies upon § 26 of that code which provides that one is not capable of committing a crime who commits an act under an ignorance or mistake of fact which disapproves any criminal intent.

Thus the sole issue relates to the question of intent and knowledge entertained by the defendant at the time of the commission of the crime charged.

Consent of the female is often an unrealistic and unfortunate standard for branding sexual intercourse a crime as serious as forcible rape. Yet the consent standard has been deemed to be required by important policy goals. We are dealing here, of course, with statutory rape where, in one sense, the lack of consent of the female is not an element of the offense. In a broader sense, however, the lack of consent is deemed to remain an element but the law makes a conclusive presumption of the lack thereof because she is presumed too innocent and naive to understand the implications and nature of her act. The law's concern with her capacity or lack thereof to so understand is explained in part by a popular conception of the social, moral and personal values which are preserved by the abstinence from sexual indulgence on the part of a young woman. An unwise disposition of her sexual favor is deemed to do harm both to herself and the social mores by which the community's conduct patterns are established. Hence the law of statutory rape intervenes in an effort to avoid such a disposition. This goal, moreover, is not accomplished by penalizing the naive female but by imposing criminal sanctions against the male, who is conclusively presumed to be responsible for the occurrence.

The assumption that age alone will bring an understanding of the sexual act to a young woman is of doubtful validity. Both learning from the cultural group to which she is a member and her actual sexual experiences will determine her level of comprehension. The sexually experienced 15-year-old may be far more acutely aware of the implications of sexual intercourse than her sheltered cousin who is beyond the age of consent. A girl who belongs to a group whose members indulge in sexual intercourse at an early age is likely to rapidly acquire an insight into the rewards and penalties of sexual indulgence.

Nevertheless, even in circumstances where a girl's actual comprehension contradicts the law's presumption, the male is deemed criminally responsible for the act, although himself young and naive and responding to advances which may have been made to him.

[COURT NOTE: "The inequitable consequences to which we may be led are graphically illustrated by the following excerpt from *State v. Snow* (Mo.1923) 252 S.W. 629 at page 632: 'We have in this case a condition and not a theory. This wretched girl was young in years but old in sin and shame. A number of callow youths, of otherwise blameless lives ... fell under her seductive influence. They flocked about her, ... like moths about the flame of a lighted candle and probably with the same result. The girl was a common prostitute ... The boys were immature and doubtless more sinned against than sinning. They did not defile the girl. She was a mere 'cistern for foul toads to knot and gender in.' Why should the boys, misled by her, be sacrificed? What sound public policy can be subserved by branding them as felons? Might it not be wise to ingraft an exception in the statute?'"]

The law as presently constituted does not concern itself with the relative culpability of the male and female participants in the pro-

hibited sexual act. Even where the young woman is knowledgeable it does not impose sanctions upon her. The knowledgeable young man, on the other hand, is penalized and there are none who would claim that under any construction of the law this should be otherwise. However, the issue raised by the rejected offer of proof in the instant case goes to the culpability of the young man who acts without knowledge that an essential factual element exists and has, on the other hand, a positive, reasonable belief that it does not exist.

The primordial concept of *mens rea,* the guilty mind, expresses the principle that it is not conduct alone but conduct accompanied by certain specific mental states which concerns, or should concern the law....

Statutory rape has long furnished a fertile battleground upon which to argue that the lack of knowledgeable conduct is a proper defense.... [The court here notes that when statutory rape originated, the age of consent was 10, but that most states have raised it to at least 16.]

[COURT NOTE: "When the law declares that sexual intercourse with a girl under the age of ten years is rape, it is not illogical to refuse to give any credence to the defense, 'I thought she was older, and I therefore did not believe that I was committing a crime when I had sexual intercourse with her.'... But when age limits are raised to sixteen, eighteen, and twenty-one, when the young girl becomes a young woman, when adolescent boys as well as young men are attracted to her, the sexual act begins to lose its quality of abnormality and physical danger to the victim. Bona fide mistakes in the age of girls can be made by men and boys who are no more dangerous than others of their social, economic and educational level.... Even if the girl looks to be much older than the age of consent fixed by the statute, even if she lies to the man concerning her age, if she is a day below the statutory age sexual intercourse with her is rape. The man or boy who has intercourse with such girl still acts at his peril. The statute is interpreted as if it were protecting children under the age of ten." (Plascowe, Sex and the Law (1951) at pages 184 and 185.)"]

There can be no dispute that a criminal intent exists when the perpetrator proceeds with utter disregard of, or in the lack of grounds for, a belief that the female has reached the age of consent. But if he participates in a mutual act of sexual intercourse, believing his partner to be beyond the age of consent, with reasonable grounds for such belief, where is his criminal intent? In such circumstances he has not consciously taken any risk. Instead he has subjectively eliminated the risk by satisfying himself on reasonable evidence that the crime cannot be committed. If it occurs that he has been misled, we cannot realistically conclude that for such reason alone the intent with which he undertook the act suddenly becomes more heinous....

At common law an honest and reasonable belief in the existence of circumstances, which, if true, would make the act for which the person is indicted an innocent act, has always been held to be a good defense.... So far as I am aware it has never been suggested that these exceptions do not equally apply to the case of statutory offenses unless they are excluded expressly or by necessary implication.

Our departure ... is in no manner indicative of a withdrawal from the sound policy that it is in the public interest to protect the sexually naive female from exploitation. No responsible person would hesitate to condemn as untenable a claimed good faith belief in the age of consent of an "infant" female whose obviously tender years preclude the existence of reasonable grounds for that belief. However, the prosecutrix in the instant case was but three months short of 18 years of age and there is nothing in the record to indicate that the purposes of the law as stated in *Ratz* can be better served by foreclosing the defense of a lack of intent. This is not to say that the granting to consent by even a sexually sophisticated girl known to be less that the statutory age is a defense.

We hold only that in the absence of a legislative direction otherwise, a charge of statutory rape is defensible wherein a criminal intent is lacking.... The judgment is reversed.

Case Discussion

What reasons does the court give for the majority view that mistake is no defense to statutory rape? Why did the court decide to change that rule and permit mistake as a defense to statutory rape? Which rule do you favor? If you would permit mistake, would you have a cut-off age, such as the court's reference to age ten? What age would you choose as a proper cut-off point? Do you think the court is right in saying that the defense of mistake should apply to all crimes? (See chapter 7 on mistake.) In *People v. Randolph,* Randolph argued that the state of Washington should adopt the rule of the *Hernandez* case. The court declined:

> It may well be ... that "(c)urrent social and moral values make more realistic the California view that a reasonable and honest mistake of age is a valid defense to a charge of statutory rape...." Nevertheless, statutory rape ... is a recognized judicial exception to the general rule that a mistake of fact is a defense to a criminal charge. We therefore disagree with the view expressed in *Hernandez* that such exception may not be sustained except by legislation so directing; rather, we believe the converse, that the exception must be sustained unless the legislature decides otherwise.... We do not think the predatory nature of man has changed in the last decade. If mistake of fact is to be the standard of permissive conduct, the legislature is the appropriate forum to indulge in that decision.[21]

Do you agree? Why? Why not?

Note Case   "On the evening of [April 14, 1985, Navarette,] ... the victim, and a third person had been drinking and driving around Ogallala, Nebraska. The defendant, who was 22 years of age, purchased the beer which was consumed by the defendant, the victim, and the third person. The victim was only 15 years of age, although he was within approximately 6 weeks of his 16th birthday.

"At about midnight the defendant and the victim were at the defendant's home. The third person had gone home. The victim was feeling the effect of the beer and went into the defendant's bedroom so that he could lie down on the bed. He awakened sometime later and found the defendant on the bed beside him. The defendant spoke with the victim for a while and then placed his hand on the victim's penis. Later the defendant put his penis in the victim's mouth and then into the victim's anus. The victim again fell asleep. When he did awaken he returned to his home but did not enter the house. The victim sat in his father's pickup truck for about an hour and then decided to report the incident to the police...."

In upholding Navarette's conviction, against Navarette's argument that to deny him the defense of mistake and remove *mens rea* as an element of statutory rape violated the Constitution, the court wrote:

> The defendant ... contends that the statute under which he was prosecuted, § 28–319(l)(c), is unconstitutional because consent and reasonable mistake concerning the victim's age are not defenses. The statute in this respect is similar to ones on statutory rape in which consent is not a defense "[M]istake or lack of information as to the victim's chastity is no defense to the crime of statutory rape." We have expressly rejected the "California Rule."...
>
> The majority of the cases hold that a defense of reasonable mistake is not constitutionally required. It is not violative of due process for the Legislature, in framing its criminal laws, to cast upon the public the duty of care or extreme caution. Nor is it unfair to require one who gets perilously close to an area of proscribed conduct to take the risk that he may cross over the line. *People v. Navarette,* 221 Neb. 171, 376 N.W.2d 8 (1985)

Criminal Sexual Conduct with Children

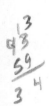

In recent years, child sex abuse has drawn much attention. Several notorious cases came to public attention, leading researchers to conclude that people in trust positions with authority over children—parents, teachers, counselors, ministers, and others—were abusing their authority by sexually violating the children under their care. The law has long taken a strong stance against such activity, as made clear not only by statutory rape but also by statutes concerning deviate sex and corrupting minors.

New developments are taking place, however, to strengthen existing law and even to create new authority to punish child sex abuse. In some cases, penalties are being made harsher for child sex abuse, and rules are being changed to make it easier for children to testify against perpetrators and to extend the law's reach beyond sexual intercourse to broad-ranging offensive touching.

It is too soon either to tell how far these developments will go or to know just where to draw the line between appropriately demonstrating affection to children and making unwanted and otherwise harmful sexual advances. Harsh penalties and fear of prosecutions ought not to offset advances made over the past three or four decades in releasing repressed healthy desires to demonstrate affection toward children. The issue is sensitive but important. It will take time to learn how to encourage healthy, affectionate demonstrations while responding to damaging sexual advances with proper legislation, prosecution, and punishment. One encouraging development is programs that guide children to discover what touching they like and do not like and that teach them to say no to offensive touching. For example, even if they are meant only to show affection and even when Mom or Dad thinks he ought to, Tommy need not accept Aunt Theresa's unwanted kisses.

Marital Rape Exception

Until recently, a man could not rape his wife, according to the **marital rape exception.** The reasons for the exception include the following: (1) when a woman marries, she consents to sex at her husband's demand, (2) permitting rape within marriage encourages unhappy wives to make false charges against their husbands, and (3) the intervention of criminal law into marital problems hinders reconciliation during marital difficulties.[22]

However warmly criminal policymakers embraced these arguments in the past, modern civil rights and feminist movements have attacked them savagely. In essence, the argument is that women are no longer possessions and that simply because women consent to marriage their husbands are not granted the right to "sex on demand." Marriage is increasingly coming to mean an equal partnership. Hence, sex practices must be negotiated and mutually agreed upon.

It is now a crime in twenty-five states for a husband to rape his wife while they are living together. New York excludes legally separated married couples from the marital exception rule. New Jersey and Oregon have gone further and abolished the marital exception completely. From 1978 to 1985, 118 husbands were prosecuted for raping their wives; 104 were convicted. Despite these efforts, it remains generally true that men cannot rape their wives.[23]

CASE

Did He Rape His Wife?

Kizer v. Commonwealth
228 Va. 256, 321 S.E.2d 291 (1984)

[The jury found Kizer guilty of rape. The judge sentenced him to twenty years in prison but suspended the last fifteen years and put Kizer on probation for life. He appealed. Justice Compton delivered the opinion.]

FACTS
Defendant and his wife, Jeri, were married in June of 1981 in Texas. The couple moved to Norfolk where defendant, age 20, was stationed aboard ship as an enlisted man in the Navy. They occupied rented quarters ashore that were leased in both names. Following the birth of a child, the couple

began having marital difficulties. In September of 1982, about six months before the incident in question, the wife returned to Texas briefly. According to her testimony, the purpose of the trip was "to visit" her parents for two weeks; the visit was not "a separation" from her husband.

During the "middle of February" 1983, about three weeks before the alleged offense, the defendant "moved back to the ship." The wife continued to reside in the apartment with the child. According to the wife's testimony, the separation occurred because "[t]he marriage was over and I did not want the marriage to be any longer." The wife added that she "wanted to be separated and in the process to file for divorce after the legal separation in Virginia." The defendant testified that the parties were not "legally separated" and that he moved to the ship "to avoid any other arguing with my wife in front of our son because we did not want to subject him to arguing between me and my wife, Jeri."

The evidence showed that the parties did not engage in sexual intercourse during the period from September 1982, when she visited her parents in Texas, until the date of the incident in question. During a portion of this time, the defendant was aboard ship at sea.

Prior to the alleged offense, the defendant filed a petition in court seeking an award of custody of his child. In addition, the parties decided in February to consult a lawyer "about getting a legal separation." As the parties were en route to an attorney's office, the wife told defendant that she had changed her mind and that she did not want to separate "right now." He said, "Are you sure?" and she responded, "Yes." They returned to their apartment. The wife testified that she decided to discontinue the trip to the attorney because the defendant had just received notification that his father was very ill and she did not want to put more "pressure" on him at that time.

The evidence showed that before the day of the alleged offense, the defendant discussed "the rape laws of Virginia" with a friend. The defendant had said that "he [the defendant] was kind of hard up for sex" and that he thought he "ought to go over there and rip her clothes off of her and take it."

On the day in question, March 6, the defendant had been visiting friends in an apartment "across the hall" from the marital home. He knocked on the door to his apartment about 6:00 p.m. and asked his wife to allow him to use the shower. She refused because she was afraid to be in the premises alone with him. The defendant insisted on gaining entry and, as the wife tried to lock the front door to the apartment, he kicked the door twice. The door "came open and the frame came off the door," according to the wife's testimony. The defendant took the child from the mother's arms and placed him on the floor. The defendant picked up the wife, carried her to the bedroom, ripped off her clothing, and forcibly had sexual intercourse with her. During this time, she was screaming, scratching, kicking, and pulling defendant's hair. At one point during the 45-minute episode, the wife broke away from the defendant and rushed to the bedroom window, screaming for help. After the assault, the wife ran from the apartment and reported the incident to a police officer who was in the area.

OPINION

On appeal, the question presented is whether, under this evidence, the Commonwealth established beyond a reasonable doubt the elements necessary to sustain a conviction for marital rape. In such a case, the prosecution, in addition to establishing a violation of the general rape statute, Code § 18.2–61, must prove beyond a reasonable doubt that the wife unilaterally had revoked her implied consent to marital intercourse. The wife's revocation of consent must be demonstrated by a manifest intent "to terminate the marital relationship." The facts necessary to show this intention to terminate must reveal that the wife: has lived separate and apart from the husband; has refrained from voluntary sexual intercourse with her husband; and, "in light of all the circumstances," has conducted herself "in a manner that establishes a de facto end to the marriage."

In the present case, the evidence shows, first, a violation of the rape statute sufficient to sustain a conviction of the defendant for the rape of a female not his wife. Second, the evidence establishes that the parties lived separate and apart. Third, the proof shows that the wife refrained from voluntary sexual intercourse with the defendant. The evidence fails, however, to show beyond a reasonable doubt the wife conducted herself in a manner that established an actual end to the marriage, in light of all the circumstances.

Significantly, the wife's marital conduct during the six-month period before the assault was equivocal, ambivalent, and ambiguous. Prior to September 1982, the parties had been having domestic difficulties but apparently had been living together as husband and wife. She left Norfolk and went to Texas to "visit" her parents. But she testified that this was not a "separation" in the divorce sense. She returned from Texas and during part of the September–January period, the husband was on shipboard duty at sea. In January, the wife left again but returned after the parties "talked." She stated at the time that she wanted to make the marriage "work." In February, she terminated a planned trip with her husband to a divorce lawyer, advising the husband that she had changed her mind and did not wish to separate "right now." Finally, about three weeks before the alleged offense, the husband began living aboard ship in port. At the time, the wife considered the marriage to be "over."

Evaluating the foregoing circumstances in the light most favorable to the Commonwealth, we think it is apparent that the wife subjectively considered the marriage fractured beyond repair when the parties separated in February. Nevertheless, we cannot say that this subjective intent was manifested objectively to the husband, in view of the wife's vacillating conduct, so that he perceived, or reasonably should have perceived, that the marriage actually was ended.

Reversed and dismissed.

Case Discussion

Why did the court reverse the jury's verdict and dismiss the rape charge against Kizer? Do you agree? What rule would you formulate for marital rape? Can you make an argument that marital rape is worse than nonmarital rape? the same as nonmarital rape? less serious? no crime at all?

Elements of Criminal Sexual Conduct

Actus Reus	*Mens Rea*	**Material Circumstances**
gender-neutral penetrations of and contacts with intimate body parts	intent to gain sexual gratification by penetration or contact	age differential between offender and victim

Criminal Sexual Conduct Statutes

Civil rights and feminist forces, along with some criminal law reform sentiment, have combined to call for abolishing existing rape and other deviate sex legislation. In its place, they recommend that legislatures create new, gender-neutral offenses. Some states have done this, enacting criminal sexual conduct laws. Michigan's 1974 statute provides, in summary, the following:

> 1st degree: This consists of "sexual penetration," defined as sexual intercourse, cunnilingus, fellatio, anal intercourse, "or any other intrusion, however slight, of any part of a person's body or of any object into the genital or anal openings of another person's body." In addition one of the following must have occurred:
>
> *1.* the defendant must have been armed with a weapon;
> *2.* force or coercion was used and the defendant was aided by another person; or
> *3.* force or coercion was used and personal injury to the victim was caused.
>
> 2nd degree: This consists of "sexual contact," defined as the intentional touching of the victim's or actor's personal parts or the intentional touching of the clothing covering the immediate area of the victim's intimate parts, for purposes of sexual arousal or gratification. "Intimate parts" is defined as including the primary genital area, groin, inner thigh, buttock, or breast. In addition, one of the circumstances required for 1st degree criminal sexual conduct must have existed.
> 3rd degree: This consists of sexual penetration accomplished by force or coercion.
> 4th degree: This consists of sexual contact accomplished by force or coercion.[24]

As the Michigan statute indicates, the new legislation purports to cover all offensive and violent sexual penetration and contact without regard to victims' and perpetrators' gender. Under the Michigan statute, what crime did the women in the following true incident commit?

Police have received a complaint from a man stating he was raped by two women. According to the complaint, the twenty-four-year-old man was driving home when he stopped to help two women who appeared to be having car trouble. He said that as he approached them, one of the women pointed a gun at him and told him to get into the back seat of their car. He said the women bound his hands with rope, pulled a ski mask over his head, and drove "about half an hour" to a house at an undetermined location. There, he said, they forced him into a bedroom and "used his body repeatedly" for "several hours." He told police he was driven back, unharmed, to his own car late that night. He gave police a sketchy description of the two women.[25]

Grading Rape

Most statutes divide rape into two degrees: simple or second-degree rape, and aggravated or first-degree rape. Aggravated rape involves at least one of the following:

☐ The victim suffers serious bodily injury.
☐ A stranger commits the rape.

☐ The rape occurs in connection with another crime.

☐ The rapist is armed.

☐ The rapist has accomplices.

☐ The victim is a minor and the rapist is several years older.

All other rapes are simple rapes for which the penalties are less severe. The criminal sexual conduct statutes have added more degrees, usually four, to accommodate the distinction between penetration and contact. Aggravated penetration constitutes first-degree criminal sexual conduct, aggravated contact second degree, simple criminal penetration third degree, and simple criminal contact fourth degree.

Summary of Rape and Criminal Sexual Conduct

Rape, a special assault, entails the specific purpose to have sexual intercourse by force and against the victim's will. Traditionally, and to a large extent even today, only men who try to force vaginal intercourse on women who are not their wives can commit rape. Because of changing moral, sexual, and social values, combined with civil rights and feminist pressures, some states have recently modified their rape laws. A few have gone far under this influence, making rape a gender-neutral crime in which a variety of sexual violations are brought together under general criminal sexual conduct statutes. Other states have made more modest changes, altering old evidence rules such as corroboration and the victim's prior sexual history. Some have abolished, or at least qualified, the marital rape exception. Taken together, these modifications indicate enhanced sensitivity in two important respects: (1) to the harms caused by a wide range of sexual assaults and (2) to the trauma suffered by victims who have the courage to bring these offensive assaults into public view. Despite these beneficial effects, however, rape laws are still more closely aligned with seventeenth-century notions than with recent reformist ideas.

Recent notorious child sex abuse cases have drawn attention to problems that arise when people in authority use their superior positions to sexually abuse children. Parents and teachers come readily to mind, but coaches, counselors, and religious leaders are also in such special positions. This area is a sensitive one, calling for careful attention. Proper policy requires that the public interest in encouraging healthy affection toward children not be thwarted. But at the same time, the equally strong public interest in preventing, discovering, and punishing damaging sexual advances toward children must also be served. It is too soon to tell how far policy makers will go toward achieving the latter without unduly impeding the former.

▼ BATTERY

Assault and battery, although frequently combined, were distinct offenses at common law. A **battery** is an unjustified offensive touching. Central to the *actus reus* of battery is body contact. An **assault** is either an attempted or a threatened battery. Assault differs from battery—it requires no physical contact; an assault is complete before the offender touches the victim.

Elements of Battery		
Actus Reus	*Mens Rea*	**Material Circumstances**
offensive unlawful touching	1. purposeful 2. knowing 3. reckless or 4. negligent	injury

The Actus Reus *of Battery*

Unjustified offensive touching constitutes the battery *actus reus*. Corporal punishment that parents or other guardians inflict to "discipline" those under their legal authority, although offensive, does not constitute battery because the law justifies it. Within that limit, offensive touching covers a wide spectrum. Brutal attacks with baseball bats, kicking with heavy boots, and staggering blows with fists obviously fall within its scope. But what about offensive touches, such as ones intended to insult (like spitting), or those with sexual overtones, such as pinching buttocks, squeezing breasts, or even putting arms around another who does not want such contacts? Criminal sexual conduct statutes make most of these contacts crimes. Cases have also held that spitting in order to insult a police officer is battery.[26]

Other unwanted and unjustified touches create problems, particularly when they cause no injury. For example, what about employers, or even companions, who tend to demonstrate their affections by throwing arms around shoulders, or grasping another's arm to make a point? Do these actions constitute battery if they have no sexual motivation, but the person being touched finds them offensive? Or, consider touching children at all, whether affectionately or sexually, who do not want to be touched. What about the child who "must" let Aunt Sylvia hug and kiss her or him in order to avoid hurting the aunt's feelings? Is this a battery? It surely is offensive to the nephew or niece who has to endure it. Just where to draw the line is difficult, but clearly battery encompasses more than blows that result in actual physical injury.

The Mens Rea *of Battery*

Existing law does not clearly specify the battery *mens rea*. At common law, battery was an injury inflicted "willfully or in anger." Modern courts and statutes extend battery *mens rea* to include reckless and negligent contacts.

Most jurisdictions either include reckless and negligent injuring within the scope of battery or create a separate offense to that effect. Louisiana, for example, provides that "inflicting any injury upon the person of another by criminal negligence" constitutes "negligent injuring." The Model Penal Code removes the *mens rea* confusion by defining battery to include "purposely, recklessly, or negligently caus[ing] bodily injury," or "negligently caus[ing] bodily injury ... with a deadly weapon."[27] The court dealt with both the *actus reus* and *mens rea* of battery in *J.A.T. v. State*.

CASE

Is "Sicking" a Dog Actus Reus?

J.A.T. v. State

212 S.E.2d 879 (Ga.1975)

Stolz, Judge

This is an appeal by a juvenile who was adjudicated delinquent and in need of treatment or rehabilitation and supervision following a hearing initiated by a petition alleging that he had committed the offense of simple battery in that he, on a certain date, did intentionally cause physical harm to another named individual by sicking his dog on him.

FACTS

Although the juvenile denied the material elements of the offense, there was evidence that he had sicked his dog on other children on previous occasions and that on the occasion in question he ran after the victim with the dog under his control on a leash yelling "sick 'em ('im?)," and that the dog began biting the victim, causing him physical harm. Although the evidence was in conflict as to whether the juvenile was holding the leash at the time the dog physically attacked the victim, this did not constitute a variance between the allegata and probata, since the petition did not contain allegations about the leash. The evidence was adequate to authorize a finding that, based upon prior custom and training, the dog was sufficiently under the juvenile's control as to respond to the stimulus of his vocal command to "sick" persons, whether he was leashed or unleashed, and that the juvenile knew or was chargeable with knowledge of this.

OPINION

The appellant contends that as a matter of law the offense of simple battery cannot be committed through the use of a dog. Code Ann. § 26–1304 (Ga.L.1968, pp. 1249, 1281) provides in part: "A person commits simple battery when he either (a) intentionally makes physical contact of an insulting or provoking nature with the person of another or (b) intentionally causes physical harm to another." The key word to be construed, therefore, is "causes."

Looking first at Georgia law, although we have found no case exactly on point construing this relatively new statute, there are, nevertheless, principles which are applicable. "In all interpretations, the courts shall look diligently for the intention of the General Assembly, keeping in view, at all times, the old law, the evil, and the remedy." Code § 102–102(9). Even under the former law, Code § 26–1408, which defined "battery" rather restrictively as "the unlawful beating of another" battery was held to be committable without direct physical contact between the parties, e.g., by use of an automobile (*Henry v. State,* 49 Ga.App. 80(3), 174 S.E. 183), a motorcycle (*Maloney v. State,* 57 Ga.App. 265, 195 S.E. 209), and a rock (*Hill v. State,* 63 Ga. 578).

It will be noted that the present statute defining simple battery, § 26–1304, is broader in its terminology than its predecessor. The word "causes," being unmodified and not defined, should be given its ordinary signification. Code § 102–102(1). Should judicial construction of that word be deemed necessary or desirable, however, this court has supplied this at least once. "When used of a person or other subject charged with an affirmative duty of care or of good conduct, so to speak, the word 'caused' implies not only active misconduct and deeds of commission, but also passive neglect, deeds of omission, and failure to exercise duties faithfully." *L. & N.R. Co. v. Warfield & Lee,* 6 Ga.App. 550(4a), 65 S.E. 308. "(C)riminal negligence may sometimes be a sufficient substitute for deliberate intention in the commission of crime." *Tift v. State,* 17 Ga.App. 663, 664(6), 88 S.E. 41.

Even if the juvenile was sicking the dog on the victim in sport, not necessarily intending to injure him, it could be found to be a battery if such action amounted to criminal negligence. Compare *Hill v. State,* 63 Ga. 578 which held that throwing a rock at another in sport, expecting him to dodge, was a battery. "Every person is presumed to intend the natural and necessary consequence of his acts." *Tift v. State.*

The dog's action was not as a matter of law such an intervening cause as would relieve its master from liability. "Generally, where there has intervened between the defendant's negligence and the injury an independent, illegal act of a third person producing the injury, and without which it would not have occurred, such independent criminal act should be treated as the proximate cause, insulating and excluding the negligence of the defendant.

"However, the above rule has been held inapplicable if the defendant (original wrongdoer) had reasonable grounds for apprehending that such criminal act would be committed. 'So far as scope of duty (or, as some courts put it, the relation of proximate cause) is concerned, it should make no difference whether the intervening actor is negligent or intentional, or criminal. Even criminal conduct by others is often reasonably to be anticipated.'" *Warner v. Arnold,* 133 Ga.App. 174, 177, 210 S.E.2d 350, 352.

Applying this to the statute, then, the act which causes the physical harm can be active or passive, and done directly or indirectly through an agency, as long as it is done intentionally, or with criminal negligence.

This construction seems to be basically consistent with authorities outside this jurisdiction. "(I)t is no longer important that the contact (in a battery) is not brought about by a direct application of force such as a blow, and it is enough that the defendant sets a force in motion which ultimately produces the result ... In order to be liable for battery, the defendant must have done some positive and affirmative act; ... The act must cause, and must be intended to cause, an unpermitted contact ... The gist of the action for battery is not the hostile intent of the defendant, but rather the absence of consent to the contact on the part of the plaintiff. The defendant may be liable where he has intended only a joke...." Prosser on Torts (4th Ed.), § 9, pp. 34–36.

In dealing with causation in fact, Prosser says: "Of all of the questions involved, it is easiest to dispose of that which has been regarded, traditionally, as the most difficult: has the conduct of the defendant caused the plaintiff's harm? This is a question of fact. It is, furthermore, a fact upon which all the learning, literature and lore of the law are largely lost. It is a matter upon which any layman is quite as competent to sit in judgment as the most experienced court. For that reason, in the ordinary case, it is peculiarly a question for the jury. Causation is a fact. It is a matter of what has in fact occurred. A cause is a necessary antecedent: in a very real and practical sense, the term embraces all things which have so far contributed to the result that without them it would not have occurred. It covers not only positive acts and active physical forces, but also pre-existing passive conditions which have played a material part in bringing about the event. In particular, it covers the defendant's omissions as well as his acts....

The defendant's conduct is a cause of the event if it was a material element and a substantial factor in bringing it about. Whether it was such a substantial factor is for the jury to determine, unless the issue is so clear that reasonable men could not differ. It has been considered that 'substantial factors' is a phrase sufficiently intelligible to the layman to furnish an adequate guide in instructions to the jury, and that it is neither possible nor desirable to reduce it to any lower terms. As applied to the fact of causation alone, no better test has been devised." Prosser on Torts, supra, § 41, pp. 237, 240. "Once it is established that the defendant's conduct has in fact been one of the causes of the plaintiff's injury, there remains the question whether the defendant should be legally responsible for what he has caused. Unlike the fact of causation, with which it is often hopelessly confused, this is essentially a problem of law." Prosser on Torts, supra, § 42, p. 244. Applying this to the case sub judice, in which a criminal offense is charged, once it is found that the juvenile's conduct has in fact been one of the causes of the victim's injury, the juvenile's legal responsibility is imposed by the criminal statute.

A number of foreign cases have recognized that animals could be used in the commission of criminal offenses. In *Dougherty v. Reckler,* 191 Iowa 1195, 184 N.W. 304, the court said that letting a vicious dog loose "negligently sets a dangerous instrumentality in operation." In *State v. Hollis,* 284 Mo. 627, 225 S.W. 952, a case involving the crime of killing animals with dogs, the court said that the offense would be shown if the dog was "set on" an animal by the owner. In *State v. Lewis,* 4 Pennewill 332, 20 Del. 332, 55 A. 3, the court found that a battery would lie where one wilfully drove a horse in contact with a person. This was so even though the accused did not have the reins. The court said that the accused was guilty if he was aiding, counseling or commanding another who was managing the horse. In *Lynch v. Commonwealth,* 131 Va. 762, 109 S.E. 427, the court quoted a definition of battery as "the actual infliction of corporal hurt on

another, wilfully or in anger, whether by the party's own hand or by some means set in motion by him."

We hold, therefore, that as a matter of law, the offense of simple battery can be committed through the use of a dog, where it is shown that the defendant's conduct was a substantial factor in the causation.

The juvenile court judge did not err in overruling the motion to quash or dismiss the petition. The petition alleged the commission of the offense of simple battery by a means contemplated by the law, as we have held in Division 1, above. Even an indictment for battery has been held not to be required to allege the exact manner and means of the battery, *Hill v. State,* 63 Ga. 578, 583, or to express the language of the charge in the exact language of the Code. *Moore v. Caldwell,* 231 Ga. 485(2), 202 S.E.2d 425. The petition was plain enough for a man of ordinary capacity to understand the nature of the offense charged. *Richardson v. State,* 231 Ga. 295(2), 201 S.E.2d 398.

The evidence construed in favor of the judgment, authorized the finding of delinquency based upon the commission of simple battery through the use of the dog.

Judgment affirmed.

Case Discussion What problem did the *actus reus* create in the case? How did the court conclude that the dog satisfied the *actus reus* requirement? Do you agree? How would you define battery *actus reus?* How does the court define the *mens rea* of battery? Would you define it that way? What facts in the case are relevant to determining J.A.T.'s *mens rea?* Do you believe he was guilty of battery? Explain your reasons why or why not?

The Harm in Battery

Battery requires some injury, at least of an emotional nature in most jurisdictions. These and batteries resulting in minor physical injury are misdemeanors in most jurisdictions. Batteries resulting in serious bodily injury are felonies. The Model Penal Code departs from existing law by requiring at least some bodily injury; offensive touching itself is not a crime.

Supporters of the code admit that insulting touching causes real psychological and emotional suffering. They maintain that tort law and informal sanctions more appropriately deal with those harms.

Some codes include provisions regarding specific harms. Recent injuries surrounding pit bulls prompted the Minnesota legislature to enact the following provision:

> 609.26   A person who causes great or substantial bodily harm to another by negligently or intentionally permitting any dog to run uncontrolled off the owner's premises, or negligently failing to keep it properly confined is guilty of a petty misdemeanor....
>
> Subd. 3.   If proven by a preponderance of the evidence, it shall be an affirmative defense to liability under this section that the victim provoked the dog to cause the victim's bodily harm.[28]

Injuries and deaths resulting from drug abuse have led the same legislature to enact the following provision:

> 609.228   Whoever proximately causes great bodily harm by, directly or indirectly, unlawfully selling, giving away, bartering, delivering, exchanging, distributing, or administering a controlled substance ... may be sentenced to imprisonment for not more than ten years or to payment of a fine of not more than $20,000, or both.[29]

The Model Penal Code grades bodily harm offenses as follows:

> § 211.1
>
> *2.* Bodily injury is a felony when
> a. such injury is inflicted purposely or knowingly with a deadly weapon; or
> b. serious bodily injury is inflicted purposely, or knowingly or recklessly under circumstances manifesting extreme indifference to the value of human life.
> c. except as provided in paragraph (2), bodily injury is a misdemeanor, unless it was caused in a fight or scuffle entered into by mutual consent, in which case it is a petty misdemeanor.

▼ ASSAULT

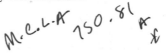

Assault includes two types of offense, attempted batteries and threatened batteries. Attempted battery assault focuses on the objective dimension to the offense, the *actus reus*. As in other attempts, attempted battery requires a specific intent to commit a battery and, in most jurisdictions, substantial steps toward carrying out the attempt without actually completing it (see chapter 5).

Elements of Assault		
Actus Reus	***Mens Rea***	**Material Circumstances**
1. attempted battery or *2.* acts threatening battery	*1.* intent to injury or *2.* intent to frighten	*1.* injury *2.* use of deadly weapon

Threatened batteries focus on the subjective dimension—the *mens rea* and the fear placed in the victim by the assaulter. Threatened battery assault, sometimes called intentional scaring, requires only that actors intend to frighten their victims, thus expanding assault beyond attempted battery. Even absent the intent to physically injure, the intent to frighten victims into believing the actor will hurt them satisfies the threatened battery assault requirement.

Victims' awareness is critical in threatened battery assault. Specifically, victims must fear an immediate battery, and that fear must be reasonable. Words alone are not assaults; threatening gestures must accompany them. This is not always just. For example, what if an assailant approaches from behind a victim, saying, "Don't move, or I'll shoot!" These words produce a reasonable fear that injury is imminent, yet they are not an assault.

Conditional threats are not immediate. The conditional threat, "I'd punch you out if you weren't a kid," is not immediate because it is conditioned on the victim's age. Therefore, no threatened battery assault has taken place. In a few jurisdictions, a present ability to carry out the threat must exist. But in most, even a person who approaches a victim with a gun he knows is unloaded, points the gun at the victim, and pulls the trigger (intending only to frighten his victim) has committed threatened battery.[30]

Threatened and attempted battery assaults address two somewhat distinct harms. Attempted battery assault deals with an incomplete or inchoate physical injury. Threatened battery assault is directed at a present psychological or emotional harm: the victim's fear. In attempted battery assault, therefore, a victim's awareness is immaterial; in threatened battery assault, it is crucial.

The Model Penal Code deals with threatened and attempted battery assaults as follows:

§ 211.1 Simple Assault.
A person is guilty of assault if he:

Words alone an not a threat

a. attempts to cause bodily injury to another; or
b. attempts by physical menace to put another in fear of imminent serious bodily harm.
   Simple assault is a misdemeanor unless committed in a fight or scuffle entered into by mutual consent, in which case the assault is a petty misdemeanor.

Historically, all assaults were misdemeanors. However, modern statutes have created several aggravated assaults that are felonies. Most common are assaults with the intent to commit violent felonies (murder, rape, and robbery, for example), assaults with deadly weapons (such as guns and knives), and assaults on police officers. The Model Penal Code has a comprehensive assault statute, integrating, rationalizing, and grading assault and battery. It takes into account *mens rea,* material surrounding circumstances, and intended harm. Note the careful attention paid to these critical elements:

§ 211.2
A person is guilty of aggravated assault if he:

a. attempts to cause serious bodily injury to another, or causes such injury purposely, knowingly or recklessly under circumstances manifesting extreme indifference to the value of human life; or

b. attempts to cause or purposely or knowingly causes bodily injury to another with a deadly weapon.

Aggravated assault under paragraph (a) is a felony of the second degree; aggravated assault under paragraph (b) is a felony of the third degree.

§ 211.3

A person commits a misdemeanor if he recklessly engages in conduct which places or may place another person in danger of death or serious bodily injury. Recklessness and danger shall be presumed where a person knowingly points a firearm at or in the direction of another, whether or not the actor believed the firearm to be loaded.

United States v. Moore deals with the established elements of assault with a deadly weapon in the context of the recent spate of cases around the country related to intentionally spreading the HIV virus that causes AIDS.

CASE

Are Teeth Deadly Weapons?

United States v. Moore
846 F.2d 1163 (8th Cir. 1988)

Timbers, Circuit Judge

FACTS

… At the time of the incident which is the subject of this appeal, Moore was an inmate at the Federal Medical Center ("FMC") in Rochester, Minnesota. On November 25 and December 3, 1986, Dr. Clifford Gastineau had Moore tested for the HIV virus because his long time heroin addiction placed him in a risk category for AIDS. In mid-December, Dr. Gastineau advised Moore that the tests were positive and that the disease could be fatal. He told Moore that the disease could be transmitted by way of blood or semen and counseled him to avoid unprotected intercourse and not to share needles, razor blades or toothbrushes.

On January 7, 1987, Lieutenant Ronald E. McCullough, a correctional officer at the FMC, called Moore to his office as part of his investigation of a report that Moore had been smoking in a non-smoking area in the FMC's medical surgical unit. Moore refused to answer questions. When McCullough told Moore he would have to be placed in seclusion and administrative detention, Moore refused to move. McCullough called for assistance. Correctional officer Timothy Voigt arrived. He told Moore to stand so that he could be handcuffed. Moore said "I won't be cuffed." McCullough called two additional correctional officers who arrived and attempted to lift Moore from his chair. Moore reacted violently. In the ensuing struggle, Moore kneed McCullough in the groin twice, attempted to bite him on the hand, and did bite him on the left knee and hip without breaking the skin. Moore held his mouth over the bite on the leg for several seconds. He also bit Voigt on the right leg, holding his mouth against the bite from five to seven seconds. Dr. Gastineaus testified that during the struggle a mild abrasion appeared at the point on Voigt's thigh where Moore had bitten him. This abrasion apparently resulted from friction with the fabric of Voigt's pants. The abrasion may have come into contact with a wet patch on Voigt's pants which possibly was made by Moore's saliva. During the struggle, Moore threatened to kill the officers.

[COURT NOTE: "The parties dispute whether this bite punctured Voigt's skin. Moore, citing Dr. Gastineau's testimony, asserts that the bite failed to penetrate the fabric of Voigt's pants. The government, citing Voigt's testimony, asserts that Moore bit deeply into Voigt's thigh, puncturing Voigt's skin in three places. Voigt's subsequent testimony indicates, however, that the bleeding at the site of this wound was due to an abrasion caused by the friction of his pants rubbing against his legs. Thus the 'puncture' wounds he describes apparently were indentations that in themselves did not cause bleeding."]

On January 10, 1987, Moore told Debra Alberts, a nurse at the FMC, that he had "wanted to hurt them bad, wanted to kill the bastards." He also said that he "hopes the wounds that he inflicted on the officers when he bit them were bad enough that they get the disease that he has."

On April 9, 1987, Moore was indicted. The indictment charged that Moore willfully had assaulted McCullough and Voigt, federal correctional officers engaged in their official duties, by means of a deadly and dangerous weapon, i.e., Moore's mouth and teeth. The indictment specifically charged that Moore was "a person then having been tested positively for the [HIV] antibody." Although Moore also had tested positive for hepatitis, the indictment did not refer to this disease.

At trial, Dr. Gastineau testified that the medical profession knew of no "well-proven instances in which a human bite has resulted in transmission of the [HIV] virus to the bitten person." He agreed with a medical manual that stated there is no evidence that AIDS can be transmitted through any contact that does not involve the exchange of bodily fluids and that, while the virus has appeared in minute amounts in saliva, it has never been shown to have been spread through contact with saliva. He said that theoretically "one cannot exclude the possibility" of transmission through biting. Later he added, however, "it seems that in medicine everything is conceivable or possible."

He testified about a case of a person who had been bitten deeply by a person with AIDS and had tested negative 18 months later. Dr. Gastineau also testified that, apart from the matter of AIDS, a human bite can be dangerous. He said that when a human bite is of a more damaging nature than the ones inflicted by Moore and "where the skin is really broken to greater depths," it can be "much more dangerous than a dog bite." He also said that "there are probably 30 to 50 variet[ies] of germs in the human mouth that together, all of them acting in concert, could cause serious infection." He characterized a human bite as "a very dangerous form of aggression" and "one of the most dangerous of all forms of bites."

On June 24, 1987, the jury found Moore guilty on both counts of the indictment. The jury had been instructed on the lesser included offense of assaulting a federal officer. The court declined to instruct the jury that the government was required to prove that AIDS could be transmitted by way of a bite in order to prove that Moore's mouth and teeth were a deadly and dangerous weapon. Moore was sentenced to concurrent five-year prison terms, which were to run consecutively to the seven-year federal prison sentence he was serving at the time of the incident.

OPINION

… The question of what constitutes a "deadly and dangerous weapon" is a question of fact for the jury. We previously have defined a "deadly and dangerous weapon" as an object "used in a manner likely to endanger life or inflict serious bodily harm." "Serious bodily harm" has been defined as something more than minor injury, but not necessarily injury creating a substantial likelihood of death.…

As a practical matter, it often is difficult to determine whether a particular object is a deadly and dangerous weapon. Almost any weapon, as used or attempted to be used, may endanger life or inflict great bodily harm; as such, in appropriate circumstances, it may be a dangerous and deadly weapon.

Moreover, the object need not be inherently dangerous, or a "weapon" by definition, such as a gun or a knife, to be found to be a dangerous and deadly weapon.

Courts frequently have considered various kinds of objects to be deadly and dangerous, including such normally innocuous objects as a chair, a walking stick, a broken beer bottle and pool cue, an automobile, and mop handles. In short, what constitutes a dangerous weapon depends not on the nature of the object itself but on its capacity, given the manner of its use, to "... endanger life or inflict great bodily harm."

As a corollary, it is not necessary that the object, as used by a defendant, actually cause great bodily harm, as long as it has the capacity to inflict such harm in the way it was used....

Courts also have held that in appropriate circumstances a part of the body may be a dangerous weapon, [including teeth, fists or feet]....

In light of the law on what may be considered a deadly and dangerous weapon, we conclude that the evidence in the instant case was sufficient to support the jury's finding that Moore used his mouth and teeth as a deadly and dangerous weapon. As stated above, Dr. Gastineau testified that a human bite is potentially "more dangerous than a dog bite"; that it is capable of causing "serious infection"; and that it can be "a very dangerous form of aggression." We reaffirm that this potential for "serious infection" is a form of "serious bodily harm.""...

We therefore hold that Dr. Gastineau's testimony, viewed in the light most favorable to the government, was substantial evidence supporting the jury's finding that Moore used his mouth and teeth in a manner likely to inflict serious bodily harm.... It may be that Moore did not transmit any of the "30 to 50" varieties of germs he might have transmitted to the officers. He nevertheless used his mouth and teeth in a way that could have transmitted disease. It was only a fortuity that he did not do so....

Although there is sufficient evidence in the record that the human mouth and teeth may be used as a deadly and dangerous weapon, we nevertheless wish to emphasize that the medical evidence in the record was insufficient to establish that AIDS may be transmitted by a bite. The evidence established that there are no well-proven cases of AIDS transmission by way of a bite; that contact with saliva has never been shown to transmit the disease; and that in one case a person who had been deeply bitten by a person with AIDS tested negative several months later. Indeed, a recent study has indicated that saliva actually may contain substances that protect the body from AIDS. *New York Times,* May 6, 1988, at A 16, col. 4. While Dr. Gastineau testified "in medicine everything is conceivable," in a legal context the possibility of AIDS transmission by means of a bite is too remote to support a finding that the mouth and teeth may be considered a deadly and dangerous weapon in this respect.

In short, we hold that the evidence was sufficient to support the finding that Moore's mouth and teeth were a deadly and dangerous weapon, regardless of the presence or absence of AIDS....

[Affirmed.]

Case Discussion   What were the critical facts in the case to establish the elements of assault with a deadly weapon? What was Moore's intent? What actions did he take to carry it out? What relevance does his testing HIV positive have to do with the case, according to the court? What is your opinion? What about a person knowing he or she is HIV positive who intentionally, knowingly, recklessly, or negligently has sex with other people? Is this simple assault? Assault with a deadly weapon? Attempted murder? Or not an offense?

Note Case   Cheryl thought her live-in boyfriend, Harrod, was at work and invited her other boyfriend, Calvin, over. Unknown to Cheryl, Harrod had left work, gone to a back room in the house, and fallen asleep. Harrod awoke and discovered Calvin. When Calvin refused to leave, Harrod threw a hammer at him, Calvin ducked, and the hammer hit the wall just over Harrod's baby son's crib. Of course Harrod assaulted Calvin, but did he assault his baby Christopher, whom he did not intend to hurt and had no idea his father threw a hammer at him? The Maryland Court of Special Appeals, reversing Harrod's conviction for assault against Christopher, held that attempted battery assault required the specific intent to harm Christopher, which Harrod lacked. *Harrod v. State,* 499 A.2d 959 (1985).

▼ FALSE IMPRISONMENT

A few states have false imprisonment statutes. California makes it a misdemeanor carrying a one-year jail term. The California Penal Code defines false imprisonment as "the unlawful violation of the personal liberty of another."[31]

Elements of False Imprisonment	
Actus Reus	*Mens Rea*
unlawful restraint of liberty or detention	specific intent to unlawfully detain and deprive another of liberty

False imprisonment is a specific intent crime. Prosecutors must prove that defendants meant to take away their victims' liberty forcibly and unlawfully. The Model Penal Code provides that such restraint, if done knowingly, is sufficient to prove false imprisonment. Motive is ordinarily not material in such cases. For example, if police officers make unlawful arrests, they can be prosecuted for false imprisonment even if they believed the arrests were lawful. Whether the error concerning an arrest was reckless, negligent, or merely honest causes problems.

Most forcible detentions or confinements are considered false imprisonment under existing law. This does not include restraints authorized by law, however, as when police officers make lawful arrests, parents restrict their children's activities, or victims detain their victimizers. False imprisonment does not require long detentions, nor does it include all detentions. The standard for criminal false imprisonment is somewhat higher than the civil requirement, which is satisfied by any confinement, however short.

The Model Penal Code requires the restraint to "interfere substantially with the victim's liberty." Although physical force often accomplishes the detention, it is not essential; threatened force is enough. Hence, the threat, "If you don't come with me, I'll break your arm," suffices. Even nonthreatening words occasionally qualify, such as when a police officer who has no right to do so orders someone on the street into a squad car, asserting, "You're under arrest."

▼ KIDNAPPING

Elements of Kidnapping		
Actus Reus	**Mens Rea**	**Material Circumstances**
1. detention and *2.* asporation or *3.* hiding in secret *4.* by force or threat of force	intent to detain and take beyond the aid of the law and friends	*1.* ransom *2.* facilitate committing another felony *3.* injury *4.* terror

Like false imprisonment, kidnapping invades privacy and takes away liberty. Kidnapping is essentially aggravated false imprisonment. As such, all kidnappings are also false imprisonments. Originally, kidnapping was the "forcible abduction or stealing away of man, woman or child from their own country." Although kidnapping was only a misdemeanor, Blackstone called it a "heinous crime" because

> it robs the king of his subjects, banishes a man from his country, and may in its consequences be productive of the most cruel and disagreeable hardships.[32]

Until recently, kidnapping was a capital offense in some jurisdictions in the United States, mainly as a result of events during the first half of the century. During Prohibition (1919 to 1933), kidnapping was prevalent in the organized crime world. One gang member might abduct a rival, "take him for a ride," and kill him. Much more frequently, rivals were captured and held hostage for ransom. Before long, law-abiding citizens were abducted, especially the spouses and children of wealthy and otherwise prominent citizens.

The most famous early case was the ransom kidnap and murder of Charles Lindbergh's son. Lindbergh was an aviator who captured Americans' hearts and imaginations when he flew solo across the Atlantic Ocean. Kidnapping was only a misdemeanor in New Jersey in 1932 when the crime occurred. The tremendous sympathy that Lindbergh's popular hero status generated and the public outrage toward what was perceived as a rampant increase in random kidnappings of America's "pillars of wealth and virtue" led legislatures to enact harsh new kidnapping statutes. These statutes are largely in force today, even though they were passed in an emotional over-reaction to a few notorious cases.[33]

Another widely publicized case breathed new life into these harsh statutes. In 1974, Patricia Hearst, heiress to newspaper tycoon William Randolph Hearst, was kidnapped. The case met with public outrage, not only because of sympathy for the prominent Hearst family but also because of shock at the psychological and physical dimensions of the crime. The kidnappers were self-styled revolutionaries called the Symbionese Liberation Army. One of the SLA's first demands was that William Randolph Hearst distribute $1 million in food to the poor of California. Later on, much to her parents' and the public's horror, Patricia Hearst converted to the SLA, participating in bank robberies to raise money for the "revolution." This all happened during a time when radicalism and violence were much feared, when the Vietnam War protest and airline hijackings for terrorist political purposes were very much on the public's mind. Hence, the public saw not only Patty Hearst's capture and her family's deep trauma but also a threat to destroy American society.

The Hearst case brought kidnapping's heinous side into bold relief. It drew together in one story capture and detention, terror, violence, and political radicalism. The details were trumpeted sensationally every day in newspapers and on radio and television. Hope that existing harsh and sweeping kidnapping legislation would be reflectively reassessed vanished in this inflamed, emotional atmosphere. President Nixon expressed his hope—a hope that many others shared—that the Supreme Court would not declare capital punishment for kidnapping to be unconstitutional. Then California Governor Reagan wished aloud that the kidnappers' demand for a free food program would set off a botulism epidemic among the poor.

Like false imprisonment, the offense from which it descended, kidnapping is a crime against personal liberty. At common law its main elements were (1) seizing, (2) confining, and (3) carrying away (asporting) (4) another person by (5) force, threat of force, fraud, or deception.

The critical difference between false imprisonment and kidnapping is the carrying away, or asportation, of victims. Since at least the eighteenth century, as Blackstone makes clear, carrying a victim into a foreign country where no friends or family could give aid and comfort, and the law could not protect the victim, added a particularly terrifying dimension to kidnapping. In the early days, the victim had to be carried at least as far as another county and usually into a foreign country.

Modern interpretations leave the asportation requirement virtually meaningless. The famous case of *People v. Chessman* illustrates how broadly asportation is interpreted by courts faced with especially revolting cases. Caryl Chessman was a multiple rapist who, in one instance, forced a young woman to leave her car and get into his, which was only twenty-two feet away. The court held that asportation's mere fact, not its distance, determined kidnapping. They upheld Chessman's conviction for kidnapping, a capital crime in California. After many years of fighting the decision, Chessman eventually was executed.[34]

Modern statutes in some states have removed the asportation requirement, usually replacing it with the requirement that kidnappers intend to confine, significantly restrain, or hold their victims in secret. The Wisconsin statute, for example, defines a kidnapper as one who "seizes or confines another without his consent and with intent to cause him to be secretly confined." Whatever the changes, the heart of the crime remains to "isolate the victim from prospect of release or friendly intervention." The court dealt with the interpretation of one of these statutes in *State v. Fulcher.*[35]

CASE

*Did He Kidnap
His Victims?*

State v. Fulcher
243 S.E.2d 338 (N.C.1978)

Lake, Justice
... Pursuant to four separate indictments, each proper in form, the defendant was found guilty of the kidnapping of each of two young women and of forcing each of them to commit with him a crime against nature. The two charges of kidnapping were consolidated for judgment and, in those cases, the defendant was sentenced to

imprisonment for 28 to 40 years. In each of the cases charging the commission of a crime against nature, the defendant was sentenced to imprisonment for 10 years, these two sentences to run consecutively with respect to each other but both to run concurrently with the sentence for kidnapping....

FACTS

On the evening of 8 September 1976, the two young women, on a vacation trip from their homes in Canada, reached and took lodging in Motel No. 6 in Winston-Salem. On previous visits to Winston-Salem, they had stayed at this motel. There were no telephones in the rooms of the motel but telephones available for use of its guests were at a well lighted alcove in or near the lobby, a well lighted hallway leading thereto from the room assigned to and occupied by the young women.

A few minutes after their occupancy of their room, at approximately 7:30 p.m., both of the young women went to the telephone alcove in an unsuccessful effort to place calls to their friends in the city. While so engaged, both of them observed the defendant, not previously known to them, using, or purporting to use, one of the other telephones in the alcove. Their attention was called to him by a comment which he made to one of them and by his general demeanor which they regarded as "strange." They remained in the telephone alcove on this occasion, some four feet from the defendant, for approximately fifteen minutes.

It was the custom of the motel, upon receipt of an incoming call for a guest, to send a messenger to the room of the guest to notify him or her of such call. At approximately 10:30 p.m., the defendant knocked at the door of the room occupied by these young women, who looked out through the curtain and observed that he was the man previously seen by them in the telephone alcove. He advised them that there was a telephone call for their room. Thereupon, one of the women went to the telephone alcove where she found one of the telephones off the hook but "dead." The

defendant was observed by her for "about a minute" in the well lighted alcove. She thanked him and returned to the room.

At approximately 11:00 p.m., the defendant again knocked at the door of the room and was once more recognized by the women, who looked through the glass window and observed him standing about six inches away and under a light over the door to the room. Again, he said there was a telephone call so, again, one of the young women went to the telephone alcove and again found the telephone "dead." The defendant was again standing in the alcove and said, "Someone is trying to play a joke on you." He then walked with the young woman back along the hallway to the door of her room. She observed that he was wearing a "big belt" from which a bunch of keys was hanging by a chain. In response to her inquiry, he said that he did not work at the motel.

Arriving at their door, she again thanked him for his trouble and thereupon "felt something" at her side. Thinking he "was trying to be fresh," she uttered an exclamation, whereupon he pushed her into the room saying: "Don't make a sound. I've got a knife." They then went into the room where the other young woman had remained and the defendant closed the door, again saying: "I've got a knife. I can kill you. Don't make a sound. Just cooperate and everything will be okay." He did, in fact, have an open knife in his hand, the blade being about four inches in length.

The defendant then compelled the two young women to lie upon one of the beds and, taking from his pocket a roll of tape, some three inches in width and metallic gray in color, he tore off strips of tape and with these bound the hands of each woman behind her back. While they were so bound, he compelled each of them, in turn, to commit an act of oral sex upon his person. In the course of this conduct one of the young women observed that the defendant had a small growth upon the side of his sex organ. The presence of such growth upon the defendant was observed and testified by a medical expert who, pursuant to an order of the court, over defendant's objection, examined the defendant during the course of the trial.

During or after the completion of the offense against the second of the young women, the first broke free from her bonds and snatched the defendant's knife. A struggle for the knife followed, during which the other young woman managed to get the door of the room open and flee down the hall to the motel lobby, whereupon the defendant fled from the room and down the hallway in the other direction, escaping from the motel.

In a matter of minutes, city police officers arrived at the motel and the women described their assailant to them in the presence of the motel manager, who immediately advised the officers that the description seemed to fit a man registered in the motel and produced the motel's registration card for the room occupied by such man, the name shown on the card being "David L. Fulcher." Over objection, this card was introduced in evidence, the manager having testified that he did not personally observe the filling out of that card by the occupant of the room, purportedly David L. Fulcher, but that it was the regular business practice of the motel to have each guest complete and sign such card, which card the motel then kept in its permanent records.

The investigating officers at once communicated with police headquarters and ascertained that the police did have a photograph of one "David L. Fulcher."... The defendant was arrested at an all-night restaurant approximately a mile from the motel....

OPINION

... G.S. 14–39(a), effective 1 July 1975, provides:

a. Any person who shall unlawfully confine, restrain or remove from one place to another, any other person 16 years of age or over without the consent of such person, or any other

person under the age of 16 years without the consent of a parent or legal guardian of such person, shall be guilty of kidnapping if such confinement, restraint, or removal is for the purpose of:

1. Holding such other person for ransom or as a hostage or using such other person as a shield or

2. Facilitating the commission of any felony or facilitating flight of any person following the commission of a felony or

3. Doing serious bodily harm to or terrorizing the person so confined, restrained or removed or any other person. (Emphasis added.)

The Court of Appeals [interpreted] ... G.S. 14–39(a) [as follows:] the statutory offense of kidnapping is not committed unless the defendant confined or restrained the alleged victim for a substantial period of time or moved the victim a substantial distance. We must, therefore, determine whether G.S. 14–39(a) is reasonably susceptible of such construction....

The present statut[e] ... plainly stat[es] ... that confinement, restraint or removal of the victim for any one of the three specified purposes is sufficient to constitute the offense of kidnapping. Thus, no asportation whatever is now required where there is the requisite confinement or restraint.... [T]he use of fraud, threats or intimidation is equivalent to the use of force or violence so far as a charge of kidnapping is concerned.

As used in G.S. 14–39, the term "confine" connotes some form of imprisonment within a given area, such as a room, a house or a vehicle. The term "restrain," while broad enough to include a restriction upon freedom of movement by confinement, connotes also such a restriction, by force, threat or fraud, without a confinement.... Such restraint, however, is not kidnapping unless it is (1) unlawful (i.e., without legal right), (2) without the consent of the person restrained (or of his parent or guardian if he be under 16 years of age), and (3) for one of the purposes specifically enumerated in the statute.

One of those purposes is the facilitation of the commission of a felony. It is self-evident that certain felonies (e.g., forcible rape and armed robbery) cannot be committed without some restraint of the victim. We are of the opinion, and so hold, that G.S. 14–39 was not intended by the Legislature to make a restraint, which is an inherent, inevitable feature of such other felony, also kidnapping so as to permit the conviction and punishment of the defendant for both crimes. To hold otherwise would violate the constitutional prohibition against double jeopardy. Pursuant to the above mentioned principle of statutory construction, we construe the word "restrain," ... to connote a restraint separate and apart from that which is inherent in the commission of the other felony....

We turn now to the application of these principles to the facts as disclosed by the record in the present case. The evidence for the State is clearly sufficient to support a finding by the jury that the defendant bound the hands of each of the two women, procuring their submission thereto by his threat to use a deadly weapon to inflict serious injury upon them, thus restraining each woman within the meaning of G.S. 14–39, and that his purpose in so doing was to facilitate the commission of the felony of crime against nature. This having been done, the crime of kidnapping was complete, irrespective of whether the then contemplated crime against nature ever occurred.

The restraint of each of the women was separate and apart from, and not an inherent incident of, the commission upon her of the crime against nature, though closely related thereto in time. Each woman was so bound, and thereby restrained, so as to reduce her ability to resist, so as to prevent her escape from the room during the commission of the crime against nature upon the other, and so as to prevent her from going to the assistance of her companion.

Thus, the restraint of each was for the purpose of facilitating the commission of the felony of crime against nature. It was also for the purpose of facilitating the flight of the defendant from the room after the perpetration of the two crimes against nature. Either such purpose satisfies the statutory definition of kidnapping....

It may well be that the Legislature, upon further consideration, may wish to amend G.S. 14–39 so as to restore to the definition of the crime of kidnapping ... asportation of the victim as essential element of the offense, leaving confinement or restraint, for the prescribed purpose, without asportation punishable as false imprisonment, but not as kidnapping. It may also wish to consider the advisability of clearly defining "remove from one place to another" so as to require more than a minor asportation, such as is sufficient for larceny at common law. That is, the Legislature may deem it advisable so to word the statute that an assailant who, with knife or gun, forces his victim from the living room of her home into the bedroom where he rapes her, or forces a merchant from the public part of his store into his office and there compels him to open his safe, will not be punishable for kidnapping in addition to the offense of rape or the offense of armed robbery.

In the present case, the defendant, in a fair and lawful trial, has been convicted of a revolting sexual offense for which the Legislature has decreed that the maximum punishment is a sentence to imprisonment for 10 years. In such case, there is the possibility of use of the kidnapping statute as a device by which to procure a sentence deemed more appropriate for the commission of the crime to facilitate which the defendant committed a confinement, restraint or removal within the literal limits of G.S. 14–39.

[Affirmed.]

Case Discussion   What are the elements in kidnapping, according to the statute in North Carolina? How does this statute modify earlier law in North Carolina? What new problems does the definition create for kidnap law? Do you agree with the changes? Why do you suppose the legislature decided to make the changes? Does the statute expand or restrict the crime of kidnapping? According to traditional kidnap law, what element is missing in Fulcher's activities? Do you think he committed the crime of kidnapping? Or just the sex offenses? Explain your answer.

M.CLA 750. 350 A

Kidnapping is usually divided into two degrees: simple and aggravated. In addition to sex offenses, such as those in the *Chessman* and *Fulcher* cases, several other circumstances aggravate simple kidnapping. The most common are (1) to obtain a hostage, (2) for ransom, (3) for robbery, (4) for murder, (5) to blackmail, (6) to terrorize, and (7) for political aims. The penalty for aggravated kidnapping is usually life imprisonment and, until recently, occasionally even death.

Recently, a new form of kidnapping has come into prominence. With increasing numbers of families separating and with the growing participation of both parents in child rearing, noncustodial parents are no longer willing to endure long periods without seeing their children. In fact, some cannot accept the noncustodial role. They take desperate measures to get their children, often illegally. The court dealt with such a kidnapping in *State v. McLaughlin.*

CASE

Can You Kidnap Your Own Child?

State v. McLaughlin
125 Ariz. 505, 611 P.2d 92 (1980)

[McLaughlin was convicted of child abduction. He appealed. Justice Hays delivered the opinion.]

FACTS

On February 18, 1977, Dr. Stephen Zang, a physician and attorney admitted to practice in both Arizona and Nevada, obtained a default divorce from his spouse, Cheryl Zang, in Las Vegas, Nevada. Pursuant to the terms of the dissolution, Dr. Zang was awarded custody of the two minor children of the marriage, subject to a right of visitation; however, the decree provided for subsequent review of the custody issue upon termination of the school semester. On

February 20, 1977, Dr. Zang and the children moved to Arizona and shortly thereafter he had the Nevada decree entered on the Arizona dockets. Although the record at this point is unclear, the transcripts do establish the existence of a written order of the Maricopa County Superior Court granting custody of the children to Dr. Zang and suspending the visitation rights of his former spouse.

Apparently dissatisfied with the custody decrees, Ms. Zang allegedly decided to covertly remove the children from Arizona and her husband's possession. In furtherance of this scheme, she contacted appellant, the owner and operator of the local security guard service, requesting protection from interference by Dr. Zang. Although again the record is not clear, it is apparent that appellant was shown at least the Nevada decree of dissolution and possibly the order of the Arizona court.

On the morning of October 12, 1977, appellant, along with two employee security guards, met with Ms. Zang and a male companion at a Phoenix restaurant in order to finalize plans to remove the Zang children from their Tempe school. Appellant outlined the proposed course of action on a napkin which was subsequently introduced into evidence. In essence, the strategy involved the blocking of Dr. Zang's driveway with a purportedly inoperative automobile and the removal of the children from the schoolyard at the first appropriate moment. Ms. Zang wore a blond wig, sunglasses and a security guard shirt supplied her by appellant as a method of concealing her identity from school officials.

Pursuant to the scheme, appellant, a guard and Ms. Zang proceeded to the school, arriving at approximately 10:30 a.m. Appellant approached the school's principal, informed her that he was seeking a younger cousin and inquired regarding the lunch hour of the second grade. Nothing more occurred until noon recess, when Ms. Zang, accompanied by one of appellant's guards, removed one of her children from the lunch line and directed him towards a waiting auto. It was only the immediate pursuit of the child's teacher and a nearby resident which prevented the successful completion of the plan and forced the parties to await the arrival of police.

OPINION

On appeal, appellant alleges that he has violated no law. He contends that jurisdiction in the Nevada divorce proceedings was fraudulently obtained and that any decree issued pursuant thereto was void and without effect. Based upon this premise, appellant would have us hold that there could thus have been no attempt at removing the youngster from a "person having lawful charge of the child" within the meaning A.R.S. § 13–841 (1956) of our previous Criminal Code. In our opinion, however, although the record before us is void of evidence other than defendant's testimony regarding the validity or invalidity of the Nevada decree, we find this contention of little significance.

A.R.S. § 13–841 provides in part: "A person who maliciously, forcibly or fraudulently takes or entices away a child under the age of seventeen years *with intent to detain and conceal the child from its parent, guardian or other person having lawful charge of the child,* shall be punished by imprisonment." (Emphasis added.)

The underscored language establishes clearly the mens rea sufficient for conviction of child abduction. There must be an intent to detain and conceal the minor from a person in lawful control. In this regard, it must thus suffice if the accused knows that he is removing the child from the custody of one who appears to have lawful custody.

[Conviction affirmed.]

Case Discussion   Do you think McLaughlin was guilty of child abduction? Should Cheryl Zang be prosecuted, too? How serious a crime do you think child abduction is under these circumstances? Is it simple kidnapping, aggravated kidnapping, or a separate, less serious offense when parents kidnap their own children?

▼ Summary ▼

Although homicide is the most serious crime against persons, it is not the only one. In fact, measured in sheer numbers, assault and battery far outnumber homicides. Although often considered one crime, battery and assault are separate offenses. Batteries are offensive touching, ranging from severe beatings to insulting contacts. Assaults are attempted batteries or threatened batteries, in which no physical contact is required to complete the crime.

Another harm to persons covered by criminal law is deprivation of liberty. Short detentions without asportations are misdemeanors called false imprisonment. More serious detentions accompanied by asportation are kidnappings, ancient offenses generally associated with carrying off important persons for ransom. Aggravated kidnapping generally involves some circumstance that generates public outrage, such as kidnappings accompanied by rape, murder, terror, and so on. Related to simple kidnapping is child abduction, a growing phenomenon as noncustodial parents are unwilling to accept separation from their children.

Restraints on liberty take three forms under existing criminal law. The misdemeanor of false imprisonment is a brief detention without asportation, the penalty for which is generally a fine or a short jail term. Simple kidnapping is a significant detention accompanied by asportation, however slight. The penalty for simple kidnapping is usually up to ten years' imprisonment. Aggravated kidnapping is reserved for cases touching off the most public outrage: kidnappings associated with murder, rape, ransom, blackmail, and terror. For aggravated kidnapping, the penalty is severe: usually life imprisonment and occasionally even death, at least until recently. A recent development, parents abducting or kidnapping their own children, has created new problems in false imprisonment and kidnapping law.

▼ *Questions for Review and Discussion* ▼

1. What is the proper scope for a law of rape? Should it be limited to sexual intercourse by force with a woman not married to the assailant? Why or why not?

2. Should all rape be a strict liability offense? Should reasonable mistake regarding age and consent constitute a defense?

3. Should the marital rape exception be abolished? Why or why not?

4. What are the main elements in the criminal sexual conduct statutes?

5. Should criminal sexual penetration be more serious than criminal sexual contact?

6. What circumstances aggravate criminal sexual conduct? Explain.

7. What are the elements of battery? What determines the definitions of simple and aggravated battery?

8. What distinguishes attempted battery assault from threatened battery assault?

9. What distinguishes assault from battery?

10. What contributions did the Model Penal Code make to assault and battery law?

11. What are the elements of false imprisonment?

12. Discuss the origins and development of kidnapping.

13. What are the elements of common-law kidnapping? In what major ways has modern law changed the definition of these elements? What is the heart of the crime of kidnapping, despite the changes?

▼ *Suggested Readings* ▼

1. Rollin M. Perkins and Ronald N. Boyce, *Criminal Law,* 3d ed. (Mineola, N.Y.: Foundation Press, 1982), pp. 197–224 and 453–77. The authors discuss all matters in this chapter, including recent developments in the law.

2. American Law Institute, *Model Penal Code and Commentaries,* vol. 1 (Philadelphia: American Law Institute, 1980), pt. II, pp. 273–439. Summarizes the legal points and the debate surrounding revision of rape laws. It is worth reading for the arguments raised for and against various definitions of the sex offenses.

3. Battelle Law and Justice Study Center, *Forcible Rape: A National Survey* (Washington, D.C.: National Institute of Law Enforcement and Criminal Justice, March 1977). An excellent study of how rape is viewed by criminal justice professionals and how rape law is enforced. This work shows rape law in action as opposed to what the books say rape law should be. It develops some important points concerning prosecutors' attitudes toward rape victims.

4. Susan Estrich, *Real Rape* (Cambridge: Harvard University Press, 1987). A stimulating history and critique of rape law in the United States with particular attention to rape by acquaintances. The author writes forcefully and convincingly, stimulating readers to think about the definition and enforcement of rape laws.

▼ *Notes* ▼

1. For the feminist position regarding the special significance of the sexual component in rape, see Diana Russell, *The Politics of Rape: The Victim's Perspective* (New York: Stein and Day, 1975); Anra Medea and Kathleen Thompson, *Against Rape* (New York: Farrar, Straus and Giroux, 1974).

2. Linda S. Williams, "The Classic Rape: When Do Victims Report?" *Social Problems* 31 (April 1984):464; Diana E. H. Russell, *Sexual Exploitation* (Beverly Hills: Sage, 1984); Judy Foreman, "Most Rape Victims Know Assailant, Don't Report to Police, Police Report Says," *Boston Globe* (April 16, 1986), p. 27; *Parade Magazine* (September 22, 1985), p. 10.

3. Sir William Blackstone, *Commentaries* (University of Chicago Press, 1979), book IV, p. 210.

4. Quoted in Blackstone, *Commentaries,* p. 215.

5. Ibid., pp. 213–14.

6. *Reynolds v. State,* 27 Neb. 90, 42 N.W. 903, 904 (Neb.1879).

7. Susan Estrich, *Real Rape* (Cambridge: Harvard University Press, 1987), pp. 40–41.

8. 127 Wis. 193, 106 N.W. 536, 538 (Wis.1906).

9. Casico v. State, 147 Neb. 1075, 25 N.W.2d 897, 900 (1947).

10. State v. Ely, 114 Wash. 185, 194 P. 988 (1921) (fraud as to nature of the act); *Moran v. People,* 25 Mich. 356 (1872) (told intercourse beneficial).

11. Satterwhite v. Commonwealth, 201 Va. 478, 111 S.E.2d 820 (1960).

12. Commonwealth v. Mlinarich, 345 Pa. Super. 269, 498 A.2d 395, 397 (1985).

13. American Law Institute, *Model Penal Code and Commentaries,* vol. 1 (Philadelphia: American Law Institute, 1980), pt. II, pp. 279–81.

14. For example, see *Minnesota Statutes Annotated* § 609.341, subd. 12 (St. Paul: West Publishing Company, 1987).

15. State v. Shamp, 422 N.W.2d 520 (Minn.App.1988).

16. Model Penal Code and Commentaries, vol. 1, pt. II, p. 281.

17. Regina v. Morgan, [1975] 2. W.L.R. 923 (H.L.).

18. State v. Reed, 479 A.2d 1291, 1296 (Me.1984).

19. Estrich, *Real Rape,* pp. 97–98.

20. State v. Bonds, 1991 W.L. 255670 (Wis.).

21. People v. Randolph, 528 P.2d 1008 (Wash.1974).

22. Model Penal Code and Commentaries, vol. 1, pt. II, pp. 42–44.

23. N.Y. Penal Law 130.00(4) (1975); New Jersey Stat.Ann. 2C:14–2 (1979); Oregon Rev. Code §§ 163.365, 163.375 (1977); statistics from J. C. Barden, "Marital Rape: Drive for Tougher Laws Is Pressed," *New York Times* (May 13, 1987), p. 10.

24. Mich.Stat.Ann. § 750(a) through (g).

25. Unidentified source.

26. State v. Humphries, 21 Wn. App. 405, 586 P.2d 130 (1978).

27. Louisiana Stat.Ann.—Rev. Stat. tit. 17—A, 14.39 (1974); American Law Institute, *Model Penal Code* (Philadelphia: American Law Institute, 1960), tentative draft no. 11.

28. Minn.Stat.Ann. § 609.26 (1987) (1989 Cumulative Supplement).

29. Ibid.

30. Encyclopedia of Crime and Justice (New York: Free Press, 1983), 1:89.

31. California, West's Ann. Penal Code, § 236 (St. Paul: West Publishing Company, 1988).

32. Blackstone, *Commentaries,* book IV, p. 219.

33. State v. Hauptmann, 115 N.J.L. 412, 180 A. 809 (1935).

34. 238 P.2d 1001 (Cal.1951)

35. Model Penal Code and Commentaries, vol. II, pp. 211–12.

Crimes Against Habitation: Burglary and Arson

▼ *Chapter Outline* ▼

I. Introduction
II. Burglary
   A. Burglary *Actus Reus*
   B. Dwelling Requirement
   C. Burglary *Mens Rea*
   D. Grading Burglary
   E. Rationale of Burglary Law
   F. Proposed Reforms to Burglary Law
III. Arson
   A. History and Rationale
   B. Burning: The Arson *Actus Reus*
   C. Arson *Mens Rea*
   D. Property in Arson
   E. Summary of Arson
IV. Summary

▼ *Chapter Main Points* ▼

1. Burglary and arson protect both personal security and property.

2. The harm in burglary stems from intrusions to homes and other structures.

3. The harm in arson is damage and destruction to homes and other property.

4. The structures subject to burglary and arson cover a broad spectrum.

5. Burglary is a specific intent crime.

6. Arson is a general intent crime.

▼ *Chapter Key Terms* ▼

surreptitious remaining—entering a structure with the intent to commit a crime inside.

unprivileged entry—entering a structure without right, license, or permission.

▼ INTRODUCTION

The ancient saying, "A home is a castle," is not merely a popular belief. Two common-law felonies, burglary and arson, were created to protect where people lived. Common-law burglary protected dwellings from intruders in the night. Arson guarded against someone "maliciously and wilfully" burning another person's home. Crimes against habitation are not merely property offenses, although to be sure homes have monetary value. Perhaps the best way to express a home's additional value is in the expression "A house is not a home." A house is the material thing worth money; a home is the haven of refuge where security and privacy from the outside world are possible.

In modern law, the ancient felonies of burglary and arson have grown far beyond their common-law origins. They have come to cover a broad spectrum and protect many interests beyond their original purposes. But they are still aimed primarily at two harms: intrusion and destruction or damage. These harms are considered serious according to most public opinion polls. Burglary, for example, is a much-feared crime. In a recent poll, nearly half the people answered that they were afraid they were going to be burglary victims, and a third believed burglars would hurt them at home during burglaries.

▼ BURGLARY

Elements of Burglary		
Actus Reus	*Mens Rea*	**Material Circumstances**
breaking and entering	intent to commit a crime	1. kind of structure 2. time of day or night 3. kind of crime intended to commit

A felon, that in the night breaketh and entereth into the mansion house of another, with intent to kill some reasonable creature, or to commit some other felony within the same, whether his felonious intent be executed or not.[1]

This was the common-law burglary definition given by the famous seventeenth-century English jurist Sir Edward Coke. Notice the principal elements in Lord Coke's definition: (1) breaking and entering, (2) dwellings, (3) in the nighttime, (4) with a purpose to commit a terrible crime inside. Based on the old English proverb, "A man's home is his castle," the idea ran deep in English law that homes deserved the law's special protection. Not even the king with all his majesty and power had the right to enter the poorest subject's meanest hovel without just cause.

Reflecting that idea, debate over unreasonable searches and seizures in homes began long before the United States Constitution's Fourth Amendment guaranteed protection against them. In 1575, for example, an irate burgess from Colchester (an English town from which many American settlers originated) successfully challenged the right of Queen Elizabeth's officers to enter his home to search for seditious libels against a local public figure. When the officers tried to enter the burgess's front door without a warrant, he met them, armed with a sword. The burgess warned that officers who had earlier tried to come in without a warrant were heavily fined in the Queen's court for trespass. At this announcement, the officers disbanded, leaving the burgess alone for the time being.

The history of burglary reaches even further back than that sixteenth-century episode. Its definition has varied greatly over the centuries, reaching far back into medieval times. Unlike Lord Coke's seventeenth-century definition, which limited the crime to homes broken into and entered with the intention to commit felonies, medieval burglary protected any place likely to attract people (churches, houses, even walled towns) against intrusions, no matter what their purpose.

Some time in the sixteenth century, the offense started to resemble Lord Coke's narrower definition. The more general trespass from medieval times became nocturnally invading a home to commit a felony. Mere intrusions without further criminal purpose became misdemeanors called trespass, for which the penalty was a fine, as opposed to capital punishment for burglary.

From Lord Coke's time to modern times, burglary gradually returned to its medieval origins. Both legislation and judicial decisions have broadened its sixteenth-century meaning. Consequently, burglary can mean entering, or even simply remaining in, any structure with four walls and a roof, and even most vehicles, with the intent to commit almost any crime. Hence, burglary, which began as a broad offense resembling criminal trespass, then narrowed to breaking into homes at night to commit felonies, gradually returned to its original broader meaning (see table 10.1).

Lord Coke's definition has seven specific elements: (1) breaking and (2) entering (3) the dwelling (4) of another (5) in the nighttime (6) with the intention of committing a felony (7) therein. The material acts in burglary are the breaking and entering, the time, and the place. The *mens rea* is the specific intent to commit some crime beyond the intrusion itself. The resulting harm is both the intrusion and the potential harm that might result if the burglar commits further crime once inside the unlawfully entered home.

The courts have liberally construed these elements, and legislatures have expanded further on these broad constructions to include intrusions across the widest possible spectrum. In other words, nocturnal intrusions

438   *Criminal Law*

Attempted B/E # 250.us
Entry w/o Breaking attempt &
Commit larceny
Atempt lacry in
a building

▼ Table 10–1 ▼
Household Burglary

	Number	Rate
Household Crimes	15,419	161
All crimes	34,404	
Completed	13,072	136.5
Attempted	2,347	24.5
Household burglary	5,148	53.8
Completed	4,076	53.8
forcible entry	1,816	19
unlawful entry without notice	2,260	23.6
Attempted forcible entry	1,072	11.2

SOURCE: *Criminal Victimization in the United States 1990,* Bureau of Justice Statistics, United States Justice Department, Washington, D.C., October 1991.

into homes are only one of a very long list of crimes constituting burglary today.

Burglary Actus Reus

At one time, breaking may have meant a violent entry, but very early on it came to include much more than knocking down doors and smashing windows. Although it meant much more than merely walking through an open door, breaking even under the common law was becoming a technicality. In the eighteenth century, Blackstone listed the following examples of breaking: "picking a lock, or opening it with a key; nay, by lifting up the latch of a door, or unloosing any other fastening which the owner has provided." Even if an outer door was left open and the felon entered through it, it was called breaking if an inner door had to be unloosened to get in.

Constructive breaking, a test often used, renders breaking's ordinary definition all but meaningless. Under certain circumstances, owners and employees who open their own doors are said to have broken in to support burglary convictions. In one case, burglars found a door locked and pretended they were there to visit the owner on official business. By this trick, they were able to get a servant to open a door. The act was considered a breaking.

It is also breaking to knock at a door and, when the owner opens it, to rush in intending to commit a felony, or to ask for a room to rent and then to enter with the intention to commit a felony. In addition to tricking owners, their employees, or other agents to secure entry, there are three other constructive breakings. They involve (1) owners or employees who open doors fearing violence, (2) employees who open doors to their accomplices, and (3) intruders who come down chimneys or enter buildings in other extraordinary ways.

The common-law requirement that the burglar break into a structure had, therefore, all but disappeared by the twentieth century. However, recent changes in the law reflect some retreat from totally eliminating breaking. Some states have introduced an **unprivileged entry** requirement. Under this innovation, anyone who enters a structure without a right, license, or permission to do so has fulfilled the burglary requirement that used to include breaking. The unprivileged entry standard creates a middle ground between requiring an actual breaking and eliminating all requirements surrounding the circumstances under which entry occurs.

The Model Penal Code burglary provision reflects this middle ground. It provides that

> [a] person is guilty of burglary if he enters a building or occupied structure, or separately secured or occupied portion thereof, with purpose to commit a crime therein, unless the premises are at the time open to the public or the actor is licensed to enter. It is an affirmative defense to prosecution for burglary that the building or structure was abandoned.[2]

Entering, like breaking, has a broad meaning in burglary law. From about 1650, partial entry was enough to satisfy the requirement. One burglar "entered" a house because his finger was inside the windowsill when he was caught. In another case, an intruder who assaulted an owner on the owner's threshold "entered" the house because his pistol crossed over the doorway. In Texas a man who never got inside a building at all, but who fired a gun into it intending to injure an occupant, "entered" by means of the bullet.[3]

The following brief burglary case summaries demonstrate how sweeping modern burglary law is. In every case, the defendant was convicted of burglary. What purposes does such an all-inclusive definition serve? What interests does it protect: persons, property, homes, or some other social interest?

☐ *State v. Hall,* 150 N.W. 97—Hall went into a tavern and had a few drinks at the bar. He later visited the men's room and took a latex vending machine off the wall. He was caught as he started to walk out with the machine under his coat.

☐ *People v. Miller,* 213 P.2d534—Miller stole a few coins from a pay telephone in a booth.

☐ *People v. Sine,* 98 N.T.S.2d588—Sine walked into a department store, intending to shoplift a few things from the counters.

☐ *Moss v. Commonwealth,* 111 S.W.2d628—Moss drove up to a gasoline station and, finding no one about, pumped gasoline from the pumps at the station's front.

☐ *People v. Buyle,* 70 P.2d955—Buyle tried to steal some goods his employer had stored in a hillside cave.

☐ *People v. Burley,* 79 P.2d148—Burley stole popcorn from a sidewalk stand.

☐ *People v. Chambers,* 228 P.2d93, Chambers passed a parked car and took a few cases of cigarettes from the trunk.

☐ *Commonwealth v. Wadley,* Philadelphia Quarter Sessions (January Term, 1951)—Wadley, a man of "low moral fibre," was on an elevated train platform one evening, watching a girl in the ticket booth who made change for commuters. When no one was around, he leered at the girl, threw a brick through the window, and climbed into the booth as the girl fled through the door. He chased and caught her, but ran away when other people appeared on the scene.

Some statutes remove the entering requirement entirely by providing that remaining in a structure satisfies the burglary act requirement. Hence, it is burglary to go into a department store during business hours and wait in a rest room until the store closes, with the intent to steal jewelry. If the remaining requirement is carried to its logical extreme, however, injustices result. For example, suppose I am invited into my friend's house, and after I am inside I notice that she has some valuable antiques. If I decide to put the antiques in my pocket when she leaves the room, I have satisfied the remaining requirement. Other states, such as North Carolina, do not even require that burglars get inside structures; it is enough that they tried. Hence, one man who got a door ajar but never set foot inside was convicted because burglary does not require entering or remaining, according to the North Carolina statute.[4]

Today's criminal law reformers believe that the sweeping modern definition illustrated in these cases distorts burglary's core idea—nighttime intrusions into homes—far beyond what it ought to mean. Historically, burglary covered an even wider spectrum. That once upon a time burglary had a broad definition, however, is not a sufficient argument to retain that definition in most modern statutes and court opinions. To determine the proper scope of burglary, it is necessary to consider what interests burglary is supposed to protect, and then define the crime according to those purposes.

The Model Penal Code and several jurisdictions take a middle ground between having strict entry requirements and eliminating entry requirements altogether. They have a standard called **surreptitious remaining**, which means entering lawfully but with the purpose to remain inside until it is not lawful to be there, in order to commit a crime. This standard reduces injustices that result from including invited guests who are clearly wanted and potential criminals who enter lawfully but stay in order to commit crimes.

CASE

Did He Enter the Office?

People v. Davis

54 Ill. App. 3d 517, 12 Ill. Dec. 362, 369 N.E.2d 1376 (1977)

[Davis was convicted of burglary and was sentenced to between six and two-thirds years and twenty years in prison. He appealed. Justice Mills delivered the opinion.]

FACTS

An information against Mr. Davis was filed charging him with the burglary of Consolidated Construction Co. in Champaign in that he knowingly and without authority "enter(ed) into part of" the building where its offices were located with the intent to commit a theft. At trial, Willie Gordon, Jr., owner and operator of Consolidated, stated that during the afternoon of May 4, 1976, he typed an estimate for a customer and left his office at 3:20 p.m. to deliver it. The building had only one public entrance and he locked it when he left. He returned to his office at 4:05 p.m. and found the door open and his typewriter missing. Gordon left the building and, in a store two doors down, found John Lee Johnson. Johnson, who used part of the building for the Community Action Depot, was asked by Gordon if he took the typewriter. Johnson told Gordon he had unlocked the outside door about 3:55 p.m. and had left the building about ten minutes before Gordon's return. Gordon returned to the office, called the police and then went out to where 5 or 6 people were standing behind a nearby store. Gordon asked if any of them had seen anyone go into the office and get the typewriter or if any of them had taken it. Defendant was the only one of the group who replied, stating he "didn't know anything about the typewriter," and that he had not seen anyone go into the office and take the typewriter. Neither defendant nor the general public had authority to be in Consolidated's office or to take the typewriter.

The connecting doorway to the area occupied by Consolidated Construction is somewhere between 5 and 15 feet wide. There is no door. Johnson and Terry Townsend, both of whom work in the front part of the building, have free access to Gordon's office. Gordon has seen members of the public come into the front part of the building. He never saw defendant with the typewriter. The front door showed no signs of forced entry.

OPINION

At common law, burglary was a crime against habitation.

The elements of burglary were "the breaking and entering of the dwelling house of another in the nighttime with the intent to commit a felony therein." The rather strict interpretation by those courts of the individual elements resulted not only from normal rules of penal construction, but also from the terminal sentence waiting for those convicted. [The] Illinois legislature has shaped what is now called "burglary" into a form unrecognizable to our common law ancestors. Gone is the element of "breaking," from which word such fine distinctions sprang. Gone too are the elements of "nighttime" and "dwelling house"; burglary is now a 24-hour crime which may be practiced upon a number of designated man-made cubicles. § 19 1(a) of the Criminal Code now states:

A person commits burglary when without authority he knowingly enters or without authority remains within a building, housetrailer, watercraft, aircraft, motor vehicle as defined in the Illinois Vehicle Code, railroad

car, or any part thereof, with intent to commit therein a felony or theft. The offense shall not include the offenses set out in Section 4–102 of the Illinois Vehicle Code (Ill. Rev. Stat. 1975, ch. 38, par. 19–1(a).)

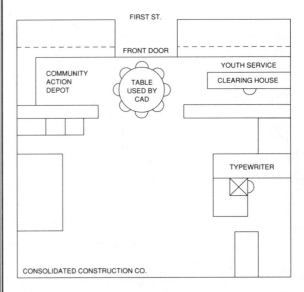

The use of force in entry has not been a necessary element of burglary in Illinois for some time. The "close" broken in the instant case was not the front door of the building; the "entry" occurred by passing through the doorway inside the building into Gordon's office area. Historically, Illinois courts have recognized that entry into certain separate areas of a building with the requisite intent could support a burglary charge. The statute implements this logic by providing entry into certain structures "or any part thereof" as an element of burglary. The charge and the state's arguments at trial in this case were directed to proof of burglary into a part of the building, namely Gordon's office area. Any discussion by the State or the defense regarding the front door is therefore immaterial to proof of burglary. The fact that Johnson left the door open merely provided a means of quicker entry to the front portion of the building.

The fact that the doorway contained no door likewise immaterial. At common law, the burglary of any interior chamber had to be pursuant to some "breaking" thereof directly requiring the existence of an interior barrier such as a hotel room door. Some recent authority indicates the requirement of an interior barrier. However, the Illinois Supreme Court in *People v. Blair* (1972), 51 Ill.2d 371, 288 N.E.2d 443, found a car wash with an open entry and exit-way to be a "building" susceptible of being entered under the burglary statute. The key to the crime is entry into the prohibited space, not whether entry was made by turning a handle, cracking a lock, or walking through an open portal. In light of *Blair* and *Shannon,* logic demands that entry into a "part" of a building through an open doorway with the requisite intent is a prohibited act under our burglary statute.

Affirmed.

Case Discussion

Illinois is one state that has abolished the entry requirement, replacing it with a remaining requirement. Is Davis really a burglar? What purpose does it serve to make him one? Does his crime have anything to do with the common-law idea that a home is a castle? If not, then how is his offense any worse than simply stealing the typewriter? Is he just "technically" a burglar? Is the surreptitious remaining requirement fairer?

Dwelling Requirement

A material circumstance in burglary concerns what broken-into, entered, or remained-in structures qualify as "dwellings." Clearly, modern law goes far beyond the common-law definition of dwelling. The structures included in burglary today stand somewhere between the sweeping medieval "any place where people are likely to congregate" and the very narrow sixteenth-century "dwelling." Even in the sixteenth century, however, dwelling did not mean only fully constructed standard houses; it meant any place a person lived, no matter how poorly constructed or squalid. In one case, the dwelling was "a sheet stretched over poles and fastened to boards nailed to posts for sides, being closed at one end and having an old door at the other."[5]

In general, any structure meant for sleeping in regularly was a dwelling at common law. Houses under construction but not yet inhabited were not dwellings, but houses that were vacant while owners were away on vacation or were completed but not yet lived in were also dwellings. Furthermore, burglary did not require people's actual presence when committed, although actual occupancy then, as now, was an aggravating circumstance.

Dwelling included more than the house itself. Anything within what used to be called the curtilage, or courtyard, was also included. Therefore, any outbuildings adjacent to a mansion or principal dwelling (such as butteries and storage areas) were included as dwellings even in the sixteenth century. Most such structures no longer exist in modern times, but they have important counterparts, such as garages.

Structures included in most modern burglary statutes cover a broad, sometimes almost limitless, spectrum. Many statutes include "any structure" or "any building." Many also include vehicles. One writer who surveyed the subject concluded that any structure with "four walls and a roof" was included. This sweeping definition has led to bizarre results. In California, for example, a person who breaks into a car and steals something from the glove compartment has committed burglary, a crime punishable by up to fifteen years in prison. If, however, the person steels the entire car, including its contents, the crime is only grand larceny, for which the maximum penalty is ten years. Similarly, stealing a chicken at a henhouse door is the misdemeanor of petty larceny, but entering a henhouse intending to steal the chicken is the far more serious felony of burglary.[6]

The Model Penal Code definition aims at limiting burglary to occupied structures. The reason for this definition, according to the Reporter, is that it covers "intrusions that are typically the most alarming and dangerous." According to Model Penal Code Section 221.0, "occupied structure" means any structure, vehicle, or place adapted for overnight accommodations of persons, or for carrying on business therein, whether or not a person is actually present.[7]

A few states follow the Model Penal Code approach and limit burglary to occupied structures, whether or not people are present when the burglary occurs.

CASE

Did He Burglarize the Garage?

People v. Jiminez
651 P.2d 395 (Colo.1982)

[The trial judge dismissed a burglary indictment against Jiminez. The prosecution appealed. Justice Lohr delivered the opinion.]

FACTS
At the defendant's request a preliminary hearing was held. The *People* presented evidence that the defendant had entered the open garage attached to the residence of Tom Tanguma, had taken Tanguma's bicycle valued at $275 from the garage, and had ridden off on the bicycle, all without permission from Tanguma. The bicycle, was not recovered. The court ruled that the proof did not establish that the garage was a dwelling within the meaning of § 18–4–203, so the burglary was only a class 4 felony.

OPINION
The pivotal question on this appeal is whether a garage attached to a residence is part of a dwelling within the meaning of § 18–4–203. We hold that it is. The burglary statute provides, in relevant part:

> A person commits second degree burglary, if he knowingly breaks an entrance into, or enters, or remains unlawfully in a building or occupied structure with intent to commit therein a crime against a person or property.

Second degree burglary is a class 4 felony, but if it is a burglary of a dwelling, it is a class 3 felony. "Dwelling" means a building which is used, intended to be used, or usually used by a person for habitation. Completing the relevant statutory definitions, "building" is defined in § 18–4–101(1), C.R.S.1973 (1978 Repl. Vol. 8) as follows:

> "Building" means a structure which has the capacity to contain, and is designed for the shelter of, man, animals, or property, and includes a ship, trailer, sleeping car, airplane, or other vehicle or place adapted for overnight accommodations of persons or animals, or for carrying on of business therein, whether or not a person or animal is actually present.

The statutory definition of dwelling comprehends an entire building. There is no room in the language of that clearly worded statute to exclude from the meaning of dwelling those parts of a residence that are not "usually used by a person for habitation." Moreover, at least some of the usual uses of a residential garage, including storage of household items, are incidental to and part of the habitation uses of the residence itself.

At the preliminary hearing the evidence was uncontroverted that the $275 bicycle was taken by the defendant without permission from the garage attached to the Tanguma residence. This established probable cause to believe that the defendant had committed the charged crimes of felony theft and burglary of a dwelling. The trial court erred, therefore, in dismissing those charges.

Reversed and remanded.

Case Discussion

The court says that the key question is whether or not an attached garage is a structure within the burglary statute's definition. It then goes on to say that garages are part of dwellings. Do you read the statute the same way? Is a garage really part of a dwelling, or just a building? In Colorado, this question is important because it is more serious to burglarize a dwelling than to burglarize other buildings. Would you decide differently if this were not an attached garage? Why is this burglary and not just stealing?

The common law required that burglars break and enter another's dwelling. As with breaking, entering, and dwelling, modern law has altered the meaning of another. It is now possible, for example, for landlords to burglarize their tenant's apartments. Some courts even say that owners can burglarize their own homes.

***

CASE

Did He Burglarize His Own Home?

People v. Gauze
15 Cal. 3d 709, 125 Cal. Rptr. 773, 512 P.2d 1365 (1975)

[Gauze was convicted of burglary. He appealed.]

FACTS
Defendant shared an apartment with Richard Miller and a third person and thus had the right to enter the premises at all times. While visiting a friend one afternoon, defendant and Miller engaged in a furious quarrel. Defendant directed Miller to "Get your gun because I am going to get mine." While Miller went to their mutual home, defendant borrowed a shotgun from a neighbor. He returned to his apartment, walked into the living room, pointed the gun at Miller and fired, hitting him in the side and arm. Defendant was convicted of assault with a deadly weapon and burglary; the latter charge was predicated on his entry into his own apartment with the intent to commit the assault.

OPINION
Common law burglary was generally defined as "the breaking and entering of the dwelling *of another* in the nighttime with intent to commit a felony." The present burglary statute, Penal Code § 459, provides in relevant part that "Every person who enters *any* house, room, apartment with intent to commit grand or petit larceny or any felony is guilty of burglary." (Italics added.)

Facially the statute is susceptible of two rational interpretations. On the one hand, it could be argued that the Legislature deliberately revoked the common law rule that burglary requires entry into the building of another. On the other hand, the Legislature may have impliedly incorporated the common law requirement by failing to enumerate one's own home as a possible object of burglary.

Common law burglary was essentially an offense "against habitation and occupancy."

... [In] proscribing felonious nighttime entry into a dwelling house, the common law clearly sought to protect the right to peacefully enjoy one's own home free of invasion. In the law of burglary, in short, a person's home was truly his castle. It was clear under common law that one could not be convicted of burglary for entering his own home with felonious intent. This rule applied not only to sole owners of homes, but also to joint occupants. The important factor was occupancy, rather than ownership.

California codified the law of burglary in 1850. That statute and subsequent revisions and amendments preserved the spirit of the common law, while making two major changes. First, the statute greatly expanded the type of buildings protected by burglary sanctions. Not only is a person's home his castle under the statute, but so, inter alia, are his shop, tent, airplane, and outhouse. This evolution, combined with elimination of the requirement that the crime be committed at night, signifies that the law is no longer limited to safeguarding occupancy rights. However, by carefully delineating the type of structures encompassed under § 459, the Legislature has preserved the concept that burglary law is designed to protect a possessory right in property, rather than broadly to preserve any place from all crime.

The second major change effected by codification of the burglary law was the elimination of the requirement of a "breaking": under the statute, every person who enters with felonious intent is a burglar. This means, at a minimum, that it no longer matters whether a person entering a house with larcenous or felonious intent does so through a closed door, an open door or a window. The entry with the requisite intent constitutes the burglary.

The elimination of the breaking requirement was further interpreted in *People v. Barry,* (1892) 94 Cal. 481, 29 P. 1026, to mean that trespassory entry was no longer a necessary element of burglary. In *Barry,* this court held a person could be convicted of burglary of a store even though he entered during regular business hours. A long line of cases has followed the Barry holding.

... [However,] the cases have preserved the common law principle that in order for burglary to occur, "The entry must be without consent." If the possessor actually invites the defendant, or actively assists in the entrance, e.g., by opening a door, there is no burglary.

Thus, § 459, while substantially changing common law burglary, has retained two important aspects of that crime. A burglary remains an entry which invades a possessory right in a building. And it still must be committed by a person who has no right to be in the building.

Applying the foregoing reasoning, we conclude that defendant cannot be guilty of burglarizing his own home. His entry into the apartment, even for a felonious purpose, invaded no possessory right of habitation; only the entry of an intruder could have done so. More importantly defendant had an absolute right to enter the apartment. This right did not derive from an implied invitation to the public to enter for legal purposes. It was a personal right that could not be conditioned on the consent of defendant's roommates. Defendant could not be "refused admission at the threshold" of his apartment, or be "ejected from the premises after the entry was accomplished." He could not, accordingly, commit a burglary in his own home.

In contrast to the usual burglary situation, no danger arises from the mere entry of a person into his own home, no matter what his intent is. He may cause a great deal of mischief once inside. But no emotional distress is suffered, no panic is engendered, and no violence necessarily erupts merely because he walks into his house. To impose sanctions for burglary would in effect punish him twice for the crime he committed while in the house. In such circumstances it serves no purpose to apply § 459.

It has been urged that the purpose of burglary laws is to protect persons inside buildings because indoor crime is more dangerous than outdoor crime. "We have often recognized that persons within dwellings are in greater peril from intruders bent on stealing or engaging in other felonious conduct." However, we have never categorized all indoor crimes to be more dangerous than all outdoor crimes. Nor would such a conclusion be relevant to the purposes of § 459. The statute protects against intruders into indoor areas, not persons committing crimes in their own homes.

To hold otherwise could lead to potentially absurd results. If a person can be convicted for burglarizing his own home, he could violate § 459 by calmly entering his house with intent to forge a check. A narcotics addict could be convicted of burglary for walking into his home with intent to administer a dose of heroin to himself. Since a burglary is committed upon entry, both could be convicted even if they changed their minds and did not commit the intended crimes.

In positing such hypotheticals, we indulge in no idle academic exercise. The differing consequences are significant, for the punishment for burglary is severe. First degree burglary is punishable by imprisonment for five years to life, while a second degree burglar is subject to imprisonment in the county jail for a one-year maximum or in state prison for one to fifteen years. (Pen. Code, § 461.) In contrast, the punishment for assault with a deadly weapon, the underlying crime committed in this case, is less severe: imprisonment in state prison for six months to life or in county jail for a maximum of one year, or a fine. (Pen. Code, § 245, subd. (a).)

For the foregoing reasons, we conclude defendant cannot be guilty of burglarizing his own home, and the judgment of conviction for burglary must therefore be reversed.

Case Discussion

The court ruled that burglary means entry without consent. Therefore, Gauze could not burglarize his own dwelling because he does not need consent to enter it. According to the court, the California legislature failed to mention "another" in the burglary statute because the legislature meant to either eliminate or incorporate the common-law requirement. If you were deciding this case, how might you find out exactly what the legislature intended when it did not mention "another"? What meaning would you give if you could not find out what the legislature intended? Would you interpret the statute broadly to include "another" or strictly to exclude it? If burglary aims to protect against threatening people's security in their homes, what meaning does that purpose require the statute to have?

The common-law nighttime requirement was based on three considerations. First, darkness facilitates committing crimes. Second, darkness hampers identifying suspects. Finally, and perhaps most important, nighttime intrusions alarm victims more than do daytime intrusions. At least eighteen states retain the nighttime requirement specifically. Most recent statutory revisions have continued to regard nighttime intrusions as an aggravating circumstance. Some proposals, however, eliminate the nighttime requirement entirely. According to a recent survey, states with these proposals include

Alaska, California, Michigan, and Vermont. Although no hard statistics are available on the point, a fair statement is that nighttime intruders are punished more severely than daytime intruders.

Burglary **Mens Rea**

Burglary is a specific intent crime. It requires not only the intent to commit the *actus reus* but also the intent to commit a crime once inside. That means breaking into, entering without privilege, and remaining surreptitiously in structures, intending to commit crimes beyond the trespass itself. Intrusions without the intention to commit additional crimes are nonetheless criminal. They are, however, only misdemeanors—criminal trespasses.

As in the other burglary elements, the list of crimes burglars must intend to commit has expanded since the sixteenth century. In Lord Coke's time, the intended crime had to be serious: murder or another heinous felony. Although some law books emphasized violent felony, the cases almost all entailed breaking and entering to steal something.

Modern statutes also concentrate on intrusions to commit theft. Many include intruding with the intent to commit "a felony or any larceny." Under these statutes, even petty theft is burglary. Hence, to enter a store intending to steal a ballpoint pen is burglary. Some jurisdictions extend the burglary *mens rea* still further, making it burglary to intrude with the intent to commit "any crime," "any public offense," and sometimes "any misdemeanor."[8]

It is not necessary to complete the intended crime in order to commit burglary. It is enough that an intent to commit crime is present at the moment entry takes place. Hence, if I break into my enemy's house intending to murder him, change my mind just inside the front door, and return home without hurting anyone, I have committed burglary. The *mens rea* of intending to commit murder is present. Burglary is complete at the moment the intrusion, however defined, occurs, so long as the intent to commit a further crime is present. Completing the intended crime, although not an element in burglary, constitutes evidence of *mens rea*. For example, if I am caught leaving a house, my arms loaded with valuable silver, jurors can infer that I entered the house in order to steal the silver.

CASE

Did He Enter Intending to Steal?

McIntosh v. State
559 S.W.2d 598 (Mo.App.1977)

[McIntosh was convicted of burglary and was sentenced to five years in prison. He appealed. Special Judge Welborn delivered the opinion.]

FACTS

The court advised the appellant that this case involved an incident of November 15, 1973 at 5228 East 40th Street in Kansas City and asked the appellant to tell what he did. The appellant responded:

Well, I went into the place. I was going with my brother. He asked me to go with him, really.

I was at home and my brother kept wanting me to go with him. And he had spotted a fellow that he thought took his coat. He told me. I didn't know. I went around, you know, to the house with him, you know, to get his coat back. I didn't know that it was going to be a burglary, but I know one thing, when he kicked the door in the officers arrived there and arrested us for the burglary, which I told them I had no idea it was anything about a burglary.

I went with him in order to get his coat—get his coat back, but otherwise I had no intention of burglarizing it.

Interrogation by the court continued:

Q. Now, you also understand, do you not, that even though you were going to get your brother's coat you didn't have any permission of the owner to break into that place, do you understand that?
A. Yes, sir.
Q. ...[Y]ou understand that the act of burglary is the breaking in, do you understand that?
A. Yes, sir.
Q. And you understand that because of that set of facts you are guilty of the charge of Burglary, do you not?

A. Yes.

OPINION

The facts recited by appellant do not amount to an admission of facts constituting the offense with which he was charged. Burglary in the second degree requires a breaking "with intent to commit a felony or to steal" § 560.045, RSMo 1969. Apparently the trial court considered that appellant had admitted a breaking and entry with intent to steal, no other criminal intent having been suggested. However, the appellant said that he went with his brother to get his coat back from "a fellow that he thought took his coat." If such were the case, there was no intent to steal because the owner of the property was asserting his right to regain its possession.

Reversed and remanded.

Case Discussion

According to McIntosh's own admission, he illegally broke and entered someone else's house. But he did not do it in order to commit a crime. He went to help his brother get his coat back, or at least what he thought was his brother's coat. According to the court, this is not burglary because McIntosh did not intend to steal the coat. Do you agree that this breaking is less serious than if McIntosh intended to steal the coat? Why or why not?

Grading Burglary

Because burglary is so broadly defined in most jurisdictions, many states divide it into several degrees. In Minnesota, for example, first-degree burglary preserves the sixteenth-century emphasis on burglary of dwellings, if another is present, if the burglar possesses a weapon, or if the burglar assaults a person within the building. Burglary of a dwelling, a bank, or a pharmacy dealing in controlled substances constitutes second-degree burglary. Third-degree burglary includes burglary of any building with an intent to steal or commit any felony or gross misdemeanor. Fourth-degree burglary includes burglary of a building with an intent to commit a misdemeanor other than theft.[9]

Despite efforts to grade burglary into degrees that reflect the broad spectrum it covers, most burglary statutes do not eliminate possible injustices. This is true in large part because burglary punishes the intrusion and not the crime for which the intrusion took place. In many cases, the penalty for burglary is much harsher than the penalty for the intended crime. The difference between a five-year sentence and a twenty-year sentence sometimes depends upon the largely metaphysical question of whether a thief intended to steal before or after entering a building.

Rationale of Burglary Law

For several centuries following 1500, burglary protected primarily security in the home from nighttime intruders. Common-law burglary did not protect other buildings considered mere real estate. Dwellings were guarded by the worst penalty—death—since burglary was a capital offense. Homes were almost sacred at common law. Invaders who threatened defenseless, sleeping families and their treasured possessions at night were specters still feared in the 1980s.

Securing homes from nighttime intruders, however, far from explains burglary's rationale under present law. Two common features in modern burglary statutes indicate that burglary aims to protect additional interests. First, trespass statutes cover the intrusion itself. Burglary requires the *mens rea* of additional criminal purpose. Second, although first-degree burglary always includes dwellings, nearly all statutes require harm, threatened harm, or the victims' presence to accompany the intrusion. Furthermore, statutes usually require other aggravating circumstances for first-degree burglary, such as an intent to commit a violent crime or an actual assault upon a person. Modern burglary, therefore, protects more than people's homes. More accurately, burglary statutes are supposed to protect homes and people, or perhaps still more precisely, people's security in their homes.

Modern burglary statutes protect at least three basic interests in society: homes, persons, and property. But what do the statutes protect these interests from? Just as burglary law protects more than one interest, it protects against more than one harm. The paramount and most ancient is intrusion itself. The misdemeanor trespass protects intrusion without further criminal purpose, a social harm widely regarded as deserving at least minor punishment. Property owners who regularly file complaints against strangers, and even against their own neighbors, resemble in that respect their sixteenth-century and even medieval ancestors who prosecuted their neighbors for trespassing even without intending to commit further crimes.

Criminal trespass is not only very old but also appears to be worldwide. The Japanese criminal code, for example, condemns "intrusion upon a habitation," defined to include human habitations, structures, or vessels, or the refusal to leave on demand, punishable by a fine or up to three years' imprisonment. Nearly all countries similarly punish intruders even when they do not intend to commit additional crimes.

Burglary reaches beyond the trespass itself. It strikes at potential harms resulting from the intrusion, specifically those that could result if intruders accomplish further criminal purposes. This unfulfilled intention lies at the core of modern burglary statutes. In this sense, burglary is an inchoate offense, an "attempt" to commit the crime the burglar intruded in order to commit.

The following possible statute might solve some of the problems of current burglary law:

1. Anyone who unlawfully enters the dwelling of another shall be subject to a fine and/or imprisonment of up to one year.

2. Anyone who, in the course of any crime punishable by one year's imprisonment or more

   a. enters the dwelling of another in which there is a person at the time, or

b. is armed with a deadly weapon, or so arms himself, or uses or attempts to use explosives, or

c. commits assault or otherwise injures another, or

d. is accompanied by confederates actually present, shall be subject to a penalty that shall not be more than double the penalty for the crime committed.

This example statute accomplishes several things. First, it separates security in homes from protecting life and property. It also takes into account elements usually included in present burglary statutes as aggravating circumstances, but it makes penalties dependent upon the crime committed rather than the trespass inherent in burglary. Attempt is removed entirely, leaving burglary's inchoate dimension to the specific attempted crime intruders intend to commit.

This solution, therefore, has many merits, but it is probably too radical. Burglary is an offense too deeply ingrained in English and American law to eradicate.

Proposed Reforms to Burglary Law

Burglary's long history demonstrates efforts to protect several basic social values: homes, personal security, and property. Because its protection covers varied interests, logic does not explain its content. Burglary statutes are thus a hodgepodge of laws covering a diversity of conduct. A nighttime prowler who breaks into a family home to commit a sexual assault on a sleeping victim does not at all resemble a casual shoplifter who goes into a department store to steal a deck of cards.

Reformers recommend changes intended to remove injustices from present burglary law. Some recommend abolishing burglary as a separate offense, for two reasons. First, attempt law can cover what is now burglary. Second, making burglary an aggravating circumstance to other crimes can deal adequately with trespassory or intrusive harms done to further other crimes. Under this scheme, criminal trespass would become the principal offense, and trespass would become a grading factor in other crimes. An approach more likely to succeed is not to abolish burglary, but to modify its present condition. Such reforms accept burglary's historical roots and deal with its wide spectrum by grading according to the values and interests it protects. The Model Penal Code provision takes this approach.[10]

> Article 221 2. Grading. Burglary is a felony of the second degree if it is perpetrated in the dwelling of another at night, or if, in the course of committing the offense, the actor:
>
>> a. purposely, knowingly or recklessly inflicts or attempts to inflict bodily injury on anyone; or
>>
>> b. is armed with explosives or a deadly weapon.
>
> Otherwise, burglary is a felony of the third degree. An act shall be deemed "in the course of committing" an offense if it occurs in an attempt to commit the offense or in flight after the attempt or commission.
>
> 3. Multiple Convictions. A person may not be convicted both for burglary and for the offense which it was his purpose to commit after the burglarious entry or for an attempt to commit that offense, unless the additional offense constitutes a felony of the first or second degree.

Both the more radical abolition and grading approach of the Model Penal Code reduce or eliminate the most serious anomalies and injustices. Under both approaches, for example, the burglary cases on page 439 either are not crimes or, if they are crimes, are graded according to the interests they are intended to protect. This is so because both schemes clearly rank homes, personal security, and property according to their seriousness; and strictly define burglary according to its seriousness.

▼ ARSON

Elements of Arson			
Actus Reus	*Mens Rea*	**Material Circumstances**	**Harm**
setting fire	intent to burn	1. kind of structure 2. amount of harm	burning

In burglary and other criminal trespasses, the harm stems from intrusions that violate homes and other structures. Arson results from damage or destruction to these and similar buildings.

750. 712 - 715

History and Rationale

> [I]f any person shall wittingly, and willingly set on fire any dwelling house, meeting house, store house or any out house, barn, stable, stack of hay, corn or wood, or any thing of like nature, whereby any dwelling house, meeting house or store house, cometh to be burnt shall be put to death, and to forfeit so much of his lands, goods, or chattels, as shall make full satisfaction, to the victim.[11]

This 1652 Massachusetts Bay Colony statute making arson a capital offense demonstrates clearly that the colonists considered arson a serious crime. Today, arson still poses a serious threat to life and property in America.

Arson kills hundreds and injures thousands of people annually. It damages and destroys more than a billion dollars in property, taxes, and lost jobs. It has also significantly increased insurance rates throughout the United States. Most states prescribe harsh penalties for arson. In North Dakota and Hawaii, the maximum penalty is ten years. In other states, such as Texas and Alabama, arson is punishable by life imprisonment.

Burning: The Arson Actus Reus

At common law, burning meant actually setting on fire. Merely setting a fire was not enough; the fire had to reach the structure and burn it. This did not mean the structure had to burn to the ground. Once it was ignited, then however slight the actual burning, arson was complete. Modern statutes generally adopt the common-law rule, and devote great efforts to determining whether smoke merely blackened or discolored buildings, whether fire scorched them, or whether fire burned only the exterior material or the wood under it.

The Model Penal Code revises the common law, providing that "starting a fire," even if the fire never touches the structure aimed at, satisfies the burning requirement. The drafters justify expanding the common-law rule on the ground that no meaningful difference separates a fire that has already started but has not yet reached the basic structure and a fire that has reached the structure but has not yet done any real damage to it.[12]

Burning also includes explosions, even though the phrase "set on fire" does not generally mean "to explode." Many statutes state explicitly that explosions are burnings for the purposes of arson law. Including explosions is based on the idea that explosions threaten equally—perhaps more—the lives, property, and security that arson was designed to protect.

CASE

Did He Burn the House?

Lynch v. State

175 Ind. App. III, 370 N.E.2d 401 (1977)

[Lynch was convicted of first-degree arson. He appealed. Judge Buchanan delivered the opinion.]

FACTS

In the early morning hours of June 18, 1975, a man identified as Lynch was seen throwing a burning object at the residence of Mr. and Mrs. Estel Barnett (Barnett). Immediately after the object struck the house flames engulfed the side of the residence. The flames lasted for several minutes and then died out. The fire department was not called.

The Barnetts, who were awakened by a passing neighbor, investigated and discovered a bottle containing flammable liquid with a cotton or cloth wick protruding from the opening. A "burn trail" extended from the lawn approximately ten feet to the house. Damage to the building's aluminum siding consisted of blistering and discoloration of the paint. The amount of the damage was Ninety-one and 29/100 ($91.29) Dollars. No other part of the house was damaged.

OPINION

The phrase "sets fire to" in the First Degree Arson statute means something less than an actual burning and therefore is not synonymous with the word "burn." The gist of Lynch's position is that he is not guilty of arson because "sets fire to" and "burns" as used in the First Degree Arson statute are synonymous, and no "burning" took place, i.e., the house was not consumed.

The statute, Ind.Code § 35–16–1–1 [10–801], provides:

> Arson in the First Degree. Any person who willfully and maliciously sets fire to or burns, or causes the setting of fire to or the burning, or who aids, counsels or procures the setting of fire to or the burning of any dwelling house, rooming house, apartment house or hotel, finished or unfinished, occupied or unoccupied; or any kitchen, shop, barn, stable, garage or other outhouse, or other building that is part or parcel of any dwelling house, rooming house, apartment house or hotel, or belonging to or adjoining thereto, finished or unfinished, occupied or unoccupied, such being the property of another; or being insured against loss or damage by fire and such setting of fire to or burning, or such causing, aiding, counselling or procuring such setting of fire to or such burning, being with intent to prejudice or fraud the insuror; or

such setting of fire to or burning or such causing, aiding, counselling or procuring such setting of fire to or such burning being with intent to defeat, prejudice or fraud the present or prospective property rights of his or her spouse, or coowner, shall be guilty of arson in the first degree, and, upon conviction thereof, shall be imprisoned in the state prison not less than five [5] years nor more than twenty [20] years, to which may be added a fine not to exceed two thousand dollars [$2,000].

Observe that the drafter used the disjunctive word "or" in separating the phrase "sets fire to" from the word "burns." If we construe "or" in its "plain, or ordinary and usual, sense" as we are bound to do, it separates two different things. "Sets fire to" and "burns" are not synonymous in this context. Traditionally the common law rigidly required an actual burning. The fire must be actually communicated to the object to such an extent as to have taken effect upon it.

Other jurisdictions have recognized the distinction between "sets fire to" and "burns" as two different concepts. To "set fire to" a structure is to "place fire upon," or "against" or to "put fire in connection with" it. It is possible to set fire to a structure which, by reason of the sudden extinction of the fire, will fail to change the characteristics of the structure. Nevertheless, it has been "set fire to."

Unlike *Lynch,* then, we cannot conclude that he is not guilty of first degree arson because there was no burning of the house. He set fire to the house by causing a flammable substance to burn thereon causing a scorching or blistering of the paint which was an integral part of the structure. The composition of the structure was changed. No more was necessary.

Thus the modern construction of statutory terms we are interpreting is that they are not synonymous, each having a separate, independent meaning, thereby eliminating any ambiguity. The judgment is affirmed.

Case Discussion   The court ruled that "burn" and "set fire to" are two different concepts; and that Lynch may not have burned the house, but he did set fire to it. Does it make a difference, really, whether Lynch burned or set fire to the house? Does the Model Penal Code provision apply here? Which is the better rule, the court's or the Code's? How much destruction would you require if you were writing an arson statute?

Arson Mens Rea

Most arson statutes follow the common-law *mens rea* requirement that arsonists maliciously and willfully burn or set fire to buildings. Some courts call the arson *mens rea* general intent. Here is one example:

> Arson is a crime of general, rather than specific, criminal intent. The requirement that defendant act "willfully and maliciously" does not signify that defendant must have actual subjective purpose that the acts he does intentionally shall produce either (1) a setting afire or burning of any structure or (2) damage to or destruction of said structure. So long as defendant has actual subjective intention to do the act he does and does it in disregard of a conscious awareness that such conduct involves highly substantial risks that will be set afire, burned or caused to be burned—notwithstanding that defendant does not "intend" such consequences in the sense that he has no actual subjective purpose that his conduct produce them—defendant acts "willfully and maliciously."[13]

Under modern decisions, such as that just quoted, defendants do not have to intend specifically to destroy buildings they set on fire or burn. It is generally considered enough if they intend to start a fire but do not intend, indeed do not even want, to burn a structure. In other words, the purpose requirement refers to the act in arson (burning or setting fire to buildings) and not to the harm (burning down or destroying buildings). Hence, a prisoner who burned a hole in his cell to escape was guilty of arson because he purposely started the fire. So, too, was a sailor who lit a match to find his way into a dark hold in a ship in order to steal rum. The criminal purpose in arson, then, is an intent or purpose to start a fire, even if there is no intent to burn a specific structure.

Burning property to defraud an insurer raises a special *mens rea* concern. The Model Penal Code divides arson into two degrees, according to defendants' culpability. Most culpable are defendants who intend to destroy buildings and not merely set fire to or burn them; these are first-degree arsonists. Second-degree arsonists are defendants who set buildings on fire for other purposes. For example, if I burn a wall with an acetylene torch because I want to steal valuable fixtures attached to the wall, I am guilty of second-degree arson for "recklessly" exposing the building to destruction even though I meant only to steal fixtures.[14]

Property in Arson

Common-law arson, like common-law burglary, protected dwellings. Modern arson law, like modern burglary law, has vastly expanded the types of structures it protects. It almost always means more than homes and sometimes even includes personal property.

The trend in modern legislation is to divide arson into three degrees. Most serious (first-degree arson) is burning homes or other occupied structures (such as schools, offices, and churches) where there is possible danger to human life. Second-degree arson includes setting fire to, or burning, unoccupied structures and perhaps vehicles (such as boats and automobiles). Third-degree arson includes setting fire to or burning personal property.

Because arson originally aimed to protect security in dwellings, setting fire to one's house was not arson. This is true in only a narrow sense today, since arson is a crime against possession and occupancy, not strictly against ownership. Hence, where owners are not in possession or do not occupy their own property, they can commit arson against it. For example, if I am a landlord and set fire to my house in order to hurt my enemy who leases it from me, I have committed arson because, although I own the house, I have transferred occupancy to my tenant enemy.

More important than this somewhat bizarre example is the significant number of owners who burn their property to collect insurance. Under common-law arson, such burnings were not arson if owners were in possession. The opportunities this provided to owners for defrauding insurance companies led to revision of the common-law rule. In most jurisdictions today, a specific provision makes it arson to burn property, whoever owns it, if done to defraud insurers.

Summary of Arson

Arson is a serious threat to at least three fundamental social interests: life, security, and property. It includes burning or setting fire to—however slightly—many structures, including houses, vehicles, and even personal property. First-degree arson includes burning homes and other occupied structures, second-degree includes burning unoccupied structures, and third-degree includes setting fire to personal property. The arson *mens rea* is general intent, meaning intent to burn but not necessarily to destroy. That is, arson requires purpose with respect to the act but generally recklessness with respect to destroying the building. Those who mean to destroy buildings are more culpable than those who recklessly destroy buildings.

One difficult problem with arson is that arsonists act for a variety of motives. There are those so consumed by rage that they burn down their enemies' homes. There are the pyromaniacs, whose neurotic or even psychotic compulsion drives them to set buildings on fire for thrill. Then there are the more rational, but equally deadly, defendants who burn down their own buildings or destroy their own property to collect insurance. Finally, the most deadly and difficult arsonist to catch is the professional torch who commits arson for hire.

Evidence indicates that professional arsonists are growing in numbers. Some even contend that arson rings are a multimillion-dollar business. Statutory provisions may not grade arson according to motive, but motive probably ought to affect sentencing. The difference between an enraged enemy and a pyromaniac on the one hand, and a calculating property owner or professional arsonist on the other, is clear.

▼ Summary ▼

Burglary and arson are both aimed at protecting homes, other occupied structures, vehicles, and many other valuable properties. Their definitions have expanded since the sixteenth century, although signs are that statutes are limiting and grading both more stringently. Both felonies protect three basic social interests: personal security, homes, and property. Burglary's harm to these interests results from intrusion; arson's harm results from damage and destruction.

The act in burglary generally includes entering another's property without privilege. Whether done at night, to homes, or to occupied structures, violence or harm to occupants aggravates the offense. The act in arson is setting fire to or burning various structures. In some cases, it even means throwing a lighted match at a structure. The *mens rea* in burglary is the specific intent to intrude in order to commit a crime. The *mens rea* in arson is the general intent to burn or set fire to various structures.

▼ Questions for Review and Discussion ▼

1. Should burglary include only breaking and entering homes at night in order to commit serious felonies?

2. If your definition is broader than that proposed in question 1, how much broader would you make it?

3. What interests should burglary law protect? Personal security? Homes? Property? All three?

4. What should constitute a burning in the law of arson?

5. Should arson be limited to intentionally burning a house?

6. How would you grade burglary? Arson?

▼ Suggested Readings ▼

1. American Law Institute, *Model Penal Code and Commentaries,* vol. 2 (Philadelphia: American Law Institute, 1980), § II, pp. 3–94. The most detailed, up-to-date survey or arson and burglary and all the offenses related to them. It compares various recent statutory developments, argues for reforms in the law, suggests grading the crimes, and includes model provisions for them. Meant for professionals, it is still worth the serious student's effort.

2. Rollin M. Perkins and Ronald N. Boyce, *Criminal Law,* 3d ed. (Mineola, N.Y.: Foundation Press, 1982), chap. 3. This book extensively surveys arson and burglary. It includes a good history, thoroughly analyzes the material elements in both arson and burglary, and analyzes recent changes in the law

3. Wayne R. LaFave and Austin W. Scott, Jr., *Handbook on Criminal Law* (St. Paul: West Publishing Co., 1972). A good analysis of burglary's material elements.

4. Janet Rosenbaum, *Burglary Statistics* (Washington, D.C.: Bureau of Justice Statistics, 1985). An excellent overview of burglary statistics—how many burglaries, reporting methods, demographic distribution, and many other interesting dimensions—that shows burglary as a social problem, not just a legal one.

5. James Inciardi, "The Adult Firesetter: A Typology," *Criminology* 8 (August 1970): 145–55. A sociologist's effort to divide arsonists into types using considerably more detail than appears in this text. Professor Inciardi discusses not only the professional torch, the pyromaniac, and the businesspeople who burn down buildings to collect insurance, but also adolescent thrill seekers, revenge-seeking firesetters, political arsonists, and others. This is an excellent article that puts arson into a broader context than a strictly legal one.

▼ Notes ▼

1. Sir Edward Coke, *The Third Part of the Institutes of the Laws of England* (London: 1797), p. 63.

2. American Law Institute, *Model Penal Code and Commentaries* (Philadelphia: American Law Institute, 1985), § 221.1.

3. Rex v. Bailey, Crown Cases Reserved (1818); Hale, *Pleas of the Crown,* p. 553 (1670); *Nalls v. State,* 219 S.W. 473 (Tex.Cr.App.1920).

4. State v. Myrick, 306 N.C. 110, 291 S.E.2d 577 (1982).

5. Rollin M. Perkins and Ronald N. Boyce, *Criminal Law,* 3d ed. (Mineola, N.Y.: Foundation Press, 1982), p. 201.

6. Note, "Statutory Burglary: The Magic of Four Walls and a Roof," *University of Pennsylvania Law Review* 100 (1951):411.

7. American Law Institute, *Model Penal Code and Commentaries,* vol. 2, pt. II, pp. 72, 6.

8. Note, "Statutory Burglary," p. 420.

9. Minn.Stat.Ann., § 609.52 (1987).

10. American Law Institute, *Model Penal Code,* tentative draft no. 11 (Philadelphia: American Law Institute, 1960).

11. William Whitmore, ed., *The Colonial Laws of Massachusetts* (Boston: 1887), p. 52.

12. Model Penal Code and Commentaries, vol. 2, pt. II, p. 3.

13. State v. O'Farrell, 355 A.2d 396, 398 (Me.1976).

14. Crow v. State, 189 S.W. 687 (Tenn.1916); *Regina v. Harris,* 15 Cox C.C. 75 (1882).

Chapter 11

Crimes against Property

▼ Chapter Outline ▼

I. Introduction
II. History of Theft
III. Larceny
    A. Larceny *Actus Reus*
    B. Larceny Material Circumstances
    C. Larceny *Mens Rea*
    D. Summary of Larceny
IV. Embezzlement
V. False Pretenses
VI. Consolidated Theft Statutes
VII. Receiving Stolen Property
VIII. Forgery and Uttering
    A. Forgery
    B. Uttering
IX. Robbery and Extortion
    A. Robbery
    B. Degrees of Robbery
    C. Extortion
X. Summary

▼ *Chapter Main Points* ▼

1. Understanding property crimes depends more on history than on logic.

2. All property crimes originated in the ancient felony of larceny, which covered only wrongfully taking the property of others.

3. Consolidated theft statutes combine wrongful takings, conversion, and deceptions leading to property misappropriations.

4. Theft law aims to protect property possession and ownership.

5. Forgery and uttering statutes protect not only property but also confidence in the authenticity of documents, which fosters smoothly operating business transactions in modern society.

6. Robbery and extortion are crimes not only against property but also against persons.

▼ *Chapter Key Terms* ▼

asportation—Carrying away another's property.

claim of right—The belief that property taken rightfully belongs to the taker.

conversion—Illegal use of another's property.

extortion—Misappropriation of another's property by means of threat to inflict bodily harm in future.

forgery—Making false writings or materially altering authentic writings.

misappropriation—Gaining possession of another's property.

robbery—Taking and carrying away another's property by force or threat of force with the intent to permanently deprive owner of possession.

theft—Consolidated crimes of larceny, embezzlement, and false pretenses.

trespassory taking—Wrongful taking required in larceny *actus reus*.

uttering—Knowing or conscious use or transfer of false documents.

▼ INTRODUCTION

Crimes against property include damage, destruction, and misappropriation. The crimes of **misappropriation,** whether temporary or permanent, include many offenses with a long history. In fact, understanding **theft**—the general term used to describe the crimes of property misappropriation—depends more on history than on logic. Larceny, embezzlement, false pretense, receiving stolen property, robbery, and extortion constitute the main common-law crimes of property misappropriation.

▼ Table 11.1 ▼
Theft

	Number	Rate
Crimes of Theft	13	63.8
All Crimes	34,404	
completed	12,155	59.8
attempted	821	4
Personal larceny with contact	637	3.1
purse snatching	165	0.8
pocket picking	472	2.3
Personal larceny without contact	12,338	60.7
Completed more than $50	6,453	31.7
Completed less than $50	4,592	22.6
Completed amount not available	514	2.5
Attempted	779	3.8

SOURCE: *Criminal Victimization in the United States 1990,* Bureau of Justice Statistics, United States Justice Department, Washington, D.C., October 1991.

Whatever variations in their material elements, all aim at the same wrong: misappropriating property. For that reason, several states have consolidated some of these crimes into one general theft offense.

▼ HISTORY OF THEFT

Larceny is the oldest crime against property. All other property misappropriation crimes originated in it. Its history demonstrates that common lawyers developed larceny to protect the ancient Anglo-Saxons' most valuable possession: livestock. People on the American frontier placed a similar value on cattle and horses. The opprobrium with which offenders against these valuable possessions were regarded still lingers in the epithet "horse thief," used today to signify a dishonest or untrustworthy person.[1]

In the beginning, the threat to peace and order created by taking another's valuable possessions was regarded as at least equal to, and probably even more important than, the misappropriation involved. People who took other people's property by stealth or force were therefore considered evil. On the other hand, cheaters were considered clever; they did not deserve the law's condemnation. Owners foolish enough to put their property into the hands of untrustworthy others did not deserve the law's support. Hence, larceny punished only those who got possession by stealth or force. Early on, larceny by force grew into a separate offense called robbery, a felony that violated both person and property.[2]

As society grew more complex, common-law larceny by stealth was too crude and simple to protect the many personal possessions and other valuable objects that clever people could get into their hands. Complex urban, commercial, and industrial society with its banks, businesses, services, and concentrated populations created a need to rely on others to carry on transactions of daily life. Owners and possessors transferred property to others voluntarily—for safekeeping, for shipping, for repair or storage—trusting caretakers to carry out the purpose for which the property was handed over.

Ordinary larceny did not cover abusing trust relationships in order to acquire the property of others, because owners relinquished possession vol-

▼ Table 11.2 ▼
Household Crimes

	Number	Rate
Household Crimes		
All Crimes	34,404	
Household larceny	8,304	86.7
Completed more than $50	4,206	43.9
Completed less than $50	3,144	32.8
Completed amount not available	419	4.4
Motor vehicle theft	1,968	20.5
Completed	1,968	12.8
Attempted	741	7.7

SOURCE: *Criminal Victimization in the United States 1990,* Bureau of Justice Statistics, United States Justice Department, Washington, D.C., October 1991.

untarily. This gap in the law led legislatures and judges to create additions to larceny and to new property offenses that would respond to the increased reliance on others in property transactions.[3]

▼ LARCENY

For at least five hundred years, larceny's material elements have included (1) wrongfully taking (2) and carrying away (3) another's (4) property (5) with the intent to permanently deprive the property's owner of its possession. Larceny is first and foremost a crime directed at possession, not necessarily ownership, and larceny law particularly aims at punishing those who take and carry away others' possessions intending to keep them permanently, not just temporarily.

Elements of Larceny		
Actus Reus	**Mens Rea**	**Material Circumstances**
1. taking and *2.* carrying away	intent to permanently deprive owner of possession	*1.* another's property *2.* value of property

Larceny Actus Reus

The larceny *actus reus* requires both taking and carrying away (asporting) another's property.

Larceny requires actors to take—that is, to gain brief control over—another person's property. Taking is central to larceny, and it includes such direct actions as picking a pocket, lifting objects from a shop, or stealing a car. Some indirect takings also qualify. For example, suppose I see an unlocked bicycle that does not belong to me parked outside a shop. I offer to sell the bicycle to an unsuspecting passerby for forty dollars. He accepts my offer, pays me the money, and gets on the bike. In most states, as soon as the passerby gets on the bike, I have taken the bike, even though I never touched it. For another example, suppose I obtain money by threat. Even if I never actually touch the money, I have still taken it.

Larceny requires that misappropriators take and carry away other people's property. Also called **asportation,** carrying away in conjunction with taking completes the larceny *actus reus.* Carrying away essentially means that misappropriators are moving property from the place they took it. Carrying a short distance satisfies the asportation requirement; a few inches suffice. The word *carry* is not used in its ordinary sense; one can carry away that which one cannot carry literally. Hence, riding a horse away, driving a car off, leading a cow away, and pulling or pushing heavy objects away all constitute carrying away.

The property must actually move from its original place. A man who picked a pocket but got the money only partway out was not guilty, because he did not carry the money away. Another man who tried to steal a barrel also was not guilty, because he had only turned the barrel on its side so he could pick it up more easily.

Larceny violates possession, and it requires that actors wrongfully dispossess property—or, as the old law says, "There must be a trespass in the taking." Problems arise when a person who takes and carries away another person's property already lawfully possesses that property. Common examples are repair shop operators who have items in their possession, parking lot attendants who have their customers' car keys, and bank tellers who are authorized to handle money. In the ordinary sense of possession, all these persons possess another's property. Therefore, they could not "take and carry away" the property wrongfully because they already have it.

The law does not define possession as simple possession alone. Instead, it looks to the nature of possession, drawing a distinction between mere custody for a particular purpose (such as when an employee possesses goods only to work on them) and legal possession (such as when someone leases a car, owns a television set, or rents a washing machine). Custodians for particular purposes can wrongfully take and carry away property they have in their possession, thereby committing larceny. Lawful possessors, however, cannot commit larceny if they take and carry away property in their possession. Possessors cannot larcenously take what they possess.

Possession is a technical concept, involving both complex history and property law questions. Distinguishing between mere custody and lawful possession is not simple, but a few rules elucidate what **trespassory taking** means. First, employees do not possess their employers' goods; they have custody. Second, those who hand over their personal property for repairs in their presence do not relinquish possession. Thus, money given to tellers or others for change does not transfer in possession, only in custody.

CASE

Did the Shoplifters Wrongfully Take the Property?

People v. Olivo
52 N.Y. 2d 309, 438 N.Y.S.2d 242, 420 N.E. 2d 40 (1981)

[Olivo and the other defendants were convicted of petit larceny. They appealed. Chief Judge Cooke delivered the opinion.]

FACTS
In *People v. Olivo,* defendant was observed by a security guard in the hardware area of a department store. Initially conversing with another person, defendant began to look around furtively when his acquaintance departed. The security agent continued to observe and saw defendant assume a crouching position, take a set of wrenches and secret it in his clothes. After again looking around, defendant began walking toward an exit, passing a number of cash registers en route. When defendant did not stop to pay for the merchandise, the officer accosted him a few feet from the exit. In response to the guard's inquiry, he denied having the wrenches, but as he proceeded to the security office, defendant removed the wrenches and placed them under his jacket. At trial, defendant testified that he had placed the tools under his arm and was on line at a cashier when apprehended. The jury returned a verdict of guilty on the charge of petit larceny. The conviction was affirmed by Appellate Term.

In *People v. Gasparik,* defendant was in a department store trying on a leather jacket. Two store detectives observed him tear off the price tag and remove a "sensormatic" device designed to set off an alarm if the jacket were carried through a detection machine. There was at least one such machine at the exit of each floor. Defendant placed the tag and the device in the pocket of another jacket on the merchandise rack. He took his own jacket, which he had been carrying with him, and placed it on a table. Leaving his own jacket, defendant put on the leather jacket and walked through the store, still on the same floor, by passing several cash registers. When he headed for the exit from that floor, in the direction of the main floor, he was apprehended by security personnel. At trial, defendant denied removing the price tag and the sensormatic device from the jacket, and testified that he was looking for a cashier without a long line when he was stopped. The court, sitting without a jury, convicted defendant of petit larceny. Appellate Term affirmed 102 Misc.2d 487, 425 N.Y.S.2d 936.

In *People v. Spatzier,* defendant entered a bookstore on Fulton Street in Hempstead carrying an attaché case. The two co-owners of the store observed the defendant in a ceiling mirror as he browsed through the store. They watched defendant remove a book from the shelf, look up and down the aisle, and place the book in his case. He then placed the case at his feet and continued to browse. One of the owners approached defendant and accused him of stealing the book. An altercation ensued and when defendant allegedly struck the owner with the attaché case, the case opened and the book fell out. At trial, defendant denied secreting the book in his case and claimed that the owner had suddenly and unjustifiably accused him of stealing. The jury found defendant guilty of petit larceny, and the conviction was affirmed by the Appellate Term.

OPINION

These cases present a recurring question in this era of the self-service store which has never been resolved by this court: may a person be convicted of larceny for shoplifting if the person is caught with goods while still inside the store? For reasons outlined below, it is concluded that a larceny conviction may be sustained, in certain situations, even though the shoplifter was apprehended before leaving the store.

The primary issue in each case is whether the evidence, viewed in the light most favorable to the prosecution, was sufficient to establish the elements of larceny as defined by the Penal Law. To resolve this common question, the development of the common-law crime of larceny and its evolution into modern statutory form must be briefly traced.

Larceny at common law was defined as a trespassory taking and carrying away of the property of another with intent to steal it. The early common-law courts apparently viewed larceny as defending society against breach of the peace, rather than protecting individual property rights, and therefore placed heavy emphasis upon the requirement of a trespassory taking.

As the reach of larceny expanded, the intent element of the crime became of increasing importance, while the requirement of a trespassory taking became less significant.

As a result, the bar against convicting a person who had initially obtained lawful possession of property faded. In *King v. Pear,* for instance, a defendant who had lied about his address and ultimate destination when renting a horse was found guilty of larceny for later converting the horse. Because of the fraudulent misrepresentation, the court reasoned, the defendant had never obtained legal possession. Thus, "larceny by trick" was born.

Later cases went even further, often ignoring the fact that a defendant had initially obtained possession lawfully, and instead focused upon his later intent. The crime of larceny then encompassed, not only situations where the defendant initially obtained property by a trespassory taking, but many situations where an individual, possessing the requisite intent, exercised control over property inconsistent with the continued right of the owner. During this evolutionary process, the purpose served by the crime of larceny obviously shifted from protecting society's peace to general protection of property rights.

Modern penal statutes generally have incorporated these developments under a unified definition of larceny (see e.g., American Law Institute, Model Penal Code [Tent Draft No. 1], § 206.1 [theft is appropriation of property of another, which includes unauthorized exercise of control]). Case law, too, now tends to focus upon the actor's intent and the exercise of dominion and control over the property. Indeed, this court has recognized, in construing the New York Penal Law, that the "ancient common-law concepts of larceny" no longer strictly apply.

This evolution is particularly relevant to thefts occurring in modern self-service stores. In stores of that type, customers are impliedly invited to examine, try on, and carry about the merchandise on display. Thus in a sense, the owner has consented to the customer's possession of the goods for a limited purpose.

That the owner has consented to that possession does not, however, preclude a conviction for larceny. If the customer exercises dominion and control wholly inconsistent with the continued rights of the owner, and the other elements of the crime are present, a larceny has occurred. Such conduct on the part of a customer satisfies the "taking" element of the crime.

It is this element that forms the core of the controversy in these cases. The defendants argue, in essence, that the crime is not established, as a matter of law, unless there is evidence that the customer departed the shop without paying for the merchandise.

Although this court has not addressed the issue, case law from other jurisdictions seems unanimous in holding that a shoplifter need not leave the store to be guilty of larceny. This is because a shopper may treat merchandise in a manner inconsistent with the owner's continued rights— and in a manner not in accord with that of prospective purchaser—without actually walking out of the store.

Under these principles, there was ample evidence in each case to raise a factual question as to the defendants' guilt. In *People v. Olivo,* defendant not only concealed goods in his clothing, but he did so in a particularly suspicious manner. And, when defendant was stopped, he was moving towards the door, just three feet short of exiting the store.

In *People v. Gasparik,* defendant removed the price tag and sensor device from a jacket, abandoned his own garment, put the jacket on and ultimately headed for the main floor of the store. Removal of the price tag and sensor device, and careful concealment of those items, is highly unusual and suspicious conduct for a shopper. Coupled with defendant's abandonment of his own coat and his attempt to leave the floor, those factors were sufficient to make out a prima facie case of taking.

In *People v. Spatzier,* defendant concealed a book in an attaché case. Unaware that he was being observed in an overhead mirror, defendant looked furtively up and down the aisle before secreting the book. In these circumstances, given the manner in which defendant concealed the book and his suspicious behavior, the evidence was not insufficient as a matter of law.

In sum, in view of the modern definition of the crime of larceny, and its purpose of protecting individual property rights, a taking of property in the self-service store context can be established by evidence that a customer exercised control over merchandise wholly inconsistent with the store's continued rights. Quite simply, a customer who crosses the line between the limited right he or she has to deal with merchandise and the store owner's rights may be subject to prosecution for larceny. Such a rule should foster the legitimate interests and continued operation of self-service shops, a convenience which most members of the society enjoy.

Accordingly, in each case, the order of the Appellate Term should be affirmed.

**Case
Discussion**
The court says that originally larceny stressed possession, but modern convenience shopping requires that the emphasis shift to intent. Do you see why the court says this? Under strict taking and carrying away requirements, do you think these defendants committed larceny? Is the court right in adopting a rule that does not require shoplifters to leave the store before they are guilty? What rule would you adopt?

———————⫸●⫷———————

In addition to temporary possession, possessions secured by trick constitute wrongful takings—larceny by trick. If a possessor gives up possession because he or she believes another's lies, the law deems it a larcenous taking and carrying away even though the possessor voluntarily relinquished possession. Hence, if I lend a valuable watch to a friend who says he is only going to borrow it for the evening but who intends to sell it to a jeweler, I have retained legal possession of the watch; my "friend" has wrongfully taken possession from me. Larceny by trick should not be confused with acquiring property by false pretenses. False pretenses requires a transfer of ownership or title, not simply a shift in possession.

Larceny law does not follow the old rhyme, "Finders keepers, losers weepers." Owners who lose their money or other property retain its possession for the purposes of larceny law. Hence, those who take and carry away lost money or other property commit larceny, assuming they do so with requisite intent.

Larceny Material Circumstances

Common-law larceny included only personal property, or "movables." Larceny was therefore limited to the misappropriation of goods and chattels. Real estate and anything attached to it—unharvested crops, uncut trees, unmined minerals, and attached fixtures—were not property within the meaning of common-law larceny. Thus, if I entered my neighbor's field, cut down growing wheat, and took and carried the wheat away, I did not commit larceny. Defining harvested crops, cut trees, and so on as movable property led to some odd results. For example, cutting down crops one day, leaving, and then returning the next day to take and carry the crops away was considered larceny.

Common-law larceny also excluded stocks, bonds, checks, and other negotiable paper. Such documents were intangible property or choses in action. This meant they were not actual property, except as paper and ink; they only represented property. Hence, they were not larcenable. Gas and electricity were also not property; nor were services and labor.

Modern statutes have drastically revised the common-law larceny definition of property. In most American jurisdictions today, minerals, crops, fixtures, trees, utilities (gas and electricity), goods and services, and other intangible property can all be taken under the law of larceny. In short, virtually all property falls within the scope of modern larceny statutes. Texas, for example, defines property to include real property; tangible or intangible personal property including anything severed from the land; and a document, including money, that represents or embodies anything of value. The statute also includes theft of service, defined as (1) labor or professional services; (2) telecommunication, public utility, and transportation services; (3) lodging, restaurant services, and entertainment; and (4) the supply of a motor vehicle or other property for use.[4]

To deal with modern forms of theft, some states have enacted elaborate statutes—such as California's computer theft statute, reproduced here:

§ 502. Definitions; computer system or network; intentional access to defraud or extort or to obtain money, property or services with false or fraudulent intent, representations or promises; malicious access, alteration, deletion, damage or disruption; violations; penalty; civil action

a. For purposes of this section:
  1. "Access" means to instruct, communicate with, store data in, or retrieve data from, a computer system or computer network.
  2. "Computer system" means a device or collection of devices, excluding pocket calculators which are not programmable and capable of being used in conjunction with external files, one or more of which contain computer programs and data, that performs functions, including, but not limited to, logic, arithmetic, data storage and retrieval, communication, and control.
  3. "Computer network" means an interconnection of two or more computer systems.
  4. "Computer program" means an ordered set of instructions or statements, and related data that, when automatically executed in actual or modified form in a computer system, causes it to perform specified functions.
  5. "Data" means a representation of information, knowledge, facts, concepts, or instructions, which are being prepared or have been prepared, in a formalized manner, and are intended for use in a computer system or computer network.
  6. "Financial instrument" includes, but is not limited to, any check, draft, warrant, money order, note, certificate of deposit, letter of credit, bill of exchange, credit or debit card, transaction authorization mechanism, marketable security, or any computer system representation thereof.
  7. "Property" includes, but is not limited to, financial instruments, data, computer programs, documents associated with computer systems and computer programs, or copies thereof, whether tangible or intangible, including both human and computer system readable data, and data while in transit.
  8. "Services" includes, but is not limited to, the use of the computer system, computer network, computer programs, or data prepared for computer use, or data contained within a computer system, or data contained within a computer network....
b. Any person who intentionally accesses or causes to be accessed any computer system or computer network for the purpose of (1) devising or executing any scheme or artifice to defraud or extort, or (2) obtaining money, property, or services with false or fraudulent intent, representations, or promises, is guilty of a public offense.
c. Any person who maliciously accesses, alters, deletes, damages, destroys or disrupts the operation of any computer system, computer network, computer program, or data is guilty of a public offense.

d. Any person who intentionally and without authorization accesses any computer system, computer network, computer program, or data, with knowledge that the access was not authorized, shall be guilty of a public offense. This subdivision shall not apply to any person who accesses his or her employer's computer system, computer network, computer program, or data when acting within the scope of his or her employment.

e. Any person who violates any provision of subdivision (b) or (c) unless specified otherwise, is punishable by a fine not exceeding ten thousand dollars ($10,000), or by imprisonment in the state prison for 16 months, or two or three years, or by both such fine and imprisonment, or by a fine not exceeding five thousand dollars ($5,000), or by imprisonment in the county jail not exceeding one year, or by both such fine and imprisonment.

f. (1) A first violation of subdivision (d) which does not result in injury is an infraction punishable by a fine not exceeding two hundred fifty dollars ($250)....

> 2. A violation of subdivision (d) which results in an injury, or a second or subsequent violation of subdivision (d) with no injury, is a misdemeanor punishable by a fine not exceeding five thousand dollars ($5,000), or by imprisonment in the county jail not exceeding one year, or by both such fine and imprisonment.
>
> 3. As used in this subdivision, "injury" means any alteration, deletion, damage, or destruction of a computer system, computer network, computer program, or data caused by the access, or any expenditure reasonably and necessarily incurred by the owner or lessee to verify that a computer system, computer network, computer program, or data was not altered, deleted, damaged, or destroyed by the access.

g. In addition to any other civil remedy available, the owner or lessee of the computer system, computer network, computer program, or data may bring a civil action against any person convicted under this section for compensatory damages, including any expenditure reasonably and necessarily incurred by the owner or lessee to verify that a computer system, computer network, computer program, or data was not altered, damaged, or deleted by the access. For the purposes of actions authorized by this subdivision, the conduct of an unemancipated minor shall be imputed to the parent or legal guardian having control or custody of the minor, pursuant to the provisions of § 1714.1 of the Civil Code. In any action brought pursuant to this subdivision, the court may award attorney's fees to a prevailing plaintiff.

h. This section shall not be construed to preclude the applicability of any other provision of the criminal law of this state which applies or may apply to any transaction.[5]

The court in *State v. McGraw* dealt with the problem of defining theft to include misappropriations by computer.

CASE

Did He "Steal" the Use of the Computer?

State v. McGraw
480 N.E. 2d 552 (Ind.1985)

[Justice Prentice delivered the opinion. Justice Pivarnik delivered a dissenting opinion.]

FACTS
Defendant was employed by the City of Indianapolis, as a computer operator. The City leased computer services on a fixed charge or flat rate basis, hence the expense to it was not varied by the extent to which it

was used. Defendant was provided with a terminal at his desk and was assigned a portion of the computer's information storage capacity, called a "private library," for his utilization in performing his duties. No other employees were authorized to use his terminal or his library.

Defendant became involved in a private sales venture and began soliciting his co-workers and using a small portion of his assigned library to maintain records associated with the venture. He was reprimanded several times for selling his products in the office and on "office time," and he was eventually discharged for unsatisfactory job performance and for continuing his personal business activities during office hours.

Defendant, at the time of his being hired by the City, received a handbook, as do all new employees, which discloses the general prohibition against the unauthorized use of city property. Other city employees sometimes used the computer for personal convenience or entertainment; and although Defendant's supervisor knew or suspected that Defendant was using the computer for his business records, he never investigated the matter or reprimanded Defendant in this regard, and such use of the computer was not cited as a basis for his discharge.

Defendant, following his discharge, applied for and received unemployment compensation benefits, over the protest of the City. He requested a former fellow employee to obtain a "print-out" of his business data and then to erase it from what had been his library. Instead, the "print-out" was turned over to Defendant's former supervisor and became the basis for the criminal charges.

OPINION

Assuming that the Defendant's use of the computer was unauthorized and that such use is a "property" under the theft statute, there remains an element of the offense missing under the evidence. The act provides: "A person knowingly or intentionally exerts unauthorized control over property of another person with intent to deprive the other of any part of its value or use, commits theft, a class

D felony." It is immediately apparent that the rest of the statute, the harm sought to be prevented, is a deprivation to one of his property or its use—not a benefit to one which, although a windfall to him, harmed nobody.

The Court of Appeals focused upon Defendant's unauthorized use of the computer for monetary gain and upon the definition of "property" as used in the statute ... which we may assume, arguendo, includes the "use" of a computer, although we think that it would be more accurate to say that the information derived by use of a computer is property. Having determined that Defendant's use was property, was unauthorized and was for his monetary benefit, it concluded that he committed a theft. Our question is, "Who was deprived of what?"...

Defendant's unauthorized use cost the City nothing and did not interfere with its use by others. He extracted from the system only such information as he had previously put into it. He did not, for his own benefit, withdraw City data intended for its exclusive use or for sale. Thus, Defendant did not deprive the City of the "use of computers and computer services" as the information alleged that he intended to do....

We have written innumerable times, that intent is a mental function and, absent an admission it must be determined by courts and juries from a consideration of the conduct and natural and usual consequences of such conduct.... It follows that when the natural and usual consequences of the conduct charged and proved are not such as would effect the wrong which the statute seeks to prevent, the intent to effect that wrong is so inferrable. No deprivation to the City resulted from Defendant's use of the computer, and a deprivation to it was not a result to be expected from such use, hence not a natural and usual consequence. There was no evidence presented from which the intent to deprive, an essential element of the crime, could be inferred....

DISSENT

I must dissent from the majority opinion wherein the majority finds that Defendant did not take property of the City "with intent to deprive the owner of said property." In the first place, intent is clearly shown in that Defendant used the City computer system for his personal business, well knowing that he was doing so and well knowing that it was unauthorized.... Time and use are at the very core of the value of a computer system. To say that only the information stored in the computer plus the tapes and discs and perhaps the machinery

involved in the computer system, are the only elements that can be measured as the value or property feature of that system, is incorrect....

... Thus, when the defendant used the computer system, putting on data from his private business and taking it out on printouts, he was taking that which was property of the City and converting it to his own use, thereby depriving the City of its use and value....

Case Discussion

Would you define the use of the computer as property? What facts would lead you to conclude that it was property? Do you think McGraw "stole" anything of value? Do you think the city lost anything of value? Should it matter? Does—or should—your definition of property depend on the purpose for which you are defining the term? Why should, or should not, that be the way to define property? Explain. Do you agree with the dissent or the majority? Was McGraw guilty of anything?

In all jurisdictions, grading depends on the value of the property taken: the higher the value of the misappropriated property, the more serious the larceny. The law determines the grade of larceny according to three criteria: (1) market value, (2) method of taking, (3) intrinsic value. Grand larceny, which is usually punishable by one year or more in prison, includes property exceeding a dollar amount, typically between $100 and $400. Property worth less than the designated amount for grand larceny is usually included in the misdemeanor of petty larceny, which is punishable by less than one year in jail or a fine, or both. The dividing line between grand and petty larceny differs from state to state. In South Carolina, for example, the critical amount is only $20; in Pennsylvania it is $2,000.

Determining property value is difficult, but generally market value governs, rather than price paid or misappropriators' evaluations. If several articles are taken from the same place at the same time, the value can be set at the aggregate value. If items are taken over an extended period from different people and different places, however, the aggregate value method cannot apply.

Market value does not always determine the gravity of theft. Pickpocketing, for example, is always a felony, and so is taking property from someone's home. These cases involve more interests than mere property; harms to both persons and habitation are present. Moreover, taking property from a person by force constitutes robbery, a serious felony. In most jurisdictions, taking and carrying away certain items is also a felony, no matter what the items' value. These items vary depending on the interests in particular jurisdictions. In Texas, for example, stealing natural oil, no matter what the value, constitutes grand larceny. California provides that grand larceny includes property valued in excess of $400, or avocados, olives, citrus or deciduous fruits, vegetables, artichokes, nuts, or other farm crops exceeding $100 in value.[6]

Larceny Mens Rea

To convict for larceny, the prosecution must prove that a defendant intended to permanently deprive the rightful possessor of the property taken and carried away. Therefore, larceny is a specific intent crime. For example, suppose I see a lawn mower on my neighbor's lawn, and I believe it is the one I loaned him last month but it is, in fact, his. If I take the mower and sell it, I have not committed larceny because I did not intend to keep his lawn mower.

Temporary misappropriations do not constitute common-law larceny. Modern statutes have filled that gap in common-law larceny by making some temporary misappropriations separate crimes. A typical case is joyriding, or taking a vehicle to drive for a short time only, fully intending to return it to its rightful possessor. The joyrider lacks the larceny *mens rea*—the intent to permanently deprive the owner of possession. Joyriding statutes make it a less serious offense than larceny to take and carry away another's vehicle with the intent to temporarily dispossess the vehicle's rightful possessor.[7]

Finally, taking property that actors believe is theirs is not larceny. Called the **claim of right,** this defense removes the *mens rea* requirement to intend to permanently dispossess rightful possessors. Most jurisdictions permit claim of right as a defense to larceny.[8]

Summary of Larceny

Larceny, the ancient common-law felony, requires (1) a wrongful taking and (2) carrying away (3) of the property (4) of another (5) with the intent to permanently dispossess the property's rightful possessor. Some modern statutes have codified common law; in these jurisdictions, the old elements remain important. These jurisdictions have added a number of other misappropriations that follow the common-law development. Some jurisdictions have consolidated several misappropriations into general theft statutes. The principal misappropriations consolidated into theft include embezzlement and obtaining property by false pretenses.

▼ EMBEZZLEMENT

Elements of Embezzlement		
Actus Reus	***Mens Rea***	**Material Circumstances**
convert	intent to permanently deprive owner of possession	*1.* another's property *2.* value of property

Historically, it was not a larcenous taking if a possessor voluntarily parted with property. For example, carriers, or persons hired to deliver owners' goods to third parties, could not "take" the goods while they were in the carriers' possession. Similarly, bank employees who removed money from an account could not "take" the money, because the owner had voluntarily deposited it. That such clearly wrongful appropriations were originally not criminal shows that larceny is an ancient crime predating carriers, banks, and other modern institutions. Statutes have altered common-law larceny so that those who acquire property lawfully—parking lot attendants, dry cleaners, auto repair people, and bank tellers—and then convert it to their own use commit embezzlement.

Embezzlers do not "take" property because they already possess it lawfully. In other words, they cannot wrongfully take what they already lawfully possess. **Conversion** replaces taking in embezzlement. Conversion can occur only after someone acquires possession lawfully. Embezzlers acquire possession for a specific purpose—to repair a watch, to dry-clean clothes, and so on—and then (convert) the property to an unlawful purpose (their own use or profit). Embezzlers stand in a trust or fiduciary relationship with rightful possessors; they possess property only for the purpose for which the rightful permanent possessor transferred it. Conversion breaches this trust.

Embezzlers or those who converted property temporarily in their possession for particular purposes, did not exist when larceny originated. They became important as society grew more complex. Larceny's trespassory taking requirement prevented the punishment of those who abused their trust and misappropriated property entrusted to them. Hence, the English Parliament created embezzlement during the period when temporary possessors, or bailees, were becoming common. With the onset of banking, industrialization, and modern society, many more embezzlement types were possible, and conversion became ever more important in misappropriation offenses. Under modern statutes, whether embezzlement and larceny or theft, either taking (larceny) or conversion (embezzlement) suffices.

▼ FALSE PRETENSES

Larceny requires a trespassory taking, and embezzlement requires the conversion of property rightfully in the converter's possession. But what about owners who part with possession because they are deceived into giving up title or ownership? Embezzlement covers only those who temporarily have a lawful right to possess and then convert property to their own use. Those

Elements of False Pretenses		
Actus Reus	*Mens Rea*	**Material Circumstances**
false representation	intent to permanently deprive owner of possession	*1.* another's property *2.* value of property

who obtain property by false pretenses have no right to possess it, and yet they do not take the property because owners willingly gave it to them. False pretenses fills the gap between larcenous takings and embezzlement that is created by deceitful misappropriation.

The *actus reus* in false pretenses replaces taking in larceny. It requires first an actual false representation, such as a promise to deliver something one cannot or does not intend to ever deliver. The law often expresses this as falsely representing a material past or existing fact. The false pretenses *mens rea* requires the specific intent to obtain title or ownership by deceit and lies—the false pretenses. A material surrounding circumstance in false pretenses is that victims must part with the possession and ownership because they believe and rely on the false representation. Suppose someone promises me he is a financial wizard when in fact he is only saying so to get my money. If I rely on his promise and transfer my money to him for investment, then the fake financial wizard obtained my money by false pretenses. Finally, the victim must actually part with the property. Note the difference between obtaining property through false pretense and through larceny by trick. In larceny by trick, the possessor must part with possession. In false pretenses, the owner must part with title or ownership.

The law on obtaining property by false pretenses aims to protect owners from several harms inflicted by cheaters and con artists who misappropriate their wealth. From early on, English criminal law tried to protect against false weights and measures because they hindered trade. It was not until 1757, however, that individuals who privately cheated other individuals out of property were made criminals. In that year, the English Parliament made it a misdemeanor to "obtain [by false pretenses] from any person or persons, money, goods, wares, or merchandizes."[9]

The extension of criminal law to include cheating has not gone without criticism. Some critics base their attack on a general reluctance to use the criminal law in any but the most extreme situations. Others feel little sympathy with victims. Taking their cue from the ancient commercial doctrine of *caveat emptor* ("Let the buyer beware"), these critics believe that "fools and their money soon part." Such criticisms are especially effective against the view that duping the public is a crime even when no one loses property. This dimension to false pretenses—humiliating and making people fools without property loss—deserves serious attention that cannot be given here. Suffice it to say that despite objections, criminal law protects property from misappropriations based on lying, cheating, deception, and other forms of false pretenses, at least under some circumstances.

Until the last twenty years, larceny, embezzlement, and obtaining property by false pretenses were distinct offenses in most criminal codes. Although all three involved misappropriation, the taking in larceny, the conversion in embezzlement, and the fraud in false pretenses were considered sufficiently different to require separate treatment under criminal codes. This view was largely due to the histories of these crimes, rather than to logic. Trespassory taking (first), conversion (later), and false pretense (last) created problems as society grew more complex during English and American history. The well-known Supreme Court justice Oliver Wendell Holmes, Jr., put it simply: "In law a page of history is worth a volume of logic."

CASE

*Did He Intend to
Deceive the Churches?*

Hixson v. State
266 Ark. 778, 587 S.W.2d 70 (1979)

*[Hixson was convicted of false pretenses mis-
appropriation. He was sentenced to twelve
years' imprisonment and fined $2,500.
Judge Howard delivered the opinion. Judge
Newbern dissented.]*

FACTS

Mrs. Rita Sue Rogers, Secretary of Trinity
Baptist Church, Fort Smith, Arkansas, testified
that on January 16, 1977, appellant entered
into an agreement with Trinity Baptist
Church and its members to take pictures of
the membership and in return for the sale of
the pictures to the members, appellant would
supply pictorial directories to the church free
of charge. The number of church directories
to be supplied was 125% of the number of
members who had their pictures taken. In
other words, the church would receive at the
rate of 125 directories for every 100 members
who purchased portraits. No money was to
be paid by the church.

The evidence clearly shows that appellant
received $1,700.00 from the membership of
Trinity, but the church has never received
any directories, although appellant promised
to deliver the directories within 60 days after
the pictures were taken. The photographing
of the membership was completed on April
3, 1977.

Mrs. Rogers further testified that the project created such interest and enthusiasm
among the members that a group of ladies
volunteered to serve as a committee to
inform the entire membership of the project
and to solicit their support; that the committee scheduled the time for the individual
and family sittings for the portraits; and that

if shut-ins already had photographs, these
photographs were to be placed in the directory for a fee of $5.00.

Mrs. Rogers also stated that appellant
delivered a $500.00 personal check to the
church, drawn on Sequoyah State Bank,
Muldrow, Oklahoma, and made payable to
Trinity Baptist Church to guarantee the
delivery of the portraits to the membership;
that when the pictures were not delivered,
as scheduled, the check was deposited for
collection, but was subsequently returned
marked "account closed."

Dan Wilmoth, a representative of Photo
World of Memphis, Tennessee, testified that
his firm specialized in photographic processing for professional photographers; that
appellant came to Memphis in April or
May, 1977, to have a roll of film developed
and that appellant advised him that appellant was just getting started in business for
himself; that appellant discussed the
prospects of Photo World printing church
directories for appellant's firm and that
while Photo World had never printed
church directories, an agreement was made
with appellant whereby Photo World would
print the directories for $1.50 a copy with a
minimum of 200 copies; that Photo World
received the necessary materials for only
one church directory and that was for
Bethany Presbyterian Church. However, Mr.
Wilmoth testified, the directory was never
printed because appellant owed Photo
World $1,200.00 for work previously done
in which Photo World received an insufficient fund check that had not been made
good; that appellant told Photo World that
appellant could not pay the $1,200.00 at
that time because appellant had paid
$5,000.00 on a property note. Mr. Wilmoth
further testified that Photo World printed its
first directory, during its 11 years of existence, in 1978.

Testifying further, Mr. Wilmoth stated that
when appellant requested Photo World to
commence work on the materials supplied
for the one church directory, appellant was
advised to "send me Three Hundred Dollars
($300.00) Cashiers' Check and I'll get it

printed for him"; that a day or two later, appellant called and stated, "hey, I can't get the money, you know, can you do it, please?" Wilmoth replied, "I'll tell you what, you send me One Hundred Fifty Dollars ($150.00) and I'll do it." Wilmoth testified he never heard anymore from appellant.

OPINION

The relevant statutory provisions that appellant was accused of violating are:

1. A person commits theft of property if he:
b. knowingly obtains the property of another person, by deception or by threat, with the purpose of depriving the owner thereof.
2. (a) Theft of property is a class B felony if: (i) the value of the property is $2,500.00 or more.

We are persuaded that it was incumbent upon the State to establish the following in order to convict the appellant-defendant of the charge brought under the above provisions:

1. That appellant-defendant, at the time he received the monies from the owners, did not intend to carry out his promise to deliver church directories to the churches and the membership thereof in return for the monies received by him.
2. That appellant-defendant knew, at the time he promised to deliver church directories to the churches and the membership thereof that the promise or representation was false and that the promise was made for the purpose of depriving the owners of their property.

Appellant argues essentially, for the reversal of his conviction, that his promise to deliver church directories within 30 to 90 days after the termination of the photographic work was "mere puffing" and, moreover, the failure of appellant to perform a "promised future act" is not criminal.

We are not persuaded by appellant's argument inasmuch as it is plain from the evidence in this record that appellant's conduct exceeded the conduct of a seller or a dealer in praising the virtues of something that he has to offer for sale and which is not calculated to, or is unlikely to deceive ordinary persons addressed. The evidence is crystal clear that the representations and promises made by appellant to deliver the church directories, which was an intricate part of the entire project and was the sole motivating factor that induced the churches and the membership to participate in the project, were false as a matter of fact and as to the value of the articles that the churches and members were to receive in return for delivering their monies to the appellant. Moreover, it is plain from this record that appellant had no experience or expertise either in photography or in the compilation of church directories; and that at the time that appellant made the promises to deliver the directories, appellant did not possess the facilities to print a directory, nor had he made arrangements with any other firm or source for the preparation of the directories.

The evidence establishes clearly that appellant made use of the funds received for purposes other than for what was promised by appellant. Consequently, the membership of the churches involved have been deprived of the use and benefit of their property; and it seems obvious that restitution is unlikely.

Affirmed.

DISSENT

The evidence of the intent of the Appellant to deceive was extremely weak. The record presented a picture of a person struggling to succeed in a business he thought would make a profit. It is true he lacked experience as a photographer, and he was an abysmal failure as a businessman, but his failure is not a crime. The majority opinion refers to instances in which he pleaded with a printer to get directories printed, and the record shows a great deal of effort expended in trying to get the directories together. The "substantial evidence" to which the majority refers is really nothing more than

Appellant's failure to deliver the directories. The argument seems to be that Appellant must have intended to deceive with respect to the agreements he entered to produce directories after he had failed so miserably to produce in accordance with some of his prior agreements. In quoting the statutory definition of "deception," the majority opin-ion leaves out the part of subsection (3)(e) of the statute which is as follows:

> Deception as to a person's intention to perform a promise shall not be inferred solely from the fact that he did not subsequently perform the promise.

Ark.Stat.Ann. § 41–2201(3) (e) (Repl.1977).

Case Discussion

The critical issue in the case is determining whether Hixson intended to deceive the churches. In other words, did he use false pretenses to get their money? He argued he was only "puffing." Does the evidence presented convince you that he meant to deceive the churches in order to get their money? Or do you think the dissent has a point? Should the criminal law punish inept people who think they can do what they cannot legally do? Does Hixson deserve twelve years in prison?

⟫●⟪

▼ CONSOLIDATED THEFT STATUTES

Critics have long recommended reforming larceny, embezzlement, and false pretenses to conform more to logic than to history. They believe that misappropriating property, whether by stealth, conversion, or deception, represents different dimensions to one general harm. In 1962, the Model Penal Code included a consolidated theft provision, one that most state laws now follow. The most common statutes consolidate larceny, embezzlement, and false pretenses into one offense called theft.

Consolidated theft statutes eliminate the largely artificial need to decide whether property was "taken and carried away," "converted," or "swindled," as traditional larceny, embezzlement, and false pretense statutes require. Joining the offenses deals more realistically with the social problem in all three: criminal property misappropriations.

Some statutes are even more ambitious than those that simply consolidate larceny, embezzlement, and false pretenses. The Model Penal Code, for example, has a single theft article that covers not only larceny, embezzlement, and false pretense but also extortion, blackmail, and receiving stolen property. Thus, the code houses all nonviolent misappropriations. Only robbery—because it refers to imminent or actual physical harm—falls under a separate provision. Other consolidated theft statutes include some or all of the following thefts: taking, conversion, deception, extortion, lost property, receiving stolen property, theft of services, failure to make required deposits, and unauthorized vehicle use.[10]

California's consolidated theft statute provides that

> every person who shall feloniously steal the personal property of another, or who shall fraudulently appropriate property which has been entrusted to him,

or who shall knowingly and designedly, by any false or fraudulent representation or pretense, defraud any other person of money, labor or real or personal property, shall be guilty of theft.[11]

Commenting on the provision, the California Supreme Court wrote:

> Included within § 484 is not only the offense of taking personal property (larceny), but also "embezzlement," theft by trick and device, and theft by false pretenses [of both personal and real property].[12]

Consolidated theft statutes reflect only in part the response of criminal law to the rapidly developing opportunities to misappropriate property. Property itself has become too restrictive to describe what constitutes value subject of misappropriation in the late twentieth century. Electronics has created not only new value but also new methods to misappropriate it. These new methods have led to legislation dealing with devices to misappropriate telephone long-distance services as well as information and services stored in electronic data banks, to mention only two.

▼ RECEIVING STOLEN PROPERTY

Elements in Receiving Stolen Property		
Actus Reus	*Mens Rea*	**Material Circumstances**
gaining control	*1.* knowingly or *2.* honestly believing	property actually stolen

In some circumstances, it is a crime not only to take, convert, and acquire the property of others by deception but also to receive property after it has been criminally misappropriated. Called receiving stolen property, this offense aims to protect against those who stand to benefit from misappropriations even though they did not wrongfully acquire others' property. Benefit does not mean simply monetary profit; receiving stolen property includes not only fences (those who trade in stolen property), but also, for example, students who steal university equipment because they need calculators, typewriters, recorders, and other equipment. Large-scale fence operations, however, account for most traffic in stolen property.

Fences have the facilities to buy, store, and market property. As go-betweens, they are as indispensable as their counterparts in legitimate operations are to farmers, manufacturers, and other producers. Large-city fences trade a remarkably large volume and variety in stolen property, ranging from narcotics and weapons to appliances and computers and even clothes. Receiving stolen property is aimed primarily at these large-scale operations.

The *actus reus* in receiving stolen property requires that property taken, converted, or acquired by deception come into the receiver's control for at least a short period. It does not mandate that the receiver personally possess the property. Hence, if I buy a stolen fur from a fence who hands it directly to my friend, I have received the fur. If my friend then gives the fur to her friend, my friend has also received the stolen fur. Included in the definition of the *actus reus* are fences as well as friends who hide stolen goods temporarily for thieves.

A material element in receiving stolen property is that the property must in fact have been criminally misappropriated—that is, taken, converted, or acquired by deception. Hence, if I think I am hiding stolen weapons but in fact the weapons were not stolen, I have not received stolen weapons.

Mens rea is difficult to establish in receiving stolen property. The culpability required varies among the states. Some jurisdictions require actual knowledge that the goods are stolen. In other jurisdictions, an honest belief that the goods are stolen suffices. In all jurisdictions, this knowledge may be inferred from surrounding circumstances, as in receiving goods from a known thief or buying goods at a fraction of their real value (for example, buying a new twelve-speed bicycle for thirty-five dollars.) Some jurisdictions reduce the *mens rea* to recklessness or even negligence. This lowered culpability requirement is often directed at likely fences, usually junk dealers and pawn shop operators.

In addition to knowledge that property was stolen, *mens rea* requires that receivers intend to permanently dispossess rightful possessors. Hence, police officers who knowingly accept stolen property and secretly place it on suspected fences in order to catch them have not received stolen property because they intend to possess it only temporarily.

CASE

Did He Receive the Stolen Guns?

State v. Davis
607 S.W.2d 149 (Mo.1980)

[Davis was convicted of receiving stolen property, was sentenced to one year in county jail, and was fined $500. He appealed. Judge Seiler delivered the opinion.]

FACTS

Appellant was the elected city marshal and police chief of Mound City in Holt County, Missouri. He used his home as his office and headquarters. Prior to his becoming police chief, appellant had worked as a security guard; he had no formal training to be a law enforcement officer.

On July 11, 1977, Bobby Hall discovered that two rifles, a German-made eight millimeter Mauser and a .22 caliber Weatherby semi-automatic, had been stolen from the gun rack of his pickup truck parked outside his father's home in a rural area three miles south of Mound City. Hall and appellant were friends, had taken trips together and purchased guns together. Hall reported the theft to appellant, but was told that he should report the theft to the sheriff since the theft occurred outside appellant's jurisdiction.

Sometime prior to September 11, 1977, two informants, appellant's wife, Kate Davis, and her employer, John King, told Deputy Patterson that they had seen two rifles, a Mauser and a .22 caliber Weatherby, at the home of appellant. Deputy Patterson told informant John King that he needed the serial numbers from the guns and requested that he secure them. King provided two serial numbers, one which matched the number of Hall's stolen Mauser rifle and a second that did not match the serial number of the stolen Weatherby rifle.

On September 12, 1977, after Patterson received a telephone call from King informing him that the rifles were still in appellant's home, Sheriff Hayzlett and Deputy Patterson obtained a search warrant to search appellant's home for the guns. Deputy Patterson called appellant on a police radio and asked him to come to a local gas station restaurant. At approximately 9:30 in the evening appellant met Deputy Patterson and Sergeant Matthews of the Highway Patrol for coffee at the restaurant. The men sat and talked for a while. After they paid for their coffee and stepped outside the restaurant, Deputy Patterson told appellant that the sheriff's office had received information that appellant had two stolen guns at his house. Appellant denied that he had the guns and walked to his police car to drive away. Deputy Patterson went to Sergeant Matthews' patrol car and called Sheriff Hayzlett on the radio. The sheriff then heard appellant call his wife over a citizen's band radio. Within three or four minutes, Sheriff Hayzlett, Deputy Patterson, Sergeant Matthews and three other Highway Patrol officers, and the county prosecutor converged according to plan upon appellant's home to execute the search warrant.

Sheriff Hayzlett and the six other law enforcement officers arrived at appellant's home and had entered it before appellant arrived on the scene. Appellant's son answered the door and said his mother was outside the building and appellant's wife subsequently entered the house through the back door. Appellant arrived moments after the arrival of the sheriff and other officers and the search of appellant's home, his bedroom in particular, commenced. No evidence of the guns was found in the house. The officers then went outside

behind the house and decided to look into the cistern, where they eventually found the guns. Appellant, his wife, and one Barbara King, who evidently arrived at appellant's home after the search began, were then arrested. It was not until the trial that the "confidential informants" who supplied the information to support the issuance of the search warrant were identified for the first time as John King and appellant's wife.

When the two guns were found it was discovered that the original scopes of the rifles were missing. One of the scopes was found on one of appellant's rifles. It was later revealed that the other scope had been traded by appellant at a sporting goods store.

At trial, appellant testified that in July of 1977 he was investigating the unsolved homicide of Chester Leggins when Bobby Hall reported the theft of the rifles to him. Several days after learning of the theft of the guns, appellant was picking up some hay they he kept for his horses at Junior Yocum's barn in Mound City. After removing several bales, appellant saw the stocks of two guns in the hay. He removed the hay covering the guns and found them to be an eight millimeter Mauser and a .22 caliber Weatherby semi-automatic. Appellant took the guns to his office at home where he hid the guns without telling anyone, even his wife, of his discovery. He testified that he considered returning the guns to the barn and staking out the area to see if anyone would come to pick them up. He said he examined and test-fired the guns in an attempt to determine whether the guns could have been used in the unsolved Chester Leggins homicide.

He stated that he never doubted that the two guns were the ones that Bobby Hall had reported as having been stolen. He explained the removal of the scopes from the rifles as an attempt to test the scopes at the homicide scene without anyone becoming aware that he had found the rifles and or that he had suspected Bobby Hall could have been involved in the homicide. He explained that he owned many rifles and scopes and that he inadvertently traded Hall's scope during one of his many gun collection trading transactions.

Appellant also testified that he and Sheriff Hayzlett had had problems in their police relations and that in the past the sheriff had taken credit for appellant's successful police work while giving appellant credit only for assisting the efforts. Because of this previous competition between the Mound City police and the Holt County sheriff, appellant said he did not report the recovery of the rifles to Sheriff Hayzlett. Appellant explained his denial to Deputy Patterson of having the guns as an angry reaction to what he felt was an insinuation that he had stolen the guns or an implication that he was under an obligation to tell the sheriff whatever information he had uncovered. Appellant said he reconsidered his position after his denial and called his wife over his citizen's band radio and told her where the guns were and instructed her to put them on the back porch. He said he had decided to take the guns to the sheriff. He could not explain why his wife threw the guns into the cistern. When appellant arrived at his home and found the sheriff, deputy sheriff, four Highway Patrol officers and the county prosecutor inside, he became angry that they were conducting the search in front of his children and he did not assist the officers in finding the guns.

On November 28, 1977, the Holt County prosecuting attorney filed an information charging that "on or about the 18th of July, 1977, in Holt County, Missouri, defendant Larry Dale Davis willfully, unlawfully and feloniously received one German Mauser rifle and one .22 caliber automatic rifle, each rifle having a scope attached and the rifles having a combined value of at least $50.00 and both rifles having been stolen from Robert Hall on or about the 11th day of July, 1977, the said Larry Dale Davis knowing at the time he received said property that the property had been stolen and the said Larry Dale Davis received the rifles with the intent to defraud Robert Hall of his lawful interest therein, in violation of V.A.M.S. § 560.270."

Accordingly, appellant was not charged with stealing the rifles on July 11th, but rather was charged with feloniously receiving them on July 18th, the day he said he found the rifles in a haystack at Junior Yocum's barn. As noted above, appellant was convicted of receiving stolen property under § 560.270, RSMo 1969 of the old criminal code.

OPINION

He [the defendant] also alleges error in the trial court's overruling his motion to quash the search warrant and the admitting into evidence of the items seized in the search.

The offense of receiving stolen property involves elements different from the offense of stealing: "a buying or receiving, from another, of property known to have been stolen, with intent to defraud." The first element has been stated variously as "the accused must receive the property in some way from another and not be the actual captor of the property" and "the property must be received in some way from another person." It is an essential element of receiving stolen property that there be at least two actors involved; the accused must receive the property from another, some person other than the owner.

In the case at bar, there is no claim that appellant stole the guns, nor evidence as to the identity of the thief, nor is there any evidence that appellant obtained the guns from another person. The only direct evidence as to appellant's coming into possession of the guns was his testimony that he recovered the guns from a haystack while acting in his official capacity as police chief of Mound City. The jury, of course, was not obligated to believe this explanation. However, the only other evidence about appellant's coming into possession of the guns is whatever follows from the facts that Mrs. Davis and her employer, King, told the deputy sheriff that they had seen two rifles at appellant's home and that when the house was searched the guns were found in the cistern, an unusual storage place. Even giving the state every legitimate inference favorable to the verdict, there is no evidence to account for the handling of the property from the time of its disappearance until it came into possession of appellant. Thus, there is no evidence of a thief or fence or anyone from whom appellant is alleged to have received the guns.

A conviction for receiving stolen property cannot stand where the evidence fails to show that defendant was the receiver rather than the taker of stolen property.

While an unexplained possession of recently stolen property can give rise to an inference that the possessor is the thief, possession of recently stolen property is no basis for an inference that the possessor received, rather than stole, the property.

The state has failed to make a case of receiving stolen property by neglecting to show that appellant received the stolen property from another with an intent to defraud.

Accordingly, the judgment must be reversed and the defendant discharged.

Under the new criminal code, the offense of receiving stolen property has been redefined and, unlike § 560.270, RSMo 1969, for which appellant was tried, now contemplates single-party transactions.

§ 560.270 was obviously intended to punish any "person who shall buy, or in any way receive any property that shall have been [previously] stolen from another." It is apparent that for there to be a "person who shall buy" previously stolen property, there must be a two-party transaction between a seller and a buyer. Likewise, in general context of the statute, any "person who shall in any way receive" from another person, denotes a two-party transfer of possession from a donor, giver, passer, etc., to a receiver, recipient, acceptor, etc. This problem appears to have been obviated by the enactment of § 570.080 RSMo 1978 (L.1977 S.B. 60, eff. 1–1–79) which provides: "1. A person commits the crime of receiving stolen property if for the purpose of depriving the owner of a lawful interest therein, he receives, retains or disposes of property of another knowing that it has been stolen, or believing that it has been stolen." The words "retains" and "disposes" can denote single-party transactions which the words in § 560.270 (now repealed) do not.

The judgment is reversed and defendant is ordered discharged.

Case Discussion The court ruled that under the old Missouri statute that governed *Davis*, receiving stolen property required two parties. In other words, Davis had to receive the property from someone, not just get it into his possession. Since the prosecution did not prove that he got the property directly from some other individual, the court overturned his conviction. Did Davis escape on a technicality? Do you think Missouri improved its receiving stolen property law when it revised it as quoted in the court's opinion? Was Davis guilty under the new statute? How serious do you think Davis's crime was if he was convicted under the new statute? What sentence would you give him if you were the judge?

▼ FORGERY AND UTTERING

Forgery includes making false legal documents or altering existing ones—such as checks, deeds, stocks, bonds, and credit cards; uttering means passing false documents on to others. Both misappropriate and destroy property. They harm not only the individuals directly involved but also society in general. Because day-to-day business in modern society relies on legal instruments for its smooth and efficient operation, impairing confidence in the authenticity of those instruments can lead to serious disruption in business, commercial, and financial transactions. It is this general harm, as much as individual losses, that forgery and uttering laws are designed to protect against.

Forgery

Elements of Forgery		
Actus Reus	*Mens Rea*	**Material Circumstances**
1. sign *2.* alter *3.* make	intent to defraud	documents of legal significance

The subject matter of **forgery** is false writing. Documents subject to forgery make up a long list, since the law defines fraudulent or false writings broadly. Many forgeries, such as forged checks, clearly and directly misappropriate property. These forgeries are obviously property offenses. Other forgeries are not so obviously harms to property. For example, a university might lose more reputation than property from forged diplomas. Injury to reputation and impairment of normal transactions make forgery more than a mere property offense.

California's approach to forgery is found in the California Penal Code, § 470.

> Every person who, with intent to defraud, signs the name of another person, or of a fictitious person, knowing that he has no authority so to do, to, or falsely makes, alters, forges, or counterfeits, any charter, letters patent, deed, lease, indenture, writing obligatory, will, testament, codicil, bond, covenant, bank bill or note, post note, check, draft, bill of exchange, contract, promissory note, due bill for the payment of money or property, receipt for money or property, passage ticket, trading stamp, power of attorney, or any certificate of any share, right, or interest in the stock of any corporation or association, or any controller's warrant for the payment of money at the treasury, county order or warrant, or request for the payment of money, or the delivery of goods or chattels of any kind, or for the delivery of any instrument of writing, or acquittance, release, or receipt for money or goods, or any acquittance, release, or discharge of any debt, account, suit, action, demand, or other thing, real or personal, or any transfer or assurance of money, certificates of shares of stock, goods, chattels, or other property whatever, or any letter of attorney, or other power to receive money, or to receive or transfer certificates of shares of stock or annuities, or to let, lease, dispose of, alien, or convey any goods, chattels, lands, or tenements, or other estate, real or personal, or

any acceptance or indorsement of any bill of exchange, promissory note, draft, order, or any assignment of any bond, writing obligatory, promissory note, or other contract for money or other property; or counterfeits or forges the seal or handwriting of another; or utters, publishes, passes, or attempts to pass, as true and genuine, any of the above named false, altered, forged, or counterfeited matters, as above specified and described, knowing the same to be false, altered, forged, or counterfeited, with intent to prejudice, damage, or defraud any person; or who, with intent to defraud, alters, corrupts, or falsifies any record of any will, codicil, conveyance, or other instrument, the record of which is by law evidence, or any record of any judgment of a court or the return of any officer to any process of any court, is guilty of forgery.[13]

California's is not the only approach to defining forgery. Other states do not list documents by name; instead, they use phrases such as "any writing," "any writing having legal efficacy or commonly relied on in business or commercial transactions," or "any written instrument to the prejudice of another's right." Either approach, however, indicates the legislatures' intention to cover written documents broadly.

The Model Penal Code drafters aimed the code's forgery provision against three harms when they wrote a sweeping forgery definition: the harms of direct property loss, damage to reputation, and impaired business and commercial confidence. Except in grading forgery, the code abandons a significant traditional requirement: that a forged document must have legal or evidentiary significance. Hence, it includes doctors' prescriptions, identification cards, diaries, and letters, not just deeds, wills, contracts, stocks, and bonds. Furthermore, documents are not the only subject matter of forgery. Coins, tokens, paintings, and antiques also fall within its scope. In fact, says the commentary to this provision, "Anything which could be falsified in respect of 'authenticity' can be the subject of forgery."[14]

Defenders of the Model Penal Code provision maintain that the grave harms caused by forgery and the difficulty in drawing meaningful distinctions between various forms of forgery justify the sweeping phrase, "any writing or object." Even critics admit that those who forge checks or fake antiques may respond more to deterrence and rehabilitation than do other criminals. There is no clear evidence that this is so, however, and some critics remain uneasy over all-encompassing forgery provisions.

Making a false document or altering an authentic one constitutes the forgery *actus reus*. Contrary to the Model Penal Code provision's apparent logic, most jurisdictions limit forgery to the making of false writings that have apparent legal significance. "Making" means making documents, in whole or in part, or altering an authentic document in any material part. Hence, if I make out and sign a check on someone else's account or a nonexistent account, with no intent to back the check myself, I have forged it because I falsified the whole check. Most existing forgery laws require that either the whole document or some material part be falsified.

Merely presenting false information on an otherwise authentic document is not forgery. Hence, if I only change the amount on a check made out and signed by the checking account's owner, I have not committed forgery because the check itself is valid. Similarly, if a properly authorized payroll clerk alters payrolls by adding hours, it is not forgery because the payroll is still valid. However, both myself and the payroll clerk may have obtained property under false pretenses. Furthermore, checks drawn on insufficient funds are not forgeries for two reasons. First, they are not false; second, unless the intention to back the checks is missing, they do not have the requisite forgery *mens rea.*

Forgery is a specific intent crime. It requires the forger to falsely write, intending to defraud others with the writing. It is not necessary to intend to defraud specific individuals; a general purpose to fraudulently use the falsified document suffices. Furthermore, forgery does not require the falsifier to intend to obtain money fraudulently. Intending to secure any advantage will do. Hence, a letter of recommendation intended to gain membership in a desirable professional organization satisfies the forgery *mens rea.*

Once documents are falsified or altered with proper fraudulent intent, forgery is complete. Forgers need not actually gain from their falsifications and fraudulent intent. The reason is that the harm of forgery lies in undermining confidence in the authenticity of documents and the consequent disruption created by such undermined confidence.

Uttering

Elements of Uttering		
Actus Reus	*Mens Rea*	**Material Circumstances**
passing	knowingly	false document

Uttering does not require making false writings or materially altering authentic ones. Rather, it means knowingly or consciously passing or using forged documents with the specific intent to defraud. Forgery means the making of false documents in order to defraud, even if the forger never defrauds anyone. Uttering, on the other hand, means passing or using documents that someone else may have falsified—even if the utterer never altered anything on the documents—and intending to defraud others with those instruments. Forgery and uttering are thus two distinct offenses. Forgery is directed at making and altering documents in order to defraud. Uttering is directed at passing and using forged documents in order to defraud.

▼ ROBBERY AND EXTORTION

Robbery and extortion are more than property crimes; they are also crimes against persons, and as such they constitute aggravated property crimes. In fact, they are violent or threatened-violent thefts. Hence, they are more serious than ordinary thefts and usually carry much heavier penalties.

Robbery

Elements of Robbery		
Actus Reus	***Mens Rea***	**Material Circumstances**
1. force or threat of immediate or imminent use of force *2.* taking *3.* carrying away	intent to permanently deprive owner of possession	*1.* another's property *2.* from person *3.* weapon *4.* injury

The principal elements of **robbery** include (1) taking and (2) carrying away (3) others' (4) property (5) from their person or in their presence (6) by immediate force or threatened immediate force (7) with the intent to permanently dispossess the rightful possessor. Hence, robbery is essentially forcible larceny from the person—an aggravated larceny because actual threatened physical harm accompanies the misappropriation of property.

Any force beyond that needed to take and carry away property satisfies the force requirement. Picking a pocket is ordinary, although aggravated, larceny and not robbery because picking pockets requires only enough force to remove the pocket's contents. But even a slight mishandling of the victim (such as shoving) makes the crime robbery, if the mishandling secures the property. Determining just how much force satisfies the requirement is a problem in robbery, because the amount of force distinguishes between robbery and the less serious larcenies from the person, of which picking pockets is most common.

Some jurisdictions require no force. Under the Arkansas Criminal Code, for example, robbery is committed "if with the purpose of committing a theft or resisting apprehension immediately thereafter ... [the criminal] employs or threatens to immediately employ physical force upon another." Under that statute, a defendant who stole a roast in a grocery store and, when caught just beyond the checkout stand, injured the apprehending officer, was found guilty of robbery, not larceny.[15]

Robbery does not require actual force; threatened force ordinarily suffices. In addition, robbers need not threaten victims themselves; threats to family members qualify as well. However, robbers must threaten to kill, or at least to do great bodily injury. Threats to property, except perhaps to a dwelling house, do not satisfy the threatened force requirement.

Most jurisdictions require that robbers threaten to use force immediately, not at some time in the future. Furthermore, victims must relinquish their property because they honestly and reasonably fear robbers' threats. Critics maintain that honest fear ought to suffice. Whether robbery requires real, honest, or reasonable fear (or a combination) bears directly on the extent to which criminal law ought to punish potential harm.

CASE

*Is Purse Snatching
Robbery?*

Commonwealth v. Jones
362 Mass. 83, 283 N.E.2d 840 (1972)

*[Jones was convicted of unarmed robbery. He
appealed. Chief Justice Tavro delivered the
opinion.]*

FACTS
On the evening of December 14, 1970, at
approximately 6:30 p.m., Mrs. Florence
Spring and her daughter, Miss Madeline
Spring, left their apartment in Dorchester to
go shopping by automobile. Each lady was
carrying a pocketbook. Florence Spring
opened both front and rear doors on the
passenger's side in search of a snow scraper
with which to remove snow from the car.
She was unable to find it. Madeline Spring
then knelt down on the front seat with feet
extended outside the car and, leaning across
the seat, she felt with her hand on the floor
for the scraper. Meanwhile, Florence Spring
opened the trunk of the car, took out a
stick, and started to clean the rear window
from the driver's side.

Madeline Spring testified that, while feeling along the floor of the front seat, she
realized she "couldn't move [her] foot," "[f]or
a minute" she was "stunned," but that then
she turned back and saw "a black face with
eyes" in the window and she "knew somebody was holding the door on [her] foot."
Miss Spring stated that she became "petrified" and screamed; that she looked up and
put her hand on the horn; and that while in
this position, she observed a "shadow [go]
by the driver's side towards the back of the
car." The door was then released and she
got out of the car. In answer to the question,
"At that time, did you observe your pocketbook?" she indicated, "No."

Mrs. Spring testified that she saw a young
man on the passenger's side by the head-
light; that this young man started across the
street but turned and approached her; and
that he "grabbed [her] pocketbook." She indicated that the pocketbook was on her arm at
the time. She described the taking as follows:
"I really couldn't tell you what he did. All I
knew he was standing there. Next thing I
knew, I felt something off my arm. I realized
my bag was gone." In answer to the question, "[H]ow did you feel?" Mrs. Spring said:
"Petrified. I was scared to death." She also
testified that, after the pocketbook was taken,
"I said it belonged to me, and I wanted it,
and he started towards the sidewalk and I
started after him with the stick in my hand."

OPINION
We begin with a general discussion of the
elements which distinguish robbery from
larceny. Under our statutes, as at common
law, in order to sustain a charge of robbery,
there must be proof of a larceny (1) "from
[the] person," and (2) "by force and violence, or by assault and putting in fear." In
other words, although it carries a separate
label, "robbery is but an aggravated form of
larceny."

The common law came to regard robbery
as a more serious offence than larceny
because of the added element of personal
violence or intimidation. The exertion of
force, actual or constructive, remains the
principal distinguishing characteristic of the
offence. Because the requirement is stated
in the disjunctive, if there is actual force,
there need be no fear (constructive force),
and vice versa. Whether actual or constructive force is employed, the degree of force is
immaterial so long as it is sufficient to obtain
the victim's property "against his will."
Similarly, in every case there must be a
causal connection between the defendant's
use of violence or intimidation and his
acquisition of the victim's property.

The element of "from the person" is the
other distinctive aspect of robbery. Although
some statutory definitions of the offence,
including our own, speak of a taking "from
[the] person" without adding "or in his presence," a larceny in the presence of the victim
is sufficient to constitute robbery. "[The

phrase 'or in his presence'] adds nothing other than emphasis because, as pointed out by Coke, where deprivation is accomplished by violence or intimidation, 'that which is taken in his presence is in law taken from his person.'" Perkins, Criminal Law (2d ed.) 282, quoting 3 Co. Inst. 69. An object is deemed to be within the presence of the victim if it is within his area of control.

The question whether the snatching or sudden taking of property constitutes robbery has arisen in other jurisdictions although not in Massachusetts. Cf. *Commonwealth v. Ordway,* 12 Cush. 270. In Kentucky, the rule is that snatching, without more, involves the requisite element of force to permit a jury verdict on a charge of robbery. See *Jones v. Commonwealth,* 112 Ky. 689, 692–695, 66 S.W. 633; *Brown v. Commonwealth,* 135 Ky. 635, 640, 117 S.W. 281. According to the rule prevailing in most jurisdictions, however, snatching does not involve sufficient force to constitute robbery, unless the victim resists the taking or sustains physical injury, or unless the article taken is so attached to the victim's clothing as to afford resistance.

We prefer the Kentucky rule on purse snatching. The majority jurisdiction rule, in looking to whether or not the victim resists, we think, wrongly emphasizes the victim's opportunity to defend himself over the willingness of the purse snatcher to use violence if necessary. See Note, 23 J.Cr.Law, 111, 115. Historically, however, the law has singled out the robber from other thieves because of his readiness to inflict bodily injury upon his victims.

In a snatching or sudden taking, so long as the victim is aware of the application of force which relieves him of his property, the crime is, at least to some degree, "against [the victim's] will." Clearly, more is involved than in a mere stealthy taking where the victim has no present realization of the theft. In the circumstances of a purse snatching, we believe the force applied is sufficient to make the crime a robbery, even though the application of force may, in practice, be so quick as to deny the victim any opportunity to resist.

We consider first the indictment arising from the taking of Florence Spring's pocketbook. Snatching necessarily involves the exercise of some actual force. For the reasons stated, supra, we hold that, where, as here, the actual force used is sufficient to produce awareness, although the action may be so swift as to leave the victim momentarily in a dazed condition, the requisite degree of force is present to make the crime robbery. In any event, Mrs. Spring testified that she was "[p]etrified." And also: "I was scared to death." Whether her fear aided the defendant in effecting the taking, or merely arose afterwards as the defendant argues, was a question properly for the determination of the jury. There is no reason for upsetting their factual determination.

Although no testimony was offered as to the precise location of Miss Spring's pocketbook at the moment of the taking, we think the evidence presented was ample to permit an inference that the pocketbook was inside the car with the victim when taken. It was not necessary that the Commonwealth show that she was physically in possession. The closing of the car door on Miss Spring's foot was sufficient evidence, coupled with the disappearance of her purse at approximately the same time, to allow the jury to infer the requisite causal relationship between the force and the taking.

Affirmed.

Case Discussion　The court admits that most jurisdictions do not call purse snatching robbery. Why does Massachusetts adopt the minority view that it is? Do you agree with the reasoning? Did Jones use force or threatened force to rob Miss Spring and Mrs. Spring? Were the women "reasonably" frightened that Jones might kill or seriously injure them? Do you think robbery ought to require honest, reasonable belief?

Degrees of Robbery

Most states have divided robbery into degrees according to injury done and force or threat used. New York, for example, grades robbery into three degrees. Robbers commit first-degree robbery if they carry deadly weapons, seriously injure victims, threaten the immediate use of dangerous instruments, or display what "appears to be a pistol, revolver, shotgun, machine gun or other firearm." In other words, play weapons suffice. Second-degree robbery occurs if robbers rob with accomplices, cause any injury, or display "what appears to be a pistol, revolver, rifle, shotgun, machine gun or firearm." Third-degree robbery is unarmed robbery or "forcible stealing"; that is, it occurs when the actor "uses or threatens the immediate use of force upon another person."[16]

Extortion

Elements of Extortion		
Actus Reus	**Mens Rea**	**Material Circumstances**
threats of future harm to person, property, or reputation	intent to permanently deprive owner of possession by threat	another's property

At common law, extortion applied only to public officials who used their influence illegally to collect fees. Most modern extortions were not known at common law, although unusually extreme threats to gain property (such as a threat to accuse another of sodomy) were considered robbery. Statutory extortion, or blackmail, resembles robbery in that it involves forcibly misappropriating property. It is distinguished from robbery by time. Generally, robbery is a threat to harm someone immediately. **Extortion,** on the other hand, involves threats to do future harm. The line between extortion and robbery is often very fine, making it difficult to distinguish between the two offenses.

Threats sufficient to constitute extortion include those (1) to inflict bodily harm in the future (remember that robbery requires an immediate threat), (2) to do damage to property, and (3) to expose victims to shame or ridicule. Extortion requires the specific intent to obtain property by threats such as those just described. Some jurisdictions require that actors actually acquire the desired property to complete extortion. Others call it extortion if actors make threats with a present intention to carry them out. In these jurisdictions, victims must actually be put in fear. Under this definition, extortion is an inchoate offense. It is a completed crime against persons, however, since fear completes the harm.

CASE

Did He Extort the Mopeds?

State v. Barber

93 N.M. 782, 606 P.2d 192 (1979)

[*Barber was convicted of extortion. He appealed. Judge Andrews delivered the opinion.*]

FACTS

On October 17, 1977, the victim, William Harris, entered into a lease with the defendant, Dan O. Barber, for the rental of commercial space in an Albuquerque shopping center. Harris began his business, selling mopeds, during the first week of November, and, although he remained "current" in his monthly rental payments, by the following summer he recognized that the moped business was not doing well. Harris then decided to move to a different location which offered more favorable rental terms. The defendant first learned of the victim's intended move while on a trip out of town and when he returned to work several days later he summoned Harris to his office for a meeting.

When Harris entered the office, the defendant asked him to sit down in a "peaceful" tone of voice, but the defendant quickly became agitated and accused Harris of skipping out on the lease and cheating the defendant out of the rent. Harris protested but the defendant called the explanation a lie. Without any provocation, the defendant struck the victim on the right side of the forehead causing him to fall and sustain lacerations on the back of the head and on the chin. The victim fell within the opening of a nearby credenza and, when he attempted to crawl to the other side, he was crudely ordered to return to his chair by the defendant. He complied with this order, resumed his seat, felt the lump on his head and asked to be taken to the hospital. The defendant replied, "you are not going anywhere until you sign this piece of paper. You are going to sell me five mopeds."

The piece of paper referred to was a previously prepared agreement which released the victim from his rental obligation totalling $1,735, in exchange for five mopeds, with an approximate wholesale value of $2,000. Harris and Barber discussed the agreement and Harris again requested that he be taken or be allowed to leave to drive to the hospital. The defendant then stated, "sit down, you are going to be alright—I'll be right back." The defendant then left the room and returned shortly with an ice pack and several paper towels for the victim's injuries. During the defendant's absence, the victim stated that he was too scared to leave, and when the defendant returned he became very red in the face, very angry. He started "screaming," "yelling" and "ranting," and when Harris thought he would be hit again, he signed the agreement. Barber dictated a release which purported to absolve him of all liability for injuries resulting from the battery which Harris wrote out and signed. The defendant then ordered Harris to unlock his store and the defendant removed the five mopeds.

OPINION

The defendant claims that the evidence (1) fails to show that a threat was made to induce the release of the mopeds; (2) fails to show that the victim consented to the transfer; and (3) fails to establish that Barber made an oral or written threat, the evidence showing only that he made threatening actions. A review of the facts recited above establishes that Harris signed the agreement to sell the mopeds under the threat of further physical injury. Mr. Harris testified:

> I started to say let's talk about this (the agreement). He became very red in the face, very angry, he started screaming, yelling and was ranting. I had no idea what he was really saying. He was very close to me, grabbed my lapel and I thought he was going to hit me again. At that point, I said, I'll sign anything, I'll sign. I'll sign anything you want.

There was substantial evidence of threat to injure.

Next, the defendant contends that the consent of the victim is the element which distinguishes extortion from the crime of robbery. Further, the defendant states that the consent of the victim was lacking in this case. The focus is on Mr. Harris' testimony during cross-examination.

Q: Mr. Harris, did you turn over the mopeds willingly?

A: No, I did not.

Q: Did you consent to Mr. Barber's taking the mopeds?

A: No, I did not consent to it.

It seems clear that the language of the New Mexico extortion statute does not require a showing of a "consented to taking." Compare *People v. Peck,* 185 P. 881 (1917)—interpreting a statute defining extortion to be "the obtaining of property from another, with his consent, induced by a wrongful use of force or fear." The difference between the statute in *People v. Peck,* supra, and the New Mexico statute is obvious. § 30–16–9, supra, does not require the victim's consent.

Finally, defendant asserts that the threat which gives rise to the extortion may be either written or oral but that there is "no authority that the threat may be by actions." The defendant concludes that when the threat is made by actions, the crime committed is robbery, not extortion.

This argument, which focuses on the type of threat to distinguish robbery vis-a-vis extortion, is unpersuasive. The short answer is that the New Mexico extortion statute is not so limited as he suggests. The statute embraces "communication or transmission of any threat to another by any means whatsoever." § 30–16–9, supra. This broad language includes both written and oral threats and also includes actions constituting threats. The type of threat made is not determinative of the crime committed. Extortion can be committed where the threat is by action.

As we have shown, defendant's arguments concerning the distinction between robbery and extortion have disregarded the statutory language in New Mexico. Robbery, as defined in § 30–16–2, N.M.S.A.1978, is an aggravated form of larceny. Robbery requires a taking. N.M.U.J.I.Crim. 16.10, N.M.S.A.1978. Extortion, as defined in § 30–16–9, supra, does not require a taking, but requires a "threat with intent thereby to wrongfully obtain anything of value or to wrongfully compel the person threatened to do or refrain from doing any act against his will." Defendant need not have actually taken the mopeds to have committed extortion. The victim need not have signed the agreement for defendant to have committed extortion. These items are evidence of defendant's intent to wrongfully obtain a thing of value; in themselves, they were not elements of the crime of extortion in New Mexico. The extortion was a completed crime when defendant's threat was communicated to the victim with the requisite statutory intent.

Affirmed.

Case Discussion   The court calls this extortion, not robbery. Do you agree that Barber threatened Harris with "future harm" in order to obtain the mopeds? Do you consider Barber's crime more or less serious than robbery? Was Harris reasonably put in fear that Barber would hurt him? The court rejects Barber's argument that consent distinguishes extortion from robbery. Does Barber have a point? Would you require consent in extortion? Why or why not? Does New Mexico regard extortion as a property offense? An offense against persons? Both?

▼ *Summary* ▼

Property misappropriation crimes originated in the ancient felony of larceny, which protected against wrongfully taking other people's possessions. Separate offenses were created primarily to keep pace with society's increasing complexity, which presented new ways to misappropriate property. Over time, the law changed piecemeal to keep pace with social and economic realities. Embezzlement protected against the wrongful conversion of property; false pretenses against deceitful misappropriations; receiving stolen property against aiding in stolen goods traffic; forgery and uttering against creating, altering, and passing false documents; and extortion against acquiring property by threatening harm in the future. These crimes responded to new ways to misappropriate property, as well as to the expanding list of larcenable items. Their creation testifies to the way criminal misappropriation law developed over the past four hundred years. History, not logic, explains the distinctions between various misappropriation offenses.

In the past twenty years, consolidated theft statutes have made criminal property misappropriation more rational. They join together what used to be larceny, embezzlement, and false pretenses into a new offense called theft. They are based on the idea that whether culprits take, convert, or use deception to acquire other people's property, misappropriation is still the core evil that the separate statutes aim to combat. Some even more ambitious statutes cover all misappropriations except robbery, using the same logic that misappropriation is the core evil behind taking, converting, deceiving, receiving, forging, uttering, and extorting. Only robbery, a crime involving imminent physical harm, stands apart.

Although larceny, embezzlement, false pretenses, and receiving stolen property protect property almost exclusively, forgery, uttering, extortion, and robbery protect other interests as well. Forgery and uttering are also aimed at protecting society in general from the disruptive effects created by impairing confidence in the authenticity of documents. Therefore, they protect not only property but also society's interest in smoothly operating business in modern, complex society. Robbery and extortion are crimes against persons as well as property, because they involve violence or threatened violence. Sometimes called aggravated larceny, their laws punish violent property misappropriations. By punishing when victims suffer fear but sustain no property loss, they demonstrate a wider application than for misappropriated property offenses.

▼ *Questions for Review and Discussion* ▼

1. What are the differences between larceny, embezzlement, and false pretenses? Should these offenses be grouped as one crime?

2. Why should receiving stolen property be a crime? Is it more serious than, equally as serious as, or less serious than theft?

3. What is the purpose of the law of forgery? Is forgery a more serious crime than theft? Why? Why not?

4. What interest does uttering protect?

5. Why are robbery and extortion aggravated misappropriations? Are they crimes against property or persons? What is the most important interest they protect?

▼ Suggested Readings ▼

1. Jerome Hall, *Theft, Law, and Society,* 2d ed. (Indianapolis: Bobbs-Merrill, 1952). An excellent demonstration of the relationship between law and society in historical development. Professor Hall convincingly shows that larceny and other misappropriation crimes grew out of English social history. This is an interesting and authoritative work written for the general reader as well as for specialists.

2. Rollin M. Perkins and Ronald N. Boyce, *Criminal Law,* 3d ed. (Mineola, N.Y.: Foundation Press, 1982), chap. 4. Surveys in detail all the property crimes, analyzes their development, discusses new developments, and presents arguments concerning most reforms.

3. Wayne R. LaFave and Austin W. Scott, Jr., *Handbook on Criminal Law,* 2d ed. (St. Paul: West Publishing Co., 1986). This book has a useful chapter on property crimes that is not quite as current as the Perkins and Boyce reading.

4. American Law Institute, *Model Penal Code and Commentaries,* vol. 2 (Philadelphia: American Law Institute, 1980), pt. II. Deals with the property crimes. This is the most comprehensive treatment of the history, contents, and recent reforms of property crimes. The commentary treats extensively its recommended consolidated theft provision, compares that provision with the state consolidated theft statutes, and discusses the influence of the Model Penal Code provision on those statutes.

▼ Notes ▼

1. Rollin M. Perkins and Ronald N. Boyce, *Criminal Law,* 3d ed. (Mineola, N.Y.: Foundation Press, 1982), chap. 4; Wayne R. LaFave and Austin W. Scott, Jr., *Handbook on Criminal Law,* 2d ed. (St. Paul: West Publishing Co., 1986), chap. 8.

2. Perkins and Boyce, *Criminal Law,* p. 289.

3. Jerome Hall, *Theft, Law, and Society,* 2d ed. (Indianapolis: Bobbs-Merrill, 1952).

4. Texas Penal Code, §§ 31.01, 31.02, 31.03. 7th ed. (St. Paul: West Publishing Co., 1988).

5. California Penal Code, tit. 13 (Added by Stats. 1979, c. 858, p. 2968, § 1. Amended by Stats. 1981, c. 837, p. 3225, § 1; Stats. 1983, c. 1092, p.——, § 292, urgency, eff. Sept. 27, 1983, operative Jan. 1, 1984; Stats. 1984, c. 949, p.——, § 2; Stats. 1985, c. 571, p.——, § 1.)

6. *California, West's Ann. Penal Code,* § 487. 1988 Compact Edition (St. Paul: West Publishing Co., 1989).

7. American Law Institute, *Model Penal Code and Commentaries,* vol. 2 (Philadelphia: American Law Institute, 1980), pt. II, 175–76.

8. Ibid., p. 151.

9. 30 Geo. II c. 24.

10. *Model Penal Code,* Arts. 223.0 to 223.9.

11. Quoted in *People v. Shirley,* 144 Cal.Rptr. 282, 289.

12. Ibid.

13. California Penal Code (1970), enacted 1872, amended by Stats. 1905, c. 515, 673, 1; Stats. 1968, c. 713, 1414, 1.

14. American Law Institute, *Model Penal Code,* tentative draft no. 11 (Philadelphia: American Law Institute, 1960).

15. Arkansas Crim.Code 41–2103 (1977); *Wilson v. State,* 262 Ark. 339, 556 S.W.2d 657 (1977).

16. *New York Penal Code,* §§ 160.00–160.15.

Crimes against Public Order and Morals

▼ *Chapter Outline* ▼

I. Introduction

II. Crimes against Public Order
  A. Driving While Intoxicated
  B. Nuisance
  C. Coarse and Indecent Language
  D. Fighting Words
  E. Threats
  F. Group Disorderly Conduct
  G. Hate Crimes
  H. Crimes of Condition

III. Public Morals Offenses
  A. Fornication and Illicit Cohabitation
  B. Prostitution
  C. Solicitation and Promotion of Prostitution
  D. Sodomy and Related Offenses

IV. Summary

▼ *Chapter Main Points* ▼

1. Crimes against public order offend society generally and often do not have individual victims.

2. Crimes against public order are punished less severely than felonies, but far more people commit them.

3. Balancing individual liberty and social order is a major challenge in public order crimes.

4. Public order offenses frequently raise constitutional questions related to due process of law, privacy, free speech, and assembly.

5. Disorderly conduct covers a broad spectrum from pubic brawling to obscene phone calls.

6. Driving while intoxicated threatens public order and safety even if it harms no specific victim.

7. The First Amendment does not protect fighting words, obscenity, or scatology.

8. Suspicious loitering and aggressive panhandling laws have replaced vagrancy, an old crime of status.

9. Objections to public order offenses are made on three levels: constitutional, principles of criminal law, and criminal policy.

10. Public morals offenses mainly involve private adult consensual sexual conduct.

11. The public morals offenses particularly prostitution and sodomy between consenting adults in private, have generated heated debate over values.

▼ *Chapter Key Terms* ▼

bias-motivated crimes—Crimes committed because of race, gender, ethnic, or religious prejudice.

due process—Constitutional protection against vague and overbroad laws.

fighting words—Words that provoke or threaten to provoke immediate violence or disorder.

hate crimes—Crimes motivated by race, gender, ethnic background, or religious prejudice.

void for overbreadth—The principle that law violates due process if it unreasonably restricts constitutional rights.

void for vagueness—The principle that law violates due process if not clearly defined.

▼ INTRODUCTION

Nothing more clearly demonstrates the breadth of American criminal law than the vast array of conduct, and until recently, conditions, that fall within the scope of crimes against public order and morals. Failing to return overdue books, parking too many vehicles in front of your house, parking a pickup truck in your own driveway, hanging clothes outside to dry, allowing your grass to grow too long, painting your house an "ugly" color—all these and more have found their way into state statutes and city ordinances. One police officer said there ought to be a billboard at his city's limits that reads: "Welcome to Bloomington, you're under arrest." Why? Because, he said, "Everything in Bloomington is a crime."

Unlike those who commit crimes against persons, habitation, and property, offenders against public order direct their conduct at no specific individual in most instances. In offenses against public morals, offenders do not intend to harm their "victims," and their victims willingly engage in the conduct with the offenders. Some people call these victimless crimes. Public order and morals offenses harm, or threaten to harm, society as a whole; we sometimes hear this idea phrased as "society is the victim." Of course, crimes against public order and morals may also harm particular individuals incidentally, but their essence lies in the harms and threats they pose to society generally.

Crimes against persons, homes, and property, to be sure, also harm society generally. In crimes that harm particular individuals—homicide, rape, assault, robbery, burglary, arson, and theft—the general harm to society rarely receives attention. This does not mean such crimes do not cause harm to society as a whole. Quite the contrary. Homicides, rapes, and other violent crimes produce personal insecurity that definitely injures society. Similarly, burglary and arson erode the confidence in homes as safe havens from intruders. Theft and other property crimes create anger and frustration in the fear of losing hard-earned money. Forgery not only harms the individuals who lose something of value but also injures society as a whole by undermining confidence in the authenticity of documents. All these crimes erode the basic mutual trust required to make modern, complex society function. These general harms to society, subordinated in serious felonies, take precedence in crimes against public order and morals.

Not everyone agrees that public order and morals offenses harm society as a whole, or if they do, that they warrant expending scarce public resources to bring the criminal law to bear on them. Critics say that only harms to specific individuals, not these "victimless crimes," deserve the attention of criminal law. Nevertheless, including public order and morals offenses in criminal law enjoys a long tradition. In fact, far more people face criminal prosecution for these crimes than for all the serious crimes receiving the most attention.[1]

Public order and morals offenses range across a wide spectrum of behavior. So pervasive is the conduct these offenses cover that they make "criminals of us all." The offenses against public order and morals not only affect more people than the crimes against specific individuals, their homes, and property, but they also raise constitutional questions. They define the permissible limits that, in the interests of public order and decency, government can place on individual rights of free speech, assembly, movement, and privacy. Their broad reach, the large numbers of otherwise law-abiding individuals they define as criminals, and the limits they place on individual freedom from government interference justify their study.[2]

Public order and morals offenses have never received systematic attention by courts, legislatures, or even scholars for that matter, due probably to the relatively mild penalties prescribed for these offenses—mainly fines and ten- to ninety-day jail terms—and to the type of people usually prosecuted for them—the poor, the young, the minorities, and dissidents on the "fringes" of respectable society. Trials are rare, convictions frequent, and appeals virtually nonexistent. Because public order and morals offenders are not politically powerful, demands for reform and even claims for attention go largely ignored.[3]

The need to reform public order and morals law is, however, great. The law defines the offenses vaguely. Disorderly conduct embraces everything from fighting to wearing masks, from bodily movements to spoken words, from actual injury to threatened injury. Because disorderly conduct is defined in all cases broadly, law enforcement officers retain the discretion to interpret informally its meaning in day-to-day practice. The public order and morals offenses also grant judges the discretion to order probation, fines, and/or jail terms for public order and morals offenders. Existing public order and morals offenses also curtail the rights to assemble, to travel about freely, and to openly express diversity that "respectable society" finds unacceptable. The public order and morals offenses raise the question: To what extent ought criminal law curtail individual freedom and spend scarce public resources in order to control and punish conduct that merely bothers or offends (or threatens to offend) "respectable" people's sensibilities as opposed to conduct that definitely injures persons, their homes, and their property?[4]

▼ CRIMES AGAINST PUBLIC ORDER

The common law, probably all law, has from its beginnings prohibited and punished conduct that either actually disturbed or threatened to disturb community tranquility. Disorderly conduct statutes, in force in every state and municipality, resemble to a surprising extent the common-law misdemeanor breach of peace. New York, California, and several other states, for example, make it a misdemeanor to willfully and wrongfully commit any act that seriously disturbs or endangers the public peace or health. Under these statutes, not only disturbing the peace but also endangering it is a crime. Thus, a man who solicited two young girls to commit sodomy was convicted under a New York statute because the court held that such an act threatened to disturb the public peace. Under a similar Kentucky statute, a man was convicted for calling another a "son of a bitch" because his act tended to provoke a breach of the peace. In these jurisdictions, disorderly conduct encompasses both actual and potential breaches of public tranquility. It is, to that extent, an inchoate offense. Some modern legislation removes potential harms from coverage, including only conduct that itself disturbs the peace (see chapter 5 on inchoate offenses).[5]

Driving While Intoxicated

Disorderly conduct covers a wide spectrum, from behavior that threatens serious physical danger to the community to minor nuisances that merely "bother" people. Brawling in public and other violent behavior create few problems either of interpretation or of obtaining broad support for including them within the scope of criminal law. Other forms of disorderly conduct create difficult definition problems. Drunk drivers kill and seriously injure thousands of individual victims (see chapter 8, vehicular homicide). Drunk drivers threaten public tranquillity even if they kill or injure no one.

The offense of driving while intoxicated is intended both to prevent injury and death, and to maintain public order and safety on the roads. Driving while intoxicated requires no *mens rea;* it is a strict liability offense. The three cases that follow deal with three common problems in the *actus reus* of driving while intoxicated: What does "driving" for purposes of the statute mean? What does "intoxicated" mean? And, how does driving while intoxicated relate to the kindred disorderly offense of being drunk in public?

CASE

Was He "Driving" or "in Control?"

State v. Block
798 S.W.2d 213 (Mo.1990)

Fenner, Judge

FACTS

On May 13, 1989, Mrs. Carol Meinders saw a vehicle on the side of the road west of her house. It was a little yellow car, but she did not know who owned or drove the car. Her husband called the Sheriff's Office or Highway Patrol, but Mrs. Meinders did not know what time it was. An officer did respond to the call, but Mrs. Meinders did not speak to the officer. Trooper James Elder with the Missouri Highway Patrol responded to the call. He had received a radio report of a car partially in the ditch in Watson, Missouri. When Trooper Elder arrived at the scene in Watson, it was about 2:00 p.m., twenty minutes after being notified. He found a small gray car completely off the roadway partially in a ditch. Block was sitting asleep behind the wheel of the car. Trooper Elder observed that the keys were in the console of the car, the vehicle was motionless and the engine was not running.

When Trooper Elder opened the car door he could smell intoxicants in the car. Block's face was somewhat flushed, his clothes were mussed and he was somewhat lethargic, his speech was slurred, his response to questions was slow and he seemed not to comprehend what Trooper Elder asked of him. Trooper Elder administered a field sobriety test which Block failed. After forming the opinion that Block was intoxicated, Trooper Elder placed him under arrest and transported him to the Sheriff's office where he was requested to submit to a breathalyzer test. Although Block consented to the breathalyzer test, he failed to blow an adequate air sample into the machine after being instructed to do so.

OPINION

… Block takes issue with this conviction alleging there was not substantial evidence to support said conviction because there was no evidence the automobile was running; there was no evidence of extra-judicial admissions by himself that he had been drinking or driving the automobile; and there was no evidence as to what time the claimed violation occurred. This court … must agree.

The applicable statutory provision [is] § 577.001, RSMo 1986, which provides, in pertinent part, as follows:

> *1.* As used in this chapter, the term "drive," "driving," "operates" or "operating" means physically driving or operating or being in actual physical control of a motor vehicle.

What constitutes "actual physical control" has been, many times, the subject of interpretation by the courts of this state. Actual

physical control was construed in *Taylor v. McNeill,* 714 S.W.2d 947, 948 (Mo.App.1986), as follows:

> existing or present bodily restraint, directing influence, domination or regulation of a vehicle and it exists even where the vehicle is motionless as long as the person is keeping the vehicle in restraint or is in a position to regulate its movements and the automobile is running. Furthermore, a finding of actual physical control is not defeated by the fact the driver is asleep.

A major factor is missing from the present situation. Here there exists no proof that the car had been running. Although the courts of this state have been called upon to determine what constitute actual physical control under similar factual scenarios as that presented herein, i.e., where the car is motionless, none have done away with the requirement that the car be running.

Independent research reveals only one Missouri case which affirmed a conviction for driving while intoxicated where a defendant was found asleep inside his car which was motionless and not running. *State v. Hoeber,* 737 S.W.2d 484 (Mo.App.1987). However, in *Hoeber,* there was significant additional evidence to support the conviction, namely that the engine compartment was warm as verified by the arresting officer, the keys to the vehicle were in the ignition, and the brake lights were on. Id. at 485. Additionally, in *Hoeber,* there was evidence that the defendant's vehicle was on the parking lot of a grocery store for no more than forty minutes and the defendant admitted he had been driving. Id. at 486.

In the present situation, there is no indication how long Block's car had been off the roadway, the engine was not running, the keys were not in the ignition and Block did not testify he had been driving. The evidence simply failed to prove up the State's case and for that reason Block's conviction for driving while intoxicated on May 13, 1989, must be reversed. Based on the foregoing, Block's judgments of conviction are hereby reversed.

DISSENT

Lowenstein, Presiding Judge, dissenting.

I respectfully dissent on the disposition of Count I. The evidence and inferences are viewed in a light most favorable to the state. *State v. Spain,* 759 S.W.2d 871, 875 (Mo.App.1988). The state may rely on sufficient circumstantial evidence to establish an element of an offense. *State v. Helm,* 755 S.W.2d 256, 259 (Mo.App.1988).

That Meinders noticed a strong odor of alcohol on Block as he sat in his vehicle just after his arrival in her back yard creates a reasonable inference, coupled with his later state of intoxication, to submit his intoxication at the time of the accident to the fact finder. That Ms. Meinders did not give an incourt opinion of intoxication is not a fatal flaw—there was ample circumstantial evidence and inferences therefrom to support a conviction. *State v. Spain.* See also *State v. Williams,* 752 S.W.2d 454 (Mo.App.1988).

This case differs from *State v. Liebhart,* 707 S.W.2d 427, 429 (Mo.App.1986), for in *Liebhart,* there was no evidence as to the time of the accident. *Domsch v. Director of Revenue,* 767 S.W.2d 121 (Mo.App.1989), does not control since the issue there was probable cause: whether the accident witness had imparted information as to the defendant's intoxication to the investigating officer who subsequently arrested the defendant for an alcohol offense. The defendant should not benefit from his leaving the scene, failure to answer his door and the trooper's taking time to obtain a warrant. I would affirm the conviction as to Count I and concur with Judge Fenner as to Count II.

CASE

Was He "Intoxicated?"

Henriott v. State

562 N.E.2d 1325 (Ind.1990)

Baker, Judge

Defendant-appellant, Larry N. Henriott (Henriott), appeals the trial court's denial of his motion to correct error which he filed following his jury convictions for DRIVING while INTOXICATED, a Class A MISDEMEANOR, and public intoxication, a Class B MISDEMEANOR. He presents three issues for our review which are:

I. Whether there was sufficient evidence to support his conviction for driving while intoxicated.
II. Whether the jury rendered inconsistent verdicts.
III. Whether there was sufficient evidence to support his public intoxication conviction.

We affirm.

FACTS

The facts most favorable to the jury's verdict reveal that on April 25, 1989, two police officers, Elbert Bays and William Carver, were dispatched to the scene of a single vehicle accident on State Road 64. When they arrived, they discovered Henriott's severely damaged pickup truck which appeared to have rolled over alongside the road. Henriott told the officers that he lost control of his truck when he swerved to avoid an automobile that was blocking the roadway. The officers did not see any automobile blocking the roadway.

As Officer Carver was talking to Henriott at the accident site, he noticed that Henriott smelled of alcoholic beverages, his face was flushed, and he was unsteady on his feet. After Officer Carver advised Henriott of Indiana's implied consent law, Henriott agreed to submit to a chemical breath test. Officer Carver took Henriott to the police station where he asked Henriott to perform two field sobriety tests. Henriott swayed when he attempted to walk heel to toe in a straight line and missed his nose when he tried to touch it with his finger. The administration of a breathalyzer test revealed Henriott had a blood alcohol content of 0.11%. Henriott testified at trial that he drank four alcoholic drinks between approximately 7:00 p.m. and midnight on the night of the accident.

Henriott was tried by a jury and convicted of driving while intoxicated and public intoxication. The jury acquitted Henriott of driving with a blood alcohol content of .10% or more.

OPINION

Henriott first challenges the sufficiency of the evidence to sustain his driving while intoxicated conviction claiming there was insufficient evidence establishing his impaired condition due to alcohol consumption. When reviewing the sufficiency of the evidence, this court will not reweigh the evidence or judge the credibility of the witnesses. We will consider only the evidence most favorable to the verdict, together with all reasonable and logical inferences to be drawn therefrom. If there is substantial evidence of probative value to support the jury's conclusion, the verdict will not be disturbed.

The statutory definition of "intoxicated" is contained in IND.CODE 9–11–1–5 which provides: "Intoxicated" means under the influence of:

1. alcohol;
2. a controlled substance;
3. any drug other than alcohol or a controlled substance; or
4. any combination of alcohol, controlled substances, or drugs;
    such that there is an impaired condition of thought and action and the loss of normal control of a person's faculties to such an extent as to endanger any person.

This court has held that the element of impairment was sufficiently established when, in addition to a blood alcohol test result in excess of .10%, the defendant ran his vehicle off the road and failed some field dexterity tests. *Clark v. State* (1987), Ind.App., 512 N.E.2d 223.

[COURT NOTE: "Henriott's attempt to distinguish *Clark* from the case at bar is unpersuasive. Henriott argues that unlike the

defendant in *Clark,* he offered an excuse for running his car off the road, that the effect of the wreck caused him dizziness and disorientation, and that the jury acquitted him of operating a vehicle with .10% or more of alcohol in his blood. This is merely an invitation for this court to reweigh the evidence which is precluded by our standard of review.

Here, Henriott ran his car off the road. He smelled of alcoholic beverages, his face was flushed, he was unsteady on his feet, and he failed two dexterity tests. Further, Henriott admitted he was drinking alcohol before the accident and the results of a breathalyzer test indicated there was alcohol in his blood."]

There was sufficient evidence of impairment to establish Henriott's intoxication.

Henriott next contends that the jury rendered inconsistent verdicts by finding him guilty of driving while intoxicated and not guilty of the lesser included offense of driving with a blood alcohol level of .10% or more. Henriott claims that the inconsistency violates his rights under the Double Jeopardy clause of the Fifth Amendment to the Untied States Constitution. Henriott fails to persuade us that the jury reached inconsistent verdicts. Henriott was convicted of DRIVING while INTOXICATED which is set forth in IND.CODE 9–11–2–2 as:

A person who operates a vehicle while intoxicated commits a Class A MISDEMEANOR.

The definition of intoxicated, as recited in § I, does not require proof of a blood alcohol content. As this court has stated, "[a] defendant may be found guilty of operating a vehicle while intoxicated irrespective of the defendant's blood alcohol content, and further, without ingesting alcohol at all." *Sering v. State* (1986), 488 N.E.2d 369. To establish the offense of DRIVING while INTOXICATED, the State is required to establish that the defendant was impaired, regardless of his blood alcohol level. *Hurt v. State* (1990), Ind.App., 553 N.E.2d 1243. As we stated ... the State adequately established the element of impairment to sustain

Henriott's conviction of DRIVING while INTOXICATED. Henriott's acquittal of driving with a blood alcohol content of .10%, or more, is not inconsistent with his conviction for DRIVING while INTOXICATED.

Henriott finally contends there was insufficient evidence to establish the offense of public intoxication. He bases his claim on the State's failure to establish his intoxication. As we have stated in the previous two sections, the State presented sufficient evidence of intoxication. Henriott's claim that his conviction should be reversed because the police failed to comply with IND.CODE 16–13–6.1–32(c) is without merit. IND.CODE 16–13–6.1–32 provides:

§ 32. Any police officer or peace officer making arrest for public intoxication may:

a. If the person is unmanageable or is causing damage to himself or others, take him into custody for criminal processing in the city lock-up or county jail; or
b. If the person is manageable and not causing damage to himself or others, issue a citation and

1. take him to his home or relatives, or a responsible person who is competent and willing to provide care, assistance, and treatment if such is in reasonable proximity; or
2. take him to an approved public or private treatment facility or to the city lock-up or county jail if no facility is available;
c. Any person to be taken to the city lock-up or county jail shall be evaluated at the earliest possible time for nonalcoholic factors which may be contributing to the appearance of intoxication.

The statute provides options to police officers for the placement of individuals who the officers arrest for public intoxication. Here, however, Henriott was not arrested for public intoxication. Rather, he was arrested for his intoxication as it related to his driving. The record reflects that the public intoxication charge was later added by the State's amendment to the Information. Accordingly, the statute does not apply.

Judgment affirmed.

Robertson and Garrard, JJ., concur.

CASE

Was He Driving While Intoxicated or Drunk in Public?

People v. Weathington
282 Cal.Rptr. 170 (Cal.1991)

Premo, Acting Presiding Justice
Defendant David Weathington appeals from conviction at jury trial of one count each of felony driving under the influence of alcohol with three or more priors for which he received a prison sentence, and misdemeanor driving on a suspended license.... [W]e affirm the judgment of conviction.

FACTS
On April 14, 1990, appellant drove into a gas station and pulled up at the full-service

bay to buy gas. He exited his car and asked the attendant, Richard Gill, to fill the gas tank and check the oil. Gill noticed a fuel line leak, so appellant moved the car away from the gas pumps to be fixed. Exiting again, appellant confided to the cashier, Chris Olsen, that he had drunk a six-pack and felt good, and inquired where he could find a liquor store. Both employees thought appellant was intoxicated: he had slurred speech and staggered when he walked.

There was a liquor store across the street; appellant went there and returned from five to ten minutes later with a wine cooler for himself and sodas for the attendants. He got into the driver's seat of the car and started drinking the cooler.

The cashier called the police, who arrived about 30 minutes later. They administered field sobriety tests and arrested appellant. Appellant admitted to consuming four beers between 9:30 a.m. and noon, the wine cooler, and complained of a bad knee when he was unable to do the balance test. A blood sample was taken; the blood alcohol level was .25. Appellant was charged with driving under the influence of alcohol with three or more priors (Veh.Code, §§ 23152, subd. (a), 23175) and driving with a suspended or revoked license (§ 14601.2, subd. (a)). The district attorney also alleged that appellant had prior convictions for driving with a suspended or revoked license (§ 14601.2, subd. (d)(2)).

§ 23175 provides for increased penalties, including a prison commitment, for persons convicted of a violation of § 23152 when the offense occurred within seven years of three or more separate violations of driving under the influence or reckless driving pursuant to § 23103.5.

Before trial commenced, appellant made a motion in limine "for the bifurcation of the trial as to the priors and concurrently for the sanitation of the complaint not to mention anything about his prior convictions." When the motions were denied, appellant admitted seven prior convictions of driving under the influence of alcohol (§ 23152, subds. (a), (b)) and six prior convictions of driving on a suspended or revoked license (§ 14601.2, subd. (a)). The jury was not informed of any of appellant's prior convictions; he stipulated that he had notice that his driver's license was suspended. Appellant was convicted and sentenced to two years in state prison for driving under the influence of alcohol with three or more priors and to a concurrent 30 days in county jail for driving with a suspended or revoked license. This appeal ensued....

OPINION

Appellant contends that since he was not under the influence of alcohol when he drove into the station, but became intoxicated while he was waiting for his car to be repaired, the court should have instructed on "the lesser related offense of being drunk and disorderly in public."

Penal Code § 647, subdivision (f), describes as misdemeanor disorderly conduct the act of being found "in any public place under the influence of intoxicating liquor, ...

in such a condition that he or she is unable to exercise care for his or her own safety or the safety of others, or by reason of his or her being under the influence of intoxicating liquor, ... interferes with or obstructs or prevents the free use of any street, sidewalk, or public way."

The underlying offense, § 23152, subdivision (a), as relevant to these facts, makes it unlawful "for any person who is under the influence of an alcoholic beverage ... to drive a vehicle." Appellant relies on *People v. Geiger* (1984) 35 Cal.3d 510, 530, 199 Cal.Rptr. 45, 674 P.2d 1303, for the proposition that fairness to the defendant requires that he receive instructions on related but not necessarily included offenses. He contends that his defense satisfies each of the three prongs of the *Geiger* test.

The first prong is that some basis must exist "other than an unexplainable rejection of prosecution evidence, on which the jury could find the offense to be less than that charged." Appellant satisfies the first prong. Support for his defense can be plucked from the testimony of the gas station employees that his driving was not erratic nor out of the ordinary, and that they did not smell alcohol on his breath, although because of his statements and other conduct they thought he was intoxicated. In addition, he explained his staggering by presenting evidence that major knee surgery in 1986 and a recent re-injury of the knee caused him to walk with a limp. To explain the slurred speech, he revealed that he had lost his partial plate which contained some of his front teeth. Finally, defense witnesses testified that he had been in their presence for some time earlier that morning before he had gone to the gas station and he had not drunk alcohol; he attributed his intoxication to "two potent wine coolers at the station." Consequently, appellant established an evidentiary basis for the instructions. "[A] defendant's right to instructions does not turn on the court's assessment of the strength of the evidence, or on whether there is a conflict in, rebuttal to, or impeachment of the *People's* evidence." (*People v. Geiger,* supra, 35 Cal.3d at p. 531, 199 Cal.Rptr. 45, 674 P.2d 1303.)

Second, *Geiger* requires that "the offense must be one closely related to that charged and shown by the evidence.... Although some evidence offered by the *People* or the defendant may indicate that the defendant has committed a crime other than that charged, instructions regarding that crime need not be given unless the evidence is also relevant to and admitted for the purpose of establishing whether the defendant is guilty of the charged offense."

The offenses are closely related. Both require a showing that the defendant is under the influence of an intoxicant, alcohol. Both require the showing of impairment of the defendant's abilities, albeit to a different level. § 23152 requires the showing that the defendant's "physical or mental abilities are impaired to such a degree that he no longer has the ability to drive a vehicle with the caution characteristic of a sober person of ordinary prudence under the same or similar circumstances." (*People v. Cortes* (1989) 214 Cal.App.3d Supp. 12, 15, 263 Cal.Rptr. 113.)

Penal Code § 647, subdivision (f), requires a showing that the defendant is unable to exercise care for his own safety or the safety of others or because of his condition, he obstructs a public way. Thus, for both offenses, the penalty attaches for misbehavior.

The Attorney General asserts that the defense never conceded that appellant was under the influence of alcohol at any place, let alone that he was unable to exercise care for his own safety on account of intoxication. However, in light of the trial court's refusal to instruct on Penal Code § 647, subdivision (f), this is not surprising. It is clear from the record that, in the words of *Geiger's* third requirement, appellant "reli[ed] on a theory of defense that would be consistent with a conviction for the related offense." Although it was error to fail to instruct on the related offense, the error "is not prejudicial if 'it is possible to determine that ... the factual question posed by the omitted instruction was necessarily resolved adversely to the defendant under other, properly given instructions....'" (*People v. Turner* (1990) 50

Cal.3d 668, 690–691, 268 Cal.Rptr. 706, 789 P.2d 887.) Such was the case here. For the jury to have acquitted on the charged offense, and to have convicted on the related offense, it would have to have found that appellant was not driving a vehicle at the time the effects of the alcohol he admitted he had drunk manifested themselves.

The question whether appellant was driving was put squarely to the jury by the instructions. The jury was told: "To constitute a violation of Vehicle Code § 23152(a)–23175, there are two essential elements: One, driving a vehicle, and, two, while under the influence of an alcoholic beverage.

> The law states that a driver is a person who drives or is in actual or is in full physical control of a motor vehicle. The word "drive" is defined to mean to cause the vehicle to be in movement. Only a slight movement of the vehicle is necessary to establish that the vehicle is being driven.
> To constitute a violation of § 23152(a)–23175 of the California Vehicle Code the law does not require that the defendant have actually been observed driving a vehicle or identified by a witness as the driver of the vehicle involved. Sufficient proof of his driving or identity as the driver may be based in whole or in part upon circumstantial evidence and the inferences reasonably drawn therefrom."

These instructions made clear beyond doubt that appellant was not guilty of driving under the influence of alcohol if he was not actually engaged in driving a vehicle at the time his abilities were impaired. In finding for the prosecution, the jury thus necessarily concluded that he was under the influence of alcohol at the time he drove the vehicle into and upon the gas station property. (Cf. *People v. Turner*, supra, 50 Cal.3d at pp. 690–691, 268 Cal.Rptr. 706, 789 P.2d 887.) The error was harmless.

Testimony regarding appellant's driving was admitted. He "pulled in [to the gas pumps] crooked, but people have done that before." He satisfactorily backed up and maneuvered the car to the other side of the pumps and to the side of the station for repairs. On the other hand, substantial evidence supported the inference that appellant was intoxicated at the time he drove into the station. The attendants testified that appellant's speech was slurred, that he had a swaying, staggering walk, that he stated that he had a six-pack earlier and he was feeling pretty good but he wanted to get something else to drink, and that even subtracting the two wine coolers appellant claimed to have drunk after he arrived at the station, his blood alcohol level was at least .19 when he arrived.

On this state of the evidence, we are certain that no reasonable juror, properly instructed on the use he or she could make of the manner in which appellant drove his car, would have entertained a reasonable doubt that he was under the influence of alcohol at the time he drove his car. Consequently, we hold the instructional error is harmless beyond a reasonable doubt and is not grounds for reversal of the conviction.

... The judgment of conviction is affirmed....

Case Discussion

What does "driving" mean for purposes of DWI law, according to the statute? Would you define it differently? What threat does Block pose to public order and safety? If you were writing a statute, would you draft it as the Missouri legislature did? Why? Why not? How would you draft the law? Would you make DWI a strict liability crime? Or would you require a *mens rea?* What culpability would you require: purpose, knowledge, recklessness, or negligence? Explain your position. Would you have degrees of DWI, such as walking toward a car drunk, getting in the driver's seat drunk, turning the key in the ignition drunk, pulling away from a parking place drunk, and driving down the highway swerving all over in the wrong direction with oncoming cars nearly colliding with the drunk-driven vehicle? Why?[6]

How does Indiana define intoxication for DWI law purposes? Do you agree with this definition? Explain your answer. Would you require a specific blood alcohol level? Would you require defendants to know they were drunk? How do you define intoxication? Can you say precisely how you know either you, your friends, and others are intoxicated? Would you aggravate the offense of driving while intoxicated depending on the degree of intoxication? For example, would it be a worse offense to drive with a blood alcohol level of 0.10 than 0.15? Why?

Why is it possible to be guilty of both driving while intoxicated and drunk in public, according to the California court? What tests does the court set up in order to determine whether the state properly charged and convicted Weathington? Would you convict him of driving while intoxicated? What evidence supports, or does not support, such a conviction? Is he guilty of being drunk in public? What facts support his guilt? Are they facts indicating a drunk-in-public *actus reus? Mens rea?* Explain.

—————⊰●⊱—————

Nuisance

The main forms of nuisance include loud noises and bad smells. Noises loud enough to disturb the public are considered criminal under existing laws. Hence, a sound truck that blares its loudspeakers in a quiet neighborhood at seven o'clock on Sunday morning falls clearly within disorderly conduct. But someone running through a neighborhood at the same time, calling out that a terrorist blew up a plane over the Atlantic Ocean, probably does not. The court dealt with the problem of noise in the common nuisance of a barking dog in *Edina v. Dreher.*

CASE

Did the Ordinance Leave the Officer Too Much Discretion?

City of Edina v. Dreher
454 N.W.2d 621 (Minn.1990)

Randall, Judge
This is an appeal from judgment against appellant for violating a city ordinance that prohibits a person from keeping an animal which by any noise disturbs the peace and quiet of persons in the vicinity. Appellant argues that the city ordinance denies him due process of law. We reverse.

FACTS
On August 14, 1989, an Edina community officer was dispatched by the police department to answer a citizen's complaint that a dog was barking at the house of appellant Roger Dreher. Upon reaching the house, the officer sat in his vehicle and from about 50 yards away listened to appellant's dog bark. Before leaving, the officer left a warning citation and a copy of Edina City Ordinance, Number 312, § 29(j) (Dec. 2, 1981), which provides:

> No person owning, operating, having charge of or occupying any building or premises shall keep or allow to be kept any animal which shall by any noise disturb the peace and quiet of any persons in the vicinity thereof.

Two days later another complaint was made about appellant's dog by a second individual. The same community officer stopped near appellant's house and listened for about 10 minutes while the dog barked. The officer testified that on this second occasion he could hear barking and also "a

howling or whining type noise." The officer further testified that it was a higher frequency and the "frequency and consistency were disturbing." He testified that the dog barked about every 10 seconds for approximately 10 minutes.

The officer then issued a formal citation to appellant for violating the Edina ordinance. At trial neither of the original complainants were called, and the city's case rested solely on the officer's testimony. After trial to the court, appellant was convicted of violating the Edina ordinance and assessed a $30 fine, plus court costs.

OPINION
Does Edina City Ordinance, Number 312, § 29(j), as applied to appellant, violate due process of law?

Appellant asserts that Edina City Ordinance, Number 312, § 29(j), is unconstitutionally vague as applied to him and thereby deprives him of due process of law.

The Edina ordinance must meet due process standards of definiteness under both the United States Constitution and the Minnesota Constitution. *State v. Newstrom,* 371 N.W.2d 525, 528 (Minn.1985). Persons of common intelligence must not be left to guess at the meaning of the ordinance nor differ as to its application. The purposes of the void for vagueness doctrine are to put people on notice of what conduct is prohibited and, more importantly, to discourage arbitrary and discriminatory law enforcement. *Kolender v. Lawson,* 461 U.S. 352, 357, 103 S.Ct. 1855, 1858, 75 L.Ed.2d 903 (1983).

When fundamental rights are not involved, as here, vagueness challenges must be examined in light of the defendant's actual conduct. *State v. Becker,* 351 N.W.2d 923, 925 (Minn.1984). Appellant must show that the ordinance "lacks specificity as to his own behavior and not as to some hypothetical situation." *State v. Kager,* 382 N.W.2d 287, 289 (Minn.Ct.App.1986), pet. for rev.

denied (Minn. April 24, 1986). Appellant must prove a constitutional violation beyond a reasonable doubt.

Respondent contends the phrase "disturb the peace and quiet" has a well accepted, generally understood meaning so that when applied to appellant's conduct, it meets the constitutional standard. We disagree. Respondent cites three cases for support.

In *State v. Johnson,* 282 Minn. 153, 163 N.W.2d 750 (1968), Vietnam war protesters disrupted the Minneapolis Aquatennial parade by climbing lamp posts, shouting, and distributing leaflets. Charged with violating a Minneapolis ordinance that punishes "conduct which disturbs the peace and quiet," the protesters challenged the ordinance on vagueness grounds.

[COURT NOTE: "The entire ordinance reads: 'No person, in any public or private place, shall engage in, or prepare, attempt, offer or threaten to engage in, or assist or conspire with another to engage in or congregate because of, any riot, fight, brawl, tumultuous conduct, act of violence, or any other conduct which disturbs the peace and quiet of another save for participating in a recognized athletic contest.'"]

The supreme court rejected the challenge, reasoning that the defendants were aware of the nature of the charged offense, that is, creating traffic congestion during a parade. *Johnson,* 282 Minn. at 159, 163 N.W.2d at 754.

Similarly, in another case, the supreme court affirmed a conviction under the same ordinance when the defendant entered a church during a reverential part of the service, berated a clergyman, and refused to leave. *State v. Olson,* 287 Minn. 300, 301–02, 178 N.W.2d 230, 231 (1970).

Finally, in 1973 the supreme court rejected a vagueness challenge to Minn.Stat. § 609.705(3), the UNLAWFUL ASSEMBLY statute, when protesters disrupted operation of a restaurant by blocking entrances and damaging property. *State v. Hipp,* 298 Minn. 81, 89–90, 213 N.W.2d 610, 615–16 (1973).

[COURT NOTE: "The statute provides in part: 'When three or more persons assemble, each person is guilty of UNLAWFUL ASSEMBLY which is a misdemeanor, if the assembly is:... Without lawful purpose, but the participants so conduct themselves in a disorderly manner as to disturb or threaten the public peace.' *Hipp,* 298 Minn. at 82, 213 N.W.2d at 612"]

Respondent's reliance on these cases is misplaced. Unlike *Johnson, Olson,* and *Hipp* where clear observable deviant conduct occurred, appellant's compliance with the ordinance hinged on the officer's personal sense of annoyance over the sound of a natural act, a dog barking. Blocking traffic, disrupting a church service, or interfering with a business are unusual acts, and may be understood by ordinary people of common intelligence as disturbing the peace. Here appellant was left to guess whether his dog's barking disturbed others in the vicinity. The ordinance provided no objective standard against which appellant could measure the level of his dog's barking.

The key words in the ordinance are "by any noise disturb the peace and quiet of any persons in the vicinity." Who does that mean? Does that include several month old babies which may easily be disturbed and cry at any strange sound? Does it include the elderly or anyone who is extremely sensitive and claims to be disturbed by any noise above the normal hum of conversation? Does it include persons who, because of their love of pets, have an extremely high tolerance for barking dogs and meowing cats, or do we go by the standards of those who strongly dislike any pet within a residential area? The ordinance as written gives no guidance to the pet owner, the neighbor, or the investigating officer as to what is allowable barking and what is not.

Besides failing to put appellant on notice of what conduct is prohibited, the ordinance invites arbitrary enforcement. A city may enforce ordinances that reasonably specify what conduct is prohibited. However, it may not enforce an ordinance "whose violation may entirely depend upon whether or not a police officer is annoyed." Yet this is precisely what this Edina ordinance does. Because the city failed to introduce any evidence from the original complainants who reported appellant's dog barking, the question whether appellant violated the ordinance depended entirely on the officer's threshold of annoyance. Under these circumstances the Edina ordinance violates appellant's right to due process of law and therefore we reverse his conviction.

[COURT NOTE: "Edina City Ordinance Number 312, § 29(k) provides that before an officer may issue a citation he must personally investigate the circumstances forming the basis of the complaint. As respondent explained it, this requirement is practical and exemplary. It puts the buffer of a police officer between two neighbors and, in theory, should help screen nuisance calls from neighbors involved in a petty backyard dispute. However, when the prosecuting authorities made the decision not to call either of the two original complainants to identify by direct evidence what they heard and observed, the city, even though encouraging politeness and good manners between neighbors, deliberately deprived itself of its best evidence. Prosecuting authorities always have the privilege of excepting witnesses from their case in chief, but they also accept the risk that their case becomes weaker."]

We note that the Washington Supreme Court recently addressed this same issue involving similar facts and a parallel ordinance. See *City of Spokane v. Fischer,* 110 Wash.2d 541, 754 P.2d 1241 (1988). In *Fischer,* the ordinance provided for conviction if a dog were permitted to "disturb or annoy another person or neighbor by frequent or habitual howling, yelping or barking." The court held the ordinance was unconstitutionally vague. It reasoned that because violation of the ordinance turned on the neighbors' level of tolerance or intolerance for barking, an average person of common intelligence could not determine prohibited conduct. We find the reasoning by the court in *Fischer* logical and persuasive, and adopt it in this case.

Edina City Ordinance, Number 312, § 29(j) is unconstitutionally vague as applied to appellant and deprives him of due process of law.

Reversed.

Case Discussion What facts support violation of the ordinance? Who determined whether the facts satisfied the ordinance's requirements? Why did the court rule that the ordinance violated the due process clause (see chapter 2, on void for vagueness)? Do you agree? Is it not easy to determine that barking dogs disturb people who hear them under the circumstances of this case? Why? Why not?

Besides brawling and making noise, nearly any mischief that imagination can create has fallen at one time or another under the disorderly conduct laws. This behavior includes making "stink bombs," lighting firecrackers on a highway, strewing garbage in an alley, and blinding motorists by shining searchlights into their windshields. A Chicago City Ordinance, called "the most charming grabbag of criminal prohibitions ever assembled," gives some idea of the number of activities encompassed by disorderly conduct:

> All persons who shall make, aid, countenance or assist in making any improper noise, riot, disturbance, breach of the peace or diversion tending to a breach of the peace, within the limits of the city; all persons who shall collect in bodies or crowds for unlawful purposes, or for any purpose, to the annoyance or disturbance of other persons; all persons who are idle or dissolute and go about begging; all persons who use or exercise any juggling or other unlawful games, all persons who are found in houses of ill-fame or gaming

houses; all persons lodging in or found at any time in sheds, barns, stables, or unoccupied buildings, or lodging in the open air and not giving a good account of themselves; all persons who shall wilfully assault another in the city, or be engaged in, aid, abet in any fight, quarrel, or other disturbance in the city; all persons who stand, loiter, or stroll about in any place in the city, waiting or seeking to obtain money or other valuable things from others by trick or fraud, or to aid or assist therein; all persons that shall engage in any fraudulent scheme, device or trick to obtain money or other valuable thing in any place in the city, or who shall aid, abet, or in any manner be concerned therein; all touts, rapers, steerers, or cappers, so called, for any gambling room or house who shall ply or attempt to ply their calling on any public way in the city; all persons found loitering about any hotel, block barroom, dramshop, gambling house, or disorderly house, or wandering about the streets either by night or day without any known lawful means of support, or without being able to give a satisfactory account of themselves; all persons who shall have or carry any pistol, knife, dirk, knuckles, slingshot, or other dangerous weapon concealed on or about their persons; and all persons who are known to be narcotic addicts, thieves, burglars, pickpockets, robbers or confidence men, either by their own confession or otherwise, or by having been convicted of larceny, burglary, or other crime against the laws of the state, who are found lounging in, prowling, or loitering around any steamboat landing, railroad depot, banking institution, place of public amusement, auction room, hotel, store, shop, public way, public conveyance, public gathering, public assembly, court room, public building, private dwelling house, house of ill-fame, gambling house, or any public place, and who are unable to give a reasonable excuse for being so found, shall be deemed guilty of disorderly conduct, and upon conviction thereof, shall be severally fined not less than one dollar nor more than two hundred dollars for each offense.[7]

Many broad and vaguely worded statutes prevent reasonable prediction of the conduct encompassed by disorderly conduct. This situation permits police and judges too much discretion to define the behavior after the fact. Because of vagueness and breadth, people charged with disorderly conduct frequently challenge statutes' constitutionality. Most commonly, statutes are attacked on the ground that they violate the United States Constitution's Fourteenth Amendment due process clause, which provides that "no state shall deprive any citizen of life, liberty or property without due process of law." The courts interpret that clause to mean that statutes are void when they violate **due process** by being too vague **(void for vagueness)** or too broad **(void for overbreadth)** to convey in advance what conduct they aim to punish. The United States Supreme Court dealt with the problem of overbreadth and void for vagueness in *Thompson v. City of Louisville*.

CASE

Was His Conduct Disorderly?

Thompson v. City of Louisville
362 U.S. 199 80 S.Ct. 624, 4 L.Ed.2d 654 (1960)

[Justice Black delivered the opinion.]

FACTS

Petitioner was found guilty in the Police Court of Louisville, Kentucky, of two offenses —loitering and disorderly conduct. The ultimate question presented to us is whether the charges against petitioner were so totally devoid of evidentiary support as to render his conviction unconstitutional under the

Due Process Clause of the Fourteenth Amendment. Decision of this question turns not on the sufficiency of the evidence, but on whether this conviction rests upon any evidence at all.

The facts ... are short and simple. Petitioner, a long-time resident of the Louisville area, went into the Liberty End Cafe about 6:20 on Saturday evening, January 24, 1959. In addition to selling food the cafe was licensed to sell beer to the public and some 12 to 30 patrons were present during the time petitioner was there. When petitioner had been in the cafe about half an hour, two Louisville police officers came in on a "routine check." Upon seeing petitioner "out there on the floor dancing by himself," one of the officers, according to his testimony, went up to the manager who was sitting on a stool nearby and asked him how long petitioner had been in there and if he had bought anything. The officer testified that upon being told by the manager that petitioner had been there "a little over a half-hour and that he had not bought anything," he accosted Thompson and "asked him what was his reason for being in there and he said he was waiting on a bus." The officer then informed petitioner that he was under arrest and took him outside. This was the arrest for loitering. After going outside, the officer testified, petitioner "was very argumentative—he argued with us back and forth and so then we placed a disorderly conduct charge on him." Admittedly the disorderly conduct conviction rests solely on this one sentence description of petitioner's conduct after he left the cafe.

The foregoing evidence includes all that the city offered against him, except a record purportedly showing a total of 54 previous arrests of petitioner.

Petitioner then put in evidence on his own behalf, none of which in any way strengthened the city's case. He testified that he bought, and one of the cafe employees served him, a dish of macaroni and a glass of beer and that he remained in the cafe waiting for a bus to go home. Further evidence showed without dispute that at the time of his arrest petitioner gave the officers

his home address; that he had money with him, and a bus schedule showing that a bus to his home would stop within half a block of the cafe at about 7:30; that he owned two unimproved lots of land; that in addition to work he had done for others, he had regularly worked one day or more a week for the same family for 30 years; that he paid no rent in the home where he lived and that his meager income was sufficient to meet his needs.

The cafe manager testified that petitioner had frequently patronized the cafe, and that he had never told petitioner that he was unwelcome there. The manager further testified that on this very occasion he saw petitioner "standing there in the middle of the floor and patting his foot," and that he did not at any time during petitioner's stay there object to anything he was doing.

There is no evidence that anyone else in the cafe objected to petitioner's shuffling his feet in rhythm with the music of the jukebox or that his conduct was boisterous or offensive to anyone present.

At the close of his evidence, petitioner repeated his motion for dismissal of the charges on the ground that a conviction on the foregoing evidence would deprive him of liberty and property without due process under the Fourteenth Amendment. The court denied the motion, convicted him of both offenses, and fined him $10 on each charge. A motion for new trial, on the same grounds, also was denied, which exhausted petitioner's remedies in the police court.

OPINION

Our examination of the record presented in the petition for certiorari convinced us that although the fines here are small, the due process questions presented are substantial and we therefore granted certiorari to review the police court's judgments.

Petitioner's conviction for disorderly conduct was under § 85–8 of the city ordinance which, without definition, provides that "[w]hoever shall be found guilty of disorderly conduct in the City of Louisville shall be fined" etc. The only evidence of "disorderly conduct" was the single statement of the policeman that after petitioner was arrested and taken out of the cafe he was very argumentative. There is no testimony that petitioner raised his voice, used offensive language, resisted the officers or engaged in any conduct of any kind likely in any way to adversely affect the good order and tranquility of the City of Louisville. The only information the record contains on what the petitioner was "argumentative" about is his statement that he asked the officers "what they arrested me for." We assume, for we are justified in assuming, that merely "arguing" with a policeman is not, because it could not be, "disorderly conduct" as a matter of the substantive law of Kentucky.

Moreover, Kentucky law itself seems to provide that if a man wrongfully arrested fails to object to the arresting officer, he waives any right to complain later that the arrest was unlawful.

Thus we find no evidence whatever in the record to support these convictions. Just as "Conviction upon a charge not made would be sheer denial of due process," so is it a violation of due process to convict and punish a man without evidence of his guilt.

The judgments are reversed and the cause is remanded to the Police Court of the City of Louisville for proceedings not inconsistent with this opinion.

Reversed and remanded.

Case Discussion

Thompson raises the common constitutional objection to disorderly conduct statutes—that they are too vague and broad to satisfy due process (see chapter 2 on void for vagueness). Do you think this case bears out the fear that police and judges abuse their discretion in disorderly conduct statutes? If Thompson's conduct was disorderly, who sets the standard for what conduct qualifies as disorderly? Was the disorderly conduct arrest and charge an excuse? If so, for what was it an excuse? Was Thompson arrested for what he did or for who he was (see Chapter 3 on *actus reus*)? Why did Thompson appeal so minor an offense to the Supreme Court? Are cases like these wasting the Court's time?

Coarse and Indecent Language

Fighting, violent behavior, and, to a lesser extent, making noise all can create physical discomfort among the general public. Disorderly conduct, however, includes not only actions causing physical discomfort but also actions that could offend public sensibilities—such as coarse and indecent language and gestures.

Statutes variously characterize language and gestures as disorderly when they are "abusive," "unnecessarily insulting," "vulgar," "unseemly," "offensive," "rude," or "obscene." In some jurisdictions, language tending to disturb suffices; other jurisdictions require that the language itself disturb. Even with the latter restriction, coarse and indecent language statutes cause problems. In the first place, vague words can lead to abuse of discretion. Rarely do statutes clarify whether merely profane language qualifies or whether obscenity is also required. Equally important, most statutes raise First Amendment free speech questions, particularly in cases involving unpopular but not necessarily offensive language or gestures. For example, calling the president of the United States a "bullshit artist" may offend the sensibilities of ordinary people. Nevertheless, the right to state an opinion about a political leader outweighs the discomfort to the public that such an utterance creates.

Statutes restricted to words that themselves disturb do not eliminate vagueness problems, abuse of discretion, and possible free speech violations. Limiting the offense to specific offensive sexual, scatological, or threatening words, and excluding words that harbor unacceptable political or religious connotations, does not satisfy some critics of coarse and offensive language laws. For example, music that arouses passions that might lead to violence in the form of suicide, crushing, and riot undoubtedly offends and can even lead to injury and death, as prominent news stories emphasize. Nonetheless, critics maintain that restrictions on such music infringe on free speech. Therefore, they recommend excluding offensive language and gestures entirely from criminal law.

Making obscene phone calls is a crime in most jurisdictions. The court dealt with the constitutional and policy implications of such laws in *State v. Hagen*.

CASE

Was His Obscene Phone Call Constitutionally Protected?

State v. Hagen
27 Ariz. App. 722, 558 P.2d 750 (1976)

[Hagen was convicted of using obscene and lewd language on the telephone and was sentenced to one year of probation. He appealed.]

FACTS
A.R.S. § 13–895A provides:

> It shall be unlawful for any person, with intent to terrify, intimidate, threaten, harass, annoy or offend, to telephone another and use any obscene, lewd or profane language or suggest any lewd or lascivious act, or threaten to inflict injury or physical harm to the person or property of any person. It shall also be unlawful to attempt to extort money or other things of value from any person, or to otherwise disturb by repeated anonymous telephone calls the peace, quiet or right of privacy of any person at the place where the telephone call or calls were received.

... [O]n or about the 19th day of March, 1975, appellant telephoned a Phoenix police officer and used obscene, lewd and profane language. Specifically he expressed a desire to engage in an act of sodomy with the Phoenix Chief of Police.

OPINION
Appellant's assertion that the statute is unconstitutionally void for vagueness was disposed of by this court in *Baker v. State* (1972), wherein the same contention was turned aside. One whose conduct is clearly proscribed by the terms of a statute may not successfully challenge it for vagueness. Here the crime and the elements comprising it are expressly set forth, and a reasonable person would not be left to speculate as to the type of activity prohibited.

Appellant also claims overbroadness because the wording of A.R.S. § 13–895A is equally applicable to constitutionally protected speech. Again we disagree. The state has a legitimate interest in prohibiting obscene, threatening, or harassing phone calls, none of which are generally thought of as protected by the First Amendment. The intrusion into the home by means of telecommunications of those individuals who intend to terrify, harass, annoy and abuse the listener by means of the language proscribed by the statute. A resort to epithets of personal abuse is not in any proper sense communication of information or opinion safeguarded by the Constitution, and its punishment as a criminal act raises no constitutional question.

By specifying the intent with which the call must be made and the nature of the language prohibited, the statute clearly demonstrates that the prohibited activities find no protection under the First Amendment. Such activities [are] not "an exercise of rights but rather [were] an abuse of rights and [entailed] a gross lack of understanding—or calloused indifference—to the simple fact that the offended parties also [had] certain rights under the same Constitution."

We cannot conceive that the State is abridging anyone's First Amendment freedom by prohibiting telephone calls that are "obscene, lewd or profane" or that threaten physical harm, provided such calls are made with the intent specified in the statute.

Judgment and sentence affirmed.

Case Discussion

The court makes clear that the Constitution does not protect all speech. Obscene phone calls are speech that the Constitution does not protect. In fact, the court goes further, concluding that Hagen's phone call violated his victim's rights. What reasons can you give for ruling that the Arizona statute on obscene telephone calls is constitutional? Are your reasons the same as the court's? What public interest does such a statute protect? Is it public order? Personal privacy? In what sense does it protect both?

⫸●⫷

Fighting Words

The First Amendment does not protect **fighting words**—words that provoke or threaten to provoke immediate violent reactions or disorder. Making fighting words a crime punishes potential harm, as opposed to actual harm (see chapter 5, on inchoate offenses). Fighting-words statutes also raise constitutional questions. To pass constitutional muster, they must balance the need for public order with the constitutional right to free speech (see Chapter 2, free speech).[8]

The use of fighting words in altercations between citizens and police require balancing public order with individual freedom. Most jurisdictions have statutes or ordinances making it a crime to obstruct police officers in their duties. Some specifically prohibit abusive language toward the police. These latter laws have drawn scrutiny from the courts on the basis of their possible interference with free speech. In these laws regarding altercations with citizens, police officers enjoy wide discretion, and judges tend to favor police versions of what happened during the altercation. As a result, convictions can result more from offending a particular officer's sensibilities than from actual or threatened public disorder. This situation can breed resentment toward law enforcement, a condition itself likely to cause public disorder.[9]

Police officers, simply by virtue of carrying out their lawful duties, provoke annoyance and occasionally even outrage. Even lawful arrests anger innocent persons. Should expressing this anger verbally be a crime because it offends a police officer? Rather than trenching on personal liberty by arrests for verbal abuse, some experts contend that officers, as professionals, ought to ignore rudeness. According to Justice Powell, in one police altercation case that reached the Supreme Court, *Lewis v. City of New Orleans:*

A properly trained officer may reasonably be expected to "exercise a higher degree of restraint" than the average citizen, and thus be less likely to respond belligerently to "fighting words."[10]

Others disagree, arguing that the police need not put up with abusive language and that permitting citizens to "get away with it" affronts public order and decency, breeding contempt for law enforcement and a corresponding increase in "real crime." In *State v. Lynch,* the Minnesota appeals court dealt with the constitutional questions of applying the fighting-words doctrine to a verbal altercation with the police.[11]

CASE

Were They "Fighting Words?"

State v. Lynch
392 N.W.2d 700 (Minn.App.1986)

Sedgwick, Judge.

Rebecca Lynch appeals from convictions of disorderly conduct and interfering with a police officer, contending she was arrested and prosecuted in derogation of her First Amendment rights. She also claims the trial court erred in denying her motions to dismiss the charges and to compel discovery of Minneapolis Police Department Internal Affairs Division files. We affirm in part and remand.

FACTS
At about 9:00 p.m. on September 3, 1985 members of the Minneapolis Police Department's "decoy unit" were on undercover patrol in North Minneapolis. Sergeant Ronald Ottoson and Officers Diaz and Thomas observed a young black male driving a scooter at a high rate of speed. The officers followed as the driver "rolled" through a stop sign, turned, and then pulled over to the curb in front of appellant's residence at 1352 Thomas Avenue North.

The policemen parked behind the stopped scooter. Ottoson got out, identified himself as a police officer, and asked the driver for his license. The driver of the scooter, Maurice Woods, did not have a required motorcycle endorsement on his license. The officers arrested Woods and placed him against their car to search him for weapons.

Appellant's son, Kevin Lynch, was standing on the boulevard and witnessed Wood's arrest. Ottoson showed Kevin Lynch his police I.D. and told him the officers were with the decoy unit. A friend of Lynch's then ran into appellant's house and told her of Woods' arrest. Woods is appellant's nephew.

Ottoson said a group of ten to fifteen people, both adults and teenagers, came out of appellant's house and moved towards the boulevard. Appellant "made no inquiry into the reasons for Woods' arrest, but instead immediately started swearing at us. Her immediate term was motherfucker and then [she] called us motherfucking pigs and stated that we had no business stopping this person for no reason at all and that the only reason we were stopping him is because he was black...."

Ottoson said appellant continued swearing and the crowd grew to "50 or 100 people or better." People were soon standing on all four corners of the intersection. Ottoson described the crowd's reaction to appellant's speech: "Her type of behavior was very excitable to the crowd and rather than having a calming effect, I felt that it had the effect of inciting the crowd. Also the yelling like this tended to draw more people to the scene."

Officer Diaz also said the crowd appeared to be getting excited and angry; some people were carrying clubs, others were swearing at the police. Ottoson called for backup; more plain clothes officers and a number of uniformed officers soon arrived.

After the backup arrived, Ottoson, another plain clothes officer, and a uniformed officer went into the crowd to arrest appellant. According to Ottoson, appellant began to struggle when informed she was under arrest: "As I attempted to place my grip upon her upper arm she immediately began to attempt to fight.... She struck out with her hand and struck [Officer Hannan] in the face. And we struggled with her and finally she was handcuffed."

Appellant was charged with interfering with a police officer, Minn.Stat. § 609.50 (1984); disorderly conduct, and simple assault; Minneapolis City Code §§ 385.190(b) (1976) and 385.90 (1981). On October 16, 1985 appellant moved to dismiss the charges on the grounds that her arrest denied her freedom of speech ... as guaranteed by the First and Fourteenth Amendments of the Constitution. That motion was denied by a Special Term court on October 21, 1985.... The jury found appellant guilty of disorderly conduct and interfering with a police officer, but not guilty of simple assault. The trial court ... sentenced appellant to a stayed term of 60 days and a fine of $110.

OPINION

Appellant ... contends that the Minneapolis disorderly conduct ordinance is unconstitutionally vague and overbroad. The ordinance provides that:

> No person, in any public or private place, shall engage in, or prepare, attempt, offer or threaten to engage in, or assist or conspire with another to engage in, or congregate because of, any riot, fight, brawl, tumultuous conduct, act of violence, or any other conduct which disturbs the peace and quiet of another save for participating in a recognized athletic contest. Minneapolis City Code § 385.90 (1981)

The supreme court has held that this language is not unconstitutionally vague. [The court did not discuss the supreme court's reasons for deciding this.]

Appellant also argues the ordinance is overbroad. A law is overbroad if it deters the exercise of First Amendment rights by unnecessarily punishing constitutionally protected along with unprotected activity. See *Matter of the Welfare of S.L.J.*, 263 N.W.2d 412, 417 (Minn.1978). Where a law is facially overbroad because it might restrict protected speech, it must be construed narrowly in order to survive a constitutional challenge. In *S.L.J.* the supreme court held the Minnesota disorderly conduct statute, Minn.Stat. § 609.72, was overbroad, but saved that statute by giving it a narrow construction:

> Although § 609.72, subd. 1(3), clearly contemplates punishment for speech that is protected under the First and Fourteenth Amendments, we can uphold its constitutionality by construing it narrowly to refer only to "fighting words." The court noted that other disorderly conduct and breach of the peace statutes should be similarly construed to punish only "fighting words."

We therefore construe the language of Minneapolis City Code § 385.90 to refer only to "fighting words." As so limited, that ordinance is not unconstitutionally overbroad.

The issue then becomes whether appellant's denunciation of police officers as "motherfucking pigs" constituted "fighting words."

[COURT NOTE: "Citizens have frequently been prosecuted for swearing at police officers. The United States Supreme Court has generally remanded such cases to state courts for reconsideration under the 'fighting words' doctrine. See e.g. *Gooding*, 405 U.S. at 519–20, n. 1, 92 S.Ct. at 1104–05 n. 1 ('white son of a bitch, I'll kill you'); *Lewis*, 415 U.S. at 131, n. 1 ('you god damn m.f. police'); but see *Chaplinsky v. New Hampshire*, 315 U.S. 568, 62 S.Ct. 766, 86 L.Ed. 1031 (1942) (upholding conviction where defendant called city marshall a 'damned fascist' and 'god damned racketeer'")].

Our supreme court has adopted the definition of "fighting words" established by the United States Supreme Court:

The real test is whether, under the facts and circumstances of this case, appellant's mere utterance of these vulgar, offensive, insulting words would "'tend to incite an immediate breach of the peace,'" *Lewis v. City of New Orleans,* 415 U.S. 130, 132, 94 S.Ct. 970, 972, 39 L.Ed.2d 214, 218; are "inherently likely to provoke violent reaction," *Cohen v. California,* 403 U.S. 15, 20, 91 S.Ct. 1780, 1785, 29 L.Ed.2d 284, 291; or "hav[e] an immediate tendency to provoke retaliatory violence or tumultuous conduct by those to whom such words are addressed," *State v. Hipp,* 298 Minn. 81, 87, 213 N.W.2d 610, 614.

The specific facts of the case are also important because, as in *Lewis,* whether words are "fighting words" depends on the circumstances surrounding their utterance. *S.L.J.,* 263 N.W.2d at 419. In *S.L.J.* the court concluded that a juvenile saying "fuck you pigs" to two police officers did not meet this standard: While it is true that no ordered society would condone the vulgar language used by this 14-year-old child, and as the court found, her words were intended to, and did, arouse resentment in the officers, the constitution requires more before a person can be convicted for mere speech. In this case, the words were directed at two police officers sitting in their squad car from a distance of 15 to 30 feet by a small, 14-year-old child who was on her way home when she turned to the officers and made

her statement. With the words spoken in retreat from more that 15 feet away rather than eye-to-eye, there was no reasonable likelihood that they would tend to incite an immediate breach of the peace or to provoke violent reaction by an ordinary, reasonable person.

Here appellant used similarly vulgar language. However, in this case there was the additional factor of the crowd drawn by the confrontation between appellant and the police. Several persons in the crowd were brandishing clubs, and the officers testified that appellant's language had the effect of inciting that crowd. Additional officers had to be summoned to protect those already present and effect appellant's arrest. The jury, which was properly instructed on the definition of "fighting words," concluded that appellant was guilty of disorderly conduct and interfering with a police officer. Under these facts and circumstances, the evidence is sufficient to support the jury's finding....

The Minneapolis disorderly conduct statute is neither vague nor overbroad as narrowly construed to punish only "fighting words." Under the facts and circumstances of this case, appellant's speech constituted "fighting words" and her prosecution did not deny her the right to freedom of assembly.

Affirmed....

Case Discussion

How does the court define "fighting words?" Why does the court say that the disorderly conduct ordinance applies to words? Does the ordinance mention words? Why were Lynch's words "fighting" words? Do you agree with the court? Should the First Amendment guarantee citizens the right to rudely disapprove what police do? Should the First Amendment ban the use of profanity and disrespect to police officers? (Review note case, chapter 2, p. 66.)

In *City of Houston v. Hill,* the United States Supreme Court addressed a similar problem, arising out of Hill's verbal abuse of a Houston police officer. The Court came to the opposite conclusion that the Minnesota court reached in *State v. Lynch*.

CASE

Did His Verbal Abuse Constitute Free Speech?

City of Houston v. Hill
482 U.S. 578 (1987)

[Justice Brennan delivered the opinion of the Court, in which Justices White, Marshall, Blackmun, and Stevens joined. Justice Blackmun filed a concurring opinion. Justice Scalia filed an opinion concurring in the judgment. Justice Powell filed an opinion concurring in the judgment in part and dissenting in part, in which Justice O'Connor joined. Chief Justice Rehnquist filed a dissenting opinion.]

FACTS

... Raymond Wayne Hill is a lifelong resident of Houston, Texas. At the time this lawsuit began, he worked as a paralegal and as executive director of the Houston Human Rights League. A member of the Board of the Gay Political Caucus, which he helped found in 1975, Hill was also affiliated with a Houston radio station, and had carried city and county passes since 1975. He lived in Montrose, a "diverse and eclectic neighborhood" that is the center of gay political and social life in Houston.

The incident that sparked this lawsuit occurred in the Montrose area on February 14, 1982. Hill observed a friend, Charles Hill, intentionally stopping traffic on a busy street, evidently to enable a vehicle to enter traffic. Two Houston police officers, one of whom was named Kelley, approached Charles and began speaking with him. According to the District Court, "shortly thereafter" Hill began shouting at the officers "in an admitted attempt to divert Kelley's attention from Charles Hill."

[COURT NOTE: "Hill testified that his 'motivation was to stop [the officers] from hitting Charles.' He also explained that 'I would rather that I get arrested than those whose careers can be damaged; I would rather that I get arrested than those whose families wouldn't understand; I would rather that I get arrested than those who couldn't spend a long time in jail. I am prepared to respond in any legal nonaggressive or nonviolent way, to any illegal police activity, at any time, under any circumstances.'"]

Hill first shouted, "Why don't you pick on somebody your own size?" "[A]re you interrupting me in my official capacity as a Houston police officer?" Hill then shouted, "Yes, why don't you pick on someone your own size?" Hill was arrested under Houston Municipal Code § 34–11(a), [which provides that it "shall be unlawful for any person to assault, strike, or in any manner oppose, molest, abuse or interrupt any policeman in the execution of his duty, or any person summoned to aid in making an arrest"]. Charles Hill was not arrested. Hill was then acquitted after a nonjury trial in Municipal Court....

Following his acquittal in the Charles Hill incident, Hill brought suit in Federal District Court for the Southern District of Texas seeking (1) a declaratory judgment that § 34–11(a) was unconstitutional both on its face and as it had been applied to him....

The District Court held ... that the ordinance was [not] unconstitutionally vague or overbroad ... because "the ordinance does not ... proscribe speech or conduct which is protected by the First Amendment." A panel of the Court of Appeals reversed, [holding that while the ordinance was not vague because it "plainly encompassed mere verbal as well as physical conduct, "it was overbroad because "a significant range of protected speech and expression is punishable and might be deterred by the literal wording of the statute"]....

The City appealed, claiming that the Court of Appeals erred in holding the ordinance overbroad.... We noted probable jurisdiction, and now affirm.

OPINION

... The City's principal argument is that the ordinance does not inhibit the exposition of ideas, and that it bans "core criminal conduct" not protected by the First Amendment. In its view, the application of the ordinance to Hill illustrates that the police employ it only to prohibit such conduct, and not "as a subterfuge to control or dissuade free expression." Since the ordinance is "content-neutral," and since there is no evidence that the City has applied the ordinance to chill particular speakers or ideas, the City concludes that the ordinance is not substantially overbroad.

We disagree with the City's characterization for several reasons. First, the enforceable portion of the ordinance deals not with core criminal conduct, but with speech.... [T]he enforceable portion of the ordinance makes it "unlawful for any person to ... in any manner oppose, molest, abuse or interrupt any policeman in the execution of his duty," and thereby prohibits verbal interruptions of police officers.

Second, contrary to the City's contention, the First Amendment protects a significant amount of verbal criticism and challenge directed at police officers. "Speech is often provocative and challenging.... But it is nevertheless protected against censorship or punishment, unless shown likely to produce a clear and present danger annoyance, or unrest." In *Lewis v. City of New Orleans,* the appellant was found to have yelled obscenities and threats at an officer who had asked appellant's husband to produce his driver's license. Appellant was convicted under a municipal ordinance that made it a crime "for any person wantonly to curse or revile or to use obscene or opprobrious language toward or with reference to any member of the city police while in the actual performance of his duty." We vacated the conviction and invalidated the ordinance as facially overbroad....

The Houston ordinance is much more sweeping than the municipal ordinance struck down in *Lewis.* It is not limited to fighting words nor even to obscene or opprobrious language, but prohibits speech that "in any manner ... interrupts" an officer. The Constitution does not allow such speech to be made a crime. The freedom of individuals to verbally oppose or challenge police action without thereby risking arrest is one of the principal characteristics by which we distinguish a free nation from a police state....

The City argues, however, that even if the ordinance encompasses some protected speech, its sweeping nature is both inevitable and essential to maintain public order.... This Houston ordinance, however, is not narrowly tailored to prohibit only disorderly conduct or fighting words.... Although we appreciate the difficulties in drafting precise laws, we have repeatedly invalidated laws that provide the police with unfettered discretion to arrest individuals for words or conduct that annoy or offend them....

Houston's ordinance criminalizes a substantial amount of constitutionally protected speech, and accords the police unconstitutional discretion in enforcement. The ordinance's plain language is admittedly violated scores of times daily, yet only some individuals—those chosen by the police in their unguided discretion—are arrested.... We conclude that the ordinance is substantially overbroad....

Today's decision reflects the constitutional requirement that, in the face of verbal challenges to police action, officers and municipalities must respond to the restraint. We are mindful that the preservation of liberty depends in part upon the maintenance of public order. But the first amendment recognizes, wisely we think, that a certain amount of expressive disorder not only is inevitable in a society committed to individual freedom, but must itself be protected if that freedom would survive. We therefore affirm the judgment of the Court of Appeals.

It is so ordered.

Case Discussion In what ways does this case differ from *State v. Lynch?* Why should the Constitution protect Hill's speech here, and not Lynch's? Do you agree that police officers—and society—have to put up with "a certain amount of expressive disorder?" Both *State v. Lynch* and *City of Houston v. Hill* demonstrate the difficulty in writing disorderly conduct laws that maintain public order without unduly restricting individual free speech. Did Hill commit a less serious offense than Lynch? Why?

Threats

Both verbal and physical threats that create public inconvenience, annoyance, or alarm, constitute a crime in most jurisdictions. Threatening is akin to, but broader than, assault. Assault protects against individual fear of serious bodily injury; threatening, a misdemeanor, aims to keep public order.[12]

CASE

*Was His Threat
Constitutional?*

Thomas v. Commonwealth

574 S.W.2d 903 (Ky.App.1978)

[Thomas was convicted of terroristic threatening, a gross misdemeanor, and was sentenced to twelve months in the county jail. Judge Hayes delivered the opinion.]

FACTS

The case for the Commonwealth was based solely on the testimony of Gladys Thomas. Mrs. Thomas on direct examination stated that on the Friday before she went to swear out the warrant that she was in her front yard cutting weeds with a butcher knife when appellant came out of the house, hit her across the back with his hand, laughed and ran into a barber shop next door. Appellant then came back laughing and hit her across the back with a belt and then ran into a liquor store about three doors down from the house. Appellant continued to aggravate Mrs. Thomas until she asked him to go and get her a coke.

Mrs. Thomas then testified thusly:

So, we went about an hour, an hour and a half after my mom left and he came in and

said, "I told you to get ready to go," and I said "I'm not going," and he grabbed me by the hair of the head and threw me against the refrigerator and said, "you are going or I will kill you and prove self-defense. This is one time everything is on my side. So, just get dressed and let's go somewhere and show everybody what a happy family we are."

Next, Mrs. Thomas gave testimony concerning the circumstances surrounding the threat which is the basis for the charge against appellant:

So, on Wednesday, he came in and he said, "I will come home. I'm coming home." I said, "you can't. You absolutely cannot. I went and applied for welfare," and he said, "I have to tell the man, Mr. Clark, that I'm here or I'll be in trouble." One thing led to another and he jumped up in the middle of the floor and said, "you and Brenda have got me against the wall. You're going to get me in trouble. I will cut both your heads off before I go back." Those are almost the exact words. And I looked around and the little girl was standing right in the screen door.

On cross-examination, Mrs. Thomas testified that this threat was made in the late afternoon and that on the next morning, on July 15, 1976, she went and got a warrant.

KRS 508.080 provides thusly:

1. A person is guilty of terroristic threatening when:

    a. He threatens to commit any crime likely to result in death or serious physical injury to another person or likely to result in substantial property damage to another person; or

b. He intentionally makes false statements for the purpose of causing evacuation of a building, place of assembly, or facility of public transportation.

c. Terroristic threatening is a Class A misdemeanor. (Enact. Acts 1974, ch. 405, § 72.)

OPINION

This court believes that KRS 508.080(1)(a) is not unconstitutionally vague and overbroad since the conduct proscribed, "threaten[ing] to commit a crime likely to result in death or serious physical injury" is not protected under either the Kentucky or United States Constitutions. Further the language of the statute is sufficiently explicit to put the average citizen on notice as to the nature of the conduct so proscribed.

The court is aware of the recent decision in *U.S. v. Sturgill,* 563 F.2d 307 (6th Cir. 1977), which invalidated KRS 525.070(1)(b) on the basis that it was unconstitutionally overbroad. KRS 525.070(1)(b) provides: "A person is guilty of harassment when with intent to harass, annoy or alarm another person he: (b) In a public place, makes an offensively coarse utterance, gesture or display, or addresses abusive language to any person present."

In *Sturgill,* the court, citing *Gooding v. Wilson,* 405 U.S. 518, 92 S.Ct. 1103, 31 L.Ed.2d 408 (1972), held that in order for a statute, which punishes spoken words only, to withstand an attack on its constitution-Δ530

ality; it must be first authoritatively interpreted by the state courts as not interfering with speech protected by the First Amendment.

This case can be distinguished from *Sturgill,* in that the language so proscribed under KRS 508.080(1)(a) is clearly without constitutional protection under the First Amendment.

… [A]pellant's assertion that the statute is defective because it does not require the defendant's threat to be serious or that it does not require an intent to actually convey a serious threat is ludicrous. When the unlawful threat is knowingly and wilfully made, the offense is complete, so that the existence of an intention to carry out the threat, or a subsequent abandonment of the bad intent with which the threat was made, is immaterial. Although idle talk or jesting will not constitute the crime, the accused cannot be regarded as having used his language only as a joke because of the fact that he may have had no intention to carry out his threat. The motive which prompts the utterance of a threat is immaterial. To bring a case within the statute no evil purpose or malice is requisite other than an intention to give utterance to words which to the accused's knowledge were in the form of, and would be naturally understood by the hearers, as being a threat.

Certainly, KRS 508.080(1)(a) does not apply in the case of idle talk or jesting. The defendant's intent to commit the crime of "terroristic threatening" can be plainly inferred from the defendant's own words and the circumstances surrounding them. All the statute requires is that the defendant threaten "to commit any crime likely to result in death or serious physical injury to another person or likely to result in substantial property damage to another person."

Case Discussion   Notice that Thomas's threat constituted the offense, not his ability or willingness to carry it out. Therefore, it is not assault, a more serious crime, from which threatening should be distinguished. The court says that Thomas was not idly jesting but was serious when he threatend his wife. Do you agree? Thomas said, and some friends testified, that when he slapped his wife's back, he was only "horseplaying." The court admitted that a Kentucky harassment statute that made it a crime to use coarse or abusive language or gestures in order to harass, annoy, or alarm another person was unconstitutionally vague. It went on to say that the threatening statute was different. Do you agree that threatening and harassment are distinguishable? How serious an offense is threatening? Should harassment be a crime as well? How serious is it?

Group Disorderly Conduct

From at least the mid-sixteenth century, English law punished three forms of group disorderly conduct: (1) unlawful assembly (three or more people gathered for an unlawful purpose); (2) rout (any movement toward completing the unlawful purpose); and (3) riot (the unlawful act in which unlawful assemblies and routs culminated). The famous Riot Act of 1714 made riot a felony if twelve or more persons rioted and failed to disperse within one hour following a warning to do so. The warning of "reading the riot act" has come down to modern times as an informal warning to calm down.

Today, all jurisdictions punish rioting and unlawful assembly. Most modern statutes follow the old practice, making unlawful assemblies, routs, and riots misdemeanors, with maximum penalties ranging from six months to a year in jail. The court in *State v. Mast* dealt with Missouri's unlawful assembly statute.

CASE

Was the Halloween Party an Unlawful Assembly?

State v. Mast
713 S.W.2d 601 (Mo.App.1986)

Dowd, Judge

Defendant, Steve Mast, appeals his jury conviction on Count I, UNLAWFUL ASSEMBLY in violation of § 574.040 RSMo (1979), a Class B misdemeanor, and on Count II, refusal to disperse from an UNLAWFUL ASSEMBLY, in violation of § 574.060 RSMo (1979), a Class C misdemeanor. On Count I, defendant was sentenced to a fine of $250.00 plus costs. On Count II, defendant was sentenced to two days in jail plus a fine of $100.00 plus costs. The information was filed in Lewis County, and after a change in venue, a jury trial was held in the Knox County Circuit Court. Defendant appeals from these convictions.

On appeal, defendant contends the evidence was insufficient to support the convictions and it was therefore error not to grant his motions for judgment of acquittal.

In testing the sufficiency of the evidence by a motion for judgment of acquittal, the evidence must be viewed in the light most favorable to the state, assuming the evidence of the state and every reasonable inference therefrom to be true, and the evidence and inferences to the contrary are disregarded. State v. Newton, *637 S.W.2d 805, 806 (Mo.App.1982).*

FACTS

On October 31, 1984, Halloween night, defendant, a student at Northeast Missouri State College in Kirksville, drove to the town of Maywood so that he could participate in the traditional Halloween gathering with his friends. Defendant was aware of Maywood's reputation for "anything goes on Halloween." He had been in Maywood on Halloween in past years, and arrived in Maywood around 5:45 p.m. with a friend, Donnie Martin. Defendant was dressed in his ROTC army fatigues and his face was covered with a black substance. Defendant had a bundle of bottle rockets in his possession and Donnie Martin carried a can of spray paint in his back pocket.

After arriving in Maywood, defendant and Donnie Martin socialized with some friends in front of a general store. Jerry Callow, the deputy sheriff, and Steve Waters, the special deputy appointed for Halloween night, warned defendant and his friends "to keep it down and keep it within reason." At that time, the officers explained to them that seven or more gathered constituted an illegal assembly, but as long as they were not doing anything but having fun, then the officers had no objections. Moreover, Waters informed defendant that it was not illegal to possess bottle rockets, but it was illegal to fire the bottle rockets. Additionally, he confiscated Donnie Martin's can of spray paint because of previous acts of vandalism.

Throughout the course of the night, different unlawful activities transpired such as: bottle rockets were set off in close vicinity to the general store's gas pumps and in the direction of the police car; Mr. Seals' house was egged and a stop sign was placed on his front porch; fire bombs and M-80s were set off; and eggs, bottle rockets, and a beer bottle were all thrown in the direction of the officers and their patrol car. In fact, Officer Callow was struck by an egg.

All of the above occurrences are not attributable to the defendant, but in the course of the evening the officers saw the defendant set off one bottle rocket away from the crowd and the buildings. The officers had difficulty identifying and determining the members of the crowd who were taking part in the unlawful activities. At one point in the evening, Deputy Callow told the crowd that they were getting unruly and committing unlawful acts, and consequently he "asked them to break it up." In response to his request, the crowd divided up into groups of four or five, but these groups did not separate far from each other and proceeded to call the officers names. After the officers departed, the crowd regrouped and continued to set off bottle rockets and fire bombs and throw eggs. Shortly after 10:30 p.m., the two officers turned on the red lights of their patrol car, drove up to the scattering crowd and made some arrests. Waters saw defendant in the middle of the crowd, immediately prior to this time, but he did not see defendant after the arrests.

OPINION

This is the first appellate attack on the present UNLAWFUL ASSEMBLY statute (§ 574.040 RSMo 1978). This statute provides in part:

> 1. A person commits the crime of UNLAWFUL ASSEMBLY if he knowingly assembles with six or more other persons and agrees with such persons to violate any of the criminal laws of this state or of the United States with force or violence.

A presumption exists "that the intent of the legislature in enacting a statute is to serve the best interests and welfare of the citizenry at large." This presumption must take into consideration the fact that the legis-lature did not intend to effect an unreasonable, oppressive or absurd result. Consequently, when interpreting § 574.040, we must determine the legislature's intent from what can be necessarily implied from the language it employed, because the legislature did not expressly state its intention. By identifying the general purposes for enacting a statute and by identifying the problem sought to be remedied, we can ascertain legislative intent.

Since § 574.040 was enacted, no Missouri case has interpreted this statute. However, other jurisdictions have addressed this issue interpreting similar statutes. The court in *Lair v. State,* 316 P.2d 225, 234 (Okla.Crim.-App.1957), defined an UNLAWFUL ASSEMBLY as being an assembly which consists of three or more persons assembled to do an unlawful act or who being assembled, attempt to do a lawful act in a violent or unlawful manner to the terror and the disturbance of the public in general. To constitute the offense of UNLAWFUL ASSEMBLY, the participants must have a common purpose and act in concert. The intent or purpose necessary to render an assembly unlawful need not exist from the onset, but may be formed either before or at the time of the assembly.

An UNLAWFUL ASSEMBLY causes a disturbance of the public order so that it is reasonable for rational, firm and courageous persons in the neighborhood of the assembly to believe the assembly will cause injury to persons or damage to property and will interfere with the rights of others by committing disorderly acts. The intent with which such persons assemble is the very offense of UNLAWFUL ASSEMBLY in that this intent is reflected by the participants' acts, conduct and language. The purpose of UNLAWFUL ASSEMBLY statutes is to discourage assemblies which interfere with the rights of others and endanger the public peace and excite fear and alarm among the people.

Even though a person does not individually commit a violent act which poses a clear and present danger of violence, this individual can be guilty of UNLAWFUL ASSEMBLY. The statutory denunciation applies to the assembly at large. Consequently, each member of an assembly need not individually commit unlawful acts to render the assembly unlawful, but a person can become a member of an UNLAWFUL ASSEMBLY by not disassociating himself from the group assembled and by knowingly joining or remaining with the group assembled after it has become unlawful. Whether a person acted knowingly and whether the necessary intent existed, are both questions of fact for the jury. Supra at 771.

If it were necessary that each member of an UNLAWFUL ASSEMBLY commit an unlawful act, before that member could be convicted then there would be no necessity to make participation in the UNLAWFUL ASSEMBLY a crime. The independent unlawful act would itself be grounds for prosecution. In short, every person who is present and cognizant of the unlawful acts being committed by the other members of the assembly can be found guilty of being unlawfully assembled.

When applying the foregoing principles to the facts in this case, we must view the evidence in a manner most favorable to the state. At its inception, the gathering in Maywood on Halloween night was a lawful assembly, however as the night progressed,

the participants' purpose in assembling changed. Undoubtedly, the assembly was disturbing the public peace and interfering with the rights of others. The persons in the neighborhood of the assembly had cause to fear the assembly would inflict damage to property and would commit disorderly acts. Throughout the evening, fire bombs, bottle rockets, M-80s, and eggs were being thrown at houses and people. Both Waters and Callow saw defendant fire a bottle rocket which is an unlawful act, according to one of the deputies. Defendant is no less guilty because he fired only one bottle rocket. Additionally, defendant drove his car across Mr. Seals' lawn.

Moreover, defendant had been in Maywood on previous Halloweens, and so he was aware of the type of activities that take place there on Halloween. Therefore, it is evident that defendant knew the purpose of the gathering on Halloween night. To be convicted of UNLAWFUL ASSEMBLY, defendant did not have to participate or encourage every harmful act which occurred that night. For that matter, defendant need not have actually committed an unlawful act. His presence alone in the UNLAWFUL ASSEMBLY was enough for conviction, because he knowingly assembled with the other members, and he was under a duty to disassociate himself from the group after other members of the group committed unlawful acts.

Defendant would have us construe the statutory section in such a manner so as to vitiate the purpose of the statute. We will favor a construction that avoids this unjust and unreasonable result. Defendant contends that no agreement existed between the group members, and consequently, he could not be guilty of participating in an UNLAWFUL ASSEMBLY. Such a narrow reading of the statute would defeat its purpose and create an absurd result by making it almost impossible to satisfy the elements of an UNLAWFUL ASSEMBLY.

Even though the group assembled did not expressly, verbally agree, their common unlawful purpose was expressed by their overt acts. Therefore, the members of the assembly intended to and in fact participated in an UNLAWFUL ASSEMBLY. The assembly members' acts, conduct and language indicated their adoption of the unlawful conduct of the other members assembled. Moreover, defendant performed an unlawful act himself so his guilt is not established by his presence alone.

The common law offense of UNLAWFUL ASSEMBLY is defined as follows:

> To constitute an offense it must appear that there was common intent of persons assembled to attain purpose ... by commission of acts of intimidation and disorder likely to produce danger to peace of neighborhood, and actually tending to inspire courageous persons with well-grounded fear of serious breaches of public peace.

The purpose of an UNLAWFUL ASSEMBLY statute is to penalize the members of assemblies when their conduct causes a disturbance or damage. The members must meet and form a common purpose to violate any of the criminal laws, but they do not have to actually violate the law. The New Missouri Criminal Code: A Manual for Court Related Personnel, § 19.5 University of Missouri—Columbia School of Law 19–3 (1978). The state has a strong and legitimate interest in protecting against criminal acts of force or violence in order to preserve public tranquility and other rights belonging to the public in general. "In furtherance of this interest, it must be able to 'nip in the bud' riots and may, therefore, regulate and proscribe UNLAWFUL ASSEMBLY." The gathering in Maywood on Halloween originally was a lawful one, but as the night progressed, the members of the assembly acted with common intent to attain a purpose which interfered with the rights of others by committing disorderly and unlawful acts.

Based on the foregoing principles, we hold there was substantial evidence to support the conviction of UNLAWFUL ASSEMBLY. Point one is denied.

Defendant's second point on appeal is that the trial court erred in denying his motion for judgment of acquittal on the charge of refusal to disperse because the evidence was manifestly insufficient to sustain a conviction. Taking the evidence in the light most favorable to the state, the evidence was sufficient to show that on Halloween night an UNLAWFUL ASSEMBLY had gathered in Maywood, and defendant had been lawfully warned to disperse. After hearing the warning, the defendant did as requested, but after a short period of time, he returned to the gathering. This evidence is sufficient to sustain his conviction for failure to disperse. Missouri's refusal to disperse statute states:

> *1.* A person commits the crime of refusal to disperse if, being present at the scene of an UNLAWFUL ASSEMBLY, or at the scene of a riot, he knowingly fails or refuses to obey the lawful command of a law enforcement officer to depart from the scene of such UNLAWFUL ASSEMBLY or riot. § 574.060 RSMo (1978).

Whether a person knowingly fails or refuses to obey the dispersal order is a question of fact for the jury. To be guilty of the charge of refusal to disperse, a person must be at the scene of an UNLAWFUL ASSEMBLY and know of the command to disperse, and still refuse to obey.

The evidence favorable to the state showed that defendant heard Callow order the crowd to disperse by telling it "to break it up." In response to this command, the gathering broke up into groups of four and five and then proceeded to regroup shortly thereafter. By regrouping, defendant in effect refused to obey the lawful command of Callow to depart from the scene of the UNLAWFUL ASSEMBLY.

Defendant alleges that the warning given was inadequate because it did not expressly order the crowd to go home or to leave town. § 574.060 does not require a warning to expressly designate a location where the crowd is to disperse. A person who "knowingly fails or refuses to obey the lawful command of a law enforcement officer to disperse from the scene of such UNLAWFUL ASSEMBLY," is guilty of this crime. § 574.060 RSMo (1978).

The warning could be reasonably understood to mean that the crowd was to leave the area. The failure of the warning to describe the area to be vacated has nothing to do with defendant's failure to comply. After Callow warned the crowd to break it up, the crowd regrouped, thus suggesting that the crowd would have disregarded the warning in any event.

Words are to be interpreted according to their plain and ordinary meaning which is the commonly accepted dictionary definition. "Break up" is defined as "to disrupt the continuity or flow or to bring to an end." Webster's Collegiate Dictionary 177 (9th ed.

1984). A person of reasonable intelligence would understand the words "break it up" to mean that he is supposed to depart from the area. In total disregard and in defiance of the command, defendant remained in the area in question. By his inaction, defendant was not complying with the command to disperse.

Defendant's second point on appeal, therefore, is denied.

For the foregoing reasons, the judgment of the trial court is affirmed.

Case Discussion

How does Missouri's unlawful assembly statute differ from the common-law definition of the offense? What facts indicate the *actus reus* and *mens rea* of unlawful assembly? Of refusal to disperse? Does Mast have a point in arguing that he was not part of an unlawful assembly, and that he did not commit the crime of refusal to disperse? Do you think Mast committed any crimes here? What were they? Why would you make them crimes? What penalty would you attach to them? What purposes would making this conduct criminal and punishing it accomplish?

In some states, aggravated rioting provisions in group disorderly conduct statutes make it a felony to carry weapons or obstruct police officers during riots.

During the 1960s and early 1970s, critics charged that modern riot legislation violated the United States Constitution. Rout, unlawful assembly, and riot violated the due process clause because they were both vague and overbroad. Courts have not sustained these charges, however. In fact, several United States Supreme Court opinions have upheld such legislation despite Justice Hugo Black's observation that the Bill of Rights was intended specifically to prevent the encroachments on free expression inherent in English riot legislation. Some critics maintain that even if modern riot legislation is constitutional, the legislation furthers an unwise public policy. They say that inchoate offense (see chapter 5 on incomplete crimes) and disorderly conduct laws deal adequately with riot, and riot needs no further special legislation. Anything more poses too great a threat to individual autonomy. Defenders maintain that our modern, pluralistic society requires special legislation to condemn and punish group disorderly conduct in order to preserve order.

The use of, and debate over, group disorderly conduct ebbs and flows according to the temper of the times. For example, riot, rout, and unlawful assembly provisions were frequently used and hotly debated during the 1960s, as they had been in earlier troubled times. When times are freer from openly expressed discontent, as were the more placid 1950s, both the use of those provisions and the debate surrounding them subside. Recently, protest has returned to the scene and controversies over abortion, CIA (Central Intelligence Agency) recruitment on college and university campuses, and the purveying of pornography amply demonstrate that group disorderly conduct law remains relevant. A panel of the Circuit Court for the District of Columbia dealt with a statute prohibiting demonstrations inside the Supreme Court building in *United States v. Wall.*

CASE

Can You Protest Inside the Supreme Court?

United States v. Wall
521 A.2d 1140 (D.C.Cir.1987)

Newman, Associate Judge: In this appeal we are asked to decide whether the statutory provision making it unlawful to "parade, stand, or move in processions or assemblages in the Supreme Court Building or grounds," 40 U.S.C. § 13k (1982), is unconstitutional as applied to conduct occurring when the Supreme Court is not in session. We hold that both the provision and its application withstand constitutional scrutiny. We reverse the trial court's ruling to the contrary.

FACTS
In January 1985, Joseph P. Wall participated in an anti-abortion demonstration which took place in front of the Supreme Court building. A crowd of approximately 50,000 demonstrators assembled in the street and sidewalk area in front of the Court, carrying placards and bullhorns, and chanting anti-abortion slogans. Eventually, a smaller group of twenty to thirty persons left the sidewalk area and proceeded to the plaza area of the Court, several of them carrying a coffin-shaped box on their shoulders. Upon reaching the plaza, the group ascended the main steps of the Courthouse until they reached a landing area, where they met a line of police officers. Approximately twenty-five feet from the top of the stairs and the front entrance to the Court, the group deposited the "coffin," knelt down, and began praying aloud. Wall was among another group of demonstrators who ascended the

steps after the coffin had been deposited; he carried a large placard and knelt down with the rest of the group to pray.

A Supreme Court police officer approached the group, and warned them three times that if they did not return to the sidewalk area, they would be arrested for violation of Title 40 of the United States Code. Although many of the participants returned to the sidewalk, Wall and a group of forty others remained kneeling on the stair landing. Following another warning (to no avail), Wall was arrested along with some forty other protestors.

Upon the conclusion of evidence, the trial court made an initial factual determination that Wall's conduct violated 40 U.S.C. § 13k, noting that Wall was "clearly actively, intentionally, knowingly, and willfully involved in a demonstration as defined by the statute and was knowingly taking part ... in it, and did walk up those steps with everyone else, with all of the placards available, and he was carrying a placard himself." Nevertheless, the court proceeded to find Wall not guilty, reasoning that the plaza area and main entrance steps of the Supreme Court constitute a public forum available for the free expression of ideas under the first amendment, so long as the Supreme Court is not in session. [No evidence was presented showing the Supreme Court was in session and the court did not decide whether the statute was constitutional applied to those facts.] Accordingly, the court held that the application of 40 U.S.C. § 13k to Wall's activity would be unconstitutional. The government appeals....

OPINION
The underlying premise of the trial court's ruling was that the plaza area and main entrance steps of the Supreme Court constitute a "public forum" for purposes of first amendment analysis. On appeal, the government argues that the area at issue is not a

public forum. In the alternative, it contends that, even if the steps and plaza are a public forum, the statute constitutes a reasonable time, place and manner restriction.

We agree that § 13k's prohibition on "parad[ing], stand[ing], or mov[ing] in processions or assemblages in the Supreme Court Building or grounds" passes muster under both the standard applicable to non-public forums and the test applied to time, place and manner restrictions permissible in public forums. Therefore, we do not find it necessary to decide in this case whether or not the Supreme Court's main entrance steps and plaza area comprise a public forum for purposes of first amendment scrutiny.

[40 U.S.C. § 13k provides in full: "It shall be unlawful to parade, stand, or move in processions or assemblages in the Supreme Court Building or grounds, or to display therein any flag, banner, or device designed or adapted to bring into public notice any party, organization, or movement."]

The Supreme Court has held that "[t]he existence of a right of access to public property and the standard by which limitations upon such a right must be evaluated differ depending on the character of the property at issue." The Court has developed a tripartite division of governmental property, while simultaneously recognizing that the types of property in fact comprise a "spectrum." At one end of the spectrum are streets and parks, the "quintessential public forums."

[COURT NOTE: "The classic statement of the quintessential public forum was given by Justice Roberts in *Hague v. CIO,* 307 U.S. 496, 515, 59 S.Ct. 954, 963, 83 L.Ed. 1423 (1939):

> Wherever the title of streets and parks may rest, they have immemorially been held in trust for the use of the public, and, time out of mind, have been used for purposes of assembly, communicating thoughts between citizens, and discussing public questions. Such use of the streets and public places has, from ancient times, been a part of the privileges, immunities, rights, and liberties of citizens. Public forum analysis, as a formula for applying different standards to governmental regulation depending upon the nature of the governmental property, is of much more

recent vintage, however. Not until the 1970's did public forum doctrine begin to be used to justify limitations on, rather than expansion of, first amendment freedoms."]

In these quintessential public forums, the state may enforce content-based regulations only if they are narrowly drawn to serve a compelling governmental interest. Content-neutral restrictions on the time, place and manner of expression, are permissible if they are narrowly tailored to serve a significant governmental interest, and leave open ample alternative channels of communication.

A second category of governmental property is property that, while not a public forum by tradition, has been designated a public forum by governmental action, usually for some limited purpose. See, e.g., *Widmar v. Vincent,* 454 U.S. 263, 102 S.Ct. 269, 70 L.Ed.2d 440 (1981) (meeting facilities provided by state university for use by student groups). In these "limited public forums," or "public forums by designation," the government is bound by the same standards that apply in traditional public forums. However, the government is not required to retain the open character of the property indefinitely. *Perry,* supra, 460 U.S. at 46, 103 S.Ct. at 955.

The third and residual category encompasses governmental property that is not a public forum either by tradition or by designation. See, e.g., *Perry,* supra, 460 U.S. at 46–48, 103 S.Ct. at 955–56 (inter-school mail system); *Cornelius v. NAACP Legal Defense and Educational Fund, Inc.,* 473 U.S. 788, 105 S.Ct. 3439, 3450–51, 87 L.Ed.2d 567 (1985) (Combined Federal Campaign federal employees' charity drive). Regulation of expression in these "nonpublic forums" is permissible so long as the regulation is both reasonable and not an effort to suppress the speaker's point of view.

[COURT NOTE: "The concept of a non-public forum implies a right to make distinctions in access on the basis of subject matter and speaker identity. These distinctions are permissible if they are reasonable in light of the purpose which the forum serves."]

Time, place and manner restrictions may also be applied to nonpublic forums.

While the standards for evaluating regulations on expression in the three types of forums are relatively clear, those for determining which type of forum describes a particular parcel of public property have been less brightly drawn. In determining whether government property has become a public forum by designation, the Court has suggested that it will consider whether the principal function of the property would be disrupted by excessive activity. Hence, the Court may make a preliminary inquiry into the compatibility between the nature of the property and the type of expression that the government is seeking to regulate. It is perhaps for this reason that the Court has observed that "the analytical line between a regulation of the 'time, place, and manner' in which First Amendment rights may be exercised in a traditional public forum, and the question of whether a particular piece of personal or real property owned or controlled by the government is in fact a 'public forum' may blur at the edges...." *United States Postal Service v. Council of Greenburgh Civic Associations,* 453 U.S. 114, 132, 101 S.Ct. 2676, 2686, 69 L.Ed.2d 517 (1981).

The difficulty of distinguishing between the categorization of the forum and the legitimacy of the regulation is especially acute in cases "falling between the paradigms of government property interests essentially mirroring analogous private interests and those clearly held in trust, either by tradition or recent convention, for the use of citizens at large." *Members of the City Council of Los Angeles v. Taxpayers for Vincent,* 466 U.S. 789, 815 n. 32, 104 S.Ct. 2118, 2134 n. 32, 80 L.Ed.2d 772 (1984). Thus, the Court has recognized that in some cases it may be "of limited utility ... to focus on whether the tangible property itself should be deemed a public forum." Id. When a regulation can be upheld as a time, place or manner restriction, the Court has not always found it necessary to consider to which type of forum the regulation is being applied. See, e.g., *Clark v. Community for Creative Non-Violence,* 468 U.S. 288, 104

S.Ct. 3065, 82 L.Ed.2d 221 (1984) (upholding ban on sleeping in Lafayette Park and national Mall area as permissible time, place, and manner restriction on demonstration, without noting the nature of the forum).

We believe that 40 U.S.C. § 13k's prohibition on processions and assemblages in the plaza area and main entrance steps of the Supreme Court is reasonable and viewpoint-neutral, and, therefore, meets the test imposed on exclusion of speakers from nonpublic forums. We also believe that the prohibition meets the more stringent test applicable to a time, place and manner restriction that may be imposed even in a public forum: that it be narrowly drawn to serve a significant governmental interest, that it be content-neutral, and that it leave open ample alternative channels of communication.

The government argues that there are two primary purposes for the statutory provision at issue here: to permit the unimpeded access and egress of litigants and visitors to the Court, and to preserve the appearance of the Court as a body not swayed by external influence.

[COURT NOTE: "The provisions and legislative history of the Act of which § 13k is a part suggest that the purpose of the Act was to provide for the protection of the building and grounds of the Supreme Court, and of persons and property therein, as well as to maintain proper order and decorum."]

We are satisfied that these are "significant" governmental interests that can support a time, place or manner restriction. In *Cameron v. Johnson,* 390 U.S. 611, 88 S.Ct. 1335, 20 L.Ed.2d 182 (1968), the Supreme Court upheld a state statute restricting persons singly or in groups from conducting picketing or mass demonstrations that obstruct or unreasonably interfere with ingress or egress from courthouses and other public buildings. In *Cox v. Louisiana,* 379 U.S. 559, 562, 85 S.Ct. 476, 479, 13 L.Ed.2d 487 (1965), the Court held that a state may adopt necessary safeguards to assure that the administration of justice is free from outside control and influence. Cox upheld a statute prohibiting picketing in or near a courthouse when done with the intent of influencing the administration of justice. We believe that preventing the appearance of such influence is also a significant governmental interest.

[COURT NOTE: "For this reason, regulation of expression outside a courthouse may be permissible where the same regulation applied to the grounds surrounding a legislature would not be. In *Jeannette Rankin Brigade v. Chief of Capitol Police,* 342 F.Supp. 575 (D.D.C.), aff'd mem., 409 U.S. 972, 93 S.Ct. 311, 34 L.Ed.2d 236 (1972), the United States District Court invalidated 40 U.S.C. § 193g, the counterpart statute to 40 U.S.C. § 13k, governing the United States Capitol grounds. The court distinguished the unique function of the judicial branch to render decisions free from the pressures of popular opinion. By contrast, explained the court, the 'fundamental function of a legislature in a democratic society assumes accessibility to such opinion.'"]

Furthermore, the prohibition is narrowly drawn to serve the interests that the government has articulated. None of its provisions appears unrelated to the ends that it was designed to serve. *Clark,* supra, 468 U.S. at 297, 104 S.Ct. at 3070. It does not prohibit all access to the Supreme Court grounds by persons not having business there. Rather, it prohibits only "parad[ing], stand[ing], or mov[ing] in processions or assemblages" therein. The statutory provision is also entirely content-neutral on its face, and there is no evidence in the record that it has been applied in a discriminatory manner.

In addition, by prohibiting processions and assemblages in the plaza and main entrance steps, the statute leaves open ample alternative channels of communication. The record reflects that Wall and the larger group of which he was a part, numbering some 50,000 persons, had been permitted to carry placards and chant slogans as long as they remained on the sidewalk and in the street in front of the Court. Hence, the demonstrators' message could be, and indeed was, communicated in other ways.

Finally, we address the trial court's conclusion that the restrictions at issue are unconstitutional as applied to Wall because they were applied when the Court was not in session. We cannot agree that the governmental interests that undergird the restriction are significantly diminished when the Justices are not actually hearing oral argument. The danger of the appearance of outside influence upon the Court is ever present. Furthermore, the building remains open for business even when oral arguments are not taking place, supporting the need to maintain the main entrance steps and plaza are clear of processions and assemblages.

Accordingly, we hold that the first clause of 40 U.S.C. § 13k, making it unlawful to "parade, stand, or move in processions or assemblages in the Supreme Court Building or grounds," is a constitutionally valid restriction on expression. The statutory provision's validity is not undermined when, as in this case, it is applied to conduct occurring when the Court is not in session.

Reversed and remanded for entry of an order consistent with this opinion.

Case Discussion Why does the court distinguish among various types of public places? Do you agree that the government has a right to pass laws restricting citizens or groups of citizens to protest in courts? Why does the court say demonstrations in legislatures differ from demonstrations in courts? Do you agree? Should the desire for decorum and looks take precedence over citizens' rights to express themselves to their government? Is this what the court is saying? Or does the law both allow protest and preserve decorum?

Hate Crimes

For a long time, both civil law and criminal law have used libel and slander laws to protect individuals from character defamation. Most of this legislation remains intact today. However, some law reformers believe that a more general harm to the community results when racial, religious, national, gender, other groups are defamed. These reformers argue that criminal law ought to protect the social cohesion that a healthy, diverse society needs in order to function smoothly and that is damaged by fomenting group hatred. Many states have enacted statutes aggravating **bias-motivated crimes.** These statutes add more severe penalties to existing crimes, such as murder, assault, trespass, and other offenses against individuals, when perpetrators committed the crimes because of racial, ethnic, or gender prejudice. Hence, gay bashing and race crimes now carry heavier penalties in many states.

Others have created specific **hate crimes,** making conduct motivated by race, gender, sexual preference, religious, and ethnic bias crimes against public order. The Supreme Court, at the time of this writing, heard arguments challenging the constitutionality of a St. Paul, Minnesota, ordinance banning cross burning. Robert Vitkora burned a cross on the lawn of Russell and Laura Jones, a black couple who had recently moved into a white middle-class neighborhood. The Minnesota Supreme Court held that the ordinance did not infringe on Vitkora's right of free expression. The Supreme Court of Georgia dealt with the constitutionality of a Georgia statute outlawing the wearing of masks in public in *State v. Miller,* a case involving a citizen who wore a KKK mask in public.[13]

CASE

Did He Have a Right to Wear His KKK Mask in Public?

State v. Miller
398 S.E.2d 547 (Ga.1990)

Clarke, Chief Justice

FACTS

Shade Miller, Jr. was arrested for violating OCGA § 16–11–38 when he appeared in public wearing the traditional regalia of the Ku Klux Klan ("Klan"), including a mask that covered his face. He admitted that he wore the mask, but challenged the constitutionality of the statute, alleging that it is unconstitutionally vague and overbroad, and violates his freedom of speech and association under the United States and Georgia constitutions. The trial court held the statute to be unconstitutional and dismissed the case. We reverse.

OPINION

… Known as the "Anti-Mask Act," OCGA § 16–11–38 provides as follows:

> a. A person is guilty of a misdemeanor when he wears a mask, hood, or device by which any portion of the face is so hidden, concealed, or covered as to conceal the identity of the wearer and is upon any public way or public property or upon the private property of another without the written permission of the owner or occupier of the property to do so.
> b. This Code section shall not apply to:
>   *1.* A person wearing a traditional holiday costume on the occasion of the holiday;
>   *2.* A person lawfully engaged in trade or employment or in a sporting activity where a mask is worn for the purpose of ensuring the physical safety of the wearer, or because of the nature of the occupation, trade or profession, or sporting activity;

3. A person using a mask in a theatrical production including use of Mardi Gras celebrations and masquerade balls; or

4. A person wearing a gas mask prescribed in emergency management drills and exercises or emergencies.

The "Anti-Mask Act" was enacted along with a "Statement of Public Policy," which reflects the General Assembly's awareness of and concern over the dangers to society posed by anonymous vigilante organizations. It reads as follows:

All persons residing in the State are entitled to the equal protection of their lives and property. The law protects all, not only against actual physical violence, but also against threats and intimidations from any person or group of persons. The General Assembly cannot permit persons known or unknown, to issue either actual or implied threats, against other persons in the State. Persons in this State are and shall continue to be answerable only to the established law as enforced by legally appointed officers. Ga.L.1951, p. 9 § 1, H.B. 12.

Miller argues first that the statute is unconstitutional as applied to him because his wearing a mask was protected symbolic speech under the federal and Georgia constitutions.

"Freedom of speech is one of this nation's most treasured rights...."

[COURT NOTE: "Miller's mask was worn solely to conceal his identity. For the purpose of this analysis we assume without deciding that Miller's wearing a mask was conduct 'sufficiently imbued with elements of communication' to implicate the First Amendment."]

However, conduct that may have some communicative element is not therefore immune from governmental regulation. Under the test enunciated in *United States v. O'Brien,* 391 U.S. 367, 376, 88 S.Ct. 1673, 1678, 20 L.Ed.2d 672 (1968), the government may regulate conduct that may have both speech and "nonspeech" elements if the regulation furthers a substantial governmental interest that is unrelated to the suppression of free expression; and the incidental restriction on First Amendment freedom is no

greater than necessary to further the governmental interest. The Anti-Mask Act meets these criteria.

We know that "[p]ublic disguise is a particularly effective means of committing crimes of violence and intimidation. From the beginning of time the mask or hood has been the criminal's dress. It conceals evidence, hinders apprehension and calms the criminal's inward cowardly fear." A nameless, faceless figure strikes terror in the human heart. But, remove the mask, and the nightmarish form is reduced to its true dimensions. The face betrays not only identity, but also human frailty. OCGA § 16–11–38 was passed in 1951. Its passage was preceded by a period of increased harassment, intimidation and violence against racial and religious minorities carried out by mask-wearing Klansmen and other "hate" organizations. These groups operated as vigilantes and were responsible for numerous beatings and lynchings. Because of the masks, victims of Klan violence were unable to assist law enforcement officers in identifying their oppressors. They were afraid, perhaps, even to report such incidents in case law enforcement officers might have been involved.

The sponsor of the Anti-Mask Act, Judge Osgood Williams, testified that prior to the passage of the act, mask-wearing had helped to create a climate of fear that prevented Georgia citizens from exercising their civil rights. "Fear," he said, "is one of the things that makes people run the other way, [puts] people in a position [so] that they won't register to vote, they won't take part in political activities...." He cited a headline from the Atlanta Constitution printed in March, 1949, that stated, "Klan Parades in Wrightsville Election Eve; 400 Registered Negroes Fail To Vote."

The statute was passed in response to a demonstrated need to safeguard the people of Georgia from terrorization by masked vigilantes.... The statute is intended to protect the citizens of Georgia from intimidation, violence, and actual and implied threats; it is also designed to assist law enforcement in apprehending criminals, and to restore confidence in law enforcement by removing any possible illusion of government complicity with masked vigilantes. The state's interests furthered by the Anti-Mask Act lie at the very heart of the realm of legitimate governmental activity....

[COURT NOTE: "We are unmoved by Miller's argument that the statute is unconstitutional because it was enacted in order to "unmask the Klan." Even if "unmasking the Klan'" is synonymous with suppressing the Klan's freedom of speech—which it is not— we reject this argument because under settled principles of constitutional law the court will not strike down an otherwise constitutional statute on the basis of an alleged illicit legislative motive."]

Further, these interests are in no way related to the suppression of constitutionally protected expression. The statute is content-neutral. It proscribes a certain form of menacing conduct without regard to the particular message of the mask-wearer. To the extent that the statute does proscribe the communicative aspect of mask-wearing conduct, its restriction is limited to threats and intimidation, which is not protected expression under the First Amendment.

Miller next contends that the statute's incidental restriction on freedom of expression is greater than necessary to protect the governmental interests at stake. We disagree. As we interpret the statute ... below, the statute's incidental restriction on expression is de minimis. The statute does not prevent Miller from appearing in public in his traditional Klan robe and pointed hat, which he points out in his brief symbolizes the "Klan's tradition of violence and terrorism." It does not prevent him from publicly proclaiming his message, from carrying any banner or flag, from wearing any badge or insignia, from handing out printed material, or from soliciting members.

The law restricts only unprotected expression—the communication of a threat; and regulates only the noncommunicative function of the mask, the concealment of the wearer's identity. In other words, the statute "seeks to proscribe conduct, not free speech, and '... that conduct—even if expressive—falls within the scope of otherwise valid criminal laws that reflect legitimate state interests in maintaining comprehensive controls over harmful, constitutionally unprotected conduct....'"

Miller next argues that the statute is unconstitutionally vague and overbroad.... Miller asserts that the statute criminalizes a substantial amount of innocent behavior, such as wearing a ski mask in mid-winter, wearing sunglasses on a sunny day, or wearing a mask to make a political point. As we interpret the statute, it does not sweep so broadly. When read with the "Statement of Public Policy," the meaning and purpose of the statute are clear. The language of the statute itself is therefore easily susceptible to a narrowing construction that avoids any constitutional overbreadth problem.

Conviction under the statute requires the state to prove that the mask is worn with an intent to conceal the identity of the wearer. Further, we construe the statute in conjunction with its policy statement to apply only to mask-wearing conduct when the mask-wearer knows or reasonably should know that the conduct provokes a reasonable apprehension of intimidation, threats or violence. So narrowed, the statute does not reach a substantial amount of constitutionally protected conduct. Miller next argues that such a narrowing construction of the statute renders it unconstitutionally vague because it requires law enforcement to cater to individuals' irrational and idiosyncratic fears. Plainly, it does not....

It is often necessary and appropriate to consider the context of certain behavior before applying a criminal statute. This does not make the statute unconstitutionally vague.... Persons of common intelligence may readily appreciate mask-wearing conduct that provokes a reasonable apprehension of intimidation, threats or impending violence in a given context. For example, a person wearing a ski-mask in mid-winter would not ordinarily warrant alarm, but a person wearing a ski-mask on a warm day and while entering a bank certainly would.

Miller next argues that the statute violates his freedom of association under the First

Amendment. He asserts that if he is not allowed to proclaim his message anonymously, fear of persecution will deter from asserting his beliefs at all. This Court and the U.S. Supreme Court have long recognized that, under certain circumstances, anonymity may be essential to the exercise of constitutional rights. In *Talley v. California*, 362 U.S. 60, 80 S.Ct. 536, 4 L.Ed.2d 559 (1960), in which the Supreme Court held unconstitutional a statute that required all hand-bills to bear the true name and address of the person sponsoring them, the Supreme Court stated:

> Anonymous pamphlets, leaflets, brochures and even books have played an important role in the progress of mankind. Persecuted groups and sects from time to time throughout history have been able to criticize oppressive practices and laws either anonymously or not at all. The obnoxious press licensing law of England, which was also enforced on the Colonies was due in part to the knowledge that exposure of the names of printers, writers and distributors would lessen the circulation of literature critical of the government.... Even the Federalist Papers, written in favor of the adoption of our Constitution, were published under fictitious names. It is plain that anonymity has sometimes been assumed for the most constructive purposes. It is equally plain, however, that anonymity has often been assumed for the most pernicious purposes. Anonymity is neither an absolute social good, nor an absolute constitutional right. Consequently, statutes that affect an individual's right to associate or to advocate anonymously are analyzed in light of the nature of the governmental interests furthered by the statute and the extent of the burden that they place on individual rights.

It is important to note that this statute ... does not require the Klan to reveal the names or addresses of any of its members. It does not prevent Klan members from joining the organization secretly or from wearing their masks when they meet on private property. It does not prevent the Klan from circulating anonymous literature, or from anonymously sponsoring signs, billboards or radio or television announcements. It only prevents masked appearance in public under circumstances that give rise to a reasonable apprehension of intimidation, threats or impending violence.

We therefore conclude that the statute's effect on the Klan's ability to advocate or proselytize anonymously is negligible. Further, we are unmoved by Miller's argument that he must appear masked in public to avoid persecution.... [T]he record in this case is devoid of any proof of any injury to or loss of a job by members of the Klan.

[COURT NOTE: "Miller's reliance on evidence that the GBI monitors or videotapes Klan meetings is unpersuasive. These practices do not constitute evidence of persecution of the Klan. Further, these practices are not mandated by the statute. Any deterrent effect they may have on the Klan's ability to associate anonymously is not at issue here. In sum, when individuals engage in intimidating or threatening mask-wearing behavior, their interest in maintaining their anonymity while in the public square must give way to the weighty interests of the State discussed above."]

Finally, Miller argues that the statute violates the Equal Protection Clause of the Fourteenth Amendment. He says that the distinctions created by the statute—allowing mask-wearing for holidays, balls and theatrical productions—discriminate unconstitutionally against mask-wearing for a political purpose. In our view, the statute distinguishes appropriately between mask-wearing that is intimidating, threatening or violent and mask-wearing for benign purposes. It would be absurd to interpret the statute to prevent non-threatening political mask-wearing, or to condone threatening mask-wearing conduct on a holiday. We eschew such a construction of the statute.

In conclusion, we hold that the Anti-Mask Act proscribes mask-wearing conduct that is intended to conceal the wearer's identity and that the wearer knows, or reasonably should know, gives rise to a reasonable apprehension of intimidation, threats or impending violence. So construed, the Act passes constitutional muster.

Judgment reversed.

CONCURRING OPINION

Hunt, Justice, concurring specially.

I agree with the majority that the Anti-Mask Act may be construed to be constitutionally permissible. I disagree, however, that this court is authorized to construe the act to impose criminal liability where the mask-wearer merely knows or reasonably should know that his conduct (in wearing a mask intended to conceal his identity) will give rise to a reasonable apprehension of intimidation, threats, or impending violence. Criminal liability should be imposed only where he intends to intimidate or to threaten or to create an environment for impending violence.

It is a long-standing rule that criminal statutes must be strictly construed against the state and liberally in favor of the accused. A reading of the Anti-Mask Act, with its Statement of Public Policy, shows the act is intended to deter threats and intimidations by persons or groups of persons wearing masks. Yet the act itself contains no requirement of mens rea connecting the mask-wearer with the conduct to be deterred (threats or intimidations). In reading an element of mens rea into the act, I believe we are required, under the rule that criminal statutes be strictly construed in favor of human liberty, to choose that most beneficial to the defendant—actual intent. Thus, I would construe the Anti-Mask Act, with its Statement of Public Policy, to require an actual intent on the part of the mask-wearer to threaten or intimidate....

DISSENT

Smith, Presiding Justice, dissenting.

"[A]bove all else, the First Amendment means that government has no power to restrict expression because of its message, its ideas, its subject matter or its content. [Cits.]" *Collin v. Smith,* 578 F.2d 1197, 1202 (7th Cir.1978) cert. denied, 439 U.S. 916, 99 S.Ct. 291, 58 L.Ed.2d 264 (1978). (Nazi party allowed to demonstrate wearing Nazi uniforms and swastikas in Skokie, Illinois, a community where many Holocaust survivors lived.) First Amendment rights are precious and fundamental. Our constitutional system protects minorities, even those with the most unpopular views. [The government cannot criminalize speech except to serve a "compelling state interest."]

The purpose of the anti-mask statute is to unmask the Ku Klux Klan; not to prevent masked crimes. The trial court found, and it is undisputed, that the statute "was written with the specific intent of unmasking the 'Klan.' Therefore, the true legislative intent was to unmask a dissident group." Judge Osgood Williams, one of the drafters of the statute and now a Superior Court judge, testified that in the twenty-eight years he has been a Fulton County Superior Court judge not one person who committed an armed robbery while wearing a mask was charged under the anti-mask statute.

The statute is not enforced against masked criminals generally; it is enforced against a dissident group. It was enacted and it is enforced as a means of preventing Klan members from appearing in public in masks. It is not the statute's ends, but its means, that is objectionable and unconstitutional.

Mr. Miller was charged with "Wearing a mask or hood which concealed his identity." He testified generally that his purpose in appearing on the courthouse square was to protest the anti-mask statute. He asserted that his identification as a Klan member could create danger for himself and his family. He was the only Klan member in Klan clothing on the square, he was not engaging in any threatening or menacing behavior, and his masked presence did not cause a breach of the peace. Under the majority opinion, his peaceful protest violates the statute because his "anonymity while in the public square must give way to the weighty interests of the State...."

The majority opinion reads an irrebuttable presumption into the statute, i.e., because of the history of the Klan, the Klan mask is irrebuttably presumed to be symbolic speech that gives rise to apprehension of intimidation, threats or impending violence. A Klan member can violate the statute during a peaceful anti-mask demonstration in which there is no evil intent or conduct on the part of the wearer. Only Klan members wearing Klan masks bear this irrebuttable presumption; other individuals or groups can hold demonstrations while wearing masks and not violate the statute because the presumption is not present.

I do not agree that the statute as written can be construed to be constitutional, but I do agree with part of Justice Hunt's concurring opinion. If a criminal intent is to be read into the statute, it must be an actual intent on the part of the actor that does not violate the actor's First Amendment rights. The majority's standard would proscribe mask-wearing conduct where the "wearer knows, or reasonably should know, [that his conduct] gives rise to a reasonable apprehension of intimidation, threats or impending violence." This standard, more appropriate to tort than criminal law, violates the First Amendment....

The majority opinion's attempt to uphold the constitutionality of the statute falls short of this requirement. Advocacy of lawless action is protected, but incitement to imminent lawless action is not. "A statute which fails to draw this distinction impermissibly intrudes upon the freedoms guaranteed by the First and Fourteenth Amendments. It sweeps within its condemnation speech which our Constitution has immunized from governmental control." The United States Supreme Court has drawn the line between ideas and overt acts. The Klan's white robes, hats, and masks may all express the idea of a threat, but ideas are protected. Only an overt act accompanied by a specific intent violates the criminal law. OCGA § 16–11–37 (Terroristic threats and acts). Certainly the state has a compelling interest in preventing intentional criminal behavior by masked individuals or groups as the mask makes identification difficult; however, the anti-mask statute as written and enforced is a content-based restriction on political speech directed to a dissident group in a public forum, and it is not narrowly tailored to serve a compelling state interest. I would find the statute unconstitutional for the reasons stated.

[COURT NOTE: "On October 12, 1990 I had the privilege of meeting with approximately 200 of south Georgia's finest high school seniors during the 'Jefferson Community Meeting on the Bill of Rights.' After a day-long discussion of Supreme Court cases … the students voted on the following question: 'Should freedom of speech include the right of Nazi and other radical groups to advocate political ideas that are contrary to society's basic beliefs and offensive to large segments of the American people?' The overwhelming majority of the students voted yes."]

Case Discussion   What exactly does the Georgia anti-mask statute intend to do? Do you think it succeeds? Do you favor legislating against wearing masks in the way Georgia does it? What purpose does such legislation serve? Do you think the law infringes on Miller's First Amendment rights? Why? Do you agree that the *mens rea* for mask-wearing should be purposeful or with specific intent as the concurring and dissenting opinions urge? Or is recklessness enough? Should negligence suffice? What about making it a strict liability crime?

Crimes of Condition

From at least the sixteenth century in England, it was a crime to be wilfully poor. Law and society distinguished sharply the "impotent poor" (those who could not work) from the "sturdy poor" (those who would not work). Poor persons who could, but would not, work were vagrants and, under old statutes, criminals. Local communities supported the impotent poor if they remained in their own neighborhoods. The assumption was that most poor people were able to work but would not. Only a few were too impotent to work. It was a crime not only to be wilfully poor but also to give money to "sturdy beggars."

Vagrancy laws came to America under the 1714 English Vagrancy Act. The statute established three vagrant categories: idle and disorderly persons, rogues and vagabonds, and incorrigible rogues. In some form, those categories remained in most modern legislation. Vagrancy was a crime of condition or status (see chapter 3 on *actus reus*). According to one judge:

> Vagrancy differs from most other offenses in the fact that it is chronic rather than acute; that it continues after it is complete, and thereby subjects the offender to arrest any time before he reforms.[14]

According to the Model Penal Code Reporter, the following conditions constituted the crime of vagrancy in

1. Living in idleness without employment or visible means of support
2. Common prostitute
3. Common drunkard
4. Common gambler
5. Keeper of house of prostitution
6. Keeper of house of gambling
7. Wanton, dissolute, or lascivious persons
8. Associate of known thieves[15]

In 1972, the United States Supreme Court addressed the constitutionality of typical vagrancy statutes and ordinances in *Papachristou et al. v. City of Jacksonville*. The vagrancy ordinance of Jacksonville, Florida, provided:

> Rogues and vagabonds, or dissolute persons who go about begging, common gamblers, persons who use juggling or unlawful games or plays, common drunkards, common night walkers, thieves, pilferers or pickpockets, traders in stolen property, lewd, wanton and lascivious persons, keepers of gambling places, common railers and brawlers, persons wandering or strolling around from place to place without any lawful purpose or object, habitual loafers, disorderly persons, persons neglecting all lawful business and habitually spending their time by frequenting houses of ill fame, gaming houses, or places where alcoholic beverages are sold or served, persons able to work but habitually living upon the earnings of their wives or minor children shall be deemed vagrants and, upon conviction in the Municipal Court shall be punished as provided for Class D offenses.

The Supreme Court held the ordinance void for vagueness (see chapter 2 on void for vagueness).[16]

Suspicious loitering and aggressive panhandling laws have replaced vagrancy statutes in some jurisdictions. These laws do not directly make the status of being poor a crime; they make the actions related to it crimes. The Model Penal Code recommends the following law:

§ 250.6. Loitering or Prowling.

A person commits a violation if he loiters or prowls in a place, at a time, or in a manner not usual for law-abiding individuals under circumstances that warrant alarm for the safety of persons or property in the vicinity. Among the circumstances which may be considered in determining whether such alarm is warranted is the fact that the actor takes flight upon appearance of a peace officer, refuses to identify himself, or manifestly endeavors to conceal himself or any object. Unless flight by the actor or other circumstance makes it impracticable, a peace officer shall prior to any arrest for an offense under this section afford the actor an opportunity to dispel any alarm which would otherwise be warranted, by requesting him to identify himself and explain his presence and conduct. No person shall be convicted of an offense under this Section if the peace officer did not comply with the preceding sentence, or if it appears at trial that the explanation given by the actor was true and, if believed by the peace officer at the time, would have dispelled the alarm.

The suspicious loitering provision reflects the drafters' effort to meet objections to existing vagrancy statutes. First, suspicious loitering is not a status; it requires an act ("loiters or prowls"). Second, loitering does not mean merely being lazy or drifting; it requires being suspicious. Hence, a known pickpocket hanging around a Greyhound bus station and a stranger in a small town lurking in an alley near a jewelry store for two hours, peering up and down the adjoining street every few minutes, are suspiciously loitering. On the other hand, punkers standing around on a street corner, with no apparent reason other than to display their wild hairstyles and clothes, are not loitering suspiciously, however, annoying their presence might be to respectable society. In the drafters' judgment, therefore, the suspicious requirement removes both the status and the *mens rea* objections to existing vagrancy laws. Because the code provision includes only suspicious conduct, constitutional objections are at least reduced, if not removed entirely.

The suspicious loitering provision does give police the power to question suspicious persons. The state can prosecute people who refuse to answer reasonable questions when there was probable cause to arrest them for suspicious loitering. Some critics object to this last part, saying it protects people who tell plausible lies but not those who tell the implausible truth. In addition, the possibility for police abuse is too great, critics say, even in this truncated vagrancy provision.

CASE

Was He Suspiciously Loitering?

Kolender, Chief of Police of San Diego v. Lawson
461 U.S. 352 103 S.Ct. 1855, 75 L.Ed.2d 903 (1983)

[Justice O'Connor delivered the Court's opinion. Berger, Brennan, Marshall, Blackmun, Powell, and Stevens joined. Justice White, with Justice Rehnquist joining, dissented.]

Appellee Edward Lawson was detained or arrested on approximately 15 occasions between March 1976 and January 1977 pursuant to Cal. Penal Code Ann. § 647(e) (West 1970). Lawson was prosecuted only twice, and was convicted once. The second charge was dismissed.

Lawson then brought a civil action in the District Court for the Southern District of California seeking a declaratory judgment that § 647(e) is unconstitutional, a mandatory injunction to restrain enforcement of the statute, and compensatory and punitive damages against the various officers who detained him. The District Court found that § 647(e) was overbroad because "a person who is stopped on less than probable cause cannot be punished for failing to identify himself." The District Court enjoined enforcement of the statute, but held that Lawson could not recover damages because the officers involved acted in the good-faith belief that each detention or arrest was lawful.... The Court of Appeals affirmed the District Court determination as to the unconstitutionality of § 647(e). The appellate court determined that the statute was unconstitutional in that it violates the Fourth Amendment's proscription against unreasonable searches and seizures, it contains a vague enforcement statute that is susceptible to arbitrary enforcement, and it fails to give fair and adequate notice of the type of conduct prohibited....

The officers appealed to this Court from that portion of the judgment of the Court of Appeals which declared § 647(e) unconstitutional and which enjoined its enforcement....

FACTS

... [T]he trial transcript contains numerous descriptions of the stops given both by Lawson and by the police officers who detained him. For example, one police officer testified that he stopped Lawson while walking on an otherwise vacant street because it was late at night, the area was isolated, and the area was located close to a high crime area. Another officer testified that he detained Lawson, who was walking at a later hour in a business area where some businesses were still open, and asked for identification because burglaries had been committed by unknown persons in the general area....

OPINION

In the courts below, Lawson mounted an attack on the facial validity of § 647(e)....;

§ 647(e) requires that an individual provide "credible and reliable" identification when requested by a police officer who has reasonable suspicion of criminal activity....

"Credible and reliable" identification is defined by the State Court of Appeal as identification "carrying reasonable assurance that the identification is authentic and providing means for later getting in touch with the person who has identified himself." In addition, a suspect may be required to "account for his presence ... to the extent that it assists in producing credible and reliable identification...." Under the terms of the statute, failure of the individual to provide "credible and reliable" identification permits the arrest.

Our Constitution is designed to maximize individual freedoms within a framework of ordered liberty. Statutory limitations on those freedoms are examined for substantive authority and content as well as for definiteness or certainty of expression.

... § 647(e), as presently drafted and as construed by the state courts, contains no standard for determining what a suspect has to do in order to satisfy the requirement to provide a "credible and reliable" identification. As such, the statute vests virtually complete discretion in the hands of the police to determine whether the suspect has satisfied the statute and must be permitted to go on his way in the absence of probable cause to arrest. An individual, whom police may think is suspicious but do not have probable cause to believe has committed a crime, is entitled to continue to walk the public streets "only at the whim of any police officer" who happens to stop that individual under § 647(e)....

Appellants stress the need for strengthened law enforcement tools to combat the epidemic of crime that plagues our Nation. The concern of our citizens with curbing criminal activity is certainly a matter requiring the attention of all branches of government. As weighty as this concern is, however, it cannot justify legislation that would otherwise fail to meet constitutional standards for definiteness and clarity. § 647(e), as presently construed, requires that "suspicious" persons satisfy some undefined identification requirement, or face criminal punishment. Although due process does not require "impossible standards" of clarity, this is not a case where further precision in the statutory language is either impossible or impractical.

We conclude § 647(e) is unconstitutionally vague on its face because it encourages arbitrary enforcement by failing to describe with sufficient particularity what a suspect must do in order to satisfy the statute. Accordingly, the judgment of the Court of Appeals is affirmed, and the case is remanded for further proceedings consistent with this opinion.

It is so ordered.

DISSENT

The majority finds that the statute "contains no standard for determining what a suspect has to do in order to satisfy the requirement to provide a 'credible and reliable' identification." At the same time, the majori-

ty concedes that "credible and reliable" has been defined by the state court to remain identification that carries reasonable assurance that the identification is authentic and that provides means for later getting in touch with the person. The narrowing construction given this statute by the state court cannot be likened to the "standardless" statutes involved in a statute that made it a crime to be a "vagrant." The statute provided:

> Rogues and vagabonds, or dissolute persons who go about begging, common gamblers,... common drunkards, common night walkers,... lewd, wanton and lascivious persons,... common railers and brawlers, persons wandering or strolling around from place to place without any lawful purpose or object, habitual loafers,... shall be deemed vagrants.

... The present statute, as construed by the state courts, does not fall in the same category.

Case Discussion Lawson is widely known as the "California Walkman," because he spends most of his free time walking, sometimes in odd places at unusual times. He is a large, imposing figure who wears his hair in dreadlocks. Why did the police arrest Lawson? Were they preventing crime, investigating crime, or harassing Lawson? What foundation did they have? Do you agree with the majority, or with the dissent's opinion? Were the Model Penal Code's efforts to draft a narrow suspicious loitering provision wasted after *Lawson v. Kolender,* which the United States Supreme Court later upheld? Or does the Model Penal Code provision overcome the objections raised to California's loitering statute? What interest is the court protecting when it strikes down a statute like the one in this case? What interests does it endanger? If you were a judge, how would you balance the interests, and how would you decide this case?

Recently, a number of jurisdictions have adopted aggressive panhandling ordinances to deal with the increasing numbers of homeless people, particularly on the streets of large cities. The Supreme Court of Washington dealt with the problem of "pedestrian interference" in *City of Seattle v. Webster.*

CASE

Did He Interfere with Pedestrians?

City of Seattle v. Webster
802 P.2d 1333 (Wash.1990)

Smith, Justice

The City of SEATTLE sought review of a King County Superior Court decision affirming the SEATTLE Municipal Court which dismissed charges against Respondent Arlander Duke Webster for violation of the SEATTLE Pedestrian Interference Ordinance, SEATTLE Municipal Code 12A.12.015(B)(1). Both courts concluded that the section of the ordinance under which respondent was charged was unconstitutionally vague and overbroad. We disagree and remand the case to the SEATTLE Municipal Court for trial.

The principal question we consider in this case is whether subsection (B)(1) of SEATTLE Municipal Code (SMC) 12A.12.015 (pedestrian interference ordinance) is unconstitutional on its face because it is vague and overbroad. We also consider whether the ordinance is unreasonable and whether it violates equal protection of the law. We answer those questions in the negative and uphold the constitutionality of the ordinance.

We reverse the Superior Court and the Municipal Court and reinstate the charge against Respondent Webster. The case should then proceed to trial in the ordinary course. Essential facts will then become of record. Respondent Webster will not be precluded from again raising the issue of constitutionality of the ordinance at a proper stage of the proceedings.

FACTS

[According to the police report, Arlander Duke Webster, a 250-pound, 6-foot, 3-inch-tall black man was] "stopping citizens on the sidewalk, blocking their path, sticking his hand out and asking 'Spare Change?' Other citizens were obstructed by the suspect and had to walk around suspect to avoid him." [The police arrested him for pedestrian interference, pursuant to a Seattle ordinance.]

Arlander Duke Webster, respondent, was charged with violating SMC 12A.12.015(B)(1), a portion of the SEATTLE "pedestrian interference ordinance," on April 10, 1988. The ordinance makes it unlawful to intentionally obstruct pedestrian or vehicular traffic. When the case was called, Respondent Webster moved for dismissal, challenging the ordinance as unconstitutionally vague, overbroad, and unreasonable and as a violation of his equal protection rights.

On May 27, 1988, the Honorable Barbara A. Madsen, SEATTLE Municipal Court, granted respondent's motion for dismissal, stating:

> [A] person could be charged with this, under this ordinance, and be doing something that no one in the world would think was unlawful conduct, including on a very nice hot sunny day being age sixteen sitting on a sidewalk watching cars go by, which of course I think that all of us have done; being a Santa Claus at Christmas time and standing ringing a bell at a front door of a department store; walking from the side of the store out to the street to see if your bus has come yet and making people walk around you.
>
> I just could imagine many, many, many, many circumstances under which it would be based on the discretion of police authority as to whether you should be charged or not based on conduct, that if you were an attractive looking person who probably was a person of some means [you] wouldn't be arrested, and if you were a scrubby looking individual looking like you didn't have the where with all [sic] for the next cup of coffee, you would be charged, or [sic] I find that unconstitutional and I would grant the defendant's motion to dismiss based on the lack of constitutionality of the ordinance.

The City of SEATTLE appealed the dismissal to the Superior Court. On November 17, 1988, the Honorable R. Joseph Wesley, King County Superior Court, affirmed the dismissal, concluding that "[t]he ordinance, SMC 12A.12.015(B)(1), is unconstitutionally vague and overbroad." On December 7, 1988, the City of SEATTLE filed a notice for discretionary review. By order dated March 6, 1990, the Court of Appeals, Division One, certified the case to this court. This court accepted certification on March 9, 1990. Because the case was dismissed before trial upon a facial challenge to the constitutionality of the ordinance, there is no factual record. The police report on the underlying charge, which is the only source of information relating to the charge, is reproduced in its entirety:

The SEATTLE "pedestrian interference ordinance," SMC 12A.12.015, adopted in October 1987, provides in relevant part:

A. The following definitions apply in this section:
  1. "AGGRESSIVELY BEG" means to beg with intent to intimidate another person into giving money or goods....
  3. "Obstruct pedestrian or vehicular traffic" means to walk, stand, sit, lie, or place an object in such a manner as to block passage by another person or a vehicle, or to require another person or a driver of a vehicle to take evasive action to avoid physical contact. Acts authorized as an exercise of one's constitutional right to picket or to legally protest ... shall not constitute obstruction of pedestrian or vehicular traffic....
B. A person is guilty of pedestrian interference if ... [that person] intentionally:
  1. Obstructs pedestrian or vehicular traffic; or
  2. AGGRESSIVELY BEGS.
C. Pedestrian interference may be punished by a fine not to exceed Five Hundred Dollars ($500.00) or by imprisonment in jail for a term not to exceed ninety (90) days or by both such fine and imprisonment....

We first consider whether SMC 12A.12.015 (B)(1) is unconstitutionally overbroad.... A law is overbroad if it sweeps within its prohibitions constitutionally protected free speech activities. The First Amendment overbreadth doctrine may invalidate a law on its face only if the law is "substantially overbroad." In determining overbreadth, "a court's first task is to determine whether the

enactment reaches a substantial amount of constitutionally protected conduct." Criminal statutes require particular scrutiny and may be facially invalid if they "make unlawful a substantial amount of constitutionally protected conduct ... even if they also have legitimate application."...

Respondent argues that "[t]he SEATTLE ordinance has a potentially enormous scope, since it is not uncommon to innocently walk, stand, sit, lie, or place an object in such a manner as to block passage of another." However, the ordinance is written to apply only to persons intentionally "block[ing] passage by another person or a vehicle" and "requir[ing] another person or a driver of a vehicle to take evasive action to avoid physical contact" by "walk[ing], stand[ing], sit[ting], l[ying], or plac[ing] an object."

The ordinance does not prohibit innocent intentional acts which merely consequentially block traffic or cause others to take evasive action. Many of those "consequential" results may arise from protected activities such as collecting signatures on a petition. In addition, "mere sauntering or loitering on a public way is lawful and the right of any man, woman, or child." Under SMC 12A.12.015(B)(1), it is not unlawful to exercise that right even though it may cause another person or driver to "take evasive action." The City of SEATTLE argues that inclusion in the ordinance of the element of specific intent saves it from being unconstitutionally overbroad. We agree.... [T]he language of SMC 12A.12.015(B)(1) clearly indicates that, before there can be a charge or conviction under the ordinance, a person must act with intent to block another's passage or with intent to cause a person or vehicle to take evasive action. The element of intent in the ordinance sufficiently narrows its scope to save SMC 12A.12.015(B)(1) against a claim of unconstitutional overbreadth.

We next consider whether SMC 12A.12.015(B)(1) is unconstitutionally vague. The due process doctrine of "void for vagueness" has two central principles. First, criminality must be defined with sufficient specificity to put citizens on notice concerning conduct they must avoid. And second, legislated crimes must not be susceptible of arbitrary and discriminatory law enforcement. A statute is unconstitutionally vague if "persons of common intelligence must necessarily guess at its meaning and differ as to its application."...

Petitioner City of SEATTLE contends that the ordinance is not unconstitutionally vague inasmuch as it includes an element of specific intent. The requirement of a specific intent to do a prohibited act may avoid those consequences to the accused which may otherwise render a vague or indefinite statute invalid.

[COURT NOTE: "SMC 12A.04.030 defines intent as follows: 'A person intends or acts intentionally or with intent to accomplish a result or to engage in conduct described by the section defining the offense, [sic] when [that person's] conscious objective or purpose is to accomplish such a result or to engage in conduct of that nature.'"]

SMC 12A.12.015(B)(1) includes an element of specific intent. The ordinance does not, as respondent and amicus claim, base criminality on the reaction of others to the presence of a person on the public sidewalks. Rather, it defines the proscribed conduct solely in reference to the person interfering with the flow of pedestrian or vehicular traffic. The question can be asked: Did that person stand, sit, walk, or place an object with the intent to cause another person or a driver of a vehicle to take evasive action?

If the answer is "yes," then the person may be properly charged under the ordinance.

SMC 12A.12.015(B)(1) provides adequate notice to persons of common understanding concerning the behavior prohibited and the specific intent required. It provides citizens, police officers and courts alike with sufficient guidelines to prevent arbitrary enforcement. It is not unconstitutionally vague.

[The court next considered claims that the ordinance] ... was reasonable... [and] ... whether it violates the equal protection rights of the homeless.... An ordinance which makes no distinction between conduct calculated to harm and conduct which is essentially innocent is an unreasonable exercise of the government's police power. This court has summarized the doctrine of "void for unreasonableness" as follows:

> An ordinance to be void for unreasonableness must be clearly and plainly unreasonable. The burden of establishing the invalidity of an ordinance rests heavily upon the party challenging its constitutionality. Every presumption will be in favor of constitutionality. And, if a state of facts justifying the ordinance can reasonably be conceived to exist, such facts must be presumed to exist and the ordinance passed in conformity therewith. These rules are more than mere rules of judicial convenience. They mark the line of demarcation between legislative and judicial functions.

We have already concluded that SMC 12A.12.015(B)(1) is not overbroad since it includes an element of specific intent. The ordinance distinguishes between conduct calculated to harm—intentionally interfering with pedestrian or vehicular traffic—and conduct which is essentially innocent—unintentionally interfering with traffic by merely being present upon a public sidewalk. Respondent has not overcome his heavy burden of proving that SMC 12A.12.015(B)(1) is "clearly and plainly unreasonable." We reject his reasonableness challenge to the ordinance.

Finally, we consider whether SMC 12A.12.015(B)(1) violates the equal protection rights of the homeless under the fourteenth amendment to the United States Constitution as argued by amicus. Citing *Massachusetts Bd. of Retirement v. Murgia*, amicus argues that the homeless should be recognized as a protected class because, among other reasons, they are "relegated to such a position of political powerlessness as to command extraordinary protection." Amicus argues, for example, that because RCW 29.07.070(4) provides that "[a]n address or post office box is required for a citizen to register to vote in Washington," the indigent homeless are thus excluded from the political process.

Respondent and amicus further argue that any pedestrian interference or begging ordinance necessarily disparately affects the homeless as a class, thus violating the equal protection rights of homeless persons. They cite no authority for this. This court has rejected an equal protection challenge to a SEATTLE ordinance because "[t]he ordinance applies equally to all persons who possess the requisite criminal intent." Similarly, in this case, the SEATTLE pedestrian interference ordinance applies equally to all persons. Nothing in the ordinance refers to economic circumstances or residential status.

Homelessness is a real national concern, particularly in metropolitan areas such as SEATTLE. We share compassion for those among us who suffer privation in the midst of plenty. However, the SEATTLE pedestrian interference ordinance with which we are here concerned is facially neutral. On the limited record before us there is no indication that Mr. Webster is indigent or homeless. His address in the police report merely indicates "transient." We cannot conclude from the limited information presented that homelessness is relevant to this case.

We have found no cases where the homeless have been judicially declared a protected class for purposes of Fourteenth Amendment analysis. While we recognize society's valid concern for the plight of the homeless, there is nothing in this record to support such a declaration in this case. SMC 12A.12.015(B)(1) withstands a facial challenge to its constitutionality.

We reverse the King County Superior Court and the SEATTLE Municipal Court and remand the case for trial....

DISSENT

Utter, Justice (concurring and dissenting).

This ordinance is overbroad without a narrowing construction. I concur in the majority's judgment on the other points raised. I write separately to urge a limiting construction and to expand on some points raised in the briefs.

Evaluation of an overbreadth claim requires the court to decide whether the ordinance before it sweeps within its prohibitions conduct protected by the First Amendment. The First Amendment protects solicitation for charitable organizations, musical performances, handing out literature, and collecting signatures for a petition. Since a person carrying out one of these activities may intend to cause a pedestrian to go around him or her, the ordinance broadly regulates a substantial amount of First Amendment conduct. Indeed, it is hard to imagine how it would be applied to any conduct not involving free speech.

The majority suggests that the intent requirement narrows the scope of the ordinance and thereby saves it from overbreadth challenge. The intent requirement does not save this ordinance absent a limiting construction.... Specific intent does not always save ordinances from overbreadth challenges.... One can intend to cause others to take evasive action while engaging in protected First Amendment speech. For example, a person may approach someone on a street to seek a signature on a petition. The majority does not confront the question of whether such an action could permissibly result in a conviction for intentionally causing another to take evasive action. Instead, the majority states that the "ordinance does not prohibit innocent intentional acts which merely consequentially ... cause others to take evasive action."...

In order to know whether this ordinance is substantially overbroad, we must know whether begging, the conduct to which it seems to be aimed, is constitutionally protected speech. Analysis of this question not only contributes to the overbreadth inquiry, it will aid trial courts in applying this ordinance to begging in a constitutional manner. I believe that begging is constitutionally protected speech, but that it is subject to reasonable time, place, and manner restrictions, like other speech. Admitting the constitutional status of begging does not involve giving beggars an unlimited right to harass potential donors. Because begging involves constitutionally protected speech, the legislation at issue requires a limiting construction in order to be upheld.... An ordinance restricting protected speech on the sidewalk must be narrowly tailored to serve a significant government interest because the sidewalks are a public forum.... The breadth of the definition of obstruction in this ordinance raises the specter of widespread unconstitutional application. It could be applied to any person who walks up to another person on the street to communicate a message, even if the person is free to walk around the speaker and the speaker does nothing to intimidate the other pedestrian....

The ordinance should be upheld, but its application limited to substantial obstruction of traffic. Trial courts may then interpret "substantial obstruction" in such a way as to keep traffic flowing without prohibiting con-

stitutionally protected speech which only annoys passersby. Because Mr. Webster has not been charged with aggressive begging, we do not pass on the constitutionality of that restriction on begging. The State's failure to charge Mr. Webster with aggressive begging indicates that he did not intimidate potential donors; rather, he obstructed traffic. This construction of the ordinance only assures that the traffic restriction is narrowly tailored to the state's interest supporting it. It does not speak to actual intimidation of potential donors.... I would hold that the ordinance is constitutional provided that it is construed to reach only substantial obstructions of traffic and remand the cause for trial.

Case Discussion   How did the court reason that the ordinance did not violate due process void for vagueness, overbreadth, unreasonableness, the equal protection clause, or free speech? Do you believe the First Amendment ought to protect free speech? Review *Young v. New York City Transit Authority,* chapter 2, pages 65–66. Do you believe that what Webster did should violate the criminal law? Why? Why not? What penalty would you put on the crime he committed, if you believe he committed one? What purposes of criminal law would it serve to make what he did a crime? To not make it a crime? What, if any, relevance does the late Justice Frankfurter's quote of Anatole France have to this case?

> [T]o sanction such a ruthless consequence ... would justify a latter-day Anatole France to add one more item to his ironic comments on the "majestic equality" of the law. "The law, in its majestic equality, forbids the rich as well as the poor to sleep under bridges, to beg in the streets, and to steal bread."

▼ PUBLIC MORALS OFFENSES

In medieval days when great rivalries existed between monarchs and churches over who had jurisdiction to hold courts and rule upon illegality, the church claimed exclusive jurisdiction over nonviolent sexual behavior, marital relations, and some other matters not relevant here. As monarchs grew stronger, royal secular courts eventually absorbed family and sex offenses into their own jurisdictions. These offenses became the modern crimes against public morals. Some modern critics maintain they should now be returned to the church, although not in the literal sense nor in the same form. These critics advocate allowing sexual behavior between consenting adults to remain a matter for private conscience and general moral persuasion.[17]

Criminal sexual conduct deals both with violent sexual attacks and with the nonviolent sexual conduct of children or others who are incompetent to decide whether they want to engage in sexual relations with others. In almost all crimes discussed in the following pages, criminal law punishes behavior between consenting adults. In other words, there is no victim in the ordinary sense of the word. Public morals offenses raise the question, what sexual conduct beyond traditional sexual intercourse between married heterosexual couples ought the criminal law to at least tolerate if not encourage? Under existing law, "normal" sexual intercourse between a husband and wife is legal, but almost everything else, even sexual intercourse between a man and a woman not married to each other, is a crime.

Nonviolent adult consensual sex offenses range across a broad spectrum. The primary statutory nonviolent sex crimes include fornication, adultery, incest, sodomy, indecent exposure, and prostitution. These crimes make it especially difficult to balance public good and individual privacy. Unlike homicide, rape, and related crimes, where broad consensus exists as to their "harmfulness," the public morals offenses enjoy no such consensus. In fact, there are two conflicting and tenaciously held positions over the role of criminal law in public morals enforcement. Hard lines divide those who believe criminal law ought to enforce morals in order to "purify" society and those who argue against the interference of criminal law in citizens' lives.[18]

Perhaps no issue in criminal policy has caused more acrimonious debate over a longer time than that of the role law should play in enforcing public morals. Two English Victorian scholars, the philosopher John Stuart Mill and the historian Sir James F. Stephen, started the debate that has raged for more than a century among theorists, lawmakers, and the public. Although the debate has many strands, it features two major positions that were well stated in the Wolfenden report, an English document recommending that sexual relations between male homosexuals and prostitution be decriminalized when they took place between two consenting adults in private. Briefly, the majority position was as follows:

> There remains one additional argument which we believe to be decisive, namely, the importance which society and the law ought to give to individual freedom of choice and action in matters of private morality. Unless a deliberate attempt is to be made by society, acting through the agency of the law, to equate the sphere of crime with that of sin, there must remain a realm of private morality and immorality which is, in brief and crude terms, not the law's business. To say this is not to condone or encourage private immorality. On the contrary, to emphasize the personal private nature of moral or immoral conduct is to emphasize the personal and private responsibility of the individual for his own actions, and that is a responsibility which a mature agent can properly be expected to carry for himself without the threat of punishment from the law.[19]

English jurist Sir Patrick Devlin rebutted the majority Wolfenden position:

> I think, therefore, that it is not possible to set theoretical limits to the power of the State to legislate against immorality. It is not possible to settle in advance exceptions to the general rule or to define inflexibly areas of morality into

which the law is in no circumstances to be allowed to enter. Society is entitled by means of its laws to protect itself from dangers, whether from within or without. Here again I think that the political parallel is legitimate. The law of treason is directed against aiding the king's enemies and against sedition from within. The justification for this is that established government is necessary for the existence of society and therefore its safety against violent overthrow must be secured. But an established morality is as necessary as good government to the welfare of society. Societies disintegrate from within more frequently than they are broken up by external pressures. There is disintegration when no common morality is observed and history shows that the loosening of moral bonds is often the first state of disintegration, so that society is justified in taking the same steps to preserve its moral code as it does to preserve its government and other essential institutions. The suppression of vice is as much the law's business as the suppression of subversive activities; it is no more possible to define a sphere of private morality than it is to define one of private subversive activity.[20]

Fornication and Illicit Cohabitation

Although pertinent legislation is rarely (if ever) enforced, extramarital and premarital sexual intercourse are crimes in many jurisdictions. A typical statute on this subject reads: "Whoever has sexual intercourse with a person he knows is not his spouse may be fined not more than $200 or imprisoned not more than 6 months or both." Other states make these acts punishable only if they are "an open and notorious relationship." Indiana, for example, specifies that "whoever cohabits with another in a state of adultery or fornication shall be fined not exceeding $500 or imprisoned in the county jail not exceeding 6 months or both."[21]

Prostitution

Prostitution has flourished throughout human history, surviving virtually unabated the condemnation of moralists in both church and state. Recent evidence suggests that about 70 percent of the male population has hired a prostitute at some time, because of physical deformity, psychological inadequacy, emotional unwillingness to make more than casual acquaintances, or other reasons that make it difficult to find suitable noncommercial sex partners. In this sense, some argue, prostitution fills a social need. Nevertheless, nearly every American state carries on the fight against prostitution.

Prostitution means to offer sex for hire. Some statutes limit criminal liability to females who offer sexual intercourse. Others extend liability to any person who offers to buy sex or who accepts such an offer. The Model Penal Code extends the meaning still further: "[A] person who engages, or offers or agrees to engage in sexual activity for hire commits a petty misdemeanor." Sexual activity, according to the code, includes "carnal knowledge, deviate sexual intercourse, and sexual contact or any lewd act," meaning, in addition to vaginal intercourse, sodomy, fellatio, cunnilingus, male prostitution, masturbation, and even voyeurism. The prostitution *mens rea* requires the purpose to sell or buy whatever sexual activity the statute includes.[22]

These definitions create problems. They exclude both sexually promiscuous people who regularly and indiscriminately engage in sex for no charge, and nonpromiscuous people who sell sex to or buy sex from one person, developing close relationships with their providers—the classic mistress and gigolo. Existing prostitution statutes aim primarily to curb promiscuity for hire—that is, situations that combine promiscuity and commercialism.

CASE

Was Cherie's Massage Prostitution?

Commonwealth v. Walter

388 Mass. 460, 446 N.E.2d 707 (1983)

[Walter was convicted of prostitution, a crime carrying a penalty of up to six months' imprisonment. She was sentenced to thirty days in jail. She appealed. Chief Justice Hennessey delivered the opinion.]

FACTS

On January 28, 1981, Officer James Walsh of the Cambridge police department received a radio call. In response, Officer Walsh changed into civilian clothes and went to the detective bureau of the Cambridge police department. There, Detective Anthony Bombino showed him a copy of an advertisement appearing in the January 27, 1981, edition of the Boston Phoenix newspaper, which read: "Swedish & Shiatsu Massage in Harvard Square Chris 661-————." The newspaper advertisement was admitted in evidence over the defendant's objection.

Officer Walsh placed a telephone call to 661-———— and asked to speak to "Chris." The person who answered the telephone stated that she was "Chris." Officer Walsh told her that he was answering the advertisement in the Boston Phoenix and that he was interested in getting a massage. "Chris" asked him if he was really interested in getting a massage, and he said, "Yes." "Chris" told him an address on Massachusetts Avenue, apartment 24, and that the massage would cost $30. Detective Bombino saw

Officer Walsh call 661-————, and heard his conversation.

Officer Walsh went to the address in an unmarked police car with Detective Bombino and two other policemen. He pressed the buzzer for apartment 24, and a woman, whom he later identified as the defendant, came to the door. He asked if she were the "Chris" with whom he had just spoken, and she said, "Yes. Why don't you come up?" He followed her to apartment 24, where he saw a man sitting in the bedroom clothed only in pants. After a brief conversation with the defendant, the man put on the rest of his clothing and left.

The defendant invited Officer Walsh into the bedroom, and told him to get undressed. She asked him for $30, which he gave her. She massaged his body generally, using her hands and some oil. During the course of the massage she removed her shirt and was naked from the waist up. She then massaged his genitals, in an act of masturbation, for about forty-five seconds. Officer Walsh then got off the bed and said he was a police officer, and that she was under arrest for prostitution. During the arrest Detective Bombino gained entry to the apartment and seized two telephones bearing the number 661-———— from the apartment.

OPINION

The defendant argues that a full body massage which includes the genitals, by use of the hands only, for a fee, is not prostitution within the meaning of the statute. In *Commonwealth v. King,* 374 Mass. 5, 12, 372 N.E.2d 196 (1977), we noted that the Legislature had not defined prostitution, and so turned to common understanding for definition of the term. We concluded that prostitution is "common indiscriminate sexual activity for hire." The defendant does not argue that her acts were not common, indiscriminate, or for hire, but rather that they were not "sexual activity." She argues that "sexual activity" is confined to coitus or oral-genital contact.

We conclude that prostitution includes performing masturbation upon a person's genitals by another's hands, for a fee. The term "sexual activity," resting as it does on the common understanding of the meaning of prostitution, and on *Commonwealth v. Cook,* supra, includes such acts. Accordingly, we reject the defendant's contention that the acts proved were not prostitution within the meaning of G.L. c. 272, § 53.

The defendant next argues that prohibition of her activities interferes with her constitutional right to privacy.... [In] *Commonwealth v. Balthazar,* 366 Mass. 298, 302, 318 N.E.2d 478 (1974), we held that G.L. c. 272, § 35, which prohibits "unnatural and lascivious acts," does not apply to private consensual conduct of adults. The defendant's prostitution conviction is based on the massage she gave Officer Walsh in her apartment.

The scope of the right to privacy under the United States Constitution is not well defined. However, whatever protection it affords to the private, sexual activities of consenting adults, we conclude that the defendant's activities were not protected, because they were performed for a fee. We will not extend a constitutional right to privacy to one who indiscriminately performs sexual acts for hire. Commercial sex is performed for profit and the sexual contact involved is incidental to that profit. The impersonal nature of the performance of commercial sex, such as was involved here, is indicated by the fact that anyone willing to pay could enter the defendant's apartment and receive a genital massage. The decision to engage in the business of sex for money is not the type of intimate, personal decision which is protected by the right to privacy.

Affirmed.

Case Discussion

The court concluded that Cherie Walter did not have a constitutional right to offer massage in her apartment. Do you believe the prostitution statute violated her right to privacy? Do you think the law should reach into an apartment where two adults willingly engage in sexual massages? If you do, what reasons can you give and what penalty would you prescribe? Do you agree that masturbation ought to be included within the meaning of prostitution? Or should prostitution include only sexual intercourse?

Solicitation and Promotion of Prostitution

Some argue that publicly soliciting sex for hire ought to be a crime, even though an agreement has not been made. Thus, prostitution and related offenses would constitute three crimes: engaging in sex for hire, offering to buy or sell sex, and publicly soliciting to buy or sell sex. In most jurisdictions, to procure, transport, or receive money for prostitution constitutes a separate offense. These jurisdictions permit multiple prosecutions for acts that are, in a sense, part of the same offense: promoting prostitution. Promoting prostitution embraces collaborating with or exploiting prostitutes. It includes transporting prostitutes, supporting houses of prostitution, living off prostitutes (pimping), and patronizing prostitution.

Several arguments support criminal penalties for prostitution. First, the following utilitarian considerations favor repressing it:

1. Prostitution spreads disease, including venereal diseases, but especially AIDS.

2. When combined with drug trade, liquor, gambling, robbery, and extortion, prostitution provides a source of power and profit for organized crime.

3. Prostitution spawns corruption and improper influence in government because politicians and law enforcement officials become easy marks for the threat of exposure.

4. Prostitution encourages sexual maladjustment, undermines the home and family, and contributes to individual moral decay.

The most potent argument favoring criminal penalties is not utilitarian, however. Moralists and religious groups have opposed commercial sex for centuries. If there is one constant theme in Western history, it is thunderous denunciation of sex for hire.

Several arguments make up the case against criminal sanctions. Most who oppose criminal penalties for prostitution recommend regulating it in other ways. In other words, to oppose making prostitution a crime does not mean supporting prostitution as a practice, at least not without qualification. Proponents argue that government's inability to effectively prosecute prostitution laws fosters extortion and results in the selective prosecution of minorities and "undesirables." Furthermore, they argue, strict enforcement cuts off an important outlet for sexual expression that might lead to more violent sex crimes. In addition, registration and mandatory health inspections can control and reduce venereal disease. Regulation also lessens the opportunities for official corruption. Finally, if prostitution were confined to specific neighborhoods—as regulation and registration permit—it would lead to more effective community health and safety.

The Wolfendon report says the following:

> Prostitution is a social fact deplorable in the eyes of moralists, sociologists and, we believe, the great majority of ordinary people. But it has persisted in many civilizations throughout many centuries, and the failure of attempts to stamp it out by repressive legislation shows that it cannot be eradicated through the agency of the criminal law. It remains true that without a demand for her services the prostitute could not exist, and that there are enough men who avail themselves of prostitutes to keep the trade alive. It also remains true that there are women who, even when there is no economic need to do so, choose this form of livelihood. For so long as these propositions continue to be true there will be prostitution, and no amount of legislation directed towards its abolition will abolish it.
>
> It follows that there are limits to the degree of discouragement which the criminal law can properly exercise towards a woman who has deliberately decided to live her life in this way, or a man who has deliberately chosen to use her services. The criminal law, as the Street Offenses Committee plainly pointed out, "is not concerned with private morals or with ethical sanctions." This does not mean that society itself can be indifferent to these matters, for prostitution is an evil of which any society which claims to be civilized should seek to rid itself; but this end could be achieved only through measures directed to a better understanding of the nature and obligation of sexual relationships and to a raising of the social and moral outlook of society as a whole. In these matters, the work of the churches and of organizations concerned with mental health, moral welfare, family welfare, child and marriage

guidance and similar matters should be given all possible encouragement. But until education and the moral sense of the community bring about a change of attitude towards the fact of prostitution, the law by itself cannot do so. In the final analysis, however, the opponents of criminal penalties for prostitution rely on more than utilitarian arguments. They also adhere to the basic libertarian view that morals are not the business of the law. The choice about whether to do a moral or an immoral thing should be left entirely to the individual, his conscience, his religion, his friends, and his family—not to the criminal law.[23]

The Model Penal Code prostitution provision falls between two extremes. The code provision keeps criminal repression but attempts to remove gross abuses in existing law. It also encompasses homosexual acts and other deviate sexual practices for hire. Penalties prescribed for prostitution are mild in contrast to those for promoting commercial sex, the latter being considered a more serious crime. Customers, called johns or tricks, as well as prostitutes are subject to prosecution under the code, and the code grades public solicitation, prostitution, and promotion.

Sodomy and Related Offenses

Large numbers of "normal" persons deviate from expressing themselves sexually through heterosexual vaginal intercourse. Heterosexual "gratification is sought and bestowed digitally, orally or by the anus." Some people even gratify their sexual desires without human contact. Some masturbate. Others turn to animals. Some only look at others or expose themselves, and still others turn to inanimate objects for gratification. Crimes such as arson and burglary provide sexual stimulation to some who commit them. Finally, substantial numbers obtain sexual gratification from members of their own gender.

For centuries, all sexual gratification except heterosexual copulation within marriage has generated substantial revulsion, at least when expressed publicly. Most religions censure sex that deviates from heterosexual vaginal intercourse in marriage. Criminal law subjects such deviation to severe punishment, according to the letter of the law, if not its actual operation. Statutes in nearly every state specify punishment for fellatio, cunnilingus, anal intercourse (sodomy), bestiality, and even masturbation. And some punishments are very harsh: ten to twenty years' imprisonment in most jurisdictions, up to maximum life imprisonment in a few.

The utilitarian reasons most often cited for making sodomy and related offenses criminal include (1) that the acts are widely disapproved and (2) that minor deviations can lead to grosser deviations and, eventually, to violent sexual aggression. Underlying these reasons, proponents believe that the state should interfere in citizens' "immoral" conduct and that criminal law is a proper instrument to enforce morality. Proponents contend that retribution, deterrence, and rehabilitation all favor punishing intentional deviate sex practices.

Not everyone agrees that criminal law should subject sodomy and related offenses to criminal penalties. Opponents maintain that enforcing sodomy law is impractical. They claim that deviate sex is not deviate in the eyes of many people, particularly those who practice it. Despite vocal opposition to such acts, normal people in substantial numbers practice fellatio, cunnilingus, and sodomy. In addition, authorities are in hopeless disagreement over the causes and "cures" for this sexual conduct. Some say the conduct constitutes an illness, others label it a congenital or hereditary defect, and still others say it is normal. The law should not interfere in conduct that punishment, deterrence, or rehabilitation cannot alter. The evidence does not support the contention either that sex offenders tend to progress from one kind of offense to another, or that criminal penalties beneficially affect sexual behavior.

Furthermore, sodomy laws are largely unenforced and unenforceable, opening the way to selective enforcement, bribery, and corruption. This wastes resources that could otherwise help respond to serious harms to persons and property, particularly since so many robberies and burglaries go unsolved. Finally, opponents assert that unenforceable laws breed contempt and resentment toward sodomy laws in particular and disrespect for law in general.

> Employment of tight-panted police officers to invite homosexual advances or to spy upon public toilets in the hope of detecting deviant behavior at a time when public solutions of serious crimes are steadily declining is a perversion of public policy both maleficient in itself and calculated to inspire contempt and ridicule.[24]

Like those who support statutes for sodomy and related offenses, opponents base their views on value-determined arguments. They are committed to the libertarian view that unless they involve violence, corrupting youth, and public nuisance, the sex lives of consenting adults are no business of the criminal law. In addition, they maintain that state interference in this area intrudes into privacy to an extent not tolerable in an enlightened free and diverse society.

Most states retain Draconian penalties for consensual sodomy, whether homosexual or heterosexual. Most even include sodomy within marriage. As most state statutes are written, any form of deviate consensual sex (that is, anything other than heterosexual vaginal intercourse) constitutes sodomy. Recently, the United States Court declared the Georgia sodomy statute constitutional in *Bowers v. Hardwick.*

CASE

Does the Law Violate His Right to Privacy?

Bowers v. Hardwick

478 U.S. 186, 106 S.Ct. 2841, 92 L.Ed.2d 140 (1986)

[Justice White delivered the opinion of the Court, in which Chief Justice Burger and

Justices Powell, Rehnquist and O'Connor joined. Chief Justice Burger and Justice Powell filed concurring opinions. Justice Blackmun filed a dissenting opinion, in which Justices Brennan, Marshall, and Stevens joined. Justice Stevens filed a dissenting opinion, in which Justices Brennan and Marshall joined.]

FACTS

[See pages 55–56 for full statement of facts.]

In August 1982, respondent was charged with violating the Georgia statute criminalizing sodomy by committing that act with another adult male in the bedroom of respondent's home. [COURT NOTE: "Ga. Code Ann. § 16–6–2 (1984) provides, in pertinent part, as follows:

a. A person commits the offense of sodomy when he performs or submits to any sexual act involving the sex organs of one person and the mouth or anus of another....
b. A person convicted of the offense of sodomy shall be punished by imprisonment for not less than one nor more than 20 years...."]

After a preliminary hearing, the District Attorney decided not to present the matter to the grand jury unless further evidence developed. Respondent then brought suit in the Federal District Court, challenging the constitutionality of the statute insofar as it criminalized sodomy. He asserted that he was a practicing homosexual, that the Georgia sodomy statute, as administered by the defendants, placed him in imminent danger of arrest, and that the statute for several reasons violates the Federal Constitution. The District Court granted the defendants' motion to dismiss for failure to state a claim....

OPINION
A divided panel of the Court of Appeals for the Eleventh Circuit reversed.... [T]he court [held] that the Georgia statute violated respondent's fundamental rights because his homosexual activity is a private and intimate association that is beyond the reach of state regulation by reason of the Ninth Amendment and the Due Process clause of the Fourteenth Amendment. The case was remanded for trial, at which, to prevail, the State would have to prove that the statute is supported by a compelling interest and is the most narrowly drawn means of achieving that end.

Because other Courts of Appeals have arrived at judgments contrary to that of the Eleventh Circuit in this case, we granted the State's petition for certiorari questioning the holding that its sodomy statute violates the fundamental rights of homosexuals. We agree with the State that the Court of Appeals erred, and hence reverse its judgment.

This case does not require a judgment on whether laws against sodomy between consenting adults in general, or between homosexuals in particular, are wise or desirable. It raises no question about the right of propriety of state legislative decisions to repeal their laws that criminalize homosexual sodomy, or of state court decisions invalidating those laws on state constitutional grounds. The issue presented is whether the Federal Constitution confers a fundamental right upon homosexuals to engage in sodomy and hence invalidates the laws of the many States that still make such conduct illegal and have done so for a very long time. The case also calls for some judgment about the limits of the Court's role in carrying out its constitutional mandate....

... [R]espondent would have us announce, as the Court of Appeals did, a fundamental right to engage in homosexual sodomy. This we are quite unwilling to do....

Striving to assure itself and the public that announcing rights not readily identifiable in the Constitution's text involves much more than the imposition of the Justices' own choice of values on the States and the Federal Government, the Court has sought to identify the nature of the rights qualifying for heightened judicial protection. In *Palko v. Connecticut,* 302 US 319, 325, 326, 92 L.Ed. (1937), it was said that this category includes those fundamental liberties that are "implicit in the concept of ordered liberty," such that "neither liberty nor justice would exist if [they] were sacrificed." A different description of fundamental liberties appeared in *Moore v. East Cleveland,* 431 US 494, (1977), where they are characterized as those liberties that are "deeply rooted in this Nation's history and tradition."

It is obvious to us that neither of these formulations would extend a fundamental right of homosexuals to engage in acts of consensual sodomy. Proscriptions against that conduct have ancient roots.... Sodomy was a criminal offense at common law and was forbidden by the laws of the original thirteen States when they ratified the Bill of Rights.... [U]ntil 1961, all 50 States outlawed sodomy, and today, 24 States and the

District of Columbia continue to provide criminal penalties for sodomy performed in private and between consenting adults. Against this background, to claim that a right to engage in such conduct is "deeply rooted in this Nation's history and tradition" or "implicit in the concept of ordered liberty" is, at best, facetious."

... Respondent, however, asserts that the result should be different where the homosexual conduct occurs in the privacy of the home. He relies on *Stanley v. Georgia,* 394 US 557 (1969), where the Court held that the First Amendment prevents convicting for possessing and reading obscene material in the privacy of his home: "If the First Amendment means anything, it means that a State has no business telling a man, sitting alone at his house, what books he may read or what films he may watch."

Stanley did protect conduct that would not have been protected outside the home, and it partially prevented the enforcement of state obscenity laws; but the decision was firmly grounded in the First Amendment. The right pressed upon us here has no similar support in the text of the Constitution, and it does not qualify for recognition under the prevailing principles for construing the Fourteenth Amendment....

Even if the conduct at issue here is not a fundamental right, respondent asserts that there must be a rational basis for the law and that there is none in this case other than the presumed belief of a majority of the electorate in Georgia that homosexual sodomy is immoral and unacceptable. This is said to be an inadequate rationale to support the law. The law, however, is constantly based on notions of morality, and if all laws representing essentially moral choices are to be invalidated under the Due Process Clause, the courts will be very busy indeed. Even respondent makes no such claim, but insists that majority sentiments about the morality of homosexuality should be declared inadequate. We do not agree, and are unpersuaded that the sodomy laws of some 25 States should be invalidated on this basis.

Accordingly, the judgment of the Court of Appeals is reversed.

CONCURRING OPINION

Chief Justice Burger, concurring.

I join the Court's opinion, but I write separately to underscore my view that in constitutional terms there is no such thing as a fundamental right to commit homosexual sodomy.... Decisions of individuals relating to homosexual conduct have been subject to state intervention throughout the history of Western Civilization. Condemnation of those practices is firmly rooted in Judeao-Christian moral and ethical standards. Homosexual sodomy was a capital crime under Roman law.... Blackstone described "the infamous crime against nature" as an offense of "deeper malignity" than rape, an heinous act "that very mention of which is a disgrace to human nature," and "a crime not fit to be named."...

DISSENT

This case is no more about "a fundamental right to engage in homosexual sodomy," than *Stanley v. Georgia,* was about a fundamental right to watch obscene movies.... Rather, this case is about "the most comprehensive of rights and the most valued by civilized men," namely, "the right to be left alone."... Like Justice Holmes, I believe that "[i]t is revolting to have no better reason for a rule of law than that so it was laid down in the time of Henry IV. It is still more revolting if the grounds upon which it was laid down have vanished long since, and the rule simply persists from blind imitation of the past." I believe we must analyze respondent's claim in the light of the values that underlie the constitutional right to privacy. If that right means anything, it means that, before Georgia can prosecute its citizens for making choices about the most intimate aspects of their lives, it must do more than assert that the choice they have made is an "abominable crime not fit to be named among Christians."...

"Our cases long have recognized that the Constitution embodies a promise that a certain private sphere of individual liberty will be kept largely beyond the reach of the government."...

Only the most willful blindness could obscure the fact that sexual intimacy is "a sensitive, key relationship of human existence, central to family life, community welfare, and the development of human personality." The fact that individuals define themselves in a significant way through their intimate sexual relationships with others suggests, in a Nation as diverse as ours, that there may be many "right" ways of conducting those relationships, and that much of the richness of a relationship will come from the freedom an individual has to choose the form and nature of these intensely personal bonds.

In a variety of circumstances we have recognized that a necessary corollary of giving individuals freedom to choose how to conduct their lives is acceptable of the fact that different individuals will make different choices.... The Court claims that its decision today merely refuses to recognize a fundamental right to engage in homosexual sodomy; what the Court really has refused to recognize is the fundamental interest all individuals have in controlling the nature of their intimate associations with others.

The behavior for which Hardwick faces prosecution occurred in his own home, a place to which the Fourth Amendment attaches special significance.... [T]he right of an individual to conduct intimate relationships in the intimacy of his or her own home seems to me to be the heart of the Constitution's protection of privacy.

Case Discussion

What major reasons did the Supreme Court give for ruling that statutes making consensual sodomy a crime do not violate the United States Constitution? Do you agree with the arguments of the majority or the dissent? Would you favor a statute making consensual sodomy within marriage a crime? Would you limit the crime to homosexual sodomy? Or, despite its constitutionality, would you oppose such a statute? Give your reasons.

▼ *Summary* ▼

Crimes against public order and morals form a large part of the criminal law. Although these crimes carry minor penalties compared with felonies, they are nevertheless important. First, they touch far more people than do felonies. Second, they lead to abuse and discrimination against undesirables. Third, they can violate both constitutional rights and basic criminal law principles. Finally, they are faulted because they curtail freedom and diversity in a complex, pluralistic society that prizes individuality.

Balancing social order with individual freedom underlies all crimes against public order. Those who favor more public order see these offenses differently from those whose priorities lie with personal freedom. Both groups enlist the Constitution for support and find arguments favoring what they consider the proper purposes, principles, and policies of criminal law. In the end, however, value choices determine whether public order takes precedence over promoting individual freedom and autonomy. Furthermore, these categories are not neatly defined. In fact, most agree that society cannot exist without order but that a society without freedom is not much worth having. Drawing the line between freedom and order, and then balancing them in order to secure, promote, and protect both, are challenges to criminal law and its administration.

Fundamental questions arise concerning the place of morals offenses in criminal law. First, there are constitutional questions: Does a provision offend the due process requirement that statutes must define clearly and specifically every offense that states wish to prosecute? Does it meet the equal protection requirement prohibiting discriminatory enforcement? Does it violate the First Amendment prohibition against free expression, the Eighth Amendment strictures against cruel and unusual punishment, and the constitutional right to privacy?

Assuming that a particular statute passes the constitutional test, still the question of whether it is wise public policy must be asked and answered. The Constitution establishes only minimum standards; as one judge said, "It doesn't pay a statute much of a compliment to say that it is not unconstitutional." If answered affirmatively, the following public policy questions would complement morals offense statutes:

1. Does the conduct offend most people, and is it not condoned by a significant number of them?
2. Does the conduct do substantial harm?
3. Can and should the harm be punished?
4. Are there no effective alternatives to the criminal sanction to deal with the problem?
5. Does the suppression of such conduct still allow enough individual autonomy?
6. Is the cost of enforcing the law reasonable in relation to the good that comes from enforcement?
7. Is fair and substantial enforcement possible?
8. Does enforcement breed respect for and acceptance of the statute in particular and the law in general?

Applied to homicide, rape, and other assaults and batteries, these questions can almost invariably be answered affirmatively. When morals offenses are considered, however, yes answers are fewer and more hesitant.

▼ *Questions for Review and Discussion* ▼

1. Do you think that threatening to breach the peace should be a crime? Explain.

2. When does free speech become fighting words?

3. Why should making threats be a crime if assault is already in the criminal law?

4. Should making obscene telephone calls be a crime? Why or why not? How serious a crime is it?

5. Do you think that engaging in altercations with the police should be a crime? Why or why not?

6. What constitutional, legal, and policy objections to vagrancy statutes can you raise? Should vagrancy be a crime? Why or why not?

7. Does suspicious loitering remove the objections raised to vagrancy?

8. What are the conflicting interests in crimes against public order? Do disorderly conduct, vagrancy, and loitering statutes effectively balance these interests?

9. What types of nonviolent private sexual conduct between consenting adults belong within the scope of criminal law? Why?

10. What are the arguments for making prostitution a crime? What are the arguments against doing so? Should solicitation and promotion of prostitution be crimes? Why or why not?

11. How would you define sodomy for the purposes of criminal law? What are the arguments in favor of having criminal penalties for sodomy? What are the arguments against doing so?

▼ *Suggested Readings* ▼

1. American Law Institute, *Model Penal Code and Commentaries,* vol. 3 (Philadelphia: American Law Institute, 1980), pt. II, pp. 309–453. A starting point for anyone interested in learning more about the crimes against public order. It summarizes existing law on the subject, criticizes it, and recommends alterations, explaining in great detail why the changes should be made.

2. Rollin M. Perkins and Ronald N. Boyce, *Criminal Law,* 3d ed. (Mineola, N.Y.: Foundation Press, 1982), pp. 477–98,. The authors discuss disorderly conduct and vagrancy. This is a good survey, including references to many more cases to read on the subject.

3. Anthony Amsterdam, "Federal Constitutional Restrictions on the Punishment of Crimes of Status, Crimes of General Obnoxiousness, Crimes of Displeasing Police Officers, and the Like," *Criminal Law Bulletin* 3 (1967):205. Amsterdam discusses all the crimes in this chapter, in addition to others, in light of their constitutionality. Although written for the professional, it repays the effort to read it.

4. William J. Chambliss, *Criminal Law in Action* (Santa Barbara, Calif.: Hamilton, 1975), pp. 9–16. A brief, interesting, and excellent history of vagrancy laws. It provokes thought about the purpose of vagrancy in criminal law as well as its development throughout the last several centuries.

5. Caleb Foote, "Vagrancy-Type Law and Its Administration," *University of Pennsylvania Law Review* 104 (1956):603–50. A first-hand account of how vagrancy is administered in a Philadelphia court. It is lively, incisive, and provocative, and clearly brings into focus not only how vagrancy laws are administered but also the underlying purposes and policies they serve.

6. Charles A. Reich, "Police Questioning of Law Abiding Citizens," *Yale Law Journal* 75 (1966):116–72. Describes one person's experience with police stops such as those associated with suspicious loitering and vagrancy. The author, a black law professor, offers his insights into his encounters with police while he walked at night to deal with his chronic insomnia.

7. Gilbert Geis, *Not the Law's Business: An Examination of Homosexuality, Abortion, Prostitution, Narcotics, and Gambling in the United States* (New York: Schocken Books, 1979). A well-written book covering the morals offenses and why they should not be within the scope of criminal law. It covers in depth many crimes from a social science point of view. Professor Geis is a senior sociologist whose ideas on the subject are well worth considering.

8. Edwin M. Schur and Hugo Adam Bedau, *Victimless Crimes: Two Sides of a Controversy* (Englewood Cliffs, N.J.: Prentice-Hall, 1974). An excellent debate over whether victimless crimes are victimless and should be criminal. Professor Schur, a senior sociology professor, explains why attempts to legislate morality fail to stop the behavior they are designed to prevent. Professor Bedau, a well-known philosophy professor, challenges the basic concept of victimless crimes. The two authors discuss the human, social, and constitutional costs of criminalizing morals offenses. This is a stimulating discussion concerning the issues brought up in the discussion of morals offenses.

▼ *Notes* ▼

1. Norval Morris and Gordon Hawkins, *The Honest Politician's Guide to Crime Control* (Chicago: University of Chicago Press, 1970), chap. 1 and 8.

2. Herbert Packer, *The Limits of the Criminal Sanction* (Palo Alto; Stanford University Press, 1968), chap. 15–17.

3. American Law Institute, *Model Penal Code and Commentaries,* vol. 3 (Philadelphia: American Law Institute, 1980), pt. II, p. 309.

4. Ibid, pp. 309–312.

5. *People v. Casey,* 188 Misc. 352, 67 N.Y.S.2d 9 (1946); *Jones v. Commonwealth,* 307 Ky. 286, 210 S.W.2d 956 (1948); Model Penal Code § 250.2 and American Law Institute, *Model Penal Code and Commentaries,* vol. 3, pt. II, pp. 348–49.

6. See James B. Jacobs, *Drunk Driving* (Chicago: University of Chicago Press, 1989), pp. 65–77.

7. *Laundry v. Daley,* 280 F.Supp. 968 (N.D.Ill.,1968); Chicago, Illinois, *Municipal Code,* chap. 193, § 1 (1905).

8. See Mark Rutzick, "Offensive Language and the Evolution of First Amendment Protection," *Harvard Civil Rights–Civil Liberties Law Review* 9 (1974):1.

9. *Model Penal Code and Commentaries,* vol. 3, pt. II, pp. 349–53.

10. 415 U.S. 130, 94 S.Ct. 970, 39 L.Ed.2d 214 (1974).

11. James Q. Wilson, *Thinking about Crime,* rev. ed. (New York: Vintage Books, 1985), p. 112.

12. *Model Penal Code and Commentaries,* vol. 3, pt. II, p. 331.

13. *Wall Street Journal* (December 2, 1991), p. A14.

14. *People v. Craig,* 152 Cal. 42, 91 P. 997 (1907); Caleb Foote, "Vagrancy-Type Law and Its Administration," *University of Pennsylvania Law Review* 104 (1956):603–50.

15. American Law Institute *Model Penal Code,* tentative draft no. 13 (1961), p. 61.

16. *Papachristou et al. v. City of Jacksonville,* 405 U.S. 156, 92 S.Ct. 839, 31 L.Ed.2d 110 (1972).

17. Morris and Hawkins, *The Honest Politician's Guide to Crime Control.*

18. Edwin M. Schur and Hugo Adam Bedau, *Victimless Crimes: Two Sides of a Controversy* (Englewood Cliffs, N.J.: Prentice-Hall, 1974).

19. Home Office, *Scottish Home Department Report of the Committee on Homosexual Offenses and Prostitution* (London: Her Majesty's Stationery Office, 1957), pp. 20–21.

20. Sir Patrick Devlin, *The Enforcement of Morals* (London: Oxford University Press, 1959), p. 48.

21. Wisconsin Stat.Ann. tit. 45, 344.15 (1958); Indiana Stat.Ann. 10–4207 (1977).

22. Article 251.2.

23. Home Office, Scottish Home Department Report, p. 247.

24. American Law Institute, "Commentary," *Model Penal Code,* tentative draft no. 4, (Philadelphia: American Law Institute, 1954), p. 276.

Constitution of the United States

We the People of the United States, in Order to form a more perfect Union, establish Justice, insure domestic Tranquility, provide for the common defence, promote the general Welfare, and secure the Blessings of Liberty to ourselves and our Posterity, do ordain and establish this Constitution for the United States of America.

Article. I.

Section. 1. All legislative Powers herein granted shall be vested in a Congress of the United States, which shall consist of a Senate and House of Representatives....

Article. II.

Section. 1. The executive Power shall be vested in a President of the United States of America. He shall hold his Office during the Term of four Years....

Article. III.

Section 1. The judicial Power of the United States, shall be vested in one supreme Court, and in such inferior Courts as the Congress may from time to time ordain and establish. The Judges, both of the supreme and inferior Courts, shall hold their Offices during good Behaviour, and shall, at stated Times, receive for their Services, a Compensation, which shall not be diminished during their Continuance in Office.

 Section. 2. The judicial Power shall extend to all Cases, in Law and Equity, arising under this Constitution, the Laws of the United States, and Treaties made, or which shall be made, under their Authority:....

 The Trial of all Crimes, except in Cases of Impeachment; shall be by Jury; and such Trial shall be held in the State where the said Crimes shall have been committed; but when not committed within any State, the Trial shall be at such Place or Places as the Congress may by Law have directed.

 Section. 3. Treason against the United States, shall consist only in levying War against them, or in adhering to their Enemies, giving them Aid and Comfort. No Person shall be convicted of Treason unless on the Testimony of two Witnesses to the same overt Act, or on Confession in open Court.

 The Congress shall have Power to declare the Punishment of Treason, but not Attainder of Treason shall work Corruption of Blood, or Forfeiture except during the life of the Person attainted.

...

Article. VI.

...

This Constitution, and the Laws of the United States which shall be made in Pursuance thereof; and all Treaties made, or which shall be made under the Authority of the United States, shall be the supreme Law of the Land; and the Judges in every State shall be bound thereby, any Thing in the Constitution or Laws of any State to the Contrary notwithstanding.

...

Amendments to the Constitution of the United States of America

Amendment I.*

Congress shall make no law respecting an establishment of religion, or prohibiting the free exercise thereof; or abridging the freedom of speech, or of the press, or the right of the people peaceably to assemble, and to petition the Government for a redress of grievances.

Amendment II.

A well regulated Militia, being necessary to the security of a free State, the right of the people to keep and bear Arms, shall not be infringed.

Amendment III.

No Soldier shall, in time of peace be quartered in any house, without the consent of the Owner, nor in time of war, but in a manner to be prescribed by law.

Amendment IV.

The right of the people to be secure in their persons, houses, papers, and effects, against unreasonable searches and seizures, shall not be violated, and no Warrants shall issue, but upon probable cause, supported by Oath or affirmation, and particularly describing the place to be searched, and the persons or things to be seized.

Amendment V.

No person shall be held to answer for a capital, or otherwise infamous crime, unless on a presentment or indictment of a Grand Jury, except in

*The first ten Amendments (Bill of Rights) were ratified effective December 15, 1791.

cases arising in the land or naval forces, or in the Militia, when in actual service in time of War or public danger; nor shall any person be subject for the same offence to be twice put in jeopardy of life or limb, nor shall be compelled in any criminal case to be a witness against himself, nor be deprived of life, liberty, or property, without due process of law; nor shall private property be taken for public use without just compensation.

Amendment VI.

In all criminal prosecutions, the accused shall enjoy the right to a speedy and public trial, by an impartial jury of the State and district wherein the crime shall have been committed; which district shall have been previously ascertained by law, and to be informed of the nature and cause of the accusation; to be confronted with the witnesses against him; to have compulsory process for obtaining witnesses in his favor, and to have the assistance of counsel for his defence.

Amendment VII.

In Suits at common law, where the value in controversy shall exceed twenty dollars, the right of trial by jury shall be preserved, and no fact tried by a jury shall be otherwise re-examined in any Court of the United States, than according to the rules of the common law.

Amendment VIII.

Excessive bail shall not be required, nor excessive fines imposed, nor cruel and unusual punishments inflicted.

Amendment IX.

The enumeration in the Constitution of certain rights shall not be construed to deny or disparage others retained by the people.

Amendment X.

The powers not delegated to the United States by the Constitution, nor prohibited by it to the States, are reserved to the States respectively, or to the people.

▼ *Glossary* ▼

ACCESSORY following a crime, the party liable for separate, lesser offenses

ACCOMPLICES before and during a crime, the parties liable as principals

ACTUAL POSSESSION on the possessor's person

ACTUS REUS the criminal act or the physical element in criminal liability

AFFIRM to uphold a trial court's decision

AFFIRMATIVE DEFENSE a defense in which the defendant bears the burden of production

ALTER EGO **DOCTRINE** the principle that high corporate officers are the corporation's brain

APPELLANT a party who appeals a lower court decision

APPELLATE COURT a court that reviews decisions of trial courts

APPELLEE the party appealed against

ASPORTATION carrying away another's property

ASSAULT an attempt to commit a battery, or intentionally putting another in fear

BATTERY offensive bodily contact

BIAS-MOTIVATED CRIMES crimes committed because of race, gender, ethnic, or religious prejudice

BURDEN OF PERSUASION the responsibility to convince the fact finder of the truth of the assertion

BURDEN OF PRODUCTION the responsibility to introduce initial evidence to support a claim

BURDEN OF PROOF the responsibility to produce the evidence to persuade the fact finder

CARNAL KNOWLEDGE sexual intercourse

CASTLE EXCEPTION defenders have no need to retreat when attacked at home

CAUSATION the substantial reason for the harm in crimes requiring a specific result

CITATION a reference to the published report of a case

CIVIL LAW the law that deals with private rights and remedies

CLAIM OF RIGHT the belief that property taken rightfully belongs to the taker

COLLATERAL ATTACK a proceeding asking an appellate court to rule against the trial court's jurisdiction to decide a question or case

COMMON LAW all the statutes and case law background of England and the colonies before the American Revolution, based on principles and rules that derive from usages and customs of antiquity

COMMON-LAW CRIMES crimes originating in the English common law

CONCURRENCE the requirement that *actus reus* must join with *mens rea* to produce criminal conduct, or to cause a harmful result

CONCURRING OPINION an opinion that joins the court's result but not its reasoning

CONSTRUCTIVE FORCE a substitute for actual force in rape cases

CONSTRUCTIVE POSSESSION legal possession or custody

CONVERSION illegal use of another's property

CRIMINAL PUNISHMENT (1) pain or other unpleasant consequence (2) inflicted for breaking a specific law and (3) administered by the state (4) for the primary purpose of hurting criminal offenders, not helping them

CRIMINAL SEXUAL CONDUCT a gender-neutral offense making both sexual penetrations and contacts crimes

CULPABILITY blameworthiness for criminal conduct based on *mens rea*

DAMAGES money awarded in civil lawsuits for injuries

DEFENDANT the person against whom a civil or criminal action is brought

DEFENSES justifications and excuses to criminal liability

DELIBERATE referring to an act committed with a cool, reflecting mind

DIMINISHED CAPACITY mental capacity less than "normal" but more than insane

DISCRETION freedom to decide outside of written rules

DISSENT the opinion of the minority of justices

DISTINGUISH CASES to find that facts differ enough from those in a prior

case to release judges from the precedent of the decision in that case

DOCTRINE OF COMPLICITY the principle regarding parties to crime

DUE PROCESS constitutional protection against vague and overbroad laws

DUE PROCESS CLAUSES government cannot deny citizens life, liberty, or property without notice, hearing, and other established procedures

DURHAM RULE, OR *PRODUCT TEST* an insanity test to determine whether a crime was a product of mental disease or defect

ELEMENTS the parts of a crime that the prosecution must prove beyond a reasonable doubt, such as *actus reus, mens rea,* causation, and harmful result

EQUIVOCALITY APPROACH the theory that attempt *actus reus* requires an act that can have no other purpose than the commission of a crime

EXCUSES wrongdoing without criminal responsibility

EX POST FACTO **LAWS** laws passed after the occurrence of the conduct constituting the crime

EXTORTION misappropriation of another's property by means of threat to inflict bodily harm in future

EXTRANEOUS FACTOR a condition beyond the attempter's control

FACTUAL CAUSATION conduct that sets a chain of events in motion

FACTUAL IMPOSSIBILITY the defense that facts make it impossible to complete a crime

FELONIES serious crimes generally punishable by one year or more in prison

FELONY MURDER a death occurring in the course of committing a serious felony other than homicide

FIGHTING WORDS words that provoke or threaten to provoke immediate violence or disorder

FORGERY making false writings or materially altering authentic writings

GENERAL DETERRENCE preventing crime by threatening potential law-breakers

GENERAL INTENT intent to commit the *actus reus*

GENERAL PRINCIPLES OF CRIMINAL LIABILITY the theoretical foundation for the elements of *actus reus, mens rea,* causation, and harm

HABEAS CORPUS PETITION a request for a court to review an individual's detention by a state or local government

HATE CRIMES crimes motivated by race, gender, ethnic background, or religious prejudice

HOLDING the legal principle or rule that a case enunciates

IMPERFECT DEFENSE defense reducing but not eliminating criminal liability

INCAPACITATION punishment by imprisonment, mutilation, and even death

INCHOATE CRIMES offenses based on crimes not yet completed

INFORMATION a document drawn up by a prosecutor formally charging a suspect with a crime

IRRESISTIBLE IMPULSE impairment of the will that makes it impossible to control the impulse to do wrong

JURISDICTION territory or subject matter under the control of a government body

JUSTIFICATIONS otherwise criminal conduct right under the circumstances

KNOWING POSSESSION awareness of the item possessed

LEGAL CAUSATION cause recognized by law to impose criminal liability

LEGAL IMPOSSIBILITY the defense that what the actor attempted was not a crime

MAJORITY OPINION the opinion of the majority of justices

MALICE AFORETHOUGHT the common-law murder *mens rea*

MALUM IN SE a crime inherently bad

MALUM PROHIBITUM a crime not inherently bad

MARITAL RAPE EXCEPTION the rule that husbands cannot rape their wives

MENS REA the mental element in crime, of which there are four mental states: purpose, knowledge, recklessness, and negligence

MERE POSSESSION possession without knowledge

MISAPPROPRIATION gaining possession of another's property

MISDEMEANOR a minor crime for which the penalty is usually less than one year in jail or a fine

MISDEMEANOR-MANSLAUGHTER RULE if death occurs during the commission of a misdemeanor, the death is an involuntary manslaughter

MITIGATING CIRCUMSTANCES facts that reduce but do not eliminate culpability

***M'Naghten* RULE, OR RIGHT-WRONG TEST** a defense pleading insanity due to mental disease or defect that impairs the capacity to distinguish right from wrong

MODEL PENAL CODE the code developed by the American Law Institute to guide reform in criminal law

MODEL PENAL CODE STANDARD the precept that attempt *actus reus* requires substantial steps that strongly corroborate the actor's purpose

MOTIVE the reason why a defendant commits a crime

NEGLIGENCE the unconscious creation of risk, or the mental state in which actors create substantial and unjustifiable risks of harm but are not aware of creating them

NULLA POENA SINE LEGE punishment without a specific law

NULLUM CRIMEN SINE LEGE no crime without a specific law

OBJECTIVE TEST external measure or reasonableness of belief

OPINION the holding and/or reasoning of a court

PARAMOUR RULE the principle that a husband discovering his wife in an adulterous act is adequate provocation

PERFECT DEFENSE a defense that leads to acquittal

PHYSICAL PROXIMITY DOCTRINE the principle that the number of remaining acts in attempt determines attempt *actus reus*

PLAINTIFF the person who sues another party in a civil action

PLURALITY OPINION an opinion that announces the result of the case but whose reasoning does not command a majority of the court

PRECEDENT prior court decisions that guide judges in deciding future cases

PREMEDITATED planned in advance

PRINCIPLE OF LEGALITY no crime or punishment without notice and hearing

PROBABLE DESISTANCE APPROACH whether the act in attempt would naturally lead to the commission of the crime

PRODUCT TEST *See* Durham rule

PROPORTIONALITY punishment in relation to the person and conduct

REASONABLE RESISTANCE STANDARD women must use the amount of force required by the totality of the circumstances surrounding sexual assault

REASONING the reasons a court gives to support its holding

RECKLESSNESS the conscious creation of substantial and unjustifiable risk; the state of mind in which actors know they are creating risks of harm

REHABILITATION prevention of crime by treatment

REMAND to send a case back to a trial court for further proceedings consistent with the reviewing court's decision

RESPONDEAT SUPERIOR the doctrine that employers are responsible for their employees' actions

RETRIBUTION punishment based on just deserts

RIGHT-WRONG TEST *See* M'Naughten rule

REVERSE to set aside the decision of the trial court

ROBBERY taking and carrying away another's property by force or threat of force with the intent to permanently deprive owner of possession

SPECIAL DETERRENCE aims at individual offenders, hoping to deter their future conduct by the threat of punishment

STARE DECISIS the principle that binds courts to stand by prior decisions and to not disturb settled points of law

STATUTES rules or doctrines enacted by legislatures

STATUTORY RAPE carnal knowledge of a person under the age of consent whether or not accomplished by force

STRICT LIABILITY liability without fault, or in the absence of *mens rea*

SUBJECTIVE TEST an internal or honest belief test

SUBSTANTIAL CAPACITY TEST insanity due to mental disease or defect impairing the substantial capacity either to appreciate the wrongfulness of conduct or to conform behavior to the law

SUPERIOR OFFICER RULE the precept that only the highest corporate officers can incur criminal liability for a corporation

SURREPTITIOUS REMAINING entering a structure with the intent to commit a crime inside

THEFT consolidated crimes of larceny, embezzlement, and false pretenses

TORT a legal wrong for which the injured party may sue the injuring party

TRESPASSORY TAKING wrongful taking required in larceny *actus reus*

UNPRIVILEGED ENTRY entering a structure without right, license, or permission

UTMOST RESISTANCE STANDARD rape victims must use all the physical strength they have to prevent penetration

UTTERING knowing or conscious use or transfer of false documents

VERBAL ACTS words

VICARIOUS LIABILITY the principle regarding liability for another based on relationship

VIOLATION a minor legal infraction subject to a small fine

VOID FOR OVERBREADTH the principle that law violates due process if it unreasonably restricts constitutional rights

VOID-FOR-VAGUENESS the principle that law violates due process if they do not clearly define crime and punishment in advance

WHARTON RULE the principle that more than two parties must conspire to commit crimes that naturally involve at least two parties

WRIT OF CERTIORARI discretionary Supreme Court order to review lower court decisions

WRIT OF PROHIBITION an order from an appellate court to a lower court ordering it to cease proceedings until the appellate court can resolve a matter not within the lower court's authority

YEAR AND A DAY RULE no act occurring more than one year and one day before death is a cause of death

▼ Index ▼

Abandonment, 203–207
Abortion, 333–337
  and defense of necessity, 253–254
ABSCAM cases, 299
Accomplices, 149
Acquaintance rape, 391
Acquittal, 233
Actual possession, 109
Actus reus
  in arson, 451–453
  in assault, 418
  in attempt, 182, 186–191
  in battery, 414, 415–417
  in burglary, 436, 438–442
  in complicity, 150–154
  in conspiracy, 208–210
  in criminal homicide, 333–341
  and criminal intent, 182, 186–191
  in criminal liability, 10, 93–114
  in criminal sexual conduct, 411
  in driving while intoxicated, 498–505
  and duress defense, 286
  in embezzlement, 471
  in extortion, 488
  in false imprisonment, 423
  in false pretense, 472, 473
  in felony murder, 352
  in forgery, 482, 483
  in homicide, 332
  in kidnapping, 424
  in larceny, 462–466
  in manslaughter, 364
  in murder, 346
  in omission, 102–109
  of parties before and during
    crime, 150–154
  in possession, 109–114
  in rape, 396–403
  in receiving stolen property, 477, 478
  in second–degree murder, 358
  in solicitation, 222–223
  status or condition as, 94–98
  in statutory rape, 405
  thoughts as, 98–99
  in uttering, 484
  in verbal acts, 102
  and voluntariness, 99–102
Adequate provocation, 365–371
Adultery, adequacy of, as
  provocation, 369–371
Affirmation, 17
Affirmative defense, 233

Age
  as aggravating circumstance, 298
  defense of, 295–299
  as factor in statutory rape, 405–408
  and *mens rea,* 295–299
  old, 298–299
Aggravated assaults, 419–420
Aggravated kidnapping, 429
Aggravated rape, 412–413
AIDS, intentional spread of HIV virus in,
  420–423
Alibi defense, 232
Alter ego doctrine, 164, 170
American Law Institute (ALI), and
  development of Model Penal
  Code, 10
Anal intercourse, 550
Animals, in criminal offenses, 415–418
Appellants, 15
Appellate cases, 15
Appellate court, 15
Appellees, 15
Aquinas, St. Thomas, 114–115
Arrest, resisting unlawful, 264–266
Arson, 436
  actus reus in, 451–453
  first–degree, 454
  history and rationale, 451
  mens rea in, 453–454
  property in, 454
  second–degree, 454
  third–degree, 454
Asportation
  in kidnapping, 425
  in larceny, 462
Assault, 413, 418–423
  actus reus in, 418
  aggravated, 419–420
  defense of consent in, 270–272
  mens rea in, 418, 419
  as provocation in manslaughter, 365
Assembly, unlawful, 521–529
Atrocious murder, 349–351
Attempt, 180–182
  actus reus in, 182, 186–191
  legal and factual impossibility, 191–202
  material elements in, 182
  mens rea in, 182, 183–185
  rationale of, 182
  renunciation, 202–207
Attempted battery, 419

Bacon, Francis, 181, 255, 256
Bacon, Nicholas, 28
Battered spouse syndrome, 323
Battery, 413
    actus reus in, 414, 415–417
    attempted, 419
    harm in, 417–418
    mens rea in, 414–417
    as provocation in manslaughter, 365
    threatened, 419
Bentham, Jeremy, 71, 74
Bestiality, 550
Bias–motivated crimes, 530
Blackmail, 488
Blackstone, William, 11, 257, 392, 424, 438
    Commentaries, 14
Bodily harm offenses, 417–418
Bracton, 181, 255
Brain death, 338, 341
Brainwashing, and defense of duress to,
    285–286
Breaking requirement in burglary, 444–446
Burden of persuasion, 233
Burden of production, 233
Burden of proof, 232, 313–319
Burglary, 8, 436–438
    actus reus in, 436, 438–442
    breaking requirement in, 444–446
    dwelling requirement, 442–446
    entry requirement in, 440–442
    grading, 448
    mens rea in, 436, 437, 447–448
    nighttime requirement in, 446–447
    proposed reforms to, law, 450–451
    rationale of law, 449–450
    remaining requirement in, 440–442
Burning, 451–453. *See also* Arson
Business crime, and vicarious
    liability, 163–169
But-for standard, 132–133

Capital cases, proportionality in, 77
Capital felonies, 24, 346
Capital murder, 332, 346, 347
Capital offense, kidnapping as, 424
Cardozo, Benjamin, 12
Carnal knowledge, 391
Cases, reading, analyzing and finding, 15–18
Castle exception, 247–250
Causation, 93, 132–140
Caveat emptor, 473
Chain conspiracies, 218
Checks, forged, 482
Child(ren)
    abduction of, 429–430
    criminal sexual conduct with, 408–409
Chronic alcoholism, and intoxication, 290
Churchill, Winston, 42

Citation, 16
Citizens, use of force by, in resisting arrest,
    264–266
Civil law, characteristics of, 8
Civil suits, defense of consent in, 270
Claim of right, 471
Clarke, Ramsey, 261
Cocaine sales, and felony murder, 352–358
Coffee, John, 363
Cohabitation, illicit, 546
Coke, Edward, 43, 255, 437
Collateral attack, 16
Common law, 11
    duress at, 280–281
    origins of criminal law, 11–13
    and self–defense, 234
Common-law accessory, 149–150
Common-law approach, to intoxication, 286
Common-law attempt, 181
Common-law burglary, 436
Common-law crimes, 11, 21–22
    abolishing, 15
    and modern criminal law, 15
    rape as, 391–392
Common-law felonies, 12
Common-law jurisdictions, 21
Common-law larceny, 466–467
Common-law misdemeanors, 12
Community service, 69
Complicity, 148
    following crime, 159–162
    and parties to crime, 148–150
    actus reus of parties before and during
        crime, 150–154
    mens rea of parties before and during
        crime, 155–159
    and vicarious liability, 162–174
Comprehensive Crime Control Act
    (1984), 314
Compulsion defense, 282–284
Computer theft, 467–470
Concurrence, 93, 131–132
Concurring opinions, 17
Condition
    as *actus reus,* 94–98
    crimes of, 535–544
Conditional threat, 419
Conflict-elitist theory, 27–28, 29
Conjunctive test of insanity, 313
Consent, 269–272
    mens rea in, 269
    in rape, 269, 392–395, 396
Consent decrees, in corporate crime, 163
Consolidated theft statutes, 476–477
Conspiracy, 207, 220–221
    actus reus in, 208–210
    material elements in, 207–208
    mens rea in, 210
    objective of, 214
    parties to, 214–220

Constitutional limits
    equal protection of the laws, 49–54
    ex post facto principle, 44
    privacy right, 54–61
    right to free speech and expressive
        conduct, 61–66
    void for vagueness, 44–49
Constructive breaking, in burglary, 438
Constructive force, in rape, 397–403
Constructive intent, 116
Constructive possession, 109–110
Conversion, 472
Corporal punishment, 414
Corporate crime
    mens rea in, 162–163
    punishing, 163
    vicarious individual liability for, 170–174
Corporate murder, 361–364
    mens rea in, 362
Cressey, Donald R., 29
Crime
    classifying and grading, 22–26
    complicity following, 159–162
    defenses to, 8–9
    parties to, 148–162
    vicarious corporate liability for real,
        169–170
Criminal codes, 13–14
Criminal court, structure of, 16
Criminal intent
    and *actus reus*, 182, 186–191
    and *mens rea*, 182, 183–185
Criminal law
    characteristics of, 7–8
    common law crimes and modern, 15
    common-law origins of, 11–13
    ethical core perspective on, 31–33
    general part of, 10
    historical perspective on, 30–31
    ideological perspective on, 27–29
    irrational forces perspective, 29–30
    purpose of, 7
    rational, 9–10
    sources of, 11–18
    special part of, 10
    variety in, 8–9
Criminal liability, 93
    actus reus in, 10, 93–114
    causation, 140
    concurrence, 131–132
    grading offenses, 140–141
    mens rea in, 93, 114–123, 127, 288
    principles of, 43
Criminal penalties, variations in, 9
Criminal punishment, 66–67
    distinction between treatment and, 67
    influence of defenses on, 233
    influence of motive on, 234
    proportionality in, 76–83
    retribution, 67, 69–71

trends in, 75–76
typical sentences in, 68–69
prevention, 71–75
Criminal sexual conduct, 390–408, 545. *See
    also* Public morals offenses; Rape
    actus reus in, 411
    with children, 408–409
    mens rea in, 411
    statutes, 411–412
Criminal trespass, 449
Culpability. *See mens rea*
    general requirements of, 116–117
    and retribution, 69–70
Cunnilingus, 550, 551

Damages, 23
Dangerous conduct rationale, 182
Dangerous person rationale, 182
Date rape, 391
Death. *See* Homicide
Death penalty, 9, 68
    constitutionality of the, 347
Defendant, 23
Defense(s), 232. *See also specific defenses*
    affirmative, 233
    common–law, 15
    to crime, 8–9
    imperfect, 233
    perfect, 233
Defense-of-others defense, 250–251
Deliberate, 347
De minimus non curat lex, 133
Democratic-consensus theory, 27–28
Depraved-heart murder, 360–361
Deterrence, 71–73
Devlin, Patrick, 545–546
Diminished capacity, 319–322. *See also*
    Insanity
Discretion, 28–29
Disorderly conduct, 505–511
Dissent, 16
Drew test of legal insanity, 312–313
Driving while intoxicated, 498–505. *See also*
    Vehicular homicide
Drug abuse
    and felony murder, 352–366
    injuries and deaths resulting from, 418
Due process, 44, 509
    and punishment for vicarious liability, 163
    and unborn child criminal statutes, 335
Duress, 280–286
    actus reus in, 286
    and brainwashing, 285–286
    mens rea in, 286
    and superior orders, 284–285
Durham rule, and insanity defense, 308–309
Durkheim, Emile, 27
Dwelling requirement, in burglary, 442–446

Economic necessity, nonacceptance of, as
    defense, 258–259
Eighth Amendment, 76
Embezzlement, 471–472
    actus reus in, 471
    mens rea in, 471
Enticement, as *actus reus,* 187
Entrapment, 299–302
    objective test of, 299
    subjective test of, 299–300
Entry requirement, in burglary, 440–442
Equal protection clause, 49
    and unborn child homicide
        statutes, 335
Equal protection of the laws, 49–54
Equivocality approach to attempt, 186
Estrich, Susan, 404
Ethical core perspective of criminal
    law, 31–33
Excusable homicides, 332
Excuses, 232
    age, 295–299
    diminished capacity, 319–322
    distinction between justification
        and, 280
    duress, 280–286
    entrapment, 299–302
    insanity, 303
        burden of proof, 313–319
        irresistible impulse test, 309–311
        right–wrong test, 303–309
        substantial capacity test, 311–313
    intoxication, 286–290
    mistake, 290–294
    syndromes, 322–324
Ex post facto laws, 43, 44
Expressive conduct, freedom of, 61–66
Extortion, 488–490
    actus reus in, 488
    mens rea in, 488
Extraneous factor, 192

Fact, mistake of, 291
Factual cause, 132–133
Factual impossibility, 192
False imprisonment, 423
    comparison of kidnapping and, 425
False pretenses, 472–476
    actus reus in, 472, 473
    distinguishing between larceny and,
        473–476
    mens rea in, 472, 473
Federal Criminal Justice Reform Act
    (1973), 32
Fellatio, 550, 551
Felonies, 24
    capital, 24
    common-law, 12
    degrees of, 25–26

Felony murder, 347, 352–358
Fence operations, 477
Fetal death, 18–21, 333–337
Feticide, 336
Fifth Amendment, due process clauses
    of, 44
Fighting words, 513–519
Fighting-words statutes, 513
Fines, 69
First Amendment
    and fighting words, 513–519
    and hate crimes, 530–535
    and obscene phone calls, 512–513
First-degree arson, 454
First-degree burglary, 448, 449
First-degree murder, 345–351
First-degree robbery, 488
Fletcher, George, 102–103, 238–239, 286
Force
    in defense of homes and
        property, 266–269
    self-defense justification of, 239–247
Forgery, 481, 482–484, 497
    actus reus in, 482, 483
    mens rea in, 482, 483–484
Fornication, 546
Fourteenth Amendment, 44–45, 49, 509
Fourth Amendment, and use of deadly
    force, 260–264
France, Anatole, 544
Fraud, sexual penetration obtained
    by, 393–395

General deterrence, 71
General intent, 115
General prevention, 71
Good and evil test of insanity, 313
Grading, of offenses, 140–141
Grand larceny, 470–471
Greylord, 299
Gross, Hyman, 280
Gross negligence, 382
    in negligent homicide, 376–377
Group disorderly conduct, 521–529

Habeas corpus petition, 16
Hadley, Joseph E., Jr., 363
Hale, Lord, 391–392
Hale, Matthew, 255, 257
Hall, Jerome, 281
Harm, principle of, 93
Hate crimes, 530–535
Hawkins, 257
Hedonism, 71
Heinous murder, 347
Historical perspective of criminal law, 30–31
Hobart, 255

Hobbes, Thomas, 256–257
Holding, 16
Holmes, Oliver Wendell, 30, 73, 183,
    207–208, 291, 473
Home, defense of, 266–269
Homeless. *See* Condition, crimes of
Homicide
    actus reus in, 332, 333
        beginning of life, 333–337
        end of life, 338–341
    causing another's death, 342–345
        year-and-a-day rule, 342–345
    criminal, 332
    excusable, 332
    justifiable, 332
    mens rea in, 332, 345
    negligent, 364, 376–382
    types and degrees of criminal, 332, 345
        atrocious murder, 349–351
        corporate murder, 361–364
        depraved–heart murder, 360–361
        felony murder, 352–358
        first-degree murder, 345–351
        manslaughter, 364–376
        negligent homicide, 376–382
        reckless murder, 360
        second-degree murder, 358–361
Homosexuality, and privacy rights, 55–56

Ideological perspective, of criminal
    law, 27–29
Immaturity. *See* Age
Imperfect defense, 233
Imperfect self-defense, 365
Implied consent law, 500
Impossibility, 191–202
    distinguishing between legal and factual,
        191–202
Imprisonment, false, 423
Incapacitation, 71, 73–74, 76
Incarceration, 68
Inchoate crimes, doctrine of, 180
Influence of defenses on punishment, 233
Information, 19
Insanity, 9, 15, 303. *See also* Diminished
        capacity
    burden of proof, 313–319
    defense of, 233
    Durham rule in, 308–309
    irresistible impulse test in, 309–311
    irresistible impulse in, 310–311
    M'Naghten rule in, 303–309
    right-wrong test in, 303–309
    substantial capacity test in, 311–313
Insulting gestures, as provocation, 365
Intent
    constructive, 116
    general, 115
    in grading offenses, 141

specific, 115
transferred, 115
Intentional scaring, 419
Intermittent confinement, 68
Intoxication, 286–290
    involuntary, 286–287
    mens rea in, 286, 287–290
    voluntary, 287–288
Involuntary acts, punishing, 102
Involuntary intoxication, 286–287
Involuntary manslaughter, 372
Irrational forces perspective of criminal law,
    29–30
Irresistible impulse in insanity defense,
    310–311
Irresistible impulse test, 309–311

Jackson, Robert, 210
Junk food syndrome, 322
Jurisdiction, 8
    common-law, 21
Justice, and retribution, 70
Justifiable homicides, 332
Justification, 232–234
    consent, 269–272
    defense of homes and property,
        266–269
    defense of others, 250–251
    distinction between excuses and, 280
    execution of public duties, 260–263
    general principle of necessity, 251–260
    resisting unlawful arrest, 264–266
    self–defense, 234–239
        definition of, 234
        elements of, 239–247
        retreat doctrine, 247–250
Juvenile court, justification of, 295

Kidnapping, 424–430
    actus reus in, 424
    aggravated, 429
    asportation in, 425
    comparison of false imprisonment
        and, 425
    mens rea in, 424
    simple, 429
Knowing possession, 109

Language, coarse and indecent, 511–513
Larceny
    actus reus in, 462–466
    asportation in, 462
    distinguishing between false pretenses
        and, 473–476
    distinguishing between robbery and,
        486–487

grand, 470–471
material circumstances in, 466–470
mens rea in, 462, 471
petty, 470
taking in, 462–466, 473
Law, mistake of, 291
Law enforcement officers
and execution of public duties
defense, 260–261
fighting words in altercations with
citizens, 513–519
and solicitation, 223
and use of entrapment, 299–302
Legal cause, 132, 133–134
Legal impossibility, 192
Legality, 43
constitutional limits to, 43
equal protection of the laws, 49–54
ex post facto prohibition, 44
right to free speech and expressive
conduct, 61–66
right to privacy, 54–61
void for vagueness, 44–49
Lewis, C. S., 75
Lex non scripta, 11
Liability, vicarious, 162–163
Life
defining the beginning of, 333–337
end of, 338–341
Life imprisonment felony, 346
Loitering laws, 536

Maakestad, William J., 362
Madison, James, 11
Majority opinion, 16–17
Mala prohibita, 24
Malice aforethought, 346, 381–382
Malum in se, 24
Malum prohibitum, 373
Manslaughter, 364–376
actus reus in, 364
definition of, 364
involuntary, 372
mens rea in, 364
voluntary, 365–372
Marital rape exception, 391, 409–411
Marijuana, possession of, 56–61
Masturbation, 550
Material element
in attempt, 182
and consent in negating, 269–272
in conspiracy, 207–208
Medical ethics
and the beginning of life, 333–337
and the end of life, 338–341
Mens rea
and age, 295–299
in arson, 451, 453–454

in assault, 418, 419
in attempt, 182, 183–185
in battery, 414–417
in burglary, 436, 437
in complicity, 155–159
in consent, 269
in conspiracy, 210–214
in corporate crime, 162–163
in corporate murder, 362
in criminal homicide, 338, 345
and criminal intent, 182, 183–185
and criminal liability, 93, 114–123,
127, 288
in criminal sexual conduct, 411
defining, 115–119
in depraved–heart murder, 361
determining, 114–115
distinguishing from motive, 234
and duress defense, 286
in embezzlement, 471
in extortion, 488
in false imprisonment, 423
in false pretense, 472, 473
in felony murder, 352
in forgery, 482, 483–484
in homicide, 332
in impaired capacity, 319–322
influence on grading, 141
in insanity defense, 302
intent in, 115–119
in intoxication, 286, 287–290
in kidnapping, 424
knowing in, 119–121
in larceny, 462, 471
in manslaughter, 364
in murder, 346
in negligence, 122–127
of parties before and during
crime, 155–159
in prostitution, 546
purpose in, 117–119
of rape, 396, 404–405
in receiving stolen property, 477, 478
in recklessness, 122–127
in second-degree murder, 358, 360
in solicitation, 223
in statutory rape, 405
and strict liability, 127–131
subjective and objective standards
for, 121–122
in uttering, 484
in vehicular homicide, 377–382
Mercy, motive of, 234
Mere possession, 109–110
Mill, John Stuart, 545
Misappropriation, 460
Misdemeanor manslaughter rule, 372
Misdemeanors, 24
common-law, 12
Misdemeanor trespass, 449

Mistake, 290–294
    as defense to statutory rape, 405–408
Mitigating circumstances, 233, 234
M'Naghten rule, 303–309
Model Penal Code, 10, 24, 76
    arson in, 452
    attempt in, 186–188
    battery in, 414, 417–418, 419
    bodily harm offenses in, 418
    and burden of proof in insanity
        defense, 314
    burglary in, 439, 440, 443, 450–451
    and choice-of-evils concept, 256
    comprehensive assault statute
        in, 419–420
    false imprisonment in, 423
    forgery in, 483
    loitering in, 536–537
    necessity provision in, 251, 252
    prostitution in, 550
    rape in, 396
    and substantial capacity test, 311
    theft in, 476
    and use of force, 241
Moral duties, failure to perform, 103
Motive, influence of, on punishment, 234
Municipal ordinances, 11
Murder. *See also* Homicide
    atrocious, 349–351
    corporate, 361–364
    depraved–heart, 360–361
    felony, 352–358
    first–degree, 345–351
    reckless, 360
    second–degree, 345, 358–361
Mutual fights, as provocations of, 365

Nader, Ralph, 363
Necessity, general principle of, 251–260
Necessity defense statutes, 251–260
Negligence, and *mens rea,* 122–127
Negligent homicide, 364, 376–382
Nesson, Charles, 310
Nighttime requirement, in burglary, 446–447
Noncustodial parents, kidnapping by,
    429–430
Nuisance, 505–511
Nulla poena sine lege, 43
Nullum crimen sine lege, 43

Objective standards, and *mens rea,* 121–122
Objective-subjective test, and use of force,
    241–242
Objective test
    of entrapment, 299–300
    of use of force, 241
    in voluntary manslaughter, 372

Obscene phone calls, 512–513
Offenses, grading, 140–141
Offensive touching, 414
Omissions, and *actus reus,* 102–109
Opinion, 17
Others, defense of, 250–251
Overboard, law as, 515

Packer, Herbert, 67, 74
Palgrave, Francis, 74
Panhandling laws, 536–544
Paramour killings, 369–371
Paramour rule, 369–371
Parties, to conspiracy, 214–220
Parties to crime, 148–150
    and *actus reus,* 150–154
    and *mens rea,* 155–159
Pedestrian interference, 539–544
Perfect defenses, 233
Personal injury law, 7
Persuasion, burden of, 233
Petty larceny, 470
Physical proximity doctrine
    in attempt, 186
Pickpocketing, 470
Plaintiff, 23
Plato, 181
Plurality opinion, 17
Police officers. *See* Law enforcement
    officers
Pornography, possession of, 55
Possession, 109–114
    actual, 109
    constructive, 109–110
    knowing, 109
    in larceny, 463
    mere, 109–110
Posttraumatic stress syndrome, 323–324
Precedent, 12
    court overrule of, 13
Premeditation, 347–349
Premenstrual syndrome, 323
Prevention, 71–75
Privacy rights, 54–61
    and sodomy and related offenses,
        551–554
Private sanctions, appropriate, 23
Probable desistance approach, 186
    to attempt, 186
Probation, 68
Production, burden of, 233
Product test, and insanity defense, 308–309
Profanity, 511–513
Property
    in arson, 454
    defense of, 266–269
Property misappropriation
    consolidated statutes, 476–477

embezzlement, 471–472
extortion, 488–490
false pretenses, 472–476
forgery, 481, 482–484
larceny, 462–471
receiving stolen property, 477–481
robbery, 485–487
theft, 461–462
uttering, 481–482, 484
Proportionality, 66
in punishment, 76–83
Prostitution, 546–548
solicitation and promotion of, 548–550
Provocation, in manslaughter, 365–372
Proximate cause, 134
Public duties, execution of, 260–263
Public morals offenses, 544–546
fornication, 546
illicit cohabitation, 546
need to reform, 497
prostitution, 546–548
sodomy, 550–554
solicitation and promotion of
prostitution, 548–550
Public order offenses, 498
coarse and indecent language, 511–513
crimes of condition, 535–544
driving while intoxicated, 498–505
fighting words, 513–519
group disorderly conduct, 521–529
hate crimes, 530–535
nuisance, 505–511
threats, 519–521
Puffing, 474–476
Punishment. *See* Criminal punishment
Purse snatching, 486–487

Racketeer Influenced and Corrupt
Organizations Act (RICO), 221
Racketeering activity, and conspiracy, 221
Rape. *See also* Criminal sexual conduct
acquaintance, 391
actus reus in, 396–403
aggravated, 412–413
consent defense in, 269, 392–395, 396
date, 391
history of, 391–396
marital exception in, 391, 409–411
mens rea in, 396, 404–405
simple, 413
statutory, 405–408
by strangers, 390–391
Rape shield statutes, 395–396
Rational criminal law, 9–10
Rationalism, 71
Reasonableness test, and use of
force, 241–242
Reasonable provocation, 371–372

Reasonable resistance standard, in rape,
393–395
Reasoning, 16
Receiving stolen property, 477–481
actus reus in, 477, 478
mens rea in, 477, 478
Reckless murder, 360
Recklessness, and *mens rea,* 122–127
Reconnoitering, 187
Rehabilitation, 71, 74–75, 76
Remaining requirement, in burglary,
440–442
Remand, 17
Renunciation, 202–207
defense of voluntary, 203–207
Respondeat superior, 166
Restitution, 68–69
Retreat doctrine, 247–250
Retribution, 67, 69–71
trends in, 75–76
Reverse, 17
Right-wrong test, 303–309
Riot, 521
Riot Act (1714), 521
Robbery, 470, 485–487
actus reus in, 485
degrees of, 388
distinguishing between larceny and,
486–487
mens rea in, 485
Rout, 521

Sayre, Francis, 114
Schwartz, Louis B., 32
Second-degree arson, 454
Second-degree burglary, 448
Second-degree murder, 345, 358–361
Second-degree robbery, 488
Self-defense, 15, 233, 234–239
definition of, 234
elements of, 239–247
imperfect, 365
necessity principle in, 252
retreat doctrine, 247–250
Sexual penetration obtained by fraud,
393–395
Shardlowe, Justice, 181
Shock probation, 68
Shoplifting, 463–466
Simple kidnapping, 429
Simple rape, 413
Sixth Amendment, 44
Social harms, nonlegal responses to, 22–23
Sodomy, 55, 488, 550, 551
Solicitation, 221–225
actus reus in, 222–223
and law enforcement officers, 223
mens rea in, 223

and promotion of prostitution, 548–550
Special deterrence, 71
Specific intent, 115
    and attempt, 183
Specific intent crime, conspiracy as, 210–11
Speech, freedom of, 61–66
Spitting, as battery, 414
Split sentences, 68
Stare decisis, 12
Status, as *actus reus,* 94–98
Statutes, 13
Statutory rape, 405–408
    actus reus in, 405
    mens rea in, 405
Stephen, James F., 67, 69, 256, 281, 349, 545
Stephenson, Robert, 363
Stolen property, receiving, 477–481
Strict liability, and *mens rea,* 127–131
Strict liability crime, forcible rape as, 404
Subjective standards, and *mens rea,*
    121–122
Subjective test
    of entrapment, 299–300
    of use of force, 241
Subject test, and entrapment, 299–300
Substantial capacity test, 311–313
Superior officer rule, 169–170
Superior orders, and defense of duress,
    284–285
Surreptitious remaining, standard in
    burglary, 440–442
Syndromes, 322–324

Taking, in larceny, 462–466, 473
Telephone, use of obscene language on,
    512–513
Theft, 460, 497
    consent defense in, 269
    consolidated statutes, 476–477
    history of, 461–462
Theft statutes, consolidated, 476–477
Third–degree arson, 454
Third–degree burglary, 448
Third–degree robbery, 488
Thoughts, as *actus reus,* 98–99
Threatened batteries, 419
Threats, 519–521
Torts, 7, 23
Transferred intent, 115–116
Treatment, distinction between criminal
    punishment and, 67

Trespasses, as provocation in
    manslaughter, 366
Trespassory taking, 463
Twinkie defense, 322–323

Uniform Brain Death Act, 338
Unlawful assembly, 521–529
Unprivileged entry, standard in burglary,
    438–439
Utility, principle of, 71–72
Utmost resistance standard, in rape,
    392–393
Uttering, 481–482, 484
    actus reus in, 484
    mens rea in, 484

Vagrancy laws, 536
Vaguely worded statutes, problem of, 509
Vagueness doctrine, 45
Vague statutes, enforcement of, 44–49
Verbal acts, and *actus reus,* 102
Vicarious liability, 162–163
    and business crime, 163–169
    corporate, for real crime, 169–170
    individual, for corporate crime, 170–174
Victim compensation, 68–69
Victims of Crime Act (1984), 69
Vietnam vet defense, 323–324
Violations, 24
Virtue testing, 301
Void for overbreadth, 509
Void for vagueness, 43, 44–49, 509,
    512–513, 536
Voluntariness, and *actus reus,* 99–102
Voluntary intoxication, 287–288
Voluntary manslaughter, 365–372

Wharton's rule, 215–217
Wheel conspiracies, 218
White–collar crime, and conspiracy, 221
Wiehofen, Henry, 70
Wild beast test, of insanity, 313
Williams, Glanville, 241–242, 256, 257, 281
Wolfendon report, 545, 549–550
Writ of prohibition, 19

Year–and–a–day rule, 342–345